D1349151

Volume Two of

THE PLAYS

OF

J. B. PRIESTLEY

By J. B. PRIESTLEY

FICTION

BRIGHT DAY
THREE MEN IN NEW SUITS
DAYLIGHT ON SATURDAY
BLACK-OUT IN GRETLEY
LET THE PEOPLE SING
THE DOOMSDAY MEN
THEY WALK IN THE CITY

FARAWAY
ANGEL PAVEMENT
THE GOOD COMPANIONS
WONDER HERO
BENIGHTED
ADAM IN MOONSHINE
JENNY VILLIERS

PLAYS

THE PLAYS OF J. B. PRIESTLEY
  VOLUME I
    Dangerous Corner
    Eden End
    Time and the Conways
    I Have Been Here Before
    Johnson Over Jordan
    Music at Night
    The Linden Tree
  VOLUME II
    Laburnum Grove
    Bees on the Boat Deck
    When We Are Married

Good Night Children
The Golden Fleece
How are They at Home?
Ever Since Paradise
THREE PLAYS
  Music at Night
  The Long Mirror
  They Came to a City
DUET IN FLOODLIGHT
CORNELIUS
THE ROUNDABOUT
AN INSPECTOR CALLS

MISCELLANEOUS

DELIGHT
POSTSCRIPTS
RAIN UPON GODSHILL
MIDNIGHT ON THE DESERT
ENGLISH JOURNEY
FOUR-IN-HAND
I FOR ONE
TALKING: AN ESSAY
OPEN HOUSE

APES AND ANGELS
SELF-SELECTED ESSAYS
THE BALCONINNY
THE ENGLISH COMIC CHARACTER
MEREDITH (E.M.L.)
PEACOCK (E.M.L.)
THE ENGLISH NOVEL
HUMOUR (E. HERITAGE SERIES)
BRIEF DIVERSIONS

THE PLAYS

OF

J. B. PRIESTLEY

VOLUME II

WILLIAM HEINEMANN LTD

MELBOURNE :: LONDON :: TORONTO

These plays are fully protected by copyright.
Applications for all professional and repertory performances
should be addressed to the Author's Agent, A. D. Peters,
10, Buckingham Street, Adelphi, London, W.C.2.
Application for amateur performances should be addressed
to Samuel French Ltd., 26, Southampton Street, Strand,
London, W.C.2.
No performance should take place until a licence has been
obtained.

FIRST PUBLISHED 1949

PRINTED IN GREAT BRITAIN
AT THE WINDMILL PRESS,
KINGSWOOD, SURREY.

CONTENTS

INTRODUCTION

THE plays in this volume are all comedies—although comedies of various kinds. James Agate, when called upon once to give a short list of his likes and dislikes, included my serious plays among his likes and my comedies among his dislikes. On the other hand, I know an equally distinguished man of the Theatre who greatly prefers my comedies to my serious plays. The playgoing public appears to have no preference one way or the other, and this seems to me very sensible of it, and here I applaud its sound judgment. There are some men who should never try to be funny and there are others who are least effective when they are in grim earnest. But most of us are somewhere between these two extremes. And for my part I would bitterly resent being compelled to restrict my writing for the stage to either one form or the other. On the whole I think I find it easier to plan and then to write a serious play than I do a comedy (and to this point I shall return), but I enjoy the actual staging of a comedy more than I do that of serious play, and if asked to produce one of my own plays I would certainly choose a comedy. Nor do I think it difficult to explain these preferences. There is about a serious play that is properly constructed a natural sweep forward, an inevitable progress, that makes it easier to write, so that often a big scene of considerable technical intricacy will almost write itself. But in the detailed presentation of a comic scene on the stage, where inflections and timing are all-important, I find myself more at home and happier on the job than I do with the more serious plays. And it is, of course, far easier to test the value of your work in comedy, if only because the laughter of the audience tells you what is happening.

There is, however, an important point to be made here. To my mind it is only in the broadest farce that "anything for a laugh" is legitimate. In the production of comedy this can be a very dangerous policy. Many productions of Shakespeare's comedies have been ruined for me by antics more suitable to the Crazy Gang at the Victoria Palace. The fun was there, of course, but it was not the fun that Shakespeare intended. For example, in the glorious orchard scene in *Henry IV: Part Two* it is easy enough to provoke laughter by turning Shallow and Silence into knockabout buffoons, but it is equally easy in this way to ruin one of the finest scenes in all comic literature. The producer of comedy should set himself the task of discovering and then exploiting to the full the particular kind of comic effect the author intended, instead of going anywhere and doing anything for a laugh. Falling about or throwing custard pies will always produce bigger laughs than the most adroit examples of mental absurdity. I delight in wild clowning myself, but it is delightful only in its own place. Actors are often at fault here, because, having been given a comic part, they feel that every laugh, no matter how obtained, is a personal contribution of value to the production in hand, whereas they may easily be sacrificing the whole structure and value of a scene, and any lasting impression it can make, by these dubious triumphs. Every comedy worth playing has its own particular atmosphere, flavour, and appeal, and these should not be sacrificed to the dangerous notion that "every laugh is worth five pounds". It is always possible that a few five-pound laughs may finally cost several thousands.

I have already suggested that—to me at any rate—the writing of a comedy is not as easy as pie. The point is worth making if only because more than once when a comedy of mine has been produced, some critics have told their readers in effect that I have merely been filling in a gap with a hasty bit of fooling, probably knocked off in a few days. Nothing could be further from the truth. I have usually spent far more time and trouble, done far more re-constructing and re-writing, demanded far more additional rehearsals, in the comedies than in the serious plays. To take two examples from the plays selected for this volume, which, incidentally, does not include all the comedies I have written and had produced: *When We Are Married* and *Ever Since Paradise*. During the provincial try-out of *When We Are Married* I wrote and re-wrote many scenes, and we were actually presenting one version of the play in the evenings while we were rehearsing an altered version of it during the day. *Ever Since Paradise* was first written in 1939; it was substantially re-written during the war; and then much of it was changed before it was finally produced in 1946, and even then, during its provincial tour, some scenes were re-written. The critic who was not amused is clearly at liberty to retort that the result was not worth all this labour. That is a matter of opinion. But, at the risk now of being accused of wasting my time and energy, I do firmly declare that no comedy of mine ever arrived in a London theatre as a hasty bit of fooling, to which not sufficient attention had been given.

These comedies, I repeat, are of various kinds, and I shall try to give some indication of how I see them myself in discussing the individual plays. But they all more or less fall into one large division of comedy, although that again can be easily sub-divided. These large divisions, I fancy, are High, Light and Broad. High Comedy, which has a particular appeal to Latin and Central European minds, has never been popular with English writers and audiences, though

I think we might fairly claim Somerset Maugham's *The Circle* as a successful example of this form. The preference here, especially among the stalls public, has been for Light Comedy, partly because it is a form that provides admirable vehicles for popular and highly skilled star performers, without whom these flimsy pieces are apt to look very thin indeed. (This is a fact that Repertory and amateur producers ignore at their peril.) It is a form of comedy that I do not much care about myself, and I have not included in this selection the two attempts of mine made some years ago. My own choice is Broad Comedy, which is stronger in situation and richer in its characterisation than Light Comedy, and more frankly farcical and less austerely intellectual in its approach than High Comedy. It is, I believe, peculiarly suitable to the English temperament, and as I consider I possess a fairly thick slab of this temperament, this is the field of comedy in which I have chosen to work. One final point: the reader who is also a London playgoer must not confuse the real existence of these plays with their life on London playbills. Thus, the earliest of them, *Laburnum Grove*, is still being widely played; and the latest, *Ever Since Paradise*, has been produced from Stockholm to Madrid and has lately enjoyed much success throughout Central Europe.

LABURNUM GROVE: This comedy of suburban life, which brought back that fine actor, Edmund Gwenn, to the stage after some years' absence in films, was originally produced at the Duchess Theatre in the autumn of 1933. It had a very long run, which I deliberately broke (for I was the management too) to send the company to New York, where the play did reasonably well. It is a great favourite with Repertory and amateur companies here, but, perhaps because it is very English in atmosphere and humour, it has not been as widely and successfully produced abroad as many of my other plays have. The droll business with the bananas, which has amused thousands of audiences and appears to remain in their memory, owes nothing to me but was a happy invention of my friend, Sir Cedric Hardwicke, who produced the play. At the time I wrote it, when I was also gathering material for *English Journey*, I was very suspicious about our financial system, if only because the banks appeared to flourish when industry was failing, and this explains certain references in the text. Frequently in the Theatre, as most people who work in it will agree, either everything goes right or everything goes wrong. With *Laburnum Grove*, which I planned in a nursing home and wrote rapidly during convalescence, everything went right. We had a good cast, headed by Edmund Gwenn and Mary Jerrold, Ethel Coleridge and Melville Cooper; and this production brought me to the Duchess

Theatre and a long and happy association with its owner, J. P. Mitchelhill.

BEES ON THE BOAT DECK: This was an attempt to write political satire in terms of farcical comedy. A few critics—I seem to remember an encouraging notice in *The Times*—saw that I was trying to do something new and rather difficult, and there were people—Humbert Wolfe was one of them—who were tremendously enthusiastic about the piece. But for most people, it did not quite come off, in spite of the fact that the production, which opened, without any preliminary tour, at the Lyric in May 1936, had an astonishing cast, which included Kay Hammond, Rene Ray, Ralph Richardson, Laurence Olivier, Raymond Huntley, Richard Goolden, John Laurie, Alan Jeayes. It was produced by Richardson and Olivier, who were my partners in the enterprise. Some good judges have told me that we made a mistake in choosing a fairly large theatre and a big realistic set, that the symbolism of the piece demanded a different type of setting and production. It has always been a favourite of mine, and I consider that one or two of its scenes contain the richest comic writing I have contrived for the stage. How it reads today, I cannot imagine, for I cannot look at the text without remembering, with pleasure and with regret, the superb acting of that unusually fine cast.

WHEN WE ARE MARRIED: Produced at the St. Martin's in October 1938, and transferred to the Prince's at the end of March 1939. It has been very popular ever since. I enjoyed writing this broadly farcical comedy because I had a lot of fun remembering and then using various aspects of West Riding life and manners known to my boyhood. The plot is nonsensical but the characters and their attitudes and their talk are all authentic. The play was magnificently cast and produced by Basil Dean, who in my opinion has a great flair for this kind of comedy. It was during the early part of its run that I had to take over, at twenty-four hours notice, the part of Henry Ormonroyd, the drunken photographer, and thus did some acting, of a sort, about which I have boasted ever since.

GOOD NIGHT CHILDREN: After a long provincial tour, this play arrived at the New Theatre in February 1942, but was withdrawn after a short run. It has at least one admirer, and a most distinguished one, namely, James Bridie, who considers it to be among the very best of its kind, really excellent vintage nonsense. The play may have all manner of faults not apparent to me, but I am certain that the chief reason why it failed to attract people in 1942 was that at that time people took their broadcasting very seriously and resented any easy mockery of radio performers and officials. Perhaps too it is one of those pieces that are too much of a private joke, with a special appeal to an inner circle, ever to be widely popular.

THE GOLDEN FLEECE: This play, which has had a curious history, has never been produced in London, because I have long felt that it would not succeed if it were produced. It was originally written just before the war and was then called *Bull Market*. I put it aside when the war came because I felt that its story of sudden vast gains in speculation would seem old-fashioned or unreal to wartime audiences, even though, as we now know, such fortunes were actually being made. But being asked to help with a new play by both the Bradford Civic Playhouse and the Glasgow Citizens Theatre, I gave both of them *Bull Market* and both of them did very well out of it. Later, after some re-writing and a change of title to *The Golden Fleece*, the play went out on tour with Betty Warren and Mervyn Johns playing the two leads, but somehow it failed to capture public interest, chiefly, I think, because audiences found the main theme incredible, and so was withdrawn. I put a great deal of work, at various times, into this play, though as a piece of writing it still remains rather rough-and-ready. I still find the story itself attractive and believe the two chief characters to be admirable playing parts; but it may well be that the film and not the Theatre is the proper medium.

HOW ARE THEY AT HOME?: This topical wartime comedy was produced at the Apollo in May 1944. But it was never intended to be a contribution to the West End Theatre. It was written specially to be performed by ENSA companies to service men overseas: hence the title. I have included it here because of its wartime topical interest, and because many of the men and women who saw performances of it during their service abroad might like to have a copy of the text. Those who played in it at the Apollo—and it had an excellent cast—are not likely to forget the warnings and buzz-bombs that punctuated most performances.

EVER SINCE PARADISE: This experimental comedy, as I have already explained, was originally written in 1939 and then much re-written at odd intervals. With some extremely adroit music by Dennis Arundell, with Ursula Jeans and Roger Livesey playing Helen and William (and all that that involved), in a production I directed myself, with much valuable help from Roger Livesey and Osmund Willson, *Ever Since Paradise* started on a long and very successful provincial tour in the summer of 1946. At the end of that tour there was no theatre for us in London, so we laid off the production for six months, and then opened at the New in June 1947. I think it is true, as several knowledgeable persons have told me, that we achieved a sparkle and gaiety in the original touring production that we never quite recaptured afterwards. Nevertheless, the reception this play had in London (though it ran for several months and made many friends) was a shock and a bitter disappointment to me. To begin with, I felt that the astonishingly versatile and brilliant performances by Ursula Jeans and Roger Livesey never received the attention and the praise they deserved. And then many of the notices were not merely inadequate but downright wilfully stupid. Let me give one example. One critic who, I know from personal observation, was not even in the auditorium during the funniest scenes of the play, condemned me—in this of all plays—for solemn preaching. Being producer as well as author, I often looked in at this play, and always the audiences appeared to be having an uproariously good time (as they have done since with it in many Continental capitals); yet it is a fact that fifty per cent of the Press was sullenly hostile. And why, I cannot imagine, unless it was because I was at least trying to do something new. One final point, which brings me back to what I said earlier about my comedies in general, is that although this play, if properly produced and acted, should often have the air of being a gay charade, it was in fact written and re-written with great care and made far greater demands on such technical knowledge as I possess than any of the other plays in this volume. But it was worth the time and trouble, not only because of all the fun we and the audiences had with it, but also because here and there it seemed to me to create a new and valuable relationship between players and audience, and because it might possibly drop a hint or two to younger and more hopeful playwrights.

J. B. PRIESTLEY

January, 1949.

LABURNUM GROVE

An Immoral Comedy in Three Acts

TO
EDMUND GWENN

CHARACTERS

(in order of appearance)

ELSIE RADFERN
MRS. (LUCY) BAXLEY
BERNARD BAXLEY
GEORGE RADFERN
HAROLD RUSS
JOE FLETTEN
MRS. (DOROTHY) RADFERN
INSPECTOR STACK
SERGEANT MORRIS

ACT I
Sunday Evening

ACT II
SCENE I. Early Monday Morning
SCENE II. Monday Afternoon

ACT III
Monday Evening

The whole action takes place in the living-room of the Radferns' house, *Ferndale*, Laburnum Grove, Shooters Green, a suburb of North London.

Laburnum Grove—Copyright, 1933, *by John Boynton Priestley.*

"Laburnum Grove" was first produced in London on November 28th, 1933, at the Duchess Theatre, with the following cast:

ELSIE RADFERN	MARGERY PICKARD
MRS. (LUCY) BAXLEY	ETHEL COLERIDGE
BERNARD BAXLEY	MELVILLE COOPER
GEORGE RADFERN	EDMUND GWENN
HAROLD RUSS	FRANCIS JAMES
JOE FLETTEN	JAMES HARCOURT
MRS. (DOROTHY) RADFERN	MARY JERROLD
INSPECTOR STACK	DAVID HAWTHORNE
SERGEANT MORRIS	DOUGLAS PAYNE

Produced by CEDRIC HARDWICKE

ACT I

The Scene is the living-room in the RADFERNS' *house, "Ferndale",
Laburnum Grove, Shooters Green—a suburb in North London.
The time is Sunday evening in late summer, still daylight at first.
On the back wall from right to left are a small window, then a door
that can lead directly into a greenhouse, then a larger window looking out on to a back garden. In the right wall, downstage, is a
door into a small hall, leading to the front door of the house and
the stairs. In the left wall is a door leading into the kitchen. Against
this wall, beyond the door, is a small sideboard with whisky decanter,
soda syphon, and several bottles of beer on it. In the corner, between the left wall and the large window, is an oval or round table,
on easy castors, that is laid for supper but is covered with two cloths.
In the opposite corner is a small table on which is a telephone, and
near it a loud-speaker and wireless set. There are one or two easy
chairs and several dining-room chairs in the room, which is brightly,
comfortably furnished in a suburban style. When the curtain rises*
MRS. BAXLEY *and* ELSIE *are discovered seated at a small card table
in the centre.* MRS. BAXLEY *is a woman in her forties, dressed in
a smart-shabby style, a mixture of silliness and calculating selfish-
ness.* ELSIE *is a pretty but rather petulant and discontented girl of
twenty or so, the kind you see in the High Street of every fairly
prosperous suburb.* ELSIE *is shuffling a pack of cards and when she
has finished she cuts them into two, towards* MRS. BAXLEY, *who
then proceeds to put them together and deal them face downward
on the table into six packs.*

MRS. BAXLEY (*as she finishes dealing the cards*): To yourself . . .
your home . . . your wish. Have you wished, Elsie?

ELSIE: Yes, auntie. Very definitely.

MRS. BAXLEY: What you do expect—what you don't expect and
what's sure to come true. Mind you, I'm not always in the mood,
you know. Sometimes I can't see things at all, and then at other times,
it's all as clear as anything, and everything I tell people comes true.
It's a gift, you know. One can't control it.

ELSIE (*with signs of excitement*): Well, you must be in the mood
to-night, Aunt Lucy.

MRS. BAXLEY: Why? What's exciting you to-night? I know there's
something.

[5]

ELSIE: I'll tell you afterwards. It would spoil it if I told you now. You must tell me things first.

MRS. BAXLEY: All right, but I hope your mother won't come back in the middle of it, because she doesn't like me to read the cards for you—she told me so, the other day.

ELSIE: Mother won't be back from Mrs. Repington's until after supper. That's why she got supper all ready (*indicating table in corner*) before she went. So you needn't worry about her.

MRS. BAXLEY: All right then.

Picks up first lot of cards and examines them, and does the same with succeeding lots throughout the speeches that follow. She assumes the usual far-away mystical air of the clairvoyant, which is in sharp and comic contrast to her tone and manner when making remarks not directly concerned with the fortune-telling.

MRS. BAXLEY: Um . . . Um . . . Well, the first thing I see, Elsie, is a great surprise. Yes, you're going to have a great surprise.

ELSIE: A surprise? When?

MRS. BAXLEY: Very soon.

ELSIE: How soon? Next week?

MRS. BAXLEY: Perhaps sooner.

ELSIE: Well, it can't be much sooner. It's Sunday night and nearly next week now.

MRS. BAXLEY: Well, it's coming very soon. And it isn't a nice surprise. I don't think you'll like it.

ELSIE (*reproachfully*): Oh—Aunt Lucy!

MRS. BAXLEY: I can't help it. I'm only telling you what's here in the cards.

ELSIE: What's it about?

MRS. BAXLEY (*brooding over more cards*): I think it's something to do with a medium-coloured man.

ELSIE (*thinking hard*): A medium-coloured man? Is he young?

MRS. BAXLEY: No, I don't think he is. Your home comes into it.

ELSIE (*disappointed*): Oh!

MRS. BAXLEY: Yes, I think the medium-coloured man must be your father.

ELSIE: Is it—is it about an engagement?

MRS. BAXLEY: No, I don't see an engagement connected with it. I think you're simply going to get a great surprise from your father.

ELSIE (*disgusted*): That's just like the cards. They're always like that. A great surprise—from Dad—of all people! I suppose the great

[6]

surprise will be that he's grown two tomatoes in his greenhouse. Or they're going to play Handel's Largo for him on the wireless. Or he can't find his pipe or one of his silly detective stories or something. Dad!

MRS. BAXLEY: Well, it's all here—quite plain.

ELSIE: Perhaps you're not in the mood to-night, auntie.

MRS. BAXLEY (*coldly*): As a matter of fact, I am seeing very clearly to-night. But it was you who asked me to read the cards, Elsie, and if you don't choose to accept what I see, I'll stop.

ELSIE: No. Sorry. Go on.

MRS. BAXLEY (*examining more cards*): Also a great surprise for two people staying in your house. And they're going to leave quite soon.

ELSIE: That must be you and Uncle Bernard. You're the only people staying in the house, besides Dad and Mother and me.

MRS. BAXLEY (*not pleased at this*): Humph! Very queer. I can't imagine what surprise we'll get and anyhow we hadn't thought of leaving you yet and nothing's been said about our going. Humph! Perhaps I'm not getting it right after all.

ELSIE: Go on. Tell me some more.

MRS. BAXLEY (*examining last lots of cards*): You're going to travel. And quite soon.

ELSIE (*excitedly*): I'm not, am I?

MRS. BAXLEY: You are. It's all here. A journey. Strange beds. Crossing water. And it'll come as a great surprise. This isn't the same surprise as the other, though. That's quite different. You're going on a long journey very soon, across water.

ELSIE: It sounds too good to be true. You're not just making this up to please me, are you?

MRS. BAXLEY (*on her dignity*): Certainly not. I never make up anything to please anybody.

ELSIE: Then it's just the cards again. They call anything a long journey, just to make it exciting. They've had me before like that. They tell you about a journey and crossing water and a strange bed and a fair woman and a dark man until you think you're in for something marvellously exciting, and then it turns out you're going to spend the night at Aunt Florrie's at Sydenham. I'll believe in this long journey when I see it. I'll bet it turns out to be like that great surprise from the medium-coloured man—just something dull about Dad.

MRS. BAXLEY (*putting the cards together*): Next time you'd better tell your own fortune. I've told you all I could see.

[7]

ELSIE: But you've missed the really important thing. Wasn't there anything about an engagement for me?

MRS. BAXLEY: Not a sign of one.

ELSIE (*triumphantly*): Well, that's where they're wrong—and it just shows you—because I'm really engaged now, and I'll be properly engaged to-night.

MRS. BAXLEY: Engaged! Well, I am surprised.

ELSIE: You don't sound very pleasantly surprised, Aunt Lucy.

MRS. BAXLEY: If you must know, I'm not.

ELSIE: Why?

MRS. BAXLEY: Because I think you're too young to be engaged.

ELSIE: I'm not too young. I'm twenty.

MRS. BAXLEY: Well, what's twenty. You're not old enough to know your own mind.

ELSIE: Yes, I am. I don't see what age has got to do with knowing your own mind. I've always been old enough to know my own mind.

MRS. BAXLEY: That's what you think. Is it that young man who was here the other night?

ELSIE: Yes, Harold Russ. And I'm bringing him here to supper to-night and he's going to ask Dad.

MRS. BAXLEY: Funny time to come, isn't it, when he's had all day to do it in?

ELSIE: He couldn't help it. He's been helping a friend of his to sell second-hand cars, and he had to take a man out in one of them to-night. He wants to start in the second-hand car business for himself, when he gets some capital.

MRS. BAXLEY: Well, I can tell you one thing, Elsie. Your Dad doesn't like him much.

ELSIE: I know that. But then Dad doesn't really know him. And you know what Dad is. If Harold was as dull as ditchwater and lived here in Laburnum Grove or somewhere in Shooters Green, and went into the City in the morning and came home at night and pottered about in a greenhouse, Dad would think he was marvellous. But just because Harold's smart and wants to get on and once laughed at Laburnum Grove and Shooters Green——

Enter BERNARD BAXLEY, *a rather glossy, shifty fellow in his forties, always either over-confident or uneasy.*

MRS. BAXLEY: Well, I don't see anything to laugh at.

BAXLEY: Who's laughing at what?

ELSIE: I'm talking about Harold Russ, uncle.

[8]

BAXLEY: Oh—your boy friend who was here the other night.

ELSIE: Yes. Dad doesn't like him because he once made fun of Laburnum Grove here and Shooters Green.

MRS. BAXLEY: And I see nothing to laugh at. It's a very nice, respectable, refined neighbourhood.

ELSIE: That's just it. It's all so deadly dull, all slippers and greenhouses. Nothing ever happens except that the people at *Ben Machree* have bought a new car or the woman at *Heather Brow* is going to have a baby.

MRS. BAXLEY: Well, wait until you're going to have a baby, you'll find it exciting enough.

BAXLEY: Ah—Elsie's like me. She doesn't care for this ultra-respectable, humdrum, suburban sort of existence. I don't mind paying it a visit—like this—just while I'm wondering what to do next, but I couldn't live in it. I want life. There's no life here. What is there here for a man who's been out East?

MRS. BAXLEY (*emphatically*): I can tell you what there is for a *woman* who's been out East—three decent meals a day and a good night's sleep.

BAXLEY: Yes, but Lucy, you never got into the life out there.

MRS. BAXLEY: Well, you didn't seem sorry to get out of it.

ELSIE: Well, I agree with Uncle Bernard. And I know Harold does too. Oh—what time is it?

BAXLEY: Just after nine.

ELSIE: I promised to meet him at the Tube station in ten minutes. I must fly. (*Hurries out.*)

BAXLEY: What's on?

MRS. BAXLEY: She's got herself engaged to that chap, and she's bringing him here so that he can ask George's permission.

BAXLEY: Oh—that's it, is it?

MRS. BAXLEY: Yes, and another thing. What he's after is borrowing some money from George to set him up in the second-hand car business.

BAXLEY: How do you know?

MRS. BAXLEY: I don't know. But it's a good guess—from something that Elsie let drop. Besides, that chap wouldn't bother asking her father's permission if he wasn't after something.

BAXLEY: Well, how does that affect us?

MRS. BAXLEY: Did you see that man——?

BAXLEY: Simpson? Yes. And they won't look at me unless I can

[9]

put down four hundred and fifty pounds, and they only give me until Wednesday.

MRS. BAXLEY: Then the sooner we ask for that four hundred and fifty pounds the better.

BAXLEY: Shall I do it direct through him or had you better try and work it through Dorothy?

MRS. BAXLEY: Not through Dorothy.

BAXLEY: Why not? After all, she's your sister.

MRS. BAXLEY: Yes, but I think she's getting a bit fed-up with us. We've been here nearly a fortnight this time, and it's the third time we've stayed with them during this last year. And she knows you've been borrowing pretty freely from George. How much have you had out of him now?

BAXLEY: Well, you know.

MRS. BAXLEY (grimly): Oh no, I don't. I only know about the amounts you've mentioned to me, that's all.

BAXLEY: Well, that's all there's been.

MRS. BAXLEY: And the rest!

BAXLEY: There might be—perhaps ten bob here and there—just something and nothing.

MRS. BAXLEY: Too many somethings and nothings. Dorothy may be my sister and easy-going as a rule, but I think she's had about enough. She's been rather sharp with both of us, I've noticed, these last few days. So you try George himself. He's good-natured enough for anything.

BAXLEY: So he ought to be. Nothing to worry about. Just stuck in the one business and let it keep him. Money for nothing. You've only got to look at him to see that it must be money for nothing. He doesn't know he's born.

MRS. BAXLEY: He ought to be married to you for a bit and then he would.

BAXLEY: All right, all right. The point is, are we going to try him to-night?

MRS. BAXLEY: We'd better try him now, before Elsie's darling Harold begins borrowing.

BAXLEY: Is Dorothy in?

MRS. BAXLEY: No, she's visiting a friend of hers, Mrs. Repington, and she won't be back until after supper. So now's the time.

BAXLEY: He's out there in the greenhouse, I suppose?

MRS. BAXLEY: Yes, call him in.

[10]

BAXLEY: Half a minute. I haven't worked out the tactics yet. Might be a good idea to sort of take a high hand with him. After all, I've seen the world, I've been somewhere, I've done something, and he hasn't. Now suppose I——

MRS. BAXLEY: Suppose you just call him in and get done with it. And if you won't, I will.

She goes towards door at back and calls:

George, George.

RADFERN (*off, at back*): All right. Just coming.

He enters through the door at the back. He is a man about fifty with nothing remarkable about his appearance, though even at the first there should be a certain quiet assurance and authority visible beneath his easy manner. At this hour, he is very much the suburban householder at ease, wearing slippers and an old coat, and smoking a pipe. He is carrying two small tomatoes in one hand, and he displays these with an air of humorous triumph.

RADFERN (*holding out tomatoes*): Look at these. What more do you want? All fresh.

MRS. BAXLEY: Charming. They look very nice, George. Won't you sit down?

RADFERN: Beautiful tomatoes. The Special Radfern brand. Apply Ferndale Nurseries, Laburnum Grove, Shooters Green. (*Looking round.*) But I thought supper was ready.

MRS. BAXLEY: No. I called you in, George, because we just wanted to have a word with you while we're by ourselves.

RADFERN: Oh—I see. Well? (*A pause.*)

MRS. BAXLEY (*impatiently*): Go on, Bernard.

BAXLEY: It's like this, old man. I've just seen this chap Simpson I mentioned to you the other day. Only time I could see him, because he's out of London all the week. I think I told you the other day— it's a marvellous opportunity.

RADFERN: Doesn't sound like one to me. When there isn't much business, I don't see that you're going to sell a lot of business supplies.

BAXLEY: You are with these things. I've worked all that out, old man. Trust me. But the point is this, they say I can have that agency —exclusive agency—if I put down four hundred and fifty pounds.

RADFERN: Put it down?

BAXLEY: Just put it down, that's all, old man. These people don't need the money, but their agent has to put down four hundred and fifty pounds.

RADFERN: But you haven't got four hundred and fifty pounds, have you, Bernard?

BAXLEY: Of course I haven't. I haven't been as lucky as you have, old man.

RADFERN: How do you know I've been lucky?

MRS. BAXLEY: He doesn't know. That's only his silly way of talking, George. We all know you've worked hard for your money.

BAXLEY: Certainly. I never suggested you hadn't. And I know you've lent me a bit already, George.

RADFERN (*good-humouredly*): About two hundred and fifty pounds, I think, Bernard.

BAXLEY: Which you'll get back, of course.

MRS. BAXLEY: Of course.

BAXLEY: But what we feel is that if you'd simply let me have this four hundred and fifty to put down——

MRS. BAXLEY: You see, it's a wonderful chance for Bernard.

BAXLEY: And I thought I'd come straight to you instead of going to Dorothy, even if she *is* Lucy's sister.

RADFERN: Quite right. We can keep Dorothy out of this. As a matter of fact, she doesn't know you owe me two hundred and fifty already.

MRS. BAXLEY (*bitterly*): And she's not the only one.

BAXLEY: Well, I don't like dragging women into these things. And I know George doesn't. Well, what about it, old man?

RADFERN (*musingly*): Four hundred and fifty. You know, it's quite a bit of money, Bernard. I'll have to think about it.

BAXLEY: There isn't much time, and I don't want to lose the chance.

RADFERN: I quite understand that, old man, but four hundred and fifty on top of the two hundred and fifty you've had already is quite a lot of money—(*Who has strolled towards the back, suddenly turning*) Look here, ask me again after supper, and I'll give you an answer.

    He goes out. BAXLEY *and* MRS. BAXLEY *watch him go, then look at one another, raising their eyebrows.*

MRS. BAXLEY: What do you think?

BAXLEY: That'll be all right. After supper, over a drink or two, I'll be able to touch him.

MRS. BAXLEY: Yes, but what about this chap of Elsie's?

BAXLEY: He'll have gone then.

MRS. BAXLEY: Listen, if they want to be alone with him *before* supper, it's better for us than if they wait.

BAXLEY: That's right. Leave 'em to it, then. After all, I got in first.

MRS. BAXLEY: This sounds like them.

Voices heard outside. Enter ELSIE, *looking very bright. She is followed by* HAROLD RUSS, *not bad-looking and smartly dressed, but with nothing in him. In twenty years' time he will look and behave exactly like* BAXLEY.

ELSIE (*happy and excited*): Harold, this is my Aunt Lucy and my Uncle Bernard. But you've all met before, haven't you?

MRS. BAXLEY (*smiling very falsely*): Yes. Last Tuesday, I think it was. What a lovely day it's been, hasn't it?

HAROLD: Yes, hasn't it? I've seen a lot of it, too. Been taking a fellow round in a car, trying to sell it to him.

BAXLEY: Any luck?

HAROLD: Shouldn't be surprised.

BAXLEY: How *is* business?

HAROLD: Not too good. How are things with you?

BAXLEY: Well, just now—I'm—er—looking round.

HAROLD: Oh—yes. I remember you telling me, the other night. Been out East, haven't you?

BAXLEY: That's right. Malay States. Singapore chiefly. Wish I'd never come back. It's a man's life out there—even yet, a man's life. Isn't it, Lucy?

MRS. BAXLEY (*tartly*): I don't know about a man's life. I know it isn't a woman's life.

BAXLEY: She wanted to get back, you see. And I thought I'd give the Old Country another chance.

ELSIE: I'd love to travel. So would you, wouldn't you, Harold?

HAROLD: Wouldn't mind. I knock up and down a bit, you know.

BAXLEY: And now you're going to pop the question to Dad, eh?

HAROLD: Hello, who's been telling you?

BAXLEY (*fatuously*): Never mind, but we know. (*To* MRS. BAXLEY) Don't we?

MRS. BAXLEY (*with ferocious parody of him*): Yes, we know.

BAXLEY: And if you two want us to leave you to it, just say the word.

ELSIE: All right. Thanks. But I think we'll wait a bit.

MRS. BAXLEY (*with dignity*): If a proper opportunity presents it-self——

[13]

RADFERN *appears in doorway at back, carrying another tomato.*

HAROLD: Good evening, Mr. Radfern.

RADFERN: Oh—good evening. And there's another one (*indicating tomatoes*), making three. Do for supper.

ELSIE (*to* MRS. BAXLEY): You see, auntie. That's the surprise in the fortune. What did I tell you? Dad and his three tomatoes.

RADFERN (*pointing to cards on table*): Oh—you've been telling fortunes again, have you? Don't you know it's unlucky to read the cards on Sunday?

MRS. BAXLEY: That's just superstition.

RADFERN: Of course it is. But then it's all superstition, isn't it, and you might as well be thoroughly superstitious while you're at it. Well, what do the cards say to-night?

MRS. BAXLEY: A great surprise for Elsie. And she's going on a long journey quite soon.

HAROLD: Oh?

ELSIE (*smiling at him*): Well, I wouldn't mind.

RADFERN: Anywhere but Laburnum Grove and Shooters Green, eh?

ELSIE: No, not anywhere. But somewhere exciting.

BAXLEY: I know what you want. You go——

RADFERN (*chiming in hastily*): Out East. And I said it first, Bernard.

ELSIE: Everybody's so smug and settled down and dull here, and so pleased with themselves.

RADFERN: Well, why shouldn't they be pleased with themselves? They've got nice peaceful homes——

ELSIE (*bitterly*): Yes, and greenhouses and wireless sets.

RADFERN (*good-humouredly*): Well, what do you want us to have —elephants and tigers and a scenic railway?

ELSIE: Yes—but it's all so—so——

HAROLD (*loftily*): Suburban.

ELSIE: Yes—suburban.

RADFERN: That's all right to me. When your mother and I came here, we thought we'd got somewhere. That's why we were so pleased with ourselves and ready to live a nice quiet life.

BAXLEY: That's all right for you, George. You've always led that sort of life. But give me—adventure.

MRS. BAXLEY (*bitterly*): Oh—and since when?

HAROLD: I know what he means. I'm just the same.

ELSIE: I am too.

RADFERN: Well, I'm not. You know, you don't get this sort of life handed to you on a plate.

ELSIE: What do you mean, Dad?

RADFERN: I mean this. Though *you* get all this handed to you on a plate—given, free, gratis, and for nothing—*I* don't. And (*pointing outside*) he doesn't and *he* doesn't.

BAXLEY (*staring fatuously*): Who doesn't?

ELSIE: I don't see what you're driving at.

RADFERN: Now listen. Here's Shooters Green, one of North London's newest suburbs. Very clean, very respectable, bright as a new pin. Nice little shops in the High Street. *Yes, Madam, shall I send it? Certainly, Madam.* Tea rooms. Picture palaces. *Good morning, Mrs. Robinson. Good evening, Mr. Johnson.* And here's Laburnum Grove, one of its best roads, very quiet, very select, best type of semi-detached villas. *Ben Machree. Craig Y Don. Mon Repos.* All nations, you see. *Heather Brow*—though there isn't any heather for miles around. And us—*Ferndale.* Nice little houses. Nice people. Quiet, respectable. No scandals. No brokers' men. No screams in the night. Morris Oxfords, little greenhouses, wireless sets.

ELSIE (*rather bitterly*): That's it. You know it all right, Dad.

HAROLD: Gosh—yes!

RADFERN (*good-humouredly*): Yes, I know it. But you don't. You're like somebody who thinks that buns grow on trees. You don't know the world. Because all this has been handed to you on a plate, you think it's been handed to everybody else——

BAXLEY: Well, hasn't it?

RADFERN: No. There are chaps who've sweated their guts out so they could settle down here. And God knows what they've risked—some of 'em. You don't know where they've been or what they've done.

BAXLEY (*with suggestion of contempt*): Well, George, I hope nobody shoots you to-morrow morning on your way to the City. I haven't noticed you running many risks.

RADFERN: Oh—me. Well, of course I'm different.

BAXLEY: You've been lucky.

MRS. BAXLEY: I'm sure George has always worked hard, even if he has been safe and comfortable in his own business.

ELSIE (*looking at her*): Er——

MRS. BAXLEY (*taking the hint*): Yes. Come on, Bernard.

BAXLEY: What for? (*As she glares at him.*) Oh—yes. Certainly.
They both go out.

RADFERN (*staring after them*): What's the matter with those two?

ELSIE: They're leaving us alone because they know we want to talk to you.

RADFERN: I see.

HAROLD: It's like this, Mr. Radfern—Elsie and I——

ELSIE: Dad, we're engaged.

HAROLD: Well, we want to be.

RADFERN: I see. (*To* ELSIE) Have you told your mother yet?

ELSIE: No, I'll tell her when she comes in, after supper.

HAROLD: Naturally I wanted to talk to you about it.

RADFERN: Quite so.

HAROLD: We'd like to get married very soon.

RADFERN: What on?

HAROLD: Well, that's the point. Of course I'd like to get a bit more settled first.

RADFERN: Let me see, aren't you helping a friend of yours to sell second-hand cars just now?

HAROLD (*loftily*): Yes. Of course that's just while I'm looking round.

RADFERN: Ah—you're looking round, are you? Like your Uncle Bernard, Elsie. He's great on looking round.

ELSIE (*impatiently*): Oh, Harold, why don't you talk to him properly. The point is, Dad, we're engaged—and Harold knows of a second-hand car business he could buy if he only had some capital——

RADFERN: Not four hundred and fifty pounds, by any chance, is it?

HAROLD: Well, it could be more and it could be a bit less. I can give you the figures.

RADFERN (*stopping him*): Not just now. I asked if it was four hundred and fifty pounds because that seems to be the popular amount to-night.

Front door bell rings loudly.

ELSIE: Oh—bother! Who can that be?

RADFERN: Probably Joe Fletten. I expected him to look in this evening.

ELSIE (*petulantly*): Why does he want to come here at this time?

He'll be coming in the middle of the night to ask about his greenhouse soon.

RADFERN: I shouldn't be surprised. Well, just let him in. (ELSIE *goes out.*) It looks as if we'll have to postpone this little talk.

HAROLD: That's all right. We could talk it over after supper perhaps.

RADFERN: Yes, perhaps we could. But it seems to me I'm going to be rather busy after supper to-night. By the way, you've never thought of becoming an agent for business supplies, have you?

HAROLD: Not my line. But I do know a car when I see one. And there's a business there just waiting to be picked up——

RADFERN: If only you can put some money down. Just put it down, eh?

HAROLD: That's all it amounts to. You see——

RADFERN (*stopping him*): After supper.

> *Enter* ELSIE, *followed by* FLETTEN, *a rather loud, jovial, middle-aged man, somewhat lower in the social scale than anybody we have met here so far. He carries his hat.*

FLETTEN: Good evening, Mr. Radfern.

RADFERN: Good evening, Joe. Thought you might be looking in.

FLETTEN (*to* HAROLD): Good evening. Seen you before here, haven't I?

HAROLD (*rather sulkily*): I believe so. Good evening.

FLETTEN: Sorry to be so late, Mr. Radfern. But that greenhouse of mine's giving me a lot of trouble, and I just wanted a tip or two about——

RADFERN (*hastily*): About your tomato plants. Come on then, I'll show you how I manage them. (*Moves towards door at back.*)

FLETTEN (*as he follows*): Shan't keep you a minute. (*Jovially to* ELSIE *and* HAROLD) This greenhouse business is a terrible hobby, I give you my word. Keeps you busy all the time, all the time.

> *They go out.*

HAROLD (*softly, grumbling*): I hope that chap's not going to stay for hours.

ELSIE (*going over to him*): No, he won't stay long. But he's an awful old nuisance, though. Comes here two or three times a week now, to look at Dad's greenhouse. Oh—Harold—I hope it'll be all right.

HAROLD: Well, it ought to be. Only—I don't think your father likes me much.

ELSIE: He will when he gets to know you better. He's just a bit stupid, that's all.

HAROLD: And I don't know that I'm very keen on *him*.

ELSIE: Oh—Dad's all right when you know him. He's dull, but he's rather nice, and he'll always do anything for me. It's mother I'm frightened of. Dad's easy.

Door into house opens and MRS. BAXLEY *peeps into the room.*

MRS. BAXLEY: Oh—all alone?

ELSIE (*not too pleased*): Yes, you can come in. (*As she comes in, leaving the door open behind her*) Mr. Fletten called and Dad's gone back into the greenhouse with him.

MRS. BAXLEY: Can't imagine what your Dad sees in that man. Common, I call him.

HAROLD: Yes, looks like a bookie's clerk.

MRS. BAXLEY (*with dignity*): I've never seen a bookie's clerk. (BAXLEY *looks in.*) All right, Bernard, you needn't stand there looking so silly. You can come in. (*He does.*) I wonder if we could get ready for supper now.

BAXLEY: That's a good idea!

ELSIE: Yes, why not?

MRS. BAXLEY: I was only thinking that if supper was here, all ready, your father might take it into his head to ask that Mr. Fletten to stay, and we don't want that, do we?

ELSIE: Good Lord, no!

HAROLD: No, don't let's have anybody else, if we can help it.

BAXLEY: Hear, hear!

ELSIE: But he won't stay, he never does. We can risk it.

MRS. BAXLEY: Come on then, Bernard. Don't just sit there.

He, MRS. BAXLEY *and* ELSIE *move the table forward, removing the small table with the cards on it, and take off the cloths.* ELSIE *can go into the kitchen for something, and* BAXLEY *can be putting the beer or whisky from the sideboard on to the table.* HAROLD *should stand up looking on in a rather lofty fashion.*

Why your Dad won't have a servant in the house, I can't imagine. He can well afford it.

BAXLEY: Two or three, I should think.

ELSIE: It's one of his little fads. Mother doesn't mind. She and the char do it easily—with my help.

MRS. BAXLEY (*sarcastically*): I'm glad you said—*with your help.*

ELSIE: It's not my fault I'm kept at home, pretending to help mother, instead of going out to work. I'd much rather go out to work.

BAXLEY: They're coming in.

Enter RADFERN *and* FLETTEN. *The supper table, now in the centre of the room, is being laid for five people. The meal consists of slices of ham and tongue, cold potatoes, stewed fruit and custard, bread and butter. To drink—whisky, beer and a jug of lemonade. During this period of the action, the light can be going rapidly.*

FLETTEN (*jovially*): Well, well, the feast is spread.

RADFERN: Have a bite with us, Joe?

FLETTEN (*moving towards door into house*): No, thank you, Mr. Radfern. Must be getting along. I'll look in to-morrow night, then.

RADFERN (*following him*): Do. Any time after eight.

FLETTEN (*turning as he reaches door, to* MRS. BAXLEY): Nice weather we're having, isn't it? I should think it is. Good night, all. Good night.

The others murmur 'good night'. RADFERN *follows him out.*

MRS. BAXLEY (*softly but with energy*): He made me jump—with his nice weather! Common, I call him.

BAXLEY (*quoting*): *The feast is spread.* That's a way to talk. Anyone would think he had never seen anybody laying a supper table before.

MRS. BAXLEY: Perhaps he hasn't.

BAXLEY: Never seen the world, that's his trouble.

ELSIE: Oh, he's just one of Dad's silly old men. If it wasn't for the greenhouse he wouldn't come here.

MRS. BAXLEY: Well, if he's what you get when you keep greenhouses I'm glad I don't keep one.

ELSIE (*softly*): Harold—remember. You must get Dad's answer to-night.

HAROLD: Yes, I know, I know.

MRS. BAXLEY: And Bernard, don't forget—after supper.

BAXLEY: Leave it to me.

Enter RADFERN, *who switches on lights at door. It is essential that the supper table should be brilliantly lit.*

RADFERN (*heartily*): Let's have some light on the subject. And plenty of it. (*Comes forward.*) Supper ready? Good! Look at those tomatoes. Home grown on the premises. They absolutely light up the table.

MRS. BAXLEY: If that's how you can go on about three tomatoes,

I'm glad you don't grow pineapples. I don't know what would happen then.

RADFERN (*looks at supper table*): Ham, tongue, salad. Beer. Everything in its place and just what I wanted. Let's get started. Come on, everybody.

> *They seat themselves in this order:* RADFERN *full facing the audience,* ELSIE *on one side of him,* MRS. BAXLEY *on the other, then* HAROLD *next to* ELSIE, *and* BAXLEY *next to* MRS. BAXLEY. RADFERN *helps them to meat, and they help themselves to salad and potatoes, making a few conventional remarks in the bustle. But when the dialogue begins, they are all quietly attentive.*

BAXLEY: This ham looks good, George.

RADFERN (*heartily*): I expect it *is* good, Bernard. You know, I don't think there's a meal in the week I enjoy more than Sunday night supper, and I couldn't tell you why. Unless it's all so nice and peaceful.

ELSIE (*with a touch of contempt*): You're all for it being nice and peaceful, aren't you, Dad?

RADFERN (*with mock humility*): I'm afraid I am. I'm not like you folks.

MRS. BAXLEY: Don't count me with them. I don't want any adventures. I want to see a regular income arriving.

HAROLD: We'd all like that.

RADFERN (*faintly sardonic*): Yes, I believe you would. But it's not so easy these days.

BAXLEY (*with loud complacency*): It's not so easy if you're straight. That's the point. I like money as much as the next man, but it's got to be clean money.

HAROLD (*in the same strain*): Of course. I'm just the same. Won't touch it if it isn't straight.

MRS. BAXLEY: Good gracious! I should think not.

BAXLEY: I've had chances of the other kind—packets of it——

RADFERN (*ironically*): No, Bernard, have you really?

BAXLEY: I have, George. But I've always turned it down. Tainted money. Wouldn't touch it.

HAROLD: Wouldn't touch it with a barge pole. I've had my chances too—you get them in our business—but I'm the same as you—wouldn't look at queer money.

ELSIE: And I hope you never will, Harold.

HAROLD: Of course I shan't.

BAXLEY (*sententiously*): It's the only thing to do, whatever happens —keep straight.

RADFERN: Well, I'm glad to hear you fellows feel like that. I used to feel like it myself in the old days.

ELSIE: What do you mean, Dad—in the old days?

RADFERN: I mean, in the days when I used to be in the wholesale paper trade.

BAXLEY: But you're still in the wholesale paper trade.

RADFERN: How do you know I am?

BAXLEY: I've always understood you were.

RADFERN: Well, I'm not. Haven't been in it for several years.

BAXLEY: But the firm's there and the office——?

RADFERN: Oh, I keep them going, but that's just a blind. Pass the mustard, will you, Elsie.

ELSIE: But I never knew you'd changed your business.

RADFERN: No? I don't think this ham's as nice as the last. I must tell your mother about it, Elsie.

ELSIE: But listen, Dad—does Mother know you're not in the paper business any more?

RADFERN: No, she doesn't. And I don't want a word of any of this repeated to her. She's a bit old-fashioned in some ways and it might give her a shock. You can ask me any questions you like, and I'll answer 'em truthfully. But not a word to her. If you can't promise that, we'll change the subject.

HAROLD and ELSIE (*together*): I promise.

MRS. BAXLEY: So do I.

BAXLEY: All right to me.

RADFERN: Honest to God? (*They murmur agreement.*) That's settled then. Not a word to her. Now what is it you'd like to know?

ELSIE: Dad, when did you leave your old business?

RADFERN: Do you remember that about four or five years ago we were very hard up?

ELSIE: Was it the year when we didn't go away for the holidays?

RADFERN: It was. We were on enough rocks without going to the seaside. We might easily have been sold up. Well, that was when I finished with the wholesale paper trade.

HAROLD: What happened?

RADFERN: Oh, I'd struggled with the business ever since I came back from the war. Slaved at it. Then the slump came. More slavery. But we had a good little connection in the fine-quality trade. And somebody wanted that, a big firm. They made me an offer. I didn't like it or the chap who made it. I turned it down, so this big firm did me in—never mind how—but they did. They won all right. Clever chap that, he's been knighted since—the dirty swine.

BAXLEY: And then—what?

RADFERN: Well, having given honesty a fair chance, I thought I'd try the other thing.

MRS. BAXLEY: The *other thing?*

RADFERN: Yes.

MRS. BAXLEY: You don't mean—dishonesty?

RADFERN: I do.

BAXLEY: You're pulling our legs.

RADFERN: Certainly not.

MRS. BAXLEY: Then you are going to tell me you're deliberately dishonest?

RADFERN: That's what I am telling you.

ELSIE: But Dad, it's ridiculous. You're talking as if you were a crook.

RADFERN (*nonchalantly*): Well, I am a crook.

MRS. BAXLEY: A crook!

RADFERN: Yes, a crook. A criminal. An enemy of society.

They all stare at him open-mouthed. ELSIE *recovers first.*

ELSIE (*getting up*): Dad, you're being funny.

BAXLEY: Course he is. That'll do now, George. We've bought it.

RADFERN (*with quiet earnestness*): I'm perfectly serious, Bernard. This isn't a joke. Have a little more salad, Elsie?

ELSIE (*staring at him, faltering*): No thanks, Dad. I—don't feel very hungry.

RADFERN: Now come along, none of that. Never let anything put you off your food—that's one of my mottoes. What do you say, Harold?

HAROLD (*dazed*): Yes—Mr. Radfern—I should think—that's a good idea.

MRS. BAXLEY (*solemnly*): George Radfern, you don't look like a crook to me.

RADFERN: Yes, but you can't judge by appearances. Why do you think Joe Fletten comes here?

MRS. BAXLEY: You mean that man who comes to talk to you about greenhouses?

RADFERN: You must be innocent if you think that Joe Fletten knows anything about greenhouses. You've only got to look at him to see he's no gardener.

MRS. BAXLEY: I suppose he's a crook too?

RADFERN: Of course he is. Very old hand, Joe. He works under me in the same organisation. (*To* MRS. BAXLEY) Have a little more tongue?

MRS. BAXLEY (*faintly*): I can't eat what I've got.

ELSIE: Dad, do you really mean all this?

RADFERN: Of course I mean it. Every penny that's come into this house for the last few years has been dishonestly earned.

BAXLEY: My God!

RADFERN (*coolly*): Tainted money. You've eaten it and drunk it and it's clothed you and housed you and taken you to the pictures and sent you to the seaside. If I'd gone on trying to make an honest living, I don't know where you'd have been now, Elsie. As it is, look at us. So nicely off that Harold here—and your Uncle Bernard here —are both hoping I'll lend them several hundred pounds each, on very doubtful security.

HAROLD: Here, I say——

ELSIE: But Dad, what do you do?

MRS. BAXLEY: Do you *burgle* places?

RADFERN: Burgle places! Certainly not. Do I look as if I burgled places?

MRS. BAXLEY: No, you don't. But then you don't look like a crook at all to me.

ELSIE (*appealingly*): You're not. Are you, Dad?

RADFERN: I've told you—I am. And one slip—just one slip, that's all—and I'd be for it.

MRS. BAXLEY (*awed*): Prison!

RADFERN: Yes, and a good long spell of it too.

ELSIE (*looking at him in awe and terror*): Dad!

BAXLEY: But look here, George, what do you do?

RADFERN: Well, you might describe it as a private policy of inflation.

ELSIE: I don't know what that means.

MRS. BAXLEY: Neither do I.

ELSIE: Do you, Harold?

RADFERN: I'm ready for a little of that stewed fruit now, Elsie. Let's put these plates on the side. (*Makes a move.*)

ELSIE (*hastily*): No, let me do it, Dad.

MRS. BAXLEY: Stewed fruit!

RADFERN: That's it, stewed fruit. What about it?

MRS. BAXLEY: This is no time for stewed fruit.

RADFERN: Yes, of course it is. When do you want it?

BAXLEY: She doesn't mean that, old man. As a matter of fact, she's very fond of stewed fruit.

RADFERN: Good, and mind you, this is real garden rhubarb.

MRS. BAXLEY: I don't want garden rhubarb—I want the truth.

RADFERN: All right, Lucy, you shall have the truth, and garden rhubarb and custard too, if you like it.

MRS. BAXLEY: Custard!

ELSIE *puts the used plates on the sideboard and then begins serving the fruit and custard.*

BAXLEY: But what about this inflation business?

RADFERN: Ah, that. Well, a lot of people think this depression in trade is chiefly due to the fact that there isn't enough money in circulation. Like playing a game with counters and finding you haven't got enough counters to go round. Our organisation—my associates and myself—have been quietly busy these last few years trying to remedy this unhappy state of things. It started in America —forging and counterfeiting bonds and notes—and then developed here, but just lately the American end has been doing badly, almost stopped. But we're doing quite nicely here, and sometimes I think that things in England would have been worse if it hadn't been for us. In fact you might say we've been doing our bit.

BAXLEY (*dazed*): Forging and counterfeiting bonds and notes!

HAROLD (*awed*): My hat!

RADFERN (*blandly*): Very interesting work. It begins as an art and ends as a profitable business.

ELSIE: But is it—serious?

HAROLD: Is it *serious!*

RADFERN: One of the most serious crimes in the calendar, Elsie. You see, the banks don't like it, and what the banks don't like must be a serious crime nowadays, like blasphemy in the middle ages.

ELSIE: And you're mixed up in it?

RADFERN: I'm engaged in it, not mixed up in it. I was able to join the organisation at first because I happened to have a supply of the right sort of paper. Since then I've been on the staff. My job now is distribution. That's what takes me away, of course. I'm off to Birmingham early to-morrow morning.

MRS. BAXLEY: What, you're going to Birmingham on this crooked work?

RADFERN: Why not? If I can do it in London, I can do it in Birmingham. There's nothing peculiarly sacred about Birmingham, is there?

ELSIE: But are the police really after you?

BAXLEY: Don't be silly, Elsie. They must be. It's a terribly serious crime, forging bonds and counterfeiting notes.

RADFERN (*calmly*): I should think we've given Scotland Yard it's biggest and most worrying case for years. After us! They're after us. Detectives, police, bank officials, magistrates, judges, the Treasury, the Army, the Navy, the Air Force. We haven't even the League of Nations on our side.

BAXLEY: But I don't see how you've managed to go on so long without being found out.

RADFERN: Partly luck, partly good management. Of course you can't really tell what's happening on the other side. They may have got the net out, and it may be closing in on us now.

Telephone bell rings, very sharp and loud.

ELSIE (*with a little scream*): Oh—what's that?

She rises, MRS. BAXLEY *half rises, and* HAROLD *pushes his chair back.*

RADFERN (*coolly*): That's the telephone. I'll answer it. Have you got a bit of cheese there for me? (*Goes to telephone.*) Hello! No . . . I'm not . . . Well, I can't help it. You've got the wrong number. (*Comes back from telephone.*) Wants to know if I'm the North London Dogs Hospital.

ELSIE: Oh—it gave me such a fright.

RADFERN: Well, I'm sorry, but after all you wanted a bit of excitement, didn't you?

BAXLEY (*solemnly*): George, that might have been somebody who was after you, tracking you down.

HAROLD: Yes, it might.

RADFERN: And then again, it might not. If tracking people down consists of ringing them up and asking if they're the Dogs Hospital, we could all be Sherlock Holmeses.

ELSIE (*eagerly*): And after all, I don't suppose they'd think of looking for crooks of any kind in a place like Shooters Green.

RADFERN: Oh—yes, they would. They haven't your ideas, Elsie. People who break the law have got to live somewhere, and why not in Shooters Green and Laburnum Grove? They took away that solicitor who used to live at *Stella Maris* and gave him a couple of years. That was a start. Probably there are one or two more of us in Laburnum Grove who'll have to go yet.

HAROLD *pushes his chair well back and rises.*

Hello, what's the matter?

HAROLD (*muttering*): I must be going.

ELSIE (*disappointed*): Harold!

HAROLD: I'm sorry but I must be going.

RADFERN (*smoothly*): What about that little talk we were going to have? Another time, eh?

ELSIE (*moving round to him*): But, Harold, you can't go like this.

HAROLD (*muttering*): I'm sorry, but it's getting late and I'm feeling very tired——

> He moves towards the door. ELSIE *intercepts him, and puts a hand on his arm.*

ELSIE: Oh—but Harold.

HAROLD (*releasing himself and suddenly raising his voice in a rather hysterical manner*): Leave me alone. I tell you I've got to go. Good night.

> He hurries out and she follows him. The other three watch them, and then stare at the door. After a moment the outer door is heard to bang. Then ELSIE, *looking tearful, opens the door and stands in the doorway.*

MRS. BAXLEY: Has he gone?

ELSIE (*tearfully*): Yes. And I'm going to bed. Good night.

RADFERN (*gravely*): Listen, Elsie——

ELSIE (*shaking her head*): No, no more now. I can't, Dad. Good night.

> *She closes the door and vanishes.*

RADFERN (*looking after her, gravely*): Poor kid, I'm afraid she's got more than she bargained for.

MRS. BAXLEY (*tartly*): We've all got more than we bargained for, if you ask me. Even the great adventurer, Bernard here.

BAXLEY (*dazed, staring at* RADFERN): Look here, George, for God's sake tell us the truth now.

RADFERN (*impressively*): I'm telling you the truth. I've not been in the wholesale paper trade for the last four years. All this (*waves his hand*) comes out of the proceeds of illegal and criminal actions. Tainted money, Bernard. And you've been enjoying it for some time, and I believe you'd like a good slice more of it, wouldn't you? Tainted money. Ill-gotten gains. And mind you're not an accessory.

BAXLEY (*frightened*): I'll see to that.

MRS. BAXLEY: This is upsetting my stomach. Why, every time I see a policeman now, I'll be frightened out of my life.

RADFERN: Oh—forget about it.

MRS. BAXLEY (*scornfully*): Forget about it! (*There is a sharp ring at the front door bell.*) What's that?

RADFERN (*coolly*): I can tell you what that is. That's Dorothy and she's forgotten her front door key again. Now don't forget. Not a word to her.

BAXLEY (*moving towards door*): Here, I'm off upstairs.

MRS. BAXLEY: So am I. I couldn't face her to-night.

BAXLEY: Let's get out of the way first.

RADFERN (*almost pushing them in front of him*): Go on then, hurry up.

> *They hurry out and he follows, stopping to light his pipe. Then he goes out and re-enters with* MRS. RADFERN, *a pleasant-looking woman in her early forties.*

MRS. RADFERN (*staring*): Hello, where is everybody?

RADFERN: I think Elsie had a bit of a tiff with that young man of hers, and went to bed early to have a little cry about it.

MRS. RADFERN: Do you think I ought to go up?

RADFERN: No, leave her alone. She'll be all right.

MRS. RADFERN: Well, where are Bernard and Lucy?

RADFERN: They've just gone to bed.

MRS. RADFERN: They went early.

RADFERN (*very innocently*): Yes, I think they must have wanted to have a talk about something.

MRS. RADFERN (*taking her things off*): Well, I must say, Dad—though Lucy is my own sister—I wouldn't be heart-broken if they'd gone upstairs to talk about leaving us. And I know you wouldn't be.

RADFERN: No, I'd get over it. (*Begins putting supper things together.*) Here, I'll give you a hand with these.

MRS. RADFERN: No, you sit down and smoke your pipe in peace, Dad. You've got to get up early in the morning to get yourself off, haven't you?

RADFERN: Yes. Early train to Birmingham.

MRS. RADFERN: Well, then. (*She begins bustling about with things, but stops to add affectionately.*) You know, Dad, I sometimes think

[27]

you're a bit too quiet and easy-going, but—dear me!—Mrs. Repington's been letting drop one or two things about *her* husband—and I was thinking on the way back I ought to be thankful I've got a nice honest, sleepy old thing like you.

RADFERN (*giving her a pat on the shoulder*): Ah—now you're talking!
The curtain falls on them as they clear the table.

END OF ACT ONE

ACT II

SCENE I

SCENE: *Same as Act one.*

TIME: *Early next morning.*

> *The room has that very early morning look about it.* ELSIE, *not yet properly dressed, is discovered bringing in the milk. Then after a few moments* BAXLEY *enters. He is wearing an old dressing gown and looks dishevelled and still sleepy.*

BAXLEY (*yawning*): Morning.

ELSIE: Morning, uncle.

BAXLEY: Thought I heard somebody moving about down here.

ELSIE: It must have been me.

BAXLEY: Of course it was you. But you're usually the last downstairs and not the first. What made you get up so early?

ELSIE: I couldn't sleep. And why are you up, uncle?

BAXLEY: Well, I couldn't sleep either. And I suddenly remembered your Dad was going to Birmingham early this morning.

ELSIE: I know. I thought I'd get up and make his breakfast.

BAXLEY: That's a new idea, isn't it?

ELSIE: Yes. But the woman we have is away—ill. So I thought I'd get up and do it.

BAXLEY: Quite right, quite right. But, you know, if he were out East, a man like your Dad could have twenty servants—thirty servants. Waited on hand and foot.

ELSIE: I know.

BAXLEY: Hand and foot.

ELSIE: He could be here, if he wanted to.

BAXLEY: I dare say, but you see now why he won't have a servant living in the house, don't you? You see?

ELSIE: Yes.

BAXLEY: He's too clever for that, much too clever. He knows what he's doing. Those his boots?

ELSIE: Yes.

BAXLEY: They could do with a bit of a rub.

ELSIE: I was going to do them.

BAXLEY: No, no, I'll give 'em a rub. It'll pass the time. Get me the polishing outfit, will you, Elsie. (*Sits down with boots, yawning, while* ELSIE *brings him the polishing outfit.*) Thanks. Now I'll make a good job of these. It'll amuse your Dad. What are you giving him for breakfast?

ELSIE: Boiled eggs. They're easiest.

BAXLEY: How does he like his eggs boiled?

ELSIE: I can't remember.

BAXLEY (*reproachfully*): You ought to remember how your own Dad likes his eggs boiled.

ELSIE: Do you remember how *your* Dad liked his eggs boiled?

BAXLEY: Don't be silly, Elsie, that's quite different. You're a girl. And, besides, it's such a long time since I lived with my old governor.

ELSIE: What did your Dad do, uncle?

BAXLEY: He used to travel the North Midlands—from Wolverhampton to Stockport—for the Wesleyan Methodist Publishing Company, selling hymn-books and Sunday school prizes. He had to look religious all the time, so he always dressed in black, and he wore a chin beard, like a Mormon. And he didn't smoke, and he didn't drink, so he used to eat a lot of cough candy. Bags of it. Absolutely stank of cough candy. I can smell it now. (*He sniffs.*) A sort of mixture of treacle and fire-lighters.

ELSIE: Was he nice?

BAXLEY: No, he was hellishly dull.

ELSIE (*plaintively*): I thought my Dad was dull. And I wish he was now.

BAXLEY: Well, he isn't.

ELSIE: I know. Uncle, do you think it's really true—what Dad told us last night?

BAXLEY: Yes. Must be.

ELSIE: But Dad! Just think of it!

BAXLEY (*irritably*): It's no good telling me to think of it, Elsie. I've been thinking about it—and talking about it—half the night.

ELSIE: I've hardly slept a wink.

BAXLEY: I'm not surprised.

ELSIE: I got so frightened in the middle of the night.

BAXLEY: Well, if you ask me, you've got something to be frightened about.

ELSIE (*in tense whisper*): Listen, uncle—if they caught him, would he really be sent to prison?

BAXLEY: I should think he would. He'd get years and years. Penal servitude.

ELSIE: But he's never done anything before.

BAXLEY: What difference does that make, when he's been doing this all the time. This is a big job. They'd drop on him like a ton of bricks.

ELSIE (*awed*): Would they?

BAXLEY (*with gloomy pride*): Go for him tooth and nail. Yes, tooth and nail. Like a ton of bricks. Penal servitude for years and years —and years.

ELSIE: But, uncle—it's awful.

BAXLEY (*solemnly beginning on other boot*): Well, speaking as a man of the world who's *seen* the world—I call that a well-polished boot! It's pretty serious—pretty serious.

ELSIE: And they've only got to catch him.

BAXLEY: Just got to lay their hands on him, once, that's all.

ELSIE *stares at him in horror.* MRS. BAXLEY *enters, half dressed and looking very worn.* ELSIE *gives a tiny scream and whirls round.*

ELSIE: Oh—auntie—you made me jump.

MRS. BAXLEY: I dare say. Anything's enough to make anybody jump, in this house. What are you up so early for?

ELSIE: I'm getting Dad's breakfast ready.

MRS. BAXLEY: Well, I thought I'd just come down to see if I could do anything for him. And what are you doing, Bernard?

BAXLEY (*very off-handedly*): Oh—just giving George's boots a bit of a rub.

MRS. BAXLEY: Be careful—or you might be cleaning my boots next. Is the tea made yet?—because I must say I could do with a cup. (*Sits down wearily.*) What a night!

BAXLEY (*irritably*): We know, we know.

MRS. BAXLEY: She doesn't know, does she? (*To* ELSIE) I haven't had such a night for years. Talked and talked about it all, then thought and thought about it all, and then when I did get a bit of sleep, I had to dream about policemen, hundreds of policemen.

ELSIE (*distressed*): Oh—don't!

BAXLEY: No. What do you want to start that for, first thing in the morning?

MRS. BAXLEY: Start what?

BAXLEY: Talking about policemen.

MRS. BAXLEY: Well, they still exist, don't they? And I know I shan't be able to look a policeman in the face.

BAXLEY: Well, why do you want to look a policeman in the face?

MRS. BAXLEY: Oh—don't you begin again. You said enough last night.

BAXLEY: Yes, when I could get a word in edgeways.

MRS. BAXLEY: It was two o'clock when I asked you to stop talking.

BAXLEY: Yes, and it was half-past two when you began again.

ELSIE (*who has gone to door into house and closed it*): Now listen —you're not to tell anybody.

BAXLEY: Not likely!

MRS. BAXLEY (*indignantly*): As if we should! It's bad enough knowing about it without telling anybody.

ELSIE: But not even mother. Don't forget.

MRS. BAXLEY: You're not going to tell me that all this has been going on all this time and your mother doesn't know anything about it?

ELSIE: I'm sure she doesn't know anything about it.

MRS. BAXLEY: Well, I can't understand why. She's my own sister, and she never seemed to me to miss much. And if she doesn't know, she ought to. If your uncle here had been up to any queer game like that, I'd have known all about it.

BAXLEY: You might—and then again you might not.

MRS. BAXLEY: What's that?

BAXLEY: I said you might—and then again you might not.

MRS. BAXLEY: Oh—and what's your funny game been then?

BAXLEY: I didn't say there'd been any funny game. I only said— if there had been, you might know—and then again——

MRS. BAXLEY: I might not. I heard you. Well, there isn't any might about it. I'd have known. And I don't see how George has kept it from Dorothy all this time.

BAXLEY (*with gloomy pride*): Ah—that's where he's been so clever, keeping it from her and from us and from everybody. That's where his cleverness comes in.

ELSIE: Yes, I suppose he must have been terribly clever all the time. And I never thought he was.

BAXLEY: Ah—I've always had my own ideas about him.

MRS. BAXLEY: Well, his being clever was never one of them.

BAXLEY: Oh, yes, it was. I've had my suspicions for some time.

[32]

MRS. BAXLEY: That's news to me.

ELSIE: The kettle! (*She hurries into the kitchen.*)

BAXLEY: He's got a lot of brains, George has.

MRS. BAXLEY: Oh?

BAXLEY: Yes. Some of the things he's said to me showed that. He didn't bother saying them to you.

MRS. BAXLEY: I see.

BAXLEY: Good.

MRS. BAXLEY: Well, it isn't good. And let me tell you he never struck me as being clever.

BAXLEY: Yes, but what do you know about it?

MRS. BAXLEY: I know this about it, that he'd have been cleverer if he'd kept all this to himself. It's bad enough telling us, but he went and told that young fellow of Elsie's. Is that clever?

BAXLEY: Yes, if he wanted to get rid of him. And I believe that's what he was after.

MRS. BAXLEY: Yes, and where's that young fellow—Harold—now?

BAXLEY: In bed, if he's any sense.

MRS. BAXLEY: You know what I mean. What's to prevent him going to the police and telling them?

BAXLEY: We had that out last night.

MRS. BAXLEY: Well, let's have it out again this morning.

BAXLEY: I tell you, he's got no real evidence, and if he went to the police, they'd laugh at him. Besides, he wouldn't go. Would you?

MRS. BAXLEY: Me! Don't be silly. I don't want to see a policeman for weeks.

ELSIE *returns with the teapot, which she places on the table.*

ELSIE: I know he likes his tea strong, anyhow.

MRS. BAXLEY (*sniffing round the pot*): That's a good thing, because by the time he comes down it'll have stewed itself as black as ink. I like my tea fresh.

ELSIE: You shall have a cup in a minute, auntie. I expect Dad will be down soon. And now I know he's so clever, I wish I didn't. I wish now I hadn't said he was dull and stupid. I wish he *was* dull and stupid again.

BAXLEY: How could he be dull again if he never was?

ELSIE (*distressed*): You know what I mean.

MRS. BAXLEY: Oh, don't bother with your uncle. He doesn't know what anybody means this morning.

[33]

ELSIE: I believe I started it last night by saying this was a dull and stupid place where nothing happened.

MRS. BAXLEY: I dare say you did—you and your young man between you.

BAXLEY: Don't be so silly. How could they start it when it's been going on for years?

MRS. BAXLEY: It was all in the cards.

BAXLEY: If it was all in the cards, why didn't you tell us then?

MRS. BAXLEY: Elsie, didn't I say your Dad was going to give us a big surprise?

BAXLEY: Well, what's the good of telling us we're going to get a big surprise, if you don't say what the surprise is?

MRS. BAXLEY: If I knew what it was, it wouldn't be a surprise, would it—cleverhead?

ELSIE: The point is, if I hadn't started talking like that, last night, we shouldn't have known all about this, and it's knowing about it that's so awful. I can't help thinking about it all the time.

MRS. BAXLEY: Same with me, just the same.

ELSIE: Besides, there's—Harold.

MRS. BAXLEY: Ah, yes. How's he going to take it?

BAXLEY: You saw how he took it last night. (*In loud complacent tone.*) You've got to look at it this way——

ELSIE: He's coming down.

MRS. BAXLEY: Shut up. He's here.

> *They all three of them are instantly expectant, rigid, like soldiers awaiting a general.* RADFERN *enters, a bustling genial figure, fully dressed except that he is wearing slippers.*

RADFERN: Good morning. Hello, what's all this? Three of you up?

BAXLEY (*respectfully*): Good morning, George.

RADFERN (*dryly*): Good morning, Bernard. I trust I see you well. And you, Lucy. Morning, Elsie.

ELSIE: Good morning, Dad.

MRS. BAXLEY (*gloomily*): How did you sleep last night, George?

RADFERN (*heartily*): How did I sleep? I slept like a top. I always do. Don't you?

MRS. BAXLEY (*reproachfully*): I didn't last night. None of us did.

RADFERN: Oh? Well, why have you all got up so early?

ELSIE: I thought I'd get your breakfast ready, Dad.

RADFERN: Very kind of you, Elsie, very kind of you. And—er— (*looks quizzically at the other two*) ——?

BAXLEY: Well, old man, I thought I'd just look down and see if there was anything I could do. Like to make myself useful at times, y'know. Knew you were going off early.

RADFERN: Aren't those my boots?

BAXLEY (*off-handedly*): Yes. Matter of fact I've just been giving them a bit of a rub.

RADFERN (*looking at them*): You've given them a very good rub, Bernard. Thank you. And what about you, Lucy?

MRS. BAXLEY (*rather defiantly*): Oh—you needn't thank me. I came down because I couldn't sleep and I wanted a cup of tea.

RADFERN: Quite right. And have you had a cup of tea?

MRS. BAXLEY: No.

RADFERN: Then give your Aunt Lucy a cup of tea—quick, Elsie.

As ELSIE *does this*, RADFERN *sits down and looks quizzically from one to the other of them.*

RADFERN: Well, well, well. My boots. Tea all ready. I call this being waited on hand and foot. This is as good as being out East, Bernard.

BAXLEY: Oh no. I was just saying, George, that a man like you—out East—would have twenty or thirty servants.

RADFERN: I wouldn't know what to do with them.

ELSIE: Dad, how do you like your eggs boiling?

RADFERN: I haven't touched a boiled egg for the last two years, Elsie. Don't agree with me.

ELSIE (*self-reproachfully*): Shows how much I've been noticing things, doesn't it?

RADFERN (*affectionately, embracing her*): Never mind.

ELSIE: What will you have for breakfast then, Dad?

BAXLEY: Want a good breakfast if you're travelling, George.

RADFERN: Oh—I always breakfast on the train. Helps to pass the time.

ELSIE: Oh—but I've made the tea.

RADFERN: That's all right. I've time for a cup of tea. Very nice.

MRS. BAXLEY: Where is it you're going, George?

RADFERN (*cheerfully*): I'm going to Birmingham for the day—on business.

MRS. BAXLEY (*bitterly*): Business!

RADFERN: That's what I said—business. You don't think I'd go to Birmingham for pleasure, do you?

[35]

MRS. BAXLEY (*still bitter*): Yes—but there's business *and* business.

RADFERN (*genially, but with point*): You mean—there's your own business—and other people's business?

MRS. BAXLEY: No, I don't.

ELSIE (*reproachfully*): You know what she means, Dad.

RADFERN (*echoing* MRS. BAXLEY): No, I don't.

BAXLEY: The queer work, that's what she means.

ELSIE: Yes—you know—crook stuff.

RADFERN: Crook stuff! Crook stuff! What a way to talk, especially early on Monday morning. Crook stuff.

MRS. BAXLEY: Well, what do you call it then?

RADFERN: Business. Not crook stuff! This comes of going so often to the pictures. What would they think if they heard you at *Ben Machree*?

ELSIE (*earnestly*): But, Dad, you told us last night.

RADFERN: Oh—so I told you last night, did I?

BAXLEY: You know very well you spilt it all last night, George. Can't get out of it now. We know.

ELSIE: And I was awake all night thinking about it. And so were Uncle Bernard and Aunt Lucy.

BAXLEY: No, not all night.

MRS. BAXLEY: Well, you never stopped talking all night. I suppose you must have been talking in your sleep.

BAXLEY: And I suppose you must have been listening in your sleep.

RADFERN: Just a minute. Here's a very good rule, if you want to have a nice quiet comfortable existence——

MRS. BAXLEY (*bitterly*): Like you, I suppose, George?

RADFERN: Yes, like me. It's a rule I've just invented, but never mind about that. Somebody's got to invent the rules some time.

BAXLEY: Quite right, old man.

RADFERN: The rule's this. Never think or talk on Monday morning about something that's been said on Sunday night.

ELSIE (*half laughing, half tearful*): Oh, Dad—that's silly.

RADFERN: No, it isn't. On Monday morning you must start with a clean slate, because you're beginning a new week.

MRS. BAXLEY (*bitterly*): Did you say—a clean slate?

RADFERN: That's what I said.

MRS. BAXLEY (*angrily*): Well, how you can talk like that, George Radfern, after all the things you told us last night and with the police

perhaps ready to march in here any minute and take us all off——
(*A thundering knock outside. She stops and gives a little scream.*)
What's that?

RADFERN (*coolly*): The postman.

ELSIE (*hastily*): I'll go.

She hurries out. RADFERN *lights his pipe.*

RADFERN (*looking at watch*): How's the time? Oh—I'm all right.

Begins putting on his boots.

BAXLEY: Is there anything I can do for you, George?

RADFERN (*respectfully*): No, I don't think so, thank you, Bernard.
You've done enough. Look at these boots. You mustn't spoil me
just because I don't make an honest living.

ELSIE *returns with three letters, two of which she places on the
table.*

ELSIE: Two for you, Dad. This is mine.

BAXLEY: Nothing for us then?

MRS. BAXLEY: Well, what should there be for us?

BAXLEY: Oh, I dunno. I thought one of the chaps might have
written.

MRS. BAXLEY: What chaps?

BAXLEY: Well—the chaps.

MRS. BAXLEY: I heard you.

BAXLEY: All right then, if you heard me, shut up.

ELSIE *opens her letter and reads it eagerly, then gives a sharp
cry of dismay.*

RADFERN: What is it?

ELSIE (*in distress*): It's from Harold. He says he won't—oh, it's
all over.

RADFERN (*going to her*): Never mind, Elsie.

ELSIE (*tearful*): Oh—but you don't understand——

RADFERN (*softly*): Listen, Elsie. Honestly, he's not worth bothering about——

ELSIE (*tearful and angry, cutting in*): It's all your fault. You've done
it. Oh!

She bursts into tears, pushes RADFERN *away and hurries towards
door into house. Before she gets there* MRS. RADFERN *appears in
doorway.*

MRS. RADFERN (*astonished*): What's the matter?

ELSIE (*in tears*): Everything.

ELSIE *pushes past and goes out.* MRS. RADFERN *stares after her for a moment, then stares at the other three.*

MRS. RADFERN: Now will anybody tell me what's happening in this house? Elsie up early. You two up. Elsie crying. What in the name of wonder is it all about?

RADFERN: Leave Elsie alone, mother. It's that blathering, weak-kneed, spineless young man of hers, Harold.

MRS. RADFERN: What's he done?

RADFERN: She's just had a letter from him. They've had some sort of quarrel. And he's just broken it off.

MRS. RADFERN: So that's it. I'd like to say something to that young man. Doesn't know his own mind.

BAXLEY: Hasn't got one. Spotted it in a minute.

MRS. RADFERN: What does he want to make her miserable like that for? Who's he—I'd like to know—to be going on shilly-shallying and quarrelling——

RADFERN: He's not worth it.

BAXLEY: Of course he isn't. I could have told you that.

MRS. BAXLEY: Pity you don't tell us all the things you know.

RADFERN: Listen, mother. Don't say anything to her. Leave her alone.

MRS. RADFERN: Well, that's all right, but I don't want her crying her eyes out all day——

RADFERN: Couldn't you take her out, for the day. Down into town—shopping—or something——?

MRS. RADFERN: I don't see how I can to-day, Dad. I've a lot to do, and I promised Mrs. Repington I'd go to the servants' registry for her this morning.

RADFERN: Well, you're not doing anything this morning, are you, Lucy?

MRS. BAXLEY (*bitterly*): No, just enjoying myself, that's all.

RADFERN: Well, enjoy yourself a bit more, and you and Bernard take Elsie into the West End. Look at the shops. Go to the pictures.

MRS. BAXLEY: And see one of these crook films, I suppose?

RADFERN (*heartily*): That's it. Find a good crook film. Be a nice change after this dull suburb. Here. (*Takes two pound notes out of his pocket book.*) Take these and help her to spend them.

MRS. BAXLEY (*taking the notes but looking at them dubiously*): All right—I suppose . . . ?

RADFERN: Go on—they won't bite you.

MRS. RADFERN: But it's too much, Dad.

RADFERN: Oh—let her spend it.

MRS. BAXLEY (*bitterly*): Plenty more where these come from, I expect.

MRS. RADFERN: Well, that's a nice way to talk, Lucy.

MRS. BAXLEY (*grimly*): I beg your pardon.

MRS. RADFERN: You'll go and make Elsie worse. I'm sure she doesn't know the value of money as it is. The way she talks sometimes, you'd think all you have to do is to pick money up in parcels.

MRS. BAXLEY (*grimly*): Indeed!

RADFERN: Good idea that. Money in parcels. What do you say, Bernard?

BAXLEY (*embarrassed*): Er—yes—quite. (*Laughs falsely.*)

RADFERN: Better than looking round, eh? Wish I knew where to pick some up.

MRS. BAXLEY: You ought to try Birmingham.

RADFERN: I think I will. Time to be off too. If anybody wants me, you can say I'll be back about eight. Joe Fletten may call round. If he does, ask him to wait.

MRS. RADFERN: What, Joe Fletten again! He'll never be out of the house soon.

MRS. BAXLEY: No, these greenhouses do seem to give a lot of trouble, don't they?

RADFERN: You're right, Lucy, they do. Well, have a good day. And keep Elsie quiet. Must go and earn an honest penny now.

MRS. BAXLEY (*in a deep disapproving tone*): A what?

RADFERN: I said an honest penny. Bye-bye.

Gives BAXLEY *and* MRS. BAXLEY *a quizzical grin, kisses* MRS. RADFERN *and then briskly departs.*

MRS. RADFERN: I don't know what brought you down so early this morning, Lucy, but you seem to have got out of the wrong side of the bed.

MRS. BAXLEY (*bristling*): Oh—and why?

BAXLEY: You know why, Lucy.

MRS. BAXLEY (*severely*): And you be quiet. (*To* MRS. RADFERN) May I ask what's the matter with you?

MRS. RADFERN: Well, George gives you two pounds to take Elsie out with—and if you ask me, it's a lot too much—and then you go and stare at him and at the money, without a word of thanks, as if—as if——

[39]

MRS. BAXLEY: As if what?

MRS. RADFERN: I don't know. As if he'd stolen it or something instead of having worked hard for years for it.

MRS. BAXLEY: I suppose he *has* worked hard for years for it?

MRS. RADFERN (*indignantly*): Of course he has. I've told you so many times.

MRS. BAXLEY: Yes, but sometimes I think he looks a bit too pleased with himself to be a man who's worked hard for years.

MRS. RADFERN: Indeed! But you see *some* men don't mind working hard.

MRS. BAXLEY: That's one at you, Bernard. I'll leave you with it.

She makes a move.

MRS. RADFERN: You can first explain what's the matter with you.

MRS. BAXLEY (*with cold dignity*): Perhaps I can get into the bathroom now.

She stalks out.

MRS. RADFERN: Now what is the matter with her? She's very queer this morning.

BAXLEY (*uneasily*): Oh—she didn't sleep so well last night.

MRS. RADFERN (*significantly*): Perhaps she could do with a change.

BAXLEY: Oh—no. Bit too much noise perhaps and not enough air.

MRS. RADFERN (*with hostility*): There's plenty of air in this house.

BAXLEY (*hastily*): Yes, but it all depends on what you're used to. Now when we were out in Singapore——

MRS. RADFERN (*coldly*): Just a minute, Bernard. You had a great time in Singapore, didn't you?

BAXLEY: Oh—yes, a great time, a great time.

MRS. RADFERN: Well, there's one thing you seem to forget about Singapore.

BAXLEY: Oh no, never forget anything about Singapore.

MRS. RADFERN: No, there's one thing you forget about it.

BAXLEY: What's that?

MRS. RADFERN: You forget that it's still there, waiting for you.

She marches towards kitchen.

BAXLEY (*puzzled*): Eh?

By the time it dawns on him, she has disappeared into the kitchen, and the curtain is rapidly falling.

SCENE II

SCENE: *Same as Act One.* TIME: *Late afternoon.*

When the curtain rises, the room is empty. On the centre table there is a book, "The Great Bank Mystery", and a work basket. MRS. RADFERN *enters and begins looking in the work basket for things, finally produces some work and sits down with it. The front door bell rings, and she goes out to open the door, and the sound of her voice and her visitor's can be heard a moment later. She returns, followed by* INSPECTOR STACK, *a plain-clothes officer, a smart-looking fellow about forty with an assured authoritative manner.* MRS. RADFERN *likes the look of him.*

STACK: Only for the day, eh?

MRS. RADFERN: Yes. Won't you sit down?

STACK: Thank you.

   They both sit.

MRS. RADFERN (*chattily*): Yes, he's gone to Birmingham on business, just for the day. He often goes there.

STACK: I see. Do you happen to know what time he'll be back to-night?

MRS. RADFERN: He said about eight o'clock.

STACK: Then if I called some time after eight, I'd catch him in.

MRS. RADFERN: Sure to. I don't think he'll be going out again. It'll be either the greenhouse or the wireless for him to-night.

STACK (*respectfully*): Very wise of him too, Mrs. Radfern. I wish they'd let me have more nice quiet evenings at home like that.

MRS. RADFERN (*enjoying the little chat*): Oh—my husband's always been quite a home bird, you know. His business takes him out, of course, and sometimes away too, but the minute he's back, all he wants are his slippers and his pipe, and a book or his greenhouse or the wireless.

STACK: Let me see, he's in the paper trade, isn't he?

MRS. RADFERN: Yes, the wholesale paper trade, not newspapers, you know, but paper for printing and writing on, and chiefly very fine-quality papers.

STACK (*blandly*): Good enough for—what shall we say?—bank notes, eh?

MRS. RADFERN: I dare say, but I don't know exactly. But I do know it's wholesale paper he's in, and always has been.

STACK: Got an office and a warehouse somewhere in the city, I suppose?

MRS. RADFERN: Oh yes. It's just off Cloth Fair, you know, by Smithfield. I remember the only time I went there, it was a very warm day and you could smell the meat in Smithfield Market—horrid it was.

STACK: I know. Never cared for that smell myself. Puts you off your beefsteaks. And he's been able to keep going all right, through all these bad times?

MRS. RADFERN: Yes, I'm sure we can't grumble. He got a bit down four or five years ago—like a lot of other people, you know— no fault of theirs at all——

STACK (*sympathetically*): Quite. Just the hard times.

MRS. RADFERN: That's it. But, however, he's picked up again wonderfully since then. I'm sure we can't grumble at all.

STACK: And I'm sure you don't grumble, Mrs. Radfern.

MRS. RADFERN: Why do you say that?

STACK (*smiling politely*): Well, you don't look the grumbling sort.

MRS. RADFERN (*pleased*): Oh, I've always believed in making the best of everything. We're only on this earth once, I always say, and so we'd better make the best of it. (*With more energy, though not at all rudely*) Though why I'm talking like this to a complete stranger, I really don't know. Let me see, you didn't give me your name, did you?

STACK: No. I'm sorry. Here's my card. (*Hands it over.*)

MRS. RADFERN (*reading*): Detective-Inspector Stack, Criminal Investigation Department, New Scotland Yard. Good gracious! Are you from Scotland Yard? A detective?

Puts card down in prominent place on the table.

STACK (*smiling*): I am. Do I look like one?

MRS. RADFERN: I'm sure I don't know. I've never seen anybody from Scotland Yard before. You certainly don't look like a policeman.

STACK: Well, that's something to be thankful for.

MRS. RADFERN: But what do you want with my husband?

STACK (*smoothly*): I'm only making a few enquiries, and Mr. Radfern's name was given to me as one of the people who might be able to give me a little information. I'm sorry to disappoint you, but it's nothing sensational. Nobody murdered. No jewels stolen. Just one of those dull routine commercial cases.

MRS. RADFERN: Well, I'm sure if my husband can help you at all, he will. And it'll amuse him meeting somebody from Scotland Yard, because he's very fond of reading these detective stories. He's just made me read one with him.

STACK: Well, I understand Mr. Radfern had some dealings with one of the firms in question, some years ago, so I thought he might be able to give me a little information. And then he gets up and down a good deal, I think, doesn't he?

MRS. RADFERN: Yes, he has to get about.

STACK: Birmingham, for instance. Of course, that's not very far, is it?

MRS. RADFERN: No, but that's about the nearest place. Sometimes he goes to Liverpool. And Newcastle.

STACK: And up into Scotland, I expect?

MRS. RADFERN: Yes, he has to go to Glasgow quite a lot.

STACK: Has he really? Still that's not so troublesome as having to go abroad, after all.

MRS. RADFERN: Oh—he has to do that sometimes, too.

STACK: Yes? Well, I'm not surprised. I used to have a friend in the same line of business and he used to have to go quite often to Amsterdam and Brussels.

MRS. RADFERN: That's just where my husband has to go sometimes. Amsterdam and Brussels. He probably knows this friend of yours.

STACK: I wouldn't be surprised if he did.

MRS. RADFERN: You must ask him, if you're calling in to-night.

STACK: I will. (*Rising.*) I won't detain you any longer, Mrs. Radfern. I'll look in again to-night, if Mr. Radfern won't mind having a private little chat with me.

MRS. RADFERN: I'm sure he won't. (*Noise of people entering house.*) Just a minute, that's my daughter and my sister and her husband coming back. Do just let me introduce you because they'll be terribly interested in meeting a detective from Scotland Yard.

> STACK *nods, smiling, and stands half facing door.* ELSIE, BAXLEY *and* MRS. BAXLEY *enter, carrying some small parcels. They stare at* STACK *but* MRS. RADFERN *begins before they have a chance to speak.*

(*Playfully.*) Now you three, I'll bet you anything you'll never guess who this is.

> All three look enquiringly at STACK.

MRS. BAXLEY (*gloomily*): Nobody I know.

BAXLEY (*hopefully*): The face is familiar.

ELSIE: No, I can't guess.

MRS. RADFERN (*pleased with herself*): Well, this is Detective Inspector Stack from Scotland Yard.

> ELSIE, BAXLEY *and* MRS. BAXLEY *instantly look the picture of dismay, alarm and horror.* ELSIE *just stifles a little scream.* BAXLEY'S *jaw drops.* MRS. BAXLEY'S *eyes nearly pop out of her head.*

You needn't look like that. If he'd come to lock you all up, you couldn't look worse. (*To* STACK) I'm sorry, If they've all been up to something, I don't know what it is.

STACK: Oh, that's nothing. We get used to people looking at us like that. Well, I'll call again to-night to see Mr. Radfern. Good afternoon.

> *Moves to the door, and* MRS. RADFERN *follows, to let him out. The other three, dumb with terror, simply stand watching them.* MRS. RADFERN *returns at once.*

MRS. RADFERN: Well, I must say you're a fine lot. It's a wonder he didn't think you were a lot of crooks or something. Such a nice man, I thought, too. Superior, and very gentlemanly manners, I'm sure. What's the matter?

ELSIE: Mother, was he really from Scotland Yard and wanting to see Dad?

MRS. RADFERN: Of course.

BAXLEY: My God! Here, Lucy, we're packing.

MRS. RADFERN: What do you mean you're packing? What's the matter?

MRS. BAXLEY: Arresting and prison and penal servitude's the matter.

ELSIE (*ready to break down*): Oh—mother!

BAXLEY (*moving towards door*): Come on, Lucy. We're getting out of this—sharp.

MRS. RADFERN (*taking a place in front of door and blocking the way*): Oh no, you're not, Bernard, not until you've told me what's wrong. What have you done?

BAXLEY (*indignantly*): Me! I've done nothing.

MRS. BAXLEY: No, don't start trying to blame it on to us now.

MRS. RADFERN: Blame what on to you?

MRS. BAXLEY: Better ask Elsie. This isn't any place for us.

MRS. RADFERN: Well, it's going to be until you tell me what it is you're all frightened of.

ELSIE: Oh—mother—it's Dad.

MRS. RADFERN: Dad!

MRS. BAXLEY (*bitterly*): Yes, Dad, your precious quiet respectable George with his honest pennies.

ELSIE: It's true, mother. He told us himself, last night.

MRS. RADFERN (*exasperated*): Told you *what*, you stupid?

MRS. BAXLEY: Told us he was a crook.

BAXLEY: And been one for years.

MRS. BAXLEY: Every penny dishonest.

BAXLEY: Working with a big gang, all the detectives after them.

MRS. BAXLEY: And proud of it, glories in it.

BAXLEY: And he'll get years and years, penal servitude.

ELSIE (*tearfully*): Oh—mother, it's true.

MRS. RADFERN (*loudly*): Stop, stop! (*They are quiet, so she continues quietly*): Now what is it you're all trying to tell me? What did Dad say to you last night?

BAXLEY: You'd better get Elsie to tell you. We're going to pack.

MRS. RADFERN: No, you're not. Nobody's leaving this room until I understand exactly what all this is about. Now who's going to tell me?

MRS. BAXLEY: Go on, Elsie. You tell her.

ELSIE: Last night, just before you came back, Dad told us that he hadn't been in the paper business for years, but that he'd been a crook.

MRS. RADFERN: He told you and Lucy and Bernard here——

ELSIE: And Harold.

MRS. RADFERN: Oh, he told Harold too, did he?

ELSIE: Yes. And he said he'd been a sort of crook for years, and that he worked for a big international gang——

BAXLEY: That started in America.

MRS. RADFERN: I see. That started in America. Go on.

ELSIE: And that they swindled banks, in America, and here in and France and all over.

BAXLEY: Counterfeiting notes and forging bonds.

MRS. BAXLEY: All sorts of dangerous dirty tricks.

ELSIE: And that the detectives had been trying for years to track down this gang but they couldn't manage it, but if he was caught, he'd get years and years of prison.

BAXLEY: And so he would too.

MRS. RADFERN: And that's what he told all the four of you, is it?

ELSIE: Yes—and mother, it's true. And that's why he has to keep

[45]

going to various places, up and down the country, and abroad. And that's why Mr. Fletten comes here such a lot, because he's working for this gang too, and he doesn't really know anything about greenhouses—that's——

BAXLEY: Just a blind, just a blind. He's taken everybody in up to now, but this time he's for it.

MRS. RADFERN: And he asked you not to tell me?

MRS. BAXLEY: Yes. Said you didn't know, and weren't to know, though I must say how he's kept it from you all this time beats me.

MRS. RADFERN: Oh—that's quite simple.

MRS. BAXLEY: Is it?

MRS. RADFERN: Certainly it is. I can explain in three seconds why he's never told me and yet told you all about it last night.

BAXLEY: Why?

MRS. RADFERN: Because he knew very well that you were four silly fools who'd believe any nonsense he told them, and he knew very well he couldn't come out with that silly stuff in front of me. Can't you see he was simply having a game with you? And serve you right too. Just because he likes to be quiet when he's at home, you've got it into your heads that he's a dull old stick. I've heard you say as much, Elsie. And you two are as bad. And as for your Harold, I know what Dad was trying to do to him—just scaring him away. (*To* ELSIE.) And is that why you had that letter from him this morning, breaking it off, and why you cried your eyes out?

ELSIE: Yes of course.

MRS. RADFERN: And why you were all so queer and said you hadn't slept last night?

MRS. BAXLEY (*with dignity*): Naturally.

MRS. RADFERN: And why you all got up so early this morning?

BAXLEY: That's it.

MRS. RADFERN: Then you're all sillier than I ever thought you were.

ELSIE: But mother, it's true.

MRS. RADFERN: Of course it isn't true. Not a word of truth in it. Do you think I wouldn't have known? How you could ever have thought it was true, I can't imagine.

BAXLEY: It's all right talking like that——

MRS. RADFERN: And now I suppose you thought that Inspector had come to arrest him. If you want to know, that Inspector was only making some enquiries about a commercial case——

BAXLEY: That's what *he* says.

MRS. RADFERN: Oh—have some sense, Bernard, even if you have been to Singapore. Do you think I'd be calmly talking about it like this if I thought for a minute Dad had ever done anything wrong?

MRS. BAXLEY: Well, you don't know he hasn't.

BAXLEY: *We* heard him last night, remember—not you.

MRS. RADFERN: I know that story he told you last night was all nonsense, just made up to tease you and frighten you.

ELSIE (*hopefully*): Oh mother, do you think it was?

MRS. RADFERN: I tell you, I *know* it was.

BAXLEY: But you can't prove it.

MRS. RADFERN (*triumphantly*): I can. (*She goes to table and picks up the book there.*) You see this book. It's called *The Great Bank Mystery.* I've just read it, and Dad's just read it. And if you want to know all the rest of that story about the international gang of bank swindlers and bond forgers that started in America, you'll find it in this book.

BAXLEY (*sitting down and mopping forehead*): Well, I'll be damned!

ELSIE (*joyfully*): Mother! (*Hugs her.*)

MRS. BAXLEY (*grumbling*): Well, that's a nice trick, frightening people with a lot of silly stuff out of a detective tale!

BAXLEY: Yes, it's a bit thick.

MRS. BAXLEY (*indignantly*): It's a lot thick.

MRS. RADFERN (*suddenly beginning to laugh*): Dad's a monkey——

MRS. BAXLEY: And I call it a foul monkey trick, too. I've had an awful day. Every time I've set eyes on a policeman I've shivered, and when I found that detective here my heart stopped and my blood went cold. I might easily be ill after this.

BAXLEY: Well, I must say it's not my idea of a joke.

MRS. RADFERN (*still laughing*): Evidently not, Bernard. But it seems to be George's. And very well he did it too, though he'll hear something from me about it when he comes back.

ELSIE (*happily*): Oh, I don't care now. Everything's different. It's been awful. I'll never say anybody's dull again—never, never, never. I don't care how dull they are. It's all nice and safe and sensible again now. Lovely.

   She hurries out.

MRS. RADFERN: Well, she's feeling a lot better already. It was silly of George to frighten her like that. Poor Elsie!

MRS. BAXLEY: And what about us, Dorothy? Weren't we frightened, too?

BAXLEY: I've been worried to death about George ever since he told us that story.

MRS. BAXLEY: So have I. And I do think, Dorothy, that George owes us some consideration after this silly trick he's played on us.

MRS. RADFERN: You do, eh?

MRS. BAXLEY: Yes, I do. He's not been as pleasant as he might have been these last few days, and I hope he'll realise now that the least thing he can do is to help Bernard to buy that little business we've talked about.

BAXLEY: Well, seeing you've mentioned it, Lucy, I might as well say that's what I feel too. He's had his fun——

MRS. RADFERN (*very quietly*): And now he must pay for it. Is that it?

BAXLEY: Oh—you can't put it like that. But you know our position, Dorothy. If George can let me have a temporary loan of a few hundreds and we can stay on here until the deal goes through——

MRS. BAXLEY: I don't think you can object to that, Dorothy. And you can tell him how much he's upset me with that silly joke of his——

MRS. RADFERN (*quietly, but decisively*): Just a minute. I want to understand you properly. You both feel that, after this, I ought to persuade George to let you have the money and I also ought to ask you to stay on until you've bought the business you're after. Is that it?

BAXLEY: Yes, that's it.

MRS. RADFERN: Well, Lucy—and Bernard—I'm going to tell you straight what I think about it. I think—you're both the limit. And I see now that Dad was right about you and I was wrong.

MRS. BAXLEY: What do you mean?

MRS. RADFERN: I mean that he was right in not wanting to put up with you any longer. You're my relations, not his. You've taken advantage of his good-nature, and so have I, through you. You've stayed here and borrowed money from him too often. He'd had enough of it when he told you that story last night. And now I've had enough of it too.

BAXLEY: But here, half a minute, what have we done?

MRS. RADFERN: You've shown me quite plainly you don't really care tuppence about him, and that you're only here to get what you can out of him. Only a few minutes ago, when you thought he was in trouble and might be arrested, what did you do? All you thought about was yourselves. You wanted to pack up and go at once. I had to stop you going out of that door. Well, now I'm not stopping you. You can pack and go as soon as you like.

> MRS. BAXLEY *and* BAXLEY *look at one another.* ELSIE *enters, and looks enquiringly from one to the other of them.*

MRS. BAXLEY: That's a nice thing to say to a sister, isn't it?

MRS. RADFERN: No, it isn't, but that's how I feel, Lucy.

BAXLEY: More shame to you. Come on, Lucy. We'll pack. I'm not staying where I'm not wanted. (*Goes to door,* MRS. BAXLEY *following. Then, turning at door.*) I'd laugh now if the old boy really was a wrong 'un all the time.

MRS. RADFERN: Well, you'll have to find something else to laugh at, Bernard.

MRS. BAXLEY (*bitterly, at door*): That oughtn't to be difficult—here.
> *They go out.*

ELSIE: Are they going?

MRS. RADFERN: Yes. I told them to. They've been sponging on Dad long enough and they're not going to get anything else out of him. Wanted to bolt as soon as they thought he was in trouble. (*As* ELSIE *goes to telephone*) What are you going to do?

ELSIE: I'm going to tell Harold it was all Dad's nonsense. At least I'm going to ask him to come here, so that I can tell him.

MRS. RADFERN: He broke it off, didn't he, after what he heard last night?

ELSIE: Yes.

MRS. RADFERN: Another one that was found out.

ELSIE: Well, mother, you can't blame him for not wanting to be engaged to the daughter of a crook.

MRS. RADFERN (*sharply, derisively*): Can't you?

ELSIE (*doing her best*): No, of course you can't.

MRS. RADFERN: *Can't you?*

ELSIE (*confusedly*): No. Yes—I suppose you can.

MRS. RADFERN: Of course you can blame him. He ought to have been ready to stick to you, whatever your father turned out to be. And you know it. I can see Dad's right about your Harold. He's a weak-kneed, shuffling boy—just out for what he can safely get.

ELSIE: You've no right to say that, mother. I don't blame Harold really for breaking it off. And anyhow he deserves another chance. I'll tell him it was all a joke.

MRS. RADFERN: If you do, I'll be ashamed of you.

ELSIE: What for?

MRS. RADFERN: Well, where's your pride?

ELSIE: I don't see where my pride comes in. After all, it *was* a joke.

MRS. RADFERN: This is where your pride comes in, or ought to come in. He's proved already that he's not sufficiently fond of you to marry you whatever your father is.

ELSIE (*hurt by this*): Don't—mother.

MRS. RADFERN: And now you want to tell him it's all right. If it was me, I wouldn't have him on those terms. You get him up here—give him a last chance if you like—but don't tell him that last night was a joke. Let him think it's still serious and then ask him if he still wants to break off the engagement finally. That'll be a fair test.

ELSIE: All right, mother, I'll do that. (*Begins dialling at telephone.*) I'll simply ask him to come and see me, and then when he comes, I won't say a word about last night's business not being true. Hello, I want Mr. Harold Russ.

MRS. RADFERN (*moving to kitchen*): And I want a cup of tea.

QUICK CURTAIN

END OF ACT TWO

ACT III

SCENE: *Same as Act Two.*

The book and the INSPECTOR'S *card are still prominent on the table in centre. In front not far from the door into the house is a fairly large suitcase, with a hat and raincoat on top of it.* BAXLEY *is discovered poking about the room, looking for something. He is out of temper, though not furiously angry.*

BAXLEY (*going to door into house and calling*): I say, Lucy. Lucy. Is my cigarette case up there? (*Pauses, listening to reply.*) It isn't. I've just looked for it. Oh, all right.

> *Gives a final glance round the room, but can't see it. Then goes over to his raincoat and carefully searches pockets. He finds the case in one of them, opens it and discovers that it is empty. He goes to the sideboard, finds a box of cigarettes there and—after one glance over his shoulder—fills his case from the box, finally lighting one. Then he puts the case in his pocket, and replaces the raincoat on the suitcase. As he does this, the front door bell rings. He hesitates a moment, then goes out, re-entering a moment later, followed by* HAROLD.

HAROLD: Isn't Elsie in?

BAXLEY: Yes, she'll be down in a minute. She's helping my wife to finish her packing.

HAROLD: What? You off?

BAXLEY: Yes. Night train to Scotland—Dundee. Got a brother there. Nothing for me down here, you know.

HAROLD (*sceptically*): No?

BAXLEY: Oh no. Not the right sort of opening. They tried to persuade me to take an agency for business supplies—exclusive agency too—chap called Simpson—I said 'What's the good of business supplies, when business itself is so bad?' That stumped him. Mind you, there's an opening there—in a small way. Might suit a youngster like yourself. But no good to me. So I'm on the move. I like to be on the move, always did. Bit of a roamer, you know, old man, bit of a roamer.

HAROLD (*sceptical*): Sez you.

BAXLEY: What's the *sez you* about. We're not doing a talkie.

HAROLD: No, but you're not going to tell me that you're clearing out so suddenly just because you like travelling.

[51]

BAXLEY: Oh?

HAROLD: No, I know why you're going, and I don't blame you.

BAXLEY: Very good of you, old man, but still I don't know what you're talking about.

HAROLD: And I think if I'd any sense, I wouldn't be here either.

BAXLEY: Of course you wouldn't. Marriage is a mug's game, you can take it from me.

HAROLD: I'm not talking about marriage.

BAXLEY: Then why shouldn't you be here?—Oh—you mean because of what he told us last night?

HAROLD: Yes, of course.

BAXLEY: And you still believe that?

HAROLD: Yes, don't you?

BAXLEY: Of course not. All a joke. Bit of leg-pulling, that's all. We're always pulling one another's legs here, you know. Sometimes I pull his leg, sometimes he pulls mine. Last night it was his turn.

HAROLD: It was his turn all right.

BAXLEY: And he's taken you in all this time. Well, you surprise me. I thought you were smart. In the second-hand car trade, too.

HAROLD: Was it a joke?

BAXLEY: Yes. All rot. Out of a book. There's the book.

HAROLD: Look here, are you sure?

BAXLEY: Well, I know a book when I see one.

HAROLD: Yes, but I mean—are you sure it did come from that book and it was a joke?

BAXLEY: I keep telling you, don't I? If you don't want to believe me, don't. It doesn't matter to me.

HAROLD: Oh well, I do believe you. Does Elsie know?

BAXLEY: Yes. She knows.

HAROLD: I suppose she's asked me to come so that she can tell me, though she could have done that on the telephone.

BAXLEY (looking cunning): Perhaps she isn't going to tell you.

HAROLD: Of course she's going to tell me. Why shouldn't she?

BAXLEY: She might be going to try you out.

HAROLD: Try me out? Oh—I see, pretend it wasn't a joke. Keep the old man's game up for him, eh?

BAXLEY: It's a possibility, isn't it?

HAROLD: Yes. Look here, don't tell her you've told me that it was all a joke.

BAXLEY: I won't tell her. I hope it works—with her and her father too. Serve 'em right.

HAROLD: What do you mean—serve them right? Do you mean I'd serve them right, because if you do, you're being very insulting.

BAXLEY: Then that isn't what I mean. (*Looks at his watch.*) Time's going on. (*Goes to door and shouts outside.*) I say, it's time we were off. . . . Well, come on, then. Oh, all right.

He goes out, and after a moment, ELSIE *enters.*

ELSIE: Hello, Harold.

HAROLD: Hello, Elsie. You see, I came as soon as I could.

He tries to kiss her, but she fends him off.

ELSIE: No, I want to talk first.

HAROLD: Oh, all right. Well, let's talk then.

ELSIE: Wait a minute. My uncle and aunt are just going.

Enter MRS. BAXLEY, *dressed for travelling and carrying a small case.*

MRS. BAXLEY: Oh—you're here again, are you?

HAROLD: Yes—do you mind?

MRS. BAXLEY: It doesn't matter to me who's here, though I know one who won't be here again for a long time—not if some people beg on their bended knees—and that's me.

ELSIE: Must you go now, Aunt Lucy?

MRS. BAXLEY: Your Uncle Bernard says so, if we're going to get that train.

ELSIE: You won't wait to say good-bye to mother? She'll be back in a minute.

MRS. BAXLEY: No, thank you. If I could wait, I wouldn't. But you can give her one message from me.

ELSIE: What's that?

MRS. BAXLEY: Just remind her, from me, that there's no smoke without fire. That's all. No smoke without fire.

Enter BAXLEY, *carrying another bag.*

MRS. BAXLEY: Here you are then. I'm all ready.

BAXLEY: What about a taxi?

MRS. BAXLEY: We're not having any taxis. We can go to the station by Tube, can't we?

BAXLEY: Yes, but what about from here to the Tube?

MRS. BAXLEY: We can walk that.

BAXLEY: Yes, but what about these bags?

HAROLD (*maliciously*): It's ten minutes' walk.

MRS. BAXLEY: Ten minutes' walk won't kill us.

BAXLEY: It won't kill you but it will kill me, carrying these bags. (*Tries them.*) This comes of giving the old country a chance. Carrying bags. It's a good job some of the chaps I knew out East can't see me now.

MRS. BAXLEY (*coldly*): What chaps?

BAXLEY! Well—the chaps—you know—out East.

MRS. BAXLEY: Anybody would think you'd been Emperor of China to hear you talk. What chaps?

BAXLEY (*shouting*): Never mind what chaps. I don't like carrying these damned bags. So there.

MRS. BAXLEY: Well, you'll have to put up with it for once. Good-bye, Elsie. (*Kisses her perfunctorily.*) And just try and be sensible, though that won't always be easy in *this* house. (*To* HAROLD.) Good-bye.

HAROLD: Good-bye.

MRS. BAXLEY (*very grimly*): Pleased to have met you. Come on, Bernard.

> *She stalks out.*

BAXLEY (*grappling with bags*): Ten minutes' walk! It's murder. I've known stronger chaps than me strain their hearts doing silly things like this.

ELSIE: Never mind, uncle, you'll be able to have a good rest in the train.

BAXLEY (*grumbling*): Good rest! It's a stopping train to Dundee. I'll be able to take root. Well, good-bye.

HAROLD: Good-bye.

ELSIE: Good-bye, uncle.

BAXLEY: Good-bye, Elsie. (*Groans.*) Good-bye.

> *Goes out, followed by* ELSIE, *with* HAROLD *going as far as the door. You hear the outer door banged to, then* ELSIE *returns.*

HAROLD: They're clearing off suddenly, aren't they?

ELSIE: Yes, as soon as they thought we were in trouble, they wanted to pack up and go, and that made mother angry——

HAROLD (*puzzled*): In trouble? You mean, because of what your father told us last night?

ELSIE: Oh—it went further than that, because they thought somebody was coming here to arrest Dad. So they wanted to go at once.

So then mother told them to go. She doesn't like people who leave you in the lurch, and (*meaningly*) I don't either.

HAROLD: But wait a minute. There isn't anybody coming here to arrest your father?

ELSIE (*watching him*): Perhaps.

HAROLD (*watching her, with faint smile*): Well—I don't care.

ELSIE (*eagerly*): Harold—do you mean that?

HAROLD (*whose tone must suggest insincerity*): Yes, I do. I really came to tell you how sorry I was—and am—about the way I went off last night and the letter I wrote to you. You see—I hadn't time to think. The whole thing completely took me by surprise.

ELSIE: You hadn't time to think about—what?

HAROLD: About you. And me. When all that stuff came out, last night, all I felt—as any honest man would—was that I must keep out of this. And for the moment—well—I suppose I mixed you up in it. I realise now that's where I was wrong. It's got nothing to do with us what your father is and does.

ELSIE: Do you really mean that, Harold?

HAROLD (*uneasily*): Yes, Elsie.

ELSIE (*gravely*): Are you sure?

HAROLD (*still uneasy*): Well—yes.

ELSIE: Think of the disgrace, though, if Dad is found out.

HAROLD (*with mock nobility*): Never mind. We'll stick it. (*Then hesitating.*) And, after all, your father was exaggerating it, wasn't he?

ELSIE: Was he?

HAROLD: You know he was. I should think he's rather a leg-puller, anyhow, isn't he?

ELSIE (*solemnly*): Oh no. Dad isn't. That's not like him at all. Now, Uncle Bernard—you know, the one who was here just now—he'd say anything for tuppence. You can't believe a word he says.

HAROLD (*uneasily*): Can't you?

ELSIE: Good Lord, no! He's an awful mischief-maker and a liar. I hope he hasn't said anything to you.

HAROLD: Er—no—of course not.

ELSIE (*watching him*): That's all right then, because you simply can't believe him. Dad's quite different.

HAROLD: Look here—I don't quite understand this.

ELSIE (*who is now standing in front of the centre table*): Well, it doesn't matter, does it? After all, the important thing is—us.

HAROLD: Oh yes—of course.

ELSIE: That's all that matters, isn't it?

HAROLD (*approaching her*): Yes.

ELSIE (*edging away*): No, I'm not going to kiss you—just yet.

HAROLD (*moving*): Oh—come on, Elsie.

ELSIE: You must remember, Harold, you upset me terribly—running away like that last night and then writing me that letter. I haven't got over it yet.

HAROLD: Well, I've told you it's all right now.

ELSIE: Yes, it may be for you, but it isn't for me. I'd given you up, you see. And it'll take me a very long time to get very fond of you all over again.

HAROLD: No, it won't.

ELSIE (*who now puts the table between them*): Yes, it will. Besides, I want to talk. And if you're kissing, you can't talk seriously.

HAROLD: Well, we don't need to talk seriously. (*They are now standing, looking at each other across the table.*) I've told you, I want you and I don't care now what your father is and does.

He catches sight of the card on the table and stares at it.

ELSIE: What's the matter?

HAROLD (*uneasily*): I suppose this is part of the joke, too?

ELSIE (*coolly*): Oh—the card. No, the man left it when he came here this afternoon.

HAROLD: An Inspector from Scotland Yard?

ELSIE: Yes, he came here this afternoon, to see Dad. And he's coming again to-night.

HAROLD: My God!

ELSIE (*watching him*): Oh—I was terribly upset at first, but I've got over it now.

HAROLD (*angrily*): Look here, what's going on here? First, your father tells us all that stuff about being a crook, and then your uncle tells me it's all a joke, and now you say there's somebody coming from Scotland Yard.

ELSIE: So uncle told you it was all a joke?

HAROLD (*sulkily*): If you must know—yes.

ELSIE: And you didn't tell me he told you. You let me think you didn't know.

HAROLD: Well, what does that matter?

ELSIE: It matters a lot.

HAROLD (*flinging away, then turning on her*): I'm fed up with this.

Is it a joke or isn't it? And if it is a joke, why did this chap from Scotland Yard come here?

ELSIE: You'd better wait and ask him. He'll be here soon.

HAROLD (*nervously*): I'm not going to wait for him, I can tell you that. It's no business of mine.

Noise outside.

ELSIE (*scornfully*): There's somebody there now. Hadn't you better go while there's time?

Enter RADFERN *and* FLETTEN.

RADFERN (*heartily*): Hello, Elsie. I found Joe Fletten here waiting on the doorstep. Hello, what's the matter?

ELSIE: I think you'd better go now, Harold.

RADFERN (*to* HAROLD, *rather grimly*): I thought you had gone—for good.

ELSIE: So did I, this morning. But I thought I'd give him another chance. And now you can tell him, Dad.

RADFERN: Tell him what?

ELSIE: You can tell him what we found out from mother this afternoon, that what you said last night was all a joke and that Harold ran away for nothing.

RADFERN: Oh—you've found that out, have you?

ELSIE: Yes, mother showed us the book—it's this one, isn't it?—you got all that stuff out of.

FLETTEN: What stuff? Or is this private and confidential?

ELSIE: No, it isn't. Dad, last night, pretended he was a crook——

FLETTEN (*humorously shocked*): Mr. Radfern, how could you!

ELSIE: And told us a lot of stuff he got out of this book. We all believed him at the time, and Harold here still thinks it's true and wants to run away.

FLETTEN (*severely to* HAROLD): Do you mean to say you could believe for one minute that my friend, Mr. Radfern, was a crook? Mr. Radfern of all people!

RADFERN: Oh, he swallowed it all right.

HAROLD (*sulkily*): And so did everybody else.

FLETTEN: Where's your intelligence, young man? Where's your what's it?—you know—sense of character. Mr. Radfern a crook! You'll be thinking I'm a crook next.

ELSIE (*demurely*): We all did.

FLETTEN: What me! Poor old Joe Fletten, who never did anybody any harm. And is this your idea of a joke, Mr. Radfern?

RADFERN: Sorry, Joe. Just a bit of fun on my part. But I thought it might catch one or two people.

FLETTEN (*severely, looking at* HAROLD): And it seems to have done.

RADFERN: Have your Aunt Lucy and Uncle Bernard gone?

ELSIE: Yes, but that was because mother told them to go.

RADFERN: That's all right, as long as they've gone.

FLETTEN (*to* HAROLD): Don't you think you might apologise to one or two of us?

HAROLD: No, I don't. (*To* ELSIE) Look here, I've had enough of this.

ELSIE (*sadly*): All right, Harold. I gave you a chance, you know. Dad was right after all. Good-bye.

HAROLD (*as if about to break out angrily*): Oh—good night.

> *Swings away and goes out quickly with* RADFERN *following him to the door.* ELSIE *remains quite still.* FLETTEN *looks at her, clears his throat as if to speak, thinks better of it and coughs instead, then hums a little. When* RADFERN *returns,* MRS. RADFERN, *dressed in her outdoor things, follows him in.*

MRS. RADFERN: Good evening, Mr. Fletten. (*To* ELSIE) So Lucy and Bernard have gone?

ELSIE: Yes, quarter of an hour ago. And so has Harold.

MRS. RADFERN: I know that. I nearly bumped into him at the front gate. Has he—gone for good?

ELSIE (*rather unhappily*): Yes. Tried and tested—and found wanting.

RADFERN: Never mind, Elsie. I'll think of something very nice to make up for it.

FLETTEN: Young man actually thought your husband and me was a pair of crooks or something. The cheek of it!

MRS. RADFERN: Oh—that was only George's nonsense, last night. And a very silly thing to do, too, Dad.

FLETTEN: I can't understand how anybody believed it for a minute.

MRS. RADFERN: Well, I must say, I'm surprised, too.

RADFERN: I did it very well.

FLETTEN (*sententiously*): Well, I wouldn't have thought you had it in you, Mr. Radfern, to play a part like that well—even for a bit of a joke. And I doubt if it's anything to joke about.

MRS. RADFERN: I rather agree with you there, Mr. Fletten.

FLETTEN (*as before*): We oughtn't to trifle with our good names— even in fun. That's what I feel.

RADFERN (*dryly*): And it does you credit.

ELSIE (*as she begins moving towards door*): As a matter of fact, it wasn't anything Dad had said, but that card that caught Harold out to-night.

RADFERN: What card?

ELSIE (*turning in doorway*): That one on the table.

    Goes out.

MRS. RADFERN (*amused*): Oh—how absurd! She means the one left by the man from Scotland Yard.

FLETTEN (*alarmed*): From where?

RADFERN (*quietly*): What's this about, then, mother?

MRS. RADFERN: Well, it's all rather amusing. It happened that a Detective-Inspector from Scotland Yard called to see you this afternoon—a very nice man indeed, and we had quite a nice little chat——

FLETTEN (*with glances of despair at* RADFERN): Did you now?

MRS. RADFERN: And he left his card. But what was so amusing was that Elsie and her aunt and uncle arrived before he'd gone and you ought to have seen their faces when I told them he was from Scotland Yard. You'd have screamed.

FLETTEN (*who is wearing the same sort of face they had*): I know I should. Oh—very amusing.

RADFERN (*putting up a good show*): Oh—yes, that's good. Ha, ha, ha!

FLETTEN (*not so good*): Isn't it? Ha, ha, ha!

RADFERN: Did he say what he'd come for?

MRS. RADFERN: Yes. Of course it was something and nothing. Just some enquiries he was making in connection with a commercial case. I told him to come back to-night. He'll be here any minute now, I expect. You ought to have a good chat.

RADFERN: I'm sure we shall.

MRS. RADFERN: Well, I'll go and take my things off and see what sort of mess Lucy and Bernard have made of their room upstairs.

    Goes out.

FLETTEN: Look here, what's the idea?

RADFERN: I don't know.

FLETTEN: I don't believe in that commercial case he's come to make a few enquiries about.

RADFERN: Neither do I.

FLETTEN: Look here, I don't like this——

RADFERN: Now don't get into a panic. Take it easy, but keep on your toes. Listen, you've got to stay here. I can't risk letting you go now. Besides, there may be a lot to do. Now the minute we hear him, I want you to go out through the greenhouse and sit on the grass on the other side, so you can't be seen.

FLETTEN: Well, somebody'll see me.

RADFERN: Yes, but this chap won't or anybody he's got with him. Doesn't matter about the neighbours. Look as if you're studying botany.

FLETTEN: I can't look as if I'm studying botany.

RADFERN: Well, look as if you're half tight and are falling asleep.

FLETTEN: I can do that all right.

Front door bell rings.

RADFERN: And don't come out until you hear me calling you, but when you do hear me calling you, don't lose a second. Understand? Outside, quick. And keep down.

FLETTEN *goes out through door at back, closing it behind him.*
RADFERN *goes through door into house, and then re-enters, followed by* STACK.

RADFERN: Take a seat, Inspector.

STACK: Thanks.

RADFERN: Have a drink?

STACK: No, thanks.

They both sit down, preferably near the table.

RADFERN: This is very interesting. I've never had the pleasure of talking to anybody from Scotland Yard before.

STACK: No, I don't suppose you have, MR. Radfern.

RADFERN: Must have a very exciting life, you chaps. Different from some of us.

STACK: It's not as exciting as people seem to think. Most of it's dull routine, and very long hours at that. Not many quiet evenings at home.

RADFERN: Ah—that's a pity.

STACK: Yes, Mrs. Radfern was telling me this afternoon that you liked to be quiet at home, with your greenhouse and so forth.

RADFERN: Yes. My wife and daughter often laugh at me. They think I'm a very dull old stick.

STACK: Still, I've known wives and children go sadly wrong about men, and think they were leading one sort of life when all the time they were leading a very different sort of life.

RADFERN: Is that so? I've never struck that myself.

STACK (*meaningly*): Really? Are you sure?

RADFERN: Well, I can't recall a case at the moment.

STACK (*meaningly*): You surprise me.

RADFERN: But if there's anything I can tell you, I'll be only too pleased, though I can't imagine why you've taken the trouble to come and see me.

STACK: Trouble's nothing to us, Mr. Radfern, if the case is big enough.

He idly reaches out for book and looks at title.

RADFERN: I can well believe that.

STACK (*holding up book*): Have you read this?

RADFERN: What is it? Oh—*The Great Bank Mystery.* Yes, I finished it yesterday.

STACK: What do you think of it?

RADFERN: Oh—very entertaining. But like most of these things, very far-fetched. Have you read it?

STACK: Yes, I have.

RADFERN: What do you think of it?

STACK: Well, as you say, it's rather far-fetched. The swindlers work on far too big a scale, to start with.

RADFERN: Yes, I should think so.

STACK: All the same, though, it reminds me of a case we've been working at now—one or other of us—for over three years.

RADFERN: Really! Now I call that interesting. And over three years, you say.

STACK: Yes, over three years. And no trouble and reasonable expense spared. Mind you, we'll win in the end. We can't lose.

RADFERN: Well, Inspector, I should hope not. We taxpayers want to see something for our money.

STACK: We're sometimes very slow——

RADFERN: But you're sure. Isn't that it?

STACK: That's it, Mr. Radfern. You see, for the last four years, at least, there's been a gang—a very clever, well-organised gang—who've been engaged in counterfeiting bank notes and Treasury notes.

RADFERN: No? I shouldn't have thought it could be done, these days.

STACK: This gang operates here in England and also abroad, chiefly from Amsterdam and Brussels. Some of the notes are printed there, some of them here. Here's one of their notes. Perhaps you'd like to see it.

Brings out pocket-book and produces pound note.

RADFERN: I would.

He brings out handkerchief and takes up note by one corner with a bit of handkerchief between his fingers and the note.

STACK: You needn't handle it as carefully as all that, Mr. Radfern.

RADFERN: Well, I thought one couldn't be too careful.

STACK (*softly*): If I wanted your fingerprints, you know, I could think of better ways of getting them.

RADFERN (*examining note, laughs*): Never occurred to me. I always thought this fingerprint business chiefly belonged to these detective yarns. Well, y'know, if this is a fake, it would take me in. I'm no expert, of course, but I'm in the paper trade, you know.

STACK (*significantly*): So I understand, Mr. Radfern.

RADFERN: I wouldn't have hesitated a minute giving anybody eight half-crowns for this chap. Isn't it marvellous what they can do. Never would have thought it!

STACK: Surprising, isn't it? Oh—they're a clever lot.

RADFERN: They must be.

STACK: Humph!

RADFERN: Humph!

STACK: They've been clever at getting the right sort of paper, and with their engraving and printing, and with the way they've distributed the slush.

RADFERN: Slush?

STACK: Slush. And the Treasury and the banks haven't given us a minute's peace about this case. But at last we're getting results.

RADFERN: Splendid!

STACK: Yes, hundreds of little details that haven't meant anything much for months are now beginning to look like something.

RADFERN: Just like a jigsaw puzzle, eh?

STACK: That's it. Of course there are still a few pieces missing, but not many—not many. It's only a matter of time now.

RADFERN: That's good, isn't it? You must be feeling very pleased with yourselves, eh?

STACK: We'd feel better still if we could just mop it all up now.

RADFERN (*sympathetically*): Of course you would.

STACK: You see—this is how it often works in these cases—I hope I'm not boring you, Mr. Radfern.

RADFERN: Not at all, Inspector. Very interesting.

STACK: It works like this. We come across a nice little nest of clues in—say—Birmingham——

RADFERN: Birmingham will do. I was there only to-day.

STACK: And among these clues is a name, just one of several names in a notebook. And that name may turn up somewhere else—perhaps in Glasgow—perhaps in Amsterdam. Well, the owner of that name is perhaps passing himself off as an ordinary respectable citizen and business man. And he thinks he's safe. Do you follow me?

RADFERN (*beaming, but with sardonic emphasis*): Yes, I should think I do. Poor devil. I can see it all. This chap imagines he's safe. And of course he isn't because you've got a lot of evidence against him.

STACK: Yes, a lot of evidence.

RADFERN (*as before, but with more emphasis*): And of course it's solid evidence, cast-iron solid evidence that wouldn't make you look silly if you took such a quiet respectable chap into a police court.

STACK (*now taking up the challenge*): No, that's not quite it, because in this instance, we haven't bothered to pile up the solid evidence yet. But we've got one or two interesting little bits. Would you like to hear them?

RADFERN: I would, Inspector.

STACK: Well—for example—we know that a member of this counterfeiting ring arrived in Glasgow from the continent on the twenty-third of last month and was met by one of his confederates here. And we're pretty sure we can prove that this quiet respectable citizen we're talking about was also there, in Glasgow, on the twenty-third of last month.

RADFERN: In Glasgow on the twenty-third of last month? You know, that reminds me of something. The twenty-third? (*He takes out pocket diary and consults it.*) Not that I was in Glasgow. As a matter of fact I was in——

STACK (*quickly, triumphantly, standing*): Newcastle. And so was this man who came from the continent. Not in Glasgow at all. That was a little trap and you walked straight into it.

RADFERN (*very calmly*): Did I? I'm afraid I don't quite follow you there, Inspector. Bit too sharp for me, I expect.

STACK (*grimly*): I shouldn't be surprised.

RADFERN: But what I was going to say was that I remember the twenty-third of last month because the Bowling Club here had an outing that day—up the river first and then finished off at the Palladium—and I was with them. About twenty of us, there were.

STACK (*disappointed*): Humph!

RADFERN (*quietly, but forcibly*): Now that's what I was meaning, you know, Inspector. Isn't that what they call an alibi? Well, you know, if I was that man and you were silly enough to rush me into court, that's the sort of thing—an alibi like that—which would make you all look very foolish, I imagine. Mind you, I know nothing about it—but I've read some of these detective tales.

STACK (*walks away, then suddenly swings round*): If you were that man we're talking about, do you know what I'd say to you?

RADFERN: I can't imagine.

STACK: I'd say to you straight out, look here, we *know* you've been in this, but as yet we can't prove it, though sooner or later we'll be able to prove it. But as the case has dragged on long enough and we want quick results, don't wait like a fool until we can put you in the dock, where nobody's going to have any mercy on you, but tell us all you know *now*—help us to clean the whole thing up—and we won't even *try* to prove anything against you.

RADFERN: Well, of course, I can't answer for this man——

STACK (*sardonically*): Never mind. Make an effort and try.

RADFERN: I fancy the first thing he'd say is that you're bluffing.

STACK: And do you know what I'd reply to that, just to show him we weren't bluffing? First, I'd simply give him two addresses: 59, Pool Road, Glasgow. And, 17, Bellingham Street, Newcastle.

RADFERN (*admiringly*): Just two addresses, like that. Isn't that interesting, now?

STACK (*grimly*): Oh—he'd find it interesting all right. Then I'd give him two names. Peter Korderman and William Frazerly. No bluffing there, you see. We know about Korderman and Frazerly.

RADFERN (*keeping it up*): You know, Inspector, this is as good as any of the films and detective tales to me. Better. It's a treat. Go on.

STACK: All right. Seeing that I'm putting some of my cards on the table, I might as well put this one. (*He produces half a playing card, the Knave of Diamonds.*) What do you think of that?

RADFERN (*examining the card*): Half a Jack of Diamonds. That's grand. But you're not going to tell me these chaps you're after use a thing like this?

STACK (*ironically*): We've got an idea they do. Sort of visiting card, you know, Mr. Radfern. Quite romantic, isn't it?

RADFERN (*shaking his head*): That's the trouble. It seems a bit too romantic to me.

STACK: What do you mean?

RADFERN (*apologetically*): Well, of course, I don't know anything about these things——

STACK (*grimly*): No, no. We know all about that.

RADFERN: But I'd say offhand that this torn card business looks like a bit of leg-pulling. Too much in the story-book style, you know. Sherlock Holmes. Edgar Wallace. I can imagine some chaps—you know, chaps who like a bit of fun—just planting something like this card on you, to keep you guessing and to amuse you. (*Gives the card back.*) And that Carl Korderman you mentioned——

STACK: Peter Korderman.

RADFERN: Peter Korderman, then. Well (*shaking his head*) he doesn't sound quite real to me, you know, Inspector. Perhaps that's another bit of leg-pulling.

STACK *stares at him speculatively, grunts, then walks away.*

STACK (*suddenly turning*): Now listen, Radfern. Let's drop this nonsense and talk straight.

RADFERN: Go on.

STACK (*accusingly*): You're in this counterfeiting game. I know damned well you are, and you know I know. That's straight talking, isn't it?

RADFERN: I don't know whether it's straight or not, but it seems to be very offensive talking.

STACK: Well, here's some more. We want convictions, of course, but what we want even more than that is to break up the ring as soon as possible, because the Treasury and the banks are at us all the time. Tell us all you know *now*, put the game into our hands, and we'll forget about you. And you know what it means if we don't forget about you. There'll be none of this my-first-offence-and-I-didn't-know-any-better humbug for you if you do find yourself in court. You'll get as much as the judge can give you, and that's plenty. Now what do you say?

RADFERN (*impressively*): This is what I say, Inspector Stack. My name is George Radfern, and I'm in the paper trade and can prove it. I live at *Ferndale*, Laburnum Grove, Shooters Green, where I'm well known as a decent respectable citizen and a householder. I've been swindled myself in my time, but if ever I've injured any man, woman or child in this country, then it's news to me. And you haven't enough evidence against me to take me to that door. And you know it.

STACK: Give me a bit more time, and I'll take you a lot further than that door.

[65]

There is a knock at the door. MRS. RADFERN *looks in, smiling.*

MRS. RADFERN: Oh—good evening, Inspector.

STACK: Good evening, Mrs. Radfern.

MRS. RADFERN: Excuse me interrupting you for a minute, but I've left my scissors down here. (*Comes in, looks for them, and finds them.*) Here they are. Are you having an interesting talk, Dad?

RADFERN: Very interesting.

MRS. RADFERN (*returning to door*): That's good. I won't interrupt again.

RADFERN: Oh, mother. You know all that stuff from the shipping companies—all those little books—that Elsie got to amuse herself with?

MRS. RADFERN: Yes, a whole heap of them. She's still got them in her bedroom.

RADFERN: Good. Well, tell her to bring them down with her when she comes. Not just yet. Later on.

MRS. RADFERN: All right. (*Nods and smiles at them both, then goes out.*)

STACK: Well, what do you say?

RADFERN: You heard me ask for all those little books from the shipping companies that my daughter's been collecting. She's always worrying me to take her away somewhere, and I think she could do with a change. So could I, and business is slack now. I've a good mind to go away on a nice long sea voyage.

STACK: Oh, you have, have you? Far?

RADFERN: Oh—I don't know. I should think so. Australia perhaps. Or the Far East. Might find something new in the way of business. And see the world, you know.

STACK: Always wanted to do it myself. I'd hate to have to stop another man going.

RADFERN: I shouldn't like to see you even try, Inspector. Just for your own sake.

STACK: Awkward things, though, ships. You can't get off them when you like, that's the trouble. And now that we've got wireless, they can't get out of hearing.

RADFERN: Yes, that's true.

STACK: An English ship, you know, is as safe to us as an English police court.

RADFERN: No! An English ship as safe as an English police

[66]

court—— Then you'll know where to find me if you want me, won't you?

STACK: I think so. Well, that's that. (*Preparing to go.*)

RADFERN: And thank you very much for calling, Inspector. I've enjoyed this. A peep behind the scenes. Something to tell my friends about.

STACK (*as he moves to door*): Good. Any friend of yours, Mr. Radfern, is interesting to me. You wouldn't like to take me round and introduce me, would you?

RADFERN: I shouldn't think that would be necessary, Inspector.

He goes out with him, leaving door behind him open. You hear them give one another ironically polite 'good nights', then you hear the sound of the front door being closed and locked. RADFERN *returns hastily and closes the sitting-room door behind him. He is now a man of rapid decisive action. He goes quickly to door at back and calls* JOE. JOE FLETTEN *comes at once, brushing his trousers with his hands, his hat on the back of his head.*

FLETTEN (*excitedly*): What's happened? What does he know?

RADFERN: Quite enough. Now listen, Joe, and keep your head screwed on. It's up to you now. Go straight to Westerburg—and it doesn't matter where he is or what he's doing, you've got to see him——

FLETTEN: I know where Westerburg is. Always at the same place, Monday nights.

RADFERN: Tell him I've had a Scotland Yard man here. They've got the Glasgow and Newcastle addresses, and they know about Korderman and Frazerly——

FLETTEN: The hell they do! We're done then.

RADFERN: No, we're not. That's all they do know *yet*. And that's got to be all too. Tell Westerburg it's Plan B now or nothing.

FLETTEN: What! Sink the plates and presses, and scatter!

RADFERN: Yes, he knows what to do. And tell him that anyhow I'm working on Plan B from to-night, and he'd better wire Amsterdam for me. And I'll ring up Middleton myself now. Have you got that?

FLETTEN: Yes.

RADFERN: And you'd better put Plan B into action yourself, Joe, if you don't want to see Maidstone and Parkhurst again.

FLETTEN: You bet your life I will.

RADFERN (*pointing to back door*): That way then, and as quick as you can. There's a narrow lane at the back. Turn to the right at the top and you're at the Tube station in three minutes. And for God's sake, make haste, but don't look as if you think the nearest bobby's going to put his hand on your shoulder. Good luck, Joe. Shan't see you for a long time—I hope.

FLETTEN: All the best, Mr. Radfern.

He hurries out at the back. RADFERN *goes to the telephone and begins dialling.*

RADFERN (*at telephone*): I want to speak to Mr. Middleton, please . . . Hello, is that you, Charlie? Yes, Radfern. Yes, everything all right at Birmingham . . . But, listen, Charlie . . .

Here MRS. RADFERN *and* ELSIE *enter. The latter is carrying a lot of shipping booklets, etc. She is listless and looks miserable.*

I've just had an Inspector from Scotland Yard . . . Yes . . . And you know how these chaps get about a bit, and he was saying that he didn't think business would be very good these next few months . . . Yes, so I thought I'd take that holiday I've been promising myself for some time . . . Yes, what we used to call Plan B—you remember our little joke . . . Holland, of course . . . All right, Charlie . . . Goodbye.

Puts down telephone.

MRS. RADFERN (*jovially*): You didn't get arrested then, Dad?

RADFERN (*in same tone*): No, just managed to escape.

MRS. RADFERN: What did the Inspector want?

RADFERN: What you said. Just making some enquiries about a commercial case he's on. Queer life they have, those chaps.

ELSIE (*joining in, but still listless*): Wouldn't suit you, Dad. Too much excitement. Not enough peace and quietness.

RADFERN: That's it.

MRS. RADFERN (*chaffing*): You didn't tell him what a tough old crook you were yourself, did you?

RADFERN: No need to. He knew it already.

ELSIE (*still listless*): What were you saying on the telephone about going away?

RADFERN (*with affectionate concern*): Look here, Elsie. You've got to brighten up, because there's a lot to do.

ELSIE (*indifferently*): What is there to do?

RADFERN: Well, one of the things you've got to do is to take your mother to Brussels to-morrow.

ELSIE (*a changed girl*): Dad! You don't mean it!

[68]

RADFERN: I do. We're going to close this house and go on our travels.

MRS. RADFERN: Good gracious me!

ELSIE: Dad!

RADFERN: Now, we've got passports.

ELSIE: Where are they marked for?

RADFERN: Everywhere. You see—we're going to close this house, pack up and go on a long sea voyage—East Indies, Far East, Australia —God knows where. Only we're starting on one of those Dutch boats.

MRS. RADFERN: Dutch boats! Why not an English boat?

RADFERN: Oh, all the best boats that go out East are Dutch. They're much more comfortable. English boats are like police courts! You and your mother are going to Brussels first, and then you're going to meet me later, over there.

MRS. RADFERN: But how are you going?

RADFERN: I'm going straight to Holland. Some business to attend to first. A friend of mine will take me.

ELSIE: But how?

RADFERN: By underground perhaps. Never mind about that.

ELSIE: Oh—I don't mind about anything. (*Embraces him.*) Mother, we're going to travel. (*Embraces her.*)

MRS. RADFERN: I hope this isn't another of your jokes, Dad?

ELSIE: Oh, Dad, I'll never forgive you if it is.

RADFERN: It isn't. You've got twenty-four hours to pack up in and close this house and get off to Brussels.

ELSIE (*babbling happily*): Then we won't go to bed at all. And let's look at these things (*holding up shipping booklets*) and then we'll have supper and begin packing. But we'll have to have some clothes, won't we, Mother, especially if we're going to hot countries, but I suppose we could get them in Brussels or wherever we're going—couldn't we go to Paris first and then we could buy some clothes there and it would be nearly as easy to get from Paris to Holland or wherever it is——

MRS. RADFERN (*loudly*): Oh, Elsie, stop it. My head's going round.

There is a ring at the front door, very loud and persistent. It startles them all.

ELSIE: I'll go.

Runs off.

MRS. RADFERN: That child's so excited she doesn't know what she's talking about.

RADFERN: Do her good.

MRS. RADFERN: It won't if she's disappointed again.

RADFERN: I'll see to that.

MRS. RADFERN: You're very masterful to-night, Dad, aren't you? What's the matter?

RADFERN: Have to assert myself sometimes, Mother.

ELSIE *returns a moment later, looking frightened.*

ELSIE: Dad, it's a police sergeant and he wants to see you.

RADFERN (*gravely, steadily*): All right.

ELSIE (*going over to him, softly*): Dad—it's not true—after all—is it?

RADFERN (*cheerfully*): That's all right, Elsie. Ask him to come in.

ELSIE *is clinging to his arm.*

MRS. RADFERN: Don't be ridiculous, Elsie. (*She goes and admits the sergeant, a heavily built, middle-aged man with a deep voice and a rather pompous manner.*)

SERGEANT MORRIS: Mr. George Radfern.

RADFERN (*steadily*): That's me, sergeant.

SERGEANT MORRIS: I think you've seen me before. I'm from the local station.

RADFERN: Know you well by sight.

SERGEANT MORRIS: I've just heard that you might be going away soon.

RADFERN: That's right. I'm seriously thinking of it, Sergeant.

SERGEANT MORRIS: Well, Mr. Cross at the end house said you'd like to be one of the patrons and vice-presidents of the new Shooters Green Football Club.

RADFERN: Oh—you've come round to make sure of my subscription.

SERGEANT MORRIS (*relieved*): That's it, Mr. Radfern. Three guineas—for a vice-president.

RADFERN (*producing money*): Must be a vice-president. There you are. There's a fiver for luck.

SERGEANT MORRIS (*who has been writing*): That's the official receipt. And thank you very much, Mr. Radfern. Good night, mum, good night, miss. Good night.

He goes out, and MRS. RADFERN *goes as far as the door behind him.* ELSIE *gives an hysterical laugh, really of relief.*

RADFERN: What are you laughing at?

[70]

ELSIE: I don't know. Everything. Oh—Dad—how long shall we be away?

RADFERN: Don't know yet. Four months. Six months.

ELSIE: Oh—what about your greenhouse?

RADFERN: Where we're going it'll be all greenhouse.

Enter MRS. RADFERN.

ELSIE: And what about Laburnum Grove?

MRS. RADFERN (*briskly*): It'll be still here when we come back.

ELSIE (*excitedly*): Let's look at all these things. (*Indicating shipping booklets.*)

MRS. RADFERN (*firmly*): It's my turn now. We don't look at anything until we've had some supper. And you can help me to get it ready for once.

ELSIE (*happily*): All right, mother. (*Hurries into kitchen, where she can be heard singing happily.*)

MRS. RADFERN (*as she removes various things and cloth from table*): And you needn't tell me you haven't been up to *something*, you know, Dad.

RADFERN (*grinning at her*): All right, Mother. I needn't tell you.

MRS. RADFERN *is spreading a tablecloth and* ELSIE *entering with some supper things and* RADFERN *smiling at them both, as the curtain slowly descends.*

END OF PLAY

BEES ON THE BOAT DECK

A Farcical Tragedy in Two Acts

CHARACTERS

(in order of their appearance)

SAM GRIDLEY, Chief Engineer, ss. *Gloriana*
ROBERT PATCH, Second Officer, ss. *Gloriana*
SLIVERS, a Local Shopkeeper
HILDA JACKSON, Gridley's Niece, a Children's Nurse
FRANCIS FLETHERINGTON, a Research Chemist
LORD COTTINGLEY, a Director of Shipping Companies
HON. URSULA MADDINGS, his Daughter
GASTER, Member of Communist Party
CAPT. MELLOCK, a Professional Fascist
SERGEANT WILKS, of the Local Police
MR. TOOKE, from Head Office

ACT I
Well deck of ss. *Gloriana*, lying in backwater of Trim Estuary,
on the South Coast. Morning of Midsummer Day.

ACT II
The same. Afternoon.

Bees on the Boat Deck—Copyright, 1936, *by John Boynton Priestley.*

First produced at the Lyric Theatre, London, on May 5th, 1936, with the following cast:

SAM GRIDLEY	RALPH RICHARDSON
ROBERT PATCH	LAURENCE OLIVIER
SLIVERS	RAYMOND HUNTLEY
HILDA JACKSON	RENEE RAY
FRANCIS FLETHERINGTON	RICHARD GOOLDEN
LORD COTTINGLEY	ALAN JEAYES
URSULA MADDINGS	KAY HAMMOND
GASTER	JOHN LAURIE
CAPTAIN MELLOCK	S. J. WARMINGTON
SERGEANT WILKS	ARTHUR HAMBLING
MR. TOOKE	FREDERICK T. COOPER

ACT I

Well deck of ss. Gloriana, *lying in backwater of Trim estuary.*

On right is superstructure, and companion-way leading to upper deck. Cabin doors above and below. Behind is rail, with place for gangway leading down to ground. At the back are branches of trees, thick with foliage. Some of these are almost over the deck. On deck are a few old deck-chairs and canvas folding chairs and a small table, all now pushed to one side. It is midsummer and the whole scene is lit with bright sunshine.

At rise, SAM GRIDLEY, *a rough-looking middle-aged man, and* BOB PATCH, *a younger, neater and rather good-looking man, are playing deck-tennis. They are wearing old flannel bags, canvas shoes and open shirts. They must play properly, with* PATCH *winning.*

GRIDLEY: Your game.

PATCH: And set. Six two.

GRIDLEY (*who is very hot, mopping his brow, etc.*): All right. Boys' game, anyhow. Boys' game.

> *They take down the net, put it away, then pull chairs forward.* GRIDLEY *puts on old chief-engineer's jacket before sitting down. He lights a pipe,* PATCH *a cigarette.* GRIDLEY *produces small volume from his pocket.*

PATCH (*noticing the book*): Not What's-his-name again!

GRIDLEY (*solemnly*): Having exercised the body, now we ought to exercise the mind. Schopenhauer. (*He pronounces it Shoppen-hawer.*)

PATCH: I'm tired of him.

GRIDLEY: Tired of him! You haven't properly started on him yet. You don't know the very beginnings of him. Let me tell you, there's things in—this—— (*Holding up book.*)

PATCH (*wearily, but good-humouredly*): I know, I know. You've told me. If I'd only been there, when the *Theodosia* went down——

GRIDLEY: You'd have known a lot more about life than you do now, laddie. What I saw that day——

PATCH: You've told me before, Sam, dozens of times. They were all screaming, fighting, knocking hell out of each other to get into the boats——

GRIDLEY: Human nature—and you can have it. All in this book, boy, all in this book. First time I ever looked into it, I said, this is the chap for me. (*Opens book and begins reading slowly.*) "Thus between desiring and attaining all human life flows on throughout. The wish is, in its nature, pain; the attainment soon begets satiety; the end was only apparent; possession takes away the charm; the wish, the need, presents itself under a new form; when it does not, then follows desolateness, emptiness . . ."

PATCH (*interrupting*): And the sooner we're dead, the better. That's what he's saying all the time, and why he takes so long to say it beats me.

GRIDLEY (*solemnly*): You haven't the mind for it yet, Bob. Schopen-hauer——

PATCH: Here, how long did *he* live?

GRIDLEY (*turning to beginning of book and reading*): Arthur Schopenhauer was born in 1788, and died in 1860.

PATCH: Seventy-two. Well, he didn't do so badly, did he? Nicely off all the time, too, I expect. Don't read me any more of that old blighter. Finish!

GRIDLEY: That's all right to me. If you haven't the mind for it, you haven't, that's all.

PATCH (*contemptuously, getting up and strolling off back right*): Mind for it!

He goes off, and GRIDLEY *settles to read, slowly and solemnly. He is disturbed by the arrival of* MR. SLIVERS, *a foolish-looking, middle-aged man, who is carrying several packages.*

SLIVERS: Good morning.

GRIDLEY: Morning, Mr. Slivers.

SLIVERS: Nice morning.

GRIDLEY: Nice morning.

SLIVERS (*coming forward*): I thought I'd bring your order here myself this morning. Gets me out o' the shop, y'know, Mr. Gridley. Makes a change. I see where it says in the paper that's what you've got to do. 'Ave a change whenever possible, it says.

GRIDLEY: Doesn't tell you to change your paper, does it? Well, what have you brought us?

SLIVERS (*now the shopkeeper, glibly*): Dozen fresh eggs, pound o' butter, same of the usual bacon——

GRIDLEY (*looking into one of the bags*): What sort of cheese is this?

SLIVERS: That's Canadian Cheddar, that is, Mr. Gridley. We're just out o' the other, but you'll find this very nice—very nice. A lot of people speak highly of that Canadian Cheddar——

GRIDLEY (*sceptically*): What people?

SLIVERS: Customers of mine, very nice people. (*Handing over package of tobacco*) And two ounces of *Hearts of Oak*. That'll set you up, won't it, Mr. Gridley. You like your pipe, don't you?

GRIDLEY: Yes.

SLIVERS (*idiotically*): That's right. Wish I could manage one. Always burns my tongue. Now, Mr. Gridley, will you tell me something?

GRIDLEY: Anything, Mr. Slivers. Just ask me, and I'll tell you. Here, put that stuff down.

> *They put packages down.* SLIVERS *sits.*

Now what is it?

SLIVERS (*earnestly*): You're not kidding me, are you?

GRIDLEY: Kidding you? What do you mean?

SLIVERS: About you—and this ship—and everything.

GRIDLEY (*calling*): Bob.

PATCH (*off, right back*): Yes?

GRIDLEY (*calling*): He's at it again. Won't believe us.

SLIVERS: Now, Mr. Gridley, did I say that? But I just wondered——

> PATCH *enters. He looks cool and neat now, is wearing a tie with his soft shirt, but no coat. He is smoking a cigarette.*

PATCH: Morning.

SLIVERS: Morning. Nice morning.

PATCH: I bet you saw that in the paper.

SLIVERS (*seriously*): No, but I see where it says there's a 'eat wave on the way.

PATCH: Shouldn't be surprised. Now what's this about you calling us a couple of liars?

SLIVERS: I never did. I thought you might 'ave been pulling my leg, that's all.

PATCH: What should we want to pull your leg for?

GRIDLEY: You haven't got the sort of leg he likes to pull.

PATCH: That'll do, Sam. (*To* SLIVERS) Now listen, this is a ship. And she's a good ship—or she was.

GRIDLEY: Still is. I don't want a better one.

PATCH: Ten thousand tons. She cost—what did she cost, Sam?

GRIDLEY: At least three hundred and fifty thousand pounds.

SLIVERS: Ah—that's money, that is.

GRIDLEY: That was. Built only in 1919. Economic speed—fourteen knots. And we have pushed her up to sixteen and a half. And she used to run, regular as clockwork, London to Cape Town, Cape Town to Durban, Durban to Melbourne, Melbourne to Sydney, Sydney to Wellington, carrying anything and anybody you wanted, as sweet and pretty as you please.

PATCH: And—get this, once and for all—for the last two years she was running, Sam Gridley here was chief engineer, and I was second officer. No deception. All perfectly straightforward. Meet the chief of the *Gloriana*. Meet the second officer. Nobody's kidding you. We're not a couple of out-of-work bookies' clerks. We're not trying to sell linoleum. This isn't a caravan. You're talking now to two officers of His Majesty's Mercantile Marine. We've served apprenticeships. We've passed examinations—all kinds of bloody examinations. We've got certificates to prove it.

SLIVERS (*rather dazed*): Yes, I expect you have.

GRIDLEY: And this ship's lying here, useless and rusting her guts out, because the White Albion Line that owns her is—like most of the shipping companies—in Queer Street. They can't afford to run her, see? She can't pay for herself, with trade as it is.

SLIVERS: Yes, but trade's better. I see where it says in the paper the depression's over. Britain back to normal, it says. Prosperity, it says, on the way.

PATCH (*savagely*): Yes, but you see, this ship's stupid. It doesn't read the paper. It doesn't know anything about that. We don't either. We're just a couple of dam' fools, you see.

GRIDLEY: Steady, boy, steady. Take it easy with Mr. Slivers. He's friendly. (*Patting* SLIVERS *on shoulder.*) Aren't you, Mr. Slivers?

SLIVERS: That's right, Mr. Gridley. Only you see—I couldn't help wondering.

GRIDLEY: You did right to wonder. You keep on wondering. If a chap isn't going to wonder nowadays, when the hell is he going to wonder? Tell me that.

PATCH: Only stop wondering about us. We explained it all before.

SLIVERS: Yes, but you see, there's some ships like this in the estuary, half a dozen of 'em between Biddington and Longport, and they just have a watchman on board . . .

GRIDLEY: Well, we're the watchmen here, see? They couldn't find us any berths, and neither could anybody else, so here we are. Seeing that nobody steals the ship.

SLIVERS: But why is she up here in this backwater, and not out there with the others?

PATCH: Because the fellow that brought her in here was crazy. Or perhaps he liked a bit of quiet fun. Anyhow, he rammed her in here, and it's my opinion the *Queen Mary* herself couldn't pull her out.

GRIDLEY: We could get her out, if she was wanted.

PATCH: Never. Couldn't be done. She's here till she rusts to pieces. Unless they'd like to dig her out and then put wheels under her and call her a roadhouse.

SLIVERS: She does look a bit funny here, doesn't she?

PATCH: Funny my foot! She doesn't make me want to laugh. She makes me want to cry. Look at them—trees. And this is a ship. Next year, if we're not careful it'll be a ruddy farm. They'll be hay-making, here.

GRIDLEY: I was up on the boat deck earlier on, Bob. Do you know what we've got there now—up on the boat deck, mind you? (*Very loudly.*) Bees. It's a fact. Bees on the boat deck.

PATCH (*to* Slivers): Now have a good laugh.

SLIVERS (*after pause, tactfully changing subject*): Er—they tell me there was a bit of a rumpus down at Longport last night. There's a by-election there, y'know.

GRIDLEY: No, I didn't know.

SLIVERS: Oh yes. Parliamentary by-election all right. Five candidates, including a Red, proper Communist he is, and a sort of Fascist chap. It was the Reds and these Fascists that had a set-to last night, they tell me. Neither of them'll get in, though. Too extreme. The good sense of the Longport voter will see to that.

PATCH: You've got that bit out of the paper too. The good sense of the Longport voter! Gert-cher!

SLIVERS: And I see where it says in the paper the Duke of Blandshire—he's got a big place about fifteen miles away from here—is giving up two of his houses——

PATCH (*sardonically*): No!

SLIVERS: Yes, can't keep them up, it says, owing to heavy taxation. It's hard lines, I say. I'm sorry for the Duke.

GRIDLEY: So am I, Mr. Slivers. It just breaks my heart to think about him, struggling on.

SLIVERS: Well, he's got his responsibilities, hasn't he? We wouldn't like it. And after all he's got a big stake in the country.

PATCH: Yes, and a lot of chips too, I'll bet. Well, what's the rest of the news? I can see you've had a good crack at the paper this morning.

SLIVERS: Oh—that Meddleworth case—you know, about who's

to keep the little boy—is held up. One of the chief witnesses has disappeared.

PATCH: Meddleworth case? Don't know anything about it. Do you, Sam?

GRIDLEY: (*who has been busy with his pipe*): No, don't know and don't care.

SLIVERS: Oh—it's a big sensation. Lot of goings on coming out. Papers are running it hard. All disgusting, y'know—but very spicy.

GRIDLEY: That'll suit you, Bob. You like it spicy.

PATCH: Got a paper with you?

As SLIVERS *hands one over, from his pocket.*

Thanks. (*Begins unfolding it.*)

GRIDLEY: Save me the cricket page, Bob.

PATCH (*now burying himself in paper*): Right.

GRIDLEY (*heartily*): Now I'll tell you what I will do, Mr. Slivers, just to show you there's no ill-feeling. If you like, you shall come below with me, and I'll let you have a peep at as neat a geared turbine job as you can ever hope to see.

SLIVERS: Engines, eh?

GRIDLEY: Yes, and engines that 'ud be ready to take you and all the other people in Biddington—yes, and all their tables and chairs and beds and bits o' things—from here to Peru next Saturday. Ready? By God, they're aching to be off again. Every time I go down I hear 'em whispering: "What about it, Sam, what about it? Come on, let's go, Sam, let's go." And you won't read about that in the paper. This way.

He holds one of the doors open. SLIVERS *rises, and they both go out.* PATCH *is reading, but is apparently disturbed by an insect, for he puts paper down, impatiently brushes something away, looks anxiously about him, then finally settles down again.* HILDA JACKSON *rather slowly and timidly boards the ship. She is a pleasant-looking girl about twenty-five, quietly and neatly dressed. She is carrying a very small case. Her manner should suggest a person of decent steady nerves who has lately been harassed almost into hysteria; she is using all her self-control.* PATCH *does not see or hear her, as she quietly comes forward. She looks at him hesitantly. She cannot see his face.*

HILDA (*timidly*): Er——

PATCH (*looking up, surprised*): Hello!

HILDA (*timidly*): Good morning.

PATCH (*getting up, staring at her in puzzled fashion, then taking up newspaper and looking at that, then looking again at her*): That's funny.

HILDA (*timidly*): Yes.

PATCH: What do you mean, "Yes"?

HILDA (*dismally*): You see—I know what you're thinking.

PATCH: Oh?

HILDA: Yes. It is me—there in the paper.

PATCH (*surprised*): It is?

HILDA: Yes.

To his astonishment, she now suddenly bursts into tears.

PATCH (*sympathetic but embarrassed*): I say, what's the matter? You mustn't do that.

HILDA (*through her sobs*): I'm sorry. But—I—can't help it.

PATCH (*fussing with her*): No, of course not. That's all right. But what's wrong, what's the matter? Look here, sit down first. Must sit down. (*Makes her sit down.*) There, that's better, isn't it?

HILDA (*trying to smile through her tears*): Yes. But I want my uncle.

PATCH (*completely puzzled by this*): Oh—you want your uncle.

HILDA: Yes.

PATCH (*regarding her with a mixture of pity and suspicion, obviously concluding that she is a bit mad*): Well—we'll have to—see what we can do. Only—don't cry. That's no good. You'll never get your uncle that way. Have—er—a cigarette.

HILDA (*drying herself*): No, thank you. I don't smoke.

PATCH (*ready to say anything now*): I don't blame you, I don't blame you at all. Pretty warm, isn't it?

HILDA: Yes. But I don't mind it.

PATCH: No, I don't. Rather like it, in fact. Now—er—about your uncle——

HILDA (*alarmed*): He's still here, isn't he?

PATCH: Still here—your uncle? (*As the light dawns*) I say—you don't mean Sam—Sam Gridley?

HILDA: Yes. He's my uncle.

PATCH (*almost shouting in his relief*): Well—for the love of Pete! And Sam's your uncle. Old Sam! Good old Sam! Yes, he's here.

HILDA (*tremendously relieved*): Oh—thank goodness!

PATCH: And I'm Bob Patch—used to be second officer with him in this ship. We're looking after her together.

[83]

HILDA: Yes, I know. And I've come here—to hide.

PATCH: Then you really are the girl—the nurse—in that Meddleworth case—the one who's disappeared.

HILDA (*in very low voice*): Yes—I'm Hilda Jackson.

PATCH: Well, I'll be—hanged! Here are you, Sam's niece—and the papers are full of you and I expect they're talking about you all over the place——

HILDA (*in low voice*): Yes, they are.

PATCH: And yet old Sam's never said a word. Not one word. D'you know, I don't believe he knows anything about the case, never heard of it. Honestly. It 'ud be just like him. Never knows what's going on. Doesn't care. And here you are—his niece.

HILDA (*hesitantly*): Yes. Do you think—I can stay here?

PATCH: Certainly you can stay here. Just the very place. They'll never find you here. Hardly anybody ever comes here anyhow. And this is the last place they'd think of looking for you. Of course you can stay. (*Pauses.*) Might have to make yourself useful, y'know.

HILDA (*eagerly*): Oh yes—I always like to do that.

PATCH: Fine. Can you cook?

HILDA: Yes—I'm rather a good cook. And I love it.

PATCH: Then you're just what we want. D'you know, I haven't tasted a pudding for weeks and weeks and weeks, and I'm very fond of puddings.

HILDA: What a shame! But isn't it rather too hot for puddings?

PATCH (*seriously*): It's never too hot for a *good* pudding. Could you do a baked jam roll?

HILDA (*smiling*): Yes, I think so.

PATCH: Couldn't be better. Old Sam likes baked jam roll, too. We've talked a lot about it lately, because we used to have a cook in this ship who was quite a fair hand at baked jam roll. Well, well, well, I call this a stroke of luck. I say, are you tired? How did you get here?

HILDA (*confidentially*): I stayed last night with a girl I know—in a little place between Portsmouth and Winchester. Then, early this morning, I got a bus half-way to Longport, then another bus there, and then another bus from Longport to that village—Biddington. You see, I thought it was safer going by bus than by train.

PATCH: I'll bet you're right, too. They may be watching the stations. You never know.

HILDA: Do you think it's wrong for me to run away, like this?

PATCH (*stoutly*): No, I don't. If you've had enough of it, why should they make you go on with it? After all, it's really nothing to do with you, who has the kid. You stay here. We'll see you're all right.

Enter GRIDLEY *and* SLIVERS, *who stares at* HILDA.

GRIDLEY (*astonished*): Aren't you—Hilda?

PATCH (*before anybody else has time to do anything*): Hoy, let me do this. Mr. Slivers, allow me to introduce my cousin, Miss Matilda —er—Robinson.

HILDA (*nervously*): How d'you do?

SLIVERS (*never taking his eyes off her, suspiciously*): Pleased to meet you. Very pleased.

PATCH (*heartily*): Well, what do you think of our engines?

SLIVERS (*still staring*): Very interesting. (*Suddenly, triumphantly, pointing at* HILDA.) I know who you are. That's it. Miss Hilda Jackson—the missing witness in the Meddleworth Case. You can't deny it, can you?

HILDA (*dismayed*) No.

GRIDLEY: What's all this about?

PATCH (*to* GRIDLEY): Just a minute. (*To others.*) Now then——

HILDA (*eagerly, to* SLIVERS): Please don't tell anybody you've seen me here, please. You can't understand how awful it's been for me. If I could have done anything for Hugh—the little boy—I'd have stayed, but they took him away and—— (*She shows signs of breaking down again.*)

SLIVERS (*who is still staring at her, rather triumphantly*): Yes, but— er—I mean to say, you're one of the chief witnesses, aren't you? And it says in the paper——

PATCH (*who has been casting unfriendly glances at* SLIVERS): Just a minute, Mr. Slivers. (*Goes up to him.*) I'd like to explain this to you. (*Dropping his voice, very confidentially*) There's a lot of things about this business you don't understand yet, see? We'll just go along here and I'll explain. (*As he leads him off, towards cabins*) Can't talk properly here, see?

They go off right. GRIDLEY *looks at* HILDA *in astonishment.*

GRIDLEY: This beats me! I don't know anything about this Meddleworth case. Where d'you come into it, Hilda?

HILDA: I was the little boy's nurse. You knew I was a children's nurse, didn't you?

GRIDLEY: Yes, your mother told me that much. But what are these Meddleworths and why are you a witness?

HILDA: They're separated. And they're very rich important people, you see, uncle. And Sir Eric Meddleworth had the boy—it was he who gave me the job—and then his wife, Lady Meddleworth, wanted Hugh, and tried to take him away. And then they went to law, and each one said the other wasn't fit to have the boy—and they were trying to prove the most horrible things about each other——

GRIDLEY (*with grim satisfaction*): Most of 'em true too, I'll be bound.

HILDA: And then the papers took it up——

GRIDLEY: I remember. They were just talking about it this morning. Spicy!

HILDA: It's not spicy. It's just horrible, dirty. And I was in the middle of it—and they were always wanting to take my photograph——

GRIDLEY: You didn't mind that. Come now. Never heard of a girl who didn't want her photograph in the papers.

HILDA: Yes, but not mixed up with all this dirt and nastiness. And the reporters wouldn't leave me alone. And in the court, they asked me the most awful questions—and wouldn't let me answer back properly—as good as told me I was a liar—and they'd taken Hugh away—and I couldn't stand it any longer. Uncle, I couldn't. Not another day of it. I'd have gone mad—had a breakdown—or something. Uncle, you do understand, don't you? (*She goes up to him.*)

GRIDLEY (*patting her on the shoulder*): Yes, yes, that's all right. You keep out of it, if you want to. Damn their eyes, I say. Yes, damn their eyes!

HILDA: I thought if I came here for a day or two, they wouldn't find me——

GRIDLEY: Don't see why they should. You stay here.

HILDA: And I can cook.

GRIDLEY: Puddings?

HILDA (*smiling*): Yes. Jam roll too.

GRIDLEY: You stay here. We'll look after you. (*He sees* PATCH *returning alone.*) Won't we, Bob? I say, we'll look after her.

PATCH: Yes. We've just started.

GRIDLEY: Where's Slivers?

PATCH (*casually*): I've locked him in Cabin A. He'll be all right. He's got his paper.

GRIDLEY (*staring*): What have you done that for?

PATCH: Had to. If we'd let him go, he'd have told everybody she was here. In half an hour the police 'ud have been here for her.

GRIDLEY *stares at* PATCH, *then at* HILDA, *in amazement.*

HILDA: It's true. I knew he was going to tell. I could see it in his eyes

PATCH: Trust him! Well, he won't blab while he's in there.

GRIDLEY, *rubbing his chin, slowly sits down.*

HILDA (*troubled*): But what are we to do? You can't keep him there long.

PATCH: We can keep him long enough to give us time to think— and you time to have a rest. That's enough to be going on with.

GRIDLEY: Well, it's plenty to be going on with. (*He whistles an ascending scale meditatively.* PATCH *answers it whistling a descending scale derisively.*) I call this a morning.

PATCH (*coolly*): It's time something happened here.

GRIDLEY: Where's the key of that cabin?

PATCH: In my pocket. Why? You're not thinking of letting the little blighter out, are you?

GRIDLEY (*dubiously*): No, not if he's going to run and tell the police about Hilda here. Certainly not. But we might make him promise——

PATCH: Promise! I wouldn't trust him ten yards. He'd let it out even if he didn't want to. Hasn't the sense to keep it to himself. Him and his papers! Forget about him. Take it easy.

HILDA (*dreamily*): I'd like to forget about everything for an hour or two, at least.

PATCH (*grinning at her*): And you're going to.

GRIDLEY: Certainly, certainly. Take it easy, girl. You're all right now.

HILDA *stretches out in her chair luxuriously. The other two also relax. The scene is very peaceful. They speak easily and quietly.*

HILDA: You don't know how wonderful it is just to rest—and be quiet.

PATCH: Quiet enough here. Too quiet.

GRIDLEY (*to* HILDA): He wants Oxford Street and Piccadilly Circus, that's what he wants. Palladiums and Corner Houses and what not. Jazz bands and girls.

PATCH (*hastily*): Not girls.

GRIDLEY (*tactlessly*): Well, you've talked enough about 'em. All colours of girls.

PATCH (*who does not want* HILDA *to hear this, and sees that she is listening carefully*): Never! But a place can be too quiet, that's all.

HILDA (*dreamily*): Not for me it can't—just now. This is perfect. So peaceful.

> *As her voice trails off into silence, there is the sound of a terrific explosion off right. Mingled with this is the noise of trees cracking, and this continues after the actual explosion. A shower of twigs falls on the deck, followed by a number of tiny twigs and a shower of leaves. HILDA gives a scream, the two men a shout. Then, in the silence, GRIDLEY whistles his scale and PATCH answers it. HILDA has risen from her chair. The two men rush to the rail now and look in the direction of the explosion.*

PATCH: There's a fellow there. See! (*Shouting to him.*) Hoy!

GRIDLEY: I don't see him. Ah yes, there he is. (*Shouting.*) Hoy!

> HILDA *joins them.*

HILDA: Oh—look! I believe he's hurt himself.

PATCH: I'll see.

> *He hurries ashore.* GRIDLEY *and* HILDA *look anxious and vaguely helpful, but do not leave the ship.*

HILDA: But what can have happened, uncle?

GRIDLEY: Looks to me as if he's been trying to blow a few trees up.

HILDA: But why should he do that?

GRIDLEY: Well—one thing or another—I dunno. Nowadays, they're just as likely to be blowing up trees as doing anything else. Don't ask me to make sense of it. I can't do it.

HILDA (*looking down*): Here they are.

GRIDLEY (*shouting*): Can you manage him? Is he bad? Oh—all right.

HILDA: Poor man! But I don't think he's badly hurt.

GRIDLEY: Looks too pleased with himself. What's he got to be pleased about? Impossible to make sense of anything!

> PATCH *returns supporting* FLETHERINGTON *with one hand and carrying in the other a small bag.* FLETHERINGTON *is between forty and fifty, with the thin eager face of an unworldly student, and a gentle high voice. He has apparently been knocked down by the explosion. He is cut and bruised in a few places, rather dirty, and his clothes have been damaged. But he is smiling.*

FLETHERINGTON: Good morning. I'm afraid I've been rather a nuisance.

GRIDLEY: Was that your explosion?

FLETHERINGTON (*smiling*): Yes.

GRIDLEY: Then you're right. You have been a nuisance.

FLETHERINGTON: I'm awfully sorry. (*To* HILDA.) I hope you weren't alarmed?

HILDA: No—not much. But—you're bleeding.

FLETHERINGTON: Oh, nothing—mere scratches, thank you.

HILDA (*rather severely*): You ought to have those cuts cleaned. If I could have some water and a clean cloth and some iodine——

PATCH: I'll find them for you. Come with me. I'd better chuck this bag down somewhere.

FLETHERINGTON: Put it down rather carefully, please.

GRIDLEY: Here, what's in that bag?

FLETHERINGTON (*coolly*): The high explosive I was testing and——

GRIDLEY: Steady with that bag, Bob. Don't drop it.

> HILDA *has recoiled in alarm.* PATCH *is regarding the bag he still holds with marked distaste.*

FLETHERINGTON (*taking the bag*): Allow me.

> PATCH *and* HILDA *go out rather hurriedly.* FLETHERINGTON *sits down and opens the bag.* GRIDLEY *watches him anxiously.*

There's no danger from the explosive itself. You can kick it about, hammer it, do what you like, it won't go off. That's one of its great advantages. But I have some detonators here—— (*He produces a small package.*) and they're very sensitive. Not powerful, of course. But if they're handled carelessly, they can take off an arm or a leg quite nicely. Where shall I put them?

GRIDLEY: Can't you throw 'em overboard?

FLETHERINGTON (*apologetically*): I'd rather not do that, you know. They'd explode at once and that would be a waste of good detonators. I'll put them here—— (*Moves across to some likely place.*) You see, it's as well to have them away from the explosive itself.

GRIDLEY: Yes. And for God's sake, see that nobody touches 'em.

FLETHERINGTON (*smiling gently; returning to his chair*): This explosive in the bag is a little discovery of mine. I'm a research chemist and I've been working on nitro compounds. Always very amusing, I think, all these coal tar derivatives. You never know what you're going to turn up—a new perfume, perhaps, a new dye, or, like this, a new explosive——

GRIDLEY (*grimly*): We're out o' luck here. I wish it 'ud been a new perfume or a new dye.

FLETHERINGTON: I made a pound or two of this explosive—they're in crystal form—at the lab, and when we came down here for our holidays, I brought the stuff with me—to try it out.

GRIDLEY (*grimly*): You have to have a bit o' fun on your holidays, haven't you?

FLETHERINGTON (*unaware of the irony*): Exactly. I've called the stuff—temporarily, anyhow—*Fletherite*. You see, my name's Fletherington. So—*Fletherite*. Rather egoistical, perhaps—— (*he smiles apologetically*)—but I think it's excusable, don't you? My wife, a very sensible woman in some respects, seemed to think so.

GRIDLEY (*who can't make this fellow out, rubbing his chin*): Oh—yes—I wouldn't let a little thing like that worry you. So long as you can blow everything up nicely.

FLETHERINGTON: As to that, I'm very pleased indeed——

> *Here* HILDA *and* PATCH *return, carrying basin of water, soap, cloth, towel and bottle of iodine, and some sticking plaster. During the dialogue that follows,* HILDA *is busy washing, drying, iodining and sticking-plastering his cuts and bruises. She should be very brisk and business-like, and handle him as if he were a rather naughty little boy, occasionally reprimanding him, as he winces or moves, with a "Now then——!"*

Oh, this is very kind of you, though you needn't have troubled. I must introduce myself. Fletherington, Francis Fletherington. Research chemist.

GRIDLEY: My niece, Miss Jackson. This is Mr. Patch, second officer in this ship. I'm Gridley, chief engineer.

FLETHERINGTON (*amiably, though inconvenienced by the first-aid*): I was just telling Mr. Gridley about this new explosive of mine, Fletherite. I only used a pinch of it—made a tiny bomb—down there, and the result was most satisfactory——

HILDA: It was beastly. And look at you!

FLETHERINGTON (*smiling*): That's the point. I grossly underestimated its power. Otherwise I shouldn't have been so near. I'm quite used to working with powerful high-explosives, of course. It completely deceived me. Most gratifying.

PATCH: I suppose if you'd blown yourself to bits, you'd have been highly delighted.

HILDA: Don't! It's so horrible. It seemed such a lovely morning too.

FLETHERINGTON: It's a beautiful morning, isn't it? I think we're going to be lucky with our holiday this year. My wife says I always choose the worst weather. This time she can't say it, can she?

HILDA: Is your wife with you?

FLETHERINGTON: Yes, we're in rooms at a farm about five miles away. Very pleasant indeed.

HILDA (*busy finishing him off*): I can't understand why she lets you go about blowing things up like that. There! You look better now.

FLETHERINGTON: I'm really much obliged, Miss—er—Jackson, and so sorry to have caused all this trouble.

PATCH (*offering case*): Cigarette?

FLETHERINGTON (*taking one*): Thank you. I don't often smoke, but I think this is quite an occasion for a little self-indulgence.

> PATCH *offers him match, and he lights the cigarette awkwardly.*
>
> PATCH *lights his own.* FLETHERINGTON *leans back and beams upon the company.*

Well, this is very pleasant, very pleasant indeed.

PATCH (*after a meaning glance at* HILDA *and* GRIDLEY): Mr. Fletherington, do you read the papers?

FLETHERINGTON: Very rarely. My wife reads them and then tells me any news that she thinks I would like to hear. This pleases her, and saves time and trouble for me. Besides, from what I can see, the popular press appears to be produced now for women, not men.

GRIDLEY: I believe you're right. Except for the sports pages. Cricket news.

FLETHERINGTON: I don't take any interest in cricket. I like to relax when I've done my work for the day.

> HILDA, *assisted by* PATCH, *begins to put the first-aid things together.*

Oh, can I help?

HILDA: Oh—no, thank you. (*To* PATCH) You needn't bother now, either. I like to be doing something. It's very restful.

> HILDA *goes out with the things.*

FLETHERINGTON: Very sensible girl, that. My wife would like her.

> FLETHERINGTON *leans back in content.* PATCH *goes and lounges by the rail at the back.*

Very odd finding oneself on a ship, like this. (*Looks about him with approval.*) Do you know what I'd like to do with this ship?

GRIDLEY (*lazily*): No.

FLETHERINGTON (*smiling*): I'd like to try a charge of my Fletherite on it. Blow it up.

GRIDLEY (*hastily*): Don't be silly——

FLETHERINGTON (*seriously*): No, no, it's just what I want. Wonderful test. Here's a fairly compact rigid steel structure, with excellent resistance. On the basis of my little experiment down there, I believe I could work out a charge of Fletherite—or perhaps two charges, detonated simultaneously—that would blow up this ship very neatly.

GRIDLEY (*heatedly*): And a damn fine thing that would be, wouldn't it? A beautiful job of work like this—planned and executed to the last inch—capable of doing her fourteen knots to-morrow from here to Honolulu—and you talk about blowing her up!

FLETHERINGTON (*blandly*): But why not? She's no use to you or anybody else, whereas she's just what I need—to try my explosive on.

GRIDLEY: She's no use here. But that's because she oughtn't to be here. Wasn't meant to be here. She ought to be out at sea, doing her work——

A whistle from PATCH *interrupts him.* PATCH *is looking out.* What's the matter?

PATCH: More people. Fellow and a girl. I'll tell Hilda to keep out of the way.

He hurries off right.

FLETHERINGTON: Why should Hild—that nice, helpful girl, I suppose—keep out of the way?

GRIDLEY (*confused*): Oh—well—likes to keep out of the way. Shy! That's what she is. Trouble with all our family. Shy!

FLETHERINGTON: I can sympathise with her. I'm shy.

GRIDLEY: You're not. Going round blowing things up! Talking about blowing this ship up!

He looks at the bag containing the explosive longingly, as if wanting to get rid of it. Then as he makes a move towards the ship's side, LORD COTTINGLEY *arrives on deck; he is a robust, well-nourished, middle-aged man, with an easy genial manner. He is very well dressed, in tweeds.*

LORD COTTINGLEY: Good morning. Beautiful morning, isn't it? I think we've met before, haven't we? (*Shaking hands with the rather dazed* GRIDLEY.) Aren't you one of the Company's officers?

GRIDLEY: Yes, sir. Gridley. Chief engineer.

LORD COTTINGLEY: Of course, of course. I'm Lord Cottingley. One of your directors up to a few weeks ago, when I resigned. Well, well, well, so this is the old *Gloriana*, eh? (*Advances towards* FLETHERINGTON, *and shakes him by the hand.*) How d'you do, my dear sir? You look as if you've been in the wars.

FLETHERINGTON: Very old wars. The people who have been in the new wars are going to look a lot worse than this.

GRIDLEY: This is Mr. Fletherington. He's been trying to blow himself up, and he'd like to blow the rest of us up now.

LORD COTTINGLEY: Ha ha, really! You must tell me about that. But where's my daughter? I came here with a daughter. (*Goes towards back and begins calling.*) Ursula. Ursula.

URSULA'S VOICE (*off, back*): All right. I'm crawling up.

> *She arrives, a handsome, weary girl, very beautifully dressed. She looks about her in disgust.*

My God! Cot, what a foul boat!

> GRIDLEY *stares at her in indignation.*

LORD COTTINGLEY: My daughter, gentlemen——

URSULA (*giving them a cursory glance. Disgusted*): How d'you do? (*To* LORD COTTINGLEY.) I thought you said this might be amusing.

LORD COTTINGLEY: Well, so it might.

URSULA: Couldn't be. I'm going.

> PATCH *enters. She brightens up at the sight of him.*

That is, when you want to go. There's no hurry. (*To* PATCH.) Hello!

PATCH (*not interested*): Hello! (*Exchanges meaning glances with* GRIDLEY.)

URSULA (*piqued at his lack of interest*): I suppose you'd be awfully bored if I asked you to show me over the ship?

PATCH: I expect you're right.

URSULA (*astonished*): What?

PATCH: I never contradict a lady.

URSULA (*disgusted*): Lady!

PATCH (*grinning*): Sorry!

URSULA: I shall go and look round myself. (*Moving.*)

GRIDLEY (*alarmed*): You wouldn't like it. Dirty. Rats——

PATCH: Mice. Spiders. Beetles——

> *As she takes no notice.*

GRIDLEY (*hurriedly*): We'd better show you what there is to see. Very little——

> *As she moves off right, they are at each side of her, carefully shepherding her.* LORD COTTINGLEY *and* FLETHERINGTON, *who have been talking quietly, can now be heard.*

LORD COTTINGLEY (*very genially*): Well, that's very interesting, very interesting indeed. I might be able to help you put your explosive on the market. That is, of course, if I were satisfied that it was all you think it is.

FLETHERINGTON (*wistfully*): I'd like to try it on this ship——

LORD COTTINGLEY (*thoughtfully*): Would you now, would you? On this ship.

FLETHERINGTON (*dreamily*): A beautiful test.

LORD COTTINGLEY (*thoughtfully*): Oh, magnificent, of course! Just what you want.

FLETHERINGTON: Yes. And you'd see for yourself then.

LORD COTTINGLEY: Exactly. And if it was *my* ship, you could do it. That is, of course, if the thing were done in such a way that the insurance people didn't object, but paid up afterwards. I couldn't exactly give you a ship this size to blow up, could I? (*Laughs heartily.*)

FLETHERINGTON: No, I suppose not. Though it might as well be blown up, it doesn't seem to be serving any useful purpose here.

LORD COTTINGLEY: Oh, quite, quite, quite. Very sharp of you to see that. You'd have a very good head for business, you know.

FLETHERINGTON: I've often thought so, but I'm not interested, don't really understand it. In fact, I let my wife, who's a very sensible woman in some respects, manage all our little business affairs at home. I find my own work very engrossing.

LORD COTTINGLEY (*smoothly*): Naturally. You're a man of science. I've had a certain amount to do with men of science—inventive geniuses like yourself—and I've always found it better for everybody if they just get on with their own work and don't bother their heads about business. They've always left that to me, and it's worked very well. A natural division of labour. After all, this is an age of specialisation.

FLETHERINGTON: Not so much as people think. Take inorganic chemistry——

LORD COTTINGLEY (*who will not have this*): Yes, you're right there, of course. We mustn't overlook that. But—er—(*dropping voice*) about this ship. Now, a wire to my broker in town, and I could find myself owner of this ship within twenty-four hours. You say you have the explosive here with you?

FLETHERINGTON: Yes—in this bag.

LORD COTTINGLEY (*drawing back*): Oh—here. Dangerous isn't it?

FLETHERINGTON: No, it has to be detonated. The detonators are over there. It wouldn't take long to fix up a couple of charges.

LORD COTTINGLEY (*thoughtfully*): Yes. Quite so. Well now, if I happened to own the ship—and then if you happened to fix up a couple of charges, as you say, and then somebody happened to come along and blew up the ship——

FLETHERINGTON (*eagerly*): Oh, but I'd have to be here myself to see what happened. Otherwise it wouldn't be a proper test at all. You'd want to see it too.

LORD COTTINGLEY (*slowly*): No. That wouldn't be absolutely necessary. In fact, it might be better if I wasn't here. What we want is somebody—well—somebody who *wants* to blow a ship up—makes no bones about it——

URSULA *comes hurrying in.*

Eh, what? What's the matter, Ursula?

URSULA (*amused*): This is getting better. There's a man locked in a cabin along there.

LORD COTTINGLEY: Nonsense! Are you sure?

URSULA: Positive, my dear. I stood just outside—after giving those two men the slip—I knew there was something queer going on —and I heard him kicking the door and shouting.

FLETHERINGTON: You're sure it wasn't a girl? Because there is one here. Nice girl. Can't remember her name, but she very kindly attended to these little cuts of mine.

URSULA (*amused*): A girl! *That* explains the good-looking boy. I thought he was very distant. He's got a girl here. Good idea too! But that was a man in the cabin.

LORD COTTINGLEY: Show me the cabin. (*To* FLETHERINGTON) Don't you come. You need a rest. Look after your explosive.

LORD COTTINGLEY *and* URSULA *hurry off right, into super-structure.*

FLETHERINGTON *picks up his bag, opens it, and is beginning to examine his explosive crystals, when* GRIDLEY *and* PATCH *hurry in, looking hot and worried, from another entrance right.*

GRIDLEY: Have you seen that damned girl?

FLETHERINGTON (*calmly*): Just gone in there with her father. To show him a cabin with a man inside it.

PATCH (*after whistling*): That's torn it.

GRIDLEY: Yes, and what the blinking blazes are we going to do to mend it? (*To* FLETHERINGTON, *who is still examining his crystals*). And don't mess about with that stuff.

FLETHERINGTON (*smiling*): Perfectly safe.

GRIDLEY: That's what *you* say, but I don't think you know what's safe and what isn't safe. Look at you! So, for God's sake, stop messing with the stuff. Put it back.

FLETHERINGTON, *still smiling, does.*

They can't let Slivers out, can they?

PATCH: No, I've got the key in my pocket. But by this time Slivers will have told 'em all about Hilda through the keyhole.

GRIDLEY: May not have done. Better wait and see. (*Sits down and mops himself and breathes heavily*). What a morning! This comes of wanting something to happen, grumbling because it's quiet. (*Shouting.*) I like it quiet. It can't be too quiet for me. If only this ship was out at sea, where she ought to be, and the engines turning over nicely and not too many passengers, I'd ask for nothing better. I wouldn't care how quiet it was, wouldn't care if not a damn thing happened for six months.

PATCH: Well, you're out of luck, Sam. It'll be a long time before this old girl goes churning through the Forties again.

FLETHERINGTON: Lord Cottingley was talking just now about buying her.

PATCH: Oh, what does that old twister want to do with her?

GRIDLEY: Wait a minute, you can't talk like that. How d'you know he's a twister?

PATCH: Ask any of 'em at Head Office. They're all twisters more or less there, but he was the king twister and that's why he had to resign. What's he want to buy her for? I don't trust him.

FLETHERINGTON: He's interested in my explosive, Fletherite.

GRIDLEY (*half humorously, half angrily*): He is, is he? I suppose he's like you, eh? Like to try it on the ship, blow her up?

FLETHERINGTON (*simply*): Yes, that's what he said.

GRIDLEY (*exploding*): What the——

> Then he stares at PATCH *and in his exasperation whistles his ascending scale, while* PATCH, *staring back, whistles his descending one.*

Either I've gone clean off my nut, or everybody else has this morning. Where's the sense of it? Now here's a ship—and when I say a ship, I mean a ship—not something you can put together in a morning, not some blankety little tuppeny ha'penny gadget, a wireless set or a gramophone, but a *Ship*—and if she was a ruddy beehive——

PATCH (*sardonically*): She *is* a beehive. Didn't you tell me there were bees up on the boat deck this morning——?

GRIDLEY (*explosively*): Bees there, and bees in our bonnets. We're all going mad. I can feel it coming. Now here's a ship——

PATCH: You've said that before, you old chump. Listen. Come here.

> They come down to talk confidentially. FLETHERINGTON *makes no attempt to listen but remains aloof and dreamy.*

Don't you see what the game is?

GRIDLEY: No, I don't.

PATCH: Well, it's the good old game. Insurance.

GRIDLEY: Insurance?

PATCH: Yes, insurance. Cottingley could buy this ship for next to nothing now. But if anything happens to her—total loss—he could collect the insurance, see?

GRIDLEY: D'you think that's it?

PATCH: I'm sure. I don't know whether it could be worked, but that's what's in his mind, you can bet your life.

GRIDLEY: But what about him? (*Indicating* FLETHERINGTON.) Is that his idea, too?

PATCH: No, he's just barmy. He wants to blow something up.

GRIDLEY (*with an angry glance at* FLETHERINGTON, *gradually raising his voice*): And he doesn't care what it is. Blow anything up. St. Paul's Cathedral. Children's Hospital. Yes, I'm talking about you, Mr. Fletherington.

FLETHERINGTON (*mildly*): And what's the matter with me?

GRIDLEY: Everything. You're all wrong. You're a nuisance. You're a menace.

FLETHERINGTON: I'm not. I'm simply a chemist, a scientist.

GRIDLEY (*bellowing*): I know, I know, and to-day you're trying to blow us up, and to-morrow you'll be trying to dose us with poison gas. What do you want to go and make the foul stuff for, eh? Before you've finished, you fellows'ull do the lot of us in.

FLETHERINGTON (*defensively*): All I do is to research——

GRIDLEY: Yes, and look at the result. Blowing us up, burning us alive, poisoning us. Just stop your damned research then.

FLETHERINGTON: Certainly not. I'm very distressed to hear you talking like this, Mr. Gridley. I've never willingly hurt anybody in my life.

GRIDLEY: No, and that's what makes it all so cock-eyed and crazy. You don't want to hurt anybody, but—by God!—you're going to. Look what you've started here this morning. I'm going to find out what those people are up to. (*Stamps off same way as* LORD COTTINGLEY *and* URSULA *went.*)

FLETHERINGTON: I'm very sorry indeed, Mr.—er——

PATCH: Patch. Patch.

FLETHERINGTON: Patch, that Mr. Gridley should think of me in this way——

PATCH: All right, never mind. Sam's very touchy, these days. After all, he's a chief engineer, not a watchman. Breaks his heart to be stuck like this in a ship that's half a market garden. You can't even see the sea from here. And he's having a worrying morning. And I'm having a worrying morning. Only I don't mind it so much. (*With abrupt change of tone.*) What do you think of that girl?

FLETHERINGTON: Lord Cottingley's daughter——?

PATCH: No, I wouldn't have her given. Seen too many bits like her. Not so high-class, of course, but with just the same carry on. No, I mean the other one—Sam's niece—Miss Jackson. Now there *is* a girl——

FLETHERINGTON: Very nice type. Where is she?

PATCH: Hiding out of the way—up in the captain's quarters, I think. I'd better go and see how she's getting on——

Turns away, but stops because he sees a new arrival, GASTER. He is a man about forty, rather tall and very thin, with the long thin neck and prominent Adam's apple of so many revolutionaries. He has rather Jewish clean-shaven features, curlyish greying hair, thick but bald in the centre, wears no hat, and is dressed in a darkish suit with no waistcoat and a rough sort of a shirt. He can wear spectacles. He has a high querulous voice. He comes aboard with a rather self-important, mysterious air.

GASTER (*to* PATCH): Good morning, Comrade.

PATCH: Morning.

GASTER: One of the party in Longport——

PATCH: What party?

GASTER: The Communist Party. He told me about this ship lying up here, and as you probably know, we're fighting a by-election in Longport and also working up a strike among the transport workers there, and so, comrade——

PATCH: Wait a minute, wait a minute. Don't keep on calling me comrade.

GASTER: Why not?

PATCH: Because I don't know you, and I'm not your comrade, see?

GASTER: But we're both workers.

PATCH (*sharply*): We're not. I'm not a worker, for one. And you're not a worker, for another. And he isn't, either.

GASTER: But you don't side with the boss class, don't help the capitalists, do you?

PATCH: No, I don't. Damn the capitalists.

GASTER: That's all right then. You're on our side. You're with the masses.

PATCH: No, I'm not. Damn the masses too. I don't know who the masses are, but to hell with them.

GASTER: We're the masses, you and I.

PATCH: You may be, but I'm not. Masses my foot! What do you take me for? I'm not your comrade and I'm not one of the masses. My name's Patch, and I'm second officer of this ship—or I was, when it *was* a ship and not a sort of roadhouse.

GASTER (*eagerly*): Yes, and why is it lying idle like this? Because the capitalist system is breaking up——

PATCH: Tell him. I know. And don't stay too long because we're very busy here this morning.

Goes off. GASTER *turns to* FLETHERINGTON, *who smiles at him.*

GASTER: Good morning, comrade. You don't look like a sailor.

FLETHERINGTON: I'm not, I'm a research chemist.

GASTER: Not a member of the party?

FLETHERINGTON: Not a member of any party. Haven't time for parties.

GASTER: All workers with hand or brain should be with us.

He has strolled over to the place where the detonators are.

FLETHERINGTON (*sharply*): Don't touch those. Detonators.

GASTER (*withdrawing*): Oh! What are they doing here?

FLETHERINGTON: I brought them. I'm trying out my new explosive, Fletherite. It's here in this bag.

GASTER (*significantly*): Oh—I see. I used to know a little about chemistry myself—before I gave up everything for party work.

FLETHERINGTON (*eagerly, approaching him*): You did, eh? Well, this will amuse you. I had been working for some time on nitro compounds. Synthetic production from benzine——

Here they are interrupted by URSULA, *who is very much the bored young female, anxious to attract the attention of males, any males.*

URSULA: I say.

They look at her without interest.

Hello, here's somebody else. Good morning.

GASTER (*not interested*): Good morning. (*To* FLETHERINGTON) You were saying?

URSULA: Rather exciting about the girl, isn't it? I saw her peeping round a corner and chased her a bit, but had to give it up. Empty ship's a marvellous place for hide-and-seek. Awfully good for a party, too. What I'm going to ask her is, what the particularly dirty work was that Sir Eric was up to? She must be in the know, eh?

FLETHERINGTON (*indifferently*): Yes. (*To* GASTER, *as they begin moving off together, to back right*) So I went through the usual ammonium nitrate treatments—the old stuff, you know—nothing new there. And then a funny thing happened. I'd sealed a small mixture in a test-tube—ordinary routine——

By this time they are off. URSULA *stares after them in disgust.*

URSULA (*staring after them*): Damned rude!

She lights a cigarette petulantly, and stares about her. She pushes a chair, kicks something, then finds the packet of detonators. She looks at it casually, throws it a little way in the air and catches it, thinking about something else. PATCH *hurries in.*

PATCH: Where the devil is everybody? (*He sees what she has got. Alarmed.*) Don't! Stop it!

URSULA (*petulantly*): What are you talking about? If you don't stop running round and shouting and being rude, I'll throw this at you.

PATCH: Oh!—for the love of Pete—put 'em down.

URSULA (*preening herself and approaching him*): Don't you think —I'm rather attractive?

PATCH: No.

URSULA: What?

PATCH: Yes.

URSULA: *Much* prettier than that nursemaid you've got along there. Aren't I?

PATCH: Yes, anything you like. Only——

URSULA: That's better. You're all so rude and inattentive here. Where shall I chuck this?

PATCH (*urgently*): Don't chuck it anywhere.

LORD COTTINGLEY *and* GRIDLEY *hurriedly enter from entrance to cabins.*

LORD COTTINGLEY: Now listen to me, Ursula—and throw that thing away——

GRIDLEY and PATCH (*urgently*): No, don't!

LORD COTTINGLEY (*gasping*): No, don't. For God's sake, child, put 'em down, but put 'em down carefully.

GRIDLEY: They're detonators.

URSULA: Well, will they break or something?

[100]

GRIDLEY (*mopping his brow*): They'll explode, blow your hands and legs off.

URSULA (*alarmed now*): Oh!

Very carefully now, watched by the men, in a dead silence, she puts the package back where she found it. LORD COTTINGLEY *breathes an audible sigh of relief.* GRIDLEY *and* PATCH *whistle.*

URSULA (*indignantly*): You might have told me!

GRIDLEY: Now wait a minute. Before we do anything else, let's get this settled. Now don't move, anybody. (*He slips into cabin entrance.*)

URSULA: Well, that's that. The next thing to do is to find that girl and get the truth out of her.

PATCH: Never mind about her.

LORD COTTINGLEY (*smoothly, but with menace*): But as law-abiding citizens, it may be our duty to notify the police that she's here.

PATCH: Don't talk rot. It's nothing to do with you.

LORD COTTINGLEY: And then there's that poor fellow you've locked in—what about him?

PATCH: We'll attend to him, thank you.

URSULA: I'd love to take you down a few pegs. You're so pleased with yourself.

GRIDLEY *enters, carrying a large piece of cardboard, on which he has written in big letters in red ink or chalk:* Danger! Don't Touch! *He puts this card in front of the detonators.*

GRIDLEY (*as he does this, muttering and groaning*): Holy Moses! What a morning! Everybody going completely and utterly bloody well barmy. No sense anywhere in anything. Human nature! I wish I was a bull in a paddock. Or a porpoise or a dolphin. Even a sea-gull, a half-starved mewing rotten seagull. (*When the placard is in position.*) There now! That's better. Isn't it—better?

LORD COTTINGLEY: Much. Very sensible thing to do.

GRIDLEY: That's what I think—very sensible.

URSULA: Anybody would imagine you'd just invented writing.

GRIDLEY (*with delusive mildness*): You know, you're an agreeable-looking girl—very agreeable-looking. I'd call you handsome. Yes, distinctly handsome. Good features, nice colouring, fine, well-built girl. Expensively educated too, I'll be bound.

LORD COTTINGLEY (*complacently*): You couldn't buy a better education. Best finishing schools in Europe. And when she came out, two years ago, she was considered the prettiest debutante of that season. She was one of the *Tatler's* lovelies.

GRIDLEY (*still mildly*): I'm sure she was, I'm sure she was. A beautiful, expensive, fashionable young lady—(*With sudden startling ferocity*) and for two pins I'd give her a belting she'd remember for the rest of her life.

URSULA (*furiously*): Well, here's one pin.

> *She walks across and gives him a hard slap on the face.* LORD COTTINGLEY *cries out in protest.* PATCH *gives a sudden hoot of laughter.* GRIDLEY *is mildly astonished.* URSULA *regards them all with contempt as she walks a few steps away from* GRIDLEY.

GRIDLEY (*briskly*): Well, we'd better get things straightened up now.

PATCH: Wait a minute, Sam. Where's that Communist chap who was here?

GRIDLEY (*exasperated*): Communist? What Communist? There aren't any Communists here. Don't be silly, Bob, don't be silly.

PATCH: I'm not being silly. I tell you there was one here a few minutes ago.

GRIDLEY: Where are they all coming from? What do they think this is—a conference?

LORD COTTINGLEY (*interested*): A Communist, eh? How do you know he was?

PATCH: Because he told me he'd come down to work for the party at the Longport election. Something about a strike too. He was a Communist all right. And a professional at that. A professional comrade.

LORD COTTINGLEY: Has he gone then?

URSULA: No, there was a rather Bolshie-looking man here talking to Mr. What's-his-name——

LORD COTTINGLEY (*interested*): Fletherington.

URSULA: Yes. They went along there together, having a good heart-to-heart talk.

PATCH: What about?

URSULA: Oh—nitrates and test-tubes and things.

> GRIDLEY *and* PATCH *exchange glances and whistles.* LORD COTTINGLEY *looks at once pleased and thoughtful.*

PATCH: I'm going to find those two.

URSULA: I shall come with you.

PATCH: What for?

URSULA: Just to annoy you.

> PATCH *moves off,* URSULA *is following him.*

LORD COTTINGLEY: Wait a minute, my dear. I may want you to take a wire for me.

GRIDLEY (*sharply*): Oh no, you don't.

LORD COTTINGLEY: Don't what?

GRIDLEY: Send a wire.

LORD COTTINGLEY: My dear sir, I don't understand you.

URSULA: Settle it between you. I'm going to annoy who-is-it— Patch. (*She goes.*)

LORD COTTINGLEY: If I choose to ask my daughter to take a telegram for me to the nearest post office, surely it isn't necessary for me to obtain your permission?

GRIDLEY (*earnestly*): Listen to me, Lord Cottingley, there isn't going to be any funny business with this ship.

LORD COTTINGLEY (*smoothly*): My dear fellow, you mustn't talk like that, really you mustn't. You're not handling a gang of trimmers or greasers now.

GRIDLEY: No, and I wish I was. It's what I ought to be doing.

LORD COTTINGLEY (*smoothly*): No doubt. For my part, I'm extremely sorry to see an officer of your experience—very valuable experience—on the shelf like this, and if there is anything I can do— as you may guess, I still have some influence in shipping circles——

GRIDLEY (*earnestly*): Why don't you buy this ship——?

LORD COTTINGLEY: I may.

GRIDLEY: Yes, but buy her to run her. I'll get you officers and crew to run her like clockwork from here to Valparaiso—chaps that are eating their hearts out, praying for a job. And there's nothing wrong with her. You've only got to spend a thousand or two on an overhaul. A beautiful ship. What do you say?

LORD COTTINGLEY (*shaking his head*): When I want an expensive hobby, I'll run a steam yacht, thank you, not a big cargo boat.

GRIDLEY: You couldn't make it pay?

LORD COTTINGLEY: Not a chance, my dear fellow. It would eat money. You might just as well take all the money you can find and throw it into the middle of the Atlantic.

GRIDLEY (*in despair*): Then—by God!—you might as well take a few thousand of us too and throw us into the middle of the Atlantic. But—I don't believe it. Look at her! (*Indicates the ship.*)

LORD COTTINGLEY (*not looking*): Yes, look at her.

GRIDLEY: Yes, but you're not looking at her. You never have looked at her properly. Sitting in offices, adding up figures, holding meetings, passing the cigars, that's not running ships.

LORD COTTINGLEY: It's the only way you can run them.

GRIDLEY: No, they're like women. You've got to love 'em and live with 'em. This ship's like a woman to me. It's not so many figures in a book—assets and debits and Judas Iscariot knows what! That's why I'm warning you. No funny business. No buying her to-day and scuttling her to-morrow.

LORD COTTINGLEY: I don't know what you mean by *scuttling her*. And in any event, Gridley, you're forgetting one thing. The moment this ship becomes my property, you've no longer any right to be here, and I can order you ashore at once.

GRIDLEY (*angrily*): And when you do that, I shall go to the nearest police station.

LORD COTTINGLEY: That's where I ought to be going now.

GRIDLEY: Why?

LORD COTTINGLEY: Aren't you forgetting your niece, Miss Jackson, known, I think, as "the missing witness"? And this man you've locked in a cabin? What about them?

> *He smiles triumphantly.* GRIDLEY *is in a fury of bewilderment and exasperation. He stamps and mutters curses.* LORD COTTINGLEY *continues smoothly.*

Now be sensible. I don't want to make trouble for either the girl or you——

GRIDLEY: I don't like the sound o' that. I've noticed people never tell you they don't want to make trouble until they're ready to start making trouble.

LORD COTTINGLEY: I've never done policeman's work and I don't mean to begin now. I believe in minding my own business.

GRIDLEY (*muttering*): Yes, but I don't like your business.

LORD COTTINGLEY: And all I ask is that you don't interfere in matters that don't concern you——

GRIDLEY: This ship does concern me.

LORD COTTINGLEY: But it won't if I buy it.

GRIDLEY: Don't call her it. She's a *she* not an *it*. And she's still the *Gloriana* to me whether you buy her or whether they sell her to the Japs to make bicycles out of. And while she's here, there's going to be no funny work with her. In fact, while your lordship's in this frame of mind, there'd better be no telegrams.

LORD COTTINGLEY: Gridley, you're forgetting yourself.

GRIDLEY: Well, that's something you'll never do.

> FLETHERINGTON *enters from right back.*

FLETHERINGTON: They're arguing about politics along there, so I left them. I can't understand why people should be always wanting to argue about politics when there are so many more interesting things to discuss.

LORD COTTINGLEY: I agree with you absolutely, my dear sir.

GRIDLEY (*looking at them with suspicion*): Too much agreement altogether about you two. (*Gloomily to* FLETHERINGTON) D'you know what I'd have done with you, if I'd had any sense?

FLETHERINGTON (*brightly*): No, Mr. Gridley?

GRIDLEY: I'd have thrown you off this ship two minutes after you came aboard. Well, I'll have that Communist off anyhow. That'll be a start. (*Goes off right back.*)

LORD COTTINGLEY (*softly*): What sort of fellow is this Communist, Mr. Fletherington?

FLETHERINGTON: Not a bad fellow at all, Lord Cottingley. He knows some chemistry, but has rather foolishly allowed himself to be drawn into his political business. Quite a fanatic.

LORD COTTINGLEY (*comfortably*): Indeed! Did you tell him about your explosive?

FLETHERINGTON: I did, and he was extremely interested. He saw the amusing side of it too.

LORD COTTINGLEY: Oh, what's that?

FLETHERINGTON: Didn't I tell you? It's very amusing. (*Laughs.*) You see, I'd been working for some time on nitro compounds. Synthetic production from benzine. Well, I'd been going through the usual ammonium nitrate treatments——

LORD COTTINGLEY (*determined to have no more of this*): Oh yes, yes, yes—I remember. Very amusing. Very, very amusing. But tell me, Mr. Fletherington, you say this Communist fellow was interested——

FLETHERINGTON: Extremely interested. He's very anxious to try it on this ship.

LORD COTTINGLEY (*amiably*): Is he now? You know, Mr. Fletherington, you've an extraordinary capacity for arousing interest, even enthusiasm, for your scientific experiments.

FLETHERINGTON: Well, his reasons, I'm afraid, are not entirely scientific, though he's genuinely interested in Fletherite. He seems to think that the blowing up of the ship could be of some political significance—though I didn't quite gather how.

LORD COTTINGLEY (*smoothly*): No doubt he feels that if his party did it, they could say it was a protest—and of course a very forcible protest—against the capitalist system, which allows these ships to remain idle——

FLETHERINGTON: That's it exactly. Does it make sense to you?

LORD COTTINGLEY: Oh yes. Although I'm a capitalist myself—and must of course publicly associate myself with the maintenance of the system—I can't help feeling there's something to be said for his point of view.

FLETHERINGTON: You ought to have a talk with him.

LORD COTTINGLEY: I shall certainly have a talk with him.

Sound of loud voices—GASTER'S *and* PATCH'S *arguing furiously off right back.* "I'll show you what I mean." "Just listen to me, will you." "Now wait a minute." GRIDLEY *can be joining in too.* But just now somebody else seems to be having a talk with him.

Enter GASTER, PATCH *and* GRIDLEY *all arguing at once.* URSULA *follows them in, looking very bored.*

GASTER (*shouting them down*): You don't know what Marx said.

PATCH: No, I don't know and I don't care. I think for myself, see?

GASTER: I can tell you exactly what he said.

PATCH (*humorously*): Why, have you got him with you?

GASTER (*simply*): Yes. (*Produces volume of Marx's* Capital *from his pocket.*)

GRIDLEY (*wonderingly*): By thunder!—he has too.

PATCH: It's his Bible.

GASTER (*as he turns the pages*): You're right. It's my Bible. Ought to be yours too.

GRIDLEY: Give me Schopenhauer.

GASTER (*still turning*): A poor bourgeois pessimist.

PATCH (*chuckling*): That's good. I must remember that.

GRIDLEY (*indignantly*): Here, wait a minute——

GASTER (*topping him*): Now listen. (*Reads.*) "If, then, the owner of money is to transform his money into capital, he must find in the commodity market a free worker, free in a double sense. The worker must be able to dispose of his labour power as his own commodity; and, on the other hand, he must have no other commodities for sale, must be 'free' from everything that is essential for the realisation of his labour power."

URSULA (*forcefully, while the others are digesting this*): Chrerrr-istmas!

She goes and sits down, disgusted with them, and lights a cigarette.

PATCH (*excitedly*): Now, wait a minute. Who's this *worker?*

[106]

GASTER: I've told you. Anybody who does not own the means of production, who is not a capitalist, who has to sell his labour.

PATCH: Well then, what about me?

GRIDLEY: Never mind about you, Bob. (*Triumphantly to* GASTER) What about a man who runs a Punch and Judy show? Is he a capitalist? Is he a worker?

GASTER (*contemptuously*): We're not talking about Punch and Judy shows.

GRIDLEY: But you said he explained everything—well, what about a man who runs a Punch and Judy show?

PATCH (*quickly*): No, Sam, you're off it, you're off it.

GRIDLEY (*loudly*): Off what?

PATCH (*shouting*): Off the argument, off the point.

GASTER (*shouting*): Of course he is.

GRIDLEY (*shouting*): What point?

LORD COTTINGLEY (*loudly, taking a hand in this*): Yes, what exactly *is* the point?

URSULA (*topping them all*): There isn't one. They don't know what they're talking about.

PATCH (*dismissing her*): I know what I'm talking about.

GRIDLEY (*almost angrily*): Well, don't I know what I'm talking about?

GASTER (*bellowing*): No. None of you know. I know because I've studied these things. It's all here in Marx. If you come here, I'll show you.

> GRIDLEY, PATCH *and* LORD COTTINGLEY *gather round him.*
> FLETHERINGTON *lingers on the stage.* URSULA *sits where she is, bored with them.*

Now read Marx for yourself.

> *As he says this, loudly,* CAPTAIN MELLOCK *appears, a sinister figure. He is a trim, athletic-looking man in his late thirties, not bad-looking in a rather hard style. He has a romantic scar on his face. He wears no hat, a dark blue uniform shirt, with a tiny Union Jack on one side and a number of military ribbons on the other, and neat dark trousers, with pockets big enough for a revolver. The whole effect is that of a Fascist uniform. He stands looking at the group, and only* URSULA *sees him at first. She brightens up at once.*

URSULA (*to the others*): Hoy! Look what's come.

> *They look at* MELLOCK *surprised.*

MELLOCK (*harshly*): Marx! Huh! Marx!

GASTER (*sharply*): What about him?

MELLOCK (*harshly*): What about you, you mean, you dirty Red. You're Gaster, aren't you? Moscow's present to Longport.

GASTER: And I suppose you're Mellock, who's been talking so big?

MELLOCK (*correcting him sharply*): Captain Mellock. Yes. Of the New British Fascisti.

GASTER (*sneering*): New British Fascisti! Boys playing at soldiers!

MELLOCK: Don't make any mistake, Gaster. We're not all boys, we're not all playing at soldiers. I'm not, for one. And I don't simply talk big. I mean what I say.

PATCH (*rudely*): Well, say it, General, and then clear off.

MELLOCK: Shut up! I'm not talking to you—yet. Listen, Gaster, I've been looking for you all morning.

GASTER: Well, you've found me.

MELLOCK: Found a whole nest of you. Party headquarters, eh?

PATCH: Can you stop being a dam' fool for just a minute——?

MELLOCK: I've told you, shut up.

GRIDLEY: Bob!

PATCH: Yes, Sam.

GRIDLEY: We've let too many of 'em come aboard already. But this is definitely one we can't have at any price.

PATCH: You're quite right, Sam. The General's out.

MELLOCK (*moving a step nearer*): I'll give you Red bastards a lesson in manners soon.

PATCH: Come on, Sam.

He and GRIDLEY *make a sharp move forward. At the same time* MELLOCK *steps back and whips out a revolver, with which he covers them.*

MELLOCK (*very harshly*): Come on, the lot of you. Hands up, and move back. Come on, come on, sharp to it. And don't think I won't shoot, because I will.

He looks as if he will. They all move back, except URSULA, *who looks on, delightedly, and are so grouped now that* GRIDLEY *and* PATCH *are separated from the others and to the left.*

URSULA: Marvellous! Am I in this too?

MELLOCK (*giving her a quick sharp look*): You will be if you don't keep quiet.

URSULA (*appreciatively*): I think you're *too* sweet.

MELLOCK (*still covering them with his gun, but concentrating chiefly on* GRIDLEY *and* PATCH): Now then—— (*Reflects.*)

PATCH: He's been too often to the pictures, that's his trouble.

MELLOCK (*sharply, to* GRIDLEY *and* PATCH): You two—who think you're damned tough—who are you?

PATCH (*promptly*): Hitler.

GRIDLEY: Mussolini. (*Goes on grumbling in muttering tone.*) Completely and utterly barmy, everything!

> PATCH *makes the beginning of a quick movement, but* MELLOCK, *who is very alert, threatens him instantly, and* PATCH *has to keep quiet.*

LORD COTTINGLEY (*at his smoothest*): Captain Mellock, I think you'd better let me explain.

MELLOCK (*giving him half an eye*): Who are you? Keep your hands up.

LORD COTTINGLEY: I'm Lord Cottingley.

MELLOCK (*surprised*): Lord Cottingley! What are you doing here?

LORD COTTINGLEY (*smoothly*): I used to be a director of the company that owns this ship. I can explain everything.

MELLOCK: Let me get rid of these two fellows, first, before there's any explaining. (*Indicating* GRIDLEY *and* PATCH.)

LORD COTTINGLEY (*comfortably*): Well, there's this hold. Send 'em down there.

GRIDLEY (*indignantly*): That's a fine idea! Hell's bells, what a morning . . . !

MELLOCK (*harshly, menacing them*): Go on. Down there.

> They have to go down into the hold, with the open hatch on the right. PATCH *gives* LORD COTTINGLEY *a very unpleasant look.*

PATCH (*to* LORD COTTINGLEY): I'll remember this—you dirty old twister.

URSULA (*with jubilant sweetness*): Good-bye—dear Mr. Patch!

PATCH (*furiously as he disappears*): Errt-cha!

LORD COTTINGLEY (*stepping forward eagerly*): I'll help you with the hatch cover.

URSULA (*gleefully*): And so will I.

> The three of them, with MELLOCK *still keeping an eye on the other two, pull down the section of the hatch cover, and fasten it.* FLETHERINGTON *steps forward to take his bag.*

MELLOCK (*sharply*): Heigh!

LORD COTTINGLEY: That's all right, Captain Mellock. Let him have it. I'll explain in a minute. These two won't give you any trouble.

MELLOCK: I don't trust Gaster a yard.

LORD COTTINGLEY: No, no, you leave this to me. You'll understand in a minute. Here, Fletherington.

He takes the bag over to FLETHERINGTON, *who has retreated back to where* GASTER *is standing. He begins whispering to them.* MELLOCK *stays where he is, watching them.* URSULA *looks at him.*

URSULA: Cigarette, Captain Mellock? (*Offers him one.*)

MELLOCK (*taking it*): Thanks. (*Lights it quickly.*)

URSULA: By the way, I'm Lord Cottingley's daughter—Ursula.

MELLOCK: I see.

URSULA: You know, I think you're rather marvellous.

MELLOCK (*indifferently*): Yes?

URSULA: What a lot of ribbons you have! Are they bogus?

MELLOCK: Course they aren't! What do you take me for? I've been soldiering one place and another, twenty years—ever since I was seventeen.

URSULA: That makes you thirty-seven, doesn't it? A nice age, I think. Young men are so feeble.

She smiles at him but he takes no notice. He is now staring at the detonator notice. He indicates it now.

MELLOCK: What's all that about?

URSULA: My dear, you mustn't bully *me* like that. As a matter of fact, they're detonators, and as I nearly blew myself up with them not long ago, that notice is there.

MELLOCK (*pleased*): Humph! Caught 'em at it. Just what we wanted.

URSULA: You haven't the faintest idea what you're talking about.

MELLOCK: I have. Don't worry.

URSULA: I'm not worrying about *that*. (*Looks at him speculatively, then drops her voice.*) Tell me. You're not one of those men who've no use for women, are you?

MELLOCK (*laughs*): Me? No fear! I've had too much use for 'em. All over the place——

URSULA: All right, I don't want to know the rest.

MELLOCK (*calling across*): Well?

LORD COTTINGLEY (*coming down a few steps*): If you'll allow these two gentlemen to finish their conversation elsewhere—they won't leave the ship—they can't, except that way—I'll explain everything——

MELLOCK: All right.

FLETHERINGTON *carrying his bag, and* GASTER *move off left.* LORD COTTINGLEY *comes down.*

LORD COTTINGLEY: Well, you seem to be a very melodramatic young man.

MELLOCK: I'm not.

LORD COTTINGLEY: What! Flourishing revolvers! Hands up! All the rest of it!

MELLOCK: That's not melodrama. I meant what I said. No pretence about it at all. I don't carry this revolver about with me for fun, any more than a navvy carries a pick and shovel about with him for fun.

URSULA (*with slight mockery*): He's a gun-man.

MELLOCK: A gun-man, if you like. Only I prefer to call myself a soldier. It's been my profession ever since I was a schoolboy. I've soldiered in France, Russia, Palestine, China and South America.

LORD COTTINGLEY: Why? Stupid life!

MELLOCK: I didn't mind it, and anyhow it was all I could do. And—don't forget—it's you people who're pretending—not me. You're pretending the world is still a nice safe place, and that the war stopped in 1918.

LORD COTTINGLEY: Well, didn't it?

MELLOCK: You bet your life it didn't. I ought to know. I've been following it round ever since.

LORD COTTINGLEY: Oh—possibly—in a few out-of-the way places. But here we've seen nothing of it.

MELLOCK: No, but you will—you will. It'll come rolling back. Otherwise, I shouldn't be here. And don't imagine I'm here for fun. I'm getting good pay and privileges, and I've been promised much better pay and privileges.

URSULA: Good!

LORD COTTINGLEY: But what are you doing here?

MELLOCK: The Reds have put up a candidate of their own for this by-election in Longport, where a lot of the scum round the docks are half Bolshie already. I'm down there—sent by our own party—to keep an eye on these Reds, especially this fellow, Gaster. That's why I followed him here in my car. And you can bet I'm not leaving until I know exactly what's going on here. So now *you* can do some explaining.

LORD COTTINGLEY (*smiling*): Looks bad, doesn't it?

MELLOCK: Well—I find you here hobnobbing with a notorious professional Red organiser—and with a lot of high explosive waiting to be used——

LORD COTTINGLEY (*smiling*): Terrible. (*Is about to go on more con-*

[111]

fidentially, when he remembers URSULA, *and turns to her.*) Wouldn't you like to go for a walk, my dear?

URSULA (*very decidedly*): No.

LORD COTTINGLEY: You'll find all this talk very boring.

URSULA: Oh—no, I won't. (*Smiles impudently at* MELLOCK, *who frowns at her.*) I wouldn't miss a word.

MELLOCK (*rather casually to* LORD COTTINGLEY): We could stick her away for half an hour or so.

URSULA (*marches up to him, very erect, defiant, feminine*): You try sticking me away somewhere! Just try it. Now!

LORD COTTINGLEY (*to* MELLOCK): Don't encourage her.

MELLOCK (*indignantly*): I'm not encouraging her. Catch me encouraging such a kid!

URSULA (*with passionate irony*): Kid! My God! You mean kiddie —don't you?

MELLOCK: Anything you like, only shut up. We want to talk.

URSULA *looks at him in disgust, goes and sits down, where she watches them as they talk.*

LORD COTTINGLEY (*confidentially*): Captain Mellock. I'm as much anti-communist as you are. In fact, I'm on your side entirely. Join your party, if you like. But this is the position. Here's a ship. Now supposing this ship was completely destroyed—blown up—by the local Communists?

MELLOCK: Now that's just the sort of thing we want to catch 'em doing.

LORD COTTINGLEY (*easily*): Of course it is. Burning the Reichstag and so forth. Always has a wonderful effect on the minds of the decent law-abiding public.

MELLOCK: After a few acts of terrorism of that sort, the public will ask for us to protect 'em. That's the strength of our position.

LORD COTTINGLEY: Of course it is.

MELLOCK: The trouble is—the poor swine here haven't the guts to be terrorists.

LORD COTTINGLEY (*softly*): That's a nuisance, of course. But— you see—here's a nice big ship, and here's some powerful new high explosive and the man who knows how it ought to be handled, and here's your friend Gaster. And then you come charging in—just at the wrong moment. (*They look meaningly at one another.*)

MELLOCK: I see.

LORD COTTINGLEY (*softly*): I thought you would.

MELLOCK: But where do I come in?

LORD COTTINGLEY: Obviously you don't yet. You go out. Though, between ourselves, I'm glad you came when you did, because we were able to get rid of those two ship's officers——

MELLOCK: Oh—those blighters we shoved in the hold?

LORD COTTINGLEY: Yes. They looked like being a nuisance, and now they're well out of the way, until we've made all our plans. Now about you. Wait a minute. (*He thinks, then looks reflectively at watch.*) You must give me an hour or so to settle things here. Lunch-time too. (*Turns to* URSULA) Ursula, would you like to take Captain MELLOCK off in search of some food and drink for us here?

URSULA: Yes. Good idea.

LORD COTTINGLEY: You could go in our car or his. Bring some decent sandwiches and some whisky, enough for four or five of us.

> Goes back to right and looks down deck for FLETHERINGTON *and* GASTER. *Gives whistle and beckons to them. Then turns to* URSULA *and* MELLOCK.

When you come back, Captain Mellock had better wait down there until you come up here and see me. (*To* MELLOCK) Safer, I think.

MELLOCK: Sounds a good scheme.

URSULA (*moving*): Come on. Let's go.

MELLOCK (*as he prepares to go*): What about—— (*Points to hatch.*)

LORD COTTINGLEY (*casually*): Oh—those fellows. They can stay where they are. And anyhow, they can't make trouble. I know something that will keep them quiet.

URSULA (*to* MELLOCK): Yes. I'll tell you about that as we go along. Serve 'em right too. Foul pair, I thought. Come on, let's go shopping.

> She and MELLOCK *go off.* LORD COTTINGLEY *looks down off right again and nods. Then comes forward and arranges three chairs together,* GASTER *and* FLETHERINGTON *enter from back right.* FLETHERINGTON *is still carrying his bag.*

GASTER: Has that Fascist bully gone?

LORD COTTINGLEY (*smoothly*): Yes—he's gone. He only needed a little talking to. And I've sent my daughter off to find us something to eat and drink.

FLETHERINGTON: That's an excellent idea. I knew there was something wrong, but couldn't think what it was. I must be hungry. I was in such a hurry to get out of the house this morning to test the Fletherite that I had no breakfast—only a cup of tea.

LORD COTTINGLEY (*the hearty chairman now*): Not enough. The inner man. Eh, Mr. Gaster? Ha ha ha ha! Well, we'll put that right.

[113]

And now this is our opportunity to have a little talk. Sit here, Mr. Fletherington, won't you? (*Indicates chair right.*) And perhaps you would like to sit here, Mr. Gaster. (*Indicates chair left.*)

> *They both sit. He takes the chair in the middle with some ceremony.*

Excellent! Capital! Well now—to business——

GASTER: Wait a minute, what about those two sailors?

FLETHERINGTON: Oh yes, I'd forgotten them.

LORD COTTINGLEY: That's all right. They're safe—though perhaps not very comfortable—in number three hold. We needn't worry about them for some time.

GASTER: Well, I shan't. Obvious counter-revolutionary types, both of them.

LORD COTTINGLEY (*the smooth chairman*): Quite so. And very acute of you, Mr. Gaster, to notice the fact so quickly. Well now, I gather that both of you—for different reasons—one scientific, the other political—have a certain interest in blowing up this ship. All right. Now there are certain questions that must be carefully considered. I might make a little agenda, eh? (*He produces a piece of paper and pencil and makes a few rapid notes.*)

GASTER (*solemnly*): I always like to have an agenda.

LORD COTTINGLEY: Very sensible of you. Now then. The first problem is undoubtedly that of time. Exactly when, gentlemen— exactly when shall the ship be blown up?

> *He looks from one to the other with a smiling alertness. They are looking thoughtful. The curtain comes down.*

END OF ACT ONE

ACT II

SCENE: *Same as before. An hour and a half later.* LORD COTTINGLEY, FLETHERINGTON *and* GASTER *are still sitting in the same chairs, but now they look hot and flustered, as if they have been arguing a long time. When the Curtain first discovers them, they are having a breathing space, as if they have just reached a deadlock and were giving themselves time to recover their breath.* LORD COTTINGLEY *mops his brow. They all start to speak, then decide to say nothing and collapse into their chairs again. Then they all speak together.*

LORD COTTINGLEY: To-morrow night is the earliest possible moment, I tell you, and I would prefer the day after——

GASTER (*at the same time*): From the point of view of the party, the sooner the better, and I say—to-night while we are certain of everything——

FLETHERINGTON (*at the same time*): I must repeat the opinion I have expressed throughout, that unless it is done as soon as possible, I cannot guarantee anything——

They all stop and look at one another, rather exhausted. LORD COTTINGLEY *holds up his hand for silence, and looks at his watch.*

LORD COTTINGLEY: Gentlemen, we've been arguing this point for over an hour. We really must get on.

GASTER: We have here, of course, comrades, three fundamentally different types of mind. Any Marxist thinker would recognise that, firstly——

LORD COTTINGLEY (*checking him*): Mr. Gaster—comrade—do you realise that if we let you go on with this, it would make the fifth lecture on Marxist philosophy you've given us during this last hour? It's too much, y'know.

FLETHERINGTON: Much too much. Now may I give you the reason why I do not want any delay? I've told you many times that I don't want one——

LORD COTTINGLEY (*wearily*): Many, many, many times, Mr. Fletherington.

FLETHERINGTON: Quite so, but so far I haven't told you why. (*Confidentially.*) It's because I'm afraid my wife would get to know—and stop it.

GASTER: But surely, comrade—you, a scientist, an intellectual—are not afraid of your wife?

[115]

FLETHERINGTON (*simply*): I am.

LORD COTTINGLEY (*to* GASTER): I take it that you aren't married?

GASTER: No, I'm not.

LORD COTTINGLEY: Obviously. You know, the amount you have to learn about everything—just the most ordinary everyday things—seems to me to have reached staggering proportions, and I see it growing every few seconds.

FLETHERINGTON: My wife——

LORD COTTINGLEY (*stopping him*): You must tell us all about Mrs. Fletherington afterwards, Mr. Fletherington. Just now we really must keep to the point.

FLETHERINGTON: But she *is* the point. Don't you see——

GASTER (*sharply*): No, I don't see. And we are wasting valuable time. Don't you agree? (*To* LORD COTTINGLEY.)

LORD COTTINGLEY: Yes, I do agree.

FLETHERINGTON (*eagerly*): Oh—I agree too, for that matter. Oh—most certainly.

GASTER (*to* LORD COTTINGLEY): To-morrow night is for you the earliest time to blow up the ship, eh?

LORD COTTINGLEY: Yes, and I'd prefer the day after to-morrow.

GASTER: To-morrow night is for me the latest time. For him too, no doubt.

FLETHERINGTON: All I wish to say is this—— (*Goes towards detonator placard.*)

LORD COTTINGLEY (*irritably*): What are you doing?

FLETHERINGTON: I might as well have these detonators. (*Takes them and puts them in his bag, which he is still holding, then comes back.*)

LORD COTTINGLEY: Then we have here the basis of a compromise——

GASTER: Correct. It would not be too late for us. On the other hand, it would give you time to order these two men off the ship——

LORD COTTINGLEY: Oh yes—but they're not the difficulty. That part of it's easy. We can ignore them.

> As he says this, PATCH *suddenly drops down on deck from some convenient part of the superstructure. He is extremely dirty and dishevelled and his clothes are torn, as if he had been crawling and climbing for the last hour. He has a stout iron bar with him, and is a very angry and formidable figure.*

PATCH (*very menacingly*): Don't move, any of you. The first man who moves, I'll flatten him with this.

FLETHERINGTON (*mildly*): But—Mr. Patch——

PATCH (*menacingly*): Don't talk either. I've been crawling and climbing for nearly an hour like a ruddy cockroach through the foulest holes in this ship, and I'm ready to kill somebody. So keep still and shut up, before I flatten you to the deck.

> *They are paralysed. He hastily goes round to the hatch, and dexterously and quickly unfastens the cover.*

PATCH (*as he removes the cover*): All right, Sam.

> GRIDLEY *climbs out, very hot and dirty, in a furious rage, also holding a thick iron rod. He is a terrifying figure. At the sight of the three standing there, he gives a great roar of inarticulate rage.*

GRIDLEY (*roaring*): Wa-a-ah! You bloody toads! You poxed-up rats! You red-eyed stinking weasels! I'll break you to pieces. I'll tear the lights and livers out of you. (*Steps forward. As they make a noisy but inarticulate protest*) I don't care who did it, you're all in it, every flaming man Jack of you.

PATCH: If they hadn't been, they'd have let us out before now. Crawling and climbing like a God-dam' cockroach, I've been!

GRIDLEY: Trying to shut us up in our own ship! Round there, Bob; they're not leaving us yet.

LORD COTTINGLEY (*to* PATCH, *who has cut off the retreat of the party to the shore*): But wait a minute, you can't do this.

PATCH (*through his teeth, menacingly, going up to him*): Who suggested putting us in the hold, eh? You'd be surprised what I could do to you—now!

FLETHERINGTON: But—Mr. Gridley——

GRIDLEY (*with passion*): You started this, by Judas. (*He goes and opens door of small store room, far side of entrance to cabins.*) Get in there.

FLETHERINGTON: But—but——

GRIDLEY (*in a violent storm, threatening him with the iron rod*): Hell's million bells! D'you want me to knock the living daylight out of you? In there!

> FLETHERINGTON, *terrified, goes in.* GRIDLEY *immediately steps across and locks the door.*

PATCH: Cabins B. and C. for these two, eh?

GRIDLEY: Yes. Rush 'em up the alleyway, boy, rush 'em up.

> *He pounces on* GASTER *and rushes him out, while* PATCH, *delighted, seizes* LORD COTTINGLEY *behind and rushes him after.*

There is a great noise off, protesting and roaring, locking of doors. Then silence. GRIDLEY *and* PATCH *return, panting and rubbing their hands.*

GRIDLEY: I don't know where that gets us—but now I feel a bit better—(*muttering*) the sons of—— (*Blows his breath out.*)

PATCH (*pugnaciously*): Yes, but where's the fellow with the blue shirt and the gun? That's the fellow I want to take a crack at. And when I see him, I'm going to chance it—rush him—gun or no gun——

GRIDLEY (*sitting down heavily*): What a day! What a day! I've not had such a day since that time when the trimmers pinched that cask o' brandy at Durban. That was a day.

PATCH: Before my time.

GRIDLEY: Dare say it was. But—bless me!—There was more sense even in that than in this. I mean to say, you knew where you were, Bob, you knew where you were. You knew what trimmers were. You knew what brandy was. You'd only to add 'em together. They were all fighting drunk, that's all. But this—it's loony from start to finish——

PATCH: Clean batty!

GRIDLEY (*in short despairing phrasing*): Blowing trees up! Reds—and blues—and revolvers—and—and—detonators—blowing ships up! Oh! (*Despairs of it.*)

PATCH (*after a pause*): Sam, we've got to work this out, and do it quick.

GRIDLEY: I know. I know.

PATCH: It's not only the ship. Don't forget—there's Hilda.

GRIDLEY: Hilda? What Hilda?

PATCH: Your niece, Hilda Jackson, you old fathead.

GRIDLEY (*wearily*): Oh!—crumpets—I'd forgotten about her. (*Remembering.*) Why—then—there's——

PATCH: Slivers. Of course there is. He's still where I put him—in Cabin A. (*Takes out key, then puts it back.*)

GRIDLEY (*muttering*): Slivers. That's right. Cabin A. Hilda. Then—— (*Mops himself, then adds solemnly*) You know, Bob, this wants thinking out.

PATCH (*irritably*): Don't tell me. That's what I'm telling you.

GRIDLEY (*reproachfully*): It doesn't matter, boy, which of us is telling which. That's a detail. The great point is—we've got to think it out.

PATCH (*his voice rising in a frenzy of irritation*): I know we have. I know we have. Don't keep telling me.

He paces about. GRIDLEY *gives him a bewildered glance, then tries hard to concentrate, beginning to reckon, quite solemnly, on his fingers.* PATCH *suddenly stops.*

PATCH: Sam!

GRIDLEY (*eagerly*): Have you got it, Bob? Have you settled it?

PATCH: No. I was going to say "Are you hungry?"

GRIDLEY (*impatiently*): Course I am. It's a long way past dinner-time. We'll just have to wait, though. (*He takes out a pipe, and sucks it without lighting it.*)

　　　PATCH *paces restlessly.*

PATCH (*stopping*): Know what I'd like to do?

GRIDLEY: No.

PATCH: Throw 'em ashore, the whole flaming lot of 'em. Just open those cabin doors—one, two, three, four—bang, boosh, bish, bash!—out!

GRIDLEY (*fired*): All right, boy, let's do it, let's do it.

PATCH: How can we, you old chump, when the first thing they'll do when they get ashore is to tell the police about Hilda?

GRIDLEY (*disappointed*): Ah—yes, of course.

PATCH: Cottingley'd do it like a shot. He's the fellow I've got it in for—the old twister. I'd like to drop him among those trees, like a dam' great acorn.

GRIDLEY: Yes, and the next minute he's off to the post office to wire his agent to buy this ship——

PATCH: Which means that we're going out and the ship's going up.

GRIDLEY: And we're not going out and the ship's not going up, or anyhow whether we go out or not, the ship's not going up.

PATCH: Fletherite there—— (*pointing to door*) started it all. If he was out o' the way, it'ud be simpler. He'd better be the first we get rid of——

GRIDLEY (*mopping himself*): Just a minute. Just a minute. This wants working out properly. What we want here is system, and that's your trouble, Bob, you haven't got system. You want to rush at it like a bull at a fence. You were just the same with Schopenhauer——

PATCH (*irritably*): Oh—for God's sake—don't start on him now——

　　　GRIDLEY *stares at him with the air of one giving a silent but terrible rebuke.* PATCH *catches it, and softens at once.*

I'm sorry, Sam.

GRIDLEY: That's all right, boy. You're worried. I'm worried.

[119]

We're both worried. We don't know where we are. Now wait——
(*Begins thinking and reckoning on fingers again.*) Here!

PATCH (*expecting a solution*): Yes?

GRIDLEY: What became of old Batten, who used to be chief in the
Moriana?

PATCH (*impatiently*): I don't know. What's he got to do with it?

GRIDLEY (*blankly*): Nothing, so far as I know. But he came into
my mind just then—old Batten of the *Moriana*——

PATCH: Well, put him out of your mind. We've got to think.

GRIDLEY: Paper and pencil might help. There's so many of 'em.

> *Is about to meditate again, when they both hear sound of cautious
> approaching steps from off back right. They look at one another,
> GRIDLEY rises quietly. They both quietly turn in direction of sound
> and make one or two quiet movements in that direction. Finally,
> HILDA's head appears cautiously round corner back right. Seeing
> only them she comes in and forward. She has made some change
> —but not an elaborate one—in her dress since Act One.*

HILDA (*quietly*): Hello! Only you two?

PATCH: Only us.

HILDA (*more confident tone now*): Do you know, I was so tired, I
fell asleep.

PATCH (*sympathetically*): I'm not surprised. Are you, Sam?

GRIDLEY: Yes.

HILDA (*to* PATCH): Oh—but what a mess you're in!

PATCH (*grinning*): What a mess we're all in!

HILDA (*penitently*): And it's all my fault, isn't it? I mean, that
man—the one you locked in the cabin——

GRIDLEY (*hesitating*): Well, yes—there's him. But—er—as a matter
of fact, he's not the only one. (*She stares at him.*) No. We've got—
er—three other chaps—er—locked in cabins.

> *To his astonishment, HILDA begins giggling softly, and sits down
> and stuffs a handkerchief in her mouth. PATCH grins in sympathy,
> but GRIDLEY regards her with annoyance. He brings PATCH away
> from her, well downstage.*

GRIDLEY: Now there's the thing I was telling you about the other
afternoon——

PATCH: What?

GRIDLEY: About women. You see, you never know how they're
going to take anything. Always contrary, see? If I'd said to her "Oh
yes—ha ha ha—you'll laugh when I tell you—we've got three other

chaps locked up here"—she'd have started crying and told me I ought to be ashamed of myself. And look at her now.

PATCH: Well, what of it? She's taking it the right way.

HILDA (*getting up*): I'm sorry, uncle. But it sounded so silly.

PATCH: If you'll excuse me, I'll get myself cleaned up a bit.

HILDA (*rather flirtatiously, for her*): Oh, we'll excuse you for that.

PATCH: Thought you would! (*To* GRIDLEY.) Shan't be two minutes. (*Goes through doorway to cabins.*)

GRIDLEY (*grumbling*): What's he want to go cleaning himself up for now?

HILDA: Because he knows he'd look nicer. He's rather good-looking, you know.

GRIDLEY (*grumpily*): I didn't know.

HILDA (*with a faint shade of tartness*): Well, I hope you know about that policeman.

GRIDLEY (*aghast*): What policeman?

HILDA: Down there in the wood. I peeped over the side and saw him. He was poking about near those damaged trees—where the explosion was—for about five minutes, then he looked as if he was coming here—and then he stopped.

GRIDLEY: What for?

HILDA (*amused*): Well—he seemed to be looking at his nose. In a little hand mirror. He was looking at his nose in it. It seemed such a silly thing for a policeman to be doing——

GRIDLEY (*with the gloomy detached air of a man who sees the whole world steadily going mad and out of control*): Yesterday I'd have agreed with you. This morning—early—I'd have agreed with you. Now—well—I'm not surprised, that's all. Just not surprised. If he took his nose off and threw it on the deck here, I wouldn't be very surprised. It's all—well—that's how it's getting. (*Suddenly shouting*) Completely and utterly barmy!

HILDA (*alarmed*): Sh-sh. He might hear you. See if he's still there.

GRIDLEY *goes to the back and cautiously looks down right over the side. Then he returns.*

GRIDLEY: That's Sergeant Wilks. He's stopped looking at his nose now, he's looking at the trees again.

HILDA (*alarmed*): Do you think he's coming here for me?

GRIDLEY: I dunno. Don't suppose he knows why he's here. Now if we'd been wanting a bit o' company, somebody fresh to talk to, and everything here'd been straight and above-board, that sergeant wouldn't have been round in a week. But to-day, of course, he must come poking round. It's my belief something somewhere (*points up, then down to suggest supernatural power*) fixes up these things. They overhear you grumbling because it's quiet, and they say "We'll fix these chaps in a proper tangle. We'll show 'em something." That's my belief. He's (*indicating back, i.e., police sergeant*) part of it. They just put it into his head to come here and tangle us up a bit more.

HILDA (*reproachfully*): Oh—uncle—you sound so hopeless.

GRIDLEY: Me! You never made a bigger mistake in your life. What, after thirty-five years in ships' engine-rooms! I've had packets like this before, girl. They won't tangle me—by thunder!

PATCH *returns, looking much cleaner and neater now.*

PATCH: Well, I feel better for that.

GRIDLEY: That's good, because you're going to need it. Do you know who's just down there—poking round? Sergeant Wilks.

PATCH *begins whistling softly.*

HILDA (*to* PATCH): I think he may be looking for me.

PATCH: He may. You'd better go below again. No—up on the bridge, that's the best. Then you can keep a look out on the path, and when you see him going, you can come out——

HILDA: All right. (*Turns to go.*)

GRIDLEY (*seriously*): And—Hilda——

HILDA (*turning*): Yes?

GRIDLEY: Just be thinking of something tasty you can make with corned beef, flour and mixed pickles——

PATCH (*solicitously crossing to her*): You'll be all right. Don't worry.

> *She goes.* PATCH *and* GRIDLEY *look at one another, then whistling softly, go together to the back and cautiously peep over the side. They instantly jump back—as if the sergeant was nearer than they expected—nod at one another—then return slowly, whistling softly again, holding themselves rather stiffly, like men who expect to get a blow in the back. They sit down carefully, light pipe and cigarette, and obviously begin making conversation for the sergeant's benefit. They have a droll false air.*

GRIDLEY: Yes, Bob.

PATCH: What, Sam?

GRIDLEY: I was thinking about corned beef. We had a cook once—before your time, Bob—it was in the old *Floriana*—who could do anything with corned beef. He'd have made you a Christmas pudding out of it. Marvel he was—with corned beef. A Sunderland man. He'd a gammy leg.

PATCH (*keeping it going*): What's that got to do with it?

GRIDLEY: What's what got to do with it?

PATCH: Gammy leg.

GRIDLEY: Well—after all—a gammy leg, y'know. How would you like to have a gammy leg?

> *The* SERGEANT *has now appeared and is slowly coming forward, a large slow man, with a very sunburnt nose. They pretend not to notice him.*

I mean to say, it wasn't in his favour, was it? All the more credit to him—I say——

> *The* SERGEANT *has now sat down, between them but a little back, and is taking off his helmet, then mopping his brow. He touches his nose tenderly.*

SERGEANT WILKS (*slowly*): Good afternoon.

PATCH: Hello—Sergeant.

GRIDLEY: Good afternoon, Sergeant Wilks.

SERGEANT WILKS: Warm again. Very warm.

GRIDLEY (*gravely*): You ought to have something on that nose, Sergeant. Have we got anything he could put on it, Bob?

PATCH: No we haven't, Sam. Nothing at all.

SERGEANT WILKS: I've got some stuff at home, thank you. My wife's uncle suffers the same way—and he sent it. Terrible lot o' bother this by-election's making in Longport. I hear they had to take several of 'em in last night. Disorderly conduct.

GRIDLEY (*solemnly*): You hear that, Bob?

PATCH: Yes, Sam.

GRIDLEY (*to* SERGEANT): He sometimes thinks he'd like to be down at Longport, but I tell him he's better off here, nice and quiet.

SERGEANT WILKS: That is so, that is so. You're all right. Very nice and quiet—peaceful——

> *At these fateful words,* GRIDLEY *and* PATCH *cringe a little and wait for something dreadful to happen, but it doesn't—to their relief. They whistle softly. Then they look at the* SERGEANT, *who is staring hard at the detonator placard. The* SERGEANT *looks slowly from the placard to them. They look at him, at the placard, and back at him.*

PATCH (*explaining it*): One of his (*indicating* GRIDLEY) little jokes. Not funny, I think.

SERGEANT WILKS (*very heavily*): Oh—well, we all like a bit o' fun sometimes.

PATCH and GRIDLEY (*together. Fatuously*): Yes. That's right.

SERGEANT WILKS: Village to-day seems to be full o' wives looking for their husbands.

GRIDLEY *and* PATCH *do not like the sound of this.*

PATCH: Oh!

SERGEANT WILKS: Yes. Lady came dashing up to me—a visitor, not a local—and said she was looking for her husband—little chap in a brown suit—spectacles—might be carrying a little black bag. Feather-something I think the name was. The way she carried on you'd have thought that instead of just giving her the slip for a bit o' fishing or something, he was going to blow the place up——

GRIDLEY: Ah!

SERGEANT WILKS: Then there's Mrs. Slivers, which reminds me. Has Mr. Slivers been here to-day?

GRIDLEY *and* PATCH *look at one another slowly.*

GRIDLEY: Has he, Bob?

PATCH: I'm just trying to think, Sam. (*To* SERGEANT) Why?

SERGEANT WILKS: His wife's in a bit of fluster about him. Spoke to me about an hour since. He set off this morning—to deliver one or two orders for the shop—and hasn't come back yet. His wife can't understand it, never known him miss his dinner before. And *she* said *he* said he was coming here. (*Stares at them.*)

PATCH (*slowly*): That's right, he *was* here this morning. You remember, Sam?

GRIDLEY: I do now, Bob. Yes, Mr. Slivers was here fairly early this morning.

PATCH: Where did he say he was going to after he left us?

GRIDLEY: Can't remember, can't remember. (*Specially to* SERGEANT) Can't remember.

SERGEANT WILKS: I see.

He walks slowly to back. GRIDLEY *and* PATCH *stand watching him, very carefully.* SERGEANT *looks over the side, down right.*

SERGEANT WILKS: Somebody seems to have been up to something along there, don't they? Trees smashed. Branches all over the place. Somebody's been up to something.

PATCH: Isn't that just what I said to you, Sam? Somebody—I said—has been up to something there.

GRIDLEY: You did. And I remember you took the very words out of my mouth.

[124]

SERGEANT WILKS (*staring steadily at them*): Mmmmm!

GRIDLEY (*cheerfully*): Yes, right out of my mouth. Well, good afternoon, Sergeant.

PATCH (*cheerfully*): Good afternoon, Sergeant. And look after that nose.

GRIDLEY (*vaguely*): And—any time y'know——

PATCH: Yes—any time——

SERGEANT WILKS (*slowly, still staring*): Mmmmm! Good afternoon!

> *They watch him go. When he has gone* PATCH *makes a loud tut-tut-ing noise. They come downstage.*

PATCH (*tut-tut-tut-ing*): What does he call himself? What a sergeant!

GRIDLEY (*indignantly*): You heard him? (*Imitating.*) Mmmm! Mmmmmm! That's what we pay 'em for.

PATCH: *And* pensions!

GRIDLEY: And what good is he?

PATCH: Useless. Here's a fellow comes and blows up half the wood down there, and all this sergeant can say is (*imitating*) "Somebody must have been up to something." (*Snorts.*)

GRIDLEY: And this poor Mrs. Slivers. She's worrying about her husband. He's not come back. He's missed his dinner.

PATCH: She's quite right to worry.

GRIDLEY: Of course she is. But what does he do? Comes round here and tells us she's in a bit of a fluster, never looks for Slivers, and goes away. Mmmmm! Mmmmm! And where does that get him? It isn't asking questions. It isn't even good manners.

PATCH: It's nothing. If he'd have had this ship to look after to-day, it would have been in bits all over the countryside now.

GRIDLEY: That's right. If he was in the fix we're in now, he wouldn't know where to start.

PATCH (*rather dubiously*): No.

GRIDLEY (*dubiously*): No.

PATCH: Well, where do we start? Because it's time we got started.

GRIDLEY: There you go. Charging at it again.

PATCH: I want to be doing something. I like action.

GRIDLEY: I know, and there's a lot o' people about like you. They all want to be doing something. Action. Only they don't stop to think what it is they want to do, and what action it ought to be. So you get 'em chasing old Jews down side-streets, chucking bombs into machines they can't mend, pulling down——

PATCH: All right, Sam, all right. Only don't forget, I've been very useful so far—if it hadn't been for me, you'd have still been down that hold——

GRIDLEY: Well, it's not my fault if I weigh fifteen stone instead of eleven, is it?

PATCH (*grinning*): Yes, you should eat less.

GRIDLEY (*indignantly*): Me! I don't eat half as much as you——

PATCH: Keep to the point, Sam. I say I've been very useful so far, and I'll be useful to the finish. It's all very well saying we must stop and think, but you haven't done any thinking yet. All you've done is—stop.

HILDA *appears, rather shyly and cautiously.*

HILDA: What happened? Did he say anything about me?

PATCH: No, he didn't. Not a word. You're all right.

HILDA (*rather disappointed*): Oh! He might have said *something*.

GRIDLEY (*with heavy irony*): Shall we call him back and tell him who you are?

HILDA: Don't be silly, Uncle.

GRIDLEY: Well, don't you begin talking like your mother.

HILDA (*to* PATCH): Tell me about all these men.

PATCH (*quickly*): Slivers is in Cabin A. Lord Cottingley—an old twister who'd like to see this ship blown up—is in B. There's a Communist, also on the blow up, in C. And there (*pointing to door*) is your friend Fletherington, the blower-up-in-chief.

HILDA: Can't you tell them you'll let them all out if they promise to say nothing about me? Then make them all go?

GRIDLEY: Oh—it's not so simple as that. In fact, it's complicated, y'know—by thunder!—it's complicated——

HILDA (*trying to be reassuring*): Perhaps it isn't—really.

GRIDLEY (*shouting*): But it is, girl, it is. Don't tell me it isn't. I *know*. I tell you, it's hellishly complicated. (*Mops himself and blows.*)

HILDA: All right, Uncle, don't shout at me. Keep cool. You'll never be able to think if you don't. Now take them one at a time——

PATCH (*admiringly*): That's the style.

GRIDLEY: Who's saying it isn't? Order, method, everything in its place, a time for everything—haven't I been advocating them things for thirty years in these ships, ever since——

PATCH (*saying it with him*): The *Theodosia* went down. All right, Sam, we know. Go on, Miss Jackson——

HILDA (*smiling*): You might as well call me Hilda, you know.

PATCH: Good! Hilda then.

GRIDLEY (*impatiently*): What does it matter what he calls you? We'll be calling you Convict Ninety-nine, if we don't get on.

HILDA (*sharply, reproachfully*): Uncle—that's not funny—it's beastly.

PATCH: Quite right, Hilda. I'm surprised at you, Sam. Talking like that to her!

GRIDLEY (*charmingly*): My dear, if I've hurt your feelings—I'm sorry. I'm a rough old devil, y'know—been knocking round in rough company for over forty years—and I'm nearly at my wits' end—you understand, don't you? (*Gives her a little hug. They are all reconciled.*)

HILDA: Well now, taking them one at a time. I should get Mr. Fletherington out of the way first. He doesn't really mean any harm, I'm sure. He's a nice little man.

GRIDLEY: He may be—but he's practically barmy——

PATCH (*eagerly*): Hilda's right, Sam. We've got Fletherington taped. We can tell him his wife's looking for him, and we can also tell him that Sergeant Wilks is asking who did the damage down there.

GRIDLEY (*enthusiastically*): That's the idea, Bob. We're getting somewhere now, making a start, anyhow.

PATCH: And he wouldn't give Hilda here away, because he liked her—you remember.

HILDA (*eagerly*): Not only that but—— I've been thinking. I'm giving you most of the trouble—really. If I went, it would be much easier. Now, isn't Mr. Fletherington staying with his wife at a farm round here? It's probably quite out of the way. If he thought it would be all right—I might go with him. He's nice, and his wife sounded nice——

GRIDLEY: That's it. Bob——

PATCH (*triumphantly*): We've got it. The rest'll be easy.

GRIDLEY: Ah—but wait a minute. There's Cottingley. As soon as we let him go—*pht!*—a telegram to London, and he's bought the ship.

PATCH: Yes, but don't you see if Fletherington's gone with his explosive, and if we've got rid of this Communist—he'll think twice about it? He only got the idea because everything was on the spot, with two mugs ready to do his dirty work for him. And he's nothing on us, because Hilda'll have gone too. There'll be only Slivers and he doesn't count.

HILDA (*to* GRIDLEY): Don't you see?

GRIDLEY: See it all. Fletherington's the man. We'll let him out.

[127]

PATCH *hurries to small door and opens it triumphantly.*

PATCH: All right, Mr. Fletherington.

No reply, nothing happens. He looks inside.

He's not there.

GRIDLEY (*roaring*): What?

PATCH: Not here. (*Goes inside, obviously to investigate.*)

GRIDLEY (*to* HILDA, *with the air of a man almost exasperated beyond speech*): Conjuring work now, see? The Great Houdini! Indian rope tricks! I thought we were being let off too easy. You see, when it starts getting out of control, it goes on. First, a bearing or two, then the valves are jammed, then the flywheel's cock-eyed, then the big shaft starts to buckle—— Do you ever read Schopenhauer?

HILDA: No.

GRIDLEY: It's all in there—though he'd never seen an engine.

PATCH (*coming down*): He'd never seen anything. If you're going to bring that old moth-eaten grouser into it, we'll get nowhere. I saw how he got out. Squeezed through the ventilator.

GRIDLEY (*full of energy again*): It's ten to one he hasn't left the ship. It's a nasty jump wherever he tries it.

PATCH: And another thing. He hasn't got his detonators. They're safe.

GRIDLEY: That's right. They're here.

Goes to detonator placard and pulls it aside.

No. Gone.

PATCH and HILDA (*together*): Gone!

GRIDLEY (*grandly defiant now*): Yes, and let 'em go. (*He sends the placard skimming off high right.*) I don't care how, when and where they've gone. For—by Moses and Jehosophat!—boy, they're not going to do it on us. If we've got to eat 'em alive, we're going to save this ship.

PATCH (*with enthusiasm*): That's the stuff. Come on. Fletherington must be somewhere about.

Enter URSULA. *She is dusty, limping and cross.*

URSULA (*unpleasantly surprised at the sight of them*): Oh!

PATCH (*aggressively*): Yes—oh! You hoped we were still down in the hold, didn't you?

URSULA: Yes.

PATCH (*glaring*): A nice girl you are!

GRIDLEY (*ogre-ishly*): Yes, we're very fond of you.

URSULA: Where is everybody?

HILDA (*calmly but promptly*): They've gone.

URSULA (*surprised*): Gone?

GRIDLEY and PATCH: Yes. Gone.

URSULA: But my father—Lord Cottingley—has he gone?

GRIDLEY and PATCH (*in cheerful sing-song*): Yes, yes. Gone.

URSULA: Damned cheek of him! (*She stares at them sceptically.*) D'you know, it wouldn't surprise me if you were all lying.

HILDA (*with virtuous indignation*): How dare you!

URSULA (*to* HILDA): Don't be silly. You must have had to do quite a lot of lying lately. The famous Meddleworth nurse! I recognised you this morning. And now you can tell me what the particularly dirty work was that Sir Eric was up to.

HILDA (*scornfully*): Don't be so disgusting.

URSULA (*cheerfully*): And don't you be such an awful little lower middle-class prig.

HILDA: After what I've just seen, I prefer to be a lower middle-class prig, thank you.

URSULA: All right. But what *have* you just seen? That's what I want to know.

HILDA (*with cutting scorn*): The court was crowded with silly girls and women, all specially dressed for the occasion.

URSULA: And that's why you didn't like 'em. Their clothes were too good.

HILDA: They were all whispering and giggling, all hoping to hear every dirty thing they'd ever dreamed of. I can't tell you how much I despised them——

URSULA: Or me.

HILDA: Or you.

URSULA: It's just envy, nurse. You'll get over it.

HILDA (*forcefully*): It's not envy. And I don't want to get over it. I hope that never in my life again have I even to look at people like you. It's time we saw that you cost more than you're worth. You're not real women, of any use to the world. You're just a set of useless, expensive mischievous—dolls. (*She turns away and marches off.*)

URSULA (*moving forward, angrily*): Hey, wait a minute! You're not going to get away with that.

She is about to make after her, but is stopped by PATCH.

PATCH: And you wait a minute. Where's your boy friend in the blue shirt?

URSULA: Captain Mellock's down there. (*Goes to side, and calls.*) Captain Mellock! Oo-oo! (*Turns.*) But he won't be too tired to handle you two again, I expect. (*Almost to herself*) And now for that blasted nursemaid.

> She goes off hurriedly, after HILDA. PATCH *and* GRIDLEY *deliberately pick up the iron bars they brought on earlier, look at them, then at one another.*

PATCH (*grinning*): For the captain?

GRIDLEY: For the noble captain.

PATCH: Length o' rope too?

GRIDLEY: No, don't think so.

> *They go slowly up to the entrance, moving so that one is at each side.*

Bob, he may use that gun.

PATCH: I know. But we can't lie down to it twice. There's a limit.

GRIDLEY: That's the answer. Spoken like a man, boy.

> *They hear him coming up the ladder and wait—on their toes. When he arrives, he is even dustier and more tired than* URSULA. *He is carrying a bottle of whisky and a packet of sandwiches. They go for him at once and though he manages to draw his gun—for he carries both parcels with one hand—they are too much for him.* GRIDLEY *has him by one arm and the back of his neck.* PATCH *is twisting the arm that holds the gun.*

PATCH: Drop the gun, or I'll break your arm into little pieces, general.

> PATCH *gets the gun. He unloads it at once, throwing the bullets away.*

GRIDLEY: Going to keep quiet now, Deadwood Dick?

MELLOCK (*wearily*): Yes. Two to one. Besides, I'm tired. Mind if I sit down?

> *He limps to a seat. The other two stand near him. He sighs and mops his brow.*

Been walking for the last hour and a half.

PATCH: Why?

MELLOCK (*wearily*): My car broke down. Don't know what was the matter with it. Don't know what's the matter with that girl either. Beats me.

PATCH: There's a lot o' things the matter with that girl. But what happened?

MELLOCK: I've been away so long, I don't know what to make of these girls. They're all new to me!

PATCH: Ask us. We know. We've had 'em as passengers.

MELLOCK: Well, to begin with I couldn't help the damned car breaking down. And at first she didn't mind. She said: "Let's go and sit in the wood."

GRIDLEY and PATCH (*together significantly*): Ah!

MELLOCK: We sat in the wood and I told her a few of my yarns. Then she suddenly lost her temper, set off walking here, and at full tilt——

PATCH: What did you do to her in the wood?

MELLOCK: Nothing.

GRIDLEY *and* PATCH *look at one another significantly.*

I don't pretend to be better than the next fellow——

PATCH (*with faint mockery*): Quite, quite.

MELLOCK: But I know when it's up to me to behave like a gentleman. I mean to say, with a fine kid like that—her father a big pot —you know——

GRIDLEY (*with ironic air of simplicity*): Yes, yes, yes.

MELLOCK: And yet she goes and loses her temper.

PATCH (*with mock sympathy*): And you'd done nothing at all.

MELLOCK: Not a thing.

PATCH (*with mock gravity*): It's what I've always said, Sam. Women—are queer.

GRIDLEY: Bob's said it, Captain. They're queer.

MELLOCK: Well, I've known a few who were all right——

PATCH (*same mocking tone*): So have we, so have we. Haven't we, Sam?

MELLOCK: But this one beats me. I don't understand how things are going here nowadays. (*Looking about him, then sharply*) How did you fellows get out? Where are the others—Lord Cottingley— that Communist chap, Gaster?

GRIDLEY *and* PATCH *eye one another across him, wondering what to invent.*

I saw a police sergeant down the road. Had he been here?

GRIDLEY *and* PATCH *nod gravely.*

Well—what's happened?

GRIDLEY (*very slowly*): Well—it's a long story.

PATCH (*very slowly*): And a very strange story—too.

GRIDLEY (*solemnly*): Ve-er-ry strange.

URSULA *enters as he speaks.*

[131]

URSULA: What is?

MELLOCK *rises.*

PATCH (*both he and* GRIDLEY *talk with an air of idiotic simplicity from now on*): We promised Sergeant Wilks—that's the policeman you saw—and a nice chap——

GRIDLEY (*solemnly*): A very nice chap indeed, Sergeant Wilks.

PATCH: We promised him not to tell anybody. I think (*confidentially*) he's frightened of a local panic. They're very nervous round here. Aren't they, Sam?

GRIDLEY: Nervous as sick kittens. And that must have been it, Bob. He's afraid there'll be a panic.

URSULA (*after exchanging look of bewilderment with* MELLOCK): What on earth are you talking about?

PATCH (*confidentially*): It didn't matter to us, you see, because whatever it turns out to be, well—we've both been vaccinated and inoculated lately. We have to be.

GRIDLEY (*following helpfully*): That's right. Regular vaccination and inoculation. And it pays in the long run. You—er—never know what's going to happen.

URSULA *and* MELLOCK *stare at them and at each other, open-mouthed.*

PATCH: Mind you, Sam, it may not be that at all. We can't tell what poor old Slivers has got——

MELLOCK: Who's Slivers?

As they do not reply, GRIDLEY *shaking his head at* PATCH, URSULA *cuts in.*

URSULA: Is he the man you had locked in that cabin? (*As they do not reply.*) He is, isn't he?

They nod.

Well, what's the matter with him?

PATCH: It was the only thing we could do, you know. Until the doctor came.

MELLOCK (*not liking this*): The doctor?

URSULA: Come on. What's the matter with him?

They are obviously reluctant to answer.

He was taken ill, wasn't he?

PATCH: All hot and flushed. Then breaking into spots.

GRIDLEY (*warningly*): Bob! You know, we promised.

URSULA: Don't be idiotic. You've got to tell us.

PATCH (*with feigned reluctance*): Spots. All over his face and hands——

GRIDLEY: You could see them coming on him, before your very eyes. About that size. (*Indicates.*) No bigger. (*Shows them.*)

PATCH: But as I said to your father and the others: "Well, it may be nothing. Just chicken-pox." We'll have to fumigate the cabin, of course——

GRIDLEY (*gravely*): We'll have to fumigate all that alleyway, Bob. But we're talking too much. You know what Wilks said——

URSULA (*to* MELLOCK): Here, I'm off. (*As he doesn't move.*) Come on. If you want to catch small-pox or scarlet fever or whatever it is, I don't. And if we hang about here they'll be coming back to fumigate us or vaccinate us or something. We'll hurry back to the wood and take your car.

MELLOCK: How can we? It won't go.

URSULA (*exploding*): Of course it will, you idiot.

MELLOCK (*shouting*): Don't call me an idiot. You know damned well it won't go.

URSULA (*shouting*): I know damned well it won't go when I turn off the ignition and take the key.

MELLOCK (*astounded*): Take the key! But you didn't.

URSULA: I did—right under your great fat silly nose. (*She takes a key out of her bag or pocket and hurls it on to the deck, then turns away and goes.*)

MELLOCK (*urgently, after picking up the key*): But where did that Communist go? I was told to look after him.

GRIDLEY: He was sure it was small-pox. Where was he going, Bob, Plymouth?

PATCH: No. Norwich.

GRIDLEY: That's it. Norwich. I know he was in a great hurry.

URSULA *hastily reappears at entrance.*

URSULA (*shouting to* MELLOCK): Are you coming, you idiot?

MELLOCK (*moving forward*): Yes, but I'll have to go to Norwich.

URSULA (*shouting as she goes*): All right then, let's go to Norwich. I've never been.

MELLOCK *hurries after her.* PATCH, *who is still holding revolver, goes to side and looks down.*

PATCH: Hoy—Mellock! You might want this.

He throws revolver over and waves good-bye, grinning.

GRIDLEY: We're on the move, boy. We're getting somewhere. I'll go look for Fletherington.

As he goes out HILDA *comes in and looks at* PATCH, *who is still staring over the side.*

HILDA: Where's that girl going?

PATCH (*grinning*): Running off with Deadwood Dick in the blue shirt, I think.

HILDA (*scornfully*): She would! She's that kind of girl.

PATCH: That's it. Hello, she's left the whisky and those packets, probably grub.

HILDA: That's the kind of girl all men seem to like.

PATCH (*investigating the packages now*): Not me. Didn't interest me in the least. Terrible type! They're sandwiches (*Examines them with interest.*)

HILDA: She was pretty, though. Don't you think?

PATCH: Yes—pretty-ish. Have a sandwich. I'm going to.

They both take and eat sandwiches.

No, I've seen too many of that sort——

HILDA (*without enthusiasm*): Oh!

PATCH: I mean—among passengers.

HILDA: Yes, of course, we all know what some girls are like when they're passengers——

PATCH (*hastily*): Don't you believe it. All exaggerated—worse—— (*he nearly says "luck", but then collects himself*)—than anything's exaggerated.

HILDA (*shyly*): I expect you know—plenty of girls——

PATCH (*shyly*): Why do you say that? You're not thinking of what Sam—your uncle—said, are you?

HILDA (*slowly*): No—but—after all, officer of a ship—and—rather good-looking—and——

PATCH: What about you, then?

HILDA (*laughing*): I'm not an officer of a ship——

PATCH: No, but you're very pretty.

HILDA: Do you think so?

PATCH: Yes, the moment I saw you.

HILDA: I'm not very pretty. And I'm not very interesting. Just—ordinary.

PATCH: No, you're not ordinary.

HILDA: Well, I do my work quite well. And I've had a very good training—Truby-King.

PATCH: I suppose—you do very well out of your job, don't you?

HILDA: Yes, not bad. I like my work too, though I shouldn't like to think I was never going to do anything but look after other people's children.

PATCH (*rather bitterly*): I've had a good training too—served my apprenticeship—passed examinations—have my master's certificate. But look at me now.

HILDA (*softly*): I know. And I think it's a shame.

PATCH: You can make more money than I can.

HILDA: That's not your fault.

PATCH: No—just my misfortune. I liked ships, you see. I was a mug. I ought to have learned to play the saxophone or to work the tote at greyhound races—something really useful.

HILDA (*troubled*): You're very bitter—aren't you?—underneath.

PATCH: I'm sorry. Got nothing to be bitter—with you—about, Hilda.

HILDA: Yes—in a way, you have, even with me. But—I don't think money ought to count—do you?

> PATCH *turns away, sharply, picks up the paper-covered whisky bottle and takes the outer wrapping off. She watches him, deeply moved, and once makes a gesture towards him. She wants to say something, do something, to comfort him, but while she hesitates* GRIDLEY *enters, from cabin entrance. He is looking much cleaner and neater than he did. As soon as he comes in,* HILDA *moves out right back.*

GRIDLEY (*heartily*): Started to look for Fletherington, but decided to clean myself up first. Feel better for it. Ready for 'em all, Bob. What are you going to do with that whisky?

PATCH (*rather gloomily*): Drink it.

GRIDLEY: No. Give it to poor old Slivers. He's been in captivity longest and a few drinks might do him a bit o'good.

PATCH: Might be useful, too. All right. (*Moving towards cabin entrance.*) Then I'll comb the ship for Fletherington. He's probably got stuck in a ventilator or a watertight door by this time.

GRIDLEY: You do that and I'll get rid of—— Now who is it we get rid of next? Cottingley?

PATCH (*moving off*): No, not before Fletherington. There's the Communist.

GRIDLEY: By criminy!—so there is. I'd forgotten about him. I'll have him out now.

> PATCH *has now gone back right.* GRIDLEY *hastens out through*

cabin entrance, and soon returns with GASTER, *who is looking hot and miserable.*

GRIDLEY (*as they enter*): Yes, you'd better get back to Longport as quick as you can. You've plenty to do there, and nothing here. There'll be no blowing up. And we've just had a police sergeant here. (*Sees the sandwiches and goes over to them.*) Now what you want before you go is a sandwich.

They both eat a sandwich.

GASTER: Did that Fascist come back?

GRIDLEY: He did, but he's gone for a razzle with Cottingley's daughter.

GASTER (*contemptuously*): That's what they would do. Well, they'd better make the most of their opportunities. They won't have 'em much longer.

GRIDLEY: It's a pity you couldn't have gone on the razzle with her instead of him. He's had too many. You've never had enough —if any. In fact, that's what's the matter with you. You've never had any fun, have you?

GASTER: How can I and my class have "fun"—as you call it— when all the time . . . ?

GRIDLEY (*interrupting*): All the time—nothing! People who want a bit o' fun, have a bit o' fun, class or no class.

GASTER (*eagerly*): We are not opposed to the people enjoying themselves. We want fun for all workers.

GRIDLEY: I know, and when they get it, what will it be? Mass physical jerks every other Tuesday in the public park.

GASTER (*after looking round, confidentially*): Comrade, you're not a right-wing swine, a rotten counter-revolutionary, I'm sure. Now this ship's nicely out of the way, yet not too far from Longport. Don't you think we might use it for party work?

GRIDLEY: No, I don't. To begin with, if I allowed that, I wouldn't be doing my duty——

GASTER (*sneering*): Your duty!

GRIDLEY: That's what I said. And don't be in such a hurry to laugh at it either. Suppose you get your revolution, what then? The first thing you'll want is a lot of people who can be relied on to do their duty—just that. And if you've laughed 'em all out of it before that, you'll find yourselves in a nice pickle. You'll be having to shoot managers and foremen in batches—Russian style!

GASTER: There are duties and duties. Our first duty is to the revolution, the proletarian state, the real community——

GRIDLEY: And anything else that's large and fine and a long way off. But what you'll want—you'll find—is a lot o' people who'll know it's their duty to keep a bearing oiled, a certain light burning, a wheel trimmed to a compass, and will see that they do their duty. Just be careful you don't throw 'em all overboard, to make room for a mob o' lazy whining sea-lawyers and Pacific Coast I.W.W. men, who can break anything and mend nothing. Don't let too much loose. When I was a young man, I was in the *Theodosia* when she went down, full o' passengers. I saw a lot let loose that time. It put twenty years on me. I used to be a clever wild young devil up to then. I thought I knew it all. That showed me what I knew.

GASTER: But I guarantee it was really the fault of the owners that ship was wrecked.

GRIDLEY: Bad owners and bad sailors, both. Don't you see, it's not just a case of the haves and the have-nots. There are men about —a few—and there are monkeys—millions of 'em. I try to be a man. If the Communist Party owned this ship, and employed me, I'd do my duty by them.

GASTER: And who does own this ship? The workers——

GRIDLEY: And who the hell are they? Don't start telling me the riveters and carpenters really own this ship——

GASTER: It was their labour——

GRIDLEY: Most of 'em wouldn't know whether they were making a ship or a skating rink. And wouldn't care. All most of them think about is beer and football, and they don't even know so dam' much about them. I don't want a party, yours or anybody else's. I don't care about capitalists and proletarians, masses and bosses, red shirts, black shirts, brown shirts, green shirts. I want to see some men about, real men who know what sense is, and duty is, and order is. (*Shouting*) I'm getting on, my time's running out, and I'm tired of living among millions of howling monkeys. For God's sake, show me some men.

A pause.

GASTER (*eagerly*): And where will you find this sense, this order, you talk about? Only——

PATCH *enters hurriedly.*

PATCH: Hoy! We're not going to have another session of Karl Marx. We've too much to do. (*Pointedly, to* GASTER) Good afternoon.

GASTER (*with dignity*): Good afternoon. (*Moves away towards exit, then turns to speak, with sincerity and passion.*) You're blind, both of you. In the end you will have to come to us. That capitalist

Cottingley will go on cheating you. That Fascist will come again and threaten you with his gun. This ship you are so anxious to protect will be taken from you. Then there will be nothing left for you but despair and death—or the living force of the revolution. Good day, comrades.

Goes out with dignity. They watch him go, impressed. Then they look at one another for a moment, whistling softly.

PATCH (*urgently*): We've found Fletherington. He'd fallen and hurt himself a bit. Hilda's giving him first aid again. And they've practically fixed it for him to take her to that farm he's staying at.

GRIDLEY (*excitedly*): We're moving, boy, we're moving. That only leaves Cottingley. Let's get Fletherington away—and Hilda—as soon as we can. Then it's all set, Bob, it's all set.

PATCH: We'll have done the lot of 'em in.

Enter FLETHERINGTON, *carrying his bag. He has two fresh pieces of sticking plaster on his face, one hand is wrapped up, and he is limping. His clothes are rather torn and dirty in places. But he is still beaming.*

FLETHERINGTON: Miss Jackson is just putting her things together. She'll be here in a moment. Very nice useful sort of girl. I'm sure my wife will be glad if we can be of any service to her.

PATCH: Well, see you go straight back to that farm. No more funny work.

GRIDLEY: No. Your wife's looking for you, y'know.

FLETHERINGTON: Yes. I remember now there was something about a picnic. She may be annoyed. I shall have to let Miss Jackson explain some of it. My wife will soon understand. She's an unusually sensible woman, really.

GRIDLEY (*briskly*): See you stick to her then. That's what we want now. Gumption! Savvy! Downright horse sense! By crikey!— there isn't much of it about. Plenty of brains, but no sense.

FLETHERINGTON (*with a sigh*): You're probably right. I myself have a fairly good brain——

PATCH (*briskly*): Put you in a lab—and no doubt you're fine. But outside it—you're practically barmy.

GRIDLEY (*briskly*): Never go out without the missis. Stick to her. Take my tip.

PATCH: Got all your explosive doings in the bag?

FLETHERINGTON (*smiling, holding the bag up*): Yes, everything.

GRIDLEY (*carefully taking the bag from him, then holding it up with both hands*): Well, watch yourself with it.

[138]

SERGEANT *moves back and towards left a few paces.*

That's right. I just want to have a word with these two officers. Mr. Patch.

Brings both of them downstage, stands between them, and addresses them confidentially.

I seem to have forced that cabin door just at the right moment, don't I? I ought to give you straight in charge—for that and for several other things. But I'll give you a last chance. As I told you before, Gridley, I believe in minding my own business. If people don't interfere with me, I won't interfere with them. Now then—leave me alone, and you're all right—which includes that girl you're hiding here. But if you won't make me that promise, then I tell that sergeant everything I know.

A pause.

PATCH (*quietly, earnestly*): Sam, I'd do a lot to keep Hilda safe.

GRIDLEY (*impatiently*): Yes, yes, so would I.

PATCH: Not as much as I would, Sam. You understand?

GRIDLEY: Yes, I see, Bob. But it's no good. It won't do. You understand too, don't you, lad?

PATCH: Yes. That's all right, Sam.

LORD COTTINGLEY: Well——?

GRIDLEY: We're making no bargains with you.

LORD COTTINGLEY: You mean——?

PATCH (*roughly*): You know what we mean. Go on and do your damnedest.

LORD COTTINGLEY (*forcefully, breaks up the group, turning and calling* SERGEANT): Sergeant, I charge these two men with forcibly keeping me here, locked in a cabin. I had to break the door down.

SERGEANT WILKS (*horrified*): No?

LORD COTTINGLEY (*continuing briskly*): They did it for two good reasons. First, they're hiding here the Jackson girl, the missing witness in the Meddleworth Case——

SERGEANT WILKS: Coo——!

LORD COTTINGLEY (*same tone*): And secondly, because they've been keeping here, also under lock and key, some local man who found the girl here—a man—er—liver—liver——

SERGEANT WILKS (*tremendously impressed*): Not Slivers?

LORD COTTINGLEY: That's the man—Slivers.

SERGEANT WILKS: And I came here and asked about that very man—just friendly, in a nice way—not an hour since. T-t-t-t. (*Produces*

[141]

THE PLAYS OF J. B. PRIESTLEY

notebook in ponderous fashion, then looks severely at GRIDLEY *and* PATCH.) This'll get you both into a lot o' trouble, a lot o' trouble. (*Solemnly*) You 'ave 'eard his lordship's charges? What is your statement in reply to same?

PATCH and GRIDLEY (*together, promptly*): Barmy!

LORD COTTINGLEY (*impatiently*): Never mind statements, man, you can get them afterwards. Search the ship. Get your evidence.

SERGEANT WILKS (*putting away notebook*): Right, your lordship.

PATCH *and* GRIDLEY *exchange glances.*

GRIDLEY: Come on. I'll take you round.

LORD COTTINGLEY: Now mind, don't let him bluff you. Artful fella, very artful fella!

> SERGEANT *goes out through cabin entrance with* GRIDLEY *close behind, and very much taking charge of him. As soon as the* SERGEANT *is off,* PATCH *quickly picks up one of the iron bars they brought on at beginning of Act and goes up to* LORD COTTINGLEY *menacingly.*

PATCH: Now listen, you old twister, you raise your voice these next two minutes, and I'll flatten you with this. For two pins I'd take a crack at you now with it. I've always wanted to set about a bad owner and this is my chance.

LORD COTTINGLEY (*who is frightened*): You—try—anything of that sort—and I've only to call the sergeant——

PATCH (*terribly ferocious*): That's just what you won't do, see? Try it, and you'll find yourself flat on that deck—out!

> HILDA *appears rather timidly from back entrance right, carrying her bag.* PATCH *motions her to leave the ship at once.* LORD COTTINGLEY *turns and sees her.*

LORD COTTINGLEY (*loudly*): There——

> PATCH *puts one hand over his mouth and holds the iron bar to his head, as if ready to lay him out with it.* LORD COTTINGLEY *grows purple.* PATCH *addresses* HILDA *with urgency.*

PATCH: Quick, Hilda. The little man's waiting for you in the wood. Hurry! And I'll see you again, won't I?

HILDA (*standing now at entrance to gangway*): If you want to— please, Bob. And you—won't—let anything—make any difference— to us, will you?

PATCH: No. Hurry. And God bless you!

> *She hurries away, and now he talks to* LORD COTTINGLEY, *still keeping his hand over* LORD COTTINGLEY'S *mouth.*

[142]

LORD COTTINGLEY (*muffled*): Let go. I can't breathe.

PATCH: Promise not to shout then.

LORD COTTINGLEY: I won't.

PATCH (*menacingly*): All right then——

LORD COTTINGLEY: Yes, I will. Damn you!

PATCH (*letting him go, politely*): Have a sandwich. They're your sandwiches. Your daughter and the Captain brought them back.

LORD COTTINGLEY: Where are they?

PATCH (*offering him sandwiches*): Here.

LORD COTTINGLEY (*irritably*): No, not the sandwiches. No—— (*as PATCH removes them*)—don't take 'em away. I'm hungry.

PATCH: Well, make up your mind then.

LORD COTTINGLEY (*taking a sandwich and eating it hungrily*): My daughter and Captain Mellock—where are they?

PATCH: They were here not half an hour ago. They wouldn't stay. Just looked in and then were off.

LORD COTTINGLEY: But they ought to have been back here hours ago.

PATCH (*with innocent air*): Yes, but their car broke down and then they sat in a wood—for quite a long time, he told me.

LORD COTTINGLEY (*who does not like the sound of this*): Sat in a wood! Did they seem—very friendly!

PATCH (*same innocent air*): Well—no, they didn't. She was calling him an idiot. And he told me he didn't know what was the matter with her.

LORD COTTINGLEY: I don't like the sound of this. Where did they go? And *why* did they go? (*As PATCH is silent*) Come along. Tell me.

PATCH: Well—er—it's awkward——

LORD COTTINGLEY (*furiously*): Mr. Patch—that girl's my daughter —the only one I've got. Now tell me the truth.

PATCH: All right, Lord Cottingley. This is exactly what happened. She made a move to go ashore and said: "Are you coming, you idiot?" And he said: "Yes, but I'll have to go to Norwich." And she said: "All right, then, let's go to Norwich. I've never been." Now those are the exact words. And off they both went.

LORD COTTINGLEY: Patch, if this is a bluff, it's a damned dirty one.

PATCH: Well, it's not a bluff.

LORD COTTINGLEY: I know the girl's crazy enough for anything— a gunman from God knows where! He can't afford to marry her.

PATCH: Marriage wasn't mentioned. I've told you all that was.

LORD COTTINGLEY (*urgently*): I know. You couldn't have invented that. Did you say they left not half an hour ago?

PATCH: Yes. You've still got time.

LORD COTTINGLEY (*impressively*): My God, I'd better have.

He is hurrying out just as WILKS *enters.*

SERGEANT WILKS (*pompously*): Your Lordship——

LORD COTTINGLEY (*hurrying off*): Brrrr! Don't bother me. I'm in a hurry.

He goes. WILKS *stares after him, then at* PATCH, *who is grinning now.*

SERGEANT WILKS: There's no girl here.

PATCH: No, of course not.

SERGEANT WILKS: But what's the matter with his lordship?

PATCH: Didn't you know?

SERGEANT WILKS: Know what?

PATCH: He's barmy.

SERGEANT WILKS: Barmy?

PATCH: Clean off his nut. I tried to tip you the wink when he was talking about charging us, but you wouldn't look at me. He'd charge anybody with anything, he would. Talks to you one minute, then the next minute he's running like the devil somewhere. Doesn't remember anything. Just runs off like a four-year-old. Oh—we know him well.

SERGEANT WILKS: Somebody ought to be looking after him—going round like that. He might have got me into trouble.

PATCH: Of course he might. That's what I always say. It isn't good enough.

SERGEANT WILKS (*looking at* PATCH *suspiciously*): Here, but what about Mr. Slivers? Is he here or isn't he?

PATCH (*hesitating*): Well, in a manner of speaking—yes. But looked at from another point of view—you might say—no.

SERGEANT WILKS: What d'you mean. Either he's here or he isn't here.

At this point SLIVERS' *voice, loud and drunken, can be heard off, coming nearer. He is singing.*

PATCH (*hearing this*): That's right. Well—he's here.

Enter SLIVERS, *who is being supported by* GRIDLEY, *who also carries the whisky bottle, now half-emptied.* SLIVERS *is very ruffled, tight, and merry in his own fashion.*

[144]

SLIVERS (*singing*):

> Whe-hen the ler-hove bird leaves its nest
> Der-hoes it fler-hy tew the East or the West——

GRIDLEY: Steady, my hearty. Steady.

SERGEANT WILKS (*astounded*): Now who'd have believed it? Never seen him this way before.

SLIVERS *laughs idiotically.*

GRIDLEY: Well, he can't be for ever just wrapping up cheese and then seeing what it says in the paper.

SLIVERS (*with drunken gravity*): Chee-sh? Didn'd I bring you shum chee-sh sh'morning? Canadian Cheddar?

PATCH: Yes, you did, old boy.

SLIVERS: Well—don'd ead id—muck!—— (*Shouting*) Muck, I shay! (*Glares defiantly at them all.*)

GRIDLEY: You see? He's got to turn into a man some time. Up to now he's been something cut out of a penny paper.

SERGEANT WILKS (*sternly to* SLIVERS): Your wife's been looking for you.

SLIVERS: Led her look. (*Impressively*) I've had mos' peculiar day. I'll tell you. Quied, ser'n'd, quied, while I tell you. Mos' peculiar. Now listen. Now then. (*Here he sticks, so appeals to* GRIDLEY.) Whad happened, Mister Grididdly?

GRIDLEY: You've been asleep in that cabin and you've been drinking whisky—this whisky.

Shows him bottle. He tries to take it.

Oh no, Mr. Slivers, my old buck, you've had enough.

SERGEANT WILKS: Too much. You'd better come along home with me.

SLIVERS: Cerdainly, cerdainly. (*Moves unsteadily over to him.*)

SERGEANT WILKS: Come on then. (*Quietly to* GRIDLEY *and* PATCH) The less said about this, the better. Respected shopkeeper—wouldn't sound well. Quite understand why you kept him close. Come along, Mr. Slivers.

SLIVERS (*solemnly*): All ri', I'm coming, but there's jus' one thing I wanda say, ser'n'd, before I go. Jus' one thing I wanda ask—jus' one——

SERGEANT WILKS: All right. Ask it then.

SLIVERS *solemnly surveys them, as if about to make some important pronouncement, then suddenly breaks into song again.*

SLIVERS (*singing*):

Whe-hen the ler-hove bird leaves its nest
Der-hoes it fly tew the East or the West——

SERGEANT *supports him firmly and half carries him off.* GRIDLEY *and* PATCH *watch them go. Then* GRIDLEY *waves a jubilant farewell with the whisky bottle over the side, while* PATCH *darts off to cabin entrance and returns at once with two glasses.*

GRIDLEY (*as* PATCH *returns*): That's the last of 'em, Bob.

PATCH: The very last of 'em, Sam.

GRIDLEY (*with growing excitement*): Boy, we've fooled 'em.

PATCH (*same mood*): Dished 'em.

GRIDLEY: Tangled 'em.

PATCH: Diddled 'em.

GRIDLEY: The whole squint-eyed——

PATCH: Fish-faced, lop-sided——

GRIDLEY: Addle-pated, crack-brained——

PATCH: Barmy lot of 'em.

GRIDLEY (*solemnly*): We drink to this, boy.

PATCH: We've earned it.

GRIDLEY: We've earned a month of it. (*Pours whisky into glasses. Holds up his own.*) The good ship *Gloriana!* (*Drinks.*)

PATCH: Here's to her next sailing! (*Drinks.*)

GRIDLEY: May we be sailing her! (*Drinks.*)

PATCH: And never miss a tide! (*Drinks.*)

GRIDLEY: And—— (*notices glass is empty.*) Oh!—well, might as well finish it now, boy, might as well finish it. We've earned it. (*Empties bottle into the two glasses, puts bottle down.*)

PATCH: And a sandwich.

Gets them. They both come down to the chairs and seat themselves luxuriously, sprawling at ease. The chairs should be so placed that there is a fair space between them, and so that neither sitter sees the back.

PATCH (*scornfully*): Blow her up! T-t-t.

GRIDLEY: Barmy, the whole lot of 'em.

They are now eating sandwiches, and taking occasional sips of whisky, very much at ease.

What a day!

PATCH: What a day!

GRIDLEY: But here she still is—the good old *Gloriana!*

PATCH: Here she still is!

GRIDLEY (*good-humouredly*): Now that it's quiet again—and the last loony's gone and we've saved the ship—you'll start grumbling again, I suppose.

PATCH: No, Sam, I shan't. I've got something—somebody—to think about now.

GRIDLEY: But mind you, though I like it quiet—when things start happening, I'm there, I'm on the spot, I'm in control——

PATCH: I didn't do so badly, either.

GRIDLEY: You didn't, Bob, you didn't. We both did well. There was our duty.

PATCH: And we did it.

GRIDLEY (*finishes eating and drinking now, and pulls out his copy of Schopenhauer*): This is what we want. Calms the mind. Gives you a big view of things. (*Begins reading.*) "The wish is, in its nature, pain; the attainment soon begets satiety; the end was only apparent; possession takes away the charm . . ."

PATCH (*interrupting very earnestly*): Sam, I'm a pal, aren't I? We've stood together, haven't we?

GRIDLEY: Yes, Bob.

PATCH: Will you do something for me, Sam? (*As* GRIDLEY *nods*) Give me that book.

   GRIDLEY, *rather surprised, hands it over.* PATCH *takes it and throws it off the ship, either back or forward, into the orchestral pit.*

GRIDLEY (*annoyed*): Here, Bob, what the——

PATCH (*earnestly*): Sam, I couldn't put up with any more of that miserable old devil. He takes the heart out of you. If you'd believed everything he wrote, you'd never have done what you have done to-day—and this ship would have been for it. He couldn't have saved a ship. He couldn't have saved a mousetrap.

GRIDLEY (*deeply reflecting, thoughtfully*): You might be right, boy, you might be right.

PATCH: I know I am. Try another chap—if only for a change.

GRIDLEY (*thoughtfully*): I might have a go at Thomas Carlyle. Old Jock MacClean, who was my first chief in the *Moriana*, used to swear by Thomas Carlyle, and he was a man, Jock MacClean. They wouldn't have talked about blowing ships up when he was about.

PATCH: They'll think twice about it next time when *we're* about.

   MR. TOOKE *has entered quietly. He is a clerkly little middle-aged man, now in rather incongruous holiday clothes. He does not see them at first, but looks about him, then notices them and comes*

[147]

forward, giving a slight cough. They turn in their chairs and stare at him.

MR. TOOKE (*standing between them*): Good afternoon. (*Smilingly*) Didn't see you at first, gentlemen. Mr. Gridley and Mr. Patch, isn't it?

GRIDLEY (*sitting up*): Yes. And I've seen you before, surely?

TOOKE (*beaming*): Of course. Don't you remember? Tooke, from Head Office.

PATCH: That's it. Mr. Tooke, from Head Office. Know you now. It was your sporting outfit that put me off.

TOOKE: Well, as a matter of fact, I'm killing two birds with one stone.

GRIDLEY: Oh? Are we the two birds?

TOOKE: Well, you see, I'm just beginning my holidays, and we've come to a little place just the other side of Longport, my wife's cousin keeps the establishment. So I said I'd come myself and bring you the message from Head Office. You're both to report there as soon as possible.

GRIDLEY: Ah!

PATCH: Oh-ho!

TOOKE (*casually now*): Yes, both go and see Commander Watson. (*Looks round.*) Quite nice here, isn't it? We've had the surveyors' reports on this ship, y'know. Quite hopeless, of course. Never ought to have been brought here.

GRIDLEY *and* PATCH, *sitting upright now, look at one another, then at* TOOKE.

GRIDLEY (*slowly*): Oh—er—what are they——

PATCH (*slowly*): Going to do with her?

TOOKE (*very casually*): Oh—blow her up, I think.

Looks at them, smiling foolishly. GRIDLEY *and* PATCH *like men exasperated beyond all speech by the insanity of things, slowly get up and do their whistling duet for the last time. As they are doing this and* TOOKE *is staring at them, his smile slowly fading into bewilderment, the curtain slowly falls.*

END OF PLAY

[148]

WHEN WE ARE MARRIED

A Yorkshire Farcical Comedy

CHARACTERS

RUBY BIRTLE
GERALD FORBES
NANCY HOLMES
ALDERMAN JOSEPH HELLIWELL
MARIA HELLIWELL
COUNCILLOR ALBERT PARKER
ANNIE PARKER
HERBERT SOPPITT
CLARA SOPPITT
MRS. NORTHROP
FRED DYSON
HENRY ORMONROYD
LOTTIE GRADY
REV. CLEMENT MERCER

The sitting-room of Alderman Helliwell's house in Cleckleywyke, a town in the West Riding, on a September evening about thirty years ago.

When we are Married—Copyright, 1938, *by John Boynton Priestley.*
Copyright, 1940, *by John Boynton Priestley.*

Produced at the St. Martin's Theatre, London, on October 11th,
1938, *with the following cast:*

RUBY BIRTLE	PATRICIA HAYES
GERALD FORBES	RICHARD WARNER
NANCY HOLMES	BETTY FLEETWOOD
HELLIWELL	LLOYD PEARSON
MRS. HELLIWELL	MURIEL GEORGE
PARKER	RAYMOND HUNTLEY
MRS. PARKER	HELENA PICKARD
SOPPITT	ERNEST BUTCHER
MRS. SOPPITT	ETHEL COLERIDGE
MRS. NORTHROP	BEATRICE VARLEY
FRED DYSON	ALEXANDER GRANDISON
HENRY ORMONROYD	FRANK PETTINGELL
LOTTIE GRADY	MAI BACON
REV. CLEMENT MERCER	NORMAN WOOLAND

Produced by BASIL DEAN

ACT I

The sitting-room in HELLIWELL'S *house, a solid detached late-Victorian house. On left (actor's left) wall is a window. Left of centre in back wall is a door to rest of house, leading directly into the hall. On right wall is a small conservatory, with door leading into this, and then into garden. The room is furnished without taste in the style of about thirty years ago. There is an upright piano. Little cupboards, drawers, small tables, etc. At rise, evening sunlight coming through window. Nobody on stage.*

We hear the front door bell ring. A moment later, RUBY BIRTLE *ushers in* GERALD FORBES. RUBY *is a very young "slavey" of the period, who looks as if her hair has just gone "up".* FORBES *is a pleasant young man, in the smart clothes of the period, and unlike* RUBY *and most of the other characters does not talk with a marked West Riding accent.*

RUBY: You'll have to wait 'cos they haven't finished their tea.

GERALD: Bit late, aren't they?

RUBY (*approaching, confidentially*): It's a do.

GERALD: It's what?

RUBY: A do. Y'know, they've company.

GERALD: Oh—I see. It's a sort of party, and they're having high tea.

RUBY (*going closer still*): Roast pork, stand pie, salmon and salad, trifle, two kinds o' jellies, lemon cheese tarts, jam tarts, swiss tarts, sponge cake, walnut cake, chocolate roll, and a pound cake kept from last Christmas.

GERALD (*with irony*): Is that all?

RUBY (*seriously*): No, there's white bread, brown bread, currant teacake, one o' them big curd tarts from Gregory's, and a lot o' cheese.

GERALD: It *is* a do, isn't it?

RUBY (*after nodding, then very confidentially*): *And* a little brown jug.

GERALD (*astonished*): A little brown jug?

RUBY (*still confidentially*): You know what that is, don't you? *Don't* you? (*Laughs.*) Well, I never did! Little brown jug's a drop

[153]

o' rum for your tea. They're getting right lively on it. (*Coolly*) But you don't come from round here, do you?

GERALD (*not disposed for a chat*): No.

A distant bell rings, not front door.

RUBY: I come from near Rotherham. Me father works in t' pit, and so does our Frank and our Wilfred.

Distant bell sounds again.

GERALD: There's a bell ringing somewhere.

RUBY (*coolly*): I know. It's for me. Let her wait. She's run me off me legs to-day. And Mrs. Northrop's in t' kitchen—she can do a bit for a change. There's seven of 'em at it in t' dining-room—Alderman Helliwell and missus, of course—then Councillor Albert Parker and Mrs. Parker, and Mr. Herbert Soppitt and Mrs. Soppitt —and of course, Miss Holmes.

GERALD: Oh—Miss Holmes *is* there, is she?

RUBY: Yes, but she's stopped eating. (*Giggles. Coolly*) You're courting her, aren't you?

GERALD (*astonished and alarmed*): What!

RUBY (*coolly*): Oh—I saw you both—the other night, near Cleckley Woods. I was out meself with our milkman's lad.

GERALD *turns away.*

Now don't look like that, I won't tell on you.

GERALD (*producing a shilling, then rather desperately*): Now—look here! What's your name?

RUBY: Ruby Birtle.

GERALD: Well, Ruby, you wouldn't like Miss Holmes to get into a row here with her uncle and aunt, would you?

RUBY: No, I wouldn't like that. But I'd like that shilling.

GERALD (*after giving it to her*): You said Miss Holmes had finished eating.

RUBY: Yes. She can't put it away like some of 'em. I'd rather keep Councillor Albert Parker a week than a fortnight. D'you want to see her?

GERALD: Yes. Could you just give her the tip quietly that I'm here—if the rest of them aren't coming in here yet?

RUBY: Not them! You'd think they'd been pined for a month—way they're going at it! I'll tell her. She'd better come round that way—through t' greenhouse——

Before she can actually move, MRS. NORTHROP, *an aggressive but humorous working-woman of about fifty puts her head in the door.*

[154]

MRS. NORTHROP (*aggressively*): Oh—'ere y'are!

RUBY (*coolly*): That's right, Mrs. Northrop.

MRS. NORTHROP (*aggressively*): I see nought right about it—you gassin' in 'ere as if you owned t' place instead o' gettin' on wi' your work. She's rung for yer twice, an' I've just taken another lot o' hot water in. Nah, come on, yer little crackpot!

> *Holds door open, and* RUBY *goes to it—turns and grins. Exit* RUBY.

MRS. NORTHROP: Aren't you t' organist at chapel?

GERALD: Yes.

MRS. NORTHROP (*cheerfully*): Ay, well, they've got it in for you.

GERALD (*astonished*): How do you know?

MRS. NORTHROP: 'Cos I 'eard 'em say so. (*Complacently*) I don't miss much.

GERALD: So that's why Mr. Helliwell asked me to come round and see him.

MRS. NORTHROP: That's right. There's three of 'em 'ere to-night, d'you see—all big men at chapel. You've been enjoyin' yerself a bit too much, I fancy, lad.

GERALD: So that's it—is it?

MRS. NORTHROP (*with very confidential air*): Ay—and d'you know what I say? I say—to 'ell with 'em!

> *Goes out, leaving* GERALD *looking a little worried. He moves about restlessly, takes cigarette-case out of his pocket mechanically, then puts it back again. He keeps an eye on the door into conservatory. After a few moments,* NANCY HOLMES, *an attractive girl in her early twenties, hurries in through this door.*

NANCY (*in breathless whisper*): Gerald!

GERALD: Nancy! (*Makes as if to kiss her.*)

NANCY (*breathlessly*): No, you mustn't, not here—no, Gerald—please——

> *But he does kiss her and no harm has been done.*

Now, listen, Gerald, and be sensible. This is serious. You know why Uncle Joe sent for you?

GERALD (*with a slight grin*): They've *got it in for* me. I've just been told.

NANCY: It's serious, Gerald. They've been grumbling about you some time, and now, as far as I can gather, one of these miserable old beasts saw you late one night—with *me*——

GERALD (*serious now*): Oh—I say—you weren't recognised, were you?

NANCY: No. But *you* were.

GERALD: Well, that's not so bad, as long as they can't drag you into it. I know how strict your aunt is, and you can't afford to quarrel with them here until we're ready to be married——

NANCY (*earnestly*): No, but you can't either, Gerald. And they're going to be very cross with you, and you'll have to be awfully careful what you say to them. And there's that beastly Councillor Parker here too, and you loathe him, don't you?

GERALD: Absolutely. And I'll loathe him more than ever now that he's full of roast pork and trifle. I think I'd better give them time to recover from that huge ghastly tuck-in they're having.

NANCY: I should. Though they've nearly finished now.

GERALD: If I clear out for half an hour or so, could you slip away too?

NANCY: I might. They don't really want me. I'm in the way. You see, it's an anniversary celebration, and I don't come into it at all.

GERALD: What are they celebrating?

Before she can reply, RUBY *opens door, announcing:*

RUBY: It's *Yorkshire Argus*—two of 'em.

GERALD *rises, moves down right.* NANCY *rises up to door.*

Enter FRED DYSON, *a cheerful, rather cheeky youngish reporter, and* HENRY ORMONROYD, *who carries a large and old-fashioned newspaperman's camera and a flash-light apparatus.* ORMONROYD *is a middle-aged man with an air of beery dignity and wears a large drooping moustache.* DYSON *walks down to* NANCY.

RUBY: This is Miss Holmes, Alderman Helliwell's niece. T'others is still having their tea.

RUBY *goes out.*

DYSON (*cheerfully*): 'Evening, Miss Holmes. (*To* GERALD) How d'you do? This is Mr. Henry Ormonroyd, our photographer.

ORMONROYD (*bowing*): Pleased to meet you, I'm sure. Delightful weather we're having for the time of year.

GERALD: Isn't it?

ORMONROYD (*profoundly*): It is.

DYSON: We seem to have come too early.

NANCY: I'm afraid you have——

ORMONROYD (*with dignified reproach*): What did I tell you, Fred? Always wanting to rush things. We could have had at least a couple more—with my friend at the *Lion*. He's a chap who used to have a very good little peppermint-rock business on the Central Pier, Black-

[156]

pool at the time I had my studio—there. Old times, y'know, Mr.—er, and happy days, happy days! (*Hums.*)

DYSON (*briskly*): All right, Henry. I'm sorry we're early. Matter of fact, I don't know yet what this is about. I just got a message from the office to come up here and bring a photographer.

NANCY: You see, it's their Silver Wedding.

DYSON: Henry, it's Alderman Helliwell's *Silver Wedding*.

ORMONROYD: Very nice, I suppose.

NANCY: Yes, but not only my uncle and aunt's. There were three couples—my uncle and aunt, Mr. and Mrs. Soppitt, Mr. and Mrs. Parker——

DYSON: Is that Councillor Albert Parker?

NANCY (*pulling a little face*): Yes. You know him?

DYSON (*gloomily*): Yes, we know him.

ORMONROYD: Every time he opens his mouth at the Town Hall, he puts his foot in it, so they call him "the foot and mouth disease". Ha. Ha. Are all three happy couples here?

NANCY: Yes, because they were all married on the same morning at the same chapel. They have a photograph—a combined wedding group. (*She goes to find it—top of piano.*)

GERALD: You'll have to interview 'em, and they'll tell you how happy they've been——

DYSON: Oh—yes. I see the idea now.

NANCY (*returning with old photograph*): Here you are. All six of them on their wedding morning. Don't they look absurd in those clothes?

ORMONROYD (*solemnly*): To you—yes. To me—no. I was married myself about that time. (*Holding photograph at arm's length*) Now, you see, Fred, what's wanted is another group in the very same positions. After twenty-five years' wear and tear. Very nice.

DYSON: You're holding it upside down.

ORMONROYD: I know, lad. I know, that's the way we always look at 'em professionally. Either flies 'ave been at this or somebody's touched up Albert Parker with a screw-driver. Well, if we're too early, we're too early. Might nip back to the *Lion*, Fred lad, eh?

ORMONROYD *takes camera from top of settee left.*

DYSON: We'll come back in about an hour.

ORMONROYD: They're keeping a very nice drop of beer down at the *Lion* now.

[157]   F*

DYSON *and* ORMONROYD *go out,* NANCY *going towards the door with them, and shutting it behind them.* GERALD *looks at the photograph, then at the back of it, and is obviously interested and amused.*

GERALD: This was when they were all married then—September the fifth, Eighty-Three?

NANCY: Yes—why? What's the matter, Gerald? (*He has started laughing.*) Gerald, what is it? Oh—don't be so mean. They'll be here in a minute.

As he shakes his head, still laughing softly, we hear voices behind door into hall.

GERALD: They're coming in. Nancy, let's dodge out that way.

Puts photograph on table behind settee right, picks up his straw hat, while she has gone to door into conservatory, and they hurry out that way, shutting door behind them.

Voices outside door into hall are louder now, and after a moment the PARKERS, *the* SOPPITTS, *the* HELLIWELLS *enter. They are dressed in their best, and obviously crammed with high tea.* ALBERT PARKER, *is a tall, thin, conceited, sententious man, his wife* ANNIE, *a hopeful kind of woman.* HERBERT SOPPITT *is a smallish neat man, clearly dominated by his wife* CLARA, *a noisy woman. The* HELLIWELLS *are high-coloured, rather bouncing, rather pompous, very pleased with themselves. Their ages are all between forty-five and fifty-five.* HERBERT SOPPITT *and* MRS. PARKER *talk a rather genteel ordinary English; the other four have pronounced north-country accents, with particularly broad "a" sounds.*

HELLIWELL (*very much the host*): Now what's wanted now's a good cigar, an' I've got the very thing. (*Goes to get box from drawer or table.*)

MARIA (*indignantly*): That Mrs. Northrop! When she's finished her washing-up to-night she goes—and goes for good.

CLARA: And quite right too! They're all the same. Answering back—if you say anything.

MARIA: Trouble with her is—she likes a drop. I've smelt it before to-day.

CLARA *sits below sofa left.* MARIA *to corner.* ANNIE *drops down right to sofa down right.*

HELLIWELL (*offering cigar-box to* PARKER): Now then, Albert! You'll find that's a good cigar, La Corona.

PARKER (*taking one*): Thanks, Joe. As you know, I don't smoke a lot, but when I do, I like a good cigar.

HELLIWELL (*offering to* SOPPITT): Herbert?

SOPPITT: I don't think—er—I will—thanks, Joe.

MARIA (*expansively*): Nay, Herbert, 'ave one o' Joe's cigars.

CLARA: If he'd had it to pay for himself, he'd have been wanting one.

SOPPITT (*rather nervously*): I think—I'd rather not smoke just now —I believe I ate too much at tea.

ANNIE (*to keep him company*): I know *I* did.

PARKER (*severely*): Yes, an' you'll be complaining before the night's out.

CLARA: An' so will Herbert.

PARKER (*complacently*): Now that's something that never bothers me.

HELLIWELL: No, we've noticed that, Albert.

PARKER (*offended*): How d'you mean?

MARIA: Go on, Albert, you know what Joe is—must 'ave his little joke.

ANNIE: I know *I* ought to have stopped long before I did—I mean, at tea—but, Maria, everything was *so* nice.

CLARA: 'Ere, 'ere.

MARIA (*complacently accepting this*): Well, I said to Joe "Now, Joe," I said, "we'll only have just the six of us, but we'll make it an occasion an' do it well while we're at it," I said. Didn't I, Joe?

HELLIWELL (*busy attending to his cigar, though he does not remove the band*): Did you?

MARIA (*indignantly*): You know very well I did.

HELLIWELL (*still not interested*): All right, you did then.

MARIA (*same indignant tone*): You know quite well I did, Joe Helliwell.

HELLIWELL (*suddenly annoyed himself*): All right, all right, all right, you did then.

CLARA (*pats MARIA'S hand*): They're all alike. Wait till somebody else's with you, and then try to make you out a liar.

PARKER (*severely*): Speak for yourself! I don't try to make my wife out a liar, do I, Annie?

ANNIE (*rather timidly, hesitantly*): Well—no—Albert, not— really——

PARKER (*very severely*): How d'you mean—*not really*—I just don't, that's all. (*Changing the subject, in rather lordly style*) A good smoke, Joe, quite a good smoke. It reminds me of that cigar Sir

[159]

Harold Watson gave me not so long since at the club. I was standing near the fireplace, and Sir Harold came up——

ANNIE (*gathering courage to interrupt*): Albert—you told them before.

PARKER (*glaring*): Well, I can tell 'em again, can't I?

SOPPITT: Maria, have you got a copy of that old photograph we had taken? I couldn't find ours.

MARIA: Yes. Where is it, Joe? (*While he looks round*) Aaa, I laugh many a time when I think o' that morning—six of us, all so nervous——

HELLIWELL: And the parson worse still. He was only like twopennorth o' copper, an' I could ha' given him a few years myself.

CLARA: I think we were about first he'd ever married.

ANNIE: I'm sure we were. I didn't feel I'd been married properly——

PARKER (*severely*): Of course you'd been married properly. If he'd been ninety and doing it all his life, you wouldn't ha' been married any better, would you?

MARIA: I've forgotten his name now. He was only a temporary, wasn't he?

SOPPITT: I remember! (*A pause.*) It was a tree. Beech.

HELLIWELL: That's right—Beech—an' he'd a funny squint. (*Has found photograph.*) And here's the old photo.

> *Hands it to his wife and the ladies look at it, with exclamations, while the men remain aloof.*

PARKER (*the business man now*): I see Crossbreds are down again.

HELLIWELL (*another business man*): Ay—and they'll stay down with Australian market as it is. If I've said it once, I've said it a thousand times—if Merinos is down and staying down, then your Crossbreds'll have to follow. Now, look at Merinos——

MARIA (*looking up to expostulate*): Here, Joe, we didn't come here to talk about Merinos. This isn't Wool Exchange. Take a look at yourselves and see what we took on.

> *He ignores her. She puts photograph on table back of settee.*

HELLIWELL: Now wait a minute. 'Ealths!

MARIA: That's right, Joe. Ring!

> HELLIWELL *rings.* MARIA *turns to others.*

We ought to do it in proper style, an' drink our healths before we go any further.

SOPPITT (*attempting a joke*): Further—where?

CLARA (*severely*): That'll do, Herbert. A bit o' fun's all right, but you go too far.

SOPPITT: I didn't mean——

CLARA (*cutting in*): That'll do.

> MRS. NORTHROP *looks in.*

MRS. NORTHROP (*aggressively*): Well?

MARIA (*rather grandly*): There's a tray with glasses on—just bring it in——

MRS. NORTHROP (*indignantly*): What—me? How many pairs of 'ands——

HELLIWELL (*peremptorily*): *Now then*—just tell thingumptyite—Ruby—to bring in the port wine.

MRS. NORTHROP: What—on top o' your tea? You'll be poorly.

> *She withdraws.* HELLIWELL *is furious.*

HELLIWELL (*angrily*): Now did you 'ear that——

MARIA (*hastily*): All right, Joe, we don't want any trouble. She goes to-night, an' she doesn't come back.

CLARA: I don't know what things are coming to! All the same! Answering back!

PARKER (*sententiously*): They're all alike, that class of people. We have the same trouble at mill. Don't know when they're well off. Idle, that's what they are—bone idle!

CLARA: *And* impudent! Back-answers!

ANNIE (*timidly*): Yes—but I suppose they don't know any better——

PARKER (*severely*): They know a lot better. And what you want to stick up for 'em for, I can't think.

HELLIWELL (*heartily*): Now then, Albert, don't start fratching, but try an' enjoy yourself for once. This is an anniversary. Which reminds me, Charlie Pearson told me, t' other day, they built a new Wesleyan Methodist Chapel up at Thornton, and they opened with an anniversary. Anyhow, this is ours, so let's have peace an' good-will all round. Now I thought we'd first drink a bit of a toast to our-selves——

MARIA: That was *my* idea.

HELLIWELL (*ignoring this, but only just*): Then I thought we'd have a bit of a chat about old times, an' then we'd settle down to a game o' Newmarket——

MARIA: That was my idea too.

HELLIWELL (*annoyed*): What the hangment does it matter whose idea it was, so long as we get on with it and enjoy ourselves!

SOPPITT: That's the great thing. (*Controlled belch. Catches his wife's eye and falters.*) Enjoy ourselves. (*Rises. Moves to door. Looks miserable and a bit sick.*)

CLARA (*severely*): I told you to leave that salmon alone.

HELLIWELL: Nay, Clara, why can't he have a bit o' salmon if he fancies it?

CLARA (*sharply*): 'Cos it doesn't fancy him, Joe Helliwell, that's why. Look at that time we all went to Scarborough!

SOPPITT (*turns*): It was Bridlington.

CLARA: It was both! And what did that doctor say? *You're digging your grave with your teeth, Mr. Soppitt.*

HELLIWELL: Hahaha!

Enter RUBY, *carrying tray with six small glasses on it, and three bottles of port.*

Here, what did you want to bring 'em all for? One bottle at a time's enough.

RUBY (*putting down tray*) Mrs. Northrop said you'd better 'ave t'lot while you was at it.

HELLIWELL: In future, just take your orders from me and not from Mrs. Northrop. Now just trot along—an' no lip. (*Starts to take cork out of bottle.*)

RUBY (*turning at door*): Mrs. Northrop says she's not coming 'ere again——

HELLIWELL (*heatedly*): We know all about it. (*Moves after her, cigar in mouth, bottle in hand.*)

MARIA (*cutting in*): Now let it be, Joe.

HELLIWELL *stands, draws cork with an effort.*

RUBY *has now gone and closed door.* HELLIWELL *begins pouring out the port.*

D'you know what we ought to do for this? We ought to get just in the same places we were in that old photo. Where is it? (*Finds it and directs them from it.*) Now here we are. (*Uses a sofa.*) I was in the middle. You were here, Clara. You this side, Annie. Now come on, Albert—behind Annie. Herbert.

MARIA *sits last. These five have now arranged themselves in grouping of old photograph.* HELLIWELL *hands them their glasses of port, then takes up a position himself.*

HELLIWELL (*facetiously*): Here's to me and my wife's husband!

MARIA: Let's have none o' that silly business, Joe!

PARKER (*solemnly*): A few serious words is what's needed.

ANNIE (*rather plaintively*): Oh—must you, Albert?

PARKER: How d'you mean—must I? What's wrong with a few serious words on an occasion like this? Marriage—is a serious business.

CLARA: That's right, Albert. Where'd we be without it?

SOPPITT: Single.

CLARA: That'll do, Herbert.

PARKER (*sententiously*): Marriage—well—marriage—to begin with, it's an institution, isn't it?

MARIA (*solemnly*): That is so. (*Sighs profoundly.*)

PARKER (*getting into his stride*): One of the *oldest* institutions. It goes back—right back to—well, it goes right back. And it's still going strong to-day. Why?

HELLIWELL (*hastily*): Well, because——

PARKER (*sharply cutting in*): Let me finish, Joe, let me finish. Now why is it still going strong to-day? Because it's the backbone of a decent respectable life.

HELLIWELL (*solemnly*): True, Albert, true.

PARKER: Where would women be without marriage?

CLARA (*sharply*): And where'd some o' you men be?

PARKER: All right, I'm coming to that.

HELLIWELL: Well, don't be too long, Albert. I want to try this port.

PARKER (*solemnly*): Marriage may be a bit more necessary to women than it is to men——

ANNIE: Why?

PARKER (*annoyed at this*): *Why?*

HELLIWELL: Children, you see, Annie.

ANNIE (*abashed*): Oh—yes—I'd forgotten. Still——

PARKER: I'm talking now, *if* you please. But if a woman wants a 'ome and security and a respectable life, *which* she gets from marriage, a man wants something to——

CLARA (*quickly*): He wants all he can get.

PARKER: He wants a nice comfortable 'ome, somebody to tell his troubles to and so forth——

HELLIWELL (*facetiously*): That's good, Albert, the *and so forth.*

PARKER: Now, Joe——

HELLIWELL: Well, cut it short——

PARKER (*slowly and solemnly*): So, as we're all gathered 'ere to celebrate the anniversary of our joint wedding day, friends, I give you—the toast of *Marriage!*

[163]

MARIA: Very nice, Albert.

They all drink.

ANNIE (*confidentially*): It'll go straight to my head. D'you remember that time at Harrogate? I could have sunk through the floor when that waiter laughed.

HELLIWELL (*producing bottle again*): Now wait a minute. That's all right as far as it goes—but—nay—damn it!——

MARIA (*reproachfully*): Joe!

HELLIWELL: We must have another toast, just for ourselves. I bet it isn't often there's three couples can meet like this who were all wed on same morning together. Now then——

Insists on filling the glasses again as they still hold them in their hands.

MARIA (*confidentially*): I don't act silly, but my face gets so red.

HELLIWELL: Now—here's to all of us—and the Reverend Mr. What's his name—Beech—who tied us up—wherever he is——

THE OTHERS: Here's to us. Here's to him. (*Etc.*)

They drink. When they have finished, front-door bell is heard.

MARIA: Front door! Who'll that be?

HELLIWELL (*rather importantly*): Well, I told *Yorkshire Argus* to send somebody round to have a word with us.

CLARA (*delighted*): What—are you going to have a piece in the papers?

PARKER: They don't want to catch us like this.

PARKER swallows rest of his port hastily. The others do the same. The group breaks up.

RUBY looks in.

MARIA: Is it *Yorkshire Argus?*

RUBY: No, it's Mr. Forbes, t'organist from t'chapel. He came afore, an' then went away again.

HELLIWELL: Tell him to wait.

RUBY goes. HELLIWELL turns to the others.

You know about this business, Albert. You too, Herbert.

SOPPITT (*hesitantly*): Yes—but—— (*crosses to HELLIWELL.*)

HELLIWELL (*sharply*): But, nothing. You're too soft, Herbert.

CLARA: I'm always telling him so.

HELLIWELL: He's chapel organist—he's paid for t'job—an' either he behaves himself properly or he goes.

PARKER (*severely*): He'll go anyhow, if I've *my* say.

ANNIE: No, Albert, he's not a bad young fellow——

PARKER: Now you shut up, Annie. You don't know half of what we know. An' I'll bet we don't know half there is to know about that chap. Never should ha' been appointed. I said so then. I say so now. I know my own mind.

ANNIE (*rebelliously*): I wish sometimes you'd keep a bit of it to yourself.

PARKER: What's that mean?

NANCY *now appears at door from conservatory.*

MARIA: Hallo, love, where've you been?

NANCY (*who seems a trifle giggly*): Just out a minute. You don't want me, do you, Auntie? Because if you don't, I thought I'd put my hat and coat on and see if Muriel Spencer's in. (*Crosses up to door.*)

MARIA (*rises*): All right. There's that Gerald Forbes waiting outside—your uncle has something to say to him—now don't go talking to him.

HELLIWELL: I should think not. Just say "Hello" or "Good evening" and leave it at that. The less you have to do with that chap the better, Nancy.

NANCY *suddenly explodes into giggles.*

Now what's funny about that?

NANCY (*still giggling*): I'm sorry, Uncle. I just remembered—something that amused me——

NANCY *goes out, giggling.*

HELLIWELL: Now what's got hold of her?

MARIA: Oh—she's at silly age. They don't know half the time whether to laugh or cry when they're that age. Now, Clara—Annie—we'll leave the men to it. I expect that's what they want——

PARKER (*solemnly*): Certainly. After all, it's chapel business.

MARIA: Well, we want to go upstairs anyhow!

HELLIWELL: That's right.

CLARA *glares at him.*

MARIA: You haven't seen what Joe bought me yet. But don't take too long over him.

PARKER: *Him!* It wouldn't take *me* long——

HELLIWELL: It'll take me less long, 'cos I don't make speeches. Here, we'll put these out o' t'way—— (*at sideboard.*)

The women go out, and HELLIWELL *puts the glasses back on the tray. A certain primness now descends on them.*

[165]

PARKER: I said from first—it's a bad appointment. To start with, he's too young.

SOPPITT (*rather timidly*): I don't think that matters much.

PARKER (*severely*): Trouble with you, Herbert, is you don't think anything matters much, and that's just where you're wrong.

HELLIWELL: Young Forbes is a southerner an' all.

PARKER (*with grim triumph*): Ah—I was coming to that.

SOPPITT: Oughtn't we to have him in?

HELLIWELL: No, let him wait a bit.

PARKER: Do him good. No, as soon as they told me he's a southerner and his name's Gerald, I said: "We don't want him." I said: "La-di-dah. That's what you're going to get from him," I said. "La-di-dah. What we want at Lane End—biggest chapel for miles—wi' any amount o' money in congregation—what we want is a bit o' good old Yorkshire organ-playing and choir training," I said. "We don't want la-di-dah." (*With awful imitation of ultra-refined accents.*) "Heow d'yew dew. Sow chawmed to meek your acquaintance. Eoh, dee-lateful wethah!" Grr. You know what I call that stuff?

SOPPITT (*who has a sense of humour*): Yes. (*Broadly.*) La-di-dah.

HELLIWELL: Albert's right. We made a mistake. Mind you, he'd good qualifications, an' he seemed a nice quiet lad. But I must say, after old Sam Fawcett, chapel didn't seem right with an organist who goes round wearing one o' these pink shirts and knitted ties and creases in his trousers——

PARKER: It's all——

Here SOPPITT *joins in.*

PARKER and SOPPITT: La-di-dah!

PARKER (*in disgusted tone*): Then look at his *Messiah!* We warned him. I said to him myself: "I know it's a Christmas piece, but you've got to get in quick, afore the others."

HELLIWELL: Right, Albert. After t'end o' November, there's been so many of 'em you might as well take your Messiah an' throw it into t'canal.

PARKER: And look what happened. Hillroad Baptist gave *Messiah.* Salem gave *Messiah.* Tong Congregational gave *Messiah.* Picklebrook Wesleyans gave *Messiah.* And where was Lane End?

SOPPITT: Well, when we did get it—It was a good one.

HELLIWELL: I'm not saying it wasn't, but by that time who cared? But anyhow all that's a detail. Point is, we can't have any carrying on, can we?

SOPPITT ((*gravely*): Ah—there I agree, Joe.

PARKER (*indignantly*): An' I should think so. Organist at Lane End Chapel *carrying on!* That sort o' game may do down south, but it won't do up 'ere.

HELLIWELL: We're all agreed on that.

SOPPITT *and* PARKER *nod.*

Right then! We'll have 'im in.

> HELLIWELL *goes to the door, the other two sitting up stiffly and looking official and important.*

(*Rather grimly through open door.*) All right, come in.

> GERALD FORBES *follows him in, closing but not latching the door behind him.* GERALD *looks cool and self-possessed, with a twinkle in his eye.* HELLIWELL *sits down and looks as official and important as the other two. All three stare severely at* GERALD, *as he sits down.* GERALD *pulls out a cigarette-case, but no sooner has he taken a cigarette from it than* ALBERT PARKER *remonstrates with him.*

PARKER (*severely*): I wouldn't do that.

GERALD (*rather startled*): Do what?

PARKER (*severely*): Well, what 'ave you got in your 'and?

GERALD (*still surprised*): This? Cigarette. Why?

PARKER: Under the circumstances, young man, don't you think it might be better—more—more suitable—more fitting—if you didn't smoke that just now?

> *The three men look at each other.*

GERALD (*with a shrug*): Oh—all right, if that's how you feel about it. (*Puts case away. A pause.*) Well? You wanted to talk about something, didn't you?

HELLIWELL (*firmly*): We did. We do.

PARKER: And if I'd 'ad *my* way, we'd have been talking to you long since.

GERALD: Well, not very long since, because I haven't been up here very long.

PARKER: No, you haven't been up here very long, and I don't think you'll be up here much longer.

HELLIWELL: Here, Albert, let *me* get a word in. Mr. Forbes, you're organist of our Lane End Chapel, and that's the biggest place o' worship round here, and this is a very respectable neighbourhood, with a lot o' money behind it. You have a paid appointment as organist and choir-master.

GERALD: Yes, though it doesn't keep me, y'know, Mr. Helliwell.

HELLIWELL: No, but because you *are* our organist, you're able to get pupils and various extra jobs, so you don't do so bad out of it, eh?

GERALD (*a trifle dubiously*): No, I'm quite satisfied—for the time being.

PARKER (*annoyed*): *You're* satisfied! For the time being! You're satisfied!

GERALD (*quietly*): That's what I said, Mr. Parker.

PARKER (*with dignity*): Councillor Parker. (*Pointing.*) Alderman Helliwell. Councillor Parker. *Mr.* Soppitt.

GERALD (*indicating himself*): Plain mud!

PARKER (*explosively*): Now listen——

HELLIWELL (*cutting in noisily*): Nay, let me finish, Albert. We want to keep calm about this—just keep calm.

GERALD: I'm quite calm.

HELLIWELL (*explosively*): You're a damn sight too calm for my liking, young man. You ought to be sitting there looking right ashamed of yourself, instead of looking—looking—well, as you do look.

GERALD: But you haven't told me what's wrong yet.

PARKER (*angrily*): Wrong? You're wrong. And carrying on's wrong.

HELLIWELL (*loftily*): In some chapels they mightn't care what you did—I don't know—but Lane End's got a position to keep up. We're respectable folk, and naturally we expect our organist to behave respectably.

SOPPITT (*apologetically*): I think you have been very careless, Mr. Forbes, and there really has been a lot of grumbling.

PARKER: For one thing—you've been seen out—late at night—wi' girls.

GERALD: Girls?

HELLIWELL: It may be t'same lass each time, for all I know, but if what I hear is true, whoever she is, she ought to be ashamed of herself. My word, if she'd owt to do wi' me, I'd teach her a sharp lesson.

PARKER: Somebody saw you once gallivanting away late at night, at Morecambe. And it gets round, y'know—oh—yes—it gets round.

GERALD (*beginning to lose his temper*): Yes, so it seems. But I didn't think you'd find it worth while to listen to a lot of silly gossip——

[168]

PARKER (*sharply*): Now don't start taking that tone——

GERALD: What tone can I take? I say, a lot of silly gossip——

SOPPITT: Now, steady, steady.

GERALD: Silly gossip. Old women's twaddle——

HELLIWELL (*heavily*): That'll do. Just remember, you're not much more than a lad yet. We're nearly twice your age, and we know what's what——

GERALD (*angrily*): Well, what is what then?

HELLIWELL (*angrily*): This is what. We're not going to have any more of this. Either behave yourself or get back to where you came from. You're not going to make us a laughing-stock and a byword in t'neighbourhood. Now this is a fair warning——

GERALD (*steadily*): I haven't done anything I'm ashamed of.

PARKER: What's that prove? If a chap's got cheek of a brass monkey, he never need do aught he's ashamed of.

SOPPITT: Careful, Albert.

PARKER: Why should I be careful? I'll tell him to his face what I've said behind his back. He never ought to have been appointed, and now he's been carrying on and not caring tuppence what respectable folk might think, he oughtn't to be given any warnings but told to get back to where he came from, and then he can carry on as much as he likes.

> Both GERALD *and* HERBERT SOPPITT *start to protest, but* HELLIWELL *loudly stops them.*

HELLIWELL: Now, Albert, we mustn't be too hard. We must give young men just another chance. (*Severely and patronisingly to* GERALD) I'm not sure I should if this were any other time. But nay—damn it this is a festive occasion an' we must take it easy a bit. So I'm giving you a last chance to mend yourself. And you can think yourself lucky catching me i' this humour. Just happens we're all celebrating anniversary of our wedding day—all three of us—ay, we've all been married twenty-five years to-day. (*Blows nose.*)

> GERALD *shakes his head rather sadly.*

What're you shaking your head about?

GERALD (*quietly, gently*): Well, you see, Mr. Helliwell—I beg your pardon, Alderman Helliwell—I'm rather afraid you haven't been married twenty-five years.

HELLIWELL (*roaring*): Do you think we can't count, lad?

GERALD (*same quiet tone*): No, I don't mean that. But I'm afraid you've only been living together all this time.

HELLIWELL (*jumping up angrily*): *Living together!* I'll knock your head right off your shoulders, lad, if you start talking like that to me.

GERALD (*also standing up*): No, no, no. I'm not trying to insult you. I mean what I say.

PARKER (*rises, angrily*): Mean what you say! You're wrong in your damned 'ead.

SOPPITT (*authoritatively, for him*): Wait a minute—Albert, Joe. We must listen. He means it.

HELLIWELL (*angrily*): Means it! Means what?

GERALD (*impressively*): If you'll just be quiet a minute I'll explain.

PARKER (*explosively*): I don't want to——

GERALD (*sharply*): I said—*quiet*.

HELLIWELL: Leave him be, Albert.

GERALD (*sits*): Thanks. Mind if I smoke now?

> *All sit. With maddening slowness,* GERALD *takes out and lights cigarette.* HELLIWELL *and* ALBERT PARKER *watch him with impatience and look as if about to explode.*

I went to North Wales for my holiday this summer——

HELLIWELL (*impatiently*): Is this part of it, 'cos *I* don't care *where* you went for your holidays!

GERALD (*calmly*): I went to North Wales, and only came back about a fortnight ago. While I was there I made the acquaintance of a parson, who'd been in Africa for the last twenty years. When he learnt that I was the organist of Lane End Chapel, Cleckleywyke, he became very excited, and then it turned out that he'd been at Lane End himself for a short time. About twenty-five years ago.

SOPPITT: What was his name.

GERALD: Beech. Francis Edwin Beech.

HELLIWELL (*boisterously*): Oh—yes—Beech! We were only talking about him to-night. We remember Mr. Beech. He married us, y'know. Yes, he married us, five-and-twenty years ago—all three couples. That's what we're celebrating——

> *His voice suddenly dies away because he realises what the other two have realised for the last minute, that there might be something wrong. So as he mutters the end of his sentence now, he glances unhappily at the others.*

Y'know—being—married—twenty-five years——

> GERALD *looks at them over his cigarette.*

PARKER (*swallowing*): Go on. Go on.

GERALD: I could see that something he remembered about Cleckleywyke and Lane End worried him. (*With obvious relish.*) You might say, gentlemen, it was *preying* on his mind, it was *gnawing* at his conscience, it was *haunting* him, it was——

HALLIWELL (*angrily*): What is this—a recitation?

GERALD: I must apologise if I'm boring you, gentlemen——

PARKER (*in sudden passion, jumps up*): La-di-dah! La-di-dah! (*As* GERALD *stares at him in astonishment.*) Now if you've anything to tell us, for God's sake tell us—and don't la-di-dah!

HELLIWELL: Quite right, Albert. (*To* GERALD, *impatiently*) Well, what did Mr. Beech say?

GERALD: He didn't *say* anything.

HELLIWELL *and* PARKER *are at once relieved and annoyed. They breathe more freely, but then feel they have been needlessly alarmed.* HERBERT SOPPITT *waits to learn more and looks steadily at* GERALD.

HELLIWELL: Well, what are you nattering on about him for——?

SOPPITT: Just a minute, Joe. (*To* GERALD) That's not all, is it?

GERALD: All? I should think not! Only you won't give me a chance. I said he didn't *say* anything, but he *wrote* something. The letter only came two days ago. I have it here. (*Produces one rather small sheet of notepaper, written on both sides. He now reads it impressively.*) From the Reverend Francis Edwin Beech. "*Dear Mr. Forbes, Before returning to Africa I feel I owe it both to you and to myself to explain what you must have found puzzling in my many references to Cleckleywyke and Lane End Chapel. Although I was only temporarily at Lane End, I could not forget it for there I was guilty of the most culpable negligence.*"

The three men look at each other.

"*I went to Cleckleywyke straight from college, and during those first few months I did not realise that there were various forms I ought to have signed, and had witnessed by church officers, so that one may be recorded as an authorised person to perform the ceremony of marriage——*"

HELLIWELL (*rises, shouting*): What? (*Grabs the letter from* GERALD, *stares at it, then reads himself, slowly.*) . . . "*the ceremony of marriage. The result was, I was not then an authorised person. Fortunately during that short period I was only called upon twice to marry people, but the first time there were no less than three hopeful young couples who imagined—poor souls—that I was joining them in holy wedlock—when —I—was completely—unauthorised—to—do—so——*"

PARKER (*yelling and snatching the letter*): Let's have a look. (*He looks and* HERBERT SOPPITT *joins him.*) It's signed all right too— Francis Edwin Beech.

GERALD: And if you compare that signature with the one in the chapel register, you'll see it's the same man. No deception.

HELLIWELL (*dazed and bitter*): Why—the bloody donkey!

HELLIWELL, PARKER *and* SOPPITT *look at each other in silent consternation.*

SOPPITT (*slowly, thoughtfully*): Why, if we've never been married at all, then——

HELLIWELL: Don't start working it out in detail, Herbert, 'cos it gets very ugly—very ugly. There's that lad o' yours at grammar school, for instance—I wouldn't like to have to give him a name now——

SOPPITT (*indignantly*): Here, steady, Joe——

HELLIWELL: Well, you see, it gets very ugly. Keep your mind off t'details.

PARKER (*bitterly*): Silver wedding!

HELLIWELL: Now don't you start neither, Albert.

PARKER (*solemnly*): Joe, Herbert, when them three poor women upstairs gets to know what they really are——

HELLIWELL (*grimly*): Then t'balloon goes up properly. Talk about a rumpus. You'll 'ear 'em from 'ere to Leeds.

PARKER (*gravely*): Joe, Herbert, they mustn't know. Nobody must know. Why—we'd be laughed right out o' town. What—Alderman Helliwell—Councillor Albert Parker—Herbert Soppitt—all big men at chapel too! I tell you, if this leaks out—we're done!

HELLIWELL: We are, Albert.

SOPPITT (*horrified*): If once it got into the papers!

HELLIWELL (*even more horrified*): Papers! Oh—Christmas!—it's got to be kept from t'papers.

GERALD, *who has been leaving them to themselves to digest this news, now turns to them again.*

GERALD (*holding out his hand*): You'd better give me that letter, hadn't you?

PARKER and HELLIWELL (*rising*): Oh no!

They stand together as if protecting it.

PARKER (*holding it out*): This letter——

HELLIWELL (*snatching it*): Here——

PARKER (*angrily*): Nay, Joe—give it back——

HELLIWELL: I'm sorry, Albert, but I don't trust nobody wi' this letter but meself. Why—it's—it's dynamite!

GERALD: Yes, but it's addressed to me, and so it happens to be my property, you know.

SOPPITT: I'm afraid he's right there!

HELLIWELL (*turning on him, annoyed*): You would have to put that in, wouldn't you? Dang me, you're in this mess just as we are, aren't you?

PARKER (*severely*): Anyhow, *we've* a position to keep up even if you haven't, Herbert.

SOPPITT (*apologetically*): I was only saying he's right when he says it's his property. We had a case——

HELLIWELL (*aggressively*): Never mind about that case. Think about this case. It's a whole truck-load o' cases, this is.

GERALD: My letter, please.

HELLIWELL (*ingratiatingly*): Now listen, lad. I know you only want to do what's right. And we happened to be a bit 'asty with you, when you first came in. We didn't mean it. Just—a way o' talking. When Herbert Soppitt there gets started——

SOPPITT (*indignantly*): What—me!

PARKER (*severely*): You were 'asty, y'know, Herbert, you can't deny it. (*To* GERALD) Mind you, I'll say now to your face what I've often said behind your back. You gave us best *Messiah* and best *Elijah* we've ever had at Lane End.

HELLIWELL: Easy, easy! Best i' Cleckleywyke! And why? I've told 'em when they've asked me. "That young feller of ours is clever," I said. "I knew he had it in him," I said.

SOPPITT (*hopefully*): Yes, you did, Joe. (*To* GERALD) And so did I. I've always been on your side.

GERALD: I believe you have, Mr. Soppitt. (*To all three of them*) You can keep that letter to-night—on one condition. That Mr. Soppitt has it.

SOPPITT (*eagerly, holding out his hand*): Thank you, Joe.

HELLIWELL (*uneasily*): What's the idea o' this?

GERALD: That happens to be the way I feel about it. Now either give it back to me at once—or hand it over to Mr. Soppitt, who'll be answerable to me for it.

SOPPITT (*eagerly*): Certainly, certainly.

HELLIWELL *silently and grudgingly hands it over.* SOPPITT *puts it carefully in his inside pocket. The others watch him like hawks. There is a pause, then we hear a knocking from upstairs.*

HELLIWELL: Knocking.

[173]

PARKER (*grimly*): I 'eard.

HELLIWELL: That means she's getting impatient.

PARKER: I expect Clara's been ready to come down for some time.

HELLIWELL (*bitterly*): They want to get on with the celebration.

PARKER (*bitterly*): Chat about old times.

HELLIWELL (*bitterly*): Nice game o' cards.

GERALD (*after a pause*): I'd better be going.

HELLIWELL (*hastily*): No, no. No. Take it easy.

PARKER: No 'urry, no 'urry at all. I expect Joe has a nice cigar for you somewhere.

HELLIWELL (*with forced joviality*): Certainly I have. And a drink of anything you fancy——

GERALD: No, thanks. And I must be going.

HELLIWELL: Now listen, lad. We've admitted we were 'asty with you, so just forget about it, will you? Now you see the mess we're in, through no fault of ours—— (*Goes up to get cigars.*)

GERALD: I do. And it *is* a mess, isn't it? Especially when you begin to think——

PARKER (*hastily*): Yes, quite so, but don't you bother thinking. Just—— (*rather desperately*) try an' forget you ever saw that letter.

HELLIWELL (*who now comes with the cigars*): We're all friends, the best of friends. Now you've got to have a cigar or two, lad—I insist—— (*he sticks several cigars into* GERALD'S *outside pocket, as he talks*) and you're going to promise us—on your word of honour—not to tell anybody anything about this nasty business, aren't you?

> *All three look at him anxiously. He keeps them waiting a moment or two.*

GERALD: All right.

> *They breathe again.* HELLIWELL *shakes his hand.*

HELLIWELL: And you won't regret it, lad.

> *The knocking from upstairs is heard again.*

PARKER (*miserably*): 'Ear that?

HELLIWELL: It's wife again.

SOPPITT (*thoughtfully*): Curious thing about wives. They're always telling you what poor company you are for them, yet they're always wanting to get back to you.

HELLIWELL (*darkly*): That isn't 'cos they enjoy your company. It's so they can see what you're doing.

PARKER: Well, what are we doing?

HELLIWELL (*sharply now*): Wasting time. (*To them*) Now listen, chaps, we're in no proper shape yet to face t'wives. They'd have it all out of us in ten minutes, and then fat'll be in t'fire.

PARKER: I know. We've got to put our thinking caps on.

SOPPITT: I suppose Mr. Beech couldn't have been mistaken, could he?

PARKER: We might take that letter and get expert advice——

HELLIWELL (*hastily*): What! An' 'ave it all over the town?

PARKER (*quickly*): We might put a case—without mentioning names——

HALLIWELL (*with decision*): I know what we'll do. We'll nip down to t'club, 'cos we can talk it over there in peace an' quiet. Come on, chaps. Just as we are, straight down t'club. (*To* GERALD) Now, young man, you promised. You won't go back on your word?

GERALD: No. You're safe with me.

HELLIWELL (*urgently*): Good lad! Now, wait till we've got off, then go out front way. Come on, Albert, Herbert, we've no time to lose an' we go this way—— (*bustling them towards exit through conservatory*) straight to t'club.

> *They go out.* GERALD *looks at his watch, smiles, lights a cigarette, then makes for door, which has never been quite closed. When he opens it suddenly,* MRS. NORTHROP, *still holding a towel and a large glass dish, which she is wiping perfunctorily, is discovered just behind door. She is in high glee and not at all abashed at being found there.*

GERALD (*with mock sternness*): Have you been listening?

MRS. NORTHROP (*who may have had a drink or two*): Listening! I should think I have been listening! I wouldn't have missed this lot even if it means 'aving earache for a week. None of 'em rightly married at all! Not one of 'em properly tied up! (*She begins laughing quite suddenly, and then goes off into peals of laughter, rolling against the door. The dish she holds seems to be in danger.*)

GERALD (*amused as he goes past her, out*): Look out—or you may break that dish.

MRS. NORTHROP (*calling to him*): Brek a dish! If I want to, I'll brek a dozen now.

GERALD (*just off, challengingly*): Not you! I dare you!

MRS. NORTHROP (*coolly*): Well, here's a start, any road. (*Tosses the dish down and it smashes noisily in hall.*)

> *We hear* GERALD *give a laughing shout, then bang the front door.*

MRS. NORTHROP *now starts laughing helplessly again, still leaning against the door.*

MRS. NORTHROP: Nay—dammit!—— (*laughing*) Oh dear—oh dear—oh dear——

She is still roaring with laughter as the curtain briskly descends.

END OF ACT ONE

ACT II

About half an hour later. The lights are on. MARIA *is drawing curtains,* ANNIE *and* CLARA *are laying out the cards and counters for Newmarket on a card-table, and they continue doing this throughout the scene that follows, chiefly counting the coloured counters and putting them into piles.*

CLARA (*with much discontent*): Well, I must say—this is a queer way o' going on.

MARIA: They'll have just gone outside to finish their smokes.

CLARA (*grimly*): When Herbert takes me out to enjoy myself, I don't expect him to be outside finishing any smokes.

ANNIE (*at table*): Perhaps they'd something they wanted to talk over.

CLARA: Well they can talk it over here, can't they?

> RUBY *enters from conservatory.*

MARIA: Well, Ruby, are they out there?

RUBY: No, they aren't.

MARIA (*sharply*): Have you looked properly?

RUBY: Well I couldn't miss three grown men in a garden that size.

MARIA: Did you look up and down the road like I told you?

RUBY: Yes, but they aren't there.

> *The three wives look at each other, puzzled.*

CLARA: Didn't you hear them go?

RUBY: No. I was back in t'kitchen all time, doing t'washing up. That Mrs. Northrop left me to it.

MARIA: Where was she then?

RUBY: Out 'ere somewhere, I fancy. I know she's gone like a dafthead, ever since she come back. Laughin' to herself—like a proper barmpot.

MARIA: Well, ask Mrs. Northrop if she knows where they went.

> RUBY *goes.*

That noise you heard upstairs was a bit o' this Mrs. Northrop's work —one o' my best dishes gone. An' Ruby says she just laughed.

CLARA: Stop it out of her wages and see if she can get a good laugh out o' that. I've no patience with 'em.

ANNIE: I thought she didn't look a nice woman.

[177]

CLARA: One o' them idle drinking pieces o' nothing from back o' t'mill.

MARIA: Well, I was in a hurry and had to have somebody. But she goes—for good—to-night.

RUBY *appears.*

RUBY: Mrs. Northrop says they wanted to have a nice quiet talk, so they went down to their club.

RUBY *disappears.*

CLARA (*angrily*): Club! *Club!*

ANNIE: And to-night of all nights—I do think it's a shame.

MARIA (*indignantly*): I never 'eard o' such a thing in me life.

CLARA (*furiously*): *Club!* I'll club him.

ANNIE: Nay, I don't know what's come over 'em.

CLARA (*angrily*): I know what'll come over one of 'em.

MARIA: Perhaps there's something up.

CLARA: Something down, you mean—ale, stout, an' whisky. Drinks all round! Money no object!

MARIA: They're 'ere.

The three of them immediately sit bolt upright and look very frosty. The men file in from the conservatory, looking very sheepish.

HELLIWELL (*nervously*): Ay—well——

MARIA (*grimly*): Well what?

HELLIWELL: Well—nowt—really.

SOPPITT (*nervously*): We didn't—er—think you'd be down yet. Did we, Joe? Did we, Albert?

HELLIWELL: No, we didn't, Herbert.

ALBERT: That's right, we didn't.

CLARA (*cuttingly*): Herbert Soppitt, you must be wrong in your head. *Club!*

ANNIE: And to-night of all nights!

HELLIWELL: Well, you see, we thought we'd just nip down for a few minutes while you were talking upstairs.

MARIA: What for?

PARKER: Oh—just to talk over one or two things.

CLARA: What things?

SOPPITT: Oh—just—things, y'know—things in general.

PARKER (*coming forward, rubbing his hands*): Well—I see the table's all ready—so what about that nice little game o' Newmarket?

[178]

CLARA: You'll get no Newmarket out o' me to-night.

ANNIE: You're—you're—selfish.

CLARA: Have you just found that out? Never think about anything but their own comfort and convenience.

MARIA: I'm surprised at you, Joe Helliwell—and after I'd planned to make everything so nice.

CLARA: Lot o' thanks you get from them! Club! (*Looking hard at* SOPPITT) Well, go on—say something.

The men look at each other uneasily. Then the women look indignantly.

ANNIE: Just think what day it is!

CLARA: And after giving you best years of our life—without a word o' thanks.

MARIA: An' just remember, Joe Helliwell, there were plenty of other fellows I could have had besides you.

ANNIE: You seem to think—once you've married us you can take us for granted.

PARKER (*uneasily*): Nay, I don't.

CLARA (*very sharply*): Yes, you do—all alike!

MARIA: If some of you woke up to-morrow to find you weren't married to us, you'd be in for a few big surprises.

HELLIWELL (*uneasily*): Yes—I dare say—you're right.

MARIA (*staring at him*): Joe Helliwell, what's matter with you to-night?

HELLIWELL (*uneasily*): Nowt—nowt's wrong wi' me, love.

CLARA (*looking hard at* SOPPITT): You'll hear more about this when I get you 'ome.

SOPPITT (*mildly*): Yes, Clara.

The women look at the men again, then at each other. Now they turn away from the men, ignoring them.

MARIA: What were you saying about your cousin, Clara?

CLARA (*ignoring the men*): Oh—well, the doctor said: "You're all acid, Mrs. Foster, that's your trouble. You're making acid as fast as you can go."

ANNIE: Oh—poor thing!

CLARA: Yes, but it didn't surprise me, way she'd eat. I once saw her eat nine oyster patties, finishing 'em up after their Ethel got married. I said: "Nay, Edith, have a bit o' mercy on your inside," but of course she just laughed.

The men have been cautiously moving to the back towards the door. As HELLIWELL *has his hand on the handle,* MARIA *turns on him.*

MARIA: And where're you going now?

HELLIWELL (*uneasily*): Into t'dining-room.

MARIA: What for?

HELLIWELL: Well—because—well—— (*Gathers boldness.*) We've summat to talk over. Albert, 'Erbert, quick!

> *They file out smartly, without looking behind them. The women stare at them in amazement. The door shuts. The women look at each other.*

MARIA: Now what's come over 'em?

ANNIE: There's something up.

CLARA: What can be up? They're just acting stupid, that's all. But wait till I get his lordship 'ome.

ANNIE: Suppose we went home now——

CLARA: No fear! That's just what they'd like. Back to t'club!

MARIA: I'd go up to bed now and lock me door, if I didn't think I'd be missing something.

ANNIE: It's a pity we can't go off just by ourselves—for a day or two.

CLARA: And what sort o' game are they going to get up to while we're gone? But I've a good mind to go in and tell mine: "Look, I've been married to you for five-and-twenty years and it's about time I had a rest."

MARIA: And for two pins I'll say to Joe: "If you got down on your bended knees and begged me to, I wouldn't stay married to you if I didn't have to."

> *Door opens slowly, and* MRS. NORTHROP *comes just inside, carrying large string bag, with clothes, two stout bottles in, etc. She is dressed to go home now.*

MRS. NORTHROP: I've done.

MARIA (*suspiciously*): It hasn't taken you very long.

MRS. NORTHROP (*modestly*): No—but then I'm a rare worker. Many a one's said to me: "Mrs. Northrop, I can't believe you've just that pair of 'ands—you're a wonder."

MARIA (*acidly*): Well, I don't think I want a wonder here, Mrs. Northrop. I'll pay you what I owe you to-night, and then you needn't come again.

MRS. NORTHROP (*bridling*): Ho, I see—that's it, is it?

MARIA: Yes, it is. I don't consider you satisfactory.

CLARA: I should think not!

MRS. NORTHROP (*annoyed*): Who's asking you to pass remarks? (*To* MARIA) And don't think I want to come 'ere again. Me 'usband wouldn't let me, anyhow, when he 'ears what I 'ave to tell him. We've always kept ourselves respectable.

MARIA: And what does that mean?

CLARA: Don't encourage her impudence.

MRS. NORTHROP: An' *you* mind your own interference. (*To* MARIA) I was beginnin' to feel sorry for you—but now——

MARIA (*coldly*): I don't know what you're talking about.

CLARA: What's she got in that bag?

MRS. NORTHROP (*angrily*): I've got me old boots an' apron an' cleanin' stuff in this bag——

MARIA: I can see two bottles there——

MRS. NORTHROP (*angrily*): Well, what if you can? D'you think you're the only folk i' Cleckleywyke who can buy summat to sup? If you must know, these is two stout empties I'm taking away 'cos they belong to me—bought an' paid for by me at Jackson's off-licence an' if you don't believe me go an' ask 'em.

MARIA (*stopping* CLARA *from bursting in*): No, Clara, let her alone —we've had enough. (*To* MRS. NORTHROP, *rather haughtily*) It's twenty-four shillings altogether, isn't it?

MRS. NORTHROP (*aggressively*): No, it isn't. It's twenty-five and six—if I never speak another word.

MARIA (*going for her purse on side-table*): All right then, twenty-five and six, but I'm going to take something off for that dish you broke——

MRS. NORTHROP (*angrily*): You won't take a damned ha'penny off!

CLARA: Language now as well as back-answers!

MARIA (*giving* MRS. NORTHROP *a sovereign*): Here's a pound and that's all you'll get.

MRS. NORTHROP (*angrily*): I won't 'ave it. I won't 'ave it.

MARIA (*leaving it on nearest table to* MRS. NORTHROP): There it is, Mrs. Northrop, and it's all you'll get. (*Sitting down in stately fashion and turning to* CLARA.) Let's see, Clara, what were you saying? (*All three women now ignore* MRS. NORTHROP, *which makes her angrier than ever.*)

MRS. NORTHROP (*drowning any possible conversation*): An' don't sit there tryin' to look like duchesses, 'cos I've lived round 'ere too long an' I know too much about yer. Tryin' to swank! Why—— (*pointing to* MARIA) I remember you when you were Maria Fawcett an' you were nobbut a burler and mender at Barkinson's afore you took up wi' Joe Helliwell an' he were nobbut a woolsorter i' them days. And as for you—— (*pointing to* CLARA) I remember time when you were weighin' out apples an' potatoes in your father's greengrocer's shop, corner o' Park Road, an' a mucky little shop it wor an' all——

MARIA (*rising, angrily*): I'll fetch my husband.

MRS. NORTHROP: He isn't your husband. I was goin' to say I'm as good as you, but fact is I'm a damn sight better, 'cos I'm a respectable married woman an' that's more than any o' you can say——

CLARA (*angrily*): Get a policeman.

MRS. NORTHROP (*derisively*): Get a policeman! Get a dozen, an' they'll all 'ave a good laugh when they 'ear what I 'ave to tell 'em. Not one o' you properly married at all. I 'eard that organist o' yours tellin' your 'usbands—if I can call 'em your 'usbands. I wor just be'ind t'door—an' this lot wor too good to miss—better than a turn at t'Empire.

CLARA (*angrily*): I don't believe a word of it.

MRS. NORTHROP: Please yourself. But 'e give 'em a letter, an' that's why they went down to t'club to talk it over—an' I can't say I blame 'em 'cos they've plenty to talk over. An' by gow, so 'ave you three. It's about time yer thought o' getting wed, isn't it?

> *They stare in silence. She gives them a triumphant look, then picks up her sovereign.*

And now you owe me another five an' six at least—an' if you've any sense you'll see I get it—but I can't stop no longer 'cos I've said I meet me 'usband down at '*Are an*' '*Ounds*, 'cos they're 'aving a draw for a goose for Cleckleywyke Tide an' we've three tickets—so I'll say *good night.*

> *She bangs the door. The three women stare at each other in consternation.*

MARIA: That's why they were so queer. I knew there was something.

CLARA (*bitterly*): The daft blockheads!

> ANNIE *suddenly begins laughing.*

CLARA: Oh—for goodness' sake, Annie Parker!

ANNIE (*still laughing*): I'm not Annie Parker. And it all sounds so silly.

MARIA (*indignantly*): Silly! What's silly about it?

CLARA (*bitterly*): Serves me right for ever bothering with anybody so gormless. Isn't this Herbert Soppitt all over! Couldn't even get us married right!

MARIA (*looking distressed*): But—Clara, Annie—this is *awful!* What are we going to do?

CLARA: I know what we're *not* going to do—and that's play *Newmarket*. (*Begins putting things away, helped by other two.*)

ANNIE: Eee—we'll look awfully silly lining up at Lane End Chapel again to get married, won't we?

CLARA (*angrily*): Oh—for goodness' sake——!

MARIA (*bitterly*): Better tell them three daftheads in t'dining-room to come in now.

CLARA: No, just a minute.

MARIA: What for?

CLARA: 'Cos I want to think, an' very sight of Herbert'll make me that mad I won't be able to think. (*Ponders a moment.*) Now if nobody knew but us, it wouldn't matter so much.

MARIA: But that fool of a parson knows——

CLARA: And the organist knows——

ANNIE: And your Mrs. Northrop knows—don't forget that—and you wouldn't pay her that five-and-six——

MARIA: Here, one o' them men must fetch her back.

CLARA: I should think so. Why, if people get to know about this —we're—we're——

RUBY (*looking in, announcing loudly*): Yorkshire Argus.

CLARA (*in a panic*): We don't want any *Yorkshire Argus* here—or God knows where we'll be——

> She is interrupted by the entrance of FRED DYSON, who has had some drinks and is pleased with himself.

DYSON (*very heartily*): Well, here we are again. At least I am. Fred Dyson—*Yorkshire Argus*. Mrs. Helliwell?

MARIA (*rather faintly*): Yes.

DYSON (*same tone*): And Mrs. Albert Parker and Mrs. Soppitt— three lucky ladies, eh?

> They are looking anything but fortunate.

DYSON: Now, you'd never guess my trouble.

ANNIE (*who can't resist it*): You'd never guess ours, either.

MARIA (*hastily*): Shut up, Annie. What were you saying, Mr. Dyson?

DYSON: I've gone and lost our photographer—Henry Ormonroyd. Brought him with me here earlier on, then we went back to the *Lion*, where he'd met an old pal. I left 'em singing *Larboard Watch* in the tap-room, not twenty minutes since, went into the private bar five minutes afterwards, couldn't find old Henry anywhere, so thought he must have come up here. By the way, where's the party?

ANNIE: This is it.

MARIA (*hastily*): Shut up, Annie. (*Rather desperately, to* DYSON) You see, my husband—Alderman Helliwell—you know him of course?

DYSON (*heartily*): Certainly. He's quite a public figure, these days. That's why the *Argus* sent me up here to-night—when he told 'em you were all celebrating your silver wedding——

CLARA (*unpleasantly*): Oh—he suggested your coming here, did he?

DYSON: He did.

CLARA (*unpleasantly*): He would!

MARIA: Well, he didn't know then—what—I mean—(*her voice alters and dies away.*)

DYSON: Our readers 'ud like to know all about this affair.

CLARA (*grimly*): An' I'll bet they would!

MARIA: Now 'ave a bit o' sense, Clara——

CLARA (*quickly*): Why, you nearly gave it away——

ANNIE (*coming in*): What on earth are you saying, you two? (*Smiles at* DYSON, *who is looking rather mystified.*) It's all right, Mr. Dyson. What Mrs. Helliwell was going to say was that there was only just us six, y'know. It wasn't a real party. Just a little—er—private—er—sort of—you know.

DYSON (*looking about him, thirstily*): I know. Just a cosy little do —with—er—a few drinks.

MARIA: That's it.

DYSON: A few drinks—and—er—cigars—and—er—so on.

> *But they do not take the hint, so now he pulls out pencil and bit of paper.*

Now, Mrs. Helliwell, wouldn't you like to tell our readers just what your feelings are now that you're celebrating twenty-five years of happy marriage?

MARIA (*her face working*): I—er—I—er——

DYSON: You needn't be shy, Mrs. Helliwell. Now, come on.

> *To his astonishment,* MARIA *suddenly bursts into tears, and then hurries out of the room.*

CLARA (*reproachfully*): Now, look what you've done, young man.

DYSON (*astonished*): Nay, dash it—what have I done? I only asked her——

ANNIE (*hastily*): She's a bit upset to-night—you know, what with all the excitement. It's no use your staying now—you'd better go and find your photographer.

CLARA (*angrily*): Now, Annie, for goodness' sake! We want no photographers here.

ANNIE (*to* DYSON): That's all right. She's upset too. Now you just pop off.

> ANNIE *almost marches* DYSON *to the door and sees him through it. We hear him go out.* CLARA *sits breathing very hard.* ANNIE *returns, leaving door open behind her.*

ANNIE: Well, we're rid of him.

CLARA: For how long?

ANNIE (*annoyed*): You can't sit there, Clara, just saying: "For how long?" as if you're paying me to manage this business. If we want it kept quiet, we'll have to stir ourselves and not sit about shouting and nearly giving it all away as you and Maria did when that chap was here.

CLARA (*bitterly*): If we hadn't said we'd marry a set o' numskulls, this would never 'ave happened. If my poor mother was alive to see this day——

> MARIA *returns, blowing her nose and sits down miserably.*

MARIA (*unhappily*): I'm sorry—Clara, Annie—but I just couldn't help it. When he asked me that question, something turned right over inside—an' next minute I was crying.

CLARA (*severely*): Well, crying's not going to get us out of this mess.

ANNIE (*sharply*): You're never satisfied, Clara. First you go on at me for laughing and now you blame poor Maria for crying——

CLARA (*loudly, sharply*): Well, what do you want to go laughing an' crying for? What do you think this is? *Uncle Tom's Cabin?*

MARIA: They're coming in.

> *The women sit back, grimly waiting.* HELLIWELL, PARKER, SOPPITT *enter, and the women look at them.*

PARKER (*uneasily*): Who was that?

> *No reply. He exchanges a glance with* SOPPITT *and* HELLIWELL.

I said, who was it came just then?

CLARA (*suddenly, fiercely*): *Yorkshire Argus!*

PARKER (*resigned tone*): They know.

ANNIE (*sharply*): Course we know.

> HELLIWELL *looks at them, then makes for the door again.*

MARIA: And where are you going?

HELLIWELL: To fetch t'whisky.

MARIA: And is whisky going to 'elp us?

HELLIWELL: I don't know about you, but it'll help me. (*Goes out.*)

MARIA (*hopefully*): It's not all a tale, is it?

PARKER: No, it's right enough. We put case to a chap at club—no names, of course—and he said it 'ad 'appened a few times—when a young parson thought he was qualified to marry folk—an' it turned out he wasn't. But of course it 'asn't happened often.

CLARA: No, but it has to 'appen to *us*. (*Fiercely to* SOPPITT) I blame you for this.

SOPPITT (*unhappily to* PARKER): Didn't I tell you she would?

CLARA (*sharply*): *She!* Who's *she?* The cat? Just remember you're talking about your own wife.

PARKER: Ah—but you see, he isn't—not now.

CLARA (*angrily*): Now, stop that, Albert Parker.

HELLIWELL *returns with large tray, with whisky, soda and glasses.*

HELLIWELL: Any lady like a drop?

MARIA: State I'm in now, it 'ud choke me.

The other women shake their heads scornfully.

HELLIWELL: Albert?

PARKER: Thanks, I think I will, Joe. (*Goes to him.*)

HELLIWELL (*busy with drinks*): 'Erbert?

CLARA (*quickly*): He mustn't 'ave any.

HELLIWELL: 'Erbert?

CLARA (*confidently*): You 'eard what I said, Herbert. You're not to 'ave any.

SOPPITT (*the rebel now*): Thanks, Joe, just a drop.

He goes up, looks at his wife as he takes his glass and drinks, then comes away, still looking at her, while she glares at him.

HELLIWELL: 'Ere, but I'd never ha' thought young Forbes ud' have gone back on his word like that, when he promised solemnly not to tell another soul.

MARIA: But he didn't tell us.

HELLIWELL (*staggered*): Eh? (*Exchanges alarmed glance with other men.*) Who did then?

MARIA: Charwoman—Mrs. Northrop. She 'eard you, behind that door.

HELLIWELL (*alarmed*): 'Ere, where is she?

MARIA: Gone.

[186]

ANNIE (*with some malice*): Maria's just given her the push.

PARKER (*angrily*): If she's gone off with this news you just might as well play it on Town Hall chimes.

HELLIWELL (*angrily*): Why didn't you say so at first? If this woman gets round wi' this tale about us, we'll never live it down. Did she go 'ome?

ANNIE: No, to the *Hare and Hounds.*

HELLIWELL (*masterfully*): Herbert, swallow that whisky quick—an' nip down to t'*Hare an' Hounds* as fast as you can go, an' bring her back——

SOPPITT: But I don't know her.

HELLIWELL: Nay, damn it, you saw her in here, not an hour since——

SOPPITT: An' she doesn't know me.

HELLIWELL: Now, don't make difficulties, Herbert. Off you go. (*Moves him towards conservatory.*) And bring her back as fast as you can and promise her owt she asks so long as you get back. (*He is now outside, shouting.*) An' make haste. We're depending on you.

> HELLIWELL *returns, blowing, carrying* SOPPITT'S *glass. He is about to drink out of this when he remembers, so takes and drinks from his own, then breathes noisily and mops his brow. They are all quiet for a moment.*

You know, Albert lad, it feels quite peculiar to me.

PARKER: What does?

HELLIWELL: This—not being married.

MARIA (*rising, solemn*): Joe Helliwell, 'ow can you stand there an' say a thing like that?

CLARA: } He ought to be ashamed of himself.
ANNIE: } I'm surprised at you, Joe.

HELLIWELL (*bewildered*): What—what are you talking about?

MARIA (*solemnly*): After twenty-five years together. Haven't I been a good wife to you, Joe Helliwell?

HELLIWELL: Well, I'm not complaining, am I?

PARKER (*tactlessly*): You've been the *same* as a good wife to him, Maria.

MARIA (*furiously*): The *same!* I haven't been the same as a good wife, I've been a good wife, let me tell you, Albert Parker.

ANNIE: } Nay, Albert!
CLARA: } (*angrily to* PARKER): I never 'eard such silly talk.

PARKER (*aggressively*): Oh—an' what's silly about it, eh?

[187]

CLARA: Everything.

HELLIWELL (*tactlessly*): Nay, but when you come to think of it—Albert's right.

PARKER (*solemn and fatuous*): We must face facts. Now, Maria, you might *feel* married to him——

MARIA (*scornfully*): *I might feel married to him!* If you'd had twenty-five years of him, you wouldn't talk about *might*. Haven't I——

HELLIWELL (*cutting in noisily*): 'Ere, steady on, steady on—with your *twenty-five years of 'im*. Talking about me as if I were a dose o' typhoid fever.

MARIA (*loudly*): I'm not, Joe. All I'm saying is——

PARKER (*still louder*): Now let me finish what I started to say. I said—you might *feel* married to him—but strictly speaking—and in the eyes of the law—the fact is, you're *not* married to him. We're none of us married.

CLARA (*bitterly*): Some o' t'neighbours ha' missed it, couldn't you shout it louder?

PARKER: I wasn't that loud.

HELLIWELL (*reproachfully*): You were bawling your 'ead off.

ANNIE: Yes, you were.

MARIA (*reproachfully*): You don't know who's listening. I'm surprised you haven't more sense, Albert.

PARKER (*irritably*): All right, all right, all right. But we shan't get anywhere till we face facts. It's not our fault, but our misfortune.

MARIA: I don't know so much about that either.

HELLIWELL: Oh? (*To* ALBERT) Goin' to blame us now.

MARIA: Well, an' why not?

HELLIWELL (*irritably*): Nay, damn it—it wasn't *our* fault.

MARIA: If a chap asks me to marry him and then he takes me to chapel and puts me in front of a parson, I expect parson to be a real one an' not just somebody dressed up.

HELLIWELL: Well, don't I?

MARIA: You should ha' found out.

HELLIWELL: Talk sense! 'Ow could I know he wasn't properly qualified?

MARIA (*sneering*): Well, it's funny it's got to 'appen to us, isn't it?

PARKER: But that's what I say—it's not our fault, it's our misfortune. It's no use blaming anybody. Just couldn't be 'elped. But fact remains—we're——

CLARA (*interrupting angrily*): If you say it again, Albert Parker, I'll throw something at yer. You needn't go on and on about it.

MARIA (*bitterly*): Mostly at top o' your voice.

PARKER (*with air of wounded dignity*): Say no more. I've finished. (*Turns his back on them.*)

    All three women look at him disgustedly. MARIA *now turns to* JOE.

MARIA: But, Joe, you're not going to tell me you feel different—just because of this—this accident?

JOE (*solemnly*): I won't tell you a lie, love. I can't help it, but ever since I've known I'm not married I've felt *most peculiar.*

MARIA (*rising, sudden temper*): Oo, I could knock your fat head off.

    MARIA *goes hurriedly to the door, making sobbing noises on the way, and hurries out.*

ANNIE (*following her*): Oh—poor Maria!

    ANNIE *goes out, closing door.*

CLARA: Well, I 'ope you're pleased with yourself now.

HELLIWELL (*sententiously*): Never interfere between 'usband and wife.

CLARA: You just said you weren't 'usband an' wife.

HELLIWELL (*angrily*): 'Ere, if I'm going to argue with a woman it might as well be the one I live with.

    HELLIWELL *hurries out. A silence.* PARKER *remains sulky and detached.*

CLARA (*after pause*): Well, after all these ructions, another glass o' port wouldn't do me any 'arm. (*Waits, then as there is no move from* PARKER) Thank you very much. (*Rises, with dignity, to help herself.*) Nice manners we're being shown, I must say. (*Fills her glass.*) I said *nice manners*, Councillor Albert Parker!

PARKER (*turning, angrily*): Now if I were poor Herbert Soppitt, I'd think twice before I asked you to marry me again.

CLARA (*just going to drink*): *Ask me again!* There'll be no asking. Herbert Soppitt's my husband—an' he stays my husband.

PARKER: In the eyes of the law——

CLARA (*cutting in ruthlessly*): You said that before. But let me tell you, in the sight of Heaven Herbert and me's been married for twenty-five years.

PARKER (*triumphantly*): And there you're wrong again, because in the sight of Heaven nobody's married at all——

    HELLIWELL *pops his head in, looking worried.*

HELLIWELL: Just come in the dining-room a minute, Albert. We're having a bit of an argument——

PARKER: Yes, Joe.

HELLIWELL *disappears.* PARKER *goes out, leaving door a little open.* CLARA, *left alone, finishes her port, then picks up the old photograph and glares with contempt at the figures on it. A house bell can be heard ringing distantly now.*

CLARA (*muttering her profound contempt at the figures in the photograph*): Yer silly young softheads! (*Bangs it down in some prominent place, face up.*)

RUBY *now looks in.*

RUBY: Mrs. Soppitt——

CLARA (*rather eagerly*): Yes?

RUBY: Mrs. Helliwell says will you go into t' dining-room.

As CLARA *moves quickly towards door,* RUBY *adds coolly:*
Aaa—they're fratchin' like mad.

CLARA *goes out quickly, followed by* RUBY. *We hear in distance sound of door opening, the voices of the three in the dining-room noisily raised in argument, the shutting of the door, then a moment's silence. Then several sharp rings at the front door. After a moment,* RUBY'S *voice off, but coming nearer.*

(*Off*) Yes, I know . . . All right . . . 'Ere, mind them things . . . This way . . .

RUBY *ushers in* ORMONROYD, *who is carrying his camera, etc., and is now very ripe.*

ORMONROYD (*advances into room and looks about him with great care, then returns to* RUBY): Nobody here. (*Gives another glance to make sure.*) Nobody at all.

RUBY: They'll all be back again soon. They're mostly in dining-room—fratchin'.

ORMONROYD: What—on a festive occasion like this?

RUBY: That's right.

ORMONROYD: Well, it just shows you what human nature is. Human nature! T-t-t-t-t. I'll bet if it had been a funeral—they'd have all been in here, laughing their heads off. (*He goes over and looks closely at the cigars.*) There isn't such a thing as a cigar here, is there?

RUBY: Yes, yer looking at 'em. D'you want one? 'Ere. (*As he lights it*) Me mother says if God had intended men to smoke He'd have put chimneys in their heads.

ORMONROYD: Tell your mother from me that if God had intended

[190]

men to wear collars He'd have put collar studs at back of their necks. (*Stares at her.*) What are you bobbing up an' down like that for?

RUBY: I'm not bobbing up an' down. It's you. (*Laughs and regards him critically.*) You're a bit tiddly, aren't yer?

ORMONROYD (*horror-struck*): Tidd-ldly?

RUBY: Yes. Squiffy.

ORMONROYD (*surveying her mistily*): What an ex't'rornry idea! You seem to me a mos' ex't'rornry sort of—little—well, I dunno, really—what's your name?

RUBY: Ruby Birtle.

ORMONROYD (*tasting it*): Umm—Ruby——

RUBY: All right, I know it's a silly daft name, you can't tell me nowt about Ruby I 'aven't been told already—so don't try.

ORMONROYD (*solemnly*): Ruby, I think you're quite ex't'rornry. How old are you?

RUBY (*quickly*): Fifteen—how old are you?

ORMONROYD (*waving a hand, vaguely*): Thousands of years, thousands and thousands of years.

RUBY (*coolly*): You look to me about seventy.

ORMONROYD (*horrified*): *Seventy!* I'm fifty-four.

RUBY (*severely*): Then you've been neglectin' yerself.

ORMONROYD *looks at her, breathing hard and noisily.*
Too much liftin' o' t' elbow.

ORMONROYD (*after indignant pause*): Do you ever read the *Police News?*

RUBY: Yes. I like it. All 'orrible murders.

ORMONROYD: Then you must have seen them pictures of women who've been chopped up by their husbands——

RUBY (*with gusto*): Yes—with bloody 'atchets.

ORMONROYD (*impressively*): Well, if you don't look out, Ruby, you'll grow up to be one of them women. (*Wanders away and then notices and takes up old photograph.*)

RUBY (*looking at it*): Aaaaa!—don't they look soft? (*Looks suspiciously at him, dubiously.*) How d'you mean—one o' them women?

ORMONROYD: Don't you bother about that, Ruby, you've plenty of time yet.

RUBY (*puzzled*): Time for what?

ORMONROYD (*intent on his art now*): Now what I'm going to do— is to take a flashlight group of the three couples—just as they were

[191]

in the old photograph. Now—let me see—— (*Very solemnly and elaborately he sets up his camera.*)

RUBY (*who has been thinking*): 'Ere, d'you mean I've plenty of time yet to grow up an' then be chopped up?

ORMONROYD (*absently*): Yes.

RUBY (*persistently*): But what would 'e want to chop me up for?

ORMONROYD: Now you sit there a minute.

RUBY: I said, what would 'e want to chop me up for?

ORMONROYD (*putting her into a chair and patting her shoulder*): Perhaps you might find one who wouldn't, but you'll have to be careful. Now you stay there, Ruby.

RUBY (*hopefully*): Are yer goin' to take my photo?

ORMONROYD (*grimly*): Not for a few years—yet—— (*Is now fiddling with his camera.*)

RUBY (*after thoughtful pause*): D'you mean you're waiting for me to be chopped up? (*Cheerfully, not reproachfully.*) Eeeee!—you've got a right nasty mind, 'aven't you? (*A pause.*) Are *you* married?

ORMONROYD: Yes.

RUBY: Yer wife doesn't seem to take much interest in yer.

ORMONROYD: How do you know?

RUBY: Well, I'll bet yer clothes hasn't been brushed for a month. (*Going on cheerfully.*) Yer could almost make a meal off yer waist-coat—there's so much egg on it. (*After pause.*) Why doesn't she tidy you up a bit?

ORMONROYD (*busy with his preparations*): Because she's not here to do it.

RUBY: Doesn't she live with yer?

ORMONROYD (*stopping to stare at her, with dignity*): Is it—er—essential—you should know all about my—er—private affairs?

RUBY: Go on, yer might as well tell me. Where is she?

ORMONROYD: Mrs. Ormonroyd at present is—er—helping her sister to run a boarding-house called *Palm View*—though the only palm you see there is the one my sister-in-law holds out.

RUBY: Where? Blackpool?

ORMONROYD: Not likely. There's a place you go to live in—not to die in. No, they're at Torquay. (*With profound scorn*) Torquay!

RUBY (*impressed*): That's right down South, isn't it?

ORMONROYD (*with mock pompousness*): Yes, my girl, Torquay is on the South Coast of Devonshire. It is sheltered from the northerly and easterly winds, is open to the warm sea breezes from the South,

and so is a favourite all-year-round resort of many delicate and refined persons of genteel society. In other words, it's a damned
miserable hole. (*Surveys his arrangements with satisfaction.*) There
we are, all ready for the three happy couples.

RUBY (*sceptically*): Did yer say 'appy?

ORMONROYD: Why not?

RUBY: Well, for a start, go an' listen to them four in t' dining-room.

ORMONROYD (*beginning solemnly*): Believe me, Rosie——

• RUBY (*sharply*): Ruby.

ORMONROYD: Ruby. Believe me, you're still too young to understand.

RUBY: I've 'eard that afore, but nobody ever tells what it is I'm
too young to understand. An' for years me brother kept rabbits.

ORMONROYD (*solemnly but vaguely*): It's not a question of rabbits
—thank God! But marriage—marriage—well, it's a very peculiar
thing. There's parts of it I never much cared about myself.

RUBY: Which parts?

ORMONROYD: Well—now I'm a man who likes a bit o' company.
An' I like an occasional friendly glass. I'll admit it—I like an occasional friendly glass.

RUBY: It 'ud be all t' same if you didn't admit it. We could tell.
(*Sniffs.*)

ORMONROYD: If these three couples here have been married for
twenty-five years and—er—they're still sticking it, well, then I call
'em three happy couples, an' I won't listen to you or anybody else
saying they're not. No, I won't have it. And if you or anybody else
says "Drink their health" I say "Certainly, certainly, with
pleasure——" (*Gives himself a whisky with remarkable speed.*)
Wouldn't dare to refuse, 'cos it would be dead against my principles.
Their very good health. (*Takes an enormous drink.*)

RUBY: Eeee!—you are goin' to be tiddly.

ORMONROYD (*ignoring this, if he heard it, and very mellow and sentimental now*): Ah—yes. To be together—side-by-side—through all
life's sunshine and storms—hand-in-hand—in good times and bad
ones—with always a loving smile—— (*Waving hand with cigar in.*)

RUBY (*coldly*): Mind yer cigar!

ORMONROYD: In sickness and in health—rich or poor—still together—side-by-side—hand-in-hand—through all life's sunshine and
storms——

RUBY (*quickly*): You said that once.

[193]

ORMONROYD: Oh—yes—it's a wonderful—it's a bee-yutiful thing——

RUBY: What is?

ORMONROYD: *What is!* Lord help us—it's like talking to a little crocodile! I say—that it's a wonderful and bee-yutiful thing to go through good times and bad ones—always together—always with a loving smile——

RUBY: Side-by-side—an' 'and-in-'and——

ORMONROYD: Yes, and that's what I say.

RUBY: Then there must be summat wrong wi' me 'cos when I've tried goin' side-by-side an' 'and-in-'and even for twenty minutes I've 'ad more than I want.

ORMONROYD (*staring at her*): Extr'ord'n'ry! What's your name?

RUBY: It's still Ruby Birtle.

ORMONROYD: Well, haven't you had a home?

RUBY: Course I've 'ad a home. Why?

ORMONROYD: You talk as if you'd been brought up in a tramshed. No sentiment. No tender feeling. No—no—poetry——

RUBY (*indignantly*): Go on. I know Poetry. We learnt it at school. 'Ere——

RUBY *recites, as* ORMONROYD *sits.*

They grew in beauty side by side,
They filled one home with glee;
Their graves are severed, far an' wide,
By mount and stream and sea.

The same fond mother bent at night
O'er each fair sleeping brow;
She 'ad each folder flower in sight—
Where are those dreamers now?

One 'midst the forest of the west,
By a dark stream is laid—
The Indian knows his place of rest
Far——

RUBY *hesitates.* CLARA *enters quietly and stares at her in astonishment.* RUBY *gives her one startled look, then concludes hurriedly.*

—Far in the cedar shade.

RUBY *hurries out.* CLARA *stands in* RUBY'S *place.* ORMONROYD, *who has turned away and closed his eyes, now turns and opens them, astonished to see* CLARA *there.*

[194]

ORMONROYD (*bewildered*): Now I call that most peculiar, *most* peculiar. I don't think I'm very well to-night——

CLARA (*same tone as* RUBY *used*): You're a bit tiddly, aren't you?

ORMONROYD: Things aren't rightly in their place, if you know what I mean. But I'll get it.

CLARA: Who are you, and what are you doing here?

ORMONROYD (*still dazed*): Henry Ormonroyd—*Yorkshire Argus*—take picture—silver wedding group——

CLARA (*firmly*): There's no silver wedding group 'll be taken *here* to-night.

ORMONROYD: Have I come to t' wrong house?

CLARA (*firmly*): Yes.

ORMONROYD: Excuse me. (*Moving to door, which opens to admit* ANNIE.)

ANNIE: Who's this?

ORMONROYD (*hastily confused*): Nobody, nobody—I'll get it all straightened out in a minute—now give me time——

ORMONROYD *goes out.*

ANNIE: Isn't he the *photographer*?

CLARA (*bitterly*): Yes, an' he's drunk, an' when I come in, Maria's servant's reciting poetry to him, an' God knows what's become of Herbert an' Albert an' that Mrs. Northrop an' (*angrily*) I'm fast losing my patience, I'm fast losing my patience——

ANNIE: Now, Clara——

MARIA *enters, rather wearily.*

MARIA: I can't knock any sense at all into Joe. Where's Herbert?

CLARA (*grimly*): Still looking for that Mrs. Northrop.

Front door bell rings.

Somebody else here now.

MARIA: Well, don't carry on like that, Clara. I didn't ask 'em to come, whoever it is.

CLARA: If you didn't, I'll bet Joe did. With his *Yorkshire Argus!*

RUBY *enters, rather mysteriously.*

MARIA: Well, Ruby, who is it?

RUBY (*lowering voice*): It's a woman.

CLARA (*hastily*): What woman?

MARIA: Now, Clara! (*To* RUBY) What sort of woman? Who is it?

RUBY (*coming in, confidentially*): I don't know. But she doesn't

[195]

look up to much to me. Paint on her face. An' I believe her 'air's dyed.

The three women look at each other.

CLARA (*primly*): We don't want that sort o' woman here, Maria.

MARIA: Course we don't—but—— (*Hesitates.*)

ANNIE: You'll have to see what she wants, Maria. It might be something to do with—y'know—this business.

CLARA (*angrily*): How could it be?

ANNIE: Well, you never know, do yer?

CLARA: Let Joe see what she wants.

MARIA: Oh—no—state of mind Joe's in, *I'd* better see her. Ask her to come in, Ruby—and—er—you needn't bother Mr. Helliwell just now.

> RUBY *goes out. The three women settle themselves, rather anxiously.* RUBY *ushers in* LOTTIE, *who enters smiling broadly.* MARIA *rises, the other two remaining seated.*

MARIA (*nervously*): Good evening.

LOTTIE: Good evening.

MARIA (*step down*): Did you want to see me?

LOTTIE (*coolly*): No, not particularly. (*She sits down, calmly, and looks about her.*)

The other three women exchange puzzled glances.

MARIA: Er—I don't think I got your name.

LOTTIE: No. You didn't get it because I didn't give it. But I'm Miss Lottie Grady.

MARIA (*with dignity*): And I'm Mrs. Helliwell.

LOTTIE (*shaking her head*): *No*, if we're all going to be on our dignity, let's get it *right. You're not Mrs. Helliwell.* You're Miss Maria Fawcett.

CLARA (*as* MARIA *is too stunned to speak*): Now just a minute——

LOTTIE (*turning to her, with mock sweetness*): Miss Clara Gawthorpe, isn't it? Gawthorpe's, Greengrocer's, corner of Park Road. (*Turning to* ANNIE) I'm afraid I don't know *your* maiden name——

ANNIE: I'm Mrs. Parker to you.

LOTTIE: Please yourself, I don't care. I'm *broadminded.* (*Surveying them with a smile.*)

CLARA (*angrily*): I suppose that Mrs. Northrop's been talking to you.

LOTTIE: Certainly. Met in the old *Hare and Hounds*, where I used to work. She's an old friend of mine.

CLARA (*angrily*): If you've come 'ere to get money out of us——

LOTTIE: Who said anything about money?

MARIA: Well, you must have some idea in coming to see us.

LOTTIE (*coolly*): Oh—I didn't come here to see any of you three.

ANNIE: Well, who did you come to see then?

LOTTIE (*smiling*): A gentleman friend, love.

CLARA (*angrily*): Gentleman friend! *You*'ll find none o' your gentleman friends in *this house*, will she, Maria?

MARIA (*indignantly*): I should think not!

ANNIE: Just a minute, Clara. I'd like to hear a bit more about this.

LOTTIE: Very sensible of you. You see, if a gentleman friend gets fond of me—then tells me—more than once—that if he wasn't married already, he'd marry me——

CLARA (*grimly*): Well, go on.

LOTTIE: Well—then I suddenly find out that he isn't married already, after all, then you can't blame me—can you?—if I'd like to know if he's still in the same mind. (*Beams upon them, while they look at each other in growing consternation.*)

CLARA (*astounded*): Well, I'll be hanged.

ANNIE: Now we *are* getting to know something.

MARIA (*flustered*): Clara—Annie. (*Pause. Suddenly to* LOTTIE) Who was it?

    Front door bell rings.

ANNIE: Just a minute, Maria, there's somebody else here now.

CLARA (*angrily*): Oh—for goodness' sake—can't you keep 'em out?

RUBY (*appearing, importantly*): The Rever-ent Clem-ent Mer-cer!

    All three wives look startled, as MERCER, *a large grave clergyman, enters, and* RUBY *retires.*

MERCER (*sympathetically*): Mrs. Helliwell?

MARIA (*faintly*): Yes?

MERCER (*taking her hand a moment*): Now, Mrs. Helliwell, although you're not a member of my congregation, I want you to realise that I feel it my duty to give you any help I can.

MARIA (*confused*): I'm afraid—I don't understand—Mr. Mercer.

MERCER: Now, now, Mrs. Helliwell, don't worry. Let's take everything calmly. May I sit down? (*Takes chair and brings it down.*)

    MERCER *sits down, smiling at them.* MARIA *sits.*

ANNIE: Did somebody ask you to come here?

MERCER: Yes, madam. A working man I know called Northrop

stopped me in the street and told me to go at once to Alderman Helliwell's house as a clergyman's presence was urgently required here. So here I am—entirely at your service.

> LOTTIE, *in danger of exploding, rises and goes quickly towards conservatory, where she stands with her back to the others.* MERCER *gives her a puzzled glance, then turns to the other three.*

Now what is it? Not, I hope, a really dangerous illness?

MARIA (*blankly*): No.

MERCER (*rather puzzled*): Ah!—I hurried because I thought there might be. But perhaps you feel some younger member of your family is in urgent need of spiritual guidance. An erring son or daughter?

> *A noise from* LOTTIE.

CLARA (*forcefully*): *No.*

MERCER (*puzzled*): I beg your pardon?

CLARA: I just said *No*. I mean, there aren't any erring sons and daughters. Just husbands, that's all.

MERCER (*rises*): Husbands?

> LOTTIE *suddenly bursts into a peal of laughter, turning towards them.* MERCER *looks puzzled at her.*

LOTTIE (*laughing*): You've got it all wrong.

MERCER (*rather annoyed*): Really! I don't see——

LOTTIE: I think they want you to marry 'em.

MERCER (*looking astounded*): *Marry them!*

ANNIE (*rising, with spirit*): 'Ere, Maria, come on, do something. (*To* MERCER) You'd better talk to Mr. Helliwell——

MARIA (*who has risen*): He's in the dining-room—just across—— (*Almost leading him out.*) Ask him if he thinks you can do anything for us—— (*Now outside room.*) Just in there—that's right——

CLARA (*to* LOTTIE): Which one was it?

> MARIA *returns, flustered, shutting door, as* LOTTIE *returns to her seat, still smiling.*

LOTTIE: I think you missed a chance there—at least, two of you did.

MARIA: Two of us!

LOTTIE: Well, you remember what I told you? (*Smiling reminiscently.*) I'd known him here in Cleckleywyke, but it was at Blackpool we really got going. He said he was feeling lonely—and you know what men are, when they think they're feeling lonely, specially at Blackpool.

CLARA (*hastily*): It couldn't have been Herbert. He's never been to Blackpool without me.

[198]

ANNIE: Yes, he has, Clara. Don't you remember—about four years since——?

CLARA (*thunderstruck*): And he said he hadn't a minute away from that Conference. I'll never believe another word he says. But your Albert was with him that time.

ANNIE (*grimly*): I know he was.

MARIA: So was Joe. Said he needed a change.

LOTTIE (*sweetly*): Well, we all like a change, don't we?

SOPPITT *enters, rather hesitantly.* CLARA *sees him first.*

CLARA (*sharply*): Now, Herbert Soppitt——

SOPPITT: Yes, Clara?

LOTTIE (*going to him*): Well, Herbert, how are you these days? (*Playfully.*) You haven't forgotten me, have you?

SOPPITT: Forgotten you? I'm afraid there's a mistake——

CLARA (*grimly*): Oh—there's a mistake all right.

MARIA: Now, Clara, don't be too hard on him. I expect it was only a bit o' fun.

SOPPITT: What is all this?

LOTTIE (*playfully*): Now, Herbert——

SOPPITT (*indignantly*): Don't call me Herbert.

CLARA (*angrily*): No, wait till I'm out o' t' way.

ANNIE: I expect he didn't mean it.

SOPPITT (*annoyed*): Mean *what?*

ALBERT PARKER *now enters, rather wearily.* SOPPITT *turns to him.*

I found that Mrs. Northrop, Albert.

LOTTIE: Oh—hello, Albert!

PARKER (*staring at her*): How d'you mean—*Hello, Albert!*

LOTTIE (*playfully*): Now, now—Albert!

PARKER *looks at her in astonishment, then at the three women, finishing with his wife.*

ANNIE (*bitterly*): Yes, you might well look at me, Albert Parker. You and your cheap holiday at Blackpool! I only hope you spent more on her than you've ever done on me.

PARKER (*vehemently*): Spent more on *her?* I've never set eyes on her before. *Who is she?*

ANNIE *and* CLARA *now look at one another, then at* MARIA, *who looks at them in growing consternation.*

MARIA: I don't believe it. I *won't* believe it.

[199]

RUBY *looks in, excitedly.*

RUBY: There's a motor-car stopping near t' front gate.

CLARA (*shouting as* RUBY *goes*): Well, tell it to go away again.

HELLIWELL *comes out of dining-room, bumping into* RUBY *as she goes out, and begins speaking early.*

HELLIWELL (*who is flustered*): What with a photographer who's drunk and a parson who's mad——! (*He sees* LOTTIE *now, and visibly wilts and gasps.*) Lottie!

MARIA (*furiously*): Lottie! So it was *you*, Joe Helliwell.

HELLIWELL: Me what?

MARIA: Who said you'd marry her——

HELLIWELL (*shouting desperately*): That was only a bit o' fun.

MARIA (*bitterly*): You and your bit o' fun!

RUBY (*importantly*): Mayor o' Cleckleywyke, *Yorkshire Argus, Telegraph and Mercury.*

MAYOR *enters, carrying case of fish slices, with* REPORTERS *behind.*

MAYOR (*pompously*): Alderman and Mrs. Helliwell, the Council and Corporation of Cleckleywyke offers you their heartiest congratulations on your Silver Wedding and with them this case of silver fish slices.

He is now offering the case to MARIA, *who has suddenly sunk down on the settee and is now weeping. She waves the case away, and the bewildered* MAYOR *now offers it to* HELLIWELL, *who has been looking in exasperation between his wife,* LOTTIE *and the* MAYOR. HELLIWELL *takes the case and opens it without thinking, then seeing what is in it, in his exasperation, shouts furiously:*

An' I told yer before, Fred—I don't like fish. (*Quick curtain.*)

END OF ACT TWO

ACT III

SCENE: *As before. About quarter of an hour later. RUBY is tidying up the room, and also eating a large piece of pasty. She continues with her work several moments after rise of curtain, then NANCY makes cautious appearance at conservatory, sees that nobody but RUBY is there, then turns to beckon in GERALD, and they both come into the room.*

NANCY: What's been happening, Ruby?

RUBY: What 'asn't been 'appening! Eee—we've had some trade on what wi' one thing an' another.

NANCY (*mischievous rather than reproachful*): You see what you've done, Gerald.

RUBY: What! He didn't start it, did he? 'Cos if he did, he's got summat to answer for.

NANCY: Did—anybody ask where I was, Ruby?

RUBY: No, an' I'll bet you could stop out all night and they'd neither know nor care.

GERALD: But what *has* been happening, Ruby?

RUBY (*confidentially*): Place 'as been like a mad-'ouse this last half-hour. To start with, mayor o' Cleckleywyke's been and gone——

NANCY: The mayor?

GERALD (*amused*): Why did they want to bring the mayor into it?

RUBY: Nobody brought him. He come of his own accord—with a case o' fish things an' wearing t' chain—like a chap in a pantymime. He soon took his 'ook. But reporters didn't——

GERALD: Reporters, eh?

RUBY: Ay, an' there were plenty of 'em an' all an' they didn't want to go, neither, not like t' mayor. So Mr. Helliwell an' Mr. Parker took 'em into t' kitchen an' give 'em bottled ale an' for all I know they may be there yet. Mrs. Helliwell's up in t' bedroom—feeling poorly—an' Mrs. Soppitt's with her. Mr. Soppitt an' Mrs. Parker's somewhere out in garden——

NANCY: I told you there was somebody there.

RUBY: Ah, but let me finish. Now there's a woman wi' dyed 'air washing herself in t' bathroom upstairs—an' nobody knows what she wants—beyond a good wash. Down in t' dining-room there's a photo-

[201]

grapher who's right tiddly tryin' to argue with gert big parson—an' I'll bet he's makin' a rare mess—an' that'll be to do next.

Exit RUBY.

GERALD: Sounds all very confused to me.

NANCY: Yes, and I'd better slip upstairs while nobody's about. Oh—Gerald.

GERALD: Nancy!

NANCY: Do you still love me?

GERALD: Yes, Nancy—still—even after a whole hour.

They kiss. Enter SOPPITT *and* ANNIE PARKER *from conservatory.*

SOPPITT: Here, I say! You two seem very friendly!

ANNIE: I believe you were the girl he was seen with.

SOPPITT: Were you?

NANCY: Yes. We're practically engaged, you know. Only—I was frightened of saying anything yet to Uncle Joe.

SOPPITT: Well, don't start to-night——

ANNIE: Why shouldn't she? He won't be quite so pleased with himself to-night as usual—just as I know another who won't.

NANCY: Good night.

ANNIE: Good night. Why don't you go outside and say good night properly? You're only young once.

NANCY *and* GERALD *exit to conservatory.*

ANNIE: Yes, you're only young once, Herbert. D'you remember that time, just after you'd first come to Cleckleywyke, when we all went on that choir trip to Barnard Castle?

SOPPITT: I do, Annie. As a matter of fact, I fancy I was a bit sweet on you then.

ANNIE: You fancy you were! I know you were, Herbert Soppitt. Don't you remember coming back in the wagonette?

SOPPITT: Ay!

ANNIE: Those were the days!

SOPPITT: Ay!

ANNIE: Is that all you can say—Ay?

SOPPITT: No. But I might say too much.

ANNIE: I think I'd risk it for once, if I were you.

SOPPITT: And what does that mean, Annie?

ANNIE: Never you mind. But you haven't forgotten that wagonette, have you?

SOPPITT: Of course I haven't.

[202]

He has his arm round her waist. Enter CLARA.

Hello, Clara.

CLARA: How long's this been going on?

ANNIE: Now, don't be silly, Clara.

CLARA: Oh—it's me that hasn't to be silly, is it? I suppose standing there with my 'usband's arm round you bold as brass, that isn't being silly, is it? I wonder what you call that sort of behaviour, then?

SOPPITT: It was only a bit of fun.

CLARA: Oh—an' how long have you been 'aving these bits o' fun —as you call them—Herbert Soppitt?

ANNIE: You've a nasty mind, Clara.

CLARA: Well—of all the cheek and impudence! Telling me I've got a nasty mind. You must have been at it some time getting Herbert to carry on like that with you. Don't tell me he thought of it himself, I know him too well.

ANNIE: Oh—don't be so stupid, Clara. I'm going into the garden. I want some fresh air.

She goes out.

CLARA: Well, Herbert Soppitt, why don't you follow her and get some fresh air, too? Go on, don't mind me. Come here.

SOPPITT *doesn't move.*

You 'eard me, come here!

SOPPITT: Why should I?

CLARA: Because I tell you to.

SOPPITT: I know. I heard you. But who do you think you are?

CLARA: Herbert Soppitt—you must have gone wrong in your head.

SOPPITT: No. Not me. I'm all right.

CLARA (*sharply*): You'd better go home now an' leave me to deal with this business here.

SOPPITT (*bravely*): Certainly not.

CLARA: In my opinion it's awkward with both of us here.

SOPPITT (*pause*): Well, *you* go home then!

CLARA: What did you say?

SOPPITT (*bravely*): I said, *you* go home. You are doing no good here.

Very angry now, she marches up to him and gives him a sharp slap on the cheek.

CLARA: Now then! (*Steps back and folds arms.*) Just tell me to go home again!

SOPPITT (*slowly, impressively, approaching her*): Clara, I always said that no matter what she did, I'd never lift a hand to my wife——

CLARA: I should think not indeed!

SOPPITT: But as you aren't my wife—what about this?

He gives her a sharp slap. She is astounded.

CLARA: Herbert!

SOPPITT (*commandingly*): Now sit down. (*Pointing.*)

She does not obey. In a tremendous voice of command.

Sit down!

She sits, staring at him. Then when she opens her mouth to speak:

Shut up! I want to think.

A silence, during which she still stares at him.

CLARA (*in a low voice*): I don't know what's come over you, Herbert Soppitt.

SOPPIT (*fiercely*): You don't, eh?

CLARA (*gaping at him*): No, I don't.

SOPPITT (*severely*): Well, you don't think I put up with women coming shouting and bawling at me and smacking my face, do you?

CLARA: Well—you've never gone on like this before.

SOPPITT: Yes, but then before you were my wife——

CLARA (*hastily*): I'm your wife now.

SOPPITT: Oh, no—you're not. (*Produces letter.*)

CLARA: Give me that letter!

SOPPITT: *Sit down*—and *shut up, woman!*

Enter ALBERT PARKER.

PARKER: Where's Annie?

SOPPITT: She's out there somewhere—why don't you look for her?

CLARA: Perhaps she's hiding her face—and if you'd seen what I'd seen to-night, Albert Parker——

SOPPITT: Hold your tongue before it gets you into mischief!

CLARA: I'm only——

SOPPITT: *Shut up.*

PARKER: Here, but wait a minute—I'd like to hear a bit more about this.

SOPPITT: Then you're going to be disappointed. (*To* CLARA) You get back to Maria Helliwell, go on!

PARKER: Here, Clara, you're not going to——

SOPPITT: YOU mind your own business! (*To* CLARA) Go on—sharp.

CLARA *exits.*

PARKER: Herbert, 'ave you been 'aving a lot to drink?

SOPPITT: I had a few, trying to find that Mrs. Northrop.

PARKER: I thought as much.

SOPPITT: And I may possibly have some more, but whether I do or not, I'll please myself—just for once—and if any of you don't like it, you can lump it.

PARKER: Where did you say my wife was?

SOPPITT: She's out there in the garden.

PARKER (*disapprovingly*): What—at this time o' night? (*Looking to garden.*)

SOPPITT: Yes—and why not?

PARKER (*with dignity*): I'll tell '*er* that. I've no need to tell you. You're not my wife.

SOPPITT: No, and she isn't, either. Don't forget that.

PARKER *goes to the door and calls.*

PARKER: Annie! Hey—Annie!

SOPPITT: Why don't you go out and talk to her, instead o' calling her like that—as if she were a dog or something?

PARKER: 'Cos standing about in damp grass this time o' night is bad for me. I don't want to start a running cold on top of all this. (*Calls again.*) Hey—Annie! (*Turns to* SOPPITT.) I came in to 'ave a few words in private with her——

SOPPITT: Oh—I'll leave you.

PARKER: In my opinion, there's been a lot too much talk among us altogether, too much noisy 'anky-panky about this daft business. You might think we were a meeting o' t' gas committee way we've gone on so far. What's wanted is a few serious words i' private between us chaps an' our wives, an' less o' this public argy-bargy an' 'anky-panky.

ANNIE PARKER *enters through conservatory.*

Ah—so there y'are.

SOPPITT (*going*): Well, best o' luck, Annie!

PARKER (*suspiciously*): How d'you mean?

SOPPITT (*turning at door*): Hanky-panky!

He goes out.

PARKER: He's 'ad a drop too much, Herbert 'as! Comes of running round the town after that charwoman!

ANNIE (*amused*): Well, Albert?

PARKER (*pompously and complacently*): Well, Annie, I'm going to set your mind at rest.

ANNIE (*demurely*): Thank you, Albert.

PARKER (*pompously and complacently*): Yes, I don't want you to be worrying. Now I think you'll admit I've always tried to do my duty as a 'usband.

ANNIE: Yes, Albert, I think you've always tried.

PARKER (*suspiciously*): What do you mean?

ANNIE (*demurely*): Why—just what you mean, Albert.

PARKER (*after another suspicious glance, returns to former tone, and is insufferably patronising*): Of course, as nobody knows better than you, I'm in a different position altogether to what I was when I first married you——

ANNIE: When you *thought* you married me, Albert.

PARKER: Well, you know what I mean! In them days I was just plain young Albert Parker.

ANNIE: And now you're Councillor Albert Parker——

PARKER: Well, an' that's something, isn't it? And it isn't all, by a long chalk. I've got on i' business, made money, come to be a big man at chapel, vice-president o' t' Cricket League, on t' hospital committee, an' so forth—eh?

ANNIE: Yes, Albert, you've done very well.

PARKER (*complacently*): I know I 'ave. An' mind you, it's not altered me much. I'm not like some of 'em. No swank about me—no la-di-dah—*I'm a plain man.*

ANNIE (*rather sadly*): Yes, Albert, you are.

PARKER (*looking at her suspiciously*): Well, what's wrong wi' it? You're not going to tell me that at your time o' life——

ANNIE (*indignantly cutting in*): My time of life!

PARKER: Well, you're no chicken, are yer? And I say, you're not going to tell me now, at your time o' life, you'd like a bit o' swank an' la-di-dah!

ANNIE (*wistfully*): I've sometimes wondered——

PARKER (*brushing this aside*): Nay, nay, nay, nobody knows better than me what you'd like. An' you know very well what a good husband I've been: steady——

ANNIE (*rather grimly*): Yes, you've been steady all right, Albert.

PARKER (*complacently*): That's what I say. Steady. Reliable. Not silly wi' my money——

ANNIE (*same tone*): No, Albert, your worst enemy couldn't say you'd ever been silly with your money.

PARKER (*complacently*): And yet at the same time—not stingy. No, not stingy. Everything of the best—if it could be managed—everything of the best, within reason, y'know, within reason.

ANNIE: Yes, within reason.

PARKER (*in a dreamy ecstasy of complacency*): Always reasonable —*and* reliable. But all the time, getting on, goin' up i' the world, never satisfied with what 'ud do for most men—no, steadily moving on an' on, up an' up—cashier, manager, share in the business— councillor this year, alderman next, perhaps mayor soon—that's how it's been an' that's how it will be. Y'know, Annie, I've sometimes thought that right at first you didn't realise just what you'd picked out o' t' lucky bag. Ay! (*Contemplates his own greatness, while she watches him coolly.*)

ANNIE (*after a pause*): Well, Albert, what's all this leading up to?

PARKER (*recalled to his argument*): Oh!—Well, yer see, Annie, I was just saying that I thought I'd been a good husband to you. An', mind yer, I don't say you've been a bad wife—no, I don't——

ANNIE (*dryly*): Thank you, Albert.

PARKER (*with immense patronage*): So I thought I'd just set your mind at rest. Now don't you worry about this wedding business. If there's been a slip up—well, there's been a slip up. But I'll see you're all right, Annie. I'll see it's fixed up quietly, an' then we'll go an' get married again—properly. (*He pats her on the shoulder.*) I know my duty as well as t' next man—an' I'll see that you're properly married to me.

ANNIE: Thank you, Albert.

PARKER: That's all right, Annie, that's all right. I don't say every man 'ud see it as I do—but—never mind—I know what my duty is.

ANNIE: And what about me?

PARKER (*puzzled*): Well, I'm telling yer—you'll be all right.

ANNIE: How d'you know I will?

PARKER (*hastily*): Now don't be silly, Annie. If I say you'll be all right, you ought to know by this time yer *will* be all right.

ANNIE (*slowly*): But I don't think I want to be married to you.

PARKER (*staggered*): *What!*

ANNIE (*slowly*): You see, Albert, after twenty-five years of it, perhaps I've had enough.

PARKER (*horrified*): 'Ad enough!

ANNIE: Yes, had enough. You talk about your duty. Well, for

twenty-five years I've done my duty. I've washed and cooked and cleaned and mended for you. I've pinched and scrimped and saved for you. I've listened for hours and hours to all your dreary talk. I've never had any thanks for it. I've hardly ever had any fun. But I thought I was your wife and I'd taken you for better or worse, and that I ought to put up with you——

PARKER (*staring, amazed*): *Put up with me!*

ANNIE (*coolly*): Yes, put up with you.

PARKER: But what's wrong with me?

ANNIE (*coolly*): Well, to begin with, you're very selfish. But then, I suppose most men are. You're idiotically conceited. But again, so are most men. But a lot of men at least are generous. And you're very stingy. And some men are amusing. But—except when you're being pompous and showing off—you're not at all amusing. You're just very dull and dreary——

PARKER: Never!

ANNIE (*firmly*): Yes, Albert. *Very* dull and *very, very* dreary and stingy.

PARKER (*staring at her as if seeing a strange woman*): 'As somebody put you up to this?

ANNIE: No, I've thought it for a long time.

PARKER: How long?

ANNIE: Nearly twenty-five years.

PARKER (*half dazed, half indignant*): Why—you—you—you little *serpent!*

ANNIE (*ignoring this*): So now I feel it's time I enjoyed myself a bit. I'd like to have *some* fun before I'm an old woman.

PARKER (*horrified*): Fun! Fun! What do you mean—fun?

ANNIE (*coolly*): Oh—nothing very shocking and terrible—just getting away from you, for instance——

PARKER (*in loud pained tone*): Stop it! Just stop it now! I think—Annie Parker—you ought to be ashamed of yourself.

ANNIE (*dreamily*): Well, I'm not. Bit of travel—and liveliness—and people that are amusing—and no wool business and town councillors and chapel deacons——

PARKER (*shouting angrily*): Why don't you dye your hair and paint your face and go on t' stage and wear tights——?

ANNIE (*wistfully*): I wish I could.

As PARKER *groans in despair at this*, RUBY *looks in*.

RUBY (*loudly and cheerfully*): Mr. Soppitt says if you haven't

finished yet yer better 'urry up or go somewhere else to 'ave it out
'cos they're all coming in 'ere.

PARKER (*angrily*): Well, we 'aven't finished.

ANNIE (*coolly*): Yes, we have.

RUBY *nods and leaves the door open.*

PARKER (*loudly*): Now listen, Annie, let's talk a bit o' sense for a
minute——

ANNIE: They'll all hear you—the door's open.

PARKER: Nay—damn it——!

Goes to shut door, but SOPPITT *and* CLARA *enter.*

SOPPITT (*amused*): Hello, Albert—what's made you look so
flabbergasted?

PARKER (*annoyed*): If I want to look flabbergasted, then I'll look
flabbergasted, without asking your advice, Herbert.

SOPPITT: Hanky-panky!

PARKER: Now shut up! 'Ere, Clara, yer wouldn't say I was stingy,
would yer?

CLARA: Well, you've never been famous for getting your hand
down, have you, Albert?

PARKER (*indignantly*): I've got my 'and down as well as t' next
man. I've always paid my whack, let me tell yer. Call a chap stingy
just because he doesn't make a big show—'cos he isn't—er——

ANNIE (*burlesqueing his accent, coolly*): La-di-dah!

SOPPITT: Now stop tormenting him, Annie.

PARKER (*indignantly*): Tormenting me! Nobody 'll torment me.
And I like that coming from *you*, Herbert, when you've been a by-
word for years.

CLARA (*angrily*): A by-word for what?

PARKER: For years.

CLARA: Yes, but a by-word for years for what?

PARKER: Oh! Hen-pecked! Ask anybody who wears trousers in
your house!

ANNIE: Albert, don't be so vulgar!

PARKER: Why, a minute since you wanted to wear tights.

ANNIE: Only in a manner of speaking.

PARKER: How can it be in a manner of speaking?—'cos either you're
wearing tights or you're not.

Enter LOTTIE *and* JOE HELLIWELL.

LOTTIE: What's this about tights?

PARKER: Now you'll clear out right sharp—if you'll take my tip.

LOTTIE: And I'll bet it's the only kind of tip you do give, too. (*To* ANNIE) He looks stingy to me!

PARKER: Stingy! If anyone says that again to me to-night—I'll—I'll give 'em jip.

Exit PARKER.

HELLIWELL: For two pins I'd either leave this house myself or else clear everybody else out. I've never seen such a place—there's folk nattering in every damn corner!

ANNIE: Where's poor Maria?

SOPPITT: Clara!

Exeunt SOPPITT, CLARA *and* ANNIE.

HELLIWELL: Now, Lottie, be reasonable. A bit o' devilment's all right, but I know you don't want to make real mischief——

LOTTIE: Where's the mischief come in? Didn't you say—more than once—that if you hadn't been married already——?

HELLIWELL (*urgently to her*): Now, you know very well that were only a bit o' fun. When a chap's on a 'oliday in a place like Blackpool an' gets a few drinks inside 'im, you know very well he says a lot o' damn silly things he doesn't mean——

LOTTIE (*indignantly*): Oh—I see. Just tellin' me the tale an' then laughing at me behind my back, eh?

HELLIWELL (*urgently*): No, I don't mean that, Lottie. Nobody admires you more than I do. You're a fine lass and a good sport. But you've got to be reasonable. Coming 'ere *like this*, when you know as well as I do, it were just a bit o' fun!

MARIA *enters. She is dressed to go out, and is carrying some housekeeping books, some keys, and several pairs of socks.*

MARIA (*at door, leaving it open; grimly*): Just a minute, Joe Helliwell!

HELLIWELL (*groaning*): Oh—Christmas! (*Then sees she has outdoor things on.*) 'Ere, Maria, where are yer going?

MARIA (*determined, but rather tearful*): I'm going back to me mother's.

HELLIWELL: *Your mother's!* Why, if you go to your mother in this state o' mind at this time o' night, you'll give her a stroke.

LOTTIE: That's right. She must be about ninety.

MARIA (*angrily*): She's seventy-two. (*Pauses.*) And mind your own *business*. I've got some of it 'ere *for you.*

LOTTIE: What do you mean?

MARIA (*indicating things she's carrying*): Some of your new business, an' see 'ow you like it. You'll find it a change from carrying on wi' men behind the bar.

HELLIWELL: What in the name o' thunder are you talking about?

MARIA: I'm talking about 'er. If she wants my job, she can 'ave it.

LOTTIE: 〕 'Ere, just a minute——
HELLIWELL: 〕 Now listen, Maria——

MARIA (*silencing them by holding up keys and rattling*): There's all t' keys, an' you'd better start knowing where they fit. (*Puts them on table behind settee.*) An' don't forget charwoman's just been sacked, an' I don't expect Ruby'll stay. You'll have to manage by yourself a bit. An' greengrocer calls at ten and the butcher calls at half-past——

HELLIWELL (*shouting*): What does it matter when t' butcher calls?

MARIA (*calmly*): I'm talking to 'er, not to you. (*To* LOTTIE, *who looks astonished*) These is the housekeeping books an' you'll 'ave to 'ave 'em straight by Friday or he'll make a rumpus. 'Ere you are.

LOTTIE (*backing away*): I don't want 'em.

HELLIWELL (*harassed*): 'Course she doesn't——

MARIA: She can't run this house without 'em. You said so yourself. (*Throws books on to settee.*)

HELLIWELL: I know I did, but it's nowt to do with 'er.

MARIA: Then what did she come 'ere for? (*To* LOTTIE, *producing socks*) An' look, 'ere's five pairs of his socks and one pair of woollens (*hangs them on back of settee*) that wants darning, and you'd better get *started* on 'em. An' upstairs you'll find three shirts and two more pairs of woollens you'll 'ave to do to-morrow, an' you'd better be thinking o' to-morrow's dinner, 'cos he always wants something *hot* an' he's very *particular*—— (*Turns towards door.*)

LOTTIE (*aghast*): 'Ere, what do you think I am?

HELLIWELL: Now, Maria, you're getting it all wrong. Nobody knows better than me what a good wife you've been. Now 'ave a bit of sense, love. It's all a mistake.

MARIA: And there's a lot of other things you'll have to manage, but while you're trying to manage them and him, too, I'll be at Blackpool.

She goes, followed by HELLIWELL.

Enter ORMONROYD.

ORMONROYD: I know that face.

LOTTIE: Harry Ormonroyd.

ORMONROYD: Lottie, my beautiful Lottie. And you haven't forgotten me?

LOTTIE: Forgotten you! My word, if you're not off I'll saw your leg off. 'Ere, you weren't going to take their photos?

ORMONROYD: Yes, group for *Yorkshire Argus*. Make a nice picture—very nice picture.

LOTTIE: Nice picture! Don't you know? Haven't they told you? (*Roars with laughter.*)

ORMONROYD: Here now, stop it, stop it. Have a drink of port.

LOTTIE: Well, I suppose I might.

ORMONROYD: Certainly, certainly. Liberty 'All here to-night.

LOTTIE: Oh—it's Liberty Hall right enough. Chin—chin.

ORMONROYD: All the best, Lottie.

LOTTIE: Nice drop of port wine this. Joe Helliwell does himself very well here, doesn't he?

ORMONROYD: Oh, yes, Lottie, you'll find everything very comfortable here. 'Ere, somebody told me you were back at the Talbot.

LOTTIE: I was up to Christmas. Who told you? Anybody I know?

ORMONROYD (*solemnly*): Yes—now just a minute. You know him. I know him. We both know him. I have him here on the tip of my tongue. Er—— (*but can't remember*) no. But I'll get him, Lottie, I'll get him.

LOTTIE: Then I had to go home. Our Violet—you remember our Violet—she married a sergeant in the Duke of Wellington's—the dirty Thirty-Thirds—and now she's in India.

ORMONROYD (*remembering, triumphantly*): Tommy Toothill!

LOTTIE: What about him?

ORMONROYD (*puzzled by this*): Nay, weren't you asking about 'im?

LOTTIE: No, I've something better to do than to ask about Tommy Toothill.

ORMONROYD (*still bewildered*): Quite so, Lottie. But what were we talking about him for? Didn't you say he'd gone to India?

LOTTIE: No, you fathead, that's our Violet. Oh—I remember, it must have been Tommy Toothill 'at told you I was working at the *Talbot*—d'you see?

ORMONROYD (*still bewildered*): Yes, I know it was. But what of it, Lottie? Aren't you a bit argumentative to-night, love?

LOTTIE (*good-naturedly*): No, I'm not, but you've had a couple too many.

ORMONROYD: Nay, I'm all right, love. 'Ere, what's happened to your Violet?

LOTTIE (*impatiently*): She married a sergeant and went to India.

ORMONROYD (*triumphantly*): Of course she did. Somebody told me—just lately.

LOTTIE: I told you.

ORMONROYD (*reproachfully*): Yes, I know—I can 'ear. But so did somebody else. I know—Tommy Toothill!

LOTTIE: You've got him on the brain. Then at Whitsun—I took a job at Bridlington—but I only stuck it three weeks. No life at all —I told 'em, I says: "I don't mind work, but I do like a bit of life."

ORMONROYD: I'm just the same. Let's 'ave a bit of life, I say. An' 'ere we are, getting down in dumps, just because Tommy Toothill's gone to India.

LOTTIE: He hasn't, you piecan, that's our Violet. Nay, Harry, you're giving me the hump.

ORMONROYD: Well, play us a tune, just for old times' sake.

LOTTIE: Aaaa, you silly old devil, I'm right glad to see you.

ORMONROYD: Good old times, Lottie, good old times.

They sing. Interrupted by entrance of HELLIWELL, PARKER *and* SOPPITT.

HELLIWELL: Now what the hangment do you think this is—a taproom? *Yorkshire Argus* wants you on telephone.

LOTTIE: Come on, love, I'll help you.

HELLIWELL: And then get off home.

ORMONROYD: See you later.

ORMONROYD *and* LOTTIE *exit.*

PARKER: Now, what's wanted now is a few serious words in private together.

HELLIWELL: Yes, yes, Albert. I know. But give a chap time to have a breather. I've just had to persuade Maria not to go back to her mother's.

PARKER: Why, what can her mother do?

HELLIWELL: Oh—don't start asking questions—just leave it, Albert, leave it, and let me have a breather.

Enter the three wives, all with hats and coats on.

ANNIE: Now then—Albert—Joe—Herbert——

HELLIWELL: What is this—an ultimatum?

MARIA: Joe Helliwell, I want you to answer one question.

[213]   H

HELLIWELL: Yes, Maria?

MARIA: Joe, do you love me?

HELLIWELL (*embarrassed*): Now what sort of a question is that to come and ask a chap—here? Why didn't you ask me upstairs?

MARIA (*solemnly*): Once and for all—do you or don't you?

HELLIWELL: Yes, of course I do, love.

MARIA: Then why didn't you say so before?

All three women sit down, take off hats.

PARKER (*as if beginning long speech*): And now we're all by our-selves it's about time we started to put our thinking caps on, 'cos we're not going to do any good running round the 'ouse argy-bargy-ing——

MARIA: That's right, Albert.

PARKER: Yes, but let me finish, Maria. We——

He is interrupted by RUBY *appearing round door.*

RUBY (*loudly, cheerfully*): She's back!

MARIA: Who is?

RUBY: That Mrs. Northrop. (*Withdraws, leaving door open.*)

HELLIWELL (*loudly, in despair*): Oh—Jerusalem—we don't want 'er ere.

MRS. NORTHROP (*appearing, still carrying bag, and flushed*): If you don't want me here why did you send 'im round chasing me and askin' me to come back? Yer don't know yer own minds two minutes to-gether. (*To* MARIA) You 'aven't settled up wi' me yet, y'know.

HELLIWELL (*annoyed*): Outside!

PARKER (*hastily, anxiously*): Half a minute, Joe, we can't 'ave her telling all she knows—we'll be t'laughing stock of Cleckleywyke to-morrow.

MRS. NORTHROP (*contemptuously*): Yer've bin that for years, lad. I'd rather ha' Joe Helliwell nor you. Joe 'as 'ad a bit o' fun in his time, but you've allus been too stingy.

PARKER (*the word again*): Stingy! If anybody says that again to me to-night, they'll get what for, an' I don't care who it is.

HELLIWELL (*to* MRS. NORTHROP): I told you—outside—sharp!

MRS. NORTHROP (*full of malice*): Suits me. I reckon naught o' this for a party. You can't frame to enjoy yourselves. But then there's one or two faces 'ere that'ud stop a clock, never mind a party. But wait till a few of 'em I know 'ears about it! You'll 'ear 'em laughing at back o' t'mill right up 'ere.

PARKER: Now we can't let her go i' that state o' mind.

CLARA: You ought to charge 'er with stealin'.

MRS. NORTHROP (*horrified*): Stealin'! Why—for two pins—I'll knock yer lying 'ead off, missis. Never touched a thing i' my life that wasn't me own!

> RUBY *looks in, and* MRS. NORTHROP *sees her.*

What is it, love?

RUBY (*loudly, chiefly to* HELLIWELL): That photographer's asleep an' snoring be telephone.

HELLIWELL (*irritably*): Well, waken him up an' tell him to go home.

> RUBY *withdraws.* MRS. NORTHROP *takes charge again.*

MRS. NORTHROP (*significantly*): An' I *could* keep me mouth shut if it were worth me while——

CLARA (*almost hissing*): That's blackmail!

SOPPITT (*hastily*): Shut up, Clara!

MRS. NORTHROP (*looking at him*): Hello, *you've* come to life, 'ave yer?

HELLIWELL (*to* MRS. NORTHROP): How much d'you want?

MARIA (*angrily*): I wouldn't give her a penny.

CLARA (*quickly*): Nor me, neither.

PARKER (*quickly*): Can we trust 'er—we've no guarantee?

SOPPITT (*quickly*): She could sign something.

ANNIE (*quickly*): That'ud be silly.

MARIA (*quickly*): Not one single penny!

HELLIWELL (*angrily*): Will you just let *me* get a word in—an' be quiet a minute? Now then——

RUBY (*looking in*): Mr. Helliwell!

HELLIWELL (*impatiently*): What?

RUBY: I wakened 'im an' told 'im to go 'ome. But 'e says 'e *is* at 'ome. (*Withdraws as* HELLIWELL *bangs and stamps in fury.*)

HELLIWELL (*at top of his voice*): What *is* this—a bloody mad-'ouse?

MERCER (*off, but approaching*): Mr. Helliwell! Please!

HELLIWELL (*groaning*): Oh!—Jehoshaphat!—another of 'em!

> MERCER *enters.*

MERCER (*sternly*): Mr. Helliwell, I cannot allow you to use such language. It's quite unnecessary.

HELLIWELL (*protesting*): You wouldn't think so if——

MERCER (*cutting in*): *Quite* unnecessary. A little patience—a little quiet consideration—that's all that is needed.

[215]

HELLIWELL: What—with folk like her? (*Pointing to* MRS. NORTHROP.)

MERCER (*surprised and disapproving*): Mrs. Northrop! What are *you* doing here?

MARIA (*quickly*): Making trouble!

MERCER (*before* MRS. NORTHROP *can speak*): Making trouble? (*He stoops a little, near her.*) And you've been drinking again.

MRS. NORTHROP (*humble, crestfallen*): Only a drop or two—just because I was a bit upset——

MERCER (*accusingly*): And then you come and make a nuisance of yourself here. *T-t-t-t-t!* What's to be done with you? I am ashamed of you after all your promises.

MRS. NORTHROP (*humble and flattering*): Oh—Mr. Mercer—you're a wonderful man—an' you're t'only preacher i' Cleckleywyke worth listening to. (*To the others, roundly*) Aaaa!—he's a fine preacher is Mr. Mercer. Like—like a—gurt lion of a man! (*To* MERCER *admiringly*) Ay, y'are that an' all.

MERCER (*briskly, masterfully*): Now, Mrs. Northrop, flattery won't help. You've broken all your promises. I'm ashamed of you.

MRS. NORTHROP (*almost tearful now*): Nay—Mr. Mercer——

MERCER: Now—go home quietly——

MARIA (*quickly*): She'll tell all the town about us.

MERCER: We cannot allow that. Mrs. Northrop, you must make me a solemn promise.

MRS. NORTHROP (*looking up at him, humbly*): Yes, Mr. Mercer.

MERCER: Now promise me, solemnly, you will tell nobody what you've heard here to-night. Now promise me.

MRS. NORTHROP (*in solemn quavering tone*): I promise. (*Making suitable gestures.*) Wet or dry . . . may I die.

MERCER: T-t-t-t-t. But I suppose that will do. Now off you go, quietly home, and be a good woman. Good night, Mrs. Northrop.

MRS. NORTHROP (*humbly*): Good night, Mr. Mercer, and thank you very much. (*Turns at door to address the company.*) Aaaa!— he's a gurt lion of a man—— (*Fiercely, a parting shot*) Worth all you lot put together.

She goes.

HELLIWELL (*with relief*): Well, we're rid o' one. (*To* MERCER) Now have you studied that letter, Mr. Mercer?

MERCER (*producing it*): I've considered it very carefully. (*Impressively*) And you know what I think?

SEVERAL OF THEM (*eagerly*): No. Tell us. (*Etc.*)

MERCER (*slowly*): This letter—in my opinion—is perfectly genuine.

HELLIWELL (*disgustedly*): I thought you were going to tell us summat we didn't know.

MERCER (*ignoring this*): I am sorry to say it—but—quite obviously —you are, none of you, really married.

PARKER (*bitterly*): 'Ere, don't rub it in. (*Hopefully*) Unless, of course, you're prepared to marry us yourself—quietly—now.

MERCER (*indignantly*): Certainly not. Quite impossible.

HELLIWELL (*impatiently*): Well—what the hangment are we going to do, then?

MERCER (*turning to him impressively*): My dear sir—— (*Then quickly*) I don't know.

HELLIWELL (*disgusted*): Oh—Christmas!

MERCER: But if you want my final opinion, I think that if there were less bad temper and bad language in this house, and a little more patience and quiet consideration, you would have a better chance of settling your affairs.

HELLIWELL (*exasperated*): And *I* think I'm getting a bit tired o' you, Mr. Mercer.

MERCER (*very angry, towering over* HELLIWELL): What! After wasting my time, you now have the audacity—— Here!

HELLIWELL *flinches, but it is the letter he is being given.* Good night, sir. Good night, ladies.

He marches out and bangs doors. HELLIWELL *breathes heavily and wipes his face.*

HELLIWELL: Well, that's another we're rid of.

PARKER (*beginning in his usual style*): And now what's wanted——

CLARA (*cutting in, mimicking him*): Is a few serious words. We know. But what's really wanted now is a bit o' brainwork, and where we're going to get it from I don't know.

HELLIWELL (*severely to* CLARA): You'll get it from me if you'll keep quiet a minute.

They concentrate hard, and now ORMONROYD, *still carrying a large glass of beer, comes in and sits down in the chair centre, while they stare at him in amazement and disgust.*

ORMONROYD (*cheerfully*): Now—let's see—what were we talking about?

PARKER (*angrily*): We weren't talking about anything to you.

ORMONROYD (*ignoring this*): I wouldn't object to a nice hand at cards. (*To* HELLIWELL, *who is looking exasperated*) I like a game o' solo, don't you?

HELLIWELL: No. And I told you to get off 'ome.

ORMONROYD (*reproachfully*): Nay, but you want your photo o' t'group, don't you?

PARKER: You'll take no photos 'ere to-night.

ORMONROYD: Now it's a funny thing you should ha' said that. I'm a chap 'at notices things—I 'ave to be in my profession—an' I've been telling meself there's people 'ere in this 'ouse to-night who isn't easy in their minds. No, there's summat a bit off 'ere—just you see.

CLARA: Oh—for goodness' sake——

ORMONROYD (*to* HELLIWELL): And people has to be easy in their minds to be photographed. Nobody ever comes with the toothache, y'know, to 'ave their photos taken.

SOPPITT (*seriously*): No, I don't suppose they do. It never occurred to me—that.

ORMONROYD: Name, sir?

SOPPITT: Soppitt.

ORMONROYD: Ormonroyd 'ere. There's thought in this face. I'd like to do it some time in a nice sepia finish. Remind me, Mr. Soppitt.

> LOTTIE *enters.*

Ah, there y'are, Lottie. Join the company.

MARIA (*to* LOTTIE): I thought you'd gone long since.

HELLIWELL: You know very well you promised to go, half an hour since.

CLARA (*rises*): We ought to put police on you.

ORMONROYD: Now what's the idea of picking on Lottie? Why don't you live and let live? We're all in the same boat. We all come 'ere and we don't know why. We all go in our turn and we don't know where. If you are a bit better off, be thankful. An' if you don't get into trouble an' make a fool of yourself, well be thankful for that, 'cos you easily might. What I say is this—we're all human, aren't we?

ANNIE: Yes, and thank you, Mr. Ormonroyd.

PARKER: What yer thanking him for? Who's he to start telling us what we ought to do?

CLARA: Impudence, I call it. (*Telephone rings.*)

ORMONROYD: Oh, me? I'm nothing much. But in case you want to be nasty, Councillor Albert Parker, just remember though I may be nothing I 'appen to work for a newspaper. Behind me stands the

Press, don't forget that, an' the Press is a mighty power in the land to-day——

RUBY *enters.*

RUBY: Telephone went and when I says: "Who is it?" chap said: "*Yorkshire Argus*—is Ormonroyd, our photographer there?" an' when I says: "Yes, he's still 'ere," he says: "Well, tell him he's sacked." You're sacked. I'm sorry.

RUBY *exits.*

ORMONROYD (*suddenly crushed*): So am I, lass. I left a bag in 'ere somewhere.

LOTTIE: You must have left it down at *Lion*, lad.

PARKER: I thought 'e couldn't carry corn.

ANNIE: Shut up, Albert.

LOTTIE: Nay, Harry, you silly old devil, it's not so bad.

ORMONROYD: It's not so good. Hard to know where to turn.

LOTTIE: Come on, lad, never say die. We've seen a bit of life an' we'll see some more before they throw us on the muck heap. (*To others*) For two pins, I'd take him away now, and leave you to settle your own troubles—if you can.

HELLIWELL: Why—what's he got to do with our troubles?

LOTTIE: Plenty. Now, Harry, tell 'em where you were married.

ORMONROYD: Nay, Lottie, they don't want to hear about my bad luck.

PARKER: We've enough of our own, without his.

ANNIE: No, Albert. Come on, Mr. Ormonroyd.

LOTTIE: Tell 'em where you were married.

ORMONROYD: Lane End Chapel—five an' twenty years since.

HELLIWELL: 'Ere, he must be in t'same boat with us then.

ORMONROYD: Just another o' my bits of bad luck.

CLARA: We can understand that all right.

LOTTIE: Yes, but Harry 'ere had separated from his wife and they wanted to be free.

HELLIWELL: Well, what were they worrying for? They were free. Parson hadn't proper qualifications.

LOTTIE: Hold on a minute . . . go on, Harry.

ORMONROYD: I know he hadn't. Wife found that out. But what she'd forgotten, till I got a copy o' t'certificate, is that in them days —twenty-five years since—chapel wedding—registrar had to be there an' all—to sign certificate.

[219]

PARKER: Joe, he's right.

ORMONROYD: I know damn well I'm right. I've been carrying certificate for months trying to find a loophole in it—see for yourself.

CLARA: Are we married after all?

HELLIWELL: Yes, of course we are. If parson didn't tie us up, registrar did—all legal—as right as ninepence.

CLARA: Aaaaa, thank God!

MARIA: Mr. Ormonroyd, this is best night's work you ever did. Thank you.

LOTTIE: Now then, Harry, buck up, lad. Why don't you take that little photo shop in Blackpool again?

ORMONROYD: Nay, it 'ud cost me about a hundred pound to start it again—and I haven't a hundred shillings—an' I know you haven't.

LOTTIE: No, but there's folk here who'd never miss it.

PARKER: 'Ere, steady.

ANNIE: Albert, stingy again?

PARKER: Nay, never—if that's how you feel——

HELLIWELL: We'll soon fix you up, Ormonroyd lad, leave it to me. By gow, you've taken a load off my mind—— Aaaaa—— Now then, everybody, let's brighten up. (*At door.*) Who'll give us a song? Ruby . . . Ruby . . . bring some more drinks, lass. Owt you've got.

ANNIE: Let's sing a bit.

ORMONROYD: Lottie's the one. Come on, Lottie, play us a tune.

CLARA: Now then, Herbert Soppitt, you see, I am your wife after all.

SOPPITT: Yes, Clara, and I hope we'll be very happy. But we won't be if you don't drop that tone of voice. I don't like it.

CLARA: Yes, Herbert.

SOPPITT *begins to sing.*

PARKER: 'Ere, Joe, you wouldn't say I was dull and dreary, would you?

HELLIWELL: Ay, a bit, Albert.

PARKER: Well, that beats me. I've always seemed to myself an exciting sort of chap. (*To* ANNIE) Anyhow, stingy or whatever I am, I'm still your husband.

ANNIE: So it looks as if I'll have to make the best of you.

MARIA: We'll all have to make the best of each other. But then, perhaps it's what we're here for.

HELLIWELL: That's right, love.

[220]

PARKER: Well, we'd better see if we can have some of this fun of yours you talk about.

ANNIE: Aaaa, it doesn't matter, Albert.

PARKER: It does. I say we'll have some fun. (*Takes her hand and begins singing. They are all singing now.*)

ORMONROYD (*loudly*): All in your places. We'll have this group yet, and to hell with the *Yorkshire Argus!* Now, steady—steady—everybody.

Enter RUBY. *The flashlight goes off and* RUBY *drops her tray. But they are all singing as curtain falls.*

END OF PLAY

GOOD NIGHT CHILDREN

A Comedy of Broadcasting

CHARACTERS

(in the order of their appearance)

JOE COSSART, engineer
EDNA DARLINGTON, a secretary
DOROTHY LIMPLE, a secretary
BRENDA GEE, a secretary
BOB DINTY, an actor
HETTY LODORE, an actress
FAIRFAX HAYCRAFT, announcer
TRISTAN SPROTT, a producer
MOYA GRONOVA, a pianist
COMMANDER COPLEY, regional director
PAULA LEEDS, a producer
MARTIN BRADBURN, a producer
PERCY KING, effects boy
DAISY PUNNET, Matthew's grand-daughter
MATTHEW PUNNET, an ancient musician
SIR REGINALD RUNTON, D.A.D.G.

ACT I
Morning

ACT II
Middle of the Afternoon

ACT III
Evening

Good Night Children—Copyright, 1949, *by John Boynton Priestley.*

First produced at the New Theatre, London, on February 5th, 1942,
with the following cast:

EDNA DARLINGTON	JOSEPHINE DENT
BRENDA GEE	PATRICIA HAYES
JOE COSSART	CHARLES LAMB
DOROTHY LIMPLE	NAN HOPKINS
BOB DINTY	FRED GROVES
HETTY LODORE	EILEEN BELDON
FAIRFAX HAYCRAFT	PATRICK LUDLOW
TRISTIN SPROTT	NAUNTON WAYNE
MOYA GRONOVA	INA DE LA HAY
COMMAND COPLEY	CHARLES MORTIMER
PAULA LEEDS	GILLIAN LIND
MARTIN BRADBURN	MANNING WHILEY
PERCY KING	GEORGE COLE
DAISY PUNNET	JEAN SHORT
MATTHEW PUNNET	MEADOWS WHITE
SIR REGINALD RUNTON	LAWRENCE HANRAY

ACT I

The Scene is the English Broadcasting Company's regional studio in the remote county of Barset. It is a large square room, handsomely fitted out in the modern style. There is a door downstage right (actors'), which leads to the main entrance to the studio. There is another door on the same side at the back that communicates with the rest of the building, the offices, etc. Also on this side is a desk, used by FAIRFAX HAYCRAFT, *the announcer. Nearer the centre is a similar desk, used by* PAULA LEEDS. *Also in the centre are a small settee and one or two chairs. Further left is a grand piano. Then downstage left are microphones and a space for broadcasting. Behind is a glass-enclosed producers' control room, with a small flight of stairs leading up to it. There are no windows in the studio.*

Before the rise of curtain the interval signal of the E.B.C. is heard from the piano—on the second E.B.C. the curtain rises—on the fourth E.B.C. the "six pips" are heard, then the telephone signal flickers.

At Rise the studio is in half darkness, interval signal going. JOE, *a middle-aged solemn engineer, enters and goes to the telephone in control cabin.*

JOE (*at telephone*): No, this isn't the South-Western Dairy Farmers —it's the English Broadcasting Company——

> EDNA, *a rather colourless secretary, enters, puts files, etc. on centre desk, switches on lights and returns to desk upstage end. She is followed in by* DOROTHY, *who is a tall, handsome, rather stupid girl.*

—yes, the *English Broadcasting Company.* . . . No, I can't get your sister an audition.

> *Puts down telephone.*

DOROTHY (*left of desk*): This is a note from Commander Copley to Miss Leeds, explaining that the workmen will be in her office to-day and to-morrow.

EDNA: Miss Leeds will be very annoyed at being out here.

DOROTHY: Why? It won't kill her.

EDNA: We have two programmes going out from here to-day— the Children's Hour this afternoon and then Mr. Sprott's Barset programme to-night. Mr. Sprott will probably want to rehearse both this morning and this afternoon. So how can Miss Leeds do any work in here? Why couldn't Commander Copley have put her——

DOROTHY *starts to go up right.*

—in one of the other two offices?

DOROTHY: Because the workmen are going to be in there, too. There's something wrong with the walls.

EDNA: There's always something wrong with something here.

DOROTHY (*right of desk*): I don't know why you people are always grumbling. I like it here, and after all I've just had two years in London—at Radio House.

EDNA: Oh—I know why *you* like it here.

DOROTHY (*haughtily*): What do you mean?

Enter BRENDA *hurriedly. She is a lively young girl.*

BRENDA: Have you got a stop-watch?

EDNA (*hastily*): Yes, and you're not going to have it. What have you done with yours?

BRENDA (*drifting slowly across stage to sofa*): It's just gone again. I think somebody eats 'em. Oh dear—I wish they'd hurry up and give me that audition—I'm so tired of being a secretary. It isn't the life for me at all.

Re-enter JOE *from control room.*

JOE (*coming down*): Rehearsal here this morning, isn't there?

BRENDA: Yes, Mr. Sprott's programme for to-night—"Down Here in Barset".

JOE (*who is testing piano, mikes, etc.*): "Down Here in Barset"! I read what it said in the *Broadcasting Times*. "Another fascinating medley of folk-lore and song from a fragrant corner of old England!" Escapism, that's what I call it. (*At large arm mike.*) Fragrant Corner! (*Turns to* EDNA) Did you read what the County Medical Officer said? No, of course you didn't. But that's what they ought to be telling the workers—what the Medical Officer said—and never mind their fascinating medleys.

DOROTHY: I don't think that's being very loyal to the E.B.C.

JOE: Now listen, Miss Limple. 'Cos you're working for Commander Copley and he seems to have taken a fancy to you, that's no reason why you should start talking like him.

DOROTHY (*haughtily*): I don't agree.

Goes out.

BRENDA: I do hate that girl. I wish she'd stayed in London.

JOE (*now sitting on stool down left*): How are the impersonations coming along, Brenda?

BRENDA (*eagerly*): I'm working on Katherine Hepburn now. I

[226]

went to see her film again, last night. I think I've got her. Listen! (*Announces herself grandly.*) My next impression is that of the famous stage and film star—Katherine Hepburn—(*does something to her hair, then acts madly at* JOE, *who does not turn a hair.*) "Aw shucks, Larry, don't take it that way—I didn't mean it that way, Larry—all I meant was just the two of us to go right away somewhere—back to your ranch if that's what you want—I want light, I want freedom, Larry, I want the great spaces, my dear—yes, the silent music of the great spaces—don't you see, Larry?" Um?

EDNA: I don't think it's quite right yet, Brenda.

JOE (*rising*): Oh—I think it's good.

BRENDA: Thank you, Joe.

JOE: Who is it you're doing?

BRENDA (*surprised*): Katherine Hepburn.

JOE (*seriously*): Never heard of her.

> *Enter* BOB DINTY. *He is a middle-aged actor and an odd mixture of jauntiness and gloom.*

BOB: Morning, girls. Morning, Joe.

> *They reply cheerfully.*

I met a fella in the *Lion* last night who distinctly remembered me in *White Cargo* at Nottingham ten years ago. Knew me at once, he said. And stood a round on it. Got my scripts, Brenda?

BRENDA (*crossing to desk*): Yes, here it is. I'm working up the Katherine Hepburn now, Mr. Dinty.

BOB: That's right, just keep working them up, Brenda. I believe you have something—(*with a wink at the others*)—if you can only bring it out.

BRENDA (*eagerly*): You wouldn't like to hear——

BOB (*looking at script, crossing to couch*): Not to-day, dear. It 'ud take my mind off my work. Hetty been in yet?

> BRENDA *sits at* HAYCRAFT'S *desk.*

EDNA: I haven't seen her.

BOB: Still shopping, I expect. (*Begins to read script.*)

JOE (*approaching confidentially*): Bob!

BOB: Yes, old boy?

JOE (*confidentially*): Did you say anything to Haycraft about me doing that bit in the Children's Hour?

BOB: Yes, I did, old boy. But he didn't seem to catch on, you know what these chaps are.

JOE (*with great dignity*): They're afraid of the big realities.

[227]

Goes up into control room.

BOB (*deep in his script*): The way they cut the fat out of these parts —it's terrible. Too much stop-watch, that's the trouble.

BRENDA (*rises and crosses right of desk*): You haven't seen a stop-watch, have you?

BOB (*gloomily*): Not yet. But it'll be there all right when we start rehearsing.

> *Enter* HETTY, *a middle-aged actress. Her line is all sympathy, sweetness and light.*

HETTY (*sweetly*): Good morning, everybody. I hope I'm not late.

EDNA: No, Hetty, Mr. Sprott's not here yet.

HETTY: Thank you, Edna. Now, Brenda, can I have a look at my scripts? Quite a busy day to-day, isn't it? (*As she gets scripts*) Thank you, Brenda. The woman at the greengrocer's was *so* interested when she knew I was working for the E.B.C. She was almost certain she recognised my voice. Wasn't that nice? (*Crossing to couch.*)

BRENDA: Yes, Miss Lodore.

> *Moving above piano.*

HETTY: She insisted on me giving her my autograph for her niece at Weston-super-Mare. (*Confidentially to* BOB) I got a lovely duck, but she'll only cook it for lunch.

BOB: I don't want it for lunch, not with two shows ahead of us. The time for roast duck is when we've done our work.

HETTY: Yes, dear, but you see—she's going out this afternoon to see her sister—you know, the one who's——

BOB: Don't tell me. Life's bad enough without knowing what's gone wrong with the landlady's sister. The point is, she won't cook it for to-night, and I won't eat it at lunch time. So where are we?

> *Enter* FAIRFAX HAYCRAFT, *tall, humourless, and still the golden-voiced announcer.*

HAYCRAFT: Good morning. Anyone asking for me?

BRENDA: No, Mr. Haycraft, But there are two letters on your desk.

HAYCRAFT: Thank you, Brenda. (*Opening letter.*)

BOB: I appeal to you, Fairfax. Would you eat roast duck just before doing two shows?

HAYCRAFT (*horrified*): Good heavens—no, Bob! Certainly not! I've always made it a rule never to eat anything hours before announcing.

HETTY (*sweetly*): Yes, but you're different. Everybody knows *your* voice. You couldn't afford to take any risks, could you?

BOB: I suppose it doesn't matter if I gurk out of a million loud-speakers.

HAYCRAFT (*referring to letters*): Really, I must say some of these listeners are very tiresome—the arrogant way in which they talk about switching you on and off.

BOB: They've been spoilt, that's why. Pay half a guinea—and then expect sixteen hours' a day continuous entertainment for a year—it's been made too cheap, that's the trouble.

HAYCRAFT: You're probably right, Bob. (*Rising.*) Oh—Hetty—while I remember——

HETTY (*crossing to him, all attention*): Yes, Fairfax?

HAYCRAFT: When I say—at the beginning of our Children's Hour programme—"But where's Aunt Hetty this afternoon?" don't reply at once.

HETTY: All right. When do I reply?

HAYCRAFT: I'll call "Aunt Hetty, Aunt Hetty!" Then I'll go on: "I say, children, this is serious. No Aunt Hetty."

HETTY: Oh, I like that, Fairfax. Gives me quite a build-up.

BOB: What's the point of giving *you* a build-up?

HAYCRAFT: Now, Bob! Then you come running in—you can do it across the mike—breathless effect—"Here I am—*so* sorry, Uncle Fairfax. Hello, children!"

HETTY (*giving her best at once*): Oh—lovely! (*Does the breathless effect.*) "Here I am—*so* sorry, Uncle Fairfax! Hello, children!"

BRENDA (*in surprising child voice*): Hello, Aunt Hetty!

    Rises and sits on "Effects box".

BOB (*disgusted*): Good God!

HETTY (*sweetly*): Very clever, Brenda——

HAYCRAFT: And then we'll go straight on, Hetty. I thought of it at breakfast this morning. It just gives a little touch of suspense, doesn't it?

HETTY: Oh—yes—beautiful touch. I'll mark it in my script. (*Does so.*)

    Enter hurriedly TRISTAN SPROTT, *a fantastic youngish man, carrying telephone with very long lead and plug. He is followed by* MOYA GRONOVA, *very dark, intense, foreign, with her music MS. He stops abruptly.*

TRISTAN (*with great energy and decision*): Good morning, play-mates! Edna, get me Lovedale 4289.

Gives telephone to EDNA.

They reply "Good morning, *Mr. Sprott*," *or* "*Tristan.*" *He sits at desk centre.*

MOYA: But—Mr. Sprott, please, *please!* I know this music is wrong. There is some mistake in the copying—or something——

TRISTAN: Tell that to Tony Winter.

MOYA (*in despair*): But he's not here—he's gone to London.

TRISTAN: London! That reminds me. Has that effects boy from London arrived yet?

EDNA: No, not yet.

BRENDA: Could I do some effects? (*Slight move down.*)

TRISTAN: The only effect I want from you, Brenda, is that of a dead silence.

MOYA: But I *know* this music is wrong—and Tony Winter is away —and to-night we go on the air with it—so?

TRISTAN: We'll see what it sounds like at rehearsal. Go and chew it over at the piano—but quietly, quietly, we're very busy. Has an old man with a serpent arrived?

HETTY: What!

TRISTAN: It isn't that kind of serpent.

HETTY: What kind of a serpent is it then?

TRISTAN: It's a musical instrument. You blow them. My "Down Here in Barset" programme to-night will be unique, and the talk of all the tap-rooms. It may initiate a great national movement back to the land. Here—(*noticing* PAULA'S *desk*) is this mine? (*Opens drawer and picks out pair of stockings.*) Oh—no, it's Paula's. Oh dear, oh dear! Does this mean she's going to sit here all day watching us rehearse? That'll be too delicious.

EDNA (*at telephone*): Lovedale 4289.

TRISTAN: Thank you very much. (*As he goes to telephone*) I knew when I woke this morning and remembered *who* I was and *where* I was that this was going to be a most peculiar day. (*He has said the last words into the telephone.*) No, peculiar day's not the name. Tristan Sprott's the name—yes, E.B.C. Now what about that old man who plays the serpent—yes, Matthew Punnet—old Matt? . . . No, not yet—and I'll have to rehearse him for *hours*. . . . Oh, his grand-daughter's bringing him, is she? Daisy Punnet. Oh yes, of course, she's in my cast too. . . . You're sure they've left?

Enter DOROTHY.

DOROTHY (*proudly*): Commander Copley wants to speak to you all.

TRISTAN: What did you say?

[230]

DOROTHY: Commander Copley's coming in to talk to you all.

TRISTAN: Don't be silly. (*Back at telephone*) No, not you—one of the girls here. Now what about the other three rustics? . . . Can't leave before five? Coming in by car, are they? Well, tell them to come straight here and ask for me. I'll have to rehearse them like fury. We're on the air at eight-fifteen. All right, I'm depending on you to get 'em off clean and sober—and of course I'm desperately obliged. Good-bye.

> *Rises, crosses up left, drops receiver on to* BOB'S *lap.*

> *Enter* JOE *up right to control cabin.*

MOYA (*at piano*): Now, Mr. Sprott, listen—*please*—and you will see what I mean——

> *She plays a rather discordant phrase or two.*

> TRISTAN *downstage end of piano.*

TRISTAN: No, that can't be right. I rather like that.

> *Picks up glass with rose in it and takes it to sofa and sits.*

MOYA: But can it possibly be music for this so sweet rural pro-gramme "Down Here in Barset"?

TRISTAN: No, Moya. Someone has blundered. Just put back the sugar into it, will you.

> BOB *replaces receiver and sits box.*

JOE (*suddenly turning, loudly*): Pure escapism, that's what I call it.

TRISTAN: Now, Joe, not so rugged, please. Besides you've not seen Matthew Punnet yet and heard his serpent.

> COMMANDER COPLEY *enters. He is a solemn but professionally "hearty" type.*

ALL: Good morning, Commander.

TRISTAN: Now let's have it straight from the shoulder.

COPLEY: You're all here, aren't you?

DOROTHY: Miss Leeds isn't here yet.

COPLEY: Oh—isn't she? Well—er—that doesn't matter, really——

TRISTAN: And no effects boy yet either.

> *Picks pencil off centre desk.*

COPLEY: They've definitely sent one down. He'll be here any minute now. (*Looks round importantly.*) Look here, I've had a memo from Radio House—it's a circular thing, asking all us regional directors to give you all a bit of a jaw——

TRISTAN (*solemnly*): Not *really* a straight-from-the-shoulder.

COPLEY: That's about it, Tristan. Now I don't mind telling you all that I'm going to say to them at Radio House that, so far as this Barset regional station's concerned, no such talk from me or anybody else is necessary. I know you're trying to pull together. We've got our jobs to do, and a pretty important job it is too when you think of the number of decent people who are regular listeners these days——

HAYCRAFT (*seriously*): Hear, hear!

TRISTAN: Hear, hear!

COPLEY: There's been a tendency lately at Radio House to regard this particular regional studio of ours—perhaps because it's one of the smallest and furthest from London—to regard it, I say, as a kind of . . . (*hesitates*.)

TRISTAN: Chain gang for the hard cases.

COPLEY: Well, not quite that—Tristan exaggerates, as usual—but perhaps rather on those lines. And what seems to some of us here in Barset a pretty bad show——

HAYCRAFT: Definitely. It's all wrong.

TRISTAN: Oh—rotten bad show, chaps!

COPLEY: But as for making any appeals for your loyal co-operation and—er—asking you to play the game, I'm not going to do it —for the simple reason that I know jolly well that here in Barset it simply isn't necessary. We all know how to work together—and to play together. As I've said before—(*leaning on desk*)——

But the entrance of PAULA LEEDS *suddenly dries him up. She is an attractive, carelessly dressed girl, with a sardonic manner.*

PAULA (*going up right*): Good morning. (*She notices her desk— and stops.*) Sorry to interrupt the prize-giving—but isn't this my desk?

COPLEY: The workmen are in your office for a day or two.

PAULA (*sitting down*): So I'm practically out in the street.

TRISTAN: And shortly you'll be in the middle of my rehearsal.

PAULA (*sitting centre desk*): I thought of that too.

COPLEY (*to* PAULA *and* TRISTAN): By the way, I forgot to say that another producer is arriving from London this morning.

PAULA (*staggered*): What—*another* producer?

TRISTAN: Perhaps he's going to relieve you or me, Paula. Who is it?

COPLEY: I don't know—and—between ourselves—I think the whole thing rather preposterous. I've had a chit saying this fella —whoever he is—arrives to-day. He's written—*Demanding a Quiet Office*.

TRISTAN: He's got a hope!

PAULA: He'll be lucky if he gets a chair.

COPLEY: Also, he wants a full-time secretary, preferably Dorothy Limple——

DOROTHY (*interested*): You didn't tell me that.

COPLEY: Oh, he isn't going to claim you—don't worry. And then he asks for specially recorded rehearsals with playbacks——

PAULA: Local auditions, I'll bet.

BOB: And a full symphony orchestra.

COPLEY: All that sort of thing. Really, it's pretty steep. We're quite capable of producing anything that's required of us here, without all this nonsense.

TRISTAN (*with mock solemnity*): Of course we are.

COPLEY: I shall send him a stiff note—a rouser.

TRISTAN: Who, Rudolph?

COPLEY: Yes, Rudolph. Well—that's all—everybody, and thank you.

TRISTAN: He's going to send Rudolph a rude one, a rouser.

COPLEY *goes out, followed by* DOROTHY.

PAULA (*with irony*): Rudolph—Rudolph? Now where have I heard that name before?

TRISTAN (*in the same vein*): Rudolph Persimmon, dear. He's the director of our Drama Department—your director—my director—have you forgotten—is it all so long ago, dear?

PAULA (*in faint, far-away tone*): I've been so long here in Barset. And he never comes here, does he?

TRISTAN: Great heaven's, girl, no! He once borrowed a fur coat and an interpreter and spent half a day in Manchester. (*Sits sofa.*) By the way, I've discovered the most fabulous ancient—straight out of Hardy—who plays the serpent. I'm practically building to-night's programme round that serpent.

PAULA: And rehearsing him first here?

TRISTAN: Of course.

PAULA: Tristan, no good'll come of this.

TRISTAN: Why not?

PAULA: You're too enthusiastic. Every time you're enthusiastic something happens.

TRISTAN: But if I'm not enthusiastic, then nothing happens. And we're not quite Civil Servants, even yet.

HAYCRAFT: Tristan, there are several questions I'd like to ask——

MOYA (*suddenly starting up from piano*): Mr. Sprott—what shall I *do* about this music—I——

TRISTAN (*with decision*): Now listen—Bob—Hetty—all of you—get your scripts. I'll want you too, Brenda. Just as yourself, y'know—no impersonations.

BOB: But where are we going, old boy?

TRISTAN: Along to the little talks studio.

BRENDA: The workmen are in there too, Mr. Sprott.

TRISTAN: Then they must clear out for half an hour.

MOYA: But there's no piano in there.

TRISTAN: You can mark your cues, and we'll have a proper run through in here later this morning. Come on, chaps—play the game for old Barset——

As he shepherds them through the door PAULA *calls him back.*

PAULA: Tristan, just a minute.

TRISTAN: Yes, blossom?

PAULA: There isn't room here for another producer. So they must be relieving one of us. Um?

TRISTAN: If one of us can go back to London—then it has to be you. I've always known that.

PAULA: I *was* going to say it could be you.

TRISTAN: You'd let me go? But why, duckie? You know you loathe it here.

PAULA: Yes, but you still believe in broadcasting. I don't think I do. So I might as well be here as anywhere else. Besides——

DOROTHY *enters with memos.*

TRISTAN: Sh! Admiralty Intelligence approaching.

DOROTHY *gives one memo to* TRISTAN, *then puts another on* PAULA'S *desk.* TRISTAN *begins reading his, while* PAULA *ignores hers and looks across at* JOE.

PAULA: Good morning, Joe. I didn't notice you.

JOE: Morning, Miss Leeds. Sorry I couldn't manage a desk phone for you, but it 'ud be more bother than it would be worth.

PAULA: It doesn't matter, thanks, Joe. I'm hardly ever rung up. I don't think anybody except my mother and the administration department knows I'm here.

TRISTAN (*picks up memo from desk*): Joe, very interesting internal memo here. Just pay attention. (*Reads*) "In future, acting assistant directors bracket unpaid bracket will be differentiated from acting assistant directors by being designed as quotation mark A stroke A

[234]

quotation mark, the A stroke A without quotation marks being reserved for acting assistant directors." See?

JOE (*cautiously*): No, I don't quite follow that, Mr. Sprott.

TRISTAN (*going*): Never mind, it gives one a lift, so to speak—helps one through the morning, doesn't it?

Exit TRISTAN.

JOE *crosses to* PAULA *at desk.*

JOE (*with great solemnity*): If you want *my* opinion, Miss Leeds—it's this. Just as there's too much escapism about a lot of our programmes, there's a bit too much red tape in the administration.

PAULA: I think you've got something there, Joe. I'd work on it.

Nods, smiles, to dismiss him.

He goes out. EDNA *now picks up the bulky MS.*

EDNA: What about this? You said you'd send it back this morning.

PAULA (*looking at it with distaste*): Oh—dear—yes. *The Fall of Jerusalem,* a radio play by the Reverend A. S. Humphrey Harborough. I know his niece. This is what you get for knowing clergymen's nieces. (*Moving to sofa.*) All right.

EDNA *rises.*

(*Dictating.*) "Dear Mr. Harborough——" or is it Dr. Harborough? —"Thank you for letting me see your *Fall of Jerusalem.* I am afraid I must return it as unfortunately it would take about two hours and a half to perform, needs about fifty actors, a full chorus and orchestra, and would cost several thousand pounds to produce, and therefore it is rather too ambitious for our present scale of production. You could, of course, send it to our director of drama at Radio House, Mr. Rudolph Persimmon, but I'm afraid he has not recovered yet from the Fall of Old Vienna as you may have noticed from his programmes——"

EDNA *giggles.*

"No, you'd better leave that out. Stop after Persimmon. "I hope Eileen is well. It's a long time since I heard from her. Yours sincerely." And make a nice parcel of it, Edna.

EDNA: I'll be awfully glad to see the last of it.

PAULA: And ask about the copyright on those four items.

As she hands over the paper, DOROTHY *enters and without speaking or smiling, rather haughtily, deposits a memo on the desk. Exit.*

Well, what's the latest from the quarter-deck? (*Reads.*) "It has been recently brought to my notice that certain members of the senior staff have lately neglected to leave telephone numbers which would find them when off duty and away from their normal base. I should also like to remind them that office hours must be more strictly observed." My God, what cheek! I thought it was some little wreath of poison ivy by the way that girl handed it out. I'm sorry—but I don't like our Commander's new secretary. I hope she's not a bosom friend of yours by this time, Edna?

EDNA: No, I think she's too jolly conceited. I wouldn't mind if it were just because she's so attractive to look at—and she is, you know——

PAULA: Oh yes, a terrific charmer.

EDNA: Well, I wouldn't mind that, but she's so pleased with herself because she's had two years in Radio House.

PAULA: I've had ten years of it in London, and I—but—perhaps I'm as bad. Oh dear!

EDNA: Oh—no—it's different for you.

PAULA (crossing to desk): Thank you, Edna. Always a comforting phrase that—different for us. I don't believe it, but I like it. (Sits desk.)

EDNA (rises): I'll get these things done upstairs—shall I?

PAULA: Do.

EDNA goes out. PAULA works quietly for a few moments.

The next time she looks up it is because MARTIN BRADBURN has entered. He is an attractive, serious, enthusiastic, untidy fellow in his early thirties. He marches in, then stops short as he notices PAULA.

MARTIN (obviously dismayed): Good lord!

PAULA (with hint of rebuke): Good morning!

MARTIN (with suggestion of apology): Oh—good morning!

PAULA (laughing): Oh—good lord! (Swings round.)

MARTIN: I didn't know you were here.

PAULA: They ought to have warned you.

MARTIN: Why ought they to have warned me?

PAULA: I don't know, but you seemed pretty taken aback. As if there'd once been something rather desperate between us. If there was, it simply escaped my memory, that's all. Perhaps it's living in the country.

MARTIN (rather confusedly): No, of course not. Stupid of me to give you that impression. The fact is, I never went to bed last night —what with one thing and another.

PAULA: I see. Well, we did have rather a row about that series we did together—when was it—two years ago? I gathered then you weren't exactly mad on me.

MARTIN: Well, you gave me to understand very plainly that *I* wasn't exactly your favourite colleague either. You ended by calling me a conceited ape.

PAULA: But that was after you'd called me a viperous virgin.

MARTIN: Did I? We did have a stinking row, didn't we? (*Sits and looks pleasantly at her.*) But—you know—there was something about you that brought out the worst in me.

PAULA: I know what you mean. It's practically hate at first sight. You seem rather more human down here, but I expect that'll soon wear off. You're not, by any chance, the producer we're expecting— a quiet office, full-time secretary, recorded rehearsals, symphony orchestras——?

MARTIN: All right, all right, I catch the note of sarcasm. But naturally I asked for a few reasonable conditions when I said I wanted to come down here——

PAULA: Wait a minute! You *asked* to come down here?

MARTIN: Yes, of course. They didn't want to let me go—Rudolph was piling the programmes on me in town—but I insisted——

PAULA: You're not wearing a hair shirt as well, are you?

MARTIN: You've got it all wrong. (*Rises, obviously embarrassed.*) Actually this is all the wildest piece of self-indulgence.

PAULA: Are you sure you've come to the right region? This is Barset, you know—B for boring, A for awful, R for rural, S for stupid——

MARTIN (*breaking in*): I wish you wouldn't be facetious all the time. I remember how it annoyed me before. Must be a complex or something.

PAULA (*quietly*): It happens to be shyness.

MARTIN (*surprised*): Good lord!

PAULA: We're not going to begin that again, are we?

MARTIN: Sorry! I was genuinely surprised.

PAULA (*rises and crosses to front of desk*): I hate to say it, but— you've been doing some lovely work, you know. I thought that liner programme was beautifully produced.

MARTIN: Oh—you heard that one, did you? But, you see, producing—in the theatre—is really my job.

PAULA: I know. But what made you insist upon doing a programme down here?

MARTIN Because I'm mad—I—(*checks himself.*)

PAULA: Well?

[237]

MARTIN: Dorothy Limple *is* here, isn't she?

PAULA: Yes. Oh!—I see.

MARTIN: Yes, I'm as mad as that. (*Rises and crosses to door and back to* PAULA.) What's she doing here?

PAULA: She's secretary to our director, Commander Copley.

MARTIN: Don't know him. What's he like?

PAULA: Oh—just a strong silent man from the blue water. No interest in drama, music, entertainment, talks—and probably hates broadcasting.

MARTIN (*grinning*): I'll bet he hates *you.*

PAULA: He does. And wonders why I was wished on him.

MARTIN: Why were you?

PAULA: I was too impertinent. At the programme meetings, when we discussed everything, but always got back to the last waltz in Old Wien, our romantic Rudolph never quite liked the look in my eye. So they said "Barset for you, my girl." And wait until you've had a few weeks down here. Love may find a way—and all that—but——

MARTIN: I'm not sure I'd call it love exactly——

PAULA: Well, you'll have plenty of time to settle all that, Bradburn. Hadn't you better report to the quarter-deck? (*Moving to desk and pushing him.*)

MARTIN (*gloomily*): Suppose I had. Where is the Admiral, Leeds?

PAULA: Through that door. (*Sits.*)

As he turns towards door DOROTHY comes through, and then stops in surprise at seeing him.

MARTIN: Dorothy!

DOROTHY: Martin! (*Stops by* HAYCRAFT'S *desk.*) Oh—this is ridiculous. I wondered if it was going to be you.

MARTIN (*going to her*): I want to explain——

DOROTHY: There's nothing to explain.

MARTIN: Of course there is.

DOROTHY: There *isn't.* And you'd no *right* to come here—it makes me—Oh—it's so stupid. *Please.*

Brushes past him. He follows her.

MARTIN: But Dorothy!——

She goes out and he follows her. PAULA with a shrug, turns to her work again. PERCY enters and collides with MARTIN. He is an imperturbable Cockney youth, and talks American slang with a

[238]

London accent. He taps PERCY *on shoulder.* PAULA *looks up and recognises him.*

PERCY: Remember me, Miss Leeds?

PAULA: Of course I do, Percy. How are you?

PERCY: Fine and dandy.

PAULA: I'm fine but I'm not dandy.

PERCY: Remember the bother we 'ad with them French Revolution noises?

PAULA: Yes, Percy, I don't know how I'd have made the French Revolution without you.

PERCY: What's it like 'ere, Miss Leeds?

PAULA: I don't think you'll enjoy it much.

PERCY: No. Country, isn't it?

PAULA: Yes, there's quite a lot of country round here, Percy, you know, fields and cows and sheep and so on.

PERCY: I thought so. Worse than Bristol.

PAULA: Oh, much worse than Bristol.

PERCY: Too slow for me, I like to step out and go places. (*Sees the piano.*) 'Ere, would you mind if I played a bit of dirt?

PAULA: No, go ahead, Percy, and express yourself.

He dashes over to the piano and plays some swing music in a fine slapdash style. He is interrupted by GRONOVA, *who rushes in.*

GRONOVA: No, no, please, please!

PERCY: Please what?

GRONOVA: Please stop this horrible playing——

PERCY: Don't you like swing?

GRONOVA: No, it is terrible!——

PERCY: Oh, classical pianist, eh?

GRONOVA: Yes, a musician—and to-day is very difficult—we are in all kinds of trouble with the programme.

PERCY: Listen, sister, you can't tell *me* anything about trouble with programmes——

GRONOVA: Then you will understand—and excuse me——

PERCY: Sure, I'll excuse you—— 'Ere, can you play Bach? (*He pronounces it—Batch.*)

GRONOVA (*all smiles*): Bach! Yes, for years I have played Bach, you like him, eh?

PERCY: I think he's a piece of cheese!

[239]

TRISTAN *enters down right hastily. He has his coat off now, and looks very wild.*

TRISTAN (*right up to* PERCY): Where is that effects boy? (*Sees* PERCY.) Ah—(*and peers at* PERCY)—there you are! I couldn't be more relieved. I suddenly thought I must have imagined you, after you just popped in and out like that.

PERCY: You wouldn't need a bit of good swing in this programme of yours, would you, Mr. Sprott?

TRISTAN: *I* would, but the programme wouldn't. It's all rural, y'know. Dainty old-world. Dear old rustic Barsetshire. What I do want is a reaper, and cider gurgling down, and the sound of darts and shove-ha'penny at the old *Brown Cow*.

PERCY (*complacently*): I've done plenty of them.

TRISTAN: I'll show you a script. Come on.

He goes out.

PERCY (*as he goes, to* PAULA): Looks like he's out on a limb, Mr. Sprott. I like your style better, Miss Leeds. You've a poker face.

Goes out.

PAULA: And bless his little heart, I say. (*Looks at* GRONOVA, *who has sat down, and plays a few notes—distressed.*) What's the matter, Moya?

GRONOVA: Everything. (*Rises.*) It is one of those days, my dear. When life is altogether too much. Not large and simple and beautiful —it is then we are happy. But small, petty, and yet—terrible. (*Sits.*) Like that awful *sweeng*. (*Rises, crosses to her.*) Yes, this sweeng— it expresses this small but terrible life we live. Yet life could so easily be large and simple and beautiful——

PAULA: No Chekhov, Moya, please! I don't like Chekhov in the morning.

GRONOVA (*back to her and leans over desk*): You pretend to be hard, Paula my darling, just to protect your real self—your lovely tender inner self.

PAULA: There might be something in that, but don't start working on it.

GRONOVA: If I were a man, my dear, I would make love to you —just to be able to pull aside that mask. I think I must take an aspirin. Have you one, please?

Crosses and sits settee right.

PAULA: Not here. (*Rises.*) Edna will have some. She lives on them in a quiet, ladylike way.

PAULA *goes to telephone.*

Miss Darlington, please! . . . Oh Edna, have you any aspirin? . . . Well, pop one in water and bring it here for Moya. Perhaps you'd better make it two.

As she turns away from the telephone, DOROTHY *enters a pace or two in front of* MARTIN, *who is still arguing with her.* DOROTHY *makes straight for the other door.*

MARTIN (*pursuing*): What's the good of telling me it's undignified? It's more than that—it's damned fatuous. But we've got to have it out—we can't go on like this.

She has gone now, and he has followed.

GRONOVA *has risen and moved a little up.*

GRONOVA (*all eyes and ears*): Did you hear him? (*Turns to* PAULA.)

PAULA (*rather grimly*): I did. (*Sits on sofa.*)

GRONOVA: He must be crrr-azy about her. That's how I like to see a man behave. (*Sits left of* PAULA.)

PAULA: Well, I don't. I take his word for it—it's not only undignified but damned fatuous. And even if it wasn't, she isn't worth it. She's been making great eyes at Copley ever since she arrived here.

GRONOVA: He is attractive to some types. To me—no.

PAULA: To me—no, too.

Enter EDNA *with glass, and memos, etc.; she gives the glass to* GRONOVA, *then gives memos to* PAULA.

GRONOVA: Thank you very much, my dear. (*Begins to drink.*)

EDNA *sits at her desk.*

PAULA (*looking at memos*): Here's news. (*Reads.*) "In succession to Brigadier Townson, Sir Reginald Runton, formerly assistant secretary to the Board of Fisheries, has now been appointed deputy-assistant director-general of the English Broadcasting Company." Isn't that nice? I don't think we've had anybody from the Fisheries before. I wonder if he'll notice any difference. (*Looks at* GRONOVA, *who is staring at her.*) What's the matter? Do you know Sir Thingumty Thing—Sir Reginald Runton?

GRONOVA (*with dramatic air*): That is what I am asking myself.

PAULA: And what are you going to reply to yourself?

GRONOVA (*to* EDNA): This Runton—it is not a common name, is it?

EDNA: No, it isn't.

GRONOVA (*to* PAULA): How strange it would be if it were him— my first delicious romance. I think I've told you something of it before.

[241]

PAULA: I only remember the one who locked you up in his castle in the Dolomites. He couldn't have ended up at the Board of Fisheries, could he?

GRONOVA: No, of course not. He was Austrian, of course. But this first one of all—when I was a girl at the Brussels Conservatoire —he was a young Englishman—and we were madly in love and ran away to the Ardennes—it was in June—a lovely June——

EDNA: But was his name Runton?

GRONOVA (*rises and crosses to* EDNA): Yes—and he had enchanting blue eyes—and a melting voice. . . .

PAULA: It must have been a lovely June that year. But was he Reginald? Did you call him your Reggie?

GRONOVA: That I can't remember. You see—he asked me to call him by the name he was known by at school and college—Topsy.

PAULA: Good lord!

GRONOVA (*dreamily*): He had beautiful fair curling hair . . . but he was jealous of my music. There was a terrible scene—oh terrrr-ible! No, no, it couldn't possibly be the same one. I'm stupid to-day. Why am I so stupid to-day? Why is life like that? (*Sits settee right.*)

PAULA: Finish your aspirin, Moya, and never mind about life. (*Looks at a letter.*) Edna—(*round to desk and sits*)—tell London I never had those sea-shanty recordings here. Tell them I never touch a sea-shanty—or a negro spiritual—or any of that gorgeous maddening Tzigane stuff, either.

EDNA (*taking* GRONOVA'S *glass*): All right. (*Rises.*) Will you sign the letter returning the script?

PAULA *does.* HAYCRAFT *enters mopping his brow delicately.* EDNA *goes out up right.* GRONOVA *gets up.*

HAYCRAFT (*going to his desk*): I don't see how Tristan can do anything about his programme until all those local people turn up.

GRONOVA (*tragically*): I have a feeling they will not turn up.

HAYCRAFT: Why shouldn't they? They always do.

GRONOVA (*moving down to door down right*): I don't know. But I have a feeling they won't. (*To door.*) So everything will be absolutely chaos.

Goes out.

HAYCRAFT (*solemnly*): It's chaos at the moment all right. And I'm afraid our Children's Hour programme isn't very much better. It's absurd when we only get it once a fortnight that wc can't organise the thing better than this. You know—(*down to* PAULA)—Paula, I *like* doing the Children's Hour.

PAULA (*turns to him*): I know you do, Fairfax.

HAYCRAFT: It's all very well for some of you people to scoff——

PAULA (*who isn't*): I'm not scoffing.

HAYCRAFT (*very much himself*): But it's the only thing I really enjoy doing nowadays. Do you remember that little series I did—*Friends in Twilight?* Just a few records and readings of selected passages suitable for a friendly twilit hour. They were an enormous success. A wealthy widow in Torquay wrote asking me to name my own terms——

PAULA: What to do?

HAYCRAFT: Oh just to go and do some more *Friends in Twilight* readings for her. I had to refuse, of course.

PAULA: Why?

HAYCRAFT: Oh—well—(*sits at his desk laughing.*)

Enter COPLEY *and* MARTIN. *They cross to downstage left.*

COPLEY (*confidentially*): Now look here, Bradburn, I don't quite understand why you've been sent down here, but of course I'll do what I can to give you everything you want. But you must understand, my dear chap, that Miss Limple's now my secretary—a very responsible job—and so you can't possibly commandeer her services. So why go on worrying her?

They stop on their return walk.

MARTIN: I'm not after her services.

COPLEY: I understood you were.

MARTIN: I'm not worrying her, as you call it, about that, but about some personal matter. You see, I saw a great deal of her in London.

COPLEY: Oh—did you? She didn't tell me that.

MARTIN: There are probably a lot of things she doesn't tell you.

COPLEY (*after pause, coldly*): Well?

MARTIN (*irritably*): Well what?

COPLEY: Is that all you've got to say?

MARTIN: What do you want—the story of my life?

COPLEY: I think I'm right in saying—you're not engaged to Miss Limple—or anything of that kind?

MARTIN: What's anything of that kind? But if you must know, I was infatuated with the girl for months—still am, apparently, or I shouldn't be here—and God knows why I *am* here——

Moves up and sits on piano stool.

[243]

Enter DAISY PUNNET, *a girl about twenty, with round red cheeks, round staring eyes, and a startling loud voice, which she never modulates, and a Barsetshire accent. She comes plump in, then stands and looks about her. The others stare at her in surprise.*

DAISY: Is my grand-dad here?

COPLEY: Oh—I say—what is this?

DAISY: I brought 'im to the door an' said, "Look grand-dad, you stay 'ere a minute while I go across to that shop for a meat pasty for your lunch," an' now I can't find 'im anywhere.

COPLEY: But—look here—this is an E.B.C. studio, y'know, missie——

DAISY: I know it is, mister. That's why we're 'ere.

HAYCRAFT (*rises and comes down to her right*): Oh—you're in Mr. Sprott's programme, are you?

DAISY (*going closer*): That's it. Oh—I say—I know *your* voice.

HAYCRAFT (*pleased*): Do you?

DAISY: Course I do. 'Eard it ever since I can remember. Aren't you the announcer, Farfax Haycraft?

HAYCRAFT: Well—yes—I am.

DAISY (*giving bag to* COPLEY *and producing autograph book*): Give me your autograph, please. It's not for us, but for my cousin Ethel—but I know she'd like yours. (*As he signs the book.*) I'll bet my grand-dad's wandering round 'ere somewhere. (*Takes bag from* COPLEY.) He's getting a bit—y'know——

MARTIN *moves down to arm of settee.*

—soft, though he'll be a good turn in your programme if you all keep right side of 'im. But y'ave to watch him.

HAYCRAFT (*the charmer*): Let's see if we can find him, shall we?

He escorts her through door.

COPLEY (*moving down left, confidentially to* MARTIN): You were saying?

MARTIN (*down to right of* COPLEY): Oh lord!—I don't know what I was saying. Can't you see the idiotic state I'm in? And been in it for weeks—ever since we had that row. And the girl isn't even intelligent!

COPLEY (*stiffly*): I've found Dorothy an extremely intelligent girl. But we're not here to discuss her.

MARTIN: We're not here to discuss anything.

They pace across and up to door then down again.

[244]

COPLEY: Yes, we are, Bradburn. Now look here, my dear chap, I can see you're a bit nervy and all that—know how you fellas get—with all this theatrical stuff you have to deal with. I'm not going to lecture you. Not my style. And your personal affairs have nothing to do with me, of course. But I'm here to run this studio—

COPLEY *stops near desk*—MARTIN *is left of him.*

to see that everybody pulls their weight and is happy about it and all that, and I simply can't have anybody barging in and upsetting everybody——

Enter BRENDA *down right.*

BRENDA (*loudly and cheerfully*): Anybody seen a stop-watch?

COPLEY (*turning*): Never mind about the stop-watch for the moment, Brenda. This is Mr. Martin Bradburn. Until Hilda comes back from her holidays or they send us somebody else, you'd better act as Mr. Bradburn's secretary.

BRENDA: What! With Mr. Sprott and Mr. Haycraft on my hands already!

COPLEY: You'll find Brenda very quick and clever, Bradburn. She's good at—er impersonations too, aren't you, Brenda? There now!

Hurries out, leaving MARTIN *and* BRENDA *staring at each other, and* PAULA *watching, amused.*

BRENDA (*wistfully*): You wouldn't like to hear one of my impersonations, would you, Mr. Bradburn?

MARTIN: Good God! He really meant it then.

Moves up to HAYCRAFT'S *desk.*

BRENDA (*in front of settee, firmly*): Beatrice Lillie.

MARTIN *sits on desk and stares at her in horror.* BRENDA *begins a quite unconvincing imitation of Beatrice Lillie.* PAULA, *taking a stop-watch from her drawer, now takes charge.*

PAULA (*below desk to* BRENDA): That'll do, Brenda. We're just not receptive this morning. But here's the stop-watch. I'll never see it again but it's probably worth it. Now run.

BRENDA *takes it and hurries out.* PAULA *sits left of sofa. Looks at him.*

MARTIN (*groaning, sits edge of desk*): I think I'm going mad. Beatrice Lillie and grand-dad and that man Copley—*my dear chap!* And I can't get a glimmer of sense out of Dorothy and until I do I don't know where I am. Why did I come here?

PAULA: Don't ask me, Bradburn.

MARTIN: All right, Leeds. If you wanted your revenge, take a good look at me now.

PAULA: I'm not the vindictive kind, strange as it may seem.

MARTIN: Is Copley like that all the time?

PAULA: Practically all the time.

MARTIN: Good lord!

PAULA: Also, he's considered rather a charmer round here.

MARTIN: Brenda?

PAULA: I don't know about poor Brenda. But there are—others.

MARTIN (*sits on settee*): No, I don't believe it. And don't tell me you aren't vindictive, Leeds.

PAULA: I'm not. Before, I always thought you clever—but insufferable. Now I see you're not so clever—but almost sufferable.

Enter DOROTHY. PAULA *sees her*. MARTIN *rises*.

And this is where I go up to my own office, even if I have to fight my way in through workmen. And—Dorothy——

DOROTHY: Well?

PAULA (*as she goes out*): Have a heart.

Goes.

MARTIN (*moving across*): Listen, Dorothy, if you won't come out——

DOROTHY: How can I? I'm the studio director's secretary and I've lots to do and——

MARTIN: All right, if you can't, you can't. But then, for God's sake, let's talk here for a minute.

DOROTHY: Can't you *wait*?

MARTIN: No, I can't. And if you were in anything like the same state of mind that I'm in, you couldn't either. Now listen—you remember what you said the last time we saw each other in London?

DOROTHY (*comes to front of desk and puts memo there*): I said a lot of things. And so did you. And some of them were pretty silly too.

MARTIN (*savagely*): All right then, let's stop being pretty silly—as you call it. Let's be tough about it, if that's what you want. Though God knows what you *do* want——

Behind settee to mike down left.

JOE *enters and goes towards mikes, etc.* MARTIN *sees him.*

Oh—for the love of Pete!

DOROTHY: Sh!

MARTIN (*in tense whisper*): Sometimes I think I simply don't see you as a real person at all.

DOROTHY (*also in tense whisper*): I shouldn't be surprised at that either.

MARTIN: It might be just a kind of image I fell in love with. I tell myself——

JOE (*shouting at mike*): How's this, Fred? Give me two buzzes if it's okay.

Only one buzz comes.

MARTIN (*trying again*): I say, I tell myself it's just a beautiful image, planted in my imagination and not a real girl, a person——

JOE (*as before*): Well, give me some more juice, Fred. Now listen —Monday, Tuesday, Wednesday, Wednesday, Thursday—the boy stood on the burning deck—is that better?

Two buzzes.

Okay, Fred, I'm coming up.

On his way out passes the other two below him and smiles at them cheerfully not noticing their tenseness at all.

JOE: We have to take advantage of these quiet spells, haven't we?

Goes out.

DOROTHY: If you want to know who's not been real in all this I can tell you—it isn't me, it's you.

MARTIN: What do you mean by that?

DOROTHY: I mean, I got sick and tired of being pulled this way and that way, never allowed to be just myself, with you always arguing and analysing and theorising, until I didn't know where I was.

Sits settee.

MARTIN: I'll bet you know where you are down here all right.

DOROTHY (*defiantly*): Yes, I do. But just as I'm beginning to settle down again, you come here and want to start all over again——

MARTIN: It isn't a question of starting all over again. You left me in a hellishly disturbed state of mind—I've not been able to work properly or think straight—so I came down——

DOROTHY: To start all over again, only worse than before.

MARTIN (*tensely*): I came to discover if I had any meaning for you—and if I had any meaning for you——

LOUD VOICE (*from Speaker*): What are you saying, Joe?

MARTIN (*trying to ignore this*): Look what happened. I was crazy about you. I couldn't——

VOICE (*from Speaker*): I thought you said you were coming up, Joe.

MARTIN (*losing his temper*): Oh—shut up!

[247]

DOROTHY *has now turned away and is making muffled sounds with her shoulders shaking.*

(*Turns back to her.*) Well, there's no need to cry.

DOROTHY (*turning*): I'm not crying. I'm laughing.

MARTIN (*angrily*): I used to have a sense of humour too.

DOROTHY: I never thought you had much.

MARTIN (*horror-struck*): What—*me*! And *you* can say that! I suppose this old sea-dog Copley supplies just about your brand of fun.

DOROTHY (*demurely*): Commander Copley says some very amusing things.

MARTIN (*groaning*): Oh!—God help us! But it serves me right, it serves me right. (*Sits beside* DOROTHY. *Collects himself, solemnly.*) Now listen, Dorothy. One last serious word——

And this is the cue for the entrance of MATTHEW PUNNET, *a very ancient be-whiskered rustic who arrives carrying a serpent of great size and blackness. His speech is almost unintelligible. At first he just comes a step inside.*

PUNNET: 'Marnin, marnin'. (*Chuckles horribly.*)

MARTIN *stares at him in horror. But there is no escape. Now the Ancient comes right in.*

Be he the E.B.C.?

MARTIN: What do you say? (*Rises and crosses to* PUNNET.)

PUNNET: Be he E.B.C.?

MARTIN *moves up a little between desk and piano, then comes back.*

DOROTHY: Yes, this is the E.B.C. studio. (*Rises.*)

PUNNET (*crossing and sits on settee, chuckling*): If he be E.B.C. I be sitting roight ahere awaitin' my tarn to play ould sarpent.

Chuckles, produces one deep note, and then waits for their applause.

DOROTHY: I think he's one of the local people for Tristan Sprott's programme.

MARTIN (*crosses to* HAYCRAFT'S *desk right*): And I think I'm going to have a nervous breakdown.

DAISY *rushes in down right, followed by* HAYCRAFT.

DAISY (*crossing to* PUNNET *and sits right of him: shouting*): He's here. Where you been, grand-dad?

HAYCRAFT: How d'you do, Mr. Punnet?

Stands right of settee.

[248]

PUNNET (*pointing to* HAYCRAFT, *but to* DAISY): He be mortal image o' Farmer Bates' cowman.

HAYCRAFT: What does he say?

DAISY (*shouting*): He says you're the image of Bates' cowman.

HAYCRAFT (*making the best of it*): And am I?

DAISY: No, he's younger than you.

> PAULA *enters up right and goes to her desk, but notices the* PUNNETS, *etc., with amusement.*

JOE'S VOICE (*from Speaker*): Mr. Sprott down there yet?

PUNNET (*rising in alarm*): Be it my tarn to play sarpent already?

DAISY: No, sit down and be quiet, grand-dad.

HAYCRAFT (*into mike, with great charm*): No, Joe, he's not here. I've been looking for him myself. Two of his cast have arrived.

JOE'S VOICE: Okay, I'll wait.

PUNNET (*indicating* HAYCRAFT): What's 'e mutterin' about?

DAISY (*humorously*): He's tellin' 'um you're going to 'ave some cider with your dinner.

MARTIN (*to* DOROTHY): This is Bedlam. Let's go out and have an early lunch.

> HAYCRAFT *sits on right arm of settee.*

DOROTHY (*coldly*): No thanks.

MARTIN: But we *must* talk.

DOROTHY: You mean, you must make a scene. Besides, I'm busy. And I happen to be working for somebody I respect. (*Turns and goes towards door.*)

MARTIN (*following*): It's our last chance, Dorothy. I mean it.

> *But she goes out, and he stays this side of door. The others are grouped round old* PUNNET, *looking at his serpent.*

> PAULA *looks at* MARTIN.

> *Enter* TRISTAN, PERCY (*to effects box*) *with scripts, etc.,* GRONOVA (*to piano*), BOB (*right of piano*), HETTY (*to chair left*), BRENDA (*to* HAYCRAFT'S *desk*). HAYCRAFT *goes behind settee.*

> TRISTAN *sees* MARTIN *as he crosses him to door.*

TRISTAN: Hello, old man.

MARTIN: Hello, Tristan.

TRISTAN: Excuse me a moment. Now just spread yourselves, playmates. What sort of rehearsal this'll be, with three of the local cast still missing, God knows, but we'll have some sort of a run-through. (*As the others get into their places, he turns to* PAULA

[249]

and MARTIN.) Paula, for the love of Pete, take him away, and then I'll be rid of you both. It's not fair, it's really not fair, you two being here. It simply isn't *done*.

MARTIN: I think I'll go and drink myself to death.

PAULA: No, you won't. You'll come out and have an early lunch with me. Only don't try and eat yourself to death. (*Rising, to door.*)

TRISTAN: That's the spirit. Off you go.

MARTIN: Nice of you. Though I'll be rotten bad company.

PAULA (*as she moves down with him*): Oh—we'll work up a cheerful little quarrel.

> *They go out.*

TRISTAN: Are you all ready? I want to try and get some sort of timing on the whole thing—and even though those three aren't here, Miss Punnet and grand-dad can get into it a bit—and we can work in the music and effects. I won't go up into the box yet. But remember next time it'll be light cues. First light for the record, Percy. Second light for you, Fairfax, for the announcement. Third light for you, Moya.

DAISY (*loudly*): What about me and grand-dad?

TRISTAN: I'll send up rockets for you two. No, that'll be all right, duckie. Watch your script with one eye and keep the other on grand-dad. Now then——

> PERCY *starts record. Fades in.*

Are you timing it, Brenda?

BRENDA: Yes, Mr. Sprott.

> *Fades out.*

TRISTAN: Fairfax—announcement.

HAYCRAFT (*in his best manner*): "Down Here in Barset"—we present another half-hour of Barsetshire humour, melody, and folk-lore, in a programme written and produced by Tristan Sprott. It's a beautiful summer night—the men have returned from the hayfields—the door of that friendly old pub *The Brown Cow* stands wide open—"Down Here in Barset".

TRISTAN: All right, Moya—Percy—give!

> MOYA *begins playing a country tune.* PERCY *makes noise suggesting bottles and glasses, etc.*

TRISTAN: Atmosphere, chaps.

> HETTY, BOB, HAYCRAFT, TRISTAN *himself and even* PERCY *and* BRENDA *laugh and chatter in a rather stagey style. In the middle*

[250]

of this, there is a queer deep note from PUNNET'S *serpent. Music stops.*

(*Shrieking.*) No, no, no. No serpent yet. The old boy's not made his entrance yet.

DAISY (*loudly*): Y'aven't to start playin' yet, grand-dad. I'll tell you when.

PUNNET (*unintelligibly*): Ef oi come 'ere to play sarpent, oi wants to play sarpent.

TRISTAN: What does he say?

DAISY: He says if he comes 'ere to play his serpent he want to play his serpent.

TRISTAN (*shouting*): Quite right, grand-dad—you've got temperament—but wait until the proper time and then you can blow your head off. Start, again everybody.

    More laughter and chatter, as before.

BOB (*in Barset style*): 'Nother point o' coider, Rose. Oi saw your young man over boi Jenkins' twenty-acre.

HETTY (*same style*): He's no young man o' moine, Charley Bragg isn't—not since Michaelmas Fair.

BOB: Didn't buy ee a praper fairing, oi'll be bound, Rose.

DAISY (*in loud, wooden tone, rise and step down*): Good evenin' all! Is moi grand-dad 'ere?

TRISTAN: No, no, no, duckie. You're much too soon.

PUNNET (*intelligible*): But oi be 'ere, girl.

DAISY: No, grand-dad. It's what I say in the piece we're doing.

TRISTAN: But you were much too early. And don't say it like that either. Do it more like this. (*Very rural but also very bright.*) "Good evenin' all! Is moi grand-dad 'ere?"

DAISY (*exactly as before*): Good evenin' all! Is moi grand-dad 'ere?

TRISTAN: Yes, a bit better, duckie. But I'll have to rehearse you later. (DAISY *sits.*) Now then, Bob, back to your fairing line.

BOB: Didn't buy ee a praper fairing, oi'll be bound, Rose.

HAYCRAFT (*surprisingly*): Oi 'eard tell on that tew, Garge.

HETTY: What yew tew 'eard tell on 'at isn't trew would fill the Barsetshire News onny Friday. What's for yew, Muster Caxton?

BOB (*in different voice, very deep*): Pint of old an' mild, Miss Nancy.

HETTY: Yes, Muster Caxton. (*Pour.*) Would yew be giving us a song to-night, Muster Caxton?

HAYCRAFT: We do be expectin' your old 'ay-makin' song to-noight, Muster Caxton.

BOB (*as* GARGE *again*): Oi'll never forget the first toime oi ever 'eard that 'ay-makin' song—dang my buttons! (*Much laughter.*) Woi, look oo's 'ere! Young Cherry Gooseman.

DAISY (*rise*): Good evenin' all. Is moi grand-dad 'ere?

Collapse of TRISTAN.

BOB (*as* GARGE): Naow, yer grand-dad's not 'ere.

HETTY (*as* ROSE): An' that's where yew be wrong, again, Garge. Ol' Gooseman's 'ere. He's asleep in the corner there.

HAYCRAFT: Woi so 'e be. An' only man in all Barset as can still play the ould sarpent.

DAISY: Moi grand-dad was the foinest sarpent player in the whole o' Barset——

TRISTAN (*rises to knees*): Not quite so loud, duckie—but a bit brighter. You see, you're frightfully proud of the fact that your grand-dad was the finest serpent player in the whole of Barset. It's kept your family going for the last sixty years.

DAISY: Me mother won't let 'im play it. (*To old* PUNNET) 'Ere, grand-dad, wake up! Y'ave to play in a minute.

TRISTAN: Let's have it again, duckie. Moi grand-dad——

PUNNET (*loudly and angrily*): Oi be woide awake naow, girl. Oi'll gi'ee a beltin' ef oi've any more o' your sauce——

DAISY: No, that's what it says in the piece, grand-dad.

> PUNNET *starts playing, to the sound of cheers and noises of glasses, etc. from* PERCY. TRISTAN *is beating time with one hand and wiping his brow with the other. The curtain comes swiftly down on the collapse of* TRISTAN.

ACT II

As before. It is now the middle of the afternoon.

At rise, PERCY KING *is playing some dashing swing, and* BRENDA *is standing near, admiring it and him and dancing. They have the studio to themselves. This performance is continued until the audience has stopped banging down the seats. It is then brought to a fine slapdash conclusion.* PERCY *breaks the music with a little dance.*

BRENDA (*coming down centre*): I think you're marvellous.

PERCY (*who does too*): Well, it's a gift reelly—(*rises*)—only you gotta practise as well, see? I nearly got into a programme—jus' before last Christmas it was—only they were frightened of over-runnin' so they cut me out.

BRENDA: I'll bet you get your chance soon, Percy.

PERCY: I'll bet I do. (*Condescending a little*) An' I'll bet you do too, Alice.

BRENDA (*like lightning*): Brenda.

PERCY (*unembarrassed*): Brenda—that's right.

BRENDA: You an' your Alices!

PERCY: 'Ere, hand out one of your impersonations.

BRENDA: All right. Who shall I do?

PERCY: Don't tell me. Let me guess—see?

BRENDA (*doubtfully, coming to front of settee*): I've never done 'em that way before. They never do 'em that way on the stage. They always *tell* you first who it is.

PERCY (*comes down and leans on desk*): Never mind—let's try it this way. Go on.

BRENDA (*changing into somebody not* BRENDA, *but God knows who*): "Good evening, my darling. You *are* my darling still, aren't you—my darling? Tired? No, I could dance the night away. I feel inspired, darling. No, it isn't champagne—I only had the tiniest sip—it's love and life—life and love——"

PERCY: It's swell. Honestly, I wouldn't have known it was you. If I'd come in at the door when you was doing it, I wouldn't 'ave known it was you.

BRENDA: Yes, but who was it?

PERCY: Jessie Matthews?

[253]

I*

BRENDA (*scornfully*): No, not a bit like her. (*Sits settee.*)

PERCY: Gertrude Lawrence?

BRENDA: No, I never seen her.

PERCY: Ginger Rogers?

BRENDA (*showing signs of distress now*): No—don't be silly. How *could* it be Ginger Rogers?

Telephone. She has to answer it.

Yes, this is the E.B.C. Who? . . . *What* emperor? . . .

She listens bewildered, but at that moment COMMANDER COPLEY *enters down right, followed by* DOROTHY.

COPLEY: What's this? Anything for me?

BRENDA (*putting hand over receiver*): Yes. It's somebody complaining about something. (*Up to piano.*)

COPLEY (*he goes and takes telephone from her*): Commander Copley here—regional director. . . . Oh yes. . . . Certainly, we're only too glad to be corrected . . . yes, I'll pass it on with pleasure, sir. . . . I see. . . . Now let me get this straight, sir—Maximilian did not assume the title of Emperor Elect until 1508, and *not* in 1506—as our speaker suggested. . . . Thank you. . . . No, I'm much obliged . . . and I'll forward the correction to the proper quarter at once. . . . *Good* afternoon.

Puts down telephone, and gives DOROTHY *a whimsical smile.*

Make a note of that, Dorothy, and send it along to Talks at Radio House. I haven't the foggiest what it's all about.

DOROTHY (*admiringly*): I don't know how you've the patience.

COPLEY (*smiling*): That's one of the things you learn in the Service. These things come in jolly useful. And that's where these chaps who've had no proper training—these temperamental Johnnies— fall down.

PERCY: Gracie Fields?

BRENDA (*suddenly furious*): No, you fathead—and I believe you're doing it on purpose.

PERCY (*staggered*): What me? Why, I only——

BRENDA (*angrily*): Oh shut up!

She hurries out and collides with BOB DINTY.

Mind where you're going—clumsy. (*She bangs out.*)

PERCY: Boy!

BOB (*who is gloomy*): What have you been doing to her?

PERCY: Nothing. She suddenly flares up——

BOB (*gloomily*): That's women, my lad. You're just beginning to get a glimpse of it. They get worse as they get older. (*He sits down heavily in settee.*)

PERCY: I've seen plenty of it. My Sis——

BOB (*cutting in*): You've seen nothing yet, my lad. Take it from me. They get worse as they get older. And it isn't their insides. They've got insides like horses.

PERCY: My Sis——

BOB (*cutting in*): Yes, like horses. Eat and drink anything.

PERCY: Horses can't eat and drink anything.

BOB: Don't argue, my lad. I'm in no mood for an argument.

Enter FAIRFAX HAYCRAFT, *who goes to his desk.*

PERCY: What about that Children's Hour stuff, Mr. Haycraft?

HAYCRAFT: Have a look in the basement. Joe Cossart might remember.

PERCY *goes out.* HAYCRAFT *now notices* BOB'S *gloom.*

What's the matter, Bob? Worrying about having two programmes to-day?

BOB: Programmes? Not me. Give me work, old boy, and I'm happy. I like work—live for it. Every good actor does. Old Thorburn—you remember old Thorburn's Shakespearean Company?—I was with him for five years—well, old Thorburn used to say, "Bob, you're a glutton for work, boy—I'll say that about you." There's no work here, Fairfax. It's child's play to a man who's been brought up in repertory. No, it's not work but the other thing that's got me down, to-day.

HAYCRAFT: What other thing?

BOB: Well, what do you think?—women.

HAYCRAFT: Oh, I see.

BOB: You go to your digs hoping for a nice quiet lunch on a busy day—and what happens? Hell breaks loose. And why? Only one answer—the women.

HAYCRAFT: What women? Who was there besides Hetty?

BOB: My wife.

HAYCRAFT: Oh—I say! She turned up then?

BOB: Yes, she does every month or two, just to see how I'm getting on. She knows about Hetty and me, of course, but that doesn't stop her coming. Embarrassing I call it, but nothing seems to embarrass women so long as their clothes don't start falling down. If I was married to a man who was living with another woman,

[255]

would I keep turning up for lunch? Of course I wouldn't—and neither would you, old man. But *they* do, think nothing of it. And you ought to have seen the way they walked into that duck we had, both Hetty and the wife.

HAYCRAFT: Didn't they leave any for you to-night?

BOB: I'll be lucky if there's a leg. Well, the first half of the lunch, while they're wolfing the duck, the wife and Hetty are taking cracks at each other all the time—you know how women are—"My dear, you're looking so tired"—"No he never cared for your acting, did he, dear?"—like a couple of talking cats round that duck. Till I got fed up and told 'em I'd like a bit of peace and quiet. That settled it. They rounded on me, then, both of 'em at once. I was a fine one to talk! You know. And no delicacy, no tact, old man, about the situation at all. Out comes everything, with me to blame all through, of course. In the end I simply couldn't stick it and walked straight out on the pair of 'em—round to the *Lion*. So—for God's sake, old man, don't leave Uncle Bob alone with Auntie Hetty this afternoon, else your Children's Hour is going to sound like a dog-fight.

Enter TRISTAN, *looking rather wild, with present in box wrapped up.*

TRISTAN: My mother's just telephoned from Leamington. She's met a theosophical Indian there who remembers her as the favourite concubine of a Chinese Emperor who flourished about two-thousand B.C. (*Crosses to settee and sits.*) No good'll come of that. Before the week's out he'll be borrowing his fare to Bombay.

BOB (*to* HAYCRAFT): You see. Nothing but trouble with 'em.

HAYCRAFT (*to* TRISTAN): Bob's had a bad time with his women-folk at lunch.

TRISTAN (*starting to untie parcel*): It's worse though when they use the telephone for all their most fantastic and revolting statements. I think the girls at the exchange listen in and then tell all bona-fide subscribers. That's why, wherever I go, I hear the unpleasant sound of only half-suppressed giggles. I ought to telephone myself to somebody, but I can't remember to whom about what. (*Has untied parcel and taken out envelope, flowers, scarf.*) What extraordinary things people do send for presents. (*Looks at envelope.*) Oh, Fairfax, this is for you.

HAYCRAFT *takes present and puts scarf round his neck.*

HAYCRAFT: I see that Sir Reginald Runton, late of the Board of Fisheries, has just been appointed our deputy-assistant director-general.

TRISTAN: Stop it, Fairfax. You sound just as if you're reading the choicest news of the Baldwin Government. You'll have us all in Westminster Abbey in a minute if you're not careful. That's what wrecked you, Fairfax. You've never been able to get Westminster Abbey out of your voice. (*Rise and move up stairs.*) I must rehearse those monstrous Punnets some time this afternoon. Then there are the other three rural druids to arrive.

BOB: You know, Tristan old man, I've never understood why you're down here doing these rustic Barset programmes.

TRISTAN (*at top of stairs*): For the same reason that Dick Hodge, who's really a farmer, is up in town doing light sophisticated metropolitan programmes like "Café Society" and—(*down stairs*)—"Company at Claridge's". If I'd turned up to Radio House covered with hayseed and reeking of manure, I'd have been in town yet, eating *supreme de volaille* and drinking *Montrachet*.

Enter EDNA.

Oh, Edna, do something for me, will you?

EDNA: Yes, what is it?

TRISTAN: That's the trouble, I can't remember. Why do I think fish comes into it?

EDNA: Do you want some fish?

TRISTAN: Good God—no! Fairfax was announcing about fish. That's it. Sir Reginald Thing, our new deputy-assistant D.G., was discovered in the Board of Fisheries. (*Giving string to* FAIRFAX.) That's yours. "Put those mackerel away," they said, "and try broadcasting. Have you ever done any? No? Good! Interested in drama, music, entertainment, news, popular talks? No? Splendid! You're just what we want." Where's Paula?

EDNA: I don't know. I came out to see, because a long telegram's just come for her.

TRISTAN: Don't tell me what it's all about.

EDNA: I'm not going to.

TRISTAN: That's right—let me guess. They want her to go to Sheffield and produce one of those stark documentaries. *Steel! Iron! Copper! Lead!* Humph?

EDNA: No, it's nothing to do with E.B.C. business. It's private.

TRISTAN (*lies on settee*): I don't like all this secrecy. No private life here.

EDNA: You mustn't be inquisitive. I can't tell you any more.

Enter GRONOVA, *looking very agitated.*

GRONOVA: A most extraordinary thing has happened to me. I'm terribly upset.

[257]

BOB (*rising*): This is where I go. (*Crossing to door.*)

GRONOVA: Why do you say that? It has nothing to do with you. Why are you so rude?

BOB: Because I've had enough of women being upset for one afternoon. I'll be in the little talks studio, Tristan, if you want me.

> *Goes out.* GRONOVA *still does her agitated act. Up to piano and down to desk.*

TRISTAN (*severely*): It would serve you jolly well right, Moya, if we just didn't ask you what was the matter. Let's not. Now as I was saying——

HAYCRAFT (*a kindly soul*): No, we want to know what happened. Go on, Moya.

GRONOVA (*dramatically to* FAIRFAX): It was a voice I overheard.

TRISTAN: That'll do, Moya. We can't have anybody in our drama department being as dramatic as that.

GRONOVA: I had to call at the hair-dresser's to arrange an appointment——

EDNA (*interested*): Which one? Maison Binns?

GRONOVA (*to* EDNA): Maison Binns, yes. Just inside there is a thin partition one side for Ladies, one for Gentlemen——

TRISTAN: Always a decent arrangement, I think.

GRONOVA: I am in the Ladies' side . . .

TRISTAN: Good!

GRONOVA: . . . making my appointment—when I hear a voice. I hear it through the partition, from the gentlemen's side. This voice, it is refusing a shampoo. "No," it is saying, "no shampoo this afternoon, thank you," it is saying. And at once I know this voice. I know it. I know it, I know it. But at once I know it.

TRISTAN (*with solemn irony*): Ah—you knew it, then?

GRONOVA: Yes, I am telling you—but at once, I knew it. This voice—it was part of my life. I could hardly wait for the stupid girl to book the appointment. I hurried to the door—(*Runs to door. Opens it*)—to see the man who owned that voice. But there was no one. (*Closes door.*) He had gone.

TRISTAN: Oh what a shame!

GRONOVA: It *is* a shame, because I cannot remember whose voice it was I heard—but I know. I *know* that it belongs to my past. My heart trembled when I heard it. And now I must wonder and puzzle my head all day. I am—*haunted*—by it. I must go out again. (*Crossing towards door.*)

HAYCRAFT: Don't be so haunted that you forget you're helping us with the Children's Hour to-day.

GRONOVA: No—of course not—I am always conscientious—my work comes first—but I must go out again—I feel stifled here——

Goes out.

HAYCRAFT: She evidently heard somebody she once knew.

TRISTAN: Think so, Fairfax? I got that idea too. Edna, I've remembered something. Ring up Philip in Manchester—and ask him to put those two Irish recordings on the train.

As EDNA is going out, DOROTHY enters, with some memos, one of which she gives to TRISTAN before giving the others to HAY-CRAFT, and busies herself at desk centre.

What have you brought us this time, Dorothy? (*Looks at memo and reads*) "Owing to copyright difficulties, until further notice no use must be made in any programme of *Hot-pants Hortense*. Don't forget that, Fairfax. That'll cramp your twilight hours a bit. (*Calling her back as she is going out*) Dorothy! (*Rises and moves to right.*)

DOROTHY (*turning*): Yes.

TRISTAN: Come here, mavourneen. There's something that's worrying me. (*As she, rather reluctantly, comes to right of him.*) My spies are telling me that young Martin Bradburn—as proud and high-stepping a cavalier as ever turned the knobs on a producer's panel—got himself sent down here to continue to pay his court to you, my haughty beauty. (*In mock bad actor's voice.*) Tell me, girl, is't true?

DOROTHY: Don't you think you ought to mind your own business?

TRISTAN: Good Lord—no! I never heard of such a loathsome idea. Come now, tell me and Uncle Fairfax the truth.

DOROTHY (*indignantly*): Well, if you must know, Martin Bradburn's been behaving like an idiot. And I've told him so. It was all off when I came down here, and now he comes charging down to try and start it all over again.

TRISTAN: Do you want me to understand, Dorothy, that the fact that he came down here specially to see you really annoys you?

DOROTHY: Yes it does. It makes me look so silly.

TRISTAN: No ordinary man, mind you—but quite a distinguished producer, distinguished in the theatre before he came to the E.B.C., a man who will go a long way—a man——

DOROTHY (*cutting in, impatiently*): Oh—what's that got to do with it?

TRISTAN (*with mock severity*): Dorothy, my famous insight into feminine psychology tells me that if that's your attitude, you must have gone and fallen for somebody else.

DOROTHY (*rather embarrassed*): Oh—don't be silly.

Goes out hastily. TRISTAN *follows her round.*

TRISTAN (*giggles*): Damn nuisance that! It's obvious Copley's her man, not Bradburn.

HAYCRAFT: Yes, but why is it a nuisance?

TRISTAN: Because if Bradburn had been happy here with his Dorothy, I was going to apply to get back to London, where I belong and where they might have allowed me to do some real broadcasting. Strange as it may seem, I didn't join the E.B.C. because I had nowhere to go, but because I believed in Radio and cared for it. It's a hell of a handicap of course, and I think it was that and not the fact that I was drunk and disorderly in the sight of the director of programmes —that got me sentenced to these salt mines.

HAYCRAFT (*rising, indignantly*): I wish you people wouldn't talk of this station as if it were a prison or something. It's as much part of the broadcasting scheme as Radio House. And I'd *rather* be here than in London——

TRISTAN: Uncle Fairfax, Uncle Fairfax, we're alone. Nobody's listening. You needn't put on that how-happy-are-the-regions act for me. You're just as much an exile as I am.

HAYCRAFT: Nonsense! They're only giving me a rest.

TRISTAN: Oh—quite, quite, quite. And when the E.B.C. get back to Westminster Abbey, they'll be asking for you. Where's Paula Leeds?

Enter MARTIN, *looking gloomy.*

Hello, you look a mite grim.

MARTIN: I feel a mite grim. Where's Paula?

HAYCRAFT (*going to door*): I thought you and she lunched together.

MARTIN: We did. But we split up an hour or two ago. She was friendly, and it was a good lunch she gave me, but somehow we couldn't get going together.

TRISTAN (*as* HAYCRAFT *goes out, crossing legs on desk*): Now why doesn't Paula give *me* lunch? I'm unusually good at being given lunch to. Did you have a row?

MARTIN: No, but we didn't tick over properly. My fault probably.

TRISTAN: Your fault certainly. Paula wouldn't ask anybody to lunch just to start a quarrel.

MARTIN: I'm worried—about various things.

[260]

TRISTAN: You realise now, of course, that you were an idiot to come down here?

MARTIN: Yes, that's fairly obvious.

TRISTAN: If I hadn't a singularly noble nature—(*moving to sofa and sitting right of* MARTIN)—I'd try to sell you the idea of staying here, so that I could get back to London. But your need is greater than mine. (*As* MARTIN *sits down and looks dejected*) Why don't you ask Copley, who doesn't want you here anyhow, to ring up Radio House and see if you can't go back? Say the place is bad for your sciatica. I've never tried them with sciatica, but I've an idea that our administration department would react very favourably towards it. It sounds such a respectable complaint.

MARTIN (*gloomily*): I suppose I've made a fool of myself but it isn't just that.

TRISTAN: Can't be. (*Leaning on* MARTIN'S *shoulder*) I rather like making a fool of myself. At least it's making *something* of yourself.

MARTIN: If that was all, I wouldn't mind. But—oh, I dunno— but nothing's *right*. And I can't put my finger on what it is that's making everything seem wrong. Good Lord—I'm beginning to sound like Hamlet.

TRISTAN: He put it better, I think. But you might try going on a blind. It removes the inhibitions, and then up from the grimy old unconscious comes the dirty dripping truth. Try a blind, Bradburn. I'll join you to-night as soon as I've taken the radio customers "down here in Barset".

MARTIN: I don't like drinking on principle——

TRISTAN: Well, pretend it's for fun then——

MARTIN: But if I still feel like this to-night, it'll probably mean a blind.

TRISTAN: Let me know. But it's a pity you don't get on with Paula.

MARTIN (*moves down, lifts* TRISTAN *up and sits left of settee*): Well, I don't. Never did. I suppose I don't like that type.

TRISTAN: She isn't a type. As a matter of fact, she's a darling— and about the best we've got in the E.B.C.

MARTIN: There's something about her—and always was—that irritates me.

TRISTAN (*considering him*): I think it's probably because she's very intelligent. You're the kind of British male who doesn't want women to be intelligent.

MARTIN (*indignantly*): Now what d'you think I am, Sprott?

TRISTAN: I didn't say *you* weren't intelligent. I said you might

[261]

be the kind of British male who doesn't want his women to be intelligent.

MARTIN: Yes, I heard, I heard, I heard . . . (*With sudden change of tone*) My God!—you might be right too. Perhaps I don't like them intelligent. If so, then this *does* serve me right.

> *He considers himself in dismay, while* TRISTAN *stares at him.* PAULA *now enters and both men stare hard at her in silence.*

PAULA (*going over to desk*): Hello! Nobody been asking for me, I suppose? (*She then notices their stares and silence.*) Why these fixed stares, gentlemen?

TRISTAN: Bradburn's staring at you because somewhere at the back of his innocent mind the dawn is breaking. *I'm* staring to remind you of a recent memo that says senior members of the staff must try to keep regular office hours. Paula, you've taken about four hours for lunch.

PAULA: No, hairdresser's, mostly.

TRISTAN (*interested*): Maison Binns?

PAULA: No, the other one. Betty and Phyllis. Ye Olde English.

MARTIN (*rousing himself*): I must see Copley.

> Goes out.

TRISTAN: He's trying to get back to London. (*Moves to left end of settee.*)

PAULA: What about his Dorothy?

TRISTAN: He's recovering.

PAULA: About time too! (*Moves up and down between desk and piano.*)

TRISTAN: Do you like him?

PAULA: He's a damn good producer. Not only for us, but he was very good in the theatre too.

TRISTAN: I know that, but do you like him?

PAULA: Not much.

TRISTAN: Do you find there's something about him that irritates you? (*Pats settee for her to sit beside him.*)

PAULA (*sits settee right*): Yes. That's very clever of you, Tristan. There always *was* something about him that irritated me.

TRISTAN: I guessed that. The trouble is, I don't think he likes intelligent women.

PAULA: I'm not surprised. He's that type.

TRISTAN: No, he isn't a type. As a matter of fact, he's really rather a darling—and of course about as good as we've got in the E.B.C.

PAULA: He can't do with me, can he?

TRISTAN: He *thinks* he can't. But secretly—he's fascinated.

PAULA: Oh—rubbish!

TRISTAN: And in the same secret way *you're* fascinated too.

PAULA (*rises and crosses to desk centre and sits*): Good lord!—what rot you talk!

TRISTAN: You see—you're beginning to say "Good lord" just as he does. Always a sure sign.

COPLEY *enters, carrying his hat and coat.*

COPLEY (*putting on coat*): Bradburn wants to go back to London now—doesn't seem to know his own mind, that chap—and of course I've no objection, so long as he can make it right with Radio House. So I've left him trying to get through to talk to 'em.

TRISTAN: Quite right, Commander. It's up to him.

COPLEY: By the way, a bloke I knew in the Service may blow in this afternoon, so if you should find anybody asking for me, tell him I'll be back in half an hour or so and keep him amused.

PAULA: How do we amuse him?

TRISTAN: We could tell him a thing or two about broadcasting.

COPLEY: Good idea! The old boy knows nothing about it, and he'll probably feel he's having the time of his life. I'll be back in time for our Children's Hour programme.

Goes out.

TRISTAN (*imitating* COPLEY): I'll be back in time for the Children's Hour programme. Why should he be back in time for the Children's Hour programme? It'll go on just the same without him.

PAULA: Just doesn't want to miss it, I suppose. A little good clean fun with the kiddies.

TRISTAN (*shaking his head, coming down to edge of piano*): You're bitter, Miss Leeds, you're very bitter. Have you ever asked yourself if you're showing a cheerful spirit of co-operation and pulling your weight in the boat?

PAULA: No, I don't talk to myself like that.

Enter EDNA, *with note-book.*

Oh—Edna—any messages for me?

EDNA: Yes. A telegram. (*Above desk.*)

TRISTAN (*crosses to desk interested*): Oh yes—that telegram.

EDNA: It's private—not E.B.C. business.

PAULA (*not unpleasantly*): In that case, Edna, we just wait until Mr. Sprott goes. (*She smiles at him.*) He'll be going any minute now.

[263]

TRISTAN (*with mock dignity*): Oh—well, if that's how you feel—of course I'll go. I have my pride. By gosh, I have my Punnets too. And I warn you that when I find 'em, I'm going to rehearse 'em in here.

PAULA: Why can't you take them into Two?

TRISTAN (*as he goes*): Because the old man would think it was all different when I brought him back in here. Must get him house-trained to this studio.

    Goes out.

EDNA (*with note-book, sits*): I took this telegram over the phone and I haven't copied it out yet.

PAULA (*a light rebuke*): Too busy?

EDNA: No, only I couldn't copy it on the machine up there without Dorothy or Brenda knowing all about it—and so——

PAULA: Yes, of course. Well, read it.

EDNA (*reading*): "Play accepted by Harland who is enthusiastic (PAULA *rises and moves round to read.*) stop good terms for immediate production West End with option New York production next season stop contract in post but could you come up as soon as possible discuss cast etc. stop any ideas for producer stop congratulations Blake." You'd like me to type this out, wouldn't you?

PAULA (*excitedly*): I'd like you to copy it in gold letters about two feet high. My goodness, Edna! (*Moves to couch.*) Harland's taken my play. *My play*, Edna!

EDNA: I know. I'm so glad. Isn't it exciting?

PAULA: Exciting? It's frightening. Harland 'll drop down dead. (*Sits couch.*) Or perhaps Blake—he's the agent, Edna—has simply gone mad. What does it say? Good terms! Immediate production West End! New York next season! Will I come up as soon as possible? Will I be found waiting on Harland's doorstep? And what was that about a producer? (*Back to* EDNA.)

EDNA (*referring to note-book*): "Any ideas for a producer?"

PAULA (*thinking hard, sits on settee*): Any ideas for a producer? How extraordinary that is!

EDNA: Why is it extraordinary?

PAULA: I'm sorry, Edna—I feel almost ready to tell you the whole story of my life, but I just can't tell you why that particular thing's extraordinary. You'll just have to take my word for it. . . . Yes, I'll do it.

EDNA: Do what? Or is that a secret too?

PAULA: Yes, that's a secret too. (*Crosses to* EDNA.) In fact, the whole thing must be. Listen, Edna—please don't tell anybody just yet. Really, not a soul. I've a special reason for asking.

EDNA: Yes, Miss Leeds, I promise. And I haven't told anybody about this telegram. I really am good at keeping secrets.

PAULA: I'm sure you're wonderful at it.

EDNA: If you become a famous dramatist, you'll have to have a secretary, won't you?

PAULA: I get the idea, and I'm sure you'd do very nicely. But I must point out that I'm an appallingly long way from anything that remotely resembles a famous dramatist. But—gosh!—Harland's taken my play—hasn't he?

EDNA: Yes, and I believe it'll be a success.

PAULA: You don't know anything about it.

EDNA: I do. I read it one afternoon when you were out. It was in the drawer of your desk.

PAULA: Well—of all the cheek!——

EDNA: Oh, but I thought it was frightfully good. You don't mind, do you?

PAULA: How can I if you think it's frightfully good. But remember —not a whisper to anybody—for all kinds of good reasons.

EDNA: I promise. Do you think I could come to the first night? If I could get leave I could——

As door opens.

PAULA (*hastily*): Sh-sh! (*Moves up.*)

HETTY *comes in, looking rather agitated.*

HETTY: Is Bob anywhere about?

PAULA: No. Do you want him?

HETTY: No, I'd like him to keep right away from me. (*To desk, looking at* PAULA *curiously.*) What's the matter with you? You're very excited about something.

PAULA: I get like this sometimes. I'm a smouldering volcano really.

HETTY: You haven't gone and fallen in love, have you?

PAULA: No, I haven't. And you don't sound as if you recommend it.

HETTY: Recommend it! I wish they'd give me the air for half an hour sometime just to tell girls the truth about this love business. But then they wouldn't believe me.

PAULA: What's poor Bob been doing this time? (*Sits arm of settee.*)

HETTY (*disgusted*): Poor Bob! You wouldn't say "poor Bob" if you'd seen the way he went on at lunch to-day. It would have served him right if I'd said to his wife, "There he is. Take him. And take him a long way off while you're about it."

PAULA: But was his wife lunching with you?

HETTY: Yes, she turns up now and again, just to see how we're getting on. And of course Bob thinks it's terrible. He's very conventional, for all his talk. (*To* EDNA) I don't know that you ought to hear all this. (*Sits at desk centre.*)

EDNA: I'll go if you want me to, Hetty, but everybody here knows all about you and Bob.

HETTY: I suppose they do. I must say, Paula, I don't blame you now for keeping so close, as if nothing ever happened to you.

PAULA: Nothing, in your sense, ever does.

HETTY: What about those long week-end leaves you're always taking?

PAULA: Ridiculous as it seems, I spend them at home with my mother.

HETTY: Ah!—if I'd known at first what I know now, I'd be telling everybody *I* spent all my spare time at home with my mother. But I was telling you about lunch to-day. (*Starts to knit.*) Well, to begin with it wasn't so bad. Maisie—that's Bob's wife—I've known her for years—we were on tour together for years—well, Maisie as usual points out all the defects in the digs, and tells us how sorry she is for us having to stay here in Barset, and be working for the E.B.C., and of course as usual I keep the ball in play, so that she gets back as good as she gives—and really we're all getting on nicely——

PAULA (*laughing*): Having a lovely cosy time, I'd say.

HETTY: Well, dear, you know how it is. She may be Bob's wife—but I know plenty about her—a lot more than Bob does—and she knows I do—so she knows too she hasn't too much room to talk—and it's all *right*—if Bob'd let it alone. I didn't want her there, specially when we were having duck and there wasn't too much of it—God knows what ducks do with themselves once you put 'em in an oven! (*Business with tape measure.*) And of course Bob, who wasn't having any, not till to-night, was watching every mouthful she ate—but really we were getting along nicely if Bob had just kept quiet.

PAULA (*amused*): Poor Bob!

HETTY: There's no "poor Bob" about it. All he'd to do was to keep quiet. But suddenly, he starts on the pair of us. Women were this, that and the other! We ought to be ashamed of ourselves! No delicacy or tact or something! All this from him, of all people, with his wife—and *me*—together there looking at him. Well, I wasn't going to stand that—and neither was Maisie, though if she'd kept out of it, we'd have done better. Then the next minute, up he jumps, bangs on the table—and upsets the gravy dish all over a clean table-cloth—shouts at the top of his voice, like a madman, and goes tearing out. And then, of course, Maisie tries to tell me that I don't know how to handle him. I'm not going to take that from her, of course, when he was never sober the last years she had him and couldn't remember his lines—so I tell her a few things—and——

> *She breaks off because* BOB *enters hastily.*

BOB (*not noticing* HETTY *at first*): Oh—I say—— (*Breaks off.*)

HETTY (*icily*): Well, what *do* you say, Bob Dinty?

BOB (*stopping near door*): Nothing—to you.

HETTY (*going forward*): Now you just listen to me.

BOB: I've something better to do.

HETTY (*hastily and angrily*): Oh—no—you haven't——

> *As she darts forward, he hastily leaves, and she goes after him.*

PAULA: Let's hope they settle all that before they turn into Aunt Hetty and Uncle Bob this afternoon, or the kiddies may smell a rat.

EDNA: Do you want to send a reply to that telegram?

PAULA (*rises*): Yes, I've been thinking about that.

> EDNA *prepares to take down the telegram.*

"Blake Play Agency"—no, he has a telegraphic address—yes, it's "Blaplay, Dover Street, W. 1." Wait a minute now. "Your exciting telegram received——" (*Breaks off.*)

> *Enter* JOE, *bringing with him old* PUNNET *and* DAISY. *The old man has no serpent with him, and looks very sleepy and very cross. As* JOE *takes them across the studio*—

JOE (*as he brings them in*): Come along, please.

PAULA: Upstairs, Edna, the circus is here.

> *They go out.* JOE *almost forcibly puts* PUNNET *into chair at* PAULA'S *desk.*

JOE: Now you're going to be all right there, and I'll find Mr. Sprott for you, and you won't have to worry any more.

> *As old* PUNNET *apparently sinks into a coma.*

Doesn't seem very lively, does he? What's the matter with him?

DAISY (*loudly*): He'd two pints o' cider with 'is dinner—an' me mother told me not to let 'im 'ave any—but soon as my back's turned, 'e gets it—'e's that artful. An' now 'e's testy as a weasel—an' gone an' lost 'is sarpent into the bargain. (*Shouting at the old man*) But where did yer leave it, grand-dad?

[267]

Old PUNNET *opens one eye, looks malevolently at* DAISY *and* JOE *and makes a deep gurring noise.*

DAISY: It's all right yer saying *gurrr,* but yer've gone an' lost yer ould sarpent, an' yer no good to the E.B.C. without yer sarpent, grand-dad.

JOE (*crosses at back to left end couch*): Percy's looking for it. He's a bright lad, Percy. He'll find it. Now you wait here.

As he starts to move settee, SIR REGINALD RUNTON *enters, very hesitantly. He is a tallish, slightish, very gentlemanly fellow in his fifties, with a timid but precise manner. A senior Civil Servant clean out of his depth. He punctuates his phrases with a little apologetic cough.*

SIR REGINALD (*to* DAISY): Oh—I say—could I see Commander Copley? (DAISY *giggles.*)

JOE (*coming forward*): What name, sir?

SIR REGINALD: Oh—er—Sir Reginald Runton.

JOE: I beg your pardon.

SIR REGINALD (*rather surprised*): Not at all, not at all.

JOE (*after a pause*): I mean, I didn't catch the name.

SIR REGINALD: Oh—sorry. (*Distinctly*) Sir Reginald Runton.

JOE (*who has never heard of him*): I see. Well, Commander Copley's out just now, but he'll be back soon. (*Moving away to left end of couch.*)

SIR REGINALD (*looking round helplessly*): Well—er—I suppose I could—er—wait somewhere. (*About to sit.*)

JOE: We're a bit short of space just now—and we've got a transmission in here soon—oh, will you give me a hand?

SIR REGINALD: Oh—yes of course. (*He does so.*)

JOE: So, as Commander Copley won't be long, what I'd suggest is that you have a walk round and then come back again in about a quarter of an hour. (PUNNET *gives loud snore.*)

SIR REGINALD: Yes—of course—probably the best thing under the circumstances——

As they move together slowly towards door——
You—er—on the staff here?

JOE: Yes, engineer.

SIR REGINALD (*with affable condescension*): Job all right, eh?

JOE: No, lousy.

They go out. DAISY *watches them and now shakes the old man, who has dropped his hat.*

DAISY (*picking up hat and giving it to him*): Grand-dad, yer be-havin' something terrible—an' what me mother'll say if she finds out, I don't know. Wake up an' behave proper!

PUNNET (*waking up*): Grrr! Woi be we a-sittin' 'ere girl? Oi want to go 'ome.

DAISY: 'Ow can we go home when yer promised to play for the E.B.C.?

PUNNET (*suddenly and viciously awake*): 'Od rabbit un! Oi says 'Od rabbit un—E.B.C. an' all.

Enter TRISTAN *and stares at* PUNNET.

'Od rabbit 'em all!

TRISTAN (*comes over to* DAISY *and bends over to look at* PUNNET): What's he saying?

DAISY: He's just a-swearin' an' carryin' on something terrible— (TRISTAN *crosses to left of desk, sits on arm of sofa and looks at* PUNNET)—the silly old turnip. He's full o' cider an' gone an' lost 'is sarpent.

TRISTAN *kneels down on sofa and leans on desk and looks at old* PUNNET *anxiously. The old man is beginning to doze off again, but manages to stare at* TRISTAN *with one malevolent eye.*

PUNNET (*only half intelligibly*): 'Tisn't 'im as be image o' Farmer Bates' cowman.

TRISTAN: What does he say?

DAISY (*loudly*): He says it isn't you that's the image o' Farmer Bates' cowman.

TRISTAN: Well, that's something, but it doesn't get us very far. Where do we go from there?

PUNNET (*with startling violence*): It be all slummerty-wummerty—ay, masters—slummerty-wummerty! (*Relapses into coma again after this effort.*)

TRISTAN: Did he say "slummerty-wummerty"?

DAISY: Yes, it's a saying of 'is when he loses 'is silly ould temper.

TRISTAN (*in comic despair*): He's right too. It *is* slummerty-wum-merty. (*Suddenly, direct to* DAISY, *solemnly*) Just go down there— (*pointing*)—and try the opening line. "Good evenin' all! Is moi grand-dad 'ere?"

DAISY (*going, as in Act I*): "Good evenin' all! Is moi grand-dad 'ere?"

TRISTAN (*in despair*): Honestly, I don't know if that's any better or not, duckie. I just don't know. It's all slummerty-wummerty with me now.

DAISY (*continuing her rehearsal*): "Moi grand-dad was the foinest sarpent player in the whole o' Barset. 'Ere, grand-dad, wake up an' give us all a tune."

TRISTAN: Yes, yes, yes. Thank you very much, duckie.

DAISY (*going back doggedly*): "Good evenin' all. Is moi' grand-dad——"

TRISTAN (*in despair*): No, no, no. Not again. I must think.

DAISY: What about?

TRISTAN: I dunno. 'Just think about my past and my future. With just a passing glance at the Gobi Desert. (*Looks in despair 'at old* PUNNET, *now dozing again.*) How is he? Any rigor mortis setting in?

> DAISY *moves to* PUNNET.
>
> *Enter* PERCY, *carrying the serpent; stands just outside door, which he has placed open.*

DAISY: Why, there's grand-dad's sarpent. Oi, grand-dad, 'e's found it. (*Round to back of* PUNNET.)

> *As* DAISY *tries to waken old* PUNNET *and* PERCY *stands like a saxophonist holding the serpent,* PAULA *and* MARTIN *enter.*

PAULA: Oh dear! Are the rustic revels still proceeding? Must we go?

TRISTAN (*in comic despair*): No, for God's sake, don't go. Everything's slipping. Just going all *slummerty-wummerty*.

MARTIN: Going what?

TRISTAN: No, no. Don't let's go into it.

PERCY (*cheerfully*): Get a load of this, Mr. Sprott. (*He sounds a deep sustained note on the serpent.*)

TRISTAN: Percy, you're a marvel. Deeper, as Shakespeare nearly said, than Punnet ever sounded.

PERCY: It's in the bag, eh, Miss Leeds?

PAULA: You've only to grow the whiskers, Percy, and then you've got something there.

TRISTAN (*suddenly decisive*): Percy—take Miss Punnet and old Mr. Punnet and the serpent into Studio Two and give them all some tea. (DAISY *and* PERCY *help* PUNNET.) Give the serpent a saucer of milk. I'll join you when I'm feeling a little stronger. Trot along, Daisy, and just keep going over your lines.

DAISY (*crossing as* PERCY *assists old* PUNNET): "Good evenin' all —is my grand-dad 'ere——"

TRISTAN: Yes, yes, Daisy, that's the idea. Only not again here. I'm not feeling very well.

Old Punnet *suddenly and angrily snatches the serpent from* Percy. *These two,* Percy *and* Daisy, *go trooping across, the old man muttering "slummerty-wummerty", etc., as he goes.* Percy *closes door.* Tristan *stretches out on two chairs, exhausted, down left. During following dialogue* Martin *sits at* Haycraft's *desk,* Paula *on arm of settee.*

Martin (*with quiet despair*): It isn't like this here all the time, is it?

Tristan (*dreamily*): Not quite all the time.

Paula (*dreamily*): Sometimes nothing happens for days and days on end. Very restful really.

Tristan: This hell on earth we're having now is due to my enthusiasm for my Barset programme. I never ought to have touched those Punnets. I freely admit it now. I was carried away by my enthusiasm.

Paula: Where's the rest of your local cast?

Tristan: They won't be here for hours. They're just ordinary plain folks, not like the mad Punnets. Are they letting you go back to London, Bradburn?

Martin: I got through to Radio House, but of course Barton and Rudolph were out. I'm going to try again later. I can't stay here. Even if I wanted to, there isn't room for me.

Paula: There really isn't room for anybody except Copley and a couple of admiring secretaries.

Enter, with the same hesitant manner, Sir Reginald.

Sir Reginald: Oh—good afternoon. Is—er—Commander Copley in?

Tristan: No, he isn't back yet. But he said you might be popping in.

Sir Reginald (*surprised*): Oh—I say—did he?

Tristan: I think he did. (*To* Paula) Didn't he?

Paula: Yes, he asked us to amuse you until he got back.

Sir Reginald (*still surprised*): Oh—really—I'm rather surprised— I didn't—er—expect——

Tristan: He said you might be interested to learn a thing or two about broadcasting.

Sir Reginald: Well—yes, of course, I would. I don't know anything about it—really—and I suppose you people——

Tristan (*grimly*): Yes, we know all about it. Don't we?

Paula (*same tone*): We do.

MARTIN: And I'll say we do.

SIR REGINALD: Yes, well—of course—I'd be delighted. Can't begin learning too soon. (*Sitting right of desk.*)

TRISTAN (*rises and sits astride front chair*): Well now, you see before you three employees of the English Broadcasting Company.

SIR REGINALD: And—er—what do you do?

PAULA: We're all producers. This is Martin Bradburn. This is Tristan Sprott. And I'm Paula Leeds.

SIR REGINALD: And—er—what do you produce?

MARTIN (*gloomily*): Jolly entertainment for the million.

TRISTAN: We're in the drama department, and—with a bunch of other people—we handle plays, poetry, readings, and a sort of hybrid product of dreary information and ham acting known in the trade as a "feature".

MARTIN (*rises, down to right of* RUNTON): Some of us were very excited, at first, by the possibilities of broadcasting as a medium. I know I thought that with such a vast audience we ought to be able to provide some fine stuff on a grand scale. I really believed the air could really be used as a sort of huge People's Theatre. Big stuff done in a big way, and handled professionally. On a kind of Reinhardt scale.

PAULA: Don't I know *that* dream? The best plays, the best actors, the best producers. We all thought that ought to be possible.

SIR REGINALD: Quite, quite. But—then—er—isn't it?

TRISTAN: Do you ever listen to our programmes?

SIR REGINALD: The 9 o'clock news occasionally . . . and some of those jolly little nature talks . . . but don't listen to much really.

TRISTAN: Well, you see, the whole thing comes out of the spout watered down for safety.

MARTIN: And for economy.

PAULA: And for stupidity.

MARTIN (*turning on* SIR REGINALD): If only the programmes weren't made up and cut into snippets for half-wits who can't concentrate for more than five minutes at a time—one half-wits' night a week would be enough, if you ask me.

PAULA: Yes, we might call it Half-wits' Night too, and that would sell it.

MARTIN: British broadcasting at present is mostly just amateurs inside having fun among themselves to amuse amateurs outside. Nobody on the staff in authority is an artist or even a good showman. They don't know what real entertainment means. Why, the stuff is stale before the public gets it.

TRISTAN: Where are the shows of yesteryear? Why, right here, in our programmes.

PAULA: And we're all typed so stupidly. Just because I'm a woman I get handed all the old lace and lavender. Any script with a sedan chair in it flies to me like a homing pigeon.

MARTIN: The trouble is, you see—by the way we're not boring you, are we?

SIR REGINALD: Not at all. Most int'r'sting. You were saying?

MARTIN: The trouble is, the English Broadcasting Company is all wrong from top to bottom. . . . It's run as a kind of Civil Service department with a bit of broadcasting tacked on as an after-thought.

TRISTAN (*rises and sits on back of sofa above* PAULA): The people who *do* the broadcasting, believe it or not, are the least important on the staff.

PAULA: If you *will* fool about with microphones in studios, you're kept in the slave class.

TRISTAN: What's really important is our enormous Organisation department, crammed with reliable chaps who work out that if a half-hour programme starts at eight, it ought to finish round about eight-thirty.

MARTIN: And they obstruct us on principle. I think most of 'em hate broadcasting and so do all they can to strangle it.

PAULA: Half the time, it's just plain jealousy, though. They think that producers have a high old time at rehearsals, drinking cham-pagne out of actors' slippers.

SIR REGINALD: Really—and of course—I don't suppose you do, do you?

PAULA: Hardly ever. But what with all this policy nonsense and organising and administering and timidity and red-tape, we're so cluttered up with these dead-heads that we can hardly breathe, let alone move.

MARTIN (*squatting beside* SIR REGINALD): Now here's something you won't believe—yet it's true and absolutely typical. A new deputy-assistant director-general—and we're stiff with deputy-assistants and assistant-deputy-assistants, and the rest of it—well, as I say, a new deputy-assistant D.G. has been appointed to lord it over us, and do you know where he comes from?

TRISTAN: And this, believe it or not, is the truth.

MARTIN (*standing right of* SIR REGINALD. *Slowly and impressively*): He comes—from the *Board of Fisheries.*

> *The three of them begin laughing.*

PAULA (*laughing*): Straight from his files on the Herring Fleet!

> *They laugh.*

SIR REGINALD (*apologetically*): Well—you know—I believe there are one or two quite intelligent—er—administrators—at the Board of Fisheries.

> *The others laugh again.*

MARTIN (*indignantly*): Yes, but what in the name of thunder do they know about broadcasting?

PAULA: I'll bet this Sir Reginald What's-it never even listens in.

TRISTAN: And any moment now he'll come bouncing in here, asking idiotic questions and then firing even more idiotic memos at us. The whole E.B.C. system is cock-eyed.

MARTIN: Half-witted.

PAULA: Wasteful, pedantic and stupid.

MARTIN (*sits right*): And that, my dear sir, is broadcasting.

SIR REGINALD (*who appears to have been cornered and overwhelmed*): Yes—I see—well, you appear to have very strong views—really I hadn't the least idea——

> HAYCRAFT *and* PERCY, *with scripts, etc., enter and cross, preparing to broadcast. The other four are grouped upstage, with* SIR REGINALD *facing the other three and with his back to studio end.* PERCY *is preparing his effects.* GRONOVA *enters hastily, without looking at* SIR REGINALD, *and takes her place at piano.* BOB *and* HETTY *now enter looking furious, and quarrelling.*

HETTY (*to her chair, reckless of being overheard*): And after all I've done for you!

BOB (*angrily*): Well, what have you done for me? You talk as if I'd been paralysed for ten years!

HETTY: You *were* paralysed half the time when I tried to make something out of you.

BOB: *You* made something out of *me!* eh?

HETTY: Oh—shut up!

BOB: And you shut up!

PAULA (*explaining sweetly*): Just Aunt Hetty and Uncle Bob getting ready for the Children's Hour.

> *As they take their places, still muttering and glowering at each other,* COPLEY *enters.*

[274]

TRISTAN (*to* SIR REGINALD): Oh, sir, here's your friend Commander Copley.

SIR REGINALD (*turning distinctly*): Oh—(*rises*)—Commander Copley—I'm Sir Reginald Runton.

COPLEY: What—our new deputy-assistant director-general?

TRISTAN (*in anguish*): Oh—slummerty-wummerty!

But GRONOVA *turns excitedly on her piano stool.*

GRONOVA (*rises*): Sir Reginald Runton?

SIR REGINALD (*surprised*): Yes. (*Turns to her.*)

GRONOVA (*joyfully*): *Topsy!*

MOYA *drops an armful of music on* TRISTAN. *He and* MARTIN *dive on floor to pick it up.*

COPLEY (*shocked*): *Topsy!*

HAYCRAFT: *Quiet, please!*

A steady red. Everybody frozen, except for their eyes, which express their bewilderment, consternation, etc. HAYCRAFT *begins in the most arch manner.*

HAYCRAFT: Hello, Children! This is Uncle Fairfax, talking to you from the Barset Regional Studio. And here's Aunt Moya, all ready at the piano—aren't you, Aunt Moya?

GRONOVA (*rather shakily*): Ye—es, Uncle Faxf—Fairfax. (*Plays a little run.*)

HAYCRAFT: And Uncle Bob's here too.

BOB (*in deep, still cross voice*): Yes, I'm here, Uncle Fairfax.

HAYCRAFT: But where's Aunt Hetty this afternoon? . . . Aunt Hetty, Aunt Hetty! . . . I say children, this is serious. No Aunt Hetty.

PERCY *now solemnly opens and closes door effect.*

HETTY (*doing running in effect*): Here I am . . . *so* sorry, Uncle Fairfax . . . Hello, children!

SIR REGINALD (*innocently forgetting*): I say—rather jolly that——!

He is immediately sh-sh'd and almost collapses.

HAYCRAFT: And now that we're all here, children, we're going to give you another adventure in our serial, *Elsie and the Pirates.* Some Pirate music please, Aunt Moya.

SIR REGINALD *offers* COPLEY *a cigarette.* GRONOVA *obliges with some pirate music. Music starts.*

You'll remember that we left the pirates all having a tremendous fight among themselves . . .

PERCY *clashes cutlasses, etc., while the cast do atmospheric noises—groans, shouts, etc.*

[275]

HETTY (*in little-girl style*): Oh dear, Elsie thought, whatever shall I do. If I run away I shall never be able to find the treasure. No, I *won't* run away. I *must* be brave.

HAYCRAFT: Just then she noticed that one of the biggest and strongest of the pirates, with an *enormous* black beard, had stopped fighting. (PERCY *stops knives.*) Perhaps because he was hurt, and was sitting groaning just near her hiding place. So she crept out.

PERCY *makes sea noise.*

BOB (*in pirate style*): Ohhh! (*Groans.*) Them tarnation old wounds o' mine is openin' agin.

HETTY (*as* ELSIE): Mr. Pirate! *Please* Mr. Pirate!

BOB (*as* PIRATE): Oo's a-whisperin'? Why—stap my vitals—if it isn't the little gal!

HETTY: Mr. Pirate, are you hurt?

BOB: I be mortal bad, missie, mortal bad. Get me a canikin o' rum, missie.

HETTY: If I do, will you help me to find the treasure? It belongs to my grandfather really, you know. And I know he'll give you a big reward, and then you needn't be a pirate any more.

PERCY *stops sea noise.*

BOB: Missie, I never wanted to be a pirate, s'elp me Bob. Bring me a swig o' rum, sharp. (*Groans.*)

PERCY *picks up, earphones off.*

HAYCRAFT: So Elsie ran below, for she knew where the rum was —for, as you know, Elsie was a clever little girl and noticed *everything*—and then she hurried back—(PERCY *taps his feet and moves to left of* BOB)—and gave the rum to Blackbeard.

BOB: Arr—bless yer little 'eart. 'Ere goes—yer 'ealth, missie.

PERCY *does loud gurgling effect.*

HETTY: What did you want to be, Mr. Blackbeard, instead of being a pirate? (PERCY *ready with knives.*)

BOB (*whispering*): A market gardener, missie, out Saffron Walden way. Now, if you promise that if I helps you to git the treasure, you'll set me up in a nice market garden out Saffron Walden way, then I'm yer man, see?

HETTY: Oh yes—I promise. And thank you! Isn't this *exciting?* (PERCY *clashes knives.*)

HAYCRAFT: But it was even *more* exciting than Elsie imagined, for just as she and Blackbeard had agreed to find the treasure together, the fighting among the pirates suddenly stopped. . . . (PERCY *stops knives and puts them down, picking up drum-stick.*)

BOB (*in another voice*): A sail! A sail!

    PERCY *now does distant gun effect. One bang on drum.*

A frigate o' the line. She's firing across our bows, an' a signalling
of us to stop.

    PERCY *does three bangs on drum.*

HETTY: Oh dear—this is going to be *very* difficult.

    GRONOVA *plays softly.*

HAYCRAFT (*very arch*): Listen again, children, in a fortnight's time
to another thrilling adventure of *Elsie and the Pirates*. And listen
to-morrow to your friends Goosie and Henny. Good night, children.

HETTY, BOB and GRONOVA: Good night, children.

HAYCRAFT (*super-arch*): Good night, children, everywhere.

    Quick curtain as red light goes out and GRONOVA *plays louder.*

END OF ACT TWO

ACT III

As before, evening.
Just before rise of curtain we hear the piano being played. Door is open.
TRISTAN *playing piano,* HETTY *at desk sitting.* BOB *down left sitting on small table.*

HETTY: Well, aren't you going to tell us what we ought to do? Do I go on living with him or don't I?

BOB (*hastily. Rises and crosses to settee*): Now just a moment; don't start making a personal favour of it like that. We agreed——

HETTY (*cutting in*): We agreed to let Tristan decide for us, so don't start arguing all over again.

BOB (*angrily*): I'm not arguing all over again. I was going to say that we'd agreed to let Tristan decide——

HETTY: Well then, why don't you shut up, and let him decide?

BOB *sits in small chair left.*

TRISTAN (*stops playing piano*): But I can't attend to your problem, can't give it my full attention, until I know what's become of those three local idiots. My programme will be on the air in an hour, and half the cast hasn't turned up. Give me a chance.

EDNA *looks in.*

(*Up to her*) Well, Edna?

EDNA: The man at the garage at Long Boopley says they left there all right, after he'd done something to the magneto. He says we haven't to worry.

TRISTAN (*cheerful now*): All right then, we won't worry.

EDNA: But I suppose I'd better ring up the other place—Bursetford—to see if they know anything about them?

TRISTAN: Yes, though they'll probably be here now before you get through. No need to worry, though, that's the point.

EDNA: A call came through from London for Sir Reginald Runton——

TRISTAN: Oh dear! Oh dear, oh dear!

EDNA: I told them to try the County Hotel. I think he's dining there——

HETTY: With Moya?

EDNA: Yes, I believe so. (*Going.*) Well, I'll ring up Bursetford.

She goes out.

TRISTAN (*sits cross-legged on floor with playing-cards. Cheerfully*): Let's hope Moya is putting in some very heavy do-you-remember-darling work on him, or some of us are sunk. But there's no need to worry about my cast. It's on its way. So now, children, I examine your problem in the spirit in which it ought to be examined. And I say to you, giving you at the same time an old man's blessing, forgive and forget. Hetty, if you take my advice you'll forgive him.

BOB: Now wait a minute. What's all this forgiving about?

HETTY (*indignantly*): You're not going to tell me now I haven't plenty to forgive. My lord, when I think——

TRISTAN (*cutting in*): Now, now, now, comrades! Not again. And to you, Bob I say—life is too short and we are creatures of sorrow—be tolerant. Hetty has her faults——

HETTY (*angrily*): It's not Hetty's faults we're talking about.

BOB: Of course it is.

HETTY: What, after the way you went on this afternoon!

BOB: There isn't a man alive who wouldn't have—— Tristan, I appeal to you . . .

TRISTAN (*cutting in*): No, no, no. Don't disappoint me. After all, life is hard, my friends. There is nothing we can do, in the end, but be kind to each other. So—forgive and forget. You two, with all your faults, were meant to cherish each other. So give him a smile, Hetty. Bob, open your arms. And bless you, my children!

BOB (*disgusted*): What is this—a musical monologue?

Moves up to piano and leans on it looking upstage.

HETTY (*rises*): I thought you'd give us a bit of sensible advice, not "Bob, open your arms". Look at him!

Sits in desk chair.

TRISTAN: But this isn't the right spirit at all. As we travel along life's highway, we must greet each moment with a smile and turn to each fellow wayfarer with loving-kindness——

HETTY (*bitterly*): Wishing you a merry Christmas and a happy New Year.

TRISTAN: Now look at me. What a day I've had so far! Including, don't forget, giving the lowdown on the whole E.B.C. to its new deputy-assistant D.G., little Reggie Runton. But am I cast down? Do I lose my bright friendly smile? Do I—— (*Breaks off because* EDNA *enters again.*)

EDNA: They got as far as Bursetford and then the car broke down again and so they gave it up as a bad job.

TRISTAN (*leaning on sofa. Horrified*): Do you mean they're not coming here?

EDNA: Yes. All three of them have gone home.

TRISTAN (*furious*): My godfathers! Completely let down! That's the last time I ever ask any of these bullock-witted rural stinkers to do anything for me, the very last time. Why was I ever condemned to do programmes in this manure-heap, tell me that? (*Sits settee. Groans.*) All right, Edna.

 She goes.

HETTY: Can we get anybody here to help us with the programme?

TRISTAN: We'll have to, that's all.

BOB: I can always do a good double.

HETTY: Your only double is whisky.

TRISTAN (*gloomily*): That's an idea—whisky. The best thing we can do now is to get screaming drunk. We'll never get through this programme sober. Let's go and join Martin Bradburn at the *Lion*. I left him there, putting 'em down steadily. And as for you two—— (*Back to cards.*)

HETTY (*after pause*): Well, what about us two?

TRISTAN (*picking up cards*): If you want *my* advice, you'll give up trying to live together. Obviously you don't really like each other. What's the use of spending your time having rows?

BOB	(*indignantly*): What d'you mean—spending our time having rows?
HETTY	(*rises. Indignantly*): Who told you we didn't like each other?

BOB: Let me tell you this, Hetty and I can get on better together than any couple I know in this barmy broadcasting company of yours.

HETTY: Yes, and we don't need drink to do it on either, do we, Bob?

BOB: No, we don't, Hetty. At least—not much. Now listen to me, Tristan; when you've seen as much of life as I have, when you've been around and seen what a miserable mess most people make of it, the last thing you'll want to do is try and separate two hard-working decent pro's who are fond of each other and know how to look after each other.

HETTY: That's right, Bob. Here!

BOB (*crosses to her*): Sorry I threw my weight about, old girl. Won't happen again.

HETTY: Never mind, Bob. It was half my fault. (*Looking indignantly.*) My word, if one took notice of *some* people!

BOB: He's young and silly. He'll *learn.*

TRISTAN: Now I only——

HETTY (*severely*): You've said enough for one night. Come on, Bob, I know you're dying for a drink.

They go out, affectionately. TRISTAN *looks after them in comic despair. On their exit* TRISTAN *crawls across to piano.*

TRISTAN *plays a few notes of* "*The Dead March*"—*then on* COPLEY'S *entrance changes to* "*A Life on the Ocean Wave*" *and stops when* COPLEY *speaks.*

COPLEY *and* DOROTHY, *dressed for going out, now enter.* COPLEY *is spreading himself on some glamorous tale of his service life. They come down centre.*

COPLEY: So I said to Jumbo, "Look here, old boy, you and I can take on a dozen of these dagoes, can't we?" And Jumbo said, "You bet your life we can, Coppo." They called me Coppo in that ship. But things weren't looking too bright. The first dago pulled out a knife. You know what these chaps are.

TRISTAN (*who wasn't asked*): Yes, by Gad, Sir! Always ready to pull out their knives, but when it comes to war, terrified of the bayonet—cold steel.

COPLEY: Well, you know, that's about it. Just show 'em the bayonet——

TRISTAN: Just show *me* the bayonet, and see what I'd do. Tristan Sprotto would run quite as fast as any dago, Coppo.

DOROTHY (*possessively*): Tell me what happened afterwards. It's frightfully exciting. But don't spoil it now.

COPLEY: No. Remind me to finish the yarn at dinner. We're going across to the *County* for a bite of food.

TRISTAN: And I'm going across to the *Lion* for a gallon of whisky.

COPLEY: Everything all right?

TRISTAN: Everything's splendid. I've carefully insulted the E.B.C. to one of its senior officials. Half my cast aren't coming at all. The other half—the mad Punnets—seem to have disappeared. We're on the air in less than forty minutes, and, if time allows, I propose to get screaming drunk.

Enter MARTIN.

MARTIN (*to* TRISTAN): I thought you were coming back to the pub.

TRISTAN: I am.

DOROTHY (*to* COPLEY): Shall we go?

MARTIN: Are you going to the pub too?

COPLEY: I'm giving Dorothy a bite of dinner at the *County*.

MARTIN (*looking carefully at them*): Do I congratulate you both?

DOROTHY *and* COPLEY *look at each other, embarrassed.*

I believe I do too!

COPLEY: Well, what do *you* say, Dorothy?

DOROTHY: Oh—all right—I suppose it was bound to come out soon.

COPLEY: We'd meant to keep it quiet for a month or two, old boy —you know, bit embarrassing for us both—but—well—seeing you've guessed it——

TRISTAN (*shaking hands with* COPLEY): I think it's wonderful.

MARTIN (*shaking hands with* DOROTHY): So do I.

TRISTAN: It's a perfect match. (TRISTAN *and* MARTIN *shake hands across centre and down.*) That's what I say, and I shall go on saying it. When people ask me what I think—and they will, you know— I shall say "I think it's a perfect match."

COPLEY (*shakes hands again with* TRISTAN): Thanks, Tristan. Flatters *me* too much, of course—but still——

MARTIN: No, I don't think it does. I might have done at one time, but now I don't.

DOROTHY (*annoyed*): You're not being insulting, by any chance, are you?

COPLEY: No, Dorothy, of course he isn't.

TRISTAN: No, Dorothy, of course he isn't. Martin couldn't insult anybody or anything—except of course the entire English Broadcasting Company—about which we'll all hear more later. (MARTIN *moves up to desk.*)

DOROTHY: All right. Come on, Arthur.

They go out, DOROTHY *with a fine possessive air.*

TRISTAN (*sits on arm of settee*): It's nice to think that Copley's called Arthur.

MARTIN: Now why didn't I realise before how terribly stupid that girl is?

TRISTAN: You weren't in a fit condition to realise it. She's one of the stupidest girls in the E.B.C. and that's saying plenty. But then you're one of those clever fellows who are idiotic when it comes to women.

MARTIN (*rising*): I was, but I'm learning. Where's Paula?

TRISTAN: Gone home long since.

MARTIN: I call that a dirty trick. (*Sits on downstage edge of desk centre.*)

TRISTAN: Why, you can't expect her to hang about here all night, on the off-chance of amusing you.

MARTIN: I oughtn't to expect it, but somehow I do. Pity she isn't more attractive.

TRISTAN: Don't be a dam' fool.

MARTIN: What does that mean?

TRISTAN: I thought you theatrical producers were supposed to have eyes.

MARTIN: Some of us have.

TRISTAN: Then take a good look at Paula next time. That is, if there is a next time, and we don't all get the sack, by special courier, to-night.

MARTIN: I suppose we might. What are you going to do then?

TRISTAN: I shall disguise myself as an Armenian astrologer and let my mother keep me. As a matter of fact, we've done nothing to deserve the sack and if we had, the E.B.C. wouldn't sack us. They'll just find some way of killing us by inches, in the decent Civil Service fashion.

Enter JOE *with record of* "*Shepherd's Hey*".

JOE: They're back, Mr. Sprott.

TRISTAN: Who is? What is?

JOE: Them Punnets.

MARTIN (*rises*): I'm going back to the pub. (*Going towards door.*)

TRISTAN: Wait for me. Order me a double horse's neck.

MARTIN *goes.*

TRISTAN (*to* JOE): How are the Punnets?

JOE: Mad as hell. They're asking for you. Shall I send 'em in?

TRISTAN: Certainly Joe, certainly. They're all I've left for to-night's programme.

JOE: D'you know what I think, Mr. Sprott?

TRISTAN: Yes, Joe. You think it's all escapist and that we ought to be doing a programme all about the town drains, with an interlude for you to tell us about your Toscanini rehearsals.

JOE (*solemnly*): Allow me to finish, Mr. Sprott. What I think is this—that the sooner these outsiders are stopped from coming in to do bits in programmes the better. There ought to be a radio trade union, and no outsiders allowed.

TRISTAN: What about Toscanini?

[283]

JOE: He'd join the union. (*Crosses and puts record in position upstage.*)

> The PUNNETS *burst in. They are carrying several awkward-shaped parcels, but no serpent. They are very angry.*

DAISY (*loudly*): My grand-dad says 'e's 'ad enough.

TRISTAN: Had enough? He hasn't begun yet.

DAISY: 'E says 'e's going 'ome. An' I'm not goin' to try an' stop 'im, becos I've 'ad enough too.

TRISTAN: But why? We've all been very nice to you, haven't we?

DAISY: No, yew 'aven't. Not a single one of you 'cept Mr. Haycraft, an' 'e's gone.

TRISTAN: But he'll be back to do the announcing——

DAISY: 'E'll do no announcin' for us, will 'e, grand-dad?

PUNNET (*winding himself up to speak, and clutching at various parcels*): Grrrrr! Oi make nuthin' of it at all, this yer E.B.C. (*Crosses to right of* TRISTAN.) Nuthin' at all, oi don't. It be all—all——

TRISTAN (*triumphantly*): I know. Slummerty-wummerty.

PUNNET (*snarling scornfully*): Neow—yew're wrong, young man. (*Loudly, to* DAISY) Daft in the 'ead, this un be, as I tould ee.

TRISTAN (*conciliatory*): Well, I may be a bit daft in the head—wouldn't be at all surprised—but this afternoon you said it was all slummerty-wummerty.

DAISY: It's worse nor that now, ain't it, grand-dad?

PUNNET (*triumphantly*): Ay. Oi've got a word for un—for all this yer foolish E.B.C. wamsy—ay, masters—for neow oi think it be all midgety-madgety. Neow more an' neow less nor midgety-madgety. (*Looks round triumphantly, as if for applause.*)

JOE (*seriously*): I ask you, Mr. Sprott, how are you going to make a revolution of the workers with types like that about?

TRISTAN (*moves a little nearer to* JOE): Well, he seems to be making one all right.

JOE: No education, that's the trouble.

DAISY: Don't you be insulting.

PUNNET (*still having trouble with his parcels, but now launched into big speeches and enjoying himself*): Eddication, young man! Oi tell ee—it be all yer mimsy-mamsy eddication an' yer midgety-madgety E.B.C. an' the like 'at's takin' the lads out o' the fields an' the maidens out o' the dairies——

TRISTAN (*helps* PUNNET *to adjust parcels, forcefully*): Now look here, grand-dad, never mind the big agricultural issue just now. The point is, you promised to help me to-night with my Barset programme and now you say you won't.

DAISY: He thinks he did it this morning.

TRISTAN: Oh—my hat! But explain, that was only a rehearsal.

JOE: We've tried him but he won't understand about rehearsals, Mr. Sprott. No education, see?

DAISY: So now he wants to go home—an' I don't blame him—the way we've been messed about to-day something shameful.

TRISTAN (*making a last attempt*): Now look here, grand-dad, I——

PUNNET (*his big speech*): Grrrr! If oi'd the care of ee, young man, oi'd grand-dad ee wi' a big stick, oi would—ay, masters, oi would —to knock parcel o' daftness out o' your head. Eddication! E.B.C., an' woirseless! Can ee do hedgin' an' ditchin'? Can ee harrow an' plough an' mow an' reap? Can ee milk a cow or calf a cow? Can ee dip a sheep or shear a sheep? Can ee ring a pig? Can ee harness an' droive a team o' horses? Who were the best bee-keeper there ever were i' North Barset?

TRISTAN: You were.

PUNNET (*triumphantly*): Wrong again, young man, for it were ould Sam'l Daggs out at Little Fitchington. Yer know nuthin' but bits o' mimsy-mamsy, midgety-madgety. (*Moves right, taking* DAISY'S *hand.* TRISTAN *follows, then* PUNNET *turns on him.*) It's the first toime yer get Matthew Punnet to yer E.B.C. an' it's the last. Oi promised to play me serpent for ee, an' oi played un this marnin', so now oi be off home. (*Crosses to door.*)

DAISY (*stopping*): But where *is* your serpent, grand-dad?

PUNNET (*passes* DAISY *across himself to door and she exits*): 'Old yer tongue, girl, an' be off home, where we belong proper. Let un keep bloody ould serpent. (*Turning in doorway to* TRISTAN.)

He goes out hurriedly.

TRISTAN: And that, Joe, just tears it. (*Staggers across to left and sits on effects box*): Now there can't be a Barset programme. The listeners will get thirty minutes of gramophone records and I shall most certainly get the boot. Well, remember me to all the boys, Joe.

JOE: Now Mr. Sprott, it isn't as bad as that. You'll manage somehow.

TRISTAN: Not this time, Joe. Sunk without a trace. I knew it this morning when I woke up. Something told me.

Enter PAULA. *She has changed her clothes, taken off her spectacles, etc., and now looks very attractive indeed.*

PAULA: Good evening, Tristan. Hello, Joe.

TRISTAN (*sadly*): Hello, Paula. You look beautiful. I feel like death.

PAULA: Tell me afterwards. I want Edna.

JOE: I'll tell her.

Goes out up right.

PAULA (*to downstage edge of piano*): What about Sir Reginald Runton?

TRISTAN: He's giving Moya dinner at the *County*, and for all I know, they may be doing a big Chekhov act together—telling each other over the prunes and custard that in a hundred years time life will be very beautiful. But what I do know is that he's talking to London, and London's talking to him.

PAULA: With certain names, no doubt, passing along the wire.

TRISTAN: No doubt, no doubt. A brewing of hell broth. Meanwhile, to give it a seasoning, there'll be no "Down Here in Barset" programme to-night.

PAULA: I've heard you say that before.

TRISTAN: But then I had most of my cast. Now I haven't any, except Hetty and Bob. And it's too late to change the script. No, it's gramophone records to-night, and curtains to-morrow.

Enter EDNA. *She is dressed to go out.*

PAULA (*crosses down to centre*): Any telegram, Edna?

EDNA: Yes, it came about half an hour ago over the telephone. (*Reads it.*) "Harland agreeable to your producer if you insist. Blake."

PAULA: Good!

TRISTAN: What *is* all this about, Paula?

PAULA: I'll explain later. Does anybody know where Martin Bradburn is?

TRISTAN: Yes, he's across at the *Lion*, doing some serious drinking.

PAULA: Edna, you're going home now, aren't you?

EDNA: Yes, unless you want me for anything.

PAULA: No, thanks. But would you mind looking in at the *Lion* on your way, and asking Martin Bradburn if he'd mind coming back here to see me about something. Say it's important.

EDNA: I'll go now.

TRISTAN: I'll be going there myself in a minute.

PAULA: No, you won't. You've a programme to do.

TRISTAN: I tell you—there can't *be* a programme——

PAULA: All right, Edna. You tell him. Good night.

[286]

EDNA (*going*): Good night, Miss Leeds.

TRISTAN: By the way, Copley and the Limple girl are tied up.

PAULA: No.

TRISTAN: Yes, definitely. Already the salad bowl from the staff and the fortnight in Torquay are stirring in the womb of Time.

PAULA: Does Martin Bradburn know?

TRISTAN: Yes. We congratulated them.

PAULA: Did he mind?

TRISTAN: No, the cure's complete.

PAULA: Thank goodness! (*Turns up to desk.*)

TRISTAN: Why?

PAULA: Well, I hate to see a man making a fool of—(*Sits at desk.*)

TRISTAN: Yes, yes. Yes, yes, yes. Quite so.

    Enter BRENDA *hurriedly and excitedly.*

BRENDA (*breathless*): Mr. Sprott!

TRISTAN (*preparing to go*): No, Brenda, a thousand times no.

BRENDA (*getting in his way*): Oh—but please listen, Mr. Sprott——

TRISTAN: The smallest imitation from you, Brenda—the tiniest flick of Beatrice Lillie or Gertrude Lawrence—at this moment, and I fell you to the ground.

BRENDA: No, please, Mr. Sprott, it's not that——

TRISTAN: What, no impersonation?

BRENDA: Yes, but——

TRISTAN: I don't care who they are, Brenda—English, American, even Chinese—I won't have 'em.

BRENDA (*pleading hard*): But this is *different*. You'll want it to-night. Listen! (*In perfect imitation of* DAISY PUNNET) "Good evenin' all. Is moi grand-dad 'ere?

TRISTAN (*impressed*): I say! That's pure Punnet. Go on.

BRENDA (*as before*): "Moi grand-dad was the foinest serpent player in the whole o' Barset. 'Ere, grand-dad, wake up an' give us all a tune."

TRISTAN: Duckie, it's perfect, but perfect. You could go straight into the programme with that.

BRENDA (*excitedly*): Well then, why can't I?

TRISTAN: You can.

BRENDA (*bubbling over*): Oh gosh! That's marvellous. I've been practising for *hours*.

TRISTAN (*who has been thinking*): No, it's no good.

BRENDA: Oh—but why?

TRISTAN: Not because of you, Brenda. You're Daisy Punnet plus that little bit of something the Punnets never had. *But*—you see, duckie—those lines of Daisy's were put into the script simply to introduce the big star act—old man Punnet's serpent-playing—a unique turn. And now the old man's gone home, all midgety-madgety.

BRENDA: Yes, but the serpent hasn't.

TRISTAN: Where is it?

BRENDA: It's still here. (*Moves to door.*)

TRISTAN: Waiting for its mate, I suppose. (BRENDA *stops.*) But, you see, these serpents don't play themselves.

BRENDA: No—but—just wait. (*Goes to door and calls*) Percy, Percy.

> *After a moment,* PERCY *enters with the serpent.*

TRISTAN (*excitedly*): Don't tell me you can play that thing, Percy?

PERCY: Listen to this, Mr. Sprott. (*Sits right below* HAYCRAFT'S *desk. He plays a short jazzy phrase.*)

PAULA: Don't swing it, Percy.

TRISTAN (*kneels on settee—triumphantly*): Oh—midgety-madgety—we can do it, we can do it. Paula.

PAULA: Yes.

TRISTAN (*calling across*): You must read the part of Nancy, assistant barmaid at the old *Brown Cow*.

PAULA: But really, Tristan, you can't drag me into your programme—especially as a Barsetshire rustic.

TRISTAN: Why not? By this time you're more a Barsetshire rustic than anyone else in the cast—you've been down here the longest.

> *Enter* MARTIN.

Bradburn, I congratulate you.

MARTIN: Why?

TRISTAN: You're going to read the part of Mr. Caxton, a regular patron of the old *Brown Cow*, in my programme to-night.

MARTIN: I'm not. (*Up to* HAYCRAFT'S *desk.*)

TRISTAN: You must. Two lines—literally. And Paula's in it too.

PAULA: I didn't say——

TRISTAN: Besides, you two fancy yourselves as people of the theatre. Well then, the show must go on. (*To* BRENDA *and* PERCY) Come on, toots, we've work to do.

> *They go out.* PERCY *closes door.* MARTIN *stares appreciatively at* PAULA. *He has come down to her left.*)

[288]

MARTIN (*admiringly*): I say!

PAULA: What do you say?

MARTIN: Why don't you always look like this?

PAULA: I try to, outside the E.B.C. I called in to collect a telegram I was expecting.

MARTIN (*disappointed*): Oh—you're going on somewhere.

PAULA: I was. To see some people I know.

MARTIN: But you asked me to come across to see you.

PAULA: Yes, did you mind?

MARTIN: No, I'm glad.

PAULA (*moves away to front of piano*): You see, I couldn't say it before, because of the telegram.

MARTIN: Where does the telegram come in?

PAULA: I'll explain later. But this really is important. (*Leans on piano—pauses, then earnestly.*) Martin, why did you leave the theatre? You were doing grand work there and you must have loved it.

MARTIN: I did love it, but I began to feel it didn't love me much.

PAULA: Not enough work?

MARTIN: Not enough regular work. And no security. I was beginning to be frightened. You see, I began producing in repertory. You know the sort of thing—eighteen hours a day, and never having time to get anything right. Then I took a chance and went to London.

PAULA: Well, then you got plenty of work.

MARTIN: I had three plays to produce in my first year. One good one—two duds. The next year, apart from some not very bright Sunday shows, I only had two to produce—one a good one, but it was a flop—and the other the usual Surrey lounge-hall bit of nonsense, which wasn't even a successful bit of nonsense. Then I'd been too pleased with myself and had rows, and, I suppose, made enemies. And then I began to get frightened. No work coming along. No money. I was broke and didn't seem to be getting anywhere at all. I'd never bothered much about broadcasting, hardly ever listened in —and thought radio drama just third-rate footling stuff.

PAULA: Which it mostly is.

MARTIN: Yes, but I happened just then to listen to an E.B.C. production of *The Wild Duck*. And it was good.

PAULA (*very quietly*): You mean the one Margaret Owen did?

MARTIN: Yes. You knew her, of course?

PAULA: She was my greatest friend. She died just after she did that production. I begged them to do a memorial programme of her work—a lot of her shows had been recorded—but of course they wouldn't. They just wanted to forget her. I never forgave them for that. It was then I stopped caring much about my work. Sorry— go on.

MARTIN (*humbly*): I've never understood you at all, have I?

PAULA: No, you don't really know anything about me. But then how could you?

MARTIN: I ought to have guessed.

PAULA (*sits on settee arm, facing* MARTIN): Please go on about yourself. This really is important.

MARTIN: Well, after hearing that production, I thought, "What's wrong with doing some of this stuff?" So I made enquiries, and they were all very nice and flattering to me at Radio House, and after a short trial trip, I signed a contract and joined the staff. That's all.

PAULA: No, it isn't. What's happened to you since?

MARTIN: Nothing very much. (*Moves down left.*) You know that part as well as I do. I can't really complain. If I haven't got on too well, I suppose it's mostly my own fault.

PAULA: No, you're wrong, it isn't really. That's what we all come to think. But it's not true. Just because, behind all their fuss and silly memos, they seem easy-going and kind and considerate.

MARTIN: That's just it. You know what a hell the theatre can be.

PAULA: Yes, but that's because it's *alive*. And this isn't. It's a nice, easy-going, kind and considerate machine—but it's still a machine. And after a time it quietly takes something vital and essential out of you.

MARTIN: Yes, I've been wondering about that. Something certainly seems to go.

PAULA: It does. I'm nearly an old stager now. Ten years of it. I've watched 'em come and go. It's not broadcasting itself. I suppose at best it's a rather limited medium, but it can be turned into something vital, moving, quite beautiful sometimes. Margaret did it. I even did it myself once or twice. What's wrong is the organisation itself, the machine. It doesn't care—and the people who run it don't care—for that precious vital impulse which makes the artist an artist. And so that impulse just fades away and dies. And that's why some of us sit about making wisecracks. If we didn't laugh so much, we might start to cry.

MARTIN: But *you* haven't given in, Paula. You couldn't talk like this if you had. You're alive all right.

PAULA: Only just. And I'm really very tough, very fierce, very determined, though I may not look it.

MARTIN: You don't—thank God!

PAULA: Besides—I've found—well—compensations.

MARTIN (*alarmed*): You're not in love with somebody?

PAULA: No, I didn't mean that.

MARTIN: You terrified me then. Listen, Paula——

PAULA: No, Martin, let's finish this first. It's most important. Never mind about regular work and security and all the rest of it. You must get out of the E.B.C.—at once, before it's too late—and you must go back to the theatre.

MARTIN: But who wants me? What am I going to do?

PAULA: You've got to take a chance on that. I may tell you that I'm going, as soon as they'll let me resign, and I don't think they'll make any difficulties about that, after what Sir Reginald Runton has told them to-night.

MARTIN: That goes for me, too.

PAULA: Yes, that goes for you too. Now you may have been forgotten in the theatre, you may have to start all over again, but that's the chance you've got to take, Martin.

MARTIN: It'll be a lot worse than you think, Paula. And I'm still almost broke.

PAULA: I dare say.

MARTIN: You wouldn't like me to kiss you, would you?

PAULA: No. One thing at a time is my motto. And you've got to decide, Martin. You've got to leap into the dark.

MARTIN (*after a pause, decisively*): I'll do it.

PAULA: That's what I wanted to hear you say, Martin. I wanted to feel you were ready to take the chance.

MARTIN: Well, I am. And a pretty thin chance it'll be.

PAULA: It's not as bad as you think. There's a play you can do at once—for Harland.

MARTIN: Harland? But how's that? Whose play is it?

PAULA: It's mine. I was determined not to tell you until you'd decided to take the chance. Harland has accepted a play of mine for production at once, and he's agreed to let you produce it if I insist. And now—I *do* insist.

MARTIN (*delighted*): Good lord, Paula—but this is marvellous. (*Moves to her.*) What a girl!

> As he advances upon her, JOE *enters.*

JOE: Ahem! The little big noise is back.

PAULA: What do you mean?

JOE: Our new D.A.D.G.—Sir Reg. So look out. (*Moving up.*) I *think*—he's bottled.

JOE *goes out.*

MARTIN: He won't have it all his own way. I'm rather bottled myself.

PAULA: Now listen, darling, there's only one thing to do. As soon as we see him, we announce that we're resigning.

MARTIN: Right. What's your play called?

PAULA (*hastily*): *The Silver Ship*—but we can talk about that afterwards.

MARTIN: I adore you.

PAULA: Good. And we can talk a lot about *that* afterwards. But just now we've got to disentangle ourselves from our E.B.C. contracts.

MARTIN: I'll bet Sir Reginald's going to throw 'em in our faces.

PAULA: Here he comes.

Enter SIR REGINALD *with* MOYA GRONOVA. *They have been dining, and both are in fine form.*

SIR REGINALD (*continuing some splendid reminiscence for the admiring* MOYA): So he said "I don't know why you should say that, Runton." So I said, "Aren't you forgetting one thing, Smithers?" "What's that?" he said. "Aren't you forgetting," I said, "that beaten copper work has been one of my hobbies for over thirty years? So I really do know what I'm talking about, old chap," I said.

GRONOVA (*earnestly*): I think you were—*splendeed.*

SIR REGINALD (*jovially*): A-ha—we—er—meet again, Miss—er—Leeds—Mr.—er—

MARTIN: Bradburn.

SIR REGINALD: Yes, of course—Bradburn. (*Sits on arm of settee.*)

GRONOVA (*sits in desk chair*): Paula, we 'ad the most wonderful deener.

PAULA: I thought you went to the *County.*

GRONOVA: We did. But to-night—it was all—*speciale.* (*Flashing a terrific glance at* SIR REGINALD.) Thanks to *you.*

SIR REGINALD (*pleased*): Well—I always say—you can get a decent dinner out of these places—if you only take a little trouble—and of course I'm an old traveller.

PAULA (*stoutly*): Sir Reginald, Martin Bradburn and I want to offer the company our resignations.

[292]

MARTIN: Thanks, Paula. (*Crosses to left of* PAULA). Yes, our resignations.

SIR REGINALD and GRONOVA *are exchanging delighted glances.*

PAULA: We're quite willing to leave at once. We'll go quietly.

GRONOVA (*to* SIR REGINALD): What did I tell you, my deear? I knew they would feel like that.

SIR REGINALD (*smiling*): You did. Well, well, well, well!

He is highly amused. PAULA *and* MARTIN *stare at him in bewilderment.*

HAYCRAFT, BOB *and* HETTY *come in. Lights are switched on left and they take up positions at studio end.*

JOE *enters up right, crosses behind piano to lower mike.* HAYCRAFT *above desk to switch on standard lamp—on his entrance he taps* GRONOVA *on shoulder, she then moves to piano and sits ready.*

MARTIN: What's the joke?

SIR REGINALD (*still amused*): It's not a joke really—but I can't help being amused by the way in which you've misjudged the—er—attitude of the company and myself. We're really not like that, y'know.

PERCY *with serpent, and then* TRISTAN, *enter.*

TRISTAN (*seeing* SIR REGINALD): Oh—help!

SIR REGINALD (*loudly*): Ah! And here's the other culprit—eh? Also ready to offer his resignation, eh? (*Moves to* TRISTAN.)

TRISTAN: Let me do my programme first. The show must go on.

SIR REGINALD! You see, I spoke to the assistant director-general at Radio House to-night, and told him frankly what you three had said about the organisation and policy of the company——

TRISTAN: All right, don't rub it in. I must go and work the panel for the last time. (*He goes into producer's box.*)

MARTIN (*to* PAULA): Everything's okay. We're fired.

PAULA: I don't know. He's got a dangerous pleasant look in his eye.

SIR REGINALD (*loudly*): Fortunately the English Broadcasting Company can appreciate frankness and forthright criticism, so I'm delighted to tell you that you've all been promoted and your contracts extended——

PAULA (*in horror*): Oh crikey! (*Sits on arm of settee.*)

MARTIN (*horrified*): What—can't we leave? (*Kneels on settee above* PAULA.)

SIR REGINALD: Certainly not. You've been promoted to the

[293]

Organisation Department. Mr. Sprott has been made Assistant Organiser of Overseas Religion.

TRISTAN (*through speaker, horrified*): *What?*

SIR REGINALD: You, Mr. Bradburn, have been appointed Controller of co-ordinated regional children's programmes.

MARTIN (*horror-struck*): Suffering Moses! (*Falls on to the settee.*)

SIR REGINALD: And you, Miss Leeds, will be director of our new Mother's Hour—"Kitchen, Kiddies and Crêpe-de-Chine".

PAULA *breaks into a peal of laughter. The red light is now flickering.* HAYCRAFT *is at the mike.*

HAYCRAFT (*sternly*): Quiet, please! (*Announces.*) "Down Here in Barset". To-night we present another half-hour of Barsetshire humour, melody and folk-lore, in a programme written and produced by Tristan Sprott. It's a beautiful summer night—the men have returned from the hayfields—the door of that friendly old pub the *Brown Cow* stands wide open—"Down Here in Barset".

MOYA *plays her tune.* PERCY *does effects. They all, except* SIR REGINALD, *now in background, produce atmosphere noises.*

BOB (*in rural voice*): 'Nother point o' coider, Rose. Oi saw your young man over boi Jenkins' twenty-acre.

HETTY (*same style*): He's no young man o' moine, Charlie Bragg isn't—not since Michaelmas Fair.

BOB: Didn't buy ee a proper fairing, oi'll be bound, Rose.

HAYCRAFT (*rural*): Oi 'eard tell on 'at tew, Garge.

PAULA (*in fine rustic fashion*): What yew tew 'eard tell on 'at isn't trew would fill the Barsetshire News onny Friday. What's for yew, Muster Caxton?

PAULA *and* MARTIN *are sharing a mike with their backs to the audience, and we see them squeezing hands behind their backs.*

MARTIN (*rural*): Pint of old an' mild, Miss Nancy.

PAULA (*as before*): Yes, Muster Caxton. Would yew be giving us a song to-noight, Muster Caxton?

HAYCRAFT: We do be expectin' your old 'ay-makin' song to-noight, Muster Caxton.

BOB: Oi'll never forget the first toime oi ever 'eard that 'ay-makin' song—dang my buttons—— (*Much laughter.*) Woi, look oo's 'ere! Young Cherry Gooseman.

BRENDA (*as* DAISY:) Good evenin' all. Is moi grand-dad 'ere?

BOB: Naow, yer grand-dad's not 'ere.

HETTY: An' that's where yew be wrong again. Garge. Ol' Gooseman's 'ere. He's asleep in the corner there.

[294]

HAYCRAFT: Woi, so 'e be. An' only man in all Barset as can still play the ould serpent.

BRENDA: Moi grand-dad was the foinest sarpent player in the whole o' Barset. 'Ere, grand-dad, wake up an' give us all a tune.

General cry of "Wake up", "Give us a tune", etc., and then PERCY *coolly begins playing a rustic tune, with just a suspicion of swing about it, while gradually the others join in with words and as they are singing the curtain comes down.*

END OF PLAY

THE GOLDEN FLEECE

A Comedy in Three Acts

THE GOLDEN FLEECE

A Comedy in Three Acts

CHARACTERS

(in the order of their appearance)

MISS WEEKS
GEORGE PRITCHET
ELSIE
MONDOVI
LADY LEADMILL
MISS SELL
TAOG
MRS. TAOG
SIR RUFUS GARRETT
LADY GARRETT
WILLIAM LOTLESS
MOLLY CUDDEN
ALEC ROTHBURY
VERONICA FRENSHAM
DR. PLUMWEATHER
PERKINS
LORD BLUEFIELD

ACT I
An evening in early autumn

ACT II
Evening, a fortnight later

ACT III
Afternoon, five days later

The Scene is the entrance lounge of the Golden Fleece Hotel, Chelmgate Spa, an inland health resort.

CHARACTERS

(in the order of their appearance)

MISS WEEKS
GEORGE PRITCHET
ELSIE
MONDOVI
LADY LEADMILL
MISS SELL
TAGG
MRS. TAGG
SIR RUFUS GARNETT
LADY GARNETT
WILLIAM LOTLESS
MOLLY CUDDEN
ALEC ROTHBURY
VERONICA FRENSHAM
DR. PLUMWEATHER
PERKINS
LORD FLEETFIELD

———

ACT I
An evening in early autumn

ACT II
Evening, a fortnight later

ACT III
Afternoon, five days later

The Scene is the entrance lounge of the Golden Fleece Hotel, Cheltingate Spa, an inland health resort.

The Golden Fleece—Copyright, 1948, *by John Boynton Priestley.*

ACT I

The Scene is the entrance lounge of the Golden Fleece Hotel, Cheltingate Spa, an inland health resort. The set is semi-circular, or a half-oval shape. Down right (actors') is a smallish door leading to a small lounge or card room. Next, right centre is the main street entrance of the hotel, big doors or a swing door set inside the big wide doorway. Next, centre back, is the curved reception desk, with registration books, pigeon-holes for letters at back, telephones, etc. On left of this, which may or may not be behind prolongation of counter, is the door that leads into the staff part of hotel and is only used by employees—called Staff Door in script. About middle of left wall is door to rest of hotel, to lift and stairs, etc.—called Main Door. Between Staff Door and Main Door, near wall can be low table with lounge behind and a small chair or two, and another near wall between Main Door and Pros. Left. Another low table with chairs should be placed a little left of centre in mid-stage. Near reception desk are usual notices of picture-houses, theatre, lectures, Royal Pump Room hours and concerts, etc. The scene should suggest a stuffy comfort, and therefore must not be too modern in decoration, though not farcically Victorian.

At rise of curtain, lights are on. It is late in the evening. MISS WEEKS, *reception clerk, in black, neat, not unattractive, about thirty, with a "refaned" manner for guests and a much more shrewd manner for others, is behind the desk, finishing up.* GEORGE PRITCHET, *a rather gloomy middle-aged waiter, is hanging about the lounge, waiting for a final order or two before going off duty, and emptying an ashtray, flicking away a bit of dust, etc.*

MISS WEEKS (*just audible*): And three—and twelve and six—fifteen and six—and eleven and six—twenty-seven shillings—one pound seven—and thirteen and nine—two pounds and ninepence—and four shillings—two pounds four and nine—two—four-nine. . . . (*Looks up some other figure in ledger.*) Five and seven—seven and nine's one and four—six and four's ten—two—ten—four. And three, eight, two. That's five—eighteen—six. You were saying . . .

She books it, and looks speculatively in the direction of GEORGE, *who takes it as encouragement to continue a conversation that was broken off.*

GEORGE (*gloomily*): Yes, two hundred pounds, that's all. Say,

[301]

twenty fivers and ten tenners. That's all they wanted, and I couldn't lay me 'ands on it. If I could, look where I'd 'ave been now.

MISS WEEKS (*carrying on*): Five—eighteen—six. Well, where would you have been?

GEORGE (*bitterly*): In Preston Pans, with a nice business of me own.

MISS WEEKS: Eight—nine—five. Nine—five—and eleven.

GEORGE: And another thing——

MISS WEEKS (*not too impatiently*): Now, just a minute. Five—and eleven—ten, two and eight—and fifteen and four—ten—eighteen. That's it. (*Gives him all her attention now.*) Well, you're not the only one. If everybody had their own, I'd have five thousand pounds— *at least*—and a third share in a wholesale butcher's in Melbourne. That's what my mother always says. Only her brother—my uncle Fred—it was his money and business—went and lost his memory just before he died—only the lawyers said we'd never prove it. So it just shows you.

GEORGE (*bitterly*): It doesn't need to show me. I've been shown. Luck! If I told you half the things that's 'appened to me, you'd call me a liar.

Telephone rings.

MISS WEEKS (*at telephone*): The Golden Fleece Hotel—yes? ("*Refaned*" now.) Who is it, please? I can't quaite catch. Yes, the lane is very bad. Oh—Mrs. Gore—yes? . . . On Saturday? Yes, of course, Mrs. Gore . . . Did you say the First Flore, Mrs. Gore? . . . Oh, Ai think so. Ai'm sure that can be arranged . . . Yes, of course, Mrs. Gore . . . On Saturday then, Mrs. Gore . . . (*Puts down telephone. In ordinary voice.*) That's that, Mrs. Gore.

GEORGE: Yes, she's stayed with us before, Mrs. Gore. (*Pleased with himself now.*) Here, did you notice that? She's stayed with us before, Mrs. Gore—eh? All you want's a bit of music to it. (*As this provokes no response.*) Don't laugh.

MISS WEEKS: I'm not going to. Takes more than that to make me laugh, this time of night.

Yawns, then begins leisurely tidying up. GEORGE goes over to Card Room door and peeps through. She looks up and sees him strolling back.

Um!

GEORGE (*going nearer, dropping voice*): Still there.

MISS WEEKS: Who are they?

GEORGE (*same tone*): Sir Something Garnett an' his wife an' that other pair—chap with no manners——

MISS WEEKS: Mr. Tagg?

GEORGE: That's right. And no class at all.

MISS WEEKS: They've plenty of money.

GEORGE (*in despair*): I dare say. Beats me how some of 'em picks it up. Luck again.

ELSIE, *a youngish chambermaid, with a hot-water bottle in her hand, looks in hastily through Staff Door.*

ELSIE (*urgently, in loud whisper*): Miss Weeks!

MISS WEEKS: Well?

ELSIE: Is Molly about?

MISS WEEKS: Haven't seen her. She's not back on duty till eleven.

ELSIE: I know—but Number Eighteen's asking for her—silly old geezer. I s'pose she wants Molly to sing her to sleep.

GEORGE: What for? You'd do for me.

ELSIE (*haughtily*): Don't be personal, please, Mr. Pritchet. (*To* MISS WEEKS) Tell Molly when she comes. Number Eighteen—S.O.S.

Withdraws hastily.

Sound of a large car outside. MISS WEEKS *and* GEORGE *look towards Street Door, and* GEORGE *moves forward, to look out.*

GEORGE (*whispering*): Don't think it's anybody new. The Old Leadmill, I think. (*Waits at door.*)

MONDOVI, *the manager, now enters through Staff Door. He is a middle-aged Italian, dressed very formally in morning coat or dinner jacket. He has a letter or two, which he tosses on desk.*

MONDOVI (*importantly*): On Tuesday—the second-floor suite— twenty-eight an' twenty-eight A—for Mistair an' Misses Baxter, of Birmingham. They are all right. Vairy reech. Nice-a people.

MISS WEEKS ("*refaned*" *again*): Yes, Mr. Mondovi. And Mrs. Gore rang up to ask for the usual first flore rooms for Saturday and the next fortnight. I said I was sure that would be quaite all raight.

MONDOVI: But of course. We know Mrs. Gor-a vairy well. Always spenda plenty money. Nice-a People—Vairy Reech. Nice-a-people.

Sound of voices outside. He looks, managerially.

Who is-a thees?

MISS WEEKS: Ai believe—Lady Leadmill.

MONDOVI *comes forward, ready to smile and rub his hands. Assisted by* GEORGE *at door,* LADY LEADMILL *makes a tremendous entrance, followed by her companion,* MISS SELL. LADY LEADMILL *is a stout, elderly woman, like a bulging-eyed, upholstered monster.*

[303]

*She has a loud, wheezing voice. They have been out to dinner, but
are well wrapped up.*

MONDOVI (*now bowing and smiling*): Good-a evenin', Lady Leadmill! You enjoy your-a evenin' away from us, eh?

LADY LEADMILL: No, I can't say I did very much, Mondovi. They
keep a very poor table up there, I must say. The veal was even worse
than yours.

MONDOVI: I 'ave spoken vairy specially to chef about-a that veal,
Lady Leadmill. An' I am so sorry about-a your evenin'.

LADY LEADMILL: Then they took us to a lecture about some place
or other. Where was it, Miss Sell?

MISS SELL: (*timidly*) The Adriatic coast, I think it was.

MONDOVI (*all interest and enthusiasm*): Oh yais, I know it well
Vairy nice-a. Spalato—Ragusa——

LADY LEADMILL (*cutting in ruthlessly*): I dare say. Couldn't make
much of it myself out. And the lantern slides were most peculiar.
Some of them had *nothing whatever* to do with it. I distinctly recognised Market Harborough once—and another time Bury St. Edmunds.
Ridiculous of the Colonel to say I dozed off. How could I have
recognised Bury St. Edmunds if I'd dozed off? Eh, Miss Sell?

MISS SELL (*timidly*): Well, I did think once . . .

LADY LEADMILL (*heartily*): Nonsense, you never thought at all.
Did you tell Horrocks to bring round the Rolls at eleven in the
morning?

MISS SELL: Yes, Lady Leadmill.

LADY LEADMILL (*to* MISS WEEKS): Where are my letters?

MISS WEEKS: Ai'm afraid there aren't any to-night, Lady Leadmill.

LADY LEADMILL: Are you sure?

MONDOVI (*fussily*): Now make-a quite-a sure there are no letters
for Lady Leadmill.

MISS WEEKS (*who has looked again, apologetically*): No, not to-
night.

MONDOVI: So sorry—not-a to-night-a.

LADY LEADMILL (*sternly*): The posts here are most peculiar.

MISS SELL (*timidly*): Yes. A letter of mine——

LADY LEADMILL (*abruptly*): Good night.

MISS SELL (*resignedly echoing*): Good night.

MISS WEEKS (*effusively*): Good night, Lady Leadmill. Good night.

MONDOVI *has gone to Main Door and now stands holding it open, bowing and smiling, as* LADY LEADMILL *sails through, followed by* MISS SELL.

MONDOVI: Good night-a, your ladyship. Goo-ood night-a. Thank-a you so much. Good night-a!

Meanwhile, GEORGE *and* MISS WEEKS *have exchanged significant looks of disgust.* MONDOVI *returns to see these. They both look at him, he looks at them, is about to say something forceful, decides not to, gives a tremendous and most significant shrug, and closes his eyes.*

I go to bed.

Marches out Staff Door.

GEORGE, *looking particularly bitter, comes nearer* MISS WEEKS.

GEORGE (*with bitter parody, softly*): Nice-a people! Vairy reech!

To show what she feels about it, MISS WEEKS *closes her ledger with a sharp-tempered bang, and continues clearing up.* GEORGE, *yawning, flicks a bit more ash off a table. From Card Room come* MR. TAGG, *about fifty-five, coarse-grained North-countryman,* MRS. TAGG, *a year or two younger and a simple woman,* LADY GARNETT, *same age but more self-confident and genteel, and* SIR RUFUS GARNETT, *a thin, worrying fellow. The men are in dinner jackets, and the women expensively but badly dressed.*

MRS. TAGG (*continuing calculations after bridge*): Now are you sure we've got it all straightened out? I know I owed fifteen and six——

LADY GARNETT: No, eighteen shillings, if you remember. So I want another half-crown.

MRS. TAGG: Oh—then I'll have to settle with you in the morning —unless you've got half a crown, Father.

TAGG *hands over half-crown to* LADY GARNETT.

SIR RUFUS: Good game, I thought.

MRS. TAGG (*hopefully*): So did I, Sir Rufus. You enjoyed it, didn't you, Father?

TAGG (*crushingly*): No, I didn't.

LADY GARNETT: Oh, come, Mr. Tagg——

TAGG (*same tone*): I'm not blaming you. But I enjoy a game o' bridge when I play with people who return my leads and don't keep their aces as if they wanted to go to bed with 'em. (*Glaring at his wife.*)

SIR RUFUS: Now, now, no post-mortems. And as the winner, I say—what about a drink?

MRS. TAGG: Oo—not for me, Sir Rufus, thank you all the same.

I ought to get to bed, because I'm supposed to be down at the Pump Room at eight o'clock every morning.

LADY GARNETT (*moving*): I think we all ought to be going to bed. So don't be long, Rufus.

SIR RUFUS: No, dear, just one for the road. Eh, Tagg?

Moves fussily, as the two women go out through Main Door. MISS WEEKS has now gone. GEORGE is anxious to get this last order in, so does not bother opening the door for the women but hovers round the men, who now sit down at one of the tables.

What's it to be, eh? Say the word.

TAGG (*bluntly*): Double 'Aig an' small Polly for me.

SIR RUFUS: An' I'll have the same, waiter.

GEORGE (*briskly*): Two double 'Aigs an' Pollies, thank you, sir.

Goes out Staff Door.

SIR RUFUS: Always enjoy a game of bridge.

TAGG: So do I when it's played properly. But my wife won't try and learn. But I was tellin' you about Fawcett. Well, he puts up sixteen thousand—that is, of his own money.

SIR RUFUS: Well, tidy little sum.

TAGG: Oh—Fawcett's worth a couple o' hundred thousand pound, if he's worth a penny. What's sixteen thousand to 'im? 'Owever, that's what he puts up, in the first place, and in the original issue that gives 'im a controlling interest.

SIR RUFUS: What—for sixteen thousand?

TAGG: Ah—but look at the way they worked it. Very clever! But then Fawcett *is* clever. I dare say he doesn't look it, but then a lot of us don't look it, yet we manage to surprise some folk.

LADY GARNETT: Rufus!

Breaks off because his wife and LADY GARNETT have returned.

TAGG: Now, what's up now?

LADY GARNETT: We can't find anybody to work the lift.

MRS. TAGG: I said I didn't mind walking up, but Lady Garnett wants the lift.

TAGG: Well, why not? We've paid for a lift, why shouldn't we 'ave it when we want it.

SIR RUFUS: Quite so. Just slackness on somebody's part. Good deal of slackness here, if you ask me.

As GEORGE enters with drinks.

Ah—there you are, waiter. Nobody working the lift, y'know. Keeping these ladies waiting. Not good enough.

[306]

TAGG: Time you brightened up, some of you.

GEORGE: Very sorry, sir, I expect the man's gone off duty. I'll tell the Night Porter. It's 'is fault really.

GEORGE *goes out hastily through Staff Door.*

SIR RUFUS: Sure you won't have anything, my dear?

LADY GARNETT (*severely*): No, and if you'd any sense, you wouldn't either, at this time of night.

TAGG (*heavily*): I like a drop o' whisky before I go to bed.

MRS. TAGG (*proudly*): Always did, didn't you, Father? (*To* LADY GARNETT) Always did.

TAGG: It 'elps to settle my stomach. (*To* LADY GARNETT, *who winces.*) Might do yours too. I over'eard you complainin' to my wife.

LADY GARNETT *closes her eyes.* GEORGE *hastily returns.*

GEORGE (*hurriedly*): He's just gone through now.

MRS. TAGG (*who is servile to waiters*): Thank you very much.

Follows after LADY GARNETT, *who is stalking out.*

The men are now attending to their drinks. GEORGE *is coming closer.*

TAGG: Well—all the best! (*Drinks.*)

SIR RUFUS: Cheers! (*Drinks.*)

TAGG: Yes—there's several of us who's a bit cleverer than we look, especially where money's concerned. We've chaps on our exchange —an' to look at 'em, yer wouldn't think they were worth ninepence —but—don't you make a mistake, some of 'em could write you a cheque for a quarter of a million——

GEORGE (*to* SIR RUFUS): Beg pardon, sir, will you be wanting anything else just now?

SIR RUFUS (*blankly*): Why should I?

GEORGE: Only you see, sir, I'm going off duty now, an' if you *don't* want anything else, perhaps you'd like to sign for these, before I'm away.

SIR RUFUS (*putting down sixpence*): There you are.

GEORGE: Thank you, sir. Good night, gentlemen.

Exits Staff Door.

SIR RUFUS (*staring after him*): Bit arbitrary, that chap, wasn't he? Pay up and let me be off—sort of thing. Eh?

TAGG: There's one or two of 'em could do with dressing down a bit. These old women spoil 'em. My wife's not much better. I keep saying to her, "We're payin' for it, aren't we? See yer get yer money's worth. And a smile an' all." That's what I tell her, but it does no good. She's too soft.

> *Enter, through Main Door,* WILLIAM LOTLESS, *the Night Porter. He is a middle-aged man, with an intelligent, humorous face, grey hair, clean-shaven, and is wearing hotel uniform.*

WILL (*richly*): Good evening, gentlemen. Very quiet to-night again, isn't it? (*Nods and smiles and is passing them.*)

SIR RUFUS: Now, just a minute.

> WILL *stops and turns.*

You're the Night Porter, aren't you?

WILL (*cheerfully*): Yes, sir. William Lotless is the name, and I've been Night Porter here for—oh!—two or three years. Anything I can do for you, sir?

TAGG: Aren't you supposed to be working that lift when the day man goes off.

SIR RUFUS: Just what I was going to ask.

WILL: Yes, that's one of my jobs. Just one of them. I also supply any drinks that may be wanted, answer the door or telephone, arrange for early morning——

TAGG: All right. All right. We don't want to know all that. What we want to know is why you weren't working that lift when Lady Garnett and my wife were waiting there, a few minutes since.

WILL (*confidentially*): Now, I'm sorry about that. But I'll explain how it is. Now the liftman goes off at eleven every night. But he takes his time from the clock along there, which is always five minutes faster than *our* clock through here. And the trouble is—well, we're both a bit stubborn about it.

SIR RUFUS: Seems a poor reason why guests should be kept waiting.

WILL: That I grant you, sir, I grant it like lightning. And if I'd *known* the ladies were waiting, I'd have been out in a flash. As I was—in a flash—when I *did* know. But, you see, George the waiter here didn't let on.

TAGG: What's he got to do with it?

WILL: Well, it's like everything else—wheels within wheels. Now when I come on duty, George has to go off, and if there are any drinks wanted I serve 'em. But you've just ordered some drinks—and—given him something for his trouble, I've no doubt——

SIR RUFUS: Matter of fact, I did.

WILL: There you are. Now George was after that tip, that's why he didn't tell me to come on duty before you'd ordered. Not that

I'm blaming him, y'know. Very natural thing to do. But I'm just explaining. I tell you, very interesting, this hotel business.

TAGG: Interesting or not, you seem to 'ave plenty to say about it.

WILL (*quietly*): No, sir. That doesn't follow. I can hold my tongue.

Moves away with dignity and goes into space behind counter. where he puts on his glasses and looks at the registration book, etc, The other two take a look at him, look at each other, rather uneasily, have a drink each.

SIR RUFUS (*after a pause*): You were saying—er——?

TAGG (*with mouth-on-one-side manner*): What I'm saying is that there's a bit too much cheek and impudence about a few of 'em round 'ere for my liking.

SIR RUFUS (*same manner*): Have a word with the manager in the morning, I think. Got rather a pull here, matter of fact, because I know Gleason well—director of the syndicate running these hotels, I think. I'll just—er——

Looks round and sees WILL looking calmly in their direction over his spectacles, and hesitates and pauses.

TAGG: What?

SIR RUFUS: Turn in, I think, eh? (*Finishes drink.*)

TAGG (*getting up*): I'm ready. (*Shouting across to desk*) Lift!

WILL *comes across.*

SIR RUFUS: I see East Africans are coming up. Nice rise to-day. Wonder if it's too late for a flutter there.

TAGG (*as they move with WILL in attendance*): No. But I got in weeks ago, an' I'm sitting tight on 'em for a bit yet.

They go out, WILL bringing up rear, smiling rather maliciously.

After a short pause, telephone on desk rings. Nothing happens. It goes on ringing. Enter, Staff Door, MOLLY CUDDEN, a pleasant-looking, good-tempered, ripe woman in a chambermaid's uniform. She is carrying a rubber hot-water bottle in cover under her arm, and a small tray with a steaming hot drink in a cup on it. She looks at the telephone, hesitates, puts down the tray, touches it, hesitates, then as it rings again and nobody else is coming, she answers it rather tentatively.

MOLLY: Golden Fleece Hotel—Mrs. Ferguson? Oh, she's feeling a lot better . . . Well, you see, I'm Molly Cudden, the chambermaid on night duty, and I've just been upstairs—and Mrs. Ferguson told me earlier to look in to see if she wanted anything—so I peeped in and she was sleeping nicely . . . Yes, I'm sure she's a lot better . . .

Oh yes, I've heard her talk about you—and her little grandson. How is he? . . . Isn't that nice? . . . Good night.

WILL (*enters as she puts down telephone*): Good evening, Molly.

MOLLY: Good evening, Will. Good job I was here to answer that. It was Mrs. Ferguson's daughter ringing up to know how she was. Well, what's amusing you, Mr. Lotless?

WILL: Oh, that rude chap—Bag or Rag or Tagg or whatever they call him—I've just taken him and another chap up in the lift, after they'd practically told me to shut up, and this Rag or Tagg's very pleased with himself because he's got a lot of East Africans——

MOLLY: East Africans? Black men?

WILL: No, shares. And though they're going up, he says he's holding on to 'em. He's clever, he is—oh—he's not going to sell yet.

MOLLY: Well, what's funny about that?

WILL (*chuckling*): The bottom'll drop out of that market very soon, you'll see, and those East Africans won't even be worth what he gave for 'em. I tell you, it took me all my time to keep my face straight when he was saying how clever he was.

MOLLY (*staring at him*): You know, I don't understand you, Mr. Lotless.

WILL: Ah—that's how it should be, Mrs. Cudden. (*Points to himself*) Mystery man.

MOLLY (*ignoring this, earnestly*): But how d'you know about all these shares an' things? Who tells you?

WILL: Nobody tells me. I work it out for myself. I've plenty of time on my hands, these nights here, an' I read all the financial pages in the papers and—well, I work it out for myself. I'm not always right—couldn't be, of course—an' some weeks I take a fairly big loss—like the week before last, I took a nasty tumble on Gold Coasts—must have been about a hundred and fifty thousand pounds down on that lot——

MOLLY (*staggered*): What are you talking about?

WILL: Oh—it's just a sort of game I play with myself, following the market. Here, look——

Brings out note-book and shows her some pages.

MOLLY (*staring*): They don't make any sense to me.

WILL (*pointing*): Now last week I'd have made about half a million —do you see?

MOLLY: But I don't see.

WILL (*showing her*): It's all there, properly worked out.

MOLLY (*staring at him now*): I do think you're a funny chap, Mr. Lotless. I mean, all this—it's all nothing, really—isn't it?

WILL (*gravely*): All imaginary, yes, of course. Just for amusement. That's the only way I'd ever do it now, I promised myself that.

MOLLY (*quickly*): Why did you—and when did you?

WILL (*holding up warning finger*): Ah! I've told you before, Molly Cudden, not to be too curious.

As she looks offended, turning away.

Now don't take offence. We have our work to do—you upstairs, me down here—and we're friends, aren't we?

MOLLY (*simply*): Yes, Mr. Lotless. I think you're a very nice man —I've never worked with a nicer in this business—and I know that really you're very clever and not a bit like an ordinary Night Porter. But, you see, when you're so different, I can't help being curious, can I?

WILL: That's all right, Molly.

MOLLY (*indicating tray*): Oh—goodness!—look at that. And Number Eighteen's waiting for it. (*Takes up tray, and prepares to go.*) Oh—Mr. Lotless——

WILL (*who has gone to clear small table*): Yes, Molly?

MOLLY (*hastily but impressively*): You remember I told you about all those papers my uncle sent—y'know, the uncle who died so sudden week before last—well, I've brought them for you to look at. Y'know, you promised you would.

WILL: Yes. Where are they?

MOLLY: I'll bring them down, when I've taken this to Eighteen and seen if Twenty-four wants her Benger's again. Shan't be long.

She hurries out with tray through Main Door.

WILL *takes glasses, etc., from counter through Staff Door and comes out with several newspapers. He goes behind desk with these and prepares to read. He can now have changed lighting, so that there is a good light on one of the tables and over the desk and not much elsewhere. He can hum or whistle softly.*

Enter from street VERONICA FRENSHAM *and* DR. ALEC ROTH-BURY. *She is a very handsome girl, about twenty-eight, extremely well-dressed—she is wearing evening clothes—and with an air of luxurious sophistication. He is about thirty, tall, intelligent, rather awkward, and wears an anything but immaculate dinner jacket. They have only met three or four times, but he is obviously in love with her, and she knows it but does not take him very seriously.*

WILL (*coming forward*): Good evening, miss. Good evening, Doctor.

ALEC: Evening, William. Any message for me?

WILL: No, sir.

ALEC: Good! Miss Frensham, have a drink.

VERONICA (*hesitating*): Well, I don't know. I'm going in the morning—and——

ALEC (*eagerly*): That's all the more reason why you ought to have a drink.

VERONICA (*smiling*): All right.

They go over to the lighted table. WILL *comes along.*
I think—a gin and lime.

ALEC: A gin and lime. And I'll have a lager, William.

WILL: One gin and lime, one lager.

Goes out Staff Door. They light cigarettes.

VERONICA (*not unpleasantly*): Well, the Wednesday dance at the Grand Hotel wasn't any improvement on the Friday dance at the Golden Fleece here, was it?

ALEC (*gloomily*): No. Hoped it might be, for your sake.

VERONICA: Why for my sake?

ALEC: I don't go to these affairs in the ordinary way. I suggested it just to have a good excuse to talk to you again—and to look at you.

VERONICA (*after slight pause*): Go on.

ALEC: Go on? I've finished.

VERONICA: No more compliments?

ALEC: Must you have compliments?

VERONICA: Not at all. I rather dislike them from the sort of men who are good at it——

ALEC: That's not me.

VERONICA: I know. They're amusing coming from you because they're so obviously against the grain. You're the kind of young doctor who loves being brutally frank—and rather rude. In fact, I heard one of these old women here—I think it was Lady Leadmill —complaining about you. She said she was going to warn your senior partner against you when he came back.

ALEC (*bitterly*): Senior partner! Don't flatter me. Old Plumweather's my boss, who pays me by the month. And the only reason why I'm able to stay in this hotel is that Plumweather stays here, keeps a consulting room here, and they put a bed for me in the little spare room next to it. Otherwise I couldn't afford it.

VERONICA: And what did you say to poor old Lady Leadmill?

[312]

ALEC: She came moaning about not being able to sleep, so I told her she was grossly over-eating.

She laughs.

No, it's not funny. It's disgusting. The old woman treats herself as if she was a Strasbourg goose. Tea and bread-and-butter at eight-thirty. At nine-thirty a large breakfast, and at eleven-thirty perhaps coffee and a cake or two. At one-thirty a three- or four-course lunch. At four-thirty she tucks into toast and sandwiches and cake. At eight-thirty she's eating a six-course dinner. At ten-thirty——

WILL *has now arrived with the drinks.*

WILL (*putting them down*): Gin and lime. Lager.

ALEC: Thanks. I'll settle with you later, William.

WILL: Certainly, sir.

Goes back to desk and buries himself behind newspaper. The other two drink.

VERONICA: But even if she does over-eat, why should you be rude to the silly old thing? What does it matter?

ALEC: It wouldn't matter if there was just one of her, but there are thousands and thousands of her—like—like stuffed old frogs—crocodiles—dinosaurs. This country's full of 'em. And there they are, doing no good to anybody, not even to themselves—and because they have the money, demanding services all day long from other people. That's what you see everywhere in this country—the living waiting upon the half-dead.

VERONICA: That's a curious thing for a doctor to say. After all, isn't he one of the living waiting on the half-dead?

ALEC: I'm not talking about the sick. I'm talking about these people who have money, appetites, prejudices, and nothing else. And I say the place is full of 'em, and we can't get on with anything worth doing because they demand our services.

VERONICA: Nobody compels you to give your services.

ALEC (*bitterly*): Oh! Now, my dear Veronica——

VERONICA (*coolly*): I am not your dear Veronica, Dr. Rothbury.

ALEC (*as before*): I know you're not, but unfortunately for my peace of mind, I've spent the last week imagining you were.

VERONICA: And you never told me! Now why have you?

ALEC (*through his teeth*): Because I seem to have been silly enough to have—what do you people call it——?

VERONICA: Oh—we people call it all sorts of things.

ALEC: Don't be so damned flippant. Just remember even if this isn't serious for you, it is for me.

[313]

VERONICA (*sharply*): Now wait a moment. (*Smiles beguilingly at him.*) Look at me.

ALEC (*groans*): I don't want to look at you. (*But he does.*) I know. You're beautiful. I've admitted it.

VERONICA: Don't be so grudging. Don't you *like* it?

ALEC (*muttering*): I do—worse luck!

VERONICA (*coolly*): All money, y'know. These clothes—and I assure you I wouldn't look at all the same in any old thing—they cost money. Figure, hands, hair, face—all cost money too. Looking really attractive is an expensive full-time job.

ALEC (*miserably*): All right, you've won. And don't think it hadn't occurred to me. I've been chewing it over for the last week and not enjoying the taste of it.

Telephone rings. WILL answers it, then calls.

WILL: It's the Cottage Hospital for you, doctor.

ALEC: Right. (*To VERONICA*) Just a minute.

Goes to telephone. She watches him, smiling a little.

Yes, Dr. Rothbury here. . . . I see . . . Yes, I'll come round.

Returns to VERONICA, who rises.

Sorry, but I'll have to go round to the hospital. Don't suppose I'll be long, if you'd care to wait.

VERONICA: Too late. And I'm catching the nine-fifteen to town in the morning. So I must say good-bye—now.

ALEC (*awkwardly*): Yes—well——

VERONICA (*smiling, holding out her hand*): Good-bye, then. And thank you—for——

ALEC (*bitterly*): Trying to entertain you—eh?

VERONICA (*coolly*): When you're older and have work you enjoy more, you won't be so arrogant and aggressive, you might——

ALEC (*roughly*): I might be like one of these bedside pussycats. (*Stares at her.*) Well, it's good-bye. And I wish now you'd never set foot in this place.

VERONICA (*a little closer, smiling provocatively*): Oh—why?

ALEC (*savagely*): All right, if you will ask for it.

Seizes her roughly and kisses her soundly.

Good-bye.

VERONICA (*coldly*): That was very stupid.

ALEC (*hastily*): I know. I am stupid. Good-bye.

He hurries out.

She watches him go, then takes bag from table rather slowly and thoughtfully, while MOLLY *enters through Main Door.*

MOLLY (*cheerfully*): Good evening, miss. I heard you'd gone.

VERONICA (*pleasantly*): No, I go in the morning. You're not on duty in the mornings this week, are you?

MOLLY: No, miss. Nights, instead. They usually give me the late turn. I don't mind it, and the younger ones hate it.

VERONICA (*who has taken five shillings out of her bag*): Thank you for looking after me so nicely.

MOLLY (*receiving tip*): Oh—thank you, miss. It was a pleasure, I'm sure. Thank you for the shoes. You gave me no trouble at all, and it's a nice change having somebody who's young an' nice-lookin' an' with all their health an' strength. I hope you'll come back here.

VERONICA (*smiling*): I'm afraid I shan't, y'know. Cheltingate isn't exactly my style.

MOLLY (*earnestly*): Well, I know it's a bit—sort of—stuffy an'—an'—purse-proud, but for all that it's very nice sometimes. Often when I've the afternoon off I just sit down in the gardens when the band's playin'—and if the sun's shining an' the flowers are out an' the birds hopping round you, it's as pretty as a picture, an' I just sit, half in a kind of dream, if you follow me—an'—well, I wouldn't want anything nicer.

VERONICA: Lovely! Good night, Molly. (*Pauses, hesitating.*) Do you know Dr. Rothbury?

MOLLY: I should think I do. Lives here, you see. Doesn't like it, you know. Wants to be off. He's a bit silly, like all young fellows, but he's a grand young man when you get to know him—very kind and clever with it too. On at the Cottage Hospital, they swear by him. (*Confidentially, but not impudently*) I think you rather fancy him yourself, don't you?

VERONICA: Good lord—no. In fact, I'm rather annoyed with him.

MOLLY: Yes, but what's that? You can be annoyed with them just because you're interested, can't you?

VERONICA: You *can*, but it doesn't follow that you are. Well, good night, Molly.

MOLLY (*holding door open*): Good night, miss.

VERONICA *goes out.*

MOLLY *comes in and in her tidy way picks the two glasses from the table and goes to counter, behind which* WILL *is still buried in his newspaper. She waits for a moment, regarding him—or what she can see of him—with humorous, affectionate impatience.*

[315]

Well, I wouldn't call you very sociable.

WILL (*lowering the paper*): I'll explain.

MOLLY: I never knew such a chap for explaining. Here, what about these? Shall I take 'em through? (*Indicating the glasses she holds.*)

WILL (*taking them*): No—and many thanks for bringing 'em, Mrs. Cudden—but they'll do here for the time being. (*Puts them down at back, then comes forward.*) I'll explain. Now—the reason I'd got so buried behind that paper wasn't that I was specially interested in it, although I see that Harrin and his gang are making a big play for Heavy Industrials and may catch a cold——

MOLLY: Now don't start on about shares and markets or I won't listen. Tell me why you were hiding behind your paper.

WILL: Because I'd been busy effacing myself. Being here on duty, of course, as I have to be, but at the same time, as you might say, being *not* here.

MOLLY: Why?

WILL: Because the handsome young lady who has just left us had been having a little private talk—a tête-à-tête—with our friend Dr. Rothbury.

MOLLY: Ah, that's why she asked about him. I'll bet you listened to all they said, you an' your newspaper! Didn't you? You ought to be ashamed. What did they say?

WILL: He's gone on her. He's smitten. He's done for. Told her so.

MOLLY (*delighted*): Isn't that nice? But I've always said about Dr. Rothbury—let the Right Girl come along—and you'll see.

WILL: I can never understand why you women want everybody sorted out in pairs and tied up and put to bed—as if you were running a lot of Noah's Arks. Nature's bad enough without all you women egging her on all the time.

MOLLY (*earnestly*): I know, but look what a lot of happiness it brings too. And I say—take a chance. For I believe in happiness, Mr. Lotless. Plenty of people don't—they pretend to but they don't, not right down inside themselves—they're against it and against people who are happy. But not me. (*Pause.*) Now what did she say?

WILL: Oh well, it didn't go your way at all, this affair didn't. So don't start fancying anything for them. It's all off. Money again, you see. He hasn't any. She's got too much.

MOLLY: Has she? News to me. An' she only gave me five shillings.

WILL: Maybe. But you ought to know by this time—the richer they are, the less they give you. And why? I'll explain.

MOLLY: You needn't. I'm thinking about them poor silly young things. If I'd known, I'd have said a lot more to her. I think it's a shame. A fine clever young man like that. An' after telling her that he worshipped the ground she walked on!

WILL: He didn't say that. I'll bet nobody's ever said that outside of a sloppy story.

MOLLY: An' that's where you're wrong again, Mr. Clever. Because it was said to me—once—years ago—when I was only a girl—by a friend of my brother's. He said he worshipped the ground I walked on.

WILL: He must have been soft in the head.

MOLLY: He was a bit. I can see him now. He had them very light eyelashes, and he was a barber and his name was Cyril. But for all that, that didn't stop him, afterwards, from marrying a widow fifteen years older than he was—she owned three grocers' shops——

Hotel internal bells rings. WILL *answers it.*

WILL (*at telephone*): Yes, madam ... I'll tell her ... (*Puts down.*) Well, there's another who worships the ground you walk on—Number Eighteen—and she wants another hot-water bottle. How many does that make?

MOLLY: Four. The poor old thing can't sleep, and she wants an excuse to tell me all over again about her daughter in India.

Moves towards Staff Door.

WILL: If she'd gone with her to India she wouldn't want so many hot-water bottles. (*Just watching* MOLLY *as she goes.*) What about those papers your uncle left you that you wanted me to go through? Where are they?

MOLLY (*hastily*): I brought them down. I'll give you 'em now.

She hurries out. He puts on his spectacles, takes out his pipe and prepares to sit not at desk, but at a table outside. MOLLY *comes out with old worn despatch case or something of the kind.*

Here you are. I expect it's all rubbish really—it looked rubbish to me—but you might have a look, Mr. Lotless. An' I'll bring some tea in when I come down.

WILL (*taking case*): That's the idea, Molly. And I'll give this stuff my very best attention.

She goes out Staff Door—while he settles down to look through case, taking papers out and preparing to examine them in a business-like fashion. Before he has done more than look at the first document, he is interrupted by the return of ALEC.

ALEC: Miss Frensham turned in, I suppose, as soon as I'd gone?

WILL: She did, doctor.

ALEC (*more to himself than to* WILL): I might write her a note.

WILL (*coolly*): I shouldn't.

ALEC: Oh—why?

WILL: If they're really interested, they always write to you. If they're not, then why should you bother writing? Besides it's only committing yourself.

ALEC (*staring*): I believe you're right, though I don't know that that's any real excuse for not minding your own business.

WILL (*coolly*): I've wondered about that myself. Never could make up my mind.

ALEC (*still staring*): Well, it's my turn to butt in now. Come here, William my friend. No, closer—that's it. Take off your glasses.

Has WILLIAM *standing before him in strong light. He now takes from his pocket about half a sheet of newspaper, folded, and puts it across the lower half of* WILLIAM'S *face, in such a way that he can look at the upper half of the face and at a photograph—of a bearded man—in the newspaper, at the same time.*

My God, I believe you are!

WILLIAM *snatches the paper, gives it a quick startled glance.*

Hey! that's not mine.

Trying to get it back.

WILL (*determined*): I don't care whose it is, you don't get it back. (*Stuffs it into his pocket.*)

ALEC (*amused, not unpleasantly*): Well, well, well!

WILL (*quietly*): I might say, I've been expecting this.

ALEC: Why?

WILL: Because the other day I caught sight of a fellow who used to be a warder at Maidstone when I was there. And he saw me too. *And* recognised me.

ALEC: He thought he did. He told me about it to-night—he's just been taken on as an orderly at the hospital—and when he described you, I thought it might be you, so he gave me that cutting and photograph so I might make sure.

WILL: I see. What's his name?

ALEC: Robbins.

WILL: That's the chap.

ALEC (*lighting a cigarette*): Better tell me the story, William. Or should I call you Mr. Blofield now?

WILL: William's my name anyhow, but I'd just as soon you didn't use it if you're going to be funny about this, doctor. It isn't very funny to me, y'know.

ALEC: Oh—come off it. I'm not getting at you. I don't give a damn about your having been in jail. You've always seemed to me a decent fellow, and that's all I care about. Tell me what happened.

WILL: In 1916, after I'd caught a packet on the Somme, I was discharged from the army and got a job in a shipping office. For the next four years that shipping business was a proper Monte Carlo, and I was good at it—I'm a born gambler, believe me, doctor—and when I jumped out before the crash, I'd got some real money to play with. By 1930 I was worth over a million—at least, on paper —but there was another slump on top of us, and I'd got to take bigger chances. I took one that didn't come off. It was a question of making some securities do more work for me than they were entitled to do, bit of conjuring and juggling really. I'd done it before, of course, but this time I wasn't quick enough. If I'd been just a shade quicker, I'd be in the House of Lords now instead of Night Porter at the Golden Fleece, Cheltingate.

ALEC: I wonder if you've missed much.

WILL: Probably not. But I'm not complaining. I'm just telling you. Well, I did five years in Maidstone. When I came out, I didn't grow my moustache and little beard again, and I changed me name to Lotless——

ALEC: Any particular reason?

WILL (grinning): Yes, because when I came out I'd a lot less than when I went in.

ALEC: Why didn't you tuck away a nice little fortune?

WILL (grimly): Because I married. Yes, as they used to say, Bill Blofield married well. Out of the top drawer. And that's where all that was left of the money went. Even before I'd landed myself at the Old Bailey, she'd been a bit—well—careless, shall we say? Then once I was inside, she ratted on me good and hard. Couldn't get a divorce so changed her name by deed-poll. I thought once, after I came out, of going down to Cannes and just quietly screwing her neck round, but then I thought, "Oh—let her rot with it. It'll never do her any good, that money."

ALEC: But how did you get here?

WILL: When I was nearly broke, I ran into a fellow who used to be a head-waiter at the Ambassador. I'd given him many a fiver. He was managing the Bournemouth Hotel belonging to this syndicate. Put me in as a porter. Then I was moved up here.

ALEC: Doesn't anybody ever spot you?

WILL: No, why should they? When you catch sight of a clean-shaven night porter called Lotless, you're not naturally reminded of a bearded speculator called Blofield, especially as he disappeared years ago. That chap Robbins is different, because he often saw me inside. You get to know faces in there all right.

ALEX: Well, prison didn't seem to do you any harm.

WILL: In a way, it did me good. I was nearly a nervous wreck when I went in, couldn't eat, couldn't sleep. When I came out, I could eat anything, sleep anywhere at any time, and was as cool as a cucumber. Bit of a philosopher, you might say. But all the same, there's a piece of you dies in those places. Five years of it puts fifty years on to you—somewhere inside you. You're not young any more. You've got your face turned towards the graveyard. Funny, but that's how it works.

ALEC: And no more gambling on the market for you, eh?

WILL: I promised myself *Never Again*. Just as I never take a drink—I don't know if you've ever noticed. I said—no more quick strong drinks—and no more conjuring tricks with paper money. But I often manipulate the market a bit just in theory, y'know, to pass the time and keep my mind lively.

Enter MOLLY, *through Staff Door, with tray with tea for two on it and a few sandwiches.*

ALEC: Hello, Molly!

MOLLY: Hello, doctor, would you like a cup of tea with us?

ALEC: No thanks, I'm turning in. Too late already, listening to William's profound discourse. I'll have a sandwich, though. (*Takes one from tray she has put down on table.*)

WILL: I was telling the doctor how I amuse myself pretending I'm on the stock market.

MOLLY (*pouring out tea*): I know. Silly, I call it.

ALEC (*eating*): I'm with you, Molly.

MOLLY: I'm not sure you've got a lot o' sense either, Dr. Rothbury. Not from something I've heard.

ALEC: Oh, what's that?

MOLLY: Never you mind.

ALEC: I don't mind. And it's time I went to bed. Good night. (*He goes upstairs.*)

WILL and MOLLY: Good night, doctor.

They now settle down cosily with their tea, with MOLLY'S *case handy.*

MOLLY: Have you looked through these yet?

WILL: I was just starting. (*Tastes tea.*) Nice cup of tea, Mrs. Cudden.

MOLLY: I'm glad you like it, Mr. Lotless.

WILL (*beginning to turn over documents*): Now then! Two receipts. Licence for a gun. Menu of the Annual Dinner at the Red Lion— good blow-out too——

MOLLY: Yes, I've heard my uncle tell of them dinners. Famous, they were.

WILL (*still examining the papers*): What was this uncle of yours?

MOLLY: He was head gamekeeper for Sir George Curtigan at Charlton Chase, and then afterwards he was a sort of bailiff. Sir George thought the world of him. I used to go an' stay when I was a kid. It was lovely. All among thick woods.

WILL (*turning the papers faster*): Nothing here, y'know. Old licences and bills and receipts—just junk, might as well be burnt. Hello! (*Stares.*) No, he sold 'em. Evidently owned a few shares in his time, your uncle.

MOLLY: Well, you see Sir George was a big man in the City——

WILL: Yes, I know he was. I remember him.

MOLLY: *You* do?

WILL: Yes, *I* do, silly as I look.

MOLLY: I didn't mean that, I——

WILL (*cutting in*): Never mind that. What about Sir George? Did he put your uncle on to things now and again?

MOLLY: Yes, that's just what I was going to tell you.

WILL (*grinning*): I know it was.

MOLLY: Well, next time when I've something of my own to tell, just let me tell it and don't take the words out of my mouth. It's most aggravating.

WILL (*still turning them over*): I'll try not to do it again. Bought himself a nice grave in good time, I see. Another blow-out at the Red Lion—steak, kidney and oyster pudding this time. County Court summons.

MOLLY: Eh?

WILL: No, not for him. Solicitor's letters—six-and-eight a time— worth nothing now. Long letter from Tasmania——

MOLLY: My Aunt Millie—his sister, you see——

WILL: Photographs now. Wedding groups——

MOLLY (*suddenly alarmed*): Here——

WILL: Why, this is you.

[321]

She gives a sharp cry and then is silent.

He looks at it quietly, then passes it over. She stares at it a moment, then turns her face away. He looks at her curiously. Then we hear that she is crying quietly.

MOLLY (*after a pause, sniffing*): I didn't know that was still there.

WILL: Sorry if I've started anything.

MOLLY: It was just—seeing myself—twenty years ago—so bright an' happy, thinking it was all going to be wonderful—silly young donkey!

WILL (*quietly*): It wasn't wonderful?

MOLLY: No—it was a proper mess.

WILL: Same here.

MOLLY (*staring*): You as well! Why, I always thought you were one o' them born bachelors.

WILL: Perhaps I was. But for all that I went and said "I will". Like you. (*Goes on turning again.*) Certificates now. Birth, marriage, death. You can burn nearly all this stuff, except the family souvenirs, if you want to keep them. Hello! (*Stares, and turns over several share certificates.*) Wait a minute, now, wait a minute!

Holds the certificates near the light and examines them carefully. Then, satisfied they are all right, looks from them to the wide-eyed MOLLY.

Great suffocating Moses! (*Then laughs from excitement.*)

MOLLY: Now what on earth's the matter with you? (*She takes up the certificates and looks at them.*) Leadenhall and Lombard Trust. A hundred shares. A hundred shares.

WILL (*trying to repress his excitement*): Yes, five hundred shares in a little company called the Leadenhall and Lombard Trust.

MOLLY (*with growing excitement*): But—are they worth something —Mr. Lotless?

WILL (*same tone*): Now a feature of these particular shares—I'll bet my boots—is that their transfer was never registered. And they're about ten years old.

MOLLY (*impatiently*): Oh don't go on talking that silly stuff. Tell me—are they worth anything? What is this company? What does it do?

WILL (*triumphantly*): I'll tell you. For the last few years the Leadenhall and Lombard Trust has been operating as a parent or holding company. (*He now takes out a pencil and begins making calculations.*

MOLLY (*impatiently*): I don't know what that means, but could I sell them and how much would I get?

[322]

WILL (*still calculating*): This kind of company simply exists to hold shares in other companies.

MOLLY (*angrily*): Stop it! What could I get? Fifty pounds? A hundred pounds?

WILL (*still busy with figures*): Don't be silly!

MOLLY (*furiously*): You pay attention and answer me.

WILL (*not noticing her*): I'm busy.

With a cry of fury she seizes the plate that held the sandwiches and breaks it over his head. He looks at her in a dazed fashion. She is penitent at once.

MOLLY (*miserably*): You see, I told you I'd a terrible temper. Nobody'll believe I have but I have. Oh—I'm sorry, William. Have I hurt you?

WILL (*still dazed*): No. I don't think so.

MOLLY (*putting a hand on his head*): It's only a little bump. No, it's quite a big one.

WILL (*still dazed, thoughtful*): I've always had that one. (*With sudden excitement now*) Listen, Molly, I want you to let me handle this business for you.

MOLLY: These shares?

WILL (*excitedly*): Yes. It's a ticklish situation. Take 'em to one of these provincial stockbrokers or solicitors, and the clever boys in London would have 'em tied in knots in no time. But this is just my line. Believe me, Molly, I'm a wizard at it. Give me a hold like this over some of those boys, and I'm Buccaneer Bill again. You'll see. Now, Molly, we've been good pals. Will you let me handle it? All for your sake. I mean it.

MOLLY (*who has never seen him like this*): Yes, of course, William. I trust you.

WILL (*jumping up*): That's a good girl. And—oh!—what a bombshell! Where's that London Telephone Directory of ours?

MOLLY (*bewildered*): But you can't start telephoning people now?

WILL (*going to office*): Can't I? Don't you worry. The Cudden-Lotless syndicate is going to conduct its operations in the market at midnight. Trunks? . . . And just watch the feathers flying! (*Chuckles as he hastily searches directory.*) Trunks. . . . Cheltingate 175 . . . a personal call for Mr. Percival Vandermore, Mayfair 67325 . . . that's it.

She stares at him as she mechanically puts together the tea things, etc.

MOLLY (*anxiously*): William?

[323]

WILL (*still searching*): Yes?

MOLLY (*anxiously*): Are you sure you're all right? I mean, you did get an awful bang on the head, didn't you?

WILL (*chuckling*): Hardly noticed it. I was too busy thinking. Just leave it all to me. (*Into telephone*) Hello, Mr. Vandermore . . . Yes, I know it's late . . . Well, it is important business . . . You see, I represent a little syndicate that owns five hundred shares in the Leadenhall and Lombard Trust . . . Oh, no, it's not impossible . . . they're here in front of me . . . the transfer wasn't registered, you see . . . yes, it does make a difference, doesn't it? . . . Oh no, you don't . . . too easy . . . you see, Vandermore, this is Bill Blofield . . . yes, that makes a difference too . . . Yes, I'm jumping in with both feet . . . No, I can't come up and you can't ring me. I'll ring you at one o'clock sharp . . . and I'll have a proposition to put to you then . . . All right then, think it over, and then we'll get down to tricks . . . all right, Vandermore, at one o'clock. . . .

> *He puts down phone and looks triumphantly at* MOLLY, *who is standing staring at him, open-mouthed, carrying tray.*

Well, Mrs. Cudden, we've started. The Cudden-Lotless syndicate is in the market.

MOLLY (*bewildered*): You know, Mr. Lotless, you seem—quite different. And who's Bill Blofield?

WILL: Oh—it's just a name I thought he'd know.

MOLLY: But you haven't told me yet if I could sell those shares and what they'd be worth.

WILL: What they're worth now is nothing to what they'll bring in before I've done with them. You wait.

MOLLY (*wistfully*): Yes. But there are some things I'd like to buy, that's all, and I just wondered if I was a bit better off, that's all.

WILL: Bit better-off?

> *House telephone rings. He answers it.*

Twenty-seven? Yes, madam. Yes, I'm sure she can. She'll bring it up in a few minutes. (*Puts it down.*) Twenty-seven can't sleep and wonders if you could make her a cup of Benger's.

MOLLY (*backing into door with tray*): Yes, of course I can. (*Hesitates, then*) How much do you think?

WILL: Only a cup.

MOLLY: No, silly, I mean me.

WILL: Oh—well, God knows what we can build it up to if I handle Vandermore and his pals properly and really get going. You don't know where it'll end. (*Casually.*) But at the moment, I suppose those shares of yours are worth about two hundred and fifty thousand pounds.

MOLLY *gives a cry as the curtain falls quickly.*

END OF ACT ONE

ACT II

SCENE: *Same as Act One.*

Late on a Friday evening, two weeks later.

At rise, full lighting on scene. This time Main Door is wide open, showing corridor to rest of hotel behind it, and through this door we hear sound of dance band, but it is obviously at the other end of the hotel. MISS WEEKS is behind her counter, as before. GEORGE is waiting. Two young couples—men in their dinner jackets, girls in simple evening clothes—are having drinks, in separate pairs, at tables near wall. Certain properties—a toy balloon, paper hat, false nose—on the tables suggest a mild spirit of carnival. The two couples converse, but cannot be heard.

GEORGE (*crossing over to* MISS WEEKS): I don't know how they're doing along there to-night, but not many of 'em's coming in here.

MISS WEEKS: They mostly go and sit out in the far lounge.

GEORGE (*bitterly*): Yes, what there is of 'em. Birthday carnival! Whose birthday?

MISS WEEKS: Oh—that's just an excuse.

GEORGE (*bitterly*): An excuse for what?

MISS WEEKS (*severely*): To try and give people an enjoyable evening and get a little extra custom.

GEORGE (*same as before*): Carnival dance! Ten bobs' worth of paper 'ats an' false noses among fifty people!

MISS WEEKS: Better than nothing. What do you want?

GEORGE: Me? I'll tell you what I want. I want to put my feet up, read an Edgar Wallace, and get down three or four bottles o' Guinness.

MISS WEEKS (*not impressed*): Well, it's a good thing we're not all alike, isn't it?

GEORGE: No, it isn't. It's a bad thing. Save a lot of bother if we were all alike. Trouble about you girls is—you don't think for yourselves.

As he is turning away from counter, MONDOVI *enters through Staff Door. He is in evening dress, and very important.*

MONDOVI: Oh!—Jorj-a—you are notta busy a moment, eh?

GEORGE: No, sir.

MONDOVI: Then take a tray-a. In there.

[326]

GEORGE *goes through Staff Door.*

Not-a finish yet. (*Referring to dancing, which can still be heard—looks at watch.*) How many in there to-night?

MISS WEEKS: Well, I'm not quite sure, Mr. Mondovi, because nearly all the outside lot come in the other way, but I think, including our own guests, about fifty.

MONDOVI: Fifty—no good! Not a complete-a wash-*out*, but no good.

MISS WEEKS: Well, you see, Mr. Mondovi, the sort of people who come to Cheltingate aren't very lively—are they?

MONDOVI (*bitterly*): I think all they want is to eat four-a big bad meals a day, to sleep, to drink-a the smelly waters.

MISS WEEKS *looks shocked.* GEORGE *enters carrying tray with bottles, glasses, etc.*

GEORGE: Here we are, sir.

MONDOVI: To the small-a private room, through the Card-a Room.

GEORGE *crosses towards Card Room.* MONDOVI *turns to* MISS WEEKS.

If one of the girls comes with-a tray tell 'er small-a private room through Card-a Room. I give my little supper in there. (*Follows* GEORGE *across.*)

They go out. Telephone rings.

MISS WEEKS (*at telephone*): Golden Fleece . . . Mr. Lotless? . . . No, he's not here yet . . . Well, you'll have to ring later.

As she puts down telephone ELSIE *enters carrying large tray with napkins covering cold food, plates, etc.*

Through the Card Room, Mr. Mondovi said.

ELSIE (*grumbling*): I call this being put on. Came down, 'cos I'd finished, an' they said, " 'Ere, take this in." They don't ask the waiters to 'elp me with my beds, do they?

As she goes across, GEORGE *comes out and holds door for her, grinning.*

GEORGE (*sardonically*): It does me good to see yer sweet smiling face.

One of the men of the two young couples beckons him across, and in dumb show he receives payment for the drink and a tip. This young couple go out through Main Door. ELSIE *comes out Card Room and crosses to* MISS WEEKS.

ELSIE (*speaking near Staff Door*): What's the idea in there?

MISS WEEKS (*in rather superior tone*): Mr. Mondovi is giving supper to a few of our guests.

ELSIE: What for? Don't they get enough to eat already?

MISS WEEKS: Just a stunt. Part of the Birthday Carnival idea. It isn't anybody's birthday, of course.

ELSIE: Oh yes, it is. It's Molly's. She told me this morning. They're doing all this (*indicating general arrangements*) for her, only they don't know it.

Now she sees SIR RUFUS *and* TAGG, *who enter slowly together through Main Door, deep in talk.* SIR RUFUS *is wearing an absurd false nose and* TAGG *a silly little hat. They have obviously forgotten about them.* ELSIE *giggles.*

Oh, crumbs! Look what's blown in!

Exit Staff Door, giggling.

SIR RUFUS (*as they come forward together*): You mean to say— they never intended to pay a dividend?

TAGG (*very solemnly*): 'Course they didn't. That was the idea from the start. And then, what 'appened?

SIR RUFUS: Well, obviously the stock went down——

TAGG: Now, who's telling this? They says: "Well, gentlemen, we've 'ad an offer from the Pranto Company to take over the property and machinery, an' it's the best we can do——"

SIR RUFUS: Yes—neat, very neat! And they're all in the Pranto concern, eh?

TAGG: They were all in the syndicate that 'as a controlling interest in the Pranto. An' they got the whole property and machinery for twenty-five thousand. I tell yer, they were clever, that lot.

SIR RUFUS: Obviously. It reminds me of a tricky little bit of business that I came across about two years ago——

TAGG: And that isn't all they did neither.

Is interrupted by MONDOVI *coming out of Card Room, all smiles and little bows.*

MONDOVI: This-a way, if you please. Lady Garnett, Mrs. Tagg, they are coming, of course?

TAGG: They're following on. And I don't mind tellin' yer I'm feeling fairly peckish.

They go into Card Room, MONDOVI *remaining at door. Second couple go out Street Door.* GEORGE *clears away their glasses.*

LADY GARNETT, *in evening dress and carrying some carnival toy, enters Main Door with* DR. PLUMWEATHER, *an elderly doctor with a very smooth manner, in a dinner jacket. They are talking very confidentially and halt in the centre to finish what they have to say before joining* MONDOVI.

DOCTOR PLUMWEATHER: I can't believe it.

LADY GARNETT: At first I didn't want to say anything, but then I felt you ought to know, Dr. Plumweather.

DR. PLUMWEATHER (*solemn whisper*): And I assure you, Lady Garnett, I'm very much indebted to you. Of course I *had* other—er —criticisms, as you can well imagine.

LADY GARNETT: Yes, I thought you would have.

DR. PLUMWEATHER (*pompously*): The fact is, Dr. Rothbury is totally unsuited to this class of work. I don't say he's lacking in general ability. He's not. I don't say he's not a hard worker. He is. But—well—he's——

LADY GARNETT (*prompting him*): Crude.

DR. PLUMWEATHER (*archly*): I won't say it, I won't say it——

LADY GARNETT (*also archly*): Etiquette?

DR. PLUMWEATHER: Etiquette, my dear lady. But—(*solemnly, confidential now*)—between ourselves, that young man won't be here much longer. I've made up my mind.

LADY GARNETT: You're very wise. Not the Cheltingate type of doctor at all, and never will be. Ah!—Now are we all here?

She has moved over towards MONDOVI, *the doctor following. They remain there at door.* LADY LEADMILL, *carrying a sausage-shaped balloon, enters, followed by* MRS. TAGG *and* MISS SELL, *who are wearing very incongruous paper hats. All are in evening dress.*

GEORGE *closes Main Door after this entrance.*

MRS. TAGG (*nervously ending a long account*): So now I rest them whenever I can.

LADY LEADMILL (*who clearly thinks nothing of* MRS. TAGG, *stopping*): Rest what?

MRS. TAGG (*whispering*): My feet.

LADY LEADMILL (*aloud, surprised*): Your *feet!*

MISS SELL (*timidly, trying to help*): Mrs. Tagg was telling us the trouble she's had with—her feet.

LADY LEADMILL (*awfully*): Indeed! Enquire if there are any letters.

MRS. TAGG (*flustered*): Oh—yes—certainly.

Turns and then sees that it is MISS SELL *who is obeying the order, going to counter.*

Oh—I see, yes—I'm sorry.

MISS SELL (*returning*): No, Lady Leadmill, no letters.

LADY LEADMILL (*sternly*): The posts here are most peculiar.

MRS. TAGG: Yes, I had a——

LADY LEADMILL: *Most* peculiar. Miss Sell, I think you've worn that paper hat quite long enough now.

MISS SELL (*snatching it off*): Oh—yes, I'd forgotten.

MRS. TAGG *takes hers off too, then looks at it admiringly and wistfully.*

LADY LEADMILL: You had better go upstairs now, Miss Sell, as you were not invited to Mondovi's little supper party——

MISS SELL: Yes, Lady Leadmill.

LADY LEADMILL: But don't go to bed, as I may want you.

MISS SELL: Yes, Lady Leadmill. Good night, Mrs. Tagg.

Goes upstairs.

MRS. TAGG: Good night, Miss Sell. (*Looking wistfully at hat.*) I think it's so pretty.

LADY LEADMILL (*sternly*): For a young girl, no doubt.

MRS. TAGG (*bravely*): Well, I'm not a young girl. (*Puts the hat on again*). But I was once.

LADY LEADMILL (*moving forward*): Indeed!

MRS. TAGG (*following on*): Yes, and sometimes even now I still feel a young girl.

She takes a pin and bursts the sausage balloon that LADY LEAD-MILL is carrying. LADY LEADMILL turns and glares suspiciously at her, while she looks innocent.

LADY GARNETT and DR. PLUMWEATHER have now gone in. LADY LEADMILL, MRS. TAGG follow, the latter closing Card Room door behind her.

GEORGE (*going over to MISS WEEKS, who is now clearing up*): See that Mrs. Tagg burst old Leadface's balloon?

MISS WEEKS (*looking up*): She didn't!

GEORGE: She did. Quite right too! She ought to 'ave 'ad her balloon busted long since.

Enter through Street Door PERKINS of the Gazette, about forty, moustache, untidy rain-coat or mac, bowler hat towards back of his head, and puffs great volume of smoke all the time from his pipe. Manner half gauche, half impudent. GEORGE sees him.
Yes, sir?

PERKINS: No, sir. Perkins of the *Gazette*. I want to have a word with this young lady.

GEORGE (*bitterly*): Good night, all.

Goes out Staff Door.

PERKINS (*announcing himself to her*): Perkins of the *Gazette*.

MISS WEEKS: What, again?

PERKINS: Well, I haven't got anywhere yet. I tried the Grand and the Queen's. Nobody there knew what I was talking about.

MISS WEEKS: Well, I told you I didn't know what you were talking about, didn't I?

PERKINS: You did. But now—I've an idea.

Pauses, but she shows no interest.

Wouldn't you like to hear what my idea is?

MISS WEEKS (*still clearing up*): No, not particularly.

PERKINS: Thanks very much. Well, my idea is—I may have been enquiring too early.

MISS WEEKS: You don't call this too early, do you? We think it's late, up here.

PERKINS: You haven't got my point. If it's all supposed to be happening late at night, none of you people on day duty might know about it, anyhow.

Enter WILL, *through Staff Door.*

WILL: Good evening, Miss Weeks.

MISS WEEKS: Good evening, William.

PERKINS (*heartily*): Good evening, William.

WILL (*administering gentle snub*): Good evening, sir.

MISS WEEKS (*finished now*): This is our Night Porter, so you'd better try him now.

WILL: What's this about?

MISS WEEKS: Don't ask me. I've given it up. Good night.

Goes, Staff Door.

WILL (*comes forward*): Well now, what can I do for you?

PERKINS: My name's Perkins and I represent the *Gazette*.

WILL: From London?

PERKINS: The London *Daily Gazette*, of course, but I'm not from London. I'm at the Manchester office. Cheltingate comes in our area, you see.

WILL: Yes, I see. Why don't you sit down?

PERKINS: Good idea! Well, our London office had got hold——
(*Sits left of table.*) Here, haven't I seen you before somewhere?

WILL (*standing*): If you've stayed at this hotel and come in late, you probably have.

PERKINS: No, never stayed here. Haven't I seen you somewhere else?

WILL: Not to my knowledge, Mr. Perkins.

PERKINS: No?

WILL: No.

They stand looking at each other, then PERKINS *crosses back and sits.*

PERKINS: Well, it doesn't matter. This is the point. (*Confidentially*) Our London office has got hold of a queer story—or the beginnings of a queer story, for that's about all it is yet—and the idea is that there's a big financial syndicate, which is crashing the market in a very grand style, operating from an hotel here in Cheltingate. (*He takes cigarette out of packet out of his pocket, then offers one to* WILL.)

WILL: Nothing surprising in that. Lot of rich men stay here, y'know.

PERKINS: Cigarette?

WILL: Oh, thank you, sir.

He fumbles in his pocket for matches.

You have to be pretty well-off before you need these waters and baths. Hot sulphur water comes in with the sur-tax.

PERKINS: Yes, but that's not all. According to our assistant City Editor, who's a bright lad and keeps his ears open, these chaps here, who are very hot stuff, do all their business late at night.

WILL: What business? Stocks and shares?

PERKINS: Yes, big gambling on the Exchange.

WILL: How can they do that late at night? The Exchange isn't open.

PERKINS: Oh—they've got people doing their buying and selling for 'em in London during the day, naturally, but *they* do *their* work —send their instructions and all that—late at night. It was a chap he knows at a big broker's who let it slip to him. So London asked me to come and get the story.

WILL: Well, all I can say is, that if anybody here was spending half the night telephoning to London—about stocks and shares or anything else—I'd be the first to know about it, wouldn't I?

PERKINS: Stands to reason. Yes.

WILL: Yes.

PERKINS: Yes.

WILL: And I can assure you—nobody comes an' asks me to get these London numbers.

PERKINS: They don't, eh?

WILL: No, they don't.

Telephone rings sharply.

Excuse me. (*Goes—at telephone*) Golden Fleece . . . Oh yes . . . yes, it is, but ring me in about an hour . . . I know, but ring me in an hour's time . . . all right. (*Puts it down, and comes back. Casually.*) Friend o' mine—wants a chat.

PERKINS: Late, isn't he?

WILL: He's another night bird, like myself.

PERKINS: You seem to me a funny sort of chap to be a night porter.

WILL: I'll explain about night porters. Sit down, won't you. There are three types.

PERKINS: It's funny how many things go in threes. I remember I once——

WILL (*firmly*): Yes, three types of night porters. First, the fellows, usually young, who take it on because they're hoping it'll lead to a day job and promotion to head porter. Second, the fellows on the other slope of the hill, who have to take night duty because they're no longer wanted during the day, so it's either that or nothing, see? Then—the third type, who *like* being night porters, just because they're odd fish, misfits, eccentrics, philosophers.

PERKINS: And you're a number three?

WILL: I'm a number three.

PERKINS: I believe you're right.

WILL: I know I'm right.

PERKINS: Three types. I'll remember that.

WILL: You might find it useful. But now—this yarn of yours, about the big financial syndicate working late at night here, well—bit thick, isn't it?

PERKINS: I don't know. Anything's possible these days. Now I've tried this place and the Grand and the Queen's——

WILL: Well, there's still the Royal and the Bristol, and the Spa Hydro, though I can't see any big financial chaps staying at the Spa Hydro.

PERKINS: Why?

WILL: It's a temperance hotel.

PERKINS: Well, I'll try the Royal and the Bristol.

MOLLY *enters, Staff Door, wearing long outdoor coat over her uniform. She does not come forward but looks at and listens to* PERKINS, *who is now going.*

[333]

WILL: No harm in doing that.

PERKINS: And if there's a story, I'll get it.

WILL: Got a nose for it, eh?

PERKINS (*confidentially*): I tell you—with me, it's a kind of—oh—sixth sense. I can smell out a good story where most fellows wouldn't know there was anything happening. I couldn't tell you how I do it.

WILL: A gift, eh?

PERKINS: Absolutely. You'll see. Watch the *Gazette*. I could have sworn I'd seen you somewhere before.

WILL: No.

PERKINS: Oh, well, good night. (*Goes out street.*)

MOLLY : Good evening, Mr. Lotless.

WILL: Good evening, Mrs. Cudden.

MOLLY: What's the matter with that chap?

WILL (*dryly*): He's a newspaper man busy taking his sixth sense round Cheltingate.

MOLLY (*rather alarmed*): Here—it's nothing to do with this—er—business of ours, is it?

WILL (*blandly*): D'you know, I think it might be.

MOLLY (*alarmed*): Well, but——

WILL (*stopping her*): You just leave his sixth sense to me. I can handle him all right. He'll never get within a mile of our story.

MOLLY (*gazing at him earnestly*): You know, William, I call you a proper mixture. One minute you seem as simple as a baby, and next minute as artful as a box of monkeys.

WILL: Well, what's wrong with that?

MOLLY: Oh!—nothing. Makes it interesting. (*Taking her coat off.*) I gave myself a treat to-night—an I'll bet you don't know why.

WILL: I do. You told me a week ago and I haven't forgotten. Many happy returns!

MOLLY (*pleased*): Well now, I never thought you'd remember.

WILL: Never forget anything with a friend in it. As a matter of fact, I've—er—got something——

MOLLY (*excitedly*): What! A present—for me!

WILL: Too early yet. Somebody might come in.

MOLLY: Yes, but you might tell me what it is.

WILL: Oh—no. Spoil it. Just wait until it's quieter.

MOLLY: Well, it couldn't be much quieter than it is now, but I suppose it is a bit too early.

He has opened the door now. Goes through and we see the light-
ing outside, which is first at full, go down to less than half, as if
he had switched off several lights. MOLLY *can put her coat away,*
behind Staff Door, now. She is back when he returns.

WILL: Where did you go? To the pictures?

MOLLY (*with enthusiasm*): Yes. A lovely film. With Robert Drake
in it. Don't you like Robert Drake?

WILL: Never seen him.

MOLLY: Haven't you? Oh—he's a wonderful man. Tall an' very
good-looking, but that's not what gets you. He's got a little smile
—sort of tender—and—and—wistful—and his eyes crinkle up. If he
turned that smile on to me, I wouldn't know what to do. And this girl
in the film was so awful to him—until right at the end, of course—
an' she was so nasty when he kept giving her this special little smile,
I could have smacked her silly little face.

WILL (*settling down*): You were jealous?

MOLLY (*indignantly*): I wasn't jealous. To begin with, I haven't
got a jealous nature. And then, who's going to be jealous about
somebody in a film? I may be a bit soft, but I'm not *that* soft. But,
you see, in this picture, he's a poor young man who has nothing left
but an old motor-car and a caravan——

Breaks off because ALEC ROTHBURY *now enters from street.*
He is in ordinary clothes—not smartly dressed but rather shabby—
and looks rather tired and depressed.

ALEC: I don't call him a poor young man if he had a car and
a caravan.

WILL: He's poor for the films. They've a very high standard of
living on the films.

ALEC: Go on about your film, Molly. Sorry I interrupted. (*Lights*
a cigarette.)

MOLLY: Well then, Robert Drake's this poor young man but really
it turns out in the end he isn't poor.

ALEC (*sardonically*): I'll bet he isn't.

MOLLY: But this girl he's in love with—*he* thinks, and you think
too till you tumble to it, she's very rich—but really she isn't, she's
just pretending. So in the end it's all right, and they get married and
sail away on his beautiful yacht. Lovely!

ALEC (*shaking his head*): No. Eh, William?

WILLIAM (*also shaking his head*): Certainly not.

MOLLY: Now what's wrong with it?

ALEC: To begin with, it doesn't sound to me in the least like real life.

MOLLY: Who said it was like real life? I don't pay a shilling to sit in the dark and look at real life. I can see real life outside the picture theatre all for nothing. I go inside to get away from real life, just for a nice change.

WILL: That's a woman for you. They can cod themselves, but they *know* when they're codding themselves. We don't, and that's our trouble.

ALEC: It's not *my* trouble. Mine is—I can see all too clearly.

MOLLY: Not you! I'll bet you can't see anything clearly, unless it's other people's measles or chicken-pox.

Hotel telephone rings. She answers it.

Yes, of course . . . coming now. (*Puts down telephone.*)

WILL: Eighteen?

MOLLY: Eighteen. Shan't be long.

Goes out Staff Door.

ALEC (*coolly*): I believe you two are up to something.

WILL: Put that right out of your head, doctor. We're not that sort at all.

ALEC: No, I didn't mean anything of that kind. But you're up to *something*. For the last fortnight or so, you've looked as thick as thieves, and there's something about you, William, a kind of cat-full-of-cream look that suggests to me you're up to something. (*As WILL is about to speak, stopping him*) I'm not asking what it is.

WILL (*dryly*): I wasn't going to tell you.

ALEC: But what I should like is a drink and a sandwich. I've had a very long and dreary day to-day, with an extra two hours I didn't expect at the hospital to-night.

WILL: You're looking a bit done in, doctor. And you can have the drink and sandwich now, if you like, but you'd do better if you waited a little longer.

ALEC: I don't see that.

WILL: I'll explain. It's Molly's birthday to-day and—er—well, a fellow I know in London has sent a wonderful hamper for her—everything of the best—champagne, game pie——

ALEC (*surprised*): For Molly?

WILL (*solemnly*): For our Molly Cudden. And why not? Can you tell me anybody here who better deserves the best for her birthday than that woman?

[336]

ALEC: Yes, me. Apart from me, nobody. But where do *I* come in?

WILL: It's a little party, and you're invited. I know she won't mind.

ALEC: And I accept your invitation with many thanks. I'm tired, but I'm not sleepy.

WILL (*challengingly*): You're depressed.

ALEC: Yes. I'm fed up.

WILL: This place?

ALEC: Partly. Though I shan't be here much longer.

WILL: Is the sack coming?

ALEC: It is.

WILL: Is that all?

ALEC: No. But it's plenty, isn't it?

WILL: Yes, but it isn't all.

ALEC: It's all you'll hear.

WILL (*quietly, innocently*): Let's see, what was the name of that girl?

ALEC (*promptly*): Veronica Frensham. Here—what girl?

Telephone rings. WILL *goes to answer it.*

WILL (*at telephone, in sharp masterful style*): Who? . . . Yes, speaking . . . Yes, yes, I know. Get in touch with Vandermore. He's ringing me later on . . . Yes, all those are being transferred . . . Oh, won't I? . . . Don't you believe it. I'll squeeze him so hard I'll have him begging for mercy by this time to-morrow night . . . All right. Tell Vandermore. (*Puts down telephone.*)

ALEC (*sardonically*): Queer business this hotel seems to do over the telephone at night!

WILL: I dare say.

ALEC: And who is Mr. Vandermore?

WILL: He's a clever gentleman in London who knows now that he isn't quite as clever as he thought he was a couple of weeks ago.

ALEC: William, you're not a downright crook, by any chance, are you?

WILL (*smiling*): In one sense I am, and then in another sense, I'm not. Excuse me, it's time we got the party going. (*Goes towards Staff Door.*) You might give me a hand, doctor.

Goes out.

ALEC (*calling*): All right, coming!

Goes towards Staff Door, but when he arrives there WILL *comes out carrying hamper and large cardboard box.* ALEC *takes the box, which is on top. They come forward.*

I hope all this is honestly come by.

WILL: In one sense it is, and then in another sense, it isn't.

Puts down hamper near table and begins unpacking it. Two or three bottles of champagne, game pie, pâté, etc., all very sumptuous.

ALEC (*as it comes out*): My hat, somebody's spent some money on this lot.

WILL: Everything of the best. Though I don't suppose this sort of tack does you any good, does it?

ALEC (*grinning*): In one sense it does, and then in another sense, it doesn't. (*Helps to put things out.*) Taken in very rare doses, it's bad for the body but good for the soul. Taken in regular doses, it's bad for both body and soul.

Enter MOLLY *through main door. She stops in surprise when she sees the table.*

MOLLY: Good gracious me! Where's all this come from?

WILL: From a friend of mine in London—as a little birthday tribute.

MOLLY: For me?

ALEC: And for me. *You*'ve invited me.

MOLLY: I'm glad to hear it. With all that lot to shift.

WILL: I'll get some glasses.

MOLLY: No, let me.

WILL (*going*): You stay there, and take it easy. It's your treat.

Goes.

MOLLY (*handling the things*): Look! It's a sort of Christmas de luxe. I never saw such a spread. And all expensive stuff too.

ALEC (*deliberately echoing* WILL): Everything of the best. But who's treated you to all this?

MOLLY: Don't ask me. You heard what William said. One of his friends in London.

ALEC: What friends?

MOLLY: Probably one of these people he's been doing business with.

ALEC: What business?

MOLLY: Here, aren't you nosey?

ALEC: Now, come on, Molly, I knew there was something on between you two. What is it?

MOLLY: I couldn't really tell you even if I wanted to. And I promised William I wouldn't.

ALEC: Has he been making some money for you?

MOLLY (*dodging this*): Do I look as if anybody's been making money for me?

ALEC: Yes, you do, with this stuff all round you.

Begins taking paper off champagne bottle.

MOLLY: We ought to have taken this round to the back. We'll look silly, won't we, if somebody comes in here.

ALEC: Nobody'll come in now. You're all right. Besides, William has to be on duty in here.

MOLLY: I hadn't thought of that. What with its being my birthday, and then Robert Drake in that film, and then all this stuff I didn't expect, I'm a bit light-headed to-night.

Enter WILL, Staff Door, with glasses, cutlery.

(*Gaily*) The doctor doesn't deserve to be in on this, he's being so nosey about everything.

WILL: We can't have that. Dr. Rothbury, you may remember those fairy tales you read as a kid where you could enjoy everything you fancied so long as you didn't start asking questions? Well, this is one of them fairy tales.

ALEC (*holding up glass*): And now a toast! Many happy returns and every good wish—to our Molly.

WILL (*same*): To our Molly Cudden—the most obliging, best-tempered, sweetest-natured woman in the whole hotel business.

They drink.

MOLLY (*embarrassed*): Now, stop that, you two, or you'll be making me go all soft—an' then I'll start crying—an' a fat lot o' supper I'll enjoy. Who'll have some of this? It looks very rich but it can't hurt us much, just for once.

Passes them things to eat.

They settle down to eat and drink, cosily.

WILL: This is living on twenty thousand a year for twenty minutes.

MOLLY (*after drinking*): Sort of gets right up your nose, doesn't it, this champagne. It's not as sweet as that my sister had after her *wedding*.

ALEC (*refills glasses. With mock gravity*): Good champagne isn't supposed to be sweet.

MOLLY: Why?

ALEC: Hanged if I know!

WILL (*solemnly*): It's the custom in England to prefer dry champagne, and in England we live not by reason, not even by instinct, but by custom.

ALEC: And that's how the people are kept quiet. Because, custom——

MOLLY: Is this going to be politics?

ALEC: Yes.

MOLLY: Well, stop it, then. No politics to-night, thank you.

ALEC: Why not?

MOLLY (*good-humouredly but firmly*): Because this is supposed to be my party, and I don't like politics, and if you two get started on 'em, I'll soon be sitting here like a stuffed dummy.

WILL (*passing food*): Have some more stuffing.

MOLLY: Thank you. Now let's just be cosy, for once. (*After pause.*) Doctor, I wonder what's become of that very good-looking girl you were so gone on. You're still gone on her, aren't you?

ALEC: Not really.

MOLLY: Go on. Written all over you. I wonder what she's doing to-night.

ALEC: She'll be pretending to be amused and trying not to yawn, in some expensive and ridiculous place.

MOLLY (*to* WILL): It's a funny thing about young men—an' I don't care who they are, doctors or anything else you like—but when they're feeling uneasy and a bit silly inside, they get all pompous.

WILL: True, true. (*To* ALEC) She's right, y'know.

ALEC. Yes, yes, I'll admit it.

WILL (*to* MOLLY): But don't be too hard on young men.

MOLLY: Me! Why, I love 'em nearly all. Bless 'em.

WILL: You don't know what it's like being a clever young fellow, like our friend here. But I do, because I was one once myself. And I say that except for those occasional times when you fancy you've got the world in your pocket, to be a clever young man is just hell.

ALEC: True, true. (*To* MOLLY) He's right, y'know.

MOLLY: And I don't believe it. Just try being a woman for half a day, an' then you'd know something. That's why we like being with men. We aren't reminded of all our miseries. I'm going to drink to women—poor things!

ALEC (*who has been opening another bottle*): Not yet. Here you are. (*Fills glasses.*)

WILL (*raising glass*): To women—excluding nagging wives, interfering spinsters, bullying rich old dowagers, cheating adventuresses, pert little minxes, and——

ALEC (*pointedly*): All girls, no matter how devilishly attractive, who put money first—and——

MOLLY: And all female hotel guests who spill powder all over their rooms and leave their stockings and knickers to soak in the washhand basins——

They all drink off. (MOLLY: *Hic!*)

Here, if I don't eat more an' drink less, I'll be tiddly. (*Suddenly notices cardboard box.*) What's in that box?

WILL (*noticing it*): I'd clean forgotten that. (*Goes to it, and begins opening it.*) It's for you.

MOLLY (*excitedly*): For me!

WILL: Birthday present.

ALEC (*dryly*): Friend in London?

WILL: Friend in London. Now, just hold your breath—oh!—and close your eyes.

As she stands with closed eyes, he goes over and puts a magnificent fur coat into her outstretched arms. She feels the thick soft fur, then opens her eyes wide in astonishment, stares at it as she holds it out to see it better.

MOLLY (*gasping*): Christmas! Oooo—look!

ALEC: We are looking. We're overwhelmed.

WILL (*complacently*): You've got something worth having there, Molly.

MOLLY (*all excitement now*): But—I mean—this can't be for me. Look at it!

WILL: Certainly it's for you. Try it on.

MOLLY: But—I've never even dreamt of ever having a coat like this. It's a real one, y'know—I mean to say—not one of these imitations you see about—absolutely real.

WILL: You can bet your life it is.

MOLLY: Yes, but—I mean—*me* in this. Why—I'd never——

ALEC: Go on. Put it on.

She does, almost like a child. Then is delighted with herself, being luxurious in it, rubbing her cheek against the collar, etc.

MOLLY (*at end of this*): How do I look in it? Silly, I expect, eh?

WILL: Silly nothing! You look grand, doesn't she?

ALEC: Straight from Bond Street.

MOLLY: You're just making game of me——

WILL: We're not. You couldn't look better.

ALEC: We can hardly believe you know us now.

MOLLY (*doing creditable imitation of fashionable woman, coming to them*): Oh—but—of course! Dr. Rothbury, I believe, isn't it? I think we met the other morning in the Pump Room, didn't we? And Mr. Lotless too! How d'you do? Such a delightful place you have heah, isn't it?

WILL (*entering into this*): Oh—frightfully jolly—Lady Bilgewater.

MOLLY (*as before*): May I join you?

WILL: Delighted, dear lady, absolutely delighted!

MOLLY (*tapping desk and imitating* LADY LEADMILL): Are there any letters for me?

WILL (*imitating* MONDOVI): Miss-a Weeks, make-a quite sure there are no letters for Lady Bilgewater——

ALEC: Not to-night, Lady Bilgewater.

MOLLY (*as* LADY LEADMILL): The posts here are most peculiar, *most* peculiar.

They all laugh uproariously

MOLLY (*very much herself again*): Well, I'm not taking it off, though it'll be just like me to go an' mess it up now. (*She stops and looks earnestly at* WILL, *and speaks with impressive seriousness.*) Now, tell me, honestly, is it all right me taking this coat?

WILL (*gravely*): If it hadn't been all right, do you think I'd have let you have it?

MOLLY: But—you didn't buy it, did you?

WILL: Me! All the money I have in the world couldn't buy the collar, let alone the coat.

MOLLY: I don't see that. Didn't I say, the other night, that you ought to take——

WILL (*hastily cutting in*): Never mind what you said. Careful now!

MOLLY (*realising* ALEC'S *presence*): Oh—yes. Sorry! Though I don't see why——

WILL (*cutting in again*): Well, I do. (*To* ALEC) Excuse me, won't you?

ALEC: Yes, but you might as well tell me.

WILL: Not just now. What we want is another toast.

ALEC (*showing slight signs of tightness*): I'll give you one. To blazes with old Plumweather!

MOLLY: No, that's not very nice. Besides, I'm sure Dr. Plumweather's done nobody any harm.

ALEC: There you're wrong. He may look a harmless old pussycat, but really he's a pest and a menace. Instead of being a man of science, which he pretends to be, he's something between an old charlatan and a rich old woman's butler. He doesn't speak or even think the truth. He doesn't care about anything but fat fees and fat dinners. He's an example of what's wrong with this pussy-footed, rich old man's country. And if you won't drink him to blazes, I will. (*Raises his glass.*) To blazes with old Plumweather, and may he soon find himself trying to remove a perforating appendix at three in the morning in a slum tenement. (*Drinks.*)

MOLLY (*also showing slight signs*): If I didn't think you were very unhappy about that Miss Frensham, I wouldn't allow you to talk like that, just when we're trying to be cheerful and cosy.

ALEC: I have a terrible contempt for your Miss Frensham——

MOLLY: Not you!

ALEC: I repeat, a terrible contempt. Charming? No doubt. Beautiful? Perhaps. But what is she really? I'll tell you. Something out of a glass case, to be bought with money. Now there's something to drink to—the end of the reign of money. Eh, William?

WILL (*fishing in hamper*): I've got something for that toast. *Brings it out, and pulls cork out as he speaks.*) Some old liqueur brandy. Just what we need now.

MOLLY: Not for me, thank you. And you two want to be careful.

ALEC: Certainly not. We've been careful too long. That's our trouble.

MOLLY (*as if suddenly remembering*): Here—William Lotless— didn't you tell me—and more than once—that you didn't drink any more?

WILL: I did. But to-night I do drink. And I give you our young medical friend's toast—to the end of the reign of money——

MOLLY: I like that from you, when you're always *talking* and *thinking* about money!

WILL (*to* ALEC): Isn't that like a woman! If you saved one from drowning, she'd remind you that you promised to keep your clothes dry. To the end of the reign of money.

ALEC: To the end of the reign of money.

MOLLY: To the reign of the end of money.

WILL: Now do you want me to explain about money?

MOLLY: } (*promptly*) No.
ALEC: } Yes.

WILL (*as if beginning lecture*): Money! Money! It's a servant that's become a master.

ALEC: True, but not very original.

WILL: Money—was intended to be simply a sign, a token, a convenience—something like a—well, a railway ticket. That's all. But what's happened to it? Got all out of hand. Become a source of power. The way we allow people to handle money as power, it's just as if we let 'em handle battleships and bombing squadrons for their own private benefit.

ALEC: You're right there, William. (*To* MOLLY) He's right there.

MOLLY: Oh—he's often right. (*To* WILL) Is that all?

WILL (*who has found a large cigar in the hamper and is now ready to light it*): All? Of course it isn't all. Now the first thing you have to do is to take most of the power away from money. In fact, private money should be just pocket money. That's the only kind of money I believe in—pocket money. Everybody should have pocket money and nobody should have any other kind.

MOLLY: What's the difference?

WILL: Pocket money is just short-range, personal money, to be spent on—whatever you fancy. You can't use it to make me do something for you in a year's time, as if you had a pistol at my head. You can't send it out to increase itself, while you sit back and watch it grow——

MOLLY: But you said the other night that's just what we were doing—I mean, in this funny business with all these shares—and now you say——

WILL: But I'm telling you now how things ought to be, not how they are. We're only doing what everybody tries to do. We're not doing anything wrong.

MOLLY: It must be wrong if you think it isn't right. (*As he tries to cut in*) No, no, no—now let me get a word in.

ALEC: Quite right. It's your birthday party—not his.

MOLLY: Now I say it's all very well, all this clever talk about how things ought to be, but if we think something's wrong, then we oughtn't to do it ourselves. Somebody's got to make a start, haven't they?

WILL: No. It's a question of a system, not just of people themselves.

MOLLY: Everything depends really just on how people treat each other. If people aren't willing, and kind, and hopeful, then it's all up. But if they are, then it's all right.

WILL: Now, you can't begin to——

MOLLY (*cutting in ruthlessly*): I can begin. (*Hic.*) I've begun. I think that where the trouble starts is that some people are dead against happiness. They can't have it themselves, so they're going to spoil it for other people. They don't like life at all, these folks—they'd

[344]

like to be safe an' dead, only they don't know it, or perhaps they never wanted to be born—an' so whenever they see a bit of life springing up, they want to tread on it. They go rolling round like —like tanks—an' God help any little piece of happiness that's in the way. Now I don't say there's a lot of these people——

ALEC: I do. Millions and millions of 'em.

WILL: I'm not sure we aren't producing more and more of 'em.

MOLLY: Now why should we be?

WILL: Because of the way most people have to live. Now take——

ALEC (*boisterously cutting in*): Take another drink. Must have a toast. (*As glasses are being filled*) My turn too.

MOLLY: Well, make it something good.

ALEC (*solemnly*): What about the Leeds and Liverpool Canal Company, coupled with the London School of Tropical Hygiene and Major Butterworth, secretary of the North Cheltingate Golf Club?

MOLLY (*seriously*): That sounds silly to me. What about Absent Friends?

WILL: I haven't any.

MOLLY: What? Not one?

WILL: Not one.

MOLLY: Well, you poor thing! (*To* ALEC) What about you? You must have plenty.

ALEC (*seriously*): Four perhaps. No—three. Well, be on the safe side, and say two.

MOLLY: Good gracious me, I've dozens an' dozens.

WILL (*cutting in solemnly, raising glass*): Molly's Absent Friends.

ALEC (*same*): Molly's Absent Friends.

MOLLY (*same*): Oh—right, then. Absent Friends—bless 'em. (*Drinks.*)

MOLLY (*hiccup*).

ALEC (*laugh*).

LADY LEADMILL: Well!

There is a sound at Card Room Door, which now opens. MONDOVI *is holding it open, and* LADY LEADMILL, LADY GARNETT, MRS. TAGG *come out, followed by* DR. PLUMWEATHER, SIR RUFUS, TAGG, *and finally* MONDOVI *himself. Time should be given for all these to emerge and fan themselves out and forward a little. They have been chattering as they come out, but surprise silences them, as it has also silenced the opposite group of three. The*

[345]

silence is finally broken by a roar of laughter from ALEC, *at whom the guests stare angrily.*

TAGG (*annoyed*): Can't see anything funny about it.

MONDOVI (*coming forward, furiously to* MOLLY *and* WILL): Funny! Eet is dis-a-graceful. What are you two doing-a here—eating-a—dreenking-a——?

ALEC: Oh—that's my fault. If it hadn't been for me——

MOLLY (*cutting in, firmly*): It's nothing to do with Dr. Rothbury. You see, it happens to be my birthday to-day—and——

WILL (*cutting in*): I'm responsible for this bit of gaiety out here, not her. It was my idea.

LADY LEADMILL (*hoping to crush him*): Indeed!

WILL (*who is still smoking his cigar*): Yes, indeed.

LADY GARNETT (*to* MOLLY): May we ask whose coat you're wearing?

MOLLY (*indignantly*): It's my own. It came as a present.

LADY GARNETT: Really!

MOLLY (*same tone as* WILL *above*): Yes, really.

TAGG: Cheeky talk now!

MRS. TAGG: Yes, but it may be her own coat——

TAGG (*rudely*): Just take a look at it, and then ask yourself how chambermaids get coats like that.

ALEC: Don't be such a lout.

TAGG: What?

WILL (*coolly*): He said "Don't be such a lout".

MONDOVI (*spluttering with rage*): Fineesh! Absolute fineesh! To-morrow—you go——

DR. PLUMWEATHER (*pompously*): Just a moment, Mondovi. Dr. Rothbury?

ALEC (*calmly*): Yes, Dr. Plumweather?

DR. PLUMWEATHER: I've been looking for a good opportunity to say something to you, and you've provided me with one.

ALEC (*to* MOLLY *and* WILL): What did I tell you? It's here—the sack.

DR. PLUMWEATHER (*annoyed*): The sack! Yes, exactly. And the sooner we part company, the better.

ALEC: I quite agree.

DR. PLUMWEATHER: And let me tell you, that until you acquire a few decent manners and a sense of proportion you won't get very far.

ALEC (*warming to it*): And let *me* tell *you*, that until you acquire more skill and honesty, which isn't likely now, you'll stay as you are.

DR. PLUMWEATHER (*angrily*): You confounded young ass!

ALEC: You pompous old donkey!

MOLLY: Hiccup!

LADY LEADMILL (*beginning in awful tones*): Young man——

ALEC: No, thank you. I haven't to listen to you any more.

MONDOVI (*who has been dancing with impatience*): Please-a, please-a, ladees an' gentlemen, let-a me speak-a for a moment, because I am vairy ashamed. Nevair, nevair does it happen with me before. You two—(*pointing to* MOLLY *and* WILL)—fineesh with this hotel—you go in the morning—out—fineesh——

SIR RUFUS: Don't blame you. Probably been helping themselves to your stuff too, eh? Champagne!

WILL (*coolly*): Bollinger '28, too. How do you like that?

LADY LEADMILL: Well, I don't propose to stay down here all night——

> *She begins moving forward.* MOLLY *hastily puts herself in front of Main Door, facing them all.*

MOLLY (*with growing agitation*): Just wait a minute. Nobody's going yet.

MONDOVI (*spluttering*): You are drunk! You are mad. Come away——

MOLLY (*stopping him with her voice*): You be quiet. William there —and I—have worked very hard at this hotel. We've always tried to be obliging and make everybody comfortable. Even if we have made a bit of a slip to-night, we haven't done anybody any harm. You wouldn't see us sacked, turned out, like this, would you?

MRS. TAGG (*timidly*): Well, I must say, speaking for myself, I don't see there's much harm——

TAGG (*in fierce whisper*): Now you shut up!

MONDOVI (*wagging threatening finger*): I tella—you—fineesh— fineesh—thees hotel—all hotels——

MOLLY: You hear him? Anybody got anything to say?

MONDOVI: Yes—feeneesh—out——

> *There is a moment's silence while* MOLLY *stares at them all.*

MOLLY (*urgently*): When I think of all that I've done—an' with never a word of complaint—an' not even asking for any thanks— why—damn your eyes, the lot of you! You'll turn us out, will you? Well, we'll see. William Lotless, you keep telling me I'm really a rich woman. Does it mean anything or have you just been having a game with me? Am I rich?

WILL (*coolly*): Certainly you are.

MOLLY: Am I rich enough to buy this hotel?

SIR RUFUS: Oh—really—this is too much!

WILL (*to* SIR RUFUS): Don't worry. You've heard nothing yet.

MOLLY (*impatiently*): Never mind him. Answer me. Can I buy this hotel?

WILL: You don't need to buy it. Say the word, and it's yours.

MONDOVI (*almost moaning*): Oh—what ees thees? All dronk-mad!

WILL (*masterfully*): You be quiet or you'll talk yourself clean out of the hotel business. (*To* MOLLY) You don't need to buy this hotel, because three days ago you—acquired a controlling interest in Spa Hotels and Catering Limited, which owns this and six other hotels.

SIR RUFUS (*as the others stare silently*): You don't expect us to believe that, do you?

WILL: You can please yourself.

TAGG: Why, there's half a million of good property in Spa Hotels Limited.

WILL (*taking papers from pocket*): Chicken-feed! Now, all of you, I know you like money, so just take a good look at Mrs. Cudden there, because if she could realise on all her holdings to-morrow she'd be worth—(*glancing at his figures*)—well—at a conservative estimate —say, one million four hundred and fifty thousand pounds.

MONDOVI (*dropping into chair*): One milli—oh!—lachrimae Christi!——

LADY LEADMILL: This is a most extraordinary business——

MOLLY (*sharply*): Yes, but the only part of it that concerns all you is this. I'm closing this hotel as soon as I can—to-morrow, if it's possible. We're not going, but you are, the whole lot of you. And as you may have a good deal of packing to do soon, don't stay up too late. Good night.

DR. PLUMWEATHER (*looking at her with interest*): Well—of course —if this is true——

LADY GARNETT (*same look and tone*): It makes rather a difference——

MOLLY (*fiercely*): Not to me it doesn't. Good night.

SIR RUFUS (*conciliatory*): But—really now——

MOLLY (*very fiercely*): I said *good night.*

Her moral superiority is so evident that they go out meekly, all but MONDOVI, *who is standing now but still dazed. As the last of the guests are going,* WILL *goes over to* MONDOVI *and taps him on the shoulder.*

WILL: You go out that way. (*Points to Staff Door.*)

MONDOVI: Meester Lotless, I deed not-a know——

WILL (*firmly*): Pop off. That way.

MONDOVI *goes.*

ALEC (*to* WILL): Look here, is it true?

WILL: Every word. I've been playing the market with some shares she had left.

MOLLY *now sits down left of table and bursts into tears.* Now why? Why?

ALEC: Just reaction. Nerves.

MOLLY (*indignantly, through her tears*): It isn't nerves. I hate them all. And now I hate myself.

ALEC (*soothingly*): Now, now, now!

WILL *has now gone to telephone.* PERKINS *enters briskly.*

MOLLY (*explosively*): I'm *ashamed* of myself. (*Cries again.*)

PERKINS: Hello! Perkins of the *Gazette.*

WILL (*now dialling at telephone*): Oh—my God!

PERKINS (*advancing*): What's all this? What's all this?

ALEC: This is one of our chambermaids. She's just heard she's worth one million, four hundred and fifty thousand pounds, has a controlling interest in Spa Hotels Limited, has just closed this hotel, is turning everybody out to-morrow, and is now enjoying a good cry.

PERKINS (*cynically*): Thanks very much. (*Indicates his leg*) And now pull that one.

ALEC (*to* WILL *jocularly*): He thinks I'm pulling his leg.

PERKINS (*with tremendous irony*): Oh no! I'm only a reporter—I believe everything. (*Chiefly to* WILL) Well, I tried the Royal and the Bristol. Nothing doing. Then it suddenly came over me—ten minutes ago—that there's nothing in it.

WILL (*still at telephone*): Sixth sense?

PERKINS: Sixth sense, old man. I said to myself, "You're wasting your time here, old man," I said. "There never was a story in Cheltingate, and there never will be. Get back to Manchester." So I'm catching the 12.45. Bye-bye, everybody. (*Hurries out.*) Bye-bye, everybody—one million four hundred—ha, ha!

WILL: Just one of the bloodhounds of the Press. (*Into phone*) Yes, I want Mr. Vandermore . . . Oh, yes, he will . . .

MOLLY: What are you going to do now?

WILL: I'm going to make some more money for you.

MOLLY (*distressed*): Oh—stop it. I don't want any more.

WILL (*telephoning*): Vandermore? . . . All right . . . Lotless here . . . Now listen to me. Don't get cold feet, Vandermore . . . I thought you were a good gambler or I wouldn't have taken you in with us . . .

MOLLY (*half crying*): You're different already. Not half so nice . . . I don't want any more.

> *He hushes her fiercely, and then concentrates, snapping out: "All right . . ." "What of it?" etc., as she dabs at her eyes and realises it is hopeless trying to stop him, and the curtain comes quickly down.*

END OF ACT TWO

ACT III

*The Scene is the same as before, a week later. Afternoon, with strong
sunlight from street and above, as if through skylight. The scene
looks different now. Clearly it is not being used as an hotel any
longer. The tables and chairs are no longer neatly arranged. The
reception desk is not in use.*

At a table just in front of desk is MISS WEEKS, *who now looks like
a busy typist in a broker's office. There is a suggestion of barricade
about the door and windows. Actually the door has its blind
drawn, but there is a peephole through the blind that* GEORGE,
*the waiter, but no longer dressed like one, uses to see who is wanting
to come in, for the door is carefully locked. Just after rise, the
telephone, now on* MISS WEEKS'S *table, rings hard. She answers
it.* GEORGE *is standing near door.*

MISS WEEKS (*at telephone*): I'm very sorry, madam, we can't . . .
No, but at present the hotel is closed . . .

GEORGE (*sardonically*): Say we can sell 'er some nice shares.

MISS WEEKS (*telephone*): . . . No, I don't know when it'll be open
again. . . . And good day to you . . . (*She dials and waits.*)

ELSIE *enters through Staff Door carrying small tea-tray.*

GEORGE: For me? Thank you, dear.

ELSIE (*contemptuously passing him*): For you! T-t-t. This is for
Mr. Lotless. (*Halting a moment, with deceptive kindness.*) Would you
like some tea?

GEORGE: Yes.

ELSIE (*crushingly*): Then go and make some.

ELSIE *goes triumphantly into Card Room.*

GEORGE (*to* MISS WEEKS): You see!

MISS WEEKS: See what?

GEORGE: That's what you get for being affable. Been my mistake
all along. Too friendly and easy-goin'. If I'd been more stand-
offish, do you know where I'd be now?

MISS WEEKS (*wearily*): Yes, with a nice little business of your own
in Preston Pans. (*Goes on with her work, ignoring his glare.*)

After a moment, we hear WILL'S *voice booming angrily from Card
Room, then* ELSIE, *looking rather scared, returns from there.*

ELSIE (*confidentially*): Isn't he in a temper?

[351]

GEORGE (*ironically*): I wouldn't be surprised.

ELSIE: Not anything like so nice as he used to be. Is he, Miss Weeks?

MISS WEEKS: He's working too hard. And he doesn't get enough sleep. Life he's leading is enough to put anybody on edge.

ELSIE: Well, I must say——

> ELSIE *breaks off because* WILL *now comes hurriedly out of Card Room. He is in his shirt sleeves, smoking a cigar, and somehow looks like a busy financier and not like a night porter at all. His manner is brusque and domineering. He throws some documents on* MISS WEEKS'S *desk.*

WILL (*curtly*): Make two copies of them. And repeat that cable to the Manhattan Trust. Have we had a wire yet from Fox giving us the Investment Corporation quotations?

MISS WEEKS (*the Secretary now*): No, Mr. Lotless.

WILL: How the devil can a fellow be expected to do business under these conditions? What we want here is a tape machine. Get a tape machine. Tell 'em I want it installed at once. Never mind what it costs. Must have one. Oh—you—Elsie—go up and tell Mrs. Cudden I want her to sign some transfers.

> *As* ELSIE *hesitates and looks uneasy.*

Well? Go on.

> *He sees three of them exchanging uneasy glances.*

Well?

MISS WEEKS (*uneasily*): Mrs. Cudden isn't here.

WILL (*astounded*): Isn't here? Where is she?

MISS WEEKS: She—went away—last night.

WILL (*furious*): Great jumping Moses! And nobody told me. (*To* ELSIE) Don't stand gaping there. Pop off.

> ELSIE *hurries off through Staff Door.*

WILL (*he takes hold of himself*): Did she say where she was going?

MISS WEEKS (*hesitating*): No, she didn't—not exactly.

WILL: What d'you mean—not exactly?

MISS WEEKS (*hesitating*): Well—I have an idea—she was going to London——

WILL: Worse and worse! Just where I didn't want her to go. Did she say what she was going to do? Bit o' shopping perhaps, eh?

MISS WEEKS: She didn't say.

GEORGE (*slowly*): I've an idea——

WILL (*brutally*): I don't believe you, but let's have it.

[352]

GEORGE: Sorry I spoke. Sorry I spoke. (*Looks as if he'll never speak again.*)

WILL: Now listen, you two, this is serious. There's millions at stake. Everything's in Molly Cudden's name, and if some people I know in London got hold of her, that 'ud be the end of me—and of you too. Look at it. Here's a woman worth millions—and as simple as a sausage—wandering about London—Oh Christmas! It's enough to give you heart disease.

GEORGE: I've an idea she went to see that Miss Frensham—you remember, that good-lookin' young piece—who was staying here a few weeks since. I saw Mrs. Cudden lookin' at the register before she went and takin' an address down—and I had a look where she'd been lookin', after she'd gone—and it seemed to me she'd been taking down that Miss Frensham's address.

WILL (*to* MISS WEEKS): Send a wire to Mrs. Cudden care o' this Miss Frensham: "Return immediately very urgent and you are badly needed here. Will Lotless." That ought to bring her back. And we've got to get her back before some o' those smooth City and West End boys get their forks into her, or we'll all be carved up. Get that wire off at once. (*He moves towards Card Room, then wheels on them, accusingly.*) Why didn't you tell me she'd gone away?

    As they don't reply.

I see. She specially asked you not to tell me, eh?

GEORGE: Yes, she did.

WILL (*bitterly*): The biggest deal I was ever in—and it's like trying to do it from an infants' school.

    There is a sharp knocking at the front door.

Who's that? Don't let any newspaper men in. Or anybody I don't know.

GEORGE (*looking through peephole*): It's Mondovi.

WILL: All right. Let him in.

    GEORGE *lets him in.* MISS WEEKS *is busy sending the wire quietly over the telephone.* MONDOVI *is in ordinary clothes and looking worried.*

MONDOVI: Ah—Meestair Lotta-less—good afternoon.

WILL (*curtly*): Afternoon, Mondovi. I told you to go up to London and see the general manager of the company for another job.

MONDOVI: Yais——

    WILL *nods and goes into Card Room.*

Thank you so much.

MISS WEEKS: Where are you staying, Mr. Mondovi?

[353]

MONDOVI (*confidentially*): Ovair at the Grand with my frien'
Pellini. An' I tella you, Mees Weeks, thatta Grand Hotel ees no
good. Tairrible!

GEORGE: It can't be much worse than this used to be.

MONDOVI: Oh—yais. Mucha worse. Tairrible! Notta comfortable—an' a vairry bada crew in the kitchen. Las night Pellini says
"I give-a you *supreme de chicken Grand Hotel*—speciality of my
chef." Alla right, I taste eet. Tairrible! At once I know. Notta
poulet—notta chicken—at all. Eet was—— (*He makes scampering
gestures with his fingers.*)

MISS WEEKS (*horrified*): Rats.

MONDOVI: Oh—no—notta rats—but—er—you know—*lapin* bunnee—yais—bunnee rabbits. (*With tremendous scorn*) Supreme de
chicken Grand Hotel—specialaite—weeth bunnee rabbits.

GEORGE (*gloomily*): One seaside place I worked in, the chicken
used to be guinea-pig. There were a lot of boys' schools in that town.

MONDOVI: So! What do you do 'ere now?

MISS WEEKS: We're a sort of mixture of millionaires and charwomen.

MONDOVI: The hotel—it is steel closed, eh?

GEORGE: That's right. And if it's a success we'll close down the
rest of the company's hotels.

MISS WEEKS: Is there anything we can do for you, Mr. Mondovi?

MONDOVI: Oh—no. I forgot my diplome—diploma, eh? It ees in
my office. And I am afraid someone might take eet.

GEORGE: What for?

MONDOVI (*pointedly*): Because wit' theese diploma a man can be
something better than a waiter—eh, Miss Weeks? Excusa me, pliss.

MONDOVI *goes through Staff Door.*

GEORGE (*doing his parody*): Nice-a people—vairry reech!

There is a pause, during which GEORGE *yawns and* MISS WEEKS
does some typing. Then the door slowly opens, and MOLLY
CUDDEN, *carrying a small case and dressed in her fur coat, enters
cautiously, after looking round.*

MOLLY (*almost whispering*): Well, I haven't been away long have
I? Did he find out I'd gone?

GEORGE: Only a few minutes since.

MOLLY: Shows what a lot of interest he takes in me, doesn't it?

MISS WEEKS: But he was furious.

MOLLY (*shrewdly*): Why? Because he missed me?

GEORGE: No, because he thought one of the other crooks would get hold of you.

MOLLY: For once I believe you're right, George. (*As she takes off her coat and puts bag down, etc.*) Well, I enjoyed that little trip, though I nearly roasted myself in that fur coat. It looks drearier than ever—shut up in here like this—not a bit of life or anything——

MISS WEEKS (*with irony*): Just making millions.

MOLLY: I've enjoyed myself more making beds. Now, you two, pop off and get some tea.

MISS WEEKS: But Mr. Lotless——

MOLLY (*cutting in, firmly*): Never mind him. Besides, I've got a tricky bit of business on, and you'll be better off if you're not mixed up in it.

GEORGE (*moving off*): Suits me.

MISS WEEKS (*rising, rather reluctantly*): Well, if you'll take the responsibility.

MOLLY: Don't worry about that. Off you pop.

GEORGE (*turning just before exit, Staff Door*): By the way, our old pal's here.

MOLLY: Who d'you mean?

GEORGE: Vairry reech, vairry nice-a people.

GEORGE *and* MISS WEEKS *go out.*

MOLLY, *who is clearly bursting with intrigue, peeps anxiously through the peep-hole, then goes towards Card Room quietly, then returns for another peep.* MONDOVI *now returns, triumphantly carrying a large framed diploma.*

MONDOVI: Ah—Meesis Cudden—you are vairry well?

MOLLY: Only just fair. Too much sitting about. What have you got there?

MONDOVI (*showing it proudly*): My diploma. You like eet?

MOLLY (*seriously*): I think it's wonderful. Fancy it saying all that about you!

MONDOVI: Thank you very much. Good afternoon, Mrs. Cudden.

MOLLY (*after short pause*): Mr. Mondovi, what's it like running an hotel?

MONDOVI: Meesis Cudden—I tella you. Running an hotel would be pairfect—eef eet was not for two things—just two things. One— the owners. The othair—the guests.

MOLLY: So—if you owned it yourself and had different kinds of guests from the usual—eh?

MONDOVI: I theenk—it would be delightful. An' I theenk I know where they have such hotels——

MOLLY (*eagerly*): Where?

MONDOVI (*pointing upward*): In heaven. Gooda afternoon, Meesis Cudden.

MONDOVI *goes.*

MOLLY: Good afternoon, Mr. Mondovi.

WILL *enters from Card Room. They look at each other a moment. He is furious. She is defiant.*

WILL: So you had to sneak out and go to London?

MOLLY: Well, why shouldn't I?

WILL (*angrily*): Because you might easily have ditched everything. Yes, ruined us both just for a damned silly woman's whim. Let me remind you of something. A month ago you were a chambermaid here and never looked like being anything else, and now you're the richest woman in England. And who did it? You didn't do it. You don't know yet what it's all about. *I* did it.

MOLLY: Nobody said you didn't.

WILL (*furious*): And all I ask, while I'm making millions for you, is that you stay here and keep quiet for a week or two. And you can't even do that! You go an' risk everything rather than do what I ask you to do! Another break like this and you might find yourself making beds again.

MOLLY (*coolly*): Well, that wouldn't kill me. Might do me a bit of good.

WILL: I'm trying to make you into something——

MOLLY (*cutting in*): Well, don't try so hard then. And another thing, Will Lotless. Stop making yourself into something I don't like. When you were nothing but the Night Porter here, you were a nice chap.

WILL: And what's the matter with me now?

MOLLY: Everything. You go shouting and stamping and swearing. You haven't got a smile for anybody. You look so worried and cross——

WILL (*shouting*): And you'd look worried and cross if you'd got the biggest financial deal of a lifetime in the balance. (*Makes gesture, and then is calmer but still sharp.*) Why did you go to London?

MOLLY: For a nice change.

WILL: Did you see that Frensham girl?

MOLLY: Yes. I knew she wasn't rich really. I told you at the time. She told me she was a secretary. And this morning she introduced me to her employer. And he insisted on coming back here with us.

WILL (*alarmed*): *What!* But who——

VERONICA FRENSHAM *and* LORD FLEETFIELD *enter through Main Door.* LORD FLEETFIELD *is elderly, tall, imposing, superbly dressed.*

VERONICA (*to* WILL): Hello, Mr. Lotless!

MOLLY (*rather nervously*): Will, this is Lord Fleetfield.

LORD FLEETFIELD (*coolly, as* WILL *glares*): No introduction necessary, Mrs. Cudden. Just as I thought. This is Mr. William Blofield.

WILL (*very fiercely, to* MOLLY): You dirty rat!

MOLLY (*furious*): Oh—you——

She marches across and slaps his face—hard, then overcome by what she has done, she turns aside and collapses into chair.

VERONICA (*indignantly to* WILL): And serves you right. What has she done?

WILL (*bitterly*): Finished me—and herself too.

MOLLY (*rising, bewildered*): I don't know what you're talking about.

LORD FLEETFIELD (*smoothly*): Perhaps I'd better explain.

WILL (*bitterly*): That's right. Enjoy yourself.

LORD FLEETFIELD: This is Mr. William Blofield. I thought I recognised his touch in these recent operations on the market. Mr. Blofield was at one time a very well-known and successful speculator. Then he was found guilty of forging securities and was sentenced to five years' imprisonment.

MOLLY (*aghast*): William!

WILL: You had to bring him here, hadn't you? Well, it's true. Blofied—ex-convict—jailbird—that's me.

MOLLY (*almost overcome, moving nearer*): William, I always knew there was *something*. Why didn't you tell me?

WILL (*waving her away, bitterly*): I'll tell you something now. Don't think Lord Fleetfield has come here and told you who I am just for the good of your health. I know *him*. And the only real difference between him and me is that I was found out—and—well, he's Lord Fleetfield.

LORD FLEETFIELD (*coolly*): Oh no, there are other differences.

WILL: Yes, and I'll tell you what they are. The game we played was just the same game, but of course he played it with more style. Nothing vulgar, nothing common, about him. In with the Right People. Decent chap, sound fella, sahib. But playing just the same game, and ten times more dangerous.

LORD FLEETFIELD: My dear Blofield, you overlook the all-important difference in method. And then perhaps people saw that when I achieved some power I made use of it with tact, courtesy, and perhaps even with some charm. Whereas you bragged and blustered and rode rough-shod. So society took advantage of the first mistake you made to hurry you out of sight and hearing. Let us, it says, at least have pleasant masters. Are you taking this down, Miss Frensham?

VERONICA (*who is*): Yes, Lord Fleetfield.

LORD FLEETFIELD: Quite right. It may come in for something.

WILL (*roughly*): All right, then take it down. I say Lord Fleet-field——

MOLLY (*urgently, cutting in*): No, stop it, William. Let me say something now. (*To* LORD FLEETFIELD) I didn't know he'd been in prison. But—but I don't see that it matters now. He did something that was wrong. He's paid for it. That's done with. Can't we all forget about it?

LORD FLEETFIELD: No, Mrs. Cudden, we can't. We have here a very serious matter. These bold piratical raids on the stock market are extremely disturbing. Two large combines in important national industries have already been badly shaken. Investors may lose confidence. Therefore it's our duty to stop such raids.

WILL (*bitterly*): In other—and plainer—words—I've been spoiling his racket, and he's not going to stand for it.

LORD FLEETFIELD (*impressively*): Certainly I'm not going to stand for it. And if we must have plain words, here they are. I can send Mr. Blofield here back to prison, and unless I can come to a friendly agreement with him during the next hour, I shall see that he goes back to prison.

WILL (*to* MOLLY): And now do you see what you've done?

MOLLY: Is it true—what he says?

WILL: Yes.

MOLLY: And is that why you had to keep it all so secret?

WILL: Yes.

MOLLY (*distressed*): You see, William, I didn't know. I didn't know. I see why you called me that. And I hit you. I'm sorry, William. I didn't know.

WILL (*bitterly*): You know now.

MOLLY (*reproachfully*): A month ago you wouldn't have talked like that. (*Then bursting out*) Oh—I think it's horrible—all of it. I wish I'd never had anything to do with it. (*To* WILL) It's spoilt you once—sending you to prison—and now it's beginning to spoil you again. (*To* LORD FLEETFIELD) And I thought you were such a nice man—and now when I bring you here, you talk about sending William to prison again. It's all horrible and *wrong*.

VERONICA (*turning to her, sympathetically*): Molly——

MOLLY: No, dear—it's all gone wrong. And I ought to try and think—and I can't—I'm so upset.

> She goes out of the group and sits down.

> LORD FLEETFIELD *and* WILL *look at her a moment, then at each other.*

WILL: Well?

> Comes down.

LORD FLEETFIELD: If you and I could talk this over quietly—away from these emotional disturbances—we might come to some amicable settlement—eh?

WILL (*curtly*): What kind of settlement will that be?

LORD FLEETFIELD: That you're out, Blofield. Out of these deals —but also—still out of prison. And that's my final word.

WILL: All right. You win. I've a room here I use as an office. Let's go in there.

> He leads the way.

> LORD FLEETFIELD *nods to* VERONICA, *so she follows him and all three go into Card Room.*

> MOLLY *sits miserably, trying to think.*

> After a moment or two, ALEC *enters, as if from hospital. He stops when he sees* MOLLY.

ALEC: Here, what's the matter, Molly?

MOLLY (*slowly coming out of her misery*): Everything. All gone wrong. I brought Lord Fleetfield here——

ALEC: What—the big financial man?

MOLLY: Yes. I thought he could help William. But now it seems he's threatening to send him to prison. And that's not what I meant at all.

ALEC: Look here, Molly. I've thought for some time you didn't realise what all this money-making does mean.

MOLLY: Are you going to start now?

ALEC: Yes.

MOLLY: Go on then. What does it mean?

ALEC: We l, it isn't just entering figures into a book and finding you've got lots and lots of money to spend. It's grabbing power, Molly.

You're playing about with people's lives—the lives of thousands and thousands of people you've never even seen.

MOLLY (*shocked*): Oh—but I never meant——

ALEC: I don't care what you meant—that's what it is. People's savings disappear. They have to give up their houses, sell their furniture. Kids have to leave school. People can't take the holidays they planned. Fellows are sacked—middle-aged men turned out of jobs.

MOLLY (*indignantly*): Stop it! I won't hear another word. D'you think if I imagined it was like that—all real—messing about with people's lives—I'd have anything to do with it? Why, I'd have burnt them shares first. Why—it's *disgraceful*.

ALEC (*grinning*): Here, steady. You could have given them to me —to help me to start that clinic.

MOLLY: That's what you want, isn't it, a clinic?

ALEC: That's all I want.

MOLLY: Oh, no, it isn't.

ALEC: What do you mean?

MOLLY: She's in there.

ALEC: Who? Not Veronica Frensham?

MOLLY (*as she begins to move towards Card Room*): Yes. She's this Lord Fleetfield's secretary.

ALEC: A secretary?

MOLLY: I told you she wasn't rich. I'll bring her out.

> *She marches into the Card Room, and then returns at once with* VERONICA.

Now then, settle it between you. And if anybody wants me, I'll be up in my room, trying to stop looking a sight. (*She is now collecting her coat, etc.*) And don't be silly, you two. Get on with it. Let's have something sensible out of all this palaver.

> *She goes out.*

VERONICA (*smiling*): Well?

ALEC: What was the idea—pretending to be rich?

VERONICA (*coolly*): Well, I get six pounds a week. Most secretaries only get about four.

ALEC: But why tell me all that nonsense?

VERONICA: I was on a holiday, and pretending to be rich and grand was part of the holiday. Besides, you were so pleased with yourself, and thought you knew everything, so I decided to take you down a peg or two.

ALEC: I don't think it was a very good joke.

VERONICA: I didn't afterwards. And I wrote about six letters to you.

ALEC (*hastily*): I never had them.

VERONICA: No, I tore them up. But I would have written finally if I hadn't suddenly discovered we were coming up here. How *are* you?

ALEC: Broke. Old Plumweather gave me the push, and all I'm doing now is a bit of work for nothing at the hospital.

VERONICA: I've been thinking a lot about you.

ALEC: I've been thinking a lot about you too. In fact, you're a damn nuisance. I think we'd better get married.

VERONICA: What—so that you can stop thinking about me?

ALEC: Yes. I want to get on with my work.

VERONICA: That's not a good enough reason. Why do you want to marry me?

ALEC: Because if I don't, I'd probably get tied up with a nurse, and I hate nurses.

VERONICA: In that case then I'd better marry you. But if I'm going to work to keep us, you'll have to get up and cook breakfast.

ALEC: What do you have for breakfast?

VERONICA: Only tea and toast.

ALEC: I can make tea and toast.

They kiss but are interrupted by LORD FLEETFIELD.

LORD FLEETFIELD (*amused*): Oh—Miss Frensham.

VERONICA (*rather confused*): Oh—Lord Fleetfield, this is Dr. Rothbury.

LORD FLEETFIELD: How d'you do? It's a pleasure to meet a young doctor who believes in the good old-fashioned treatment. Now where is Mrs. Cudden?

ALEC: She's upstairs. I'll tell her. Don't go away.

He hurries out. LORD FLEETFIELD *looks quizzingly at* VERONICA.

LORD FLEETFIELD: I hope his intentions are dishonourable.

VERONICA: They're not. We're engaged.

LORD FLEETFIELD: I congratulate him, though I suppose no woman is as good a wife as she is a secretary. Being a secretary seems to bring out the best in a woman, and being a wife doesn't.

WILL *now appears from Card Room, carrying some documents.*

LORD FLEETFIELD: Ah, Blofield. I've sent for Mrs. Cudden, we'll explain to her the arrangement we've come to.

[361]

WILL: She won't know what we're talking about.

LORD FLEETFIELD: Still the same blunt outspoken fellow, Blofield. What were you in this hotel before you broke into the market again?

WILL: Night Porter.

LORD FLEETFIELD: That must have made a late arrival here something of an ordeal for any sensitive guest.

WILL: Don't you believe it. I was a good night porter. Wasn't I, Miss Frensham?

VERONICA: You were sweet. I think the only night porter I've ever really liked.

WILL: You see?

LORD FLEETFIELD: How do you account for your success as a night porter?

WILL: I'll explain. I hadn't much power and I'd few worries, so it wasn't hard to be pleasant. In many ways it's a more satisfying job than juggling with money. For one thing, you've more time to think—and you're not so frightened of thinking. Wouldn't suit you, though. Head waiter would be more in your line.

LORD FLEETFIELD: You're probably right. Almost the only men in London I still respect are one or two head waiters.

He sees MOLLY *entering. She looks better than she did.*

Now, Mrs. Cudden. We're all ready. Do sit down.

He fusses her into a chair. Then he and VERONICA *sit, but not* WILL.

MOLLY: Sit down, William.

WILL (*curtly*): I'm all right.

MOLLY: Oh dear, you're not going to sulk, are you?

LORD FLEETFIELD (*as* WILL *is about to reply*): No, Blofield, let me say something. Mrs. Cudden, we've come to a sensible friendly agreement, and I must tell you that throughout our friend has asked for nothing for himself and has only been trying to safeguard your interests.

MOLLY (*warmly*): William!

WILL: All right. I don't want any votes of thanks now. Let me explain what's happened. I don't go to jail, *that's* settled.

LORD FLEETFIELD (*firmly*): Quite definitely settled, whatever else happens.

MOLLY: That's all right then.

WILL: These chaps get what they want—control of the power we hold, but they'll guarantee you all the money you want to spend.

[362]

You can have ten fur coats and a diamond suit-case. It'll be wonderful. (*He begins to walk away.*)

MOLLY (*rising*): I don't won't ten fur coats and a diamond suit-case, you fathead. And where are you going?

WILL (*turning*): I'm going to pack my bag.

> *Stalks out.* MOLLY *is undecided for a moment whether to call him back, but then decides not to.*

LORD FLEETFIELD: Yes, you've only to sign the necessary documents, which give us the controlling interest we need, and then you can forget all about us. You can draw as much money as you please. And enjoy yourself. Buy what you like. Entertain. Travel.

MOLLY: I see.

LORD FLEETFIELD (*impressively*): There you are, Mrs. Cudden. It's an odd thought—and you might take this down, Miss Frensham—that if you and Blofield could have gone on a little longer, then without leaving this hotel you could have thrown your shadow across the world. The fate of whole industries would have been in your hands. You could have controlled commodity markets and, if you wished, created famines. You could have dominated the political life of people at the other end of the world. The fate of millions and millions of people you have never seen might have been in your hands. A remarkable position to be in. Though of course I've had some experience of it for some time now.

MOLLY: Then you ought to be ashamed of yourself. I call it disgraceful.

LORD FLEETFIELD: What?

MOLLY (*with growing feeling*): Yes, disgraceful! But I felt it wrong from the start. I watched it spoiling him—yes, and beginning to spoil me. No proper work to do! Just gambling! And all that power. Sitting here interfering with other people's lives, miles away. I don't want to be mucking people's lives up for money, and I don't see why you should either. No, I'm not signing your papers.

LORD FLEETFIELD (*astonished*): But, Mrs. Cudden, I don't think you realise the seriousness of the situation. These enormous interests can't be left to look after themselves.

MOLLY: These enormous interests, as you call 'em, aren't going to be left to look after themselves. The doctor explained what I could do, and a solicitor's coming to straighten it all out for me. I don't know much about these things, but I do know it isn't right that one person should be able to interfere with and mess about the lives and happiness of thousands of other people.

LORD FLEETFIELD: Perhaps not. But under the present system——

MOLLY (*cutting in*): We'd better put a stop to the present system. And I'll make a start by giving all this controlling business to the people whose lives are mixed up in it, to the people of England.

LORD FLEETFIELD: In other words, you'll hand over your interest to the government, in the form of a public trust?

MOLLY: Yes, that's it.

LORD FLEETFIELD: And do you suppose the government will manage these affairs any better than my friends and I would?

MOLLY: Well, if they don't, we can change the government, can't we?

LORD FLEETFIELD (*smiling*): Possibly, though my friends and I generally have a hand in changing governments too.

MOLLY: I dare say. But you won't have this lot—(*waving papers*)—to help you to do it. I've made up my mind about that.

VERONICA: But, Molly, don't you want anything for yourself?

MOLLY: Yes, I was coming to that. Out of all this lot, I just want two things. I want enough to keep and run this hotel—on my own lines. And I want enough money to provide young Dr. Rothbury a clinic.

VERONICA: Darling! That's perfect. (*To* LORD FLEETFIELD) She can do that, can't she?

LORD FLEETFIELD: Certainly. The solicitor can arrange that.

VERONICA: Oh, Molly, that's wonderful.

LORD FLEETFIELD: Well, I've accomplished the more important half of my task, so I can't grumble. (*Rising.*) By the way, do you know if my old friend Lady Leadmill is still staying up here?

MOLLY: Yes, she was staying here until we closed, and now she's across at the Grand.

LORD FLEETFIELD: Then I'll go to the Grand too, Miss Frensham. Report to me there in the morning. Good-bye, Mrs. Cudden.

MOLLY: Good-bye, Lord Fleetfield. Pleased to have met you.

LORD FLEETFIELD: Delighted to have met you. Most unusual experience. And—about this hotel of yours——

MOLLY: Yes?

LORD FLEETFIELD: Don't let your Night Porter read the financial Press.

He goes, the three of them having been standing near front door MOLLY *and* VERONICA *now come down.*

MOLLY: My dear, fancy me going on like that. I don't know whether to laugh or cry. Telling 'em all straight. Though I wouldn't have known how to do it if it hadn't been for the doctor—your young man.

VERONICA (*excitedly*): Who's going to have this clinic. Where is he?

MOLLY: He was only waiting till we'd finished. Didn't want to butt in, he said.

ALEC *pops his head in through Main Door.*

ALEC: Hoy, Veronica! I want you.

VERONICA: Hoy yourself! You can't talk to me like that.

MOLLY (*delighted*): Course he can. Go on. Pop off.

VERONICA (*as she moves off*): Well, this time perhaps. But I don't propose to be talked to like that all the time.

Suddenly running off, with enormous enthusiasm, crying, partly off.

Darling, you're to have that clinic. We'll have a flat on the top floor.

MOLLY *listens, smiling, then sighs as she sits down.* WILL *now enters through Staff Door, dressed in a neat but shabby suit and carrying an old suitcase. He looks at her. She looks at him and rises slowly.*

MOLLY (*reproachfully*): William! William!

He stops but says nothing.

And where d'you think you're going?

WILL: What does that matter? I'm not wanted here any more.

MOLLY: Who says so?

WILL: You said so.

MOLLY: I didn't.

WILL: You as good as said so. But there's one thing I want to tell you before I do go, Molly Cudden.

MOLLY: There's several things I want to tell you, William Lotless.

WILL: Well, listen to me first. Don't think I went back into the market again just to make some easy money. Not this time. What do I want now with a lot o' money? Wouldn't know what to do with it. I went back into the game to try and beat the smart boys again—see? And I did it. Don't forget that—I did it.

MOLLY: I know you did, William. But it was spoiling you again. And you weren't happy.

WILL: That's nothing. Ex-convicts my age don't expect to be happy. That's at least something they learn. But anyhow, I had my flutter, and I know what the game's worth. If people had had any sense, they'd have stopped us years since. But then people haven't any sense.

[365]

MOLLY: Don't you think I've any sense?

WILL: Not much. You had a bit when you were still a chamber-maid. It's a funny thing. I've never been a chap to bother a lot with women. But every time I've been badly let down it's been by a woman.

MOLLY: And *I* suppose *I* let you down, eh?

WILL: You've said it, not me. What did you ask from Fleetfield —a couple o' yachts?

MOLLY: No. And I didn't sign anything either.

WILL (*astonished*): *What!*

MOLLY: It's all going into a public trust. All I asked for myself was enough money to give Dr. Rothbury a clinic, and enough to run a little business of my own. You wouldn't like a job in it, would you?

WILL (*picking up his case*): No, thanks. I can manage without any pension. And I don't want any woman to keep me.

MOLLY (*going over to him to stop him going*): William, William, come here. Who's talking about keeping you, you silly old chump? Now answer me one question. Do you like working in hotels of this sort?

WILL: No.

MOLLY: Why?

WILL: You ought to know. Because I don't take to most of the people who use this sort of hotel. Too many idle greedy-guts.

MOLLY (*artfully*): The trouble about you is that you just criticise. I'll bet you've got no ideas of your own about running an hotel.

WILL (*indignantly*): Of course I have! What d'you think I've been doing with my brains for the last couple of years? I'm a man of ideas.

MOLLY (*artfully again*): That's what *you* say!

WILL: Certainly it's what I say. Running an hotel! Why, give me a place I could take a real interest in—and——

MOLLY (*cutting in, firmly*): You're engaged.

WILL: What? Where?

MOLLY: Here, as manager.

WILL: What—is this the business you're going to run?

MOLLY: Yes, but it'll be a new kind of hotel for Cheltingate, for people who've been working too hard and not just eating too much, for men who are some use in the world, for women who deserve to be waited on for a change—for real people. Everything must be good but not too expensive. That means I need a man of ideas to run it. But of course if you don't feel up to it——

WILL (*cutting in, vehemently*): Don't be silly, woman, don't be silly. I'm the one man in England who could tackle this job for you. Good ideas! I've got thousands of 'em. Why, look here——

> *Produces a note-book with great zest. Enter, through Staff Door,* MISS WEEKS *and* GEORGE.

MISS WEEKS: Mr. Lotless——

MOLLY: And we shall want you, Miss Weeks——

WILL: Senior receptionist.

GEORGE: And what about me?

> *A knock or ring outside.*

WILL: See who's there.

> GEORGE *lets in* LADY LEADMILL, *looking more monstrous than ever, followed by* MISS SELL.

LADY LEADMILL (*in tremendous voice*): Where is Lord Fleetfield? I was informed he was here.

MOLLY: He was here, but he went to the Grand to look for you.

LADY LEADMILL: Indeed. Any letters for me here that you've failed to forward?

MISS WEEKS: No, Lady Leadmill.

LADY LEADMILL (*going towards desk, suspiciously*): Are you sure?

MISS WEEKS: Absolutely positive.

LADY LEADMILL (*sternly*): I prefer to make sure. The posts here are *most* peculiar. And several letters are missing.

MOLLY (*confidentially to* MISS SELL *aside*): Here's a chance for you to get away from that old crocodile. Come and work for us here.

MISS SELL (*eagerly*): Oh—could I? Oh—that would be wonderful. But——

LADY LEADMILL (*marching majestically towards door*): Miss Sell.

MOLLY (*to the hesitating* MISS SELL): This is your chance—your only chance——

LADY LEADMILL (*commandingly at door*): Miss Sell.

MISS SELL (*after giving* MOLLY *a pathetic little smile*): Yes, Lady Leadmill.

> *She hurries out after her.*

WILL: And that's half England.

MOLLY: Well, I'm disappointed. It oughtn't to be like that.

WILL: Well, it is. Millions and millions of Miss Sells——

> *Telephone rings.* MISS WEEKS *answers it.*

MISS WEEKS (*telephone*): Yes? . . . Oh yes, Mrs. Gore . . . I'll just see, Mrs. Gore. (*To* MOLLY, *covering telephone*) Mrs. Gore wants to know if she can stay. She's very rich.

MOLLY: If she's very rich, tell her we don't want her. (*To* WILL) I'm disappointed.

WILL: But look.

MISS SELL *re-enters, looking excited and defiant, her hat rather askew, and carrying* LADY LEADMILL'S *umbrella, now broken, which she tosses on to the table.*

MISS SELL: When do I start?

MOLLY (*laughing*): Hurray!

WILL: You start now. Now look here——

Laughing and eager they all gather round WILL *and his notebook and talk all at once as curtain comes down.*

END OF PLAY

HOW ARE THEY AT HOME?

A Topical Comedy in Two Acts

CHARACTERS
(in the order of their appearance)

KENTON, an old butler
HILDA PACKET, from the factory
EILEEN STOCKS, from the factory
SAM CAWTHRA, a factory foreman
LOTTA SCHULBERG, an operatic cook
LADY (FRANCES) FARFIELD
PAULINE CHESTER, a Land Girl
MAJOR GEORGE WEBBER, U.S. Army
RAYMOND KILLIGREW, a Civil Servant
COMMODORE PENTWORTHY, of the B.L.A.D.S.
GROUP-CAPT. EDWARD CAMYON, R.A.F.
SQUADRON-LDR. TONY ACTON, R.A.F.
CORPORAL HERBERT PACKET, Hilda's brother

———

The Scene is Farfield Hall, Fassington, in the North Midlands, on a Saturday night in Spring, 1944.

How are they at Home?—Copyright, 1945, by Samuel French, Ltd.

*First produced at the Apollo Theatre, London, on May 4th, 1944, with
the following cast:*

HILDA PACKET	ANGELA WYNDHAM LEWIS
KENTON	CHARLES GROVES
EILEEN STOCKS	PATRICIA LAFFAN
SAM CAWTHRA	GEORGE CARNEY
LOTTA SCHULBERG	HELLA KURTY
LADY FARFIELD	JANE CARR
PAULINE CHESTER	JENNIFER GRAY
MAJOR GEORGE WEBBER	JOHN SALEW
RAYMOND KILLIGREW	HENRY HEWITT
COMMODORE PENTWORTHY	MIGNON O'DOHERTY
GROUP-CAPTAIN EDWARD CAMYON	RALPH TRUMAN
SQUADRON-LEADER TONY ACTON	NOEL DRYDEN
CORPORAL PACKET	JOHN SLATER

ACT I

The Scene is the lounge hall of a fairly large country house. It is a lofty and imposing room, though it has obviously seen much better days. At back are very tall windows, through which park-like grounds can be seen. Left centre (actors' left) are large double doors which are main entrance to the room from outside. On left wall is a massive fire-place, and downstage left is a small door leading to kitchen, etc. Right centre shows foot of handsome old staircase, which curves up, out of sight. On right wall is large door leading to drawing-room, etc. A fairly long table of refectory type occupies centre of stage, and this can have two long forms with it. Other small tables, easy chairs, etc. A telephone. Some vague family portraits and a few stuffed heads of animals on walls. A camp bed and a pile of blankets in one corner. The place is not dirty but it is dingy, untidy and dilapidated, though the general impression is rather of a cheerful bohemianism than of a depressing decay. At rise of curtain, KENTON, who is a very old butler, shabby and senile and almost out of his wits but still vaguely impressive, is making an effort to lay the table. The door down left into kitchen is open, and through it we hear the wireless playing a Viennese waltz and the still excellent voice of LOTTA SCHULBERG singing to it. KENTON listens to this, with a kind of droll despair, then does his best to get on with his work. Bell rings. KENTON goes to answer door, then returns followed by HILDA, a lively North-country girl, and EILEEN, a shy pretty girl.

HILDA (*cheerfully*): She *is* expecting us, y'know.

KENTON: Yes, miss. I'll tell her ladyship you've arrived.

HILDA: Tell her it's Hilda and Eileen. You 'aven't seen Mr. Cawthra—that's our foreman—'ave you?

KENTON: No, miss. But I remember her ladyship saying that there would be three guests this evening.

HILDA: Mr. Cawthra's the other one. I say—are you a butler?

EILEEN (*embarrassed*): Shut up—Hilda!

HILDA: You don't mind me asking, do yer? Are you a butler?

KENTON (*gravely*): Yes, miss.

HILDA (*delighted*): Well, I've always wanted to see one. I've seen dozens on the pictures. Well, will you tell her we've come.

KENTON: Certainly, miss, I'll inform her ladyship without delay.

He goes out down left. HILDA *looks after him delightedly.*

HILDA: "I'll inform her ladyship without delay." He talks just like 'em too. You'd think he was doing it on purpose.

EILEEN: Perhaps he is.

HILDA: Well, I don't see any point in 'olding these things any longer. Let's put 'em down 'ere.

Makes a move towards centre table.

EILEEN (*nervously*): I suppose we've come to the right place.

HILDA: Don't be dotty, Eileen. Course we 'ave. You 'eard him say so. Three guests—that's us two and old Sam. (*Looks round happily.*) There's always a room like this in them mystery plays. The body'll be in the libr'ry. That'll be through 'ere. (*She has gone down to door right and now opens it.*)

EILEEN: Hilda, you mustn't.

HILDA: There's only a sort of posh passage. (*Coming in again.*) Fancy old Farfy livin' 'ere!

EILEEN (*shocked*): You won't have to call her that here.

HILDA (*pleasantly*): Well, she can't expect me to start any of this ladyship business, not after workin' with 'er in the Assembly shop for the last eighteen months.

EILEEN: Well, I don't suppose she will—but—after all—it is different for her here, isn't it?

Sound of LOTTA *singing loudly and gaily from the kitchen.*

HILDA: Just listen to that. Proper singing too. I wonder who that is. (*She now goes towards kitchen door.*)

EILEEN (*alarmed again*): No, Hilda, honestly you mustn't.

KENTON *comes out down left.*

KENTON: 'Er ladyship will be free shortly—and asks if you would like to see the house.

The singing stops.

HILDA: Well, this is it, isn't it?

EILEEN: She means—have a look round, doesn't she?

KENTON: Yes, miss. Farfield 'All 'as many features of interest.

HILDA: All right. And anyhow I'd like to have a wash.

KENTON: Certainly miss. The main staircase is this way.

He ushers them upstairs ceremoniously. LOTTA *recommences singing off, down left. After a moment or two there are several rings at the front door. Then* SAM CAWTHRA *enters, rather cautiously. He is carrying some bottles of beer, etc., and smoking a pipe.*

[374]

SAM (*calling, not too loudly*): 'Ullo! 'Ullo! Anybody at 'ome?

He puts down the beer, etc., on table, then hears LOTTA *singing.*
He opens door down left and calls through.

Ah say! Is this Farfield 'All? Heigh! 'Ave Ah come to t'right shop?

He steps back a pace or two, and LOTTA *enters down left through*
open door. She is wearing apron, etc., for cooking.

LOTTA: Oh—hello!

SAM: 'Ow d'yer do?

LOTTA: You have not been sent to be billeted here?

SAM: No, no, don't worry. Ah'm only 'ere just for t'evening—
that is—if this is Farfield 'All.

LOTTA: Yes it is. Oh—you are from the factory where Lady
Farfield works?

SAM: That's right. T'aircraft factory. Sam Cawthra's my name.

LOTTA: Yes, yes—of course—I have heard Lady Farfield speak of
you, Mr. Cawthra. And the two girls have already arrived.

SAM (*pointing to the table*): Ah thought they must 'ave. We've
brought you a few things.

LOTTA (*going to table*): Oh—but how wonderful! All these nice
things. They will make a great difference to the supper. It will be
a real celebration.

SAM: Well, that's the idea, isn't it?

LOTTA: Yes, of course. Beer too!

SAM: Ay, an' it's not a bad drop o' stuff either for war-time. An'
Ah don't know about you, but after cycling five or six mile Ah'm
parched an' could tak' a glass this minute. What about you?

LOTTA: Yes—I think that would be very nice—Mr. Cawthra. Here
are some mugs. (*One of them begins to pour out the beer.*) Thank
you. But oh!—how stupid of me. I must introduce myself. Lotta
Schulberg, once of the Vienna Volksopera—and now—well, an exile,
you know. Years ago, I was—what you call a star—in Vienna. And
now I do the house-keeping and cooking here.

SAM (*shaking hands*): Good for you!

LOTTA: That is very nice of you—Mr. Cawthra.

SAM: An' you've kept yer voice an' all. Ah 'eard yer. An' Ah
knaw a bit o' good singing when Ah 'ear it. Yorkshire, yer knaw.
An' Ah'd like to 'ear some more later on.

LOTTA: That would be a very great pleasure for me. Not because
I want—as you say—to show off—but because when I sing—I forget.
Friends who are dead or have vanished come alive again—I see their

faces—I hear their voices—and the theatres, the cafés, the lovely old streets—of my city—they are alight again—but no—forgive me —I am being stupid——

SAM: No, you're not. You're all right. Well—— (*raising his glass*) 'ere's to us an' to 'ell with 'Itler. (*They both drink.*)

LOTTA (*fiercely*): He has always been in hell—and that is why he destroys other people's happiness. I should like to have come with Lady Farfield to make airplanes with you—but that was not possible —so—I do the cooking. Perhaps one day I shall sing again in Vienna —if not—then I do something else—more cooking, perhaps. It does not matter so long as *they*—the Nazi cheats and murderers—and all the people like them—have gone—and all nice simple friendly people —in Yorkshire—in Austria—anywhere—everywhere—can get to know each other and understand each other——

SAM: That's right. An' just let anybody try an' stop us, that's all. We're getting our monkey up——

LOTTA (*baffled*): Your monkey up?

SAM: Nay, don't bother with it. Leave it. (*Looking round.*) Well, Ah'd think twice afore Ah'd want to live 'ere. Tak' a bit o' lightin' an' warmin' an' cleanin', this place. No great shakes really, is it, when you tak' a good look at it? The wife would want to 'ave a do at this if it were 'ers.

LOTTA: But it is impossible to know where to begin, with a house this size and no staff at all—except one old man. And we have had dozens and dozens of people billeted on us.

HILDA *and* EILEEN *now come down, with* KENTON.

SAM: Ah—'ere's the girls.

KENTON: I will see if her ladyship is disengaged now. (*To* SAM) Good evening, sir. Are you a member of the—er—factory party?

SAM: That's right. What about you?

KENTON: Kenton, sir. 'Er ladyship's butler.

SAM: Ah see. Well, Ah don't think yer'll need to do much buttlin' for us to-night. We can buttle for ourselves. Big place you've got 'ere, isn't it?

KENTON: Yes, sir. We used to keep quite a large establishment 'ere at Farfield 'All, but of course, sir, times 'ave changed.

SAM: They 'ave, an' they'll do a lot more changing afore we've finished. But don't let us keep yer, if yer busy.

KENTON: Thank you, sir. I will inform 'er ladyship of your arrival.

Goes out down left.

LOTTA (*laughing*): Her ladyship, at this minute, is finishing cleaning her auto-cycle. Poor old Kenton!

HILDA: I can't get over 'im.

SAM: Takes it all seriously, doesn't 'e? Owerdoin' it, Ah'd say.

LOTTA (*confidentially*): You must not mind him, please. You see, he is very old, and he has been the butler here for a long, long time —and now he forgets and does not understand what is happening— and sometimes he thinks this war is the last war, and sometimes he forgets about any war, and often he thinks nothing has changed.

SAM: They might ha' found room for 'im in t'House of Commons. But I must introduce yer.

LOTTA (*smiling at the girls*): Lotta Schulberg—once of the Viennese Volksopera—now—in the kitchen——

SAM: This is one of our Assembly girls—Eileen——

LOTTA: You have beautiful eyes.

EILEEN (*abashed but delighted*): Go on—I haven't—have I?

LOTTA: But of course—and you ought to *use* them. Has nobody ever told you? What a waste! Also, you have a sensitive refined nature. Sometimes I know at once about a person. I am rather psychic, you know. (*To* SAM) Are you psychic, Mr. Cawthra?

SAM: No, whenever I know at once about anybody, Ah'm always wrong. And this is another of our Assembly girls——

HILDA: I'm Hilda. What have I got?

LOTTA (*who doesn't know*): You have—(*she pauses impressively*)— very good luck—I think.

HILDA: Well, I doubt that.

EILEEN (*hastily*): Oh you can't say that, Hilda—look at last Tuesday——

HILDA: Never mind about last Tuesday—look at last Saturday— do you call that luck? Six miles to a dance—and it was the wrong night.

EILEEN: But that was only an accident——

HILDA (*loudly*): Well, if you 'ave good luck, you don't 'ave accidents——

Telephone rings. LOTTA *goes to answer it.*

LOTTA (*at telephone*): This is Farfield Hall—yes? All right—I wait——

HILDA: Eileen, look!

EILEEN (*turning*): What?

HILDA (*pointing*): All them animals' 'eads.

[377]

LOTTA (*still at telephone, but to* HILDA): They are awful, aren't they, those stupid animals? (*Into telephone*) No, I am not talking to you—I am waiting——

SAM: Big game 'unting, that's what that is. One o' the favourite pursuits o' the leisure class at one time—big game 'unting. Ol' Musso an' Fatty Goering wouldn't look bad up there wi' glass eyes in.

LOTTA (*into telephone*): Yes . . . Farfield Hall—yes . . . Ministry of *What?* . . . is there such a Ministry? (*Laughs.*) Well, I think it is very comical . . . Well, what is it you want? . . . No, Mr. Fleming is *not* here any more . . . Yes, he was . . . *everybody* has been billeted here . . . but he left yesterday . . . Yes, I saw him go . . . And goodbye to *you.*

Puts down telephone and turns to visitors, smiling.

Why are they always so stupid, those girls on the telephones of ministries? And now I must take these beautiful presents into the kitchen and prepare for supper. But first I wish to tell you we are all so proud—so very proud—that Lady Farfield is now a *charge-hand*. It is wonderful. I said at once we must have a little party—to celebrate. A charge-hand.

SAM: That's right. And not done by influence, y'know.

LOTTA (*proudly*): No, no—not at all. She has worked her way right from the bottom right up to the top.

SAM: Well, not quite to the top. But Ah knaw what yer mean.

LOTTA: And I tell you this. Do not be afraid.

SAM: All right, Ah won't be. But why?

LOTTA: Lady Farfield will be strict—but just. She will give you your orders—so——

SAM (*aghast*): Give *me* orders!

HILDA (*impressively*): He's the *foreman.*

LOTTA (*impressed*): Oh—I am sorry—of course—the *foreman.*

SAM: All right, yer needn't look at me now as if I wor Stafford Cripps. But Ah 'ave bin on t'job a long time. Ah wor putting planes together when some of yer 'adn't started undressing yer dolls.

LOTTA (*gaily*): For me—I wish it was true. But now I really must return to the kitchen. (*Taking up things.*)

EILEEN: Can I help you with supper? I'd quite like to.

LOTTA (*going down left with things*): Yes, certainly, thank you, in a little while perhaps. But you would like to see Lady Farfield first, of course. (*She is now at door, opening it.*) Here she is.

She holds door open and LADY FARFIELD *enters, still in greasy overalls.*

LADY FARFIELD: Hello, hello, everybody!

SAM, HILDA, EILEEN: Hello, (etc.).

LOTTA: Look what nice things they have brought us for supper.

LADY FARFIELD: Oh—I say—how marvellous.

LOTTA: Now—I make something—very good. You'll see. For how many?

LADY FARFIELD: Just us—and Pauline—and Kenton, I hope.

LOTTA: I hope too. But I doubt it. Somebody always arrives. We have had everybody now except the Red Army and the Jugoslavian Partisans.

She goes out. LADY FARFIELD *smiles at the visitors.*

LADY FARFIELD: I'm so sorry to have kept you waiting, but I did want to finish cleaning my auto-bike. Well, what do you think of this place?

HILDA: Big, isn't it?

SAM: And it 'ud tak' some keeping up.

LADY FARFIELD: Yes, it's big—and it just can't be kept up. I told you it's hopelessly untidy and neglected, so I won't apologise. It looks awful and I can't help it. Before the war there were ten servants here. Now there's a woman from the village who comes in occasionally—Lotta, who's sweet and a great help but can't be expected to start scrubbing—and poor old Kenton——

SAM: An' 'e's a bit barmy, isn't 'e?

LADY FARFIELD: I suppose so. He never knows quite what's happening. And then—apart from Pauline, the Land Girl, that's the lot. To keep this huge place going—I ask you!

EILEEN: And then you have people billeted on you all the time, don't you?

LADY FARFIELD: We've had thousands of them. You heard what Lotta said. Half the United Nations war effort seems to have been through this house. You could look round at the damage and write the history of the war from it. We started, in 1939, with fifty women and children from Sheffield. When they went back home, the battalion headquarters of the Loamshire Light Infantry arrived. After them, the Polish Air Force. Then—let me think—yes, sixty-two women and children from Bootle. After that, Anti-Aircraft and Searchlights. Then a company of A.T.S. Then the Civil Service, mostly with colds. Then—some assorted Americans—with the Bob Hope and other programmes in full blast, day and night. But now—at last—nobody. Just ourselves to-night. Isn't that wonderful? The last four people who were billeted on us left yesterday, so to-night we have the place to ourselves. That's why I was so anxious for us to have our little party. And here we are!

KENTON *enters from down left with tray, bottle of sherry and glasses.*

Thank you, Kenton. I thought we'd have a quick drink—it's real sherry—and then I'd rush off and change. Will you pour out the drinks, Mr. Cawthra——

SAM (*correcting her*): Sam.

LADY FARFIELD: Sam. No, don't you bother, Kenton.

Telephone rings sharply. KENTON *goes to answer it, as the others cluster round the drinks, and* EILEEN *and* HILDA *light cigarettes.*

KENTON (*at telephone*): Farfield Hall—yes . . . I will see if 'er ladyship can speak to you . . . What name?

LADY FARFIELD: Who is it?

KENTON (*vaguely*): A person wishes to speak to you, me lady, on official business.

LADY FARFIELD (*going over*): Oh dear—I don't like the sound of this. (*At telephone*) Yes—Lady Farfield speaking . . . Oh, *no!* Oh dear, dear, dear, dear . . . Why? Because we hoped not to have anybody at least just for this week-end . . . We've had *everybody* all the time . . . No, if you can't, you can't . . . Of course. Who are they? Two Air Force officers possibly? Well, that's all right——

HILDA (*with enthusiasm*): Certainly it's all right.

LADY FARFIELD: But there's some doubt about them, you say? . . . I see, these other two are certain . . . Not women, I hope— wanting cups of tea and hot-water bottles . . . Oh I see . . . An American officer, yes. And who else? (*Delighted*) A *servant?* (*Dashed*) Oh—a *Civil* Servant . . . Ministry of Reconstruction . . . To-night? Any time now? . . . No, only I'm giving a little party for a few friends . . . Very well, we'll do our best . . . Yes, I know, but you can't cook and eat ration cards, can you?

Puts down telephone and looks at the others with droll despair. Let's hope they're both so tired they'll go straight to bed.

KENTON: More guests, me lady?

LADY FARFIELD: Yes. Two gentlemen for certain—to-night.

KENTON: Very good, me lady. Shall I give instructions for two of the bachelor rooms in the East Wing to be got ready for the gentlemen?

LADY FARFIELD (*half laughing, but touched*): No, Kenton, you must try and remember that you can't give instructions because there isn't anybody left to give instructions to.

KENTON (*confused*): I'm sorry, me lady—I was forgetting——

LADY FARFIELD (*gently*): I know. It doesn't matter. But you're forgetting too that we haven't been able to use the East Wing for the last two years, not since we had those incendiaries. No, I'll see to their rooms.

KENTON: Yes, me lady. (*Goes out down left.*)

EILEEN: We can help with the rooms.

HILDA: If you'll show us where they are.

LADY FARFIELD: That's sweet of you. It would be a help. I hoped we'd have the place to ourselves to-night. Just for once.

HILDA: What'll the Civil Servant be like?

LADY FARFIELD: Probably dull but harmless. Let's hope he'll creep away with a good book. As for the American officer, he might be terribly nice——

HILDA: I know—like Gary Cooper.

LADY FARFIELD: Yes, he *might*. Then again, he might be very dull, one of the slow boring kind. On the other hand, he might be a bit *too* lively—you know——

SAM: I've seen 'em.

HILDA (*eagerly*): What about those Air Force chaps they're sending?

LADY FARFIELD: Two officers may have to be sent up here from the Experimental Station, but it isn't certain, so don't count on it.

HILDA: I don't care. I like sergeants best. They're not so fancy, and you can understand what they're talking about.

LADY FARFIELD: I really must change—and get those beds made up.

EILEEN: We'll help you.

LADY FARFIELD: Come on, then. Sam, you must amuse yourself for a few minutes. But Pauline ought to be coming in any time now.

SAM: Who's Pauline?

LADY FARFIELD: She's our Land Girl. Rather peculiar but quite a nice child really. You have a talk to her.

The three women go upstairs, leaving SAM with his pipe. He looks round, notices the stuffed heads, and is particularly fascinated by a very ugly buffalo head—or something of the sort. He takes a chair to stand on, and has a close look at it. Slowly he lifts a hand to touch its nose—the action being in full view of the audience. Meanwhile, PAULINE CHESTER, in Land Girl uniform and carrying a basket of vegetables, etc., has entered. She is a rather small girl, in her early twenties, quite attractive, but with a precise, didactic though calm manner that is quaint and incongruous. When she sees what he is up to, she quietly goes up to him unnoticed.

PAULINE: I shouldn't do that if I were you.

SAM (*surprised, turning on his chair*): Do what?

PAULINE: Feel its nose. You were going to feel its nose, weren't you?

SAM (*slightly embarrassed*): Well—as a matter o' fact—I did just want to see what it felt like. No 'arm in that, is there?

PAULINE: No. But I did that with one of them when I first came here—it was a buffalo shot in Uganda in 1909.

SAM: Well, what 'appened?

PAULINE: The whole beastly thing came down and nearly smothered me. They can't take it, y'know. Everything here is very ramshackle and dilapidated. Including this chair, actually——

SAM (*with touch of alarm*): Oh—is it? (*Gets down at once. Then he grins at* PAULINE.) You're Pauline the Land Girl, eh?

PAULINE: Yes. Who are you?

SAM: Sam Cawthra—foreman of Assembly—where Lady Farfield works.

PAULINE: I see. You're not billeted here, are you?

SAM: No. Just 'ere for t'evening. Bit of a party.

PAULINE: Yes, Lady Farfield said something about it. Can I get you anything?

SAM: Well, I'll 'ave another drink o' this beer I brought. I reckon nowt o' sherry an' suchlike.

PAULINE: Neither do I. We'll both have some beer. Then I'll drop these vegetables and eggs into the kitchen.

SAM: Eggs, eh?

PAULINE: Three. But one of them's rather odd. Actually, I think the hen that laid it—Red Lizzie—is going mad.

SAM: 'Ow can yer tell?

PAULINE: By her general behaviour. I hope you're not hungry.

SAM: Well, I'm fairly peckish. Why? (*She drinks.*) Cheers. All the best! (*Drinks, then surveys her with interest.*) Yer know, I'd call you a pretty cool card. How d'yer like being a Land Girl?

PAULINE: Until I came here I didn't like it. Not because I minded the work, but I hate farmers. I was with three before I got this job, and they all hated me, and I hated them.

[382]

SAM: What's wrong with 'em?

PAULINE (*coolly*): Greedy, selfish, miserable old blighters. After the war, we ought to take a few out and shoot 'em.

SAM (*aghast*): *Shoot 'em!*

PAULINE: Yes, shoot 'em. And a few fat old business men. Make all the difference.

SAM: Mak' plenty o' difference, no doubt—but nay—dash it—yer can't start shootin' folk like that.

PAULINE: Why not? Thousands of nice young men, who've never done anybody any harm, are being shot and drowned and burnt to death. Why shouldn't we shoot a few nasty old men, who are always doing everybody harm?

SAM: Ay—but—there's a lot o' difference between chaps bein' killed in a war an' then just shootin' people 'cos you don't like 'em.

PAULINE: I don't see any, except it would do some real good killing off a few of these nasty old men who are so greedy and selfish and stupid.

SAM: My word—you're a bloodthirsty young woman an' no mistake. Where were you brought up?

PAULINE (*rather primly*): I was brought up chiefly by a maiden aunt in Cheltenham.

SAM: You've gone a long way since then. I should think Russia's about your style now.

PAULINE (*coolly*): If this country doesn't improve, I shall go to Russia—if they'll have me—and work on a collective farm.

SAM: But 'aven't yer got a young man?

PAULINE: No, so far I haven't bothered. But I've been thinking lately that perhaps it's time I looked around for one.

SAM: 'E'll 'ave to be careful after yer do find 'im. One wrong move an' you'll be shooting '*im*. Well, there's one or two chaps comin' to-night so yer'd better look 'em over. One's an American officer.

PAULINE: Americans don't attract me. Their attitude towards sex is so adolescent.

SAM: 'Ere, are there any more Land Girls like you? I thought we were seein' summat these days in t'factory, but we know nowt.

PAULINE: You're not being rude now, are you?

SAM: Bless yer 'eart, no! I was just talkin' free-an'-easy, like I would to any chap I was 'aving a glass o' beer wi'. Nay, nay, don't tak' offence.

PAULINE: No, of course I won't. But I'm not very good at telling whether people are being rude or just rather matey. And you seemed

[383]

such a nice man at first that I was disappointed. (*Now she smiles at him.*) But now it's all right.

SAM: Course it is. The best o' friends.

They shake hands solemnly. HILDA *now comes hurrying down the stairs, calling across to* SAM *as she reaches lower steps.*

HILDA (*calling*): Mr. Cawthra—Sam!

SAM (*rising*): Well, what is it?

HILDA: You understand about putting beds together—nuts and bolts an' all that—don't yer?

SAM (*moving*): Course I do. Am I wanted upstairs?

HILDA: Yes, and I'm not. Straight along at the top—you'll 'ear 'em talking.

He goes up and she comes across to PAULINE.

You're Pauline, the Land Girl, aren't yer?

PAULINE: Yes. Will you have some beer?

HILDA: No, I think I'll take a drop more of this sherry wine, if you don't mind. My name's Hilda Packet, and I work with Lady Farfield and Sam at the factory. There's two of us come with 'im —two girls, I mean—'cos we all started about the same time as Lady Farfield in one of the machine shops—an' then we all went to Assembly —so we're sort of friends, yer see—well, as a matter of fact, the one upstairs, Eileen, and me—we're very great friends. 'Ere, are yer interested, 'cos I can shut up if you're not?

PAULINE: No, I love it. You see, I spend all day with hens and geese and cabbages, and you don't get a word out of them. Go on about you and Eileen. Where do you live?

HILDA (*immediately in full flood again*): Oh—we're in the same billet—Mrs. Batsby's. 'Er 'usband used to keep a garage, but that's gone now and 'e's at the factory too—so Mrs. Batsby looks after five of us—'er an' 'er sister—the sister's older than Mrs. Batsby—old maid she is—and nosey!—she's awful. The minute you're out, she's runnin' through everything you've got—an' no shame about it neither. "You'll catch your death o' cold, wearin' them things underneath," she'll say. An' another time, she says, "I wouldn't have nothing to do with that chap you've got the photo of," she says. "That corporal, I mean—'e's up to no good, I can tell by his photo." An' I says, "Well, if you must know, that's my own brother 'Erbert—an' in future you mind yours an' I'll mind mine." Oo, I was that mad at 'er.

PAULINE: And was it your brother's photograph?

HILDA: Just as luck would 'ave it, yes it *was* our 'Erbert's photo. But after that I gave it to Eileen, 'cos 'er an' 'Erbert started writin' to each other. They've never seen each other, but I'd told 'im about 'er—'cos she's my friend—an' she knows all about 'im. An' one day she says, "I wish I'd a soldier in Africa or somewhere to write to" —'cos Eileen's very shy, an' doesn't bother much with boys—says she doesn't care about 'em, but yer know how much that's worth— so I says—yer know, just for a bit o' fun—I says, "Well, write to our 'Erbert—yer can 'ave 'im for me." So she did, an' 'e writes back, an' now they've been at it for months—writin' an' writin'—though God knows what they wrote about. I don't see 'ow they can find enough to write about, not when they've never seen each other— do you?

PAULINE: Yes. If I once started writing to a boy, I could write reams and reams and reams.

HILDA: What about?

PAULINE: Oh—everything. About what I do here—about Horace the old gander and Red Lizzie the mad hen—and about the Ministry of Agriculture and Reconstruction and the Coming Revolution.

HILDA: Oh—you're one o' these brainy ones, aren't you?

PAULINE (*firmly*): Yes I am. I have a lot of time to think while I'm working, and I've thought about *everything*.

HILDA: Well, I suppose it's all right if yer fancy it. I can't be bothered. Eileen tried it one time—read books an' all that—an' talked to Miss Wilson—our welfare officer—but when she started writin' to our 'Erbert, she packed it up an' just thought about 'im instead, though 'ow she can do that for long beats me, knowin' 'Erbert. But I believe if anything 'appened to 'im, she'd 'ave a broken 'eart. I'll bet you don't believe in broken 'earts, do yer?

PAULINE: No, I don't.

HILDA: I bet yer don't believe in 'ardly anything, do yer?

PAULINE (*in calm oracular manner*): I believe in the triumphant destiny of Man.

HILDA: Crumbs! Is that all?

PAULINE (*same manner*): No, I believe in the irresistible forward march of Man towards a classless world of peace, prosperity and justice.

HILDA: Go on! 'Ere, what man's this?

PAULINE: Just Man. All men.

HILDA: Well, they'll 'ave to be a lot diff'rent from the men I know. Anyhow, be a bit careful what you say to Eileen.

PAULINE: I'm never careful what I say to anybody. Don't believe in it.

HILDA: And I'll bet yer don't.

PAULINE: But I won't hurt her feelings, if that's what you mean.

HILDA: Peculiar sort o' girl you are. Do yer talk to boys like this?

PAULINE: Certainly. I've only one way of talking. But I'm not always thinking about boys. I believe you are. You ought to be married.

HILDA: Are you telling me!

There is a sound of a car arriving outside.

That's a car. Somebody's come. Let's have a look.

They go to window at back and look left.

PAULINE (*as she looks*): American Army car. It must be the American officer who's coming to stay.

HILDA (*also looking*): I wonder what he's like.. Oh!—— (*disappointed.*) That must be 'im, getting out. 'E's rather old, isn't 'e? Specs too. Oh—I don't think much of 'im.

PAULINE (*moving down*): We must let Kenton attend to this. I shall go in the kitchen and help Lotta. You'd better come too.

HILDA (*moving too*): All right. So long as it's not peelin' potatoes.

Front door bell is heard and KENTON *comes out left.*

PAULINE: There's an American officer at the door, Kenton.

KENTON: Thank you, miss.

PAULINE *and* HILDA *exit down left.*

WEBBER'S VOICE (*off*): Say, is this Farfield Hall?

KENTON: Yes, sir. This is Lady Farfield's residence.

WEBBER'S VOICE (*off*): Fine! (*Calling back to driver*) Okay, Joe —this is it. Pick me up in the morning, will you? Yeah, about quarter to nine. Good night.

As WEBBER *comes in, sound of car going off.* MAJOR GEORGE WEBBER *is a fairly plump, clean-shaven, colourless type of Middle-Western American, wearing large octagonal spectacles, in his early forties. He is a pleasant man with a slow solemn manner. He is carrying some brand-new luggage.*

WEBBER *enters, followed by* KENTON *with suitcases.*

WEBBER: I'm Major Webber—George Webber. I've been sent along here by headquarters.

KENTON (*polite, resigned*): Yes, sir.

WEBBER (*delighted by the thought*): Now—to me—you look like a butler.

KENTON (*mildly surprised*): Yes, sir.

[386]

WEBBER: Well, well, well! It took a war to bring me over here to meet a butler. How are you?

Holds out a hand, which KENTON, *after some hesitation, shakes.*

What's your name?

KENTON: Kenton, sir.

WEBBER: What comes before it—Joe, Jack, Sam?

KENTON: As a matter of fact, sir, my Christian name is—Frederick.

WEBBER: Fine! Shall I call you Frederick—or just Fred?

KENTON: Neither, sir, if you don't mind——

WEBBER: Now—go on—I don't need any of this feudal stuff—I'm just a plain democrat——

KENTON (*with dignity*): Sir, when I am on duty, I am accustomed to being addressed as Kenton. Only close relations and old friends would call me Frederick or Fred. And if I may say so without giving offence, sir—should you insist upon calling me Frederick or Fred, then you are not only ignoring the custom of this and other English gentlemen's houses, but you are also intruding into my private life, sir.

WEBBER (*slowly*): Do I understand what you're talking about?

KENTON (*looking him in the eye, slowly*): I think so, sir.

WEBBER: Okay—Kenton. (*Looking around*) Well, well, you got quite a place here, haven't you? One of the stately homes of England.

KENTON: Yes, sir.

WEBBER: I guess nobody's going to run a home like this on a nigger and a boy.

KENTON: A nigger and a boy? Certainly not, sir. The staff here, sir, is ten indoor servants, and five outdoor.

WEBBER (*both shocked and delighted*): Ten indoor servants and five outdoor! Well, sir—we've been asked not to criticise—but I must say I just don't know how you folks justify such a use of man-power at a time like this.

KENTON (*ignoring this*): When the late master—afterwards Sir Robert—celebrated his twenty-first birthday, sir, we sat down twenty-five in the servants' hall—and three hundred of the tenantry had their supper in the grounds.

WEBBER: Tenantry, eh? Just old feudal customs still going on. And twenty-five sitting down in the servant's hall, eh? When was this—since the war began?

KENTON: In nineteen-hundred and three, sir.

[387]

WEBBER: Oh—way back. That's different. Still—— (*shaking his head.*) Ten indoor servants—five outdoor——

KENTON (*proudly*): It takes three to polish the silver properly.

WEBBER (*shaking his head*): Fiddling while Rome burns.

KENTON (*same manner*): When the Hunt meets here and we have a Hunt Breakfast——

WEBBER: Hunt Breakfast! Now, do you mean red coats and packs of dogs——

KENTON (*reproachfully*): 'Ounds, sir—not dogs.

WEBBER: Hounds or dogs, I'd think you folks would be too busy these days to waste time, money and man-power on keeping up these feudal customs. I'm just a plain American——

KENTON (*politely, but with touch of irony*): Yes, sir.

WEBBER: And I'm here to defend the American way of life. I'm from the Middle West, Kenton—Indiana—and out there we're just plain folks.

KENTON: Quite different 'ere, sir. But you'll soon get used to it.

WEBBER: Well, it'll certainly be most interesting to get acquainted with some of your old-world aristocratic customs. Mrs. Webber'll get a kick out of it.

KENTON: Who will get a kick, sir?

WEBBER: Mrs. Webber.

KENTON: No lady of that name 'ere, sir.

WEBBER: No, no, I know there isn't, but my name's Webber and Mrs. Webber's my wife. Say, I'd better go up to my room and wash up. Where is it?

KENTON (*rather confused*): I'm not quite certain yet, sir. I'll 'ave to enquire. I did give instructions that two of the bachelor apartments in the East Wing were to be made ready for you and the other gentleman, but I am now under the impression, sir, that those instructions have been countermanded. Perhaps you will take a seat, sir, while I enquire.

WEBBER: Be glad to.

He sits down and lights a cigarette while KENTON *slowly goes upstairs. After a moment,* LOTTA *peeps out of doorway left, sees* WEBBER, *and comes in smiling. He notices her, and politely rises and holds his cigarette in his hand.*

LOTTA: Good evening. How do you do?

WEBBER: Fine, thanks! I'm Major Webber, just arrived. The butler told me to wait till he found out about my room.

[388]

LOTTA: He will probably forget to come back. I am Lotta Schulberg. Did you know Vienna in the old days?

WEBBER: No, this is my first trip to Europe. You from Vienna?

LOTTA: Yes, I used to play leading roles with the Vienna Volksopera. Do smoke, please. Is that a nice American cigarette you are smoking?

WEBBER (*producing packet*): Certainly is. Will you have one?

LOTTA: Thank you very much. You know, I adore American cigarettes.

WEBBER: Well, take the whole pack——

LOTTA: Oh—no—I could not do that—— (*She takes the packet and puts it in her pocket.*)

WEBBER (*heartily*): Go on. Glad for you to have them. Mrs. Webber's going to get a big surprise when I write and tell her I've met a Viennese operatic star. You staying here too?

LOTTA (*as she lights a cigarette from his lighter*): Oh yes—I am the cook. Supper will be ready in twenty minutes. Good-bye for the present.

She goes off down left humming gaily as she smokes and WEBBER *stares after her in astonishment. He has no sooner returned to his seat, than* SAM, *smoking a pipe and in his shirt-sleeves and holding a large spanner, comes down nearly to the bottom of the stairs and calls.*

SAM: Oy!

WEBBER (*turning, surprised*): Me?

SAM: Ay. Sorry yer've bin kept waiting, but them iron bedsteads wor in a 'ell of a tangle an' I've only just sorted 'em out. Shan't be long now, though. 'Ave a drop o' that beer if yer fancy it.

WEBBER: Not right now, but thanks all the same.

SAM: An' d'yer mind answerin' t'door if t'other chap comes 'cos I've got old Whoosit 'elpin' me.

WEBBER (*puzzled but helpful*): Be glad to, though I don't know my way around here. Say, are you another butler?

SAM (*aghast*): Me! I'm t'foreman from Assembly shop in t'aircraft factory. Butler!

He goes upstairs and WEBBER *is left absolutely bewildered. Before he has recovered from his surprise,* PAULINE *enters briskly.*

PAULINE: How do you do? Is it Lebber or Webber?

WEBBER: Webber.

PAULINE: Lotta wasn't sure. I'm Pauline Chester—member of the Women's Land Army attached to the estate here.

WEBBER (*shaking hands*): Fine! I hear you girls are doing a great job.

PAULINE (*very briskly*): Britain now produces two-thirds of the food she needs. Six million more acres have been ploughed up. The agricultural production per head is now probably the highest in the world. After the revolution, when we have collective farming, it will be higher still.

WEBBER (*doing his best*): But are you going to have a revolution?

PAULINE (*calmly*): Certainly. If it comes soon it can be peaceful. If we wait, then it will be sudden, violent—and bloody. And I don't care which.

    Makes as if to come towards stairs.

WEBBER: Now wait a minute, Miss Chester——

PAULINE: Call me Pauline, if you like. Everybody does.

WEBBER: Okay. Pauline then——

PAULINE (*holding up a finger*): But no reactionary talk, no Wall Street stuff——

WEBBER (*exasperated but not out of temper*): Say, wait a minute. What about your fifteen servants?

PAULINE: Fifteen servants?

WEBBER: Yeah. Ten indoors, five outdoors—three to clean the silver——

PAULINE: Where?

WEBBER: Why, right here.

PAULINE: There aren't any servants here. (*Smiling calmly at him.*) Excuse me!

    She goes quickly upstairs. He has not recovered from this fresh shock when the front door bell peals loudly. After a moment's hesitation, he goes towards the main doors at back and opens them just in time to admit RAYMOND KILLIGREW, *who comes staggering in with an immense double armful of old luggage, including two violin cases and bags, etc.* KILLIGREW *is a carelessly dressed, scholarly-looking and somewhat eccentric man in his fifties, with a quick staccato way of talking. He dumps the bags, etc., down and goes out for another load, talking rapidly and loudly all the time. His second load consists of string quartette scores, tied in bundles.*

KILLIGREW: Farfield Hall, eh? I was lucky—very lucky. Local farmer gave me a lift, otherwise might not have been here for hours. Int'resting fellow in his way too. Gave me some useful information. Didn't know the American Army was here. But no reason why they

[390]

shouldn't be, of course. Damned heavy, these things. Quartette scores. Take 'em with me everywhere. Well, well, here we are.

He lights his pipe and looks round cheerfully.

Untidy—rather dirty—I imagine—and obviously neglected—but probably got very good acoustic properties. My name's Killigrew.

KILLIGREW: I'm Major Webber.

KILLIGREW: How d'you do? Billeted here?

WEBBER: Yeah. But only just arrived. That's my baggage. And —say—I don't seem to get the hang of it here at all.

KILLIGREW: New to the country perhaps?

WEBBER: Yeah. Only landed last week. But as I was saying, I just don't seem to get the hang of it——

KILLIGREW *(cutting in ruthlessly)*: You soon will. Don't worry. Play the fiddle or the 'cello?

WEBBER *(surprised)*: No, I don't.

KILLIGREW: Pity. Always hoping to make a up string quartette. That's why I carry the scores round with me. Farmer gave me one possible name, though—got the telephone number somewhere——

WEBBER *(while* KILLIGREW *is searching)*: There's an operatic singer in the kitchen.

KILLIGREW: Let her stay there. Detest opera. Cheap hysterical muck, most of it. Ah, here it is. Telephone anywhere? Yes, I see.

Goes over to it at once, glancing at the number.

Oh—Fassington Two Five Three, please . . . Yes . . . All right . . .

WEBBER *(as* KILLIGREW *waits)*: I didn't know they billeted civilians in this country.

KILLIGREW: Certainly. We've billeted millions—war workers, land girls, civil servants. I'm a Civil Servant. Ministry of Reconstruction. New Ministry. I used to be with the Board of Trade.

WEBBER: Is that so, Mr. Killigrew? What did you do there?

KILLIGREW: Closed things down. Thousands of businesses——

WEBBER *(awed)*: Closed 'em down?

KILLIGREW: Yes, thousands of 'em. *(At telephone)* Oh—is that Mr.—er—Bramley? . . . Well, my name's Killigrew, and I'm staying at Farfield Hall . . . and I'm told you have two daughters who play the viola and the 'cello respectively and I want to get some string quartettes going . . . Oh, they are . . . both of 'em, eh? Yes, good girls, but that doesn't help me. Do you happen to know any other people who play the fiddle round here? All right, thanks very much . . . *(To* WEBBER) Gone to ask his wife. Both his daughters are Wrens. What were we saying?

WEBBER: You were telling me that you are in this new Ministry of Reconstruction, Mr. Killigrew, which interests me quite a lot. Tell me, what do you people propose to do?

KILLIGREW: We don't know yet. There are two schools of thought. One school says "Go straight on. Make a peace effort just as we made a war effort." The other school of thought, if you can call it thought—— (*To telephone*) Hello, yes? . . . But how old? . . . Eighty? . . . No use, I'm afraid . . . Yes, Fraser?—Cornland Three Four? . . . What's the other name? . . . Henniman . . . Not on the telephone . . . I see . . . Well, thanks very much. Good-bye.

Puts down telephone and lights his pipe again.

I'll try that number later. The other fellow isn't on the telephone, and they don't think he's played for years. But you never know. What were you asking me?

WEBBER: This other school of thought, as you called it—y'know, about Reconstruction.

KILLIGREW: Oh—yes. Well, their bright idea is to put everything back to where it was before the war.

WEBBER: And can you do it?

KILLIGREW: My dear sir—here are some eggs all scrambled in the pan—and here, on the side, are all the empty shells—and all they ask you to do is to unscramble the eggs and put 'em all back neatly in their shells. And while they're about it, they might as well ask us to put the eggs back into the hens.

WEBBER: Say—Mr. Killigrew—you're not my idea of a British Civil Servant.

KILLIGREW: Why? Too short, too tall, too old, too young, too fat, too thin—what?

WEBBER: Well, there you go. I expected you'd be kinda slow and pompous. But you think and talk fast—more like a business man.

KILLIGREW (*horrified*): Business man! Good heavens! (*Looks about him.*) Where is everybody? We must see about our rooms.

Enter HILDA *from kitchen with some things for the table— bread, etc.* KILLIGREW *sees her.*

Oh—good evening. I'm Mr. Killigrew. Billeted here. Where is everybody? What about our rooms? What happens?

HILDA (*sharp but not bad-tempered*): What 'appens? Well, for one thing, I come out for the evening, after working 'ard all the week, an' I find myself 'elping to get supper ready. Rest o' the party's upstairs putting yer beds up. (*To* WEBBER) I say, what are you?

WEBBER (*rather startled*): Me—well, what do you think I am?

[392]

HILDA: I can never tell by them things you wear what you Americans are. I was out with one of your boys one night and I asked 'im to tell me, but 'e couldn't keep 'is mind on it.

WEBBER (*laughing*): Well, our boys certainly take some holding, when there's a pretty girl around.

HILDA (*direct, not coquettish*): Would you call me pretty?

WEBBER: Certainly would. And I'm a major—Major Webber, Surveying Department, U.S. War Department.

HILDA: Oh—surveying. I thought you looked a bit old to be a real soldier.

To KILLIGREW, *who is sniffing curiously at the sherry bottle.*
What you sniffing at that for? D'yer want some?

KILLIGREW: What's it supposed to be?

HILDA: Sherry wine.

KILLIGREW: Most peculiar.

HILDA: Want some?

KILLIGREW: No, thanks.

WEBBER: I've got a bottle of Scotch in my bag, Mr. Killigrew, and I'll be glad if you'll join me in a drink when I get it out.

KILLIGREW: Delighted.

HILDA: Well, don't finish it between yer 'cos we're supposed to be 'aving a bit of a party 'ere—to celebrate——

KILLIGREW: What are you celebrating?

HILDA: Lady Farfield—she lives 'ere, y'know—an' she works with us at factory, an' she's just been made a charge-'and.

WEBBER (*astounded*): A charge-hand?

HILDA: Yes, an' not before time neither. Y'ought to 'ave seen some o' the charge 'ands we've 'ad, specially down in the machine shop! They didn't know whether it was Christmas or Tuesday, some of 'em didn't.

WEBBER (*earnest and bewildered*): I don't get the hang of this at all. I thought Lady Farfield was a member of your old privileged classes——

HILDA: If yer'd seen 'er coming through 'ere 'alf an hour since, after she'd been cleanin' her auto-bike, in 'er mucky old overall, yer'd 'ave thought she was Black Jack from the boiler 'ouse. Supper'll be on in a minute or two. Yer'd better get washed.

She marches off into kitchen.

WEBBER (*bewildered*): Mr. Killigrew, all this is new to me, and will you do me a favour and put me wise to what's going on around here——

KILLIGREW (*surprised at his bewilderment*): Nothing special, is there? A little party of some kind. Saturday night, y'know. Don't suppose they'll keep it up late or make too much noise—so I shouldn't worry.

WEBBER (*in despair*): No, you've got me wrong. But what about —well, that butler—and three men to clean the silver—and Hunt Breakfasts——?

KILLIGREW: Hunt Breakfast? Can't have a Hunt Breakfast, my dear chap. Be reasonable. Lucky to have any kind of breakfast. I haven't drawn a bacon ration for months. Always in the wrong place. Ah—here we are.

> He says this because he sees LADY FARFIELD *coming to the bottom of the staircase.* LADY FARFIELD *is now properly dressed and looks a fine handsome woman. Behind them are* EILEEN *and* SAM, PAULINE *and* KENTON.

Lady Farfield?

LADY FARFIELD (*smiling*): Yes. I'm so sorry you've been kept waiting.

KILLIGREW: Not at all. Hope we're not a nuisance, arriving so unexpectedly. My name's Killigrew. And this is Major Webber.

LADY FARFIELD (*shaking hands*): How d'you do?

WEBBER (*who has not recovered yet*): Very pleased to meet you, Lady Farfield, and I feel it's a great privilege to stay in your lovely home.

LADY FARFIELD: I'm afraid it's not very lovely now, but it was once.

WEBBER: And I'll bet you get quite a nostalgia for the good old days, don't you?

LADY FARFIELD: Very rarely. They were much more comfortable, of course, but they were often very dull. And whatever we are now, we're certainly not dull. Now come along, everybody. Let me introduce you. Major Webber and Mr. Killigrew—Miss Eileen Stocks and Mr. Sam Cawthra, who work with me—and that's Miss Pauline Chester, our Land Girl. And Kenton you've met already. Now let's get all these things upstairs so that you'll be in time for supper.

> KILLIGREW *and* WEBBER *take some of their things and* SAM *and* KENTON *take the rest.*

EILEEN: What shall I do?

LADY FARFIELD: Well, if you feel you must do something, will you go into the kitchen and help Lotta—I think Hilda's there. Pauline can help me to finish laying the table.

EILEEN (*preparing to go*): I wish I knew how to cook.

LADY FARFIELD: You can learn how to cook.

EILEEN: I'd like to. It must be awful getting married if you don't know how to cook.

She goes into kitchen. LADY FARFIELD *and* PAULINE *finish laying the table.*

LADY FARFIELD: Poor Eileen's mind is rather running on marriage —because of Hilda's brother, who hasn't even seen her yet.

PAULINE (*calm and clear*): I think I shall marry somebody.

LADY FARFIELD (*amused*): Do you mean—just anybody?

PAULINE: Oh no—that would be stupid, of course. In fact, I shall select the young man very carefully.

LADY FARFIELD: Have you found him yet?

PAULINE: No, I've only just made up my mind about it.

LADY FARFIELD: Well, I think it's better to fall in love first.

PAULINE: I don't see why you shouldn't marry first, while you're still clear-headed and know what you're doing, and then fall in love with the man afterwards. Do you mind if I ask you something?

LADY FARFIELD: No, Pauline.

PAULINE: Well—I know you lost your husband—Sir Michael, wasn't it?—since the war. But you never seem to talk about him. Were you very much in love with him?

LADY FARFIELD: No. I was very fond of him, of course. We had a happy marriage on the whole. But he was older than I was—and —well, before that, there had been somebody else I was in love with —only we had a stupid quarrel—so I married Sir Michael. I'd better luck than I deserved, but it isn't really a good idea—to marry one man just because you're angry with another one. Don't ever do it, Pauline.

PAULINE: I wouldn't, you know. I think I'd marry the one I was angry with, and then take it out of him afterwards.

LADY FARFIELD: You might not want to, then.

PAULINE: Then that would be all the better, because I don't really believe in taking it out of people. I don't believe in quarrelling with people I like either.

LADY FARFIELD: Who does? But when you're in a highly emotional state—and are very excited about somebody—it's easy to quarrel. You wait, my dear. You won't always be so cool, calm and collected.

PAULINE: I didn't used to be, y'know, but when I decided to be a Land Girl and take to the good brown earth and the beasts and the fowls and the vegetables, I also decided at the same time to be calm and quiet and *firm*——

Telephone rings.

LADY FARFIELD: Oh dear—now what is it this time?

PAULINE: If you don't answer it, then it won't matter what it is.

HILDA *comes in with a dish of some kind—e.g. salad or vegetables.*

HILDA: Telephone.

LADY FARFIELD: We're wondering whether to answer it.

PAULINE: And I say—*don't.*

HILDA (*shocked*): Oo—but you must answer the telephone, mustn't you? If I'd one, I'd never dare not to answer it.

LADY FARFIELD (*as she goes*): I rather agree with you, Hilda. It simply *demands* to be answered. (*At telephone*) Yes . . . speaking . . . Who? . . . Oh, is she? . . . Any minute, eh? All right, thank you.

Puts down telephone and looks at both girls.

What a nuisance! "Commodore Pentworthy is on her way, apologises for having been detained, but will now be here at any minute." I'd clean forgotten she was coming for supper to-night. Oh dear— oh dear!

PAULINE: Is that the terrible woman in uniform who came here once before, the one I had the stinking row with?

LADY FARFIELD: That's the one. And to-night, Pauline, there mustn't be a stinking row.

HILDA: I never 'eard of a woman Commodore before.

LADY FARFIELD: Phyllis Pentworthy is my husband's cousin, and years ago she organised a mysterious little gang called the British Ladies Auxiliary Defence Squadron—otherwise the *Blads.*

HILDA: What do they do?

LADY FARFIELD: I've never been able to find out, except I know that they wear uniform and salute each other—but they're so old-established and grand and exclusive that they've never been merged into the Waaf or the Wrens.

PAULINE: If you ask me, they're just barmy.

LADY FARFIELD: They occupy a dreary old mansion called Brindle-well Priory, about twenty miles from here. And Phyllis Pentworthy is their chief officer, and calls herself Commodore—though nobody knows why.

PAULINE: She's a frightful reactionary.

LADY FARFIELD: Not really. She's just idiotic. But whatever she is, she's on her way here—and we'll have to make the best of her.

PAULINE: I ought to warn you—that somebody told me her gang were being turned out of Brindlewell Priory, and she's probably plotting to billet the lot of them here——

LADY FARFIELD (*alarmed*): Oh—no! Don't say that. She hinted at it the other day at the telephone, and I told her this house was most unsuitable. I laid it on thick.

HILDA (*as she goes towards kitchen*): Then this time we'll 'ave to lay it on still thicker.

PAULINE: You can't tell that Commodore female anything. She's just a woman Blimp in solid ivory.

LADY FARFIELD (*surveying the table*): Well, we're not going to wait for her.

PAULINE: We ought to open this wine somehow.

LADY FARFIELD: Kenton'll do it. He'll love opening it. The poor old thing doesn't get much of a chance these days to show what he can do. Now then—I wonder if Lotta is ready. (*She goes down nearer kitchen, calling.*) Lotta! Lotta!

HILDA *returns, leaving the door open behind her, and bringing in more things.*

HILDA: She's ready now. She's just dishing up the stew.

LADY FARFIELD: And I'll bet there's everything in that stew but the kitchen stove.

HILDA: No, there's some of the kitchen stove in it too. She's been telling me about their opera company in Vienna. Some real daft goings on. When I tell me mother an' our 'Erbert, they won't believe a word I say.

Enter LOTTA, *triumphantly carrying a large dish of stew.*

LOTTA: Now we are ready. It is a new kind of stew—with bits of yesterday's rabbit and the American Pork Luncheon meat—and beetroot and cabbage——

LADY FARFIELD: It smells nice, Lotta.

LOTTA: Yes, somehow it smells better than it tastes.

HILDA: That's the beans. Yer've 'ad 'em near moth balls.

KENTON *enters from kitchen carrying a large gong and stick, followed by* EILEEN.

PAULINE: Kenton's going to have a lovely time now. You can go upstairs with it to-night, Kenton.

LADY FARFIELD: And after that, please draw the curtains everywhere, will you, Kenton?

KENTON: Yes, me lady. Can I sound the gong now, me lady?

LADY FARFIELD: Yes, we're ready.

[397]

KENTON, *with great pomp, begins sounding the gong, and goes upstairs with it.*

HILDA (*shouting above gong*): Proper warnin' I call it.

LADY FARFIELD: You can begin serving, Lotta. And we'd better light up here. Will you and Hilda do the curtains, Pauline?

She switches on the lights while PAULINE *and* HILDA *draw the curtains at back.* EILEEN *and* LOTTA *are dishing out the food. There is now the sound of a car outside.*

HILDA (*calling from curtains*): There's a car.

LADY FARFIELD: That'll be the Commodore.

EILEEN: Who's that?

PAULINE (*grimly*): You'll see.

Sound of front door bell.

I'll go.

She does and ushers in COMMODORE PHYLLIS PENTWORTHY, *who is a determined-looking, square, middle-aged woman, dressed in a very imposing uniform suggesting a general in some exotic revolutionary war. She has a gruff staccato voice and a curt, military, aggressive manner.*

COMMODORE PENTWORTHY (*striding in*): Hello, Frances! Sorry if I'm late.

LADY FARFIELD: No, that's all right.

COMMODORE PENTWORTHY: Lucky to get here at all really. Having to move headquarters. Not sure yet where we're going. Had to leave this telephone number with my A.D.C., though the girl's a perfect *fool.* Think I know some of these people, don't I?

PAULINE (*pointedly*): You've met me before.

COMMODORE PENTWORTHY: Have I?

LADY FARFIELD: And you know Lotta. And this is Eileen Stocks and this is Hilda Packet, who work with me.

COMMODORE PENTWORTHY: How d'you do?

LADY FARFIELD: Have a drink, won't you, Phyllis?

COMMODORE PENTWORTHY: Thanks. Don't mind a short drink.

SAM *has now arrived downstairs.*

LADY FARFIELD: This is Mr. Cawthra, our foreman—Commodore Pentworthy.

COMMODORE PENTWORTHY: How d'you do?

SAM (*looking her over*): Just middlin'. Commodore, eh? New to me. What's—er—what's yer regiment—like?

COMMODORE PENTWORTHY (*curtly*): I'm Commodore of the Blads.

[398]

LADY FARFIELD, *who has been pouring out sherry, hands glass to* COMMODORE.

SAM (*surprised*): Lads. What lads? D'yer mean—like Boys Brigades?

COMMODORE PENTWORTHY: Certainly not. Blads. Stands for British Ladies' Auxiliary Defence Squadron. Oldest of the women's defence services.

SAM: Is that so? What d'yer do?

COMMODORE PENTWORTHY: Well, we're really just headquarters now. Plenty of difficult administrative work to do, of course. Not a bad sherry this, Frances.

LADY FARFIELD: So glad. Have some more?

COMMODORE PENTWORTHY: Just a spot.

SAM: That officer and the Civil Servant's just coming down.

COMMODORE PENTWORTHY: What officer's this you're talking about?

LADY FARFIELD: One of our two new billetees—arrived to-night. American.

COMMODORE PENTWORTHY (*dismissing the whole U.S.A.*): Oh— American.

SAM (*with mock anxiety*): They're all right, aren't they—Americans?

COMMODORE PENTWORTHY: All right in their place. I say, Frances, how many rooms have you got here? Must have scores—surely.

LADY FARFIELD: Yes, Phyllis, but they're hopeless. Haven't been used for years. *Can't* be used for years, most of them.

COMMODORE PENTWORTHY: Possibly not, by civilian standards. But my girls are used to roughing it.

LADY FARFIELD (*alarmed*): Now, now, Phyllis, you couldn't possibly move your gang in here—simply don't think of it.

PAULINE (*loudly*): One whole wing has been damaged by incendiaries.

LADY FARFIELD: Oh yes—no good at all.

COMMODORE PENTWORTHY: Like to see for myself. Mind if I look round afterwards?

LADY FARFIELD: Yes I do. You simply couldn't dream of moving in here—ah, at last!

WEBBER *and* KILLIGREW, *who have tidied up and had a drink, followed by* KENTON, *now arrive.* WEBBER *is carrying an open bottle of whisky.*

WEBBER: I apologise if we're late.

LADY FARFIELD: No, you're just in time. Phyllis, this is Major Webber——

WEBBER: Pleased to meet you.

LADY FARFIELD: Mr. Killigrew. Commodore Pentworthy.

KILLIGREW: How d'you do?

LADY FARFIELD: Shall we all sit down? Supper's getting cold. Will you sit at the head of the table, Sam? Mr. Killigrew, Commodore, and Major Webber next.

WEBBER: Say that's quite a uniform. Kind of Waaf, I guess.

COMMODORE PENTWORTHY: Then you guess wrong. British Ladies' Defence Squadron . . . much older than the Waaf—or the Wrens. Much higher standard too.

PAULINE: Higher standard of what?

They take their places at the table.

LADY FARFIELD: Hilda, will you serve the salad? Pauline, pass the bread. Oh—Kenton—would you like to open that bottle of wine?

KENTON: Certainly, me lady.

KENTON *takes it and opens it in the background.*

WEBBER (*hospitably*): Here's some good Scotch, if anybody prefers it. How about you—er—Commodore?

COMMODORE PENTWORTHY: Glass of wine for me, thank you.

WEBBER: Lady Farfield?

LADY FARFIELD: No, thank you. But I'm sure Mr. Killigrew would like some.

KILLIGREW: I've had one taste of it already, but I won't say No to another. Any of your girls play the fiddle, Commodore?

COMMODORE PENTWORTHY: Not to my knowledge. Don't encourage that sort of thing. Physical jerks. Saluting drill. Get 'em out in the open and keep 'em busy.

PAULINE: Busy at what?

LADY FARFIELD: I hope nobody minds this stew. It seems to me —rather—mixed.

LOTTA (*almost tearfully*): It is terrible. One of my worst.

PAULINE: The tinned herring fishcakes were the worst. Sometimes during the night I can still taste them.

LOTTA: Darling, they were simply a bad *idea.* Are you a musician, Mr. Killigrew?

KILLIGREW: Play the fiddle, when I have a chance to. Quartettes mostly.

LOTTA (*gaily*): That is wonderful. After supper, I could sing the waltz from *Fledermaus*, and you could improvise an obbligato on your violin.

KILLIGREW: Don't like that sort of stuff, I'm afraid.

LOTTA (*disappointed*): Oh!

PAULINE: But even if you don't like it, perhaps the rest of us do, and surely you wouldn't object to doing one small thing to please the rest of the party.

KILLIGREW (*who can take it*): Telling me now I'm a selfish old highbrow, are you?

LADY FARFIELD (*hastily*): Oh no, I'm sure she wasn't.

KILLIGREW: Yes, she was. And she's right—I am. But remember, madam, I don't get much time to myself. Been working twelve—sometimes fourteen—hours a day for the last four years—and no extra pay, remember—no overtime—no nice canteens and extra rations—blitz, black-out, everything. However, as this is a party, I'll play anything you want me to. There!

WEBBER (*solemnly*): Mr. Killigrew, I think that's a pretty swell attitood.

COMMODORE PENTWORTHY (*loud, challenging*): Most of these war factory workers have been so well off they'll be sorry when the war's over.

SAM: That's nobbut true of a few. Rest 'as got 'usbands or sweethearts away, and they're as anxious as you for t'war to be ower—'appen a bit more anxious.

LADY FARFIELD: And it's not true they've been so well off. Getting up in the dark, perhaps travelling miles—then working all day in a machine shop—then getting back home in the dark, too tired to do anything—month after month, year after year—away from your husband, perhaps away from your children—doing hard monotonous work—often living with people who don't want you there—I don't think that's being well off.

HILDA: If it is, then they're not doin' so bad in Dartmoor.

COMMODORE PENTWORTHY: Yes. But most of them are not in the least patriotic. I know that for a fact.

SAM: 'Appen not what you'd call patriotic—flag-wavin'—King-and-country stuff—upper-class fancy work. But for all that, they've always wanted this country to come through. After Dunkirk, I saw 'em work till they dropped at their benches——

WEBBER: That's what they told us on the other side. And it sure is a great story—yes *sir*—a great story. That—and the Battle of

Britain—and the bombing of London. We had it over the radio every night.

KILLIGREW: I'd just as soon have a blitz as the radio every night. And I've had my share of air raids. Without wishing to boast, I must point out that I'm probably the only man in history who was ever blown clean out of his chair while practising the second violin part of the first movement of Beethoven's A-minor quartette, Opus One hundred and thirty-two.

LOTTA (*suddenly pointing at* KILLIGREW *and giving a scream of laughter*): Of course—I see now—you are really a comical man—a droll.

KILLIGREW: Good heavens!

KENTON *has gone round serving those who wanted it, and are not taking whisky or beer, with wine. There has also been some changing of plates, etc., with perhaps* LOTTA *and* PAULINE *or* HILDA *leaving the table.*

COMMODORE PENTWORTHY: You been over here long, Major Webber?

WEBBER: No, I haven't. Only landed a few days ago.

COMMODORE PENTWORTHY: Indeed! What d'you think of it here?

WEBBER: Oh—you seem to me to have done a swell job, though of course I haven't quite got the hang of things around here. One minute I imagine you British are going on in the same old way, and then the next minute—why—I begin to think you're having a kind of revolution.

COMMODORE PENTWORTHY (*shocked*): Revolution! Certainly not. Simply tryin' to do our best for the national cause. Got into uniform —obeyin' orders—and so on. Nothing to do with revolution. No sign of one, eh, Mr. Killigrew?

KILLIGREW: Words, words, words! Depends upon what you mean by revolution. Suggest we drop the subject.

WEBBER: Have you ever been to America, Commodore?

COMMODORE PENTWORTHY: Yes, once. Didn't take to it.

WEBBER: That's too bad. Why didn't you?

COMMODORE PENTWORTHY: I object to taxi drivers calling me "Sister"——

WEBBER: Aw—well—they don't mean anything by it——

COMMODORE PENTWORTHY: I didn't imagine they did mean anything by it. But I didn't like it. Then again, the hotels and houses were too hot, the waiters inefficient, and there were no egg cups, no toast racks, and my shoes were never cleaned.

WEBBER (*polite but annoyed*): Say—listen——

LADY FARFIELD (*cutting in*): Now Major Webber, you simply mustn't mind what Mrs.—I mean Commodore Pentworthy says. And, Phyllis, we can't have you talking like that. Remember, this is a special little party——

HILDA: Yes, an' Sam wants to say something. Go on, yer promised.

SAM (*rising slowly*): Well—er—friends—when I thought there was just goin' to be a few of us from t'factory, I'd agreed to say a few words—proposin' a 'ealth really—to celebrate t'occasion. Yer see, we're 'ere to-night to celebrate t'promotion o' Lady Farfield. She's just bin made a charge-'and—see? Nah that mightn't sound so much to some of yer, but we think she's done very well—an' I'll tell yer for why. An' mind yer, I speak as an old 'and, havin' bin in t'industry a good long time. But Lady Farfield, she wor new to it, o' course. It wor as strange to 'er as knitting a pair o' socks 'ud be to me—in fact, worse, 'cos I could at least try me 'and at that in private at 'ome. Well, she started down in t'machine shop, same as t'others—ay, an' 'ad plenty o' mucky little jobs an' all, 'cos there's one or two of 'em down there as I know that 'ud go out o' their way to give somebody like 'er muckiest job, d'yer see?——

EILEEN (*with unexpected vehemence*): Yes, they would too. Stinkers!

COMMODORE PENTWORTHY (*with a look*): What did you say?

PAULINE (*loud and clear*): She said "Stinkers". And quite right too.

SAM (*with good-natured reproach*): Now oo's talkin'—me or you lot? Any'ow, point is—Lady Farfield worked 'er way up to Assembly, which is best shop we 'ave, an' now she's a charge-'and. An' I say we ought to drink 'er 'ealth. Nah—then——

He raises his glass and the others, except LADY FARFIELD, rise and raise their glasses—murmuring the usual phrases. As they resume their seats, there is much applause, especially from the younger ones. LOTTA suddenly bursts into noisy sobs.

LOTTA (*through her sobs*): I am so sorry—but this reminds me so much—of—of—the old days—oh——

She runs to the kitchen, still sobbing.

PAULINE: I never knew such a one for being reminded.

LADY FARFIELD: Poor Lotta!

SAM: 'Ere, we want a speech from you.

Cries of "Yes, go on"—"Speech!", etc.

LADY FARFIELD (*rising*): Oh—well—thank you very much, Sam—

[403]

and all of you. I'm really very proud—and grateful. I haven't always liked it at the factory——

HILDA: I should think not!

LADY FARFIELD: All the people there aren't like you three—worse luck—but though I only went at first because I was desperate for something useful to do, I'm glad now that I did. I've met people —and made friends—that I couldn't have known before. I understand a lot of things—important things—that I didn't begin to understand before. I can face the future properly and in the right spirit. I feel that—in my own very humble way—now I can help—and not hinder—the new England most of us want. That's all.

Some applause as she sits down.

KILLIGREW: A most admirable little speech, if you'll allow me to say so, Lady Farfield.

WEBBER: Swell! I'd like to send a copy of it to Mrs. Webber.

LADY FARFIELD: But I haven't a copy of it, I only said the first thing that came into my head.

COMMODORE PENTWORTHY: And I must say, Frances, that I don't agree with you.

LADY FARFIELD: About what?

COMMODORE PENTWORTHY: Woman in your position could have found something more important and useful to do than going to a factory. You remember, I suggested your joining the Blads.

LADY FARFIELD: No, Phyllis, I don't believe I could have done anything more useful——

COMMODORE PENTWORTHY: Nonsense! Woman with your background! When any half-witted girl can look after those machines——

HILDA: 'Ere, 'alf a minute with yer 'alf-witted girls.

WEBBER: Well, I've seen something of mass production back home, and I can see what the Commodore's getting at. You see——

SAM (*cutting in*): Now 'old on a minute. Nobody's goin' to tell me she'd ha' bin more useful swaggerin' round in a uniform, playin' at female soldiers——

COMMODORE PENTWORTHY (*thundering*): Who's talking about playin' at female soldiers?

SAM (*who can't be intimidated*): I am. What we needed most of all for this war wor production—planes, tanks, guns an' suchlike—an' that's what the machines wor turnin' out. If uniforms could beat 'Itler, then Poles an' French 'ud ha' beaten 'im afore we started. But yer needed armaments an' machines to mak' them armaments an' folk to look after the machines.

WEBBER: Yeah—but everybody can't be——

HILDA (*cutting in*): No, Sam's right.

PAULINE (*quickly*): And even if he isn't, *she's* wrong.

LADY FARFIELD (*hastily*): Now, Pauline, be quiet.

KILLIGREW: But though you may need production first, man-power must be used properly, and a woman who——

COMMODORE PENTWORTHY (*cutting in, loudly*): I say, a woman with your social background and experience could have employed herself to better advantage. Otherwise what's the use of a good social background and experience?

PAULINE (*loud and rude*): Well, what *is* the use of it?

HILDA: Girls I know in the Ats and Waaf spend half their time sitting about——

KILLIGREW: That's not the point, young woman. Kindly stick to the point.

WEBBER: Quite so. Question of use of man-power. You don't want a square peg in a round hole.

COMMODORE PENTWORTHY: Exactly. Why a square peg in a round hole?

PAULINE: Why pegs in holes at all anyhow?

COMMODORE PENTWORTHY (*crushingly*): We're trying to be serious, if you don't mind.

SAM (*cutting in*): Well, just get back to my point——

WEBBER (*cutting in*): No, you made your point——

LADY FARFIELD (*cutting in*): Look here, this doesn't really matter——

KILLIGREW (*cutting in*): No, but if we're going to argue, we might as well argue properly. Now I contend——

COMMODORE PENTWORTHY: If you'll kindly not interrupt for one moment——

EILEEN (*topping them all*): Oh—please be quiet!

COMMODORE PENTWORTHY (*outraged*): I beg your pardon!

EILEEN (*bravely*): Oh—I didn't mean you specially. I meant every-body. We're all beginning to make silly quarrelling noises, that's all, and it simply isn't worth it.

COMMODORE PENTWORTHY (*to crush her*): Indeed?

EILEEN (*not crushed*): Yes—indeed.

The telephone rings. KENTON *emerges from the background.*

KENTON: Shall I answer the instrument, me lady?

[405]   o

LADY FARFIELD (*rising*): No, I'll answer it. And you'll all *have* to be quiet for a minute. It's difficult to hear if you're not. (*At telephone*) Yes . . . speaking . . . Oh they are, are they? . . . Had dinner? . . . Well, I'm glad of that because there isn't much left . . . I see. All right, thank you. (*Puts down telephone, to others*) Those two Air Force officers are on their way here. I suppose they're the same two they mentioned earlier, though she didn't say so.

HILDA: Hurray!

LADY FARFIELD: Come from overseas too. Now we'll have to hurry. Some of us will have to get their rooms ready. Pauline and Sam and I had better do that. Major Webber and Mr. Killigrew, you two had better go along to the drawing-room—we'll join you there afterwards—might have some music—and dancing perhaps——

HILDA: That's the stuff.

LADY FARFIELD: Phyllis, you needn't do anything, of course.

COMMODORE PENTWORTHY (*firmly*): I should like to go round the house again, Frances, and see what accommodation you really have——

LADY FARFIELD: All right, if you must—but don't dream of dumping any of your girls on me here. Now then—Eileen, Hilda—will you help Kenton to clear—and Lotta to wash up. I hope Lotta's recovered. We really must be nice and friendly and cheerful—for the sake of these boys.

> KENTON *exits down left with a tray.* HILDA *follows him with another.*

SAM: Come on, Pauline, back to the furniture job——

> *They go upstairs with* LADY FARFIELD. EILEEN *goes on clearing, but leaving the bottles and a few glasses.* WEBBER *lights a cigar and* KILLIGREW *a pipe. They have now withdrawn from table, and the* COMMODORE *lights a cigarette and joins them.*

COMMODORE PENTWORTHY (*to the two men*): Look here—I'll show you where the drawing-room is. Along here. I might as well start on the ground floor. My headquarters are over at Brindlewell Priory, but we're being turned out this week-end. Frightful nuisance. Follow me.

> *They go out by the door down right. Re-enter* HILDA *with tray.*

HILDA (*as she clears*): When she come out with that about 'alf-witted girls looking after machines, I could 'ave slapped her big fat silly face.

EILEEN (*as she clears*): Still, you must admit that some of our girls are almost half-witted, you know, Hilda.

HILDA: All right. But I'll bet they're no worse than what some

[406]

of 'ers are—all dressed up to look like somebody shoutin' outside a picture theatre. (*Imitating commissionaire*) "Standin' Only In the One an' Threes. Seats at 'Alf a Crown". That's what she oughta be doin'—wi' that uniform on.

EILEEN (*bashfully sentimental*): I wonder what your Herbert's doin' to-night, Hilda?

HILDA: Writin' a letter to you, I should think. 'E'll ha' got to page twenty by now. An' my mother could never get ten words out of 'im. Even that time 'e won four-pound-five at dogs, 'e wouldn't tell it to her properly.

EILEEN: He's told *me* all about that night.

HILDA: I'll bet 'e 'as.

EILEEN: I wish I'd sent the other photo to him now—y'know, the one half sideways. It's a lot nicer.

HILDA: Yes, but the other one's more like you.

EILEEN: Now don't say, that, Hilda. I get so worried about it, wondering what he'll think when he does see me.

HILDA: Don't you bother about 'Erbert. I know 'im. He'll 'ave to think you're wonderful now that 'e's used all that paper an' pencil on you. 'E never did like wasting anything.

EILEEN (*indignantly*): He's not mean.

HILDA: I never said 'e was, though I can't say 'e ever gave 'is little sister much. But what I want to know now is—what these Air Force chaps'll be like.

EILEEN: I don't care about them.

HILDA: No, you don't 'cos you've got our 'Erbert. But I could do with a bit of Air Force attention for a change. Will they be our sort, like them sergeants who come round the factory that time? Or will they be like them officers who came round that other time—that very 'igh-class bunch, you remember? (*Imitates them*) They 'alf-closed their eyes an' stroked their fancy moustaches an' went round sayin' "Wizard—absolutely wizard!" But when they thought we couldn't 'ear 'em, they were mutterin' to each other, "Black show, old boy."

> They go into the kitchen, leaving door ajar, and through it we can hear music, LOTTA singing, laughter. Sound of car arriving. Ring at bell. KENTON comes out slowly and answers it, admitting two R.A.F. officers. The first, GROUP-CAPTAIN EDWARD CAMYON, D.S.O., is a well-set up man about the same age as LADY FARFIELD. The other, SQUADRON-LEADER TONY ACTON, D.F.C., is a high-spirited younger man who wears one of the fancy moustaches.

[407]

Both men are very sun-burned as if newly come from overseas. They have bags with them.

CAMYON: I think you've had a message about us from the R.A.F. Experimental Station.

KENTON: Yes, sir, we 'ad a message and 'er ladyship's expecting you gentlemen. I'll inform 'er of your arrival. We 'ave—er—various guests to-night——

TONY: Yes, sounds quite like a party.

KENTON: Yes, sir. Oh—we 'ave very big parties 'ere at the Hall at times, sir. Bands playin', dancin', singing'. Sometimes I'll 'ave as many as a dozen extra waiters in, as well as our own ten indoor staff. Yes, sir. Very big parties. I'll inform 'er ladyship.

KENTON *goes upstairs. There is a louder burst of music, song, laughter from kitchen, at this moment. After taking this in,* CAMYON *turns indignantly to* TONY.

CAMYON (*angrily*): What did I tell you?

TONY: Yes, sir, black show! How's the head now, sir?

CAMYON: Not so good. Well, you see what it's like at home. You saw last night in town, at the filthy little night club you insisted on our going to——

TONY: I took a poor view of that, as you know, sir.

CAMYON: All right. That's bad enough. But we come down here —and what's happening? This Lady Whatsit has nothing better to do than throw a party. You can hear 'em. Listen to 'em. And that old fool of a butler says they're always throwing parties. Bands! Dozen extra waiters. Ten indoor staff. By thunder, Acton, it makes my blood boil. There weren't any bands and extra waiters for our chaps who went to Berlin and never came back. And think of our fellows in Italy and the Middle East and India—worrying about how they are at home, longing to get back—and some of these people here —damned empty-headed, stupid, rich women——

TONY: Couldn't agree with you more, sir. Black show! Not that I can't take a party——

CAMYON: Of course, of course. No objection to people enjoying themselves when they've earned it. But this sort of thing is a damned disgrace. These women have no imagination, no sense, no decency. They don't realise what's happening in the world. They don't even care. I've been out of this country four years and this is what I come back to find. Parties! Extravagance! Rows of servants! Callous idiocy!

TONY: Yes, sir, doesn't look too good. Take a poor view of it myself, sir. But from what I've heard, I think it must be exceptional.

CAMYON: Doubt it, Acton. But exceptional or not, it's damned disgraceful. I've half a mind to tell this fool of a woman here—what's her name—Lady Fairfield—Farfield—or whatever she calls herself—just what I think about her and then walk straight out of her house.

TONY: Serve her right, sir. But where do we walk to?

CAMYON (*irritably*): What does that matter?

TONY: Well, sir, isn't a bed for miles, they said at the station.

CAMYON (*angrily*): Filled up with dance bands and waiters and lounge lizards, I suppose. Well, I suppose we can put up with the idiotic antics of these people for one night, but I don't propose——

TONY (*hastily*): Somebody coming, sir.

> LADY FARFIELD, *with* PAULINE *behind her, now comes down the stairs.*

LADY FARFIELD (*advancing*): Good evening. I'm sorry to have kept you waiting, but I was just—— (*Then she recognises him.*) Edward!

CAMYON (*staggered*): *Frances!* Are *you* Lady Farfield?

LADY FARFIELD: Yes. Didn't you know?

CAMYON (*bitterly*): No, but I might have known, I ought to have guessed.

LADY FARFIELD (*annoyed by his tone*): What on earth do you mean?

CAMYON (*loudly and angrily*): I might have known, after being overseas for years, and coming back home to a place like this where people can still give parties every night, and fling money away, and keep rows of servants waiting on them, and generally behaving like callous idiots, that somebody like you would be mixed up in it——

LADY FARFIELD (*cutting in, furious*): Just a minute! I don't know what you're talking about, and I don't believe you do either, Edward Camyon. But of all the pompous, pig-headed, insufferable—why, for years I've waited for this.

CAMYON (*aggressively*): For what?

LADY FARFIELD (*advancing on him*): This!

> *She gives him a loud slap on the face. Then stands glaring at him. He stands amazed.* PAULINE *gives a little gurgle of delight.*

TONY (*in a kind of loud dazed murmur*): Black show, chaps! Black show!

> LOTTA *and the music from the kitchen swell up magnificently as they stand there and the curtain falls.*

END OF ACT ONE

ACT II

At rise, LOTTA *is discovered arranging drinks—*MAJOR WEBBER'S *whisky, beer, a jug of lemonade, and a jug of sinister reddish liquid —and glasses either on the centre table or the small serving table.* MAJOR WEBBER *is good-naturedly giving her a hand and can be handing over some drink or glasses when we discover them. Dance music heard off.*

LOTTA: Thank you, Major Webber. But please go on with your story. It is so interesting to me—this American business life.

WEBBER: Well, so I said to them, "Gentlemen, I want you to bear in mind that we have right here one of the biggest canning plants east of Chicago, and also that we're turning out more windshield wipers and other automobile accessories than any other city in the state, and that——

LOTTA (*who is really bored by this stuff*): Yes, it must be a wonderful life. So rich, so exciting, so—*strong!*

WEBBER: Well, yes, certainly is—in a way——

LOTTA: But for a woman—no. No, no, no, no. (*Smiling at him. And after all I am a woman.*

WEBBER: Sure thing! Well, then I said to them, "Another point I'd like you gentlemen to bear in mind," I said, "and I'm not going to try teach you anything about business conditions in general, but I'm a real-estate man and I'm here in my own home town—yes, sir——"

LOTTA: One minute, please. You 'ave not heard me sing properly yet, of course, but you have heard me a little. You like my singing?

WEBBER: Swell. So I said, "Now gentlemen——"

LOTTA (*cutting in*): This dress—it is nothing, of course—just for the kitchen. But all the same, it is rather pretty, eh?

WEBBER: Swell. So I said, "And don't forget another thing, gentlemen. This town is producing right now a bigger and better assortment of patent steel fasteners than any place between Pittsburgh and Kansas City——"

LOTTA (*cutting in*): No, no.

WEBBER: Why yes, we were doing just that thing. We were producing bigger and better——

LOTTA (*cutting in*): No, I mean—oh, you would not understand. But I am so glad you had so many steel fasteners!

[410]

HILDA *looks in through doorway to drawing-room.*

HILDA: Hey, Major Webber, I thought you wanted to do some dancing.

WEBBER: I'm raring to go.

HILDA: Well, come on then.

She withdraws. WEBBER *turns to* LOTTA.

WEBBER: You coming along?

LOTTA: No, thank you. Not just now.

WEBBER: See you later then. Pardon me!

He goes through door to drawing-room. LOTTA *gives a last look round at her drink arrangements, then sits down and sighs, obviously bored and rather melancholy. After a moment or two, SAM comes down the stairs, comfortably smoking his pipe.*

LOTTA: Mr. Cawthra—this party of ours—where is it? What has happened to it?

SAM: Well, yer might say it finished afore it got properly started. Though Ah'm not grumbling. Ah'm feeling all right.

LOTTA: Well, I am not feeling all right. I feel—very disappointed —rather sad. What about the two Air Force officers?

SAM: Well, after that Group-Captain got 'is face slapped, 'e stamps up to 'is room an' says 'e's stoppin' there. Won't 'ave nowt to do wi' this carry-on at all. An' 'e gave that young Squadron-Leader orders to stop in 'is room too, an' 'ave nowt to do wi' us. So we've lost t'Air Force.

LOTTA: But why does not Lady Farfield come and settle everything and make everybody happy?

SAM: 'Cos as soon as she'd slapped 'er old friend's face, she run straight up to 'er room an' locked 'erself in to 'ave a good cry.

LOTTA (*thoughtfully*): So! They knew one another before the war. And now, when they meet again, she slaps his face and goes to her room to cry. Then I think she must still love him at least a little.

SAM (*dryly*): I suppose if she'd knocked 'im silly an' then screamed the place down, she'd 'ave loved 'im a lot, eh?

LOTTA (*seriously*): Yes, of course.

SAM: The gentle sex!

LOTTA (*tenderly reminiscent*): I remember one of my lovers—oh, I adored that man—he was our leading baritone—and every time I saw him I wanted to take him and beat him and pull his hair out by the handful. Sometimes I did too—and then he would twist my arms until I screamed. (*Dreamily*) It was wonderful—love in Spring in Vienna—wonderful!

SAM: All right so long as yer wor i' good training for it. Well, that's all I can tell yer about this party, except that that female General-Admiral is still upstairs making a list o' t'rooms.

LOTTA: I do not care about that woman. She is all wrong.

SAM: Ay, though if she ever retires on a pension, she might mak' a good time-keeper.

LOTTA (*ignoring this, with decision*): But then all of us are all wrong. Look at me!

SAM: I see nowt wrong wi' *you.*

LOTTA: Yes, yes, everything is wrong. These clothes! When I still have some beautiful dresses. All these girls. They too should be wearing beautiful feminine things—romantic, seductive, glamorous—and then these men would not behave so badly—you would see.

SAM: I don't know that the men 'ave been behavin' badly. Unless you're goin' to blame that Group-Captain for puttin' his face in the way of Lady Farfield's 'and.

Enter HILDA *and* EILEEN *through door right, looking rather bored. Dance music has stopped now.*

HILDA: Well, I must say it's turning out a dam' dull party. I've already had enough of dancing with that American officer. Yer go bouncing round on 'is tunic as if he'd just given 'imself another medal. What is there to drink?

LOTTA: Anything here. But—— (*she indicates a dark red liquid in a glass jug*) I would not touch that stuff. There were two bottles from the chemist—and the labels came off—and I think I have used the wrong one.

EILEEN (*smelling it*): Smells to me like liniment.

LOTTA: If that is the liniment, then Kenton has been rubbing his back with black-currant juice.

HILDA: We'll give Commodore Pentworthy a nice stiff glassful o' this. That's something to look forward to, but we could do with a few more ideas.

LOTTA (*impressively*): I have a nice idea. But I must talk first to Lady Farfield.

Enter KILLIGREW *and* PAULINE *from down right, deep in talk.*

KILLIGREW (*obviously concluding an account of his troubles*): So I ask you, what is a man to do?

PAULINE (*calmly*): You ought to shoot a few of them.

KILLIGREW (*seriously*): The idea's attractive—but quite apart from the fact that there might be a question or two in the House, my department has no authority or machinery for shooting people. It would have to be referred to the Ministry of Home Security and the War Office.

PAULINE: Well then, choose fifty of the worst of the big fat crooks, and send them up to the coldest moors to make roads.

KILLIGREW: Then you'd have to come to some arrangement with the Ministry of Works or Planning. Or one of the local authorities —and you know what *they* are. But you're a very fierce young woman, aren't you?

PAULINE: Yes. And it's time somebody was fierce.

KILLIGREW: You'll feel better when you've a husband and a baby or two, y'know.

PAULINE: When I have a baby or two, I'll be *fiercer still*.

Enter LADY FARFIELD, *who looks rather pale and miserable. She comes down rather cautiously, obviously ready to retreat if* CAMYON *is about. When she sees he is not, she comes in, watched by the others.*

LADY FARFIELD (*almost whispering*): Is he—still—up in his room?

SAM: Yes, for all Ah know.

LADY FARFIELD: I was a fool to lose my temper like that. And after all this time! Poor Edward! He looked rather sweet too.

SAM: Well, 'e's stayin' in 'is room—an' I could 'ear 'im tellin' that Squadron-Leader that 'e'd better stay in 'is room too.

PAULINE (*angrily*): Then I think he's a mean pig. That Squadron-Leader looked heavenly. And unless he's completely riveted to somebody else, I'd made up my mind to take possession of him.

SAM: Yer'll 'ave to look sharp. I 'eard Group-Captain shoutin' that they'd leave first thing in t'mornin'——

LADY FARFIELD (*annoyed*): Then I'm not a bit sorry for him. Jumping to idiotic conclusions and then refusing to budge. I'd like to make him look really silly——

LOTTA (*calling her away from others*): Frances!

LADY FARFIELD (*going to her*): What is it, Lotta?

LOTTA (*confidentially*): I think this is the man you told me about, once—your first love—eh?

LADY FARFIELD (*same tone*): Yes, it is.

LOTTA: You were in love—but you quarrelled, eh?

LADY FARFIELD: Yes. And look at him! He's just as hasty and obstinate as ever. Worse, in fact.

LOTTA: But I think you are still in love with him—a little—eh?

LADY FARFIELD (*hastily*): Certainly not.

[413]   o*

LOTTA: But you ran away—and cried——

LADY FARFIELD: I was upset—naturally—besides, one can't help remembering. But now I'm absolutely furious with him. I'd like—to make him look completely idiotic. (*Hesitates, as if reflecting, and looks now at the others speculatively.*) There ought to be something we could do. What's happening down here?

SAM: Nowt.

HILDA: We're bored, and Lotta's going on about dresses an' glamour and stuff.

LOTTA (*impressively*): I say it is all our fault. The men do not care —they are sulky—they are stupid—there is no nice party—why? Because we are not truly feminine any more. They come from a war —for years they see nothing but men, men, men, guns, machines, more men, men, men—and what do they see here? We are not mysterious. We are not romantic. We are not glamorous any more. We are—— (*with a big, contemptuous gesture, indicating* PAULINE) —like that.

PAULINE (*loudly*): All right, but just you try being a romantic and glamorous Land Girl and see where it gets you.

LOTTA: I understand that perfectly, my dear Pauline, but you need not be a Land Girl to-night.

PAULINE: I don't want to be, not with that heavenly Squadron-Leader about. But what can we do?

LOTTA (*impressively*): Frances, I appeal to you.

LADY FARFIELD: What do you want *me* to do?

LOTTA: You still have some beautiful things. So have I—a few old costumes I saved. Let us go and make ourselves mysterious and beautiful. Even if none of these idiot men ever notice, we will have had some fun.

HILDA: I'm all for it, though I bet nothing fits me—and then I shan't look beautiful—and not even mysterious.

LADY FARFIELD: It might be fun. And—I have an idea—— *She breaks off, and holds up her hand.*) Sh! (*They are all still. She whispers*) I thought I heard them. One of you go and see.

HILDA (*quietly*): That's me. (*Hurries quietly to stairs and creeps up.*)

LADY FARFIELD (*whispering*): I want them to see us later, but not now. If they are coming down, we must hide. Unless they are coming to apologise.

SAM (*whispering*): I'll bet it's too early for any apologising.

LADY FARFIELD: Then be ready to hide—behind that door—if I give the signal. (HILDA *returns.*) Well, Hilda?

HILDA (*whispering*): They're either coming down quietly—or playin' at Red Indians.

LADY FARFIELD (*whispering*): Let's hide then. Hurry!

They hurry quietly across to door right leaving the door slightly ajar—to show that they are peeping and listening. ACTON *comes cautiously downstairs. He is still in uniform. He looks around and then steals to the telephone. He glances at a note-book and picks up the phone.*

ACTON (*at telephone*): Morbury Eight Nine Two.

While he is waiting, not looking toward door right, the door opens a little wider. Hearing it move, he turns round, but as he turns, the door almost closes again.

Wing-Commander Fawcett, please . . . I'm speaking for Group-Captain Camyon . . . Yes . . .

Here, if it holds, he can go through the same business as before with door right.

Wing-Commander Fawcett? Squadron-Leader Acton here, sir . . . if you don't mind waiting a moment, sir, I'll get Group-Captain Camyon.

Puts down receiver and hurries across to stairs and calls up cautiously.

All right, sir. Nobody here, and he's on the line.

CAMYON *now comes down, less cautiously than* ACTON, *and goes to telephone, with* ACTON *in attendance.*

CAMYON (*at telephone*): Fawcett? Camyon here. You were telling me this afternoon that you needed a good-sized country house or two to requisition. Well, there's one here. Yes, Farfield Hall. Occupied by people who don't seem to realise, even now, that we've had a war on our hands for the last few years. . . . Yes, that's the type —silly extravagant callous women . . . All right . . . Ring me back in about half an hour.

Puts down telephone, and regards ACTON *sternly.*

And now I'm going back to my room—and you're going back to yours, my lad.

ACTON: Yes, sir.

CAMYON: No nonsense now. This is serious.

ACTON: Understand absolutely, sir. Black show.

CAMYON (*sharply*): Come on then.

He walks briskly towards the stairs, followed by ACTON. *As they go, the door right slowly opens. As soon as they have gone,* LADY FARFIELD, PAULINE, LOTTA, HILDA, EILEEN, SAM *and* KILLIGREW *come through hastily but quietly.*

[415]

LADY FARFIELD (*who is really angry*): I'm absolutely furious.

PAULINE: So am I. Did you hear him ordering the Squadron-Leader to stay in his room too? Pig!

LADY FARFIELD: Well, did you hear what he said about us on the telephone? Silly extravagant callous women!

LOTTA: What did I tell you? No glamour, y'see.

LADY FARFIELD: Now if we could only get him downstairs again at the right moment.

SAM: I'll bet they'll both be down again soon.

KILLIGREW: We can always invent a message to bring them down, if necessary.

LADY FARFIELD (*who is thinking*): Yes. Mr. Killigrew, you'll have to help us.

KILLIGREW: Certainly. Only I'd like to do a little telephoning first.

LADY FARFIELD: There'll be no hurry for you. I'll have to find the things first. But come up as soon as you've done your telephoning. The rest of us must go through the kitchen and up the back stairs. And we'll collect Kenton—we'll need him. Come along.

As they go, all but KILLIGREW.

If Edward Camyon is determined to make a fool of himself again, I'll jolly well see that he does it properly this time. Pompous obstinate idiot!

As they go out door left the telephone rings.

KILLIGREW (*calling to* LADY FARFIELD): Leave this to me. And I'll join you later when I've done my telephoning.

He goes to the telephone.

Yes, Farfield Hall . . . Who? . . . Oh yes, Commodore Pentworthy —yes, she's here—doing a survey of the house, I believe—or perhaps firing rocket guns from the roof. Anyhow, she'll be hard to find . . . Yes, yes, I'll take a message . . . Yes, Yes, I've got that. (*Impatiently*) Yes, yes, the message is perfectly simple, young woman. Clear the line please.

He waits a moment, glancing at his note-book.

I want Cornland Three Four . . . Yes, I'll hang on . . .

COMMODORE PENTWORTHY *comes downstairs, closing a large official note-book.*

COMMODORE PENTWORTHY (*curtly*): Is Lady Farfield down here?

KILLIGREW: No.

COMMODORE PENTWORTHY: Has she gone out?

KILLIGREW: No.

COMMODORE PENTWORTHY: Where is she then?

KILLIGREW: I've no idea.

She makes a "humph!" sound, and so he makes another one, rather louder. She stares at him suspiciously.

COMMODORE PENTWORTHY (*importantly*): Well, wherever she is, I want to tell her that it's absurd of her to pretend that she hasn't ample accommodation here. Some of the rooms in the East Wing may seem useless by civilian standards—but my girls in the British Ladies Auxiliary Squadron are accustomed to roughing it.

KILLIGREW: I'll bet they are.

COMMODORE PENTWORTHY: What?

KILLIGREW: A message has just come through for you. Your headquarters has sent the car back for you. All very urgent.

COMMODORE PENTWORTHY: Urgent. Then I ought to have been told at once.

KILLIGREW: You have been told at once. (*Into telephone*) Hello . . . yes. Cornland Three Four——

COMMODORE PENTWORTHY (*going nearer*): I must telephone to my headquarters immediately. I must know exactly what has happened. This is important official business——

KILLIGREW (*angrily*): Do be quiet, I can't hear what they're saying at the exchange——

COMMODORE PENTWORTHY (*angrily*): I will *not* be quiet.

KILLIGREW (*shouting*): How can I hear what the girl's saying— (*Into telephone*)—no, not you——

COMMODORE PENTWORTHY (*loudly*): I say this is important official business and I must ask you to let me have the telephone——

KILLIGREW: Will you be quiet?

COMMODORE PENTWORTHY: No, my call is particularly important —really urgent.

KILLIGREW (*into telephone*): Oh—all right.

He puts down the receiver and the COMMODORE, *glaring at him, goes at once to take up the telephone.*

COMMODORE PENTWORTHY (*still glaring at* KILLIGREW): Brindle-well Four Five.

To KILLIGREW, *who is now looking at the drinks, before helping himself.*

I don't suppose the call you want to make is of any great importance.

KILLIGREW: Certainly it is. I'm trying to get a string quartette together.

[417]

COMMODORE PENTWORTHY (*outraged*): You call *that* important—at a time like this?

KILLIGREW (*giving himself a drink*): Most decidedly. A man must have a little order, sense and beauty somewhere in his life these days, and I find 'em in string quartettes.

COMMODORE PENTWORTHY (*indignantly*): I shall complain of your attitude—— (*Breaks off to talk into telephone*) Oh—Millicent—what has happened? No, the car hasn't arrived yet, I'm waiting for it now. Now tell me exactly what's happened . . .

KILLIGREW (*while she is listening*): Going to be long with that telephone?

COMMODORE PENTWORTHY (*at telephone*): Yes, certainly, if necessary this place would do. I've counted more than thirty rooms that could be used at a pinch . . . No, don't be *absurd*, Millicent. Just a minute. (*Calling across severely to* KILLIGREW) What did you say?

KILLIGREW: I said—are you going to be long with that telephone?

COMMODORE PENTWORTHY: As long as I please. (*At telephone*) Yes, yes, Millicent—everything must be ready. We may have to move at once. Yes, *to-night*. Of course I shall come straight back. When the car is here to take me . . . Well, give yourself an aspirin.

She puts down the telephone, still glaring at KILLIGREW, *who now takes himself and his drink back to the telephone.*

KILLIGREW (*at telephone*): Cornland Three Four.

Enter WEBBER *from down right, carrying a large book.*

COMMODORE PENTWORTHY: Where is Lady Farfield, Major Webber?

WEBBER: I haven't seen her around since supper, Commodore. I've been along there looking at this book—some mighty nice pictures of the neighbourhood.

COMMODORE PENTWORTHY: I'm waiting for my car.

WEBBER: Well, join me in a drink while you're waiting, Commodore.

KILLIGREW (*at telephone*): All right, I *am* waiting.

COMMODORE PENTWORTHY (*pointing to the red stuff*): I'll have some of that fruit cup, thank you.

WEBBER (*holding up the jug*): Is this fruit cup?

KILLIGREW (*still at telephone but calling across*): Looks to me like blood and soda. (*Into telephone*) No, I wasn't swearing at you, but I may start in a minute . . . You just get me Cornland Three Four.

COMMODORE PENTWORTHY (*who has her drink now*): Well—cheers!

WEBBER: Here's to us, Commodore!

[418]

*She takes a good drink, watched anxiously by the other two.
She closes her eyes a moment, in delight or anguish, before returning
manfully to the surface.*

How is it, Commodore?

COMMODORE PENTWORTHY (*blinking*): Obviously not made of
fresh fruit—that's too much to expect these days—but very refresh-
ing, a jolly good drink. I think I'll have a little more, please, Major
Webber.

WEBBER (*taking her glass*): Sure thing!

KILLIGREW (*into telephone*): Yes, it *is* Mr. Fraser I'm wanting.
Old Mr. Fraser or young Mr. Fraser? I don't care.

   The COMMODORE'S *second good pull at the drink has not been
   without its effect.*

COMMODORE PENTWORTHY (*sternly*): If you want *my* opinion, I
think we're becoming too soft. Yes, slack and soft. We British are
getting too slack and soft. You Americans, Major Webber—so far
as I can see—are even worse—*pampered!*

KILLIGREW (*calling across from telephone*): You ought to try the
Russians.

COMMODORE PENTWORTHY (*with dignity*): I have no wish to try
the Russians. Or to have anything to do with the Russians. I cannot
help remembering that many of the Russians are Bolsheviks.

WEBBER: You've got something there, Commodore.

KILLIGREW (*calling across*): What do you expect them to be—
members of the Primrose League? (*Into telephone*) Oh, Mr. Fraser
—my name's Killigrew and I'm staying at Farfield Hall——

COMMODORE PENTWORTHY (*on top of his remarks into telephone*):
In any case, this is not a question that any mere civilian can attempt
to discuss with any authority, if only because he lacks the necessary
experience——

KILLIGREW (*who is trying to hear on telephone*): Oh—be quiet a
minute.

COMMODORE PENTWORTHY (*angrily*): I will *not* be quiet. Why
should I?

KILLIGREW (*angrily*): Because I'm trying to hear what this chap's
saying—and the line's bad. (*Into telephone*) Yes, yes . . . now,
Mr. Fraser, I understand you play the 'cello. . . .

COMMODORE PENTWORTHY: Really—the 'cello—at a time like this!

KILLIGREW (*loudly into telephone*): Oh—your son. Well, is he
there? All right, I'll wait. . . .

COMMODORE PENTWORTHY (*angrily*): Lord Chipping Norton is

a member of the government and he also happens to be an old friend of mine. I'm inclined to make a serious complaint to him about your extraordinary conduct and attitude, Mr. Killigrew.

KILLIGREW (*still at telephone, coolly*): Make fifty complaints to Lord Chipping Norton if you like, madam. I don't care a fig for Lord Chipping Norton, who, incidentally, is a most inefficient junior minister and not likely to be in the government much longer. (*Into telephone*) Hello, hello!

WEBBER (*moving towards door right and laughing*): Say—why didn't somebody tell me about you British? Back home we've never had the right idea about you, and Mrs. Webber will never believe me when I tell her.

Sound of car outside.

COMMODORE PENTWORTHY (*preparing to go*): That must be my car.

WEBBER: Well, pleased to have met you, Commodore.

COMMODORE PENTWORTHY: You may see me again, unless my head-quarters staff have been able to cope with this emergency.

KILLIGREW (*turning, at telephone*): Quiet, *please*. I can't hear a word this chap's saying——

COMMODORE PENTWORTHY: I don't think it necessary that you should. *Fiddler!*

She marches out main door. WEBBER *laughs and goes out down right, taking his book and drink with him.* KILLIGREW *is still at telephone.*

KILLIGREW (*telephone*): I hear you play the 'cello, Mr. Fraser . . . That doesn't matter, everybody has to make a start sometime . . . Yes, I've plenty of scores . . . Now what about a viola player and a second fiddle? . . . What's her telephone number? . . . Yes, I'll wait . . .

COMMODORE PENTWORTHY *now returns, looking disappointed and cross, followed slowly by* CORPORAL HERBERT PACKET, HILDA'S *brother. He is, in fact, a larger male version of her. The most noticeable thing about him is an enormous slow grin that lights up his weatherbeaten face.*

COMMODORE PENTWORTHY (*sternly*): Are you *sure* the car was not sent for me?

HERBERT (*who is rather bewildered*): Yes, sir.

COMMODORE PENTWORTHY: Ma'am.

HERBERT: What?

COMMODORE PENTWORTHY (*snapping*): Don't call me *Sir* but *Ma'am*.

HERBERT (*with his grin*): Oh—I see—ma'am.

[420]

COMMODORE PENTWORTHY: Well, what about the car?—because I'm expecting one——

HERBERT: That car belonged to a farmer who gave me a lift—like——

COMMODORE PENTWORTHY: But who sent you here, Corporal?

HERBERT: Well, nobody sent me—miss—ma'am. I come on me own—like. (*Does his grin.*)

COMMODORE PENTWORTHY (*irritated*): But have you any right to come here on your own?

KILLIGREW (*from telephone*): Why shouldn't he?

COMMODORE PENTWORTHY (*to* KILLIGREW): This is a service matter. Don't interfere. (*To* HERBERT) Now then, Corporal.

KILLIGREW: Just a minute. (*Into telephone*) I see—she'll ring me here . . . Farfield Hall, eh? Good man! Splendid, splendid! (*Puts down telephone and looks delighted.*) Never picked up a 'cello so quickly. And I'm on the track of a viola. Don't let anybody say the Civil Service can't work fast.

COMMODORE PENTWORTHY (*impatiently*): Well, Corporal?

HERBERT: Well, y'see—er—ma'am—I was brought 'ome on a job —an' got a bit of leaf—like—all sudden, y'see. Well, I goes to see my sister an' 'er friend—an' woman where they stop tells me they've come on 'ere—so I get talkin' about it to a farmer in a pub—an' 'e gives me a lift 'ere—I 'ope it's right place—Farfield 'All.

KILLIGREW: That's right, Farfield Hall.

HERBERT (*producing his grin*): Okey dokey!

He grins from one to the other and lounges a bit.

COMMODORE PENTWORTHY (*sharply*): Come, come, Corporal. Smarten yourself up. I wouldn't allow any of my girls to behave like this. Wearing the King's uniform—you must be soldierly—smart and soldierly.

HERBERT (*apologetic but easy*): That's right. I used to be right smart an' soldierly at beginning, after I'd done me trainin'. But I wor at Dunkirk an' dropped a bit of it there—like. An' then I went to the desert an' up through Tunis an' Sicily an' into Italy. An' what wi' one thing an' another, yer get right out o' practice—an' start behavin' natural—you're so busy fighting——

KILLIGREW (*approvingly*): Quite right, Corporal.

They exchange grins. COMMODORE PENTWORTHY *looks sharply at them both, then moves away.*

Can you drink beer?

HERBERT: Can a duck swim?

[421]

KILLIGREW (*handing him a glass*): Here you are, then.

HERBERT (*taking it*): Thank you very much, sir. All the best! (*Drinks.*)

KILLIGREW: Is your sister called Hilda?

HERBERT: That's right. Hilda Packet. An' 'er friend's called Eileen.

KILLIGREW: They're here. I'll go up and tell them you've arrived. You wait down here, Corporal.

> KILLIGREW *goes upstairs.* HERBERT *stands with his beer, near the table.* COMMODORE PENTWORTHY *looks impatiently at her watch.* HERBERT *looks at her drolly. Sound of car, then ring at bell.*

COMMODORE PENTWORTHY (*eagerly*): That *must* be my car.

> *She goes out, and we hear the front door slam and then the car move off.* HILDA *now comes hurrying downstairs.*

HILDA (*delightedly*): 'Erbert! (*She hurries over to him and kisses him.*) Well, well—— (*Looking him over*) Same old 'Erbert.

HERBERT (*grinning*): Same old 'Ilda!

HILDA: 'Ave yer been 'ome to see Mother yet?

HERBERT: No, I come 'ere first. But don't you tell 'er I did.

HILDA: She'll be that mad if she knows.

HERBERT: Well, don't tell 'er then. I come 'ere first 'cos it's nearer the depot.

HILDA: Yes, an' 'cos yer wanted to 'ave a look at yer precious Eileen—I know. But why didn't yer tell us you were comin'?

HERBERT: 'Cos I didn't know. They suddenly brought a dozen of us back—six sergeants an' six corporals—in a bomber—to do some instructin'—and then afore we started they said we could 'ave a week's leaf. So yer see, 'Ilda, I went to that Mrs. Batsby's where you're billeted—an' she says, "Oh, they've gone out for the evenin'," she says—"to that Lady Farfield's at Farfield 'All," she says—an' then she tells me where it is—an' a farmer gives me a lift—an' 'ere I am.

HILDA: An' I must say, 'Erbert, you're lookin' right well.

HERBERT (*grinning*): You're not lookin' so bad yerself, 'Ilda.

HILDA: I'm all right.

HERBERT: 'Aven't got a steady chap yet, eh?

HILDA (*sharply*): No, but I've 'ad plenty o' chances, an' you needn't think I 'aven't. Course I've gone to dances an' the pictures with one or two now an' again, but that's not the same thing. An' if yer really want to know—I'll tell yer something.

HERBERT (*as she hesitates*): Well—go on.

HILDA (*solemnly*): I'm waitin' a bit afore I get a steady chap.

HERBERT: What are yer waitin' for?

HILDA: I'm waitin' till some o' the real boys get back—the boys who've done the fightin' for us.

HERBERT: That's right, 'Ilda. Them's the real bloody lads. We 'ave a sergeant—comes from Newcastle—an' 'e saw that little photo I 'ave of you—an' after that 'e kept askin' me about yer, an' askin' to 'ave another look at the photo. I'll tell yer about 'im after.

HILDA: I'll see yer do. If 'e's not married or anything.

HERBERT: No, 'e's not.

HILDA: You 'aven't got a photo of 'im, 'ave yer?

HERBERT: Course I 'aven't. I don't carry sergeants' photos round wi' me. But 'is name's Jack Philips—an' 'is old man keeps a pub in Newcastle—— 'Ere—(*dropping his voice*)—where's Eileen?

HILDA (*dropping her voice too*): She's 'ere. Yer'll see 'er in a minute.

HERBERT: That's the idea.

HILDA (*very earnestly*): An' let me tell yer something, 'Erbert Packet. Eileen's a bit shy an' gets silly ideas sometimes—like we all do—but she's a grand girl, Eileen is, an' thinks a lot about you. More than you're worth.

HERBERT. Well, I think a lot about 'er too. Though it's funny never 'aving really seen 'er—like. An' yet feelin' I know 'er right well—better than anybody in a way—like——

HILDA: Don't kid yerself. Letters aren't people. Yer've got to be with 'em—an' look at 'em—an' listen to 'em—an' see 'ow they behave—before you really know 'em. But Eileen's all right, I can tell you.

HERBERT: Well, you ought to know, 'Ilda.

HILDA: I should think I ought. When a girl works with another girl, an' then shares a room in a billet, there isn't much that girl doesn' know about the other one, I can tell yer. My word, if it were some of 'em, I could make your 'air stand on end. If chaps only knew! But Eileen's different. An' you be nice to 'er or yer'll 'ear something from me. An' don't stay too long down 'ere.

HERBERT: What for?

HILDA: 'Cos we're 'aving a bit o' fun—dressin' up an' pretendin' we're all grand or something. (*Breaks off and whispers*) This is Eileen.

[423]

EILEEN *comes slowly and shyly downstairs. The other two watch her.*

HILDA (*slowly, impressively*): Eileen, this is 'Erbert.

EILEEN (*slowly advancing*): Hello!

HERBERT (*with his grin*): Hello!

HILDA (*looking drolly from one to the other*): Well, this is where I get out. But don't just stare at each other. Get it over. An' don't be too long about it neither.

She goes upstairs. The other two, painfully shy, do not even look at each other for a moment. The scene that follows must be played with great delicacy and restraint, with no broadening for easy laughs.

EILEEN (*slowly*): You didn't say you were coming on leave.

HERBERT: No, I didn't know. I said I might be sent 'ome to do some instructin'—remember?

EILEEN: Yes, I remember you said that. I was—hoping—you might be.

HERBERT: An' then—it come quite sudden—same as everything does in the army—like I told you.

EILEEN: Yes. Nothing happens an' then suddenly a lot happens all at once, eh?

HERBERT (*with his grin*): That's right—Eileen.

EILEEN (*after a pause*): I expect it seems all different—here at home—doesn't it?

HERBERT: No—not so very different—and any'ow it's 'ome—an' that's all right. . . .

EILEEN (*slowly, softly*): I expect—I look different to what you thought I'd look—don't I?

HERBERT (*cautiously looking*): No, yer don't. I think yer look just like your photo—yer know, that one yer sent . . .

EILEEN: Yes. But after, I thought I oughtn't to have sent it. It wasn't very good of me.

HERBERT: No, yer look just like it. Only——

EILEEN (*anxiously*): Only what?

HERBERT: Only—yer a bit taller than I thought—like——

EILEEN: Oh—does that matter?

HERBERT: No, of course it doesn't. Besides—I think—well, you look a lot prettier—like——

EILEEN (*delighted*): Oh Herbert—do I?

HERBERT: Yes, yer do. (*Pause.*) Eileen.

[424]

EILEEN: Yes, Herbert?

HERBERT (*slowly*): Did yer mean all them things yer said in your letters?

EILEEN (*softly*): Yes, I did.

HERBERT: Do you still—I mean—like—now that you've seen me an' I'm 'ere an' not out there——?

EILEEN (*looking at him*): I do, Herbert—if you do.

HERBERT: Yes, I do. I mean, I'd like us to get married—an'——

EILEEN: And have a home of our own.

HERBERT: Yes, a 'ome of our own. I've thought a lot about that, Eileen.

EILEEN: So have I. Wouldn't it be wonderful?

HERBERT: Yes. But I don't know when that'll be.

EILEEN: No, but we've waited so long, we can wait a bit longer.

HERBERT (*dubiously*): Yes. Some of our chaps say they'll make it all right for us—like—yer know, there'll be 'omes an' jobs. But a lot o' the chaps say it'll be just like last time—that when we've done the fightin' an' there's no more danger—then we can go an' whistle——

EILEEN (*roused*): That's what happened to my Dad. But it won't be like last time.

HERBERT: 'Ow d'yer know?

EILEEN (*with sudden fierceness*): Because we won't let it be, that's why. This is our country, isn't it? You've gone and fought for it. And I've left home and worked for it. We've given years out of our life to keep it safe, haven't we? All right then. You want a steady job, and I want a home of my own. And we're going to get 'em, and nobody's going to stop us this time.

With abrupt change of mood and tone, hesitantly.

Herbert—now that you've seen me—do you think—it'll be all right?

HERBERT: 'Ow d'yer mean—all right?

EILEEN: Do you think—you could love me?

HERBERT (*ashamed of this*): Well—yes, I do, Eileen.

EILEEN (*with relief*): Then that's all that matters.

She looks at him, smiling, and he takes a step towards her, and is clearly about to take her in his arms and kiss her, when MAJOR WEBBER *enters down right.*

WEBBER: Well, well, well! Hello, another visitor, eh?

EILEEN: Yes, this is Hilda's brother, Herbert. He's—my young man.

[425]

WEBBER (*heartily*): Say, that's fine. We must have a drink on this.

HILDA *hurries downstairs, putting her head round.*

HILDA (*hurriedly calling*): Come, you two, you're wanted upstairs —quick. Yes, both of you.

WEBBER (*puzzled*): What's going on around here?

HILDA (*cheerfully*): You stay there—and you'll see. And when it happens, just keep quiet. Come on, you two, 'urry up. (*She looks upstairs.*) Oh—there's somebody coming. We'll go round the other way.

> She hurries downstairs and bustles them off with her through kitchen. WEBBER *stares after them, then gives himself a drink. After a moment,* TONY ACTON *comes cautiously downstairs. He is now dressed in a sports coat and flannel trousers. He looks about him carefully, sees* WEBBER *with the glass in his hand, and cautiously comes down.*

WEBBER: (*cordially*) Hello! Come right in.

TONY: Thanks.

WEBBER: My name's Webber—George Webber.

TONY: Mine's Acton.

WEBBER: Have some Scotch?

TONY: No, thanks. But I wouldn't mind some beer if there's any going.

WEBBER: Why not? Help yourself.

TONY: Thanks. (*Takes some beer.*) I'm not supposed to be down here—but—er—I ran out of matches——

WEBBER: I can let you have some matches. Don't need 'em. Got a good lighter. (*Throws some matches on the table.*)

TONY: Thanks. Cheers! (*Drinks.*)

WEBBER: Cheers! (*Drinks, then regards* TONY *curiously while latter is lighting a cigarette.*) Mr. Acton, did you say you're not supposed to be down here?

TONY: Yes.

WEBBER: You mean—downstairs here—where we are?

TONY (*smiling*): That's it. Here.

WEBBER (*rather puzzled*): Well, I'm sorry to hear that, Mr. Acton.

TONY: Don't bother about it, Major. It's of no importance at all.

WEBBER: You're staying here, I guess.

TONY: Well, I'm staying here the rest of to-night—with luck. You live here?

WEBBER: Just arrived this evening.

TONY: Did you? So did I. (*Looks about him, then more confidentially.*) Rum show, isn't it?

WEBBER: Now that's very interesting to me, Mr. Acton. Because I said to myself, "George Webber, you're just being plain stoopid."

TONY: Oh—why did you say that to yourself?

WEBBER: Well, because I couldn't get the hang of things around here. First I thought this, and then I thought that. But I reckon that right now I'm getting things under control—yes, *sir*.

TONY: I wish I could say the same.

WEBBER: You from the factory, Mr. Acton?

TONY: What factory?

WEBBER: Why, the aircraft factory where Lady Farfield and these girls work.

TONY (*astonished*): Lady Farfield — you mean — this woman here——?

WEBBER: She's the only one around here, isn't she?

TONY: I wouldn't know, old boy, I really wouldn't know. I haven't anything under control to-night. If it's the one I mean, I suppose she goes over there occasionally and cuts the cake or presents the prizes—eh?

WEBBER: No, *sir*. She worked a long time at the bench, and now she's a charge-hand. The other folks she's asked in work with her —including the foreman.

TONY (*with extreme scepticism*): You wouldn't be pulling my leg by any chance, would you? I think not. Oh no. All right, we've had that. Now ask me what I'm doing.

WEBBER (*rather surprised*): Just what I was wondering. That's why I asked if you were from the factory.

TONY (*smoothly and confidentially*): The answer is No. There's no real money in this war work, old boy. I'm in the Black Market. Doing a nice big deal at the moment in clothes coupons.

WEBBER (*unpleasantly surprised*): Clothes coupons?

TONY: That's the idea. Not forged, y'know. Oh—no, quite genuine. Of course I wouldn't like to say how the fella managed to lay his hands on quarter of a million——

WEBBER (*same tone*): Quarter of a million!

TONY (*confidentially*): And a few over, old boy, quite a few over. But they're outside the deal. The little woman wants a few new outfits—you know how they are.

> He winks at WEBBER, who stares at him aghast. While they
> are staring at each other, CAMYON, still in uniform, comes very

cautiously downstairs. When he sees only ACTON *and* WEBBER, *he looks relieved, but when* ACTON *sees him,* ACTON *looks embarrassed.*

CAMYON (*rather gruffly*): What are you doing down here?

TONY (*apologetically*): Had to come down, sir. Hadn't any matches.

CAMYON: Hm. I looked into your room—so had to come down to see what you were up to.

TONY: Quite so, sir. Er—this is Major Webber—Group-Captain Camyon.

CAMYON: How d'you do?

WEBBER: Pleased to meet you, Group-Captain. You look as if you've come from overseas.

CAMYON: I have. Only got back yesterday. After four years.

WEBBER: Fine! There must be quite a lot you can tell us that I'd be very glad to know, Group-Captain. Have some Scotch?

CAMYON: No thanks.

WEBBER: It's good Scotch. I was darned lucky to get it.

CAMYON: Oh—it's yours, is it?

WEBBER: Yes, *sir*.

CAMYON: Oh—then I'll change my mind—thanks—and have some. I thought it probably belonged to—er—the house.

As WEBBER *pours out the whisky,* TONY, *who is obviously uncomfortable, strolls with assumed nonchalance away from the table, examining the animals' heads, etc.* WEBBER *sees this as an opportunity to have a private word with* CAMYON *about him.*

CAMYON (*receiving whisky*): Thanks. I could do with this. Good luck! (*Drinks.*)

WEBBER (*very confidentially*): Group-Captain, you seem to know that young man.

CAMYON: Yes I do. Why?

WEBBER (*carefully*): Well—I'm nothing but a stranger around here, and we've been warned not to interfere—but I feel it's my dooty to tell you that that young man says he's operating the Black Market.

CAMYON (*astonished*): The Black Market!

WEBBER (*gravely*): Yes, *sir*. Illegal trading in clothes coupons— hundreds of thousands of 'em. Boasts of it——

CAMYON: Nonsense! He's my Squadron-Leader, who came back with me. (*Calling sharply*) Acton.

TONY (*turning and advancing*): Sir!

[428]

CAMYON: What the blazes do you mean by talking nonsense about the Black Market to this officer?

TONY (*embarrassed*): Well—sir—we were just chatting——

WEBBER (*amused*): And you were just joshing me, eh? Well, I ought to have known. Okay, Squadron-Leader, don't apologise.

CAMYON: It won't do, though. To begin with, it's bad manners —and it might be dangerous. What's the idea?

TONY (*apologetically*): I'm sorry, sir—but, you see, he began pulling my leg, so I thought I'd better not be too stand-offish—I know how the Americans like a bit of leg-pulling—so I pulled his.

WEBBER (*heartily*): That's all right with me, Squadron-Leader. But—say—I didn't do any leg-pulling. I was only telling you about the folks here.

TONY: I know. And didn't you tell me that Lady Farfield was entertaining a few girl chums from the aircraft factory, where she's just been made a charge-hand?

WEBBER (*firmly*): I certainly did.

CAMYON: Oh well, then you did start it, Major, and you can hardly blame him. I might have done the same myself. After all, we British have to prove we have some sense of humour.

TONY: Just what I thought, sir. Couldn't let the old side down, I thought. Had to do something.

CAMYON: Quite. Mind you, Major Webber, this doesn't mean I'm defending these people here. They'd no business to amuse themselves filling you up with all that stuff about being factory hands when in fact they're keeping a houseful of servants and throwing great idiotic parties. I could hear 'em upstairs giggling and running up and down the corridors and screaming their silly heads off.

TONY: So could I, sir. Black show, I thought.

CAMYON: Couldn't be worse. (*To* WEBBER, *who is gaping at them*) But don't imagine everybody's like this over here. You just happen to have struck a bad patch, I imagine, that's all. So have we. It happens not to seem particularly funny to me—for a special reason——

TONY (*seriously*): She slapped his face, you know. I hope you don't mind my mentioning it, sir.

CAMYON: Yes, of course I do, you ass.

WEBBER (*bewildered*): Who slapped your face?

CAMYON: Lady Farfield. She happens to be — er — an old friend——

WEBBER (*cutting in, urgently*): Now wait a minute. Let's try and straighten this out. I guess that old butler showed you in, didn't he?

TONY: He did.

WEBBER: And you listened to him, didn't you?

CAMYON: We couldn't help it.

WEBBER (*firmly*): Well, so did I! And I found out afterwards it was a lot of hooey—yes, *sir*.

CAMYON: Hooey!

WEBBER (*triumphantly*): Nothing else but. The old man's really talking about the past. He's so old he keeps forgetting.

> CAMYON *exchanges a startled glance with* TONY.

I was here at supper. There are two of us—a Civil Servant and myself—who are billeted here—and then there are a few folks from the factory—a foreman and a couple of factory girls——

TONY: Hoy, you're not starting that all over again, are you?

WEBBER (*earnestly*): But it's true. I assure you I never was more serious in my life.

CAMYON (*slowly*): I don't know what to make of this.

TONY: Don't want to butt in, sir, but did you notice that little Land Girl on the stairs when we first came in? Very serious type, I thought, and didn't seem to fit in with our notion of the place at all. Been on my mind, that girl. Perhaps we've been all wrong, sir.

WEBBER: Sure you have. And our hostess has been doing a swell job. Given up her old privileges. No class distinctions. Democracy with its sleeves rolled up.

CAMYON: My God, Tony, if we have been wrong, we've made precious idiots of ourselves. Or at least, *I* have.

WEBBER: Don't worry. We'll all be having a good laugh over it soon.

> *Sound of women's voices—light laughter and chatter—can now be heard from upstairs.*

TONY: Listen! They're coming down.

WEBBER (*beaming*): Now you'll see. Just a little bunch of factory folks. Foreman. Kids from the factory in their old clothes. Fighting democracy. You'll see. And get your apology ready—you're going to need it.

> *They look expectantly towards stairs. There arrives, very impressively, the following procession: first, old* KENTON, *who is wearing a scarlet coat, and is carrying a large branched candlestick. Then follow, in close order,* LADY FRANCES, LOTTA, PAULINE, (*who wears a full loose dress*), EILEEN *and* HILDA, *and they are*

*all wearing dresses—one or two modern, others period—that
enhance their respective personalities, and they all look very
feminine, romantic, glamorous, and give the impression of being
haughtily conscious of this. Behind them comes* KILLIGREW, *carrying his violin, and wearing full evening dress, the jacket of which
is too tight for him. Behind him come* SAM *and* HERBERT, *who have
been rigged up fancifully and rather sketchily but still impressively
as footmen, and carry tray with glasses and a bottle of champagne,
etc. The procession moves in slowly, ignoring the men, until the
women are grouped round the piano.*

WEBBER (*bowled over*): Boy—oh boy!

TONY (*also bowled over*): Crrr-ikey!

CAMYON (*to* WEBBER, *with furious irony*): Just a little bunch of
homely folks! Kids from the factory in their old clothes! Democracy
in its shirt-sleeves winning the war!

WEBBER (*earnestly*): I assure you, Grou——

CAMYON (*through his teeth*): Oh—stop acting the goat!

LADY FARFIELD (*across from piano, where ladies are*): Edward—I
beg your pardon—Group-Captain Camyon——

CAMYON (*curtly from fireplace*): Well?

LADY FARFIELD (*with touch of mockery*): As the very sight of us
seems to annoy you so much—and the music may annoy you still
more—there's no need for you to stay down here, you know. You
have my permission to return to your room.

CAMYON (*curtly*): Thank you, Frances—I beg your pardon, Lady
Farfield—but if you've no strong objection—I prefer to stay here.
I'm expecting an important telephone call.

LADY FARFIELD: About requisitioning a house, perhaps?

CAMYON: Yes. But don't let me interrupt your—er—music.

LADY FARFIELD (*smiling and playing*): We don't propose to.

*They begin singing a Viennese light opera song, just a short snatch
of it. During this,* PAULINE *can come nearer to* TONY *and smile
at him, and finding her irresistible he moves towards her, only to
be called back by a stern look and a warning* "Acton!" *from his
chief at the fireplace. As the singing ends.*

LADY FARFIELD (*still idly playing*): Kenton, the champagne.

KENTON: Yes, me lady.

He begins serving the champagne, as the music drifts dreamily on.

CAMYON (*with angry irony to* WEBBER): Just a few little factory
girls straight from the benches!

WEBBER: Certainly looks a swell bunch—yes, *sir*. Surprised me.

[431]

Always had a notion your British women didn't care how they looked——

CAMYON (*almost bursting with fury*): Dammit, sir—will you—kindly—drop it. (*Turns away.*)

TONY (*to* WEBBER, *whispering*): Turn it up, old boy. Or Groupie'll go up in flames.

WEBBER: But I tell you——

TONY (*reproachfully*): No, no, old boy. We bought it. Wizard girl there, though.

KENTON (*approaching them*): Champagne, sir?

WEBBER (*taking one*): You bet! Thanks.

KENTON (*to* TONY): And you, sir?

TONY (*taking one, promptly*): Certainly.

CAMYON (*turning, sternly*): Leave that stuff alone, Acton.

TONY: Certainly, sir. (*To* KENTON, *severely, returning glass*) Certainly not.

KENTON (*to* CAMYON): Champagne, sir?

CAMYON (*grimly*): Yes. (*He takes the glass and flings the contents impressively on the floor. A cry from the girls.*) Now what do you think of that?

KENTON (*sturdily*): Not much, sir. This is the very last bottle in my cellar, and probably the last I'll ever see. No, sir, I don't think much of that.

LADY FARFIELD (*standing up from piano*): All right, Kenton, thank you. We shan't need you any more.

KENTON: Thank you, me lady.

He goes off down left.

LADY FARFIELD (*calling across to* CAMYON): That was unpardonable.

CAMYON (*stiffly*): It was. I'll apologise to your butler if I see him again. After all, one can't blame an old servant for the faults of his employer.

LADY FARFIELD (*with irony*): Very considerate of you!

They now play and sing again, preferably something light, charming, mocking. As the music dies down——

LADY FARFIELD: Herbert—cigarettes for the gentlemen.

The embarrassed and grinning HERBERT *comes down with a small tray with twenty cigarettes on it.*

HERBERT: Er—cigarettes?

CAMYON (*sternly*): Come here. And take the grin off your face.

HERBERT: Yes, sir.

CAMYON (*indignantly*): A great healthy chap like you playing the flunkey at a time like this! What have *you* been doing the last few years? Handing round cigarettes and folding table napkins?

HERBERT (*equally indignant*): Me? I've just come back from the Eighth Army. 'Ere, I've 'ad enough o' this.

He puts down the little tray and hurries across to the stairs, but turns as he reaches them.

But don't forget them's my twenty Players. (*He goes upstairs.*)

CAMYON (*to* TONY *and* WEBBER): Eighth Army! Twenty Players! What *is* this?

LADY FARFIELD (*mockingly*): Just a little musical evening. Come on girls.

ACTON *starts to dance with* PAULINE, CAMYON *turns and sees him.* LADY FARFIELD *plays and all sing, applause.*

CAMYON: Acton!

ACTON *leaves* PAULINE. WEBBER *rises and dances with her.*

KILLIGREW (*who has been tuning his fiddle*): Quiet, please!

LADY FARFIELD: Now for some real music. (*With air of hostess with treat*) Madame Lotta Schulberg, the famous soubrette of the Vienna Volksopera has very kindly consented to sing to us.

Some applause.

WEBBER (*whispering to* CAMYON): She's the cook really.

CAMYON (*with fierce irony*): And you're the Fairy Queen.

WEBBER (*earnestly*): Now—no kidding—I——

CAMYON (*cutting in roughly*): Oh—for God's sake—drop it.

LADY FARFIELD *at the piano with* KILLIGREW *behind her with his violin, the three girls picturesquely grouped round and* LOTTA *in front. She sings a number from light opera. As she finishes the telephone rings.*

TONY: Shall I answer it, sir? (*Moves towards the phone.*)

LADY FARFIELD (*rises*): Please do.

KILLIGREW (*to* LADY FARFIELD): My G string's gone. Have another somewhere upstairs but it may take some finding. So——

He smilingly waves a hand, as if in farewell, as he goes to staircase. Then turns there and calls across to LOTTA.

Any chance of early tea in the morning?

LOTTA (*firmly*): No chance at all.

KILLIGREW: It's about eighteen months since I had any early

[433]

morning tea. (*Smiling across at* CAMYON) You've probably had gallons—um?

CAMYON (*angrily*): I never touch the stuff.

As KILLIGREW *vanishes, the telephone rings again.*

EILEEN: We ought to go upstairs and change. Come on, Hilda.

LOTTA: I will go with you—and put these dresses away.

HILDA (*as they go to stairs, turning to* CAMYON): But one day factory girls'll look like queens—and don't you try to stop it.

CAMYON: Who said I wanted to stop it!

HILDA, EILEEN, LOTTA *go upstairs. The telephone rings again.*

LADY FARFIELD (*in large clear tone*): Come along, Pauline, we'll go along to the drawing-room—and let Group-Captain Camyon take his call.

CAMYON (*ironically*): Thank you!

LADY FARFIELD (*looking at him from near door*): But be careful now, Edward. Or I swear I'll never speak to you again.

She sweeps out, with PAULINE. *Telephone rings again.* WEBBER, *who has been holding door open for* LADY FARFIELD, *shuts it and comes in. He,* SAM, TONY *watch* CAMYON, *who after some hesitation goes to telephone.*

CAMYON (*at telephone*): Yes, Group-Captain Camyon here . . . What? . . . Who d'you want to talk to? . . . What? . . . Here . . . Wait—— Gone. (*To the others*) Some nonsense about a farmer and some fiddles. What is this—a madhouse?

WEBBER (*roaring with laughter*): That'll be Killigrew and his string quartettes. Well, well, well!

CAMYON (*bewildered*): Who's Killigrew—this fiddler chap here?

WEBBER (*still laughing*): Yes. One of your prominent Civil Servants. Ministry of Reconstruction.

CAMYON: Now are you starting all over again——?

WEBBER (*still laughing*): But I've told you the exact truth the whole time. (*To* SAM, *who has now taken off his footman's coat, and is lighting his pipe.*) Sam—you'd better tell him.

SAM: Now tak' it easy, Group-Captain Camyon. This is no madder nor most 'ouses. We're all bit barmy these days any'ow.

WEBBER (*laughing*): I'll say we are.

TONY (*to* WEBBER): That's all right, old boy, but you're not carrying the can. Let's get all this buttoned up.

CAMYON: Now wait a minute. What kind of a footman are you?

SAM: No kind. Don't be daft. Ah'm foreman at factory where we make the new Prestons.

CAMYON: The new Prestons! I was coming over to your place.

SAM: Ah know, Ah know. An' me an' you's met before.

CAMYON (*staring at him*): So we have. I thought I'd seen you somewhere——

SAM: About twelve year since, an' you wor a Squadron-Leader then an' yer come to t'old Kestrel Five factory. Sam Cawthra.

CAMYON: Sam Cawthra—yes, I remember. But what on earth are you doing here?

SAM: Oh we're 'avin' a little party—so we 'ad a bit o' fun wi' yer——

CAMYON: Bit of fun! Now look here, Sam, let's get this straight. Have Lady Farfield and those girls really been working with you?

SAM: Ay, an' good workers an' all. Charge-'and now, Lady Farfield is.

CAMYON: But they looked——

SAM (*cutting in*): They looked as if they'd gone upstairs an' put some fancy clothes on. That's all. And—damn it—yer can't expect 'em to wear mucky overalls an' corduroy pants all the time.

TONY: Sir, we've bought it.

CAMYON: My God—I've made an ass of myself.

SAM: Well, yer not first an' yer won't be t'last.

CAMYON: No, but this is serious. (*Turning to* WEBBER) I'm sorry, Major Webber.

WEBBER: Think nothing of it. Enjoyed every minute of it. Why, I haven't laughed so much in years—— (*Looks as if he's about to start laughing again.*)

TONY: Easy, old boy. We've had it now.

PAULINE *enters from drawing-room.*

PAULINE (*calmly*): Sorry to intrude. But I'm thirsty.

As she goes to drinks, TONY *and* WEBBER *go too.*

TONY: Of course. Good scheme! What'll you have?

SAM (*taking* CAMYON *downstage*): No, don't worry, there's no real 'arm done.

CAMYON (*quietly but urgently*): No, but you see, we quarrelled before the war—and I was in the right then, and she knew it but wouldn't admit it. And now that she's put me nicely in the wrong, she's never going to look at me again.

SAM: Ah can see yer know nowt about women. It's just when yer in the right that they can't forgive yer. Now that yer in the wrong, all yer 'ave to do is just to say 'ow sorry you are an' what a lot yer think about 'er—an' Bob's yer uncle. (*Moving him towards door down right.*) An' this is yer chance.

CAMYON (*hesitates a second, then bracing*): Thanks, Sam. I'll try.

SAM *makes for the stairs.*

SAM: We'll 'ave to be settin' off 'ome soon. Well, go on. Up the Air Force!

He goes upstairs, leaving PAULINE *and* TONY *obviously wishing to be rid of* WEBBER.

WEBBER (*obviously beginning to settle down*): Well, well! Turned out quite a party after all. Yes, *sir!*

PAULINE (*gravely regarding him*): Major Webber. You're looking very, very tired now. You really are.

WEBBER (*concerned*): Is that so?

PAULINE (*gravely*): Yes, it is. I think you ought to go to bed—and never mind about us.

TONY: Good scheme! You look all in, sir. Probably had a long day.

WEBBER: Well, I have had quite a long confused kinda day. May take me some time, I guess, to get the hang of things in this little neck of the woods.

PAULINE: Major Webber, I think you're very sweet.

WEBBER (*smiling*): Well, that's fine. You're a pretty cute trick yourself, Miss Pauline. And I'll turn in, I guess. Good night.

TONY *and* PAULINE: Good night.

WEBBER (*turning on stairs*): I'll get around to it in time.

He goes upstairs.

TONY: Mind you, I know how he feels.

PAULINE: Why do you?

TONY: Well, what with last night——

PAULINE (*sternly*): Were you *drinking?*

TONY: Well—we had a can or two.

PAULINE: Any girls?

TONY: No—no—chaps—just chaps.

PAULINE: Well, pull yourself together, because I want to talk to you seriously. You're not, I hope, the type of officer who is looking forward to nothing after the war but the secretaryship of a second-rate golf club in a decaying society—are you?

TONY: Good lord—no. Hate golf. And I'm full of plans and ambition and all that—you'd be surprised.

PAULINE: That's settled then. We can talk about your plans afterwards. In the meantime I shall call you Tony and you can call me Pauline.

TONY (*sincerely*): Thanks very much, Pauline.

KENTON (*entering from kitchen*): Beg pardon, miss. But is her ladyship in the drawing-room?

PAULINE: She is, and you mustn't disturb her. There isn't anything more for you to do. Just go straight upstairs to your little room and have one of your interesting dreams.

KENTON: Thank you, miss. I 'ad one last night, miss. I dreamt I took my old aunt, who used to keep the draper's, to the races at Goodwood.

PAULINE: Well, to-night you try and get her into the Royal Enclosure at Ascot.

KENTON (*with a sudden smile—the first*): Thank you, miss. And —good luck!

> *He goes back into kitchen.*

PAULINE (*cool and clear*): Well, Tony, I've decided to take a deep personal interest in you.

TONY: Wizard! Absolutely wizard!

PAULINE: But first, I want to know why you keep staring at me in a puzzled rather than a fascinated manner.

TONY: Well—look here—you *are* the little Land Girl I saw when I first came in, aren't you?

PAULINE: Why? Does it matter?

TONY: It does rather. She completely bowled me over.

PAULINE (*indignantly*): So much for glamour. Look!

> *She begins hastily pulling off her dress.*

TONY (*in alarm*): Hoy! Steady! Whoa!

> PAULINE *now shows herself in her Land Girl's uniform. She smoothes her hair back to what it was before.*

PAULINE (*holding dress over her arm*): Well, here you are, idiot. Specimen of the Women's Land Army—Second World War.

TONY (*lost in admiration*): What a girl! You've got everything.

> *While they gaze at each other,* CAMYON *and* LADY FARFIELD *enter from drawing-room.*

PAULINE (*hastily*): I must take this dress upstairs. You can come with me, if you like.

They begin to move towards the stairs.

CAMYON (*with mock severity*): Where are you going, Acton?

PAULINE (*coolly*): I've asked Squadron-Leader Acton to go with me as I'm very nervous at night.

LADY FARFIELD (*laughingly*): Pauline!

TONY: That's right, sir. Nervous type.

CAMYON (*grinning*): Go on. (*As the two youngsters hurry off, he turns to* LADY FARFIELD.) And another thing, Frances, I had a splitting bad headache.

LADY FARFIELD (*coldly*): Well, you shouldn't drink too much.

CAMYON: I haven't been drinking too much. You see, I got rather a nastly little crack on the head a few months ago and though it's healed now, it troubles me at times, and especially after travelling.

LADY FARFIELD (*concerned*): Oh—Edward, why didn't you tell me?

CAMYON: Hadn't a chance to. (*Moves towards her.*) But never mind that. What I really wanted to say was—not only was I wrong to-night, for which I apologise all over again, but also I was badly wrong before the war. I'm sorry.

LADY FARFIELD: I'm not so sure you were.

CAMYON: Oh yes, I was. And please say you forgive me. And don't forget I've already paid heavily for my stupidity.

LADY FARFIELD: How?

CAMYON: By having lost you for all this time. And to-night—when I saw you—at last—you took my breath away.

LADY FARFIELD: I certainly took your breath away—slapping you like that. And probably now that I'm a manual worker I don't know my own strength. I'm sorry, Edward.

CAMYON: I asked for it. But please remember, Frances, I've been away overseas for four years, working with men who are wondering all the time about their womenfolk.

LADY FARFIELD (*gravely*): You tell them that we women at home work for them, pray for them, and think of nothing else, deep down, but the time when it'll be over and they're all back. And that's our real life.

CAMYON (*slowly*): I suppose I've no right even to ask, now. But —are you waiting for somebody like that?

LADY FARFIELD (*half-smiling*): No, Edward—not now.

CAMYON (*about to embrace her*): Frances—darling!

[438]

LADY FARFIELD: Darling!

Sound of factory party and HERBERT *coming downstairs.*

LADY FARFIELD: Oh damn! They're all coming down. But Edward, there's something I want to hear you say to other people before you talk to me.

As HILDA, EILEEN, SAM *and* HERBERT *come down.*

I suppose you ought to go really, but it seems a pity.

HILDA: Yes, it does. 'Ere, we've got our bikes, but what about 'Erbert?

EILEEN: I've fixed up to borrow one for him here.

HILDA (*to* HERBERT): You see—got somebody to look after you now.

SAM (*to* LADY FARFIELD): Well, thank you very much. Ah've 'ad a good evening, Ah don't know about t'others.

EILEEN (*shy and happy*): We all have. Haven't we, Herbert?

HERBERT (*grinning*): That's right. Except for that footman business.

CAMYON: Sorry about that, Corporal.

HERBERT: No 'arm done, sir. And—er—Lady Farfield, I wish you'd keep them twenty Players—like—just for what you've given me to-night——

LADY FARFIELD (*surprised*): But I haven't given you anything, have I?

HERBERT (*indicating* EILEEN): Well—look what I've got.

EILEEN (*confused but radiant*): Oh—'Erbert!

CAMYON: Quite right, Corporal. Ladies, I seem to have misjudged you all. I'm sorry. But you shouldn't have looked so gorgeous.

HILDA (*to* LADY FARFIELD): There! You see, he's nice really.

SAM: Come on.

CAMYON: Good night, Sam, see you at the factory in the morning.

Chorus of good-byes, thank you's, etc., as they all go up to main door. Enter LOTTA *right.*

LADY FARFIELD: And are you nice really, Edward? (*To* LOTTA) You need not sit up, Lotta.

LOTTA (*picks up tray*): I know. I go to the kitchen to make some porridge. Always I forget the porridge. Good night. (*Exit* LOTTA.)

LADY FARFIELD (*moving to settee*): And now that we've got this place to ourselves at last, let's be quiet and peaceful.

CAMYON (*sitting beside her*): I'm all for it, Frances. I've had quite a day.

LADY FARFIELD: So have I, darling. So let's make the best of it. Just relax and be quiet.

CAMYON: Enjoy our bit of luck. You know, I'm not bad-tempered really. A peaceful quiet chap when I'm allowed to be.

LADY FARFIELD: Perhaps we're all peaceful quiet chaps when we're allowed to be, darling. (*There is a loud ringing at the front door.*) Oh—my goodness!

> *Before they can move, door bursts open and three people carrying instruments and scores burst in. An elderly man with a beard, a stout middle-aged woman and a queer-looking young girl.*

ELDERLY MAN (*loud rural voice*): Evening, all! This is it, isn't it? Farfield Hall. Mr. Killi—summat or other—asked for us to come. Onny time, he said, an' sooner the better, I thought. So we are here, though I don't know what use young Lucy'll be——

> KILLIGREW, *armed with his fiddle and scores, dashes downstairs, while the others stare, amazed.*

KILLIGREW (*in tremendous form*): Hello, hello, hello! Happened to have my head out of the window and saw you arriving in your gig or trap or whatever it is. Delighted to see you—Mr. er—— (*consults his note-book*) Mr. Bramley——

ELDERLY MAN: No.

KILLIGREW: No, of course not. Mr.—er—Fraser——

ELDERLY MAN: No.

KILLIGREW: I mean, Mr. Henniman——

ELDERLY MAN: No.

KILLIGREW: Never mind. Delighted to see you. (*Indicating girl*) Looks a bit young for the Mozart—but we'll manage——

> *There is now a tremendous sound of lorries arriving, female voices shouting, etc.*

> COMMODORE PENTWORTHY *bursts in, with uniformed girls behind her, carrying files, etc.*

COMMODORE PENTWORTHY (*in loud official tone*): I'm billeting the whole of my headquarters here. There's nowhere else—and I warned you, Frances.

LADY FARFIELD (*protesting loudly*): Phyllis, you can't all descend on us like this.

COMMODORE PENTWORTHY (*ignoring them, in commanding tones*): All right, Millicent, unload as quickly as possible. Straight up the stairs, girls. Office files and equipment before personal luggage. Come along, girls, sharp now—tell the lorries to clear the doorway as soon as possible——

As she goes on giving loud orders, LADY FARFIELD *and* LOTTA *keep on protesting,* PAULINE *bursts into a scream of laughter, in which* TONY *joins, while* CAMYON *joins* LADY FARFIELD *in protesting. The din outside gets louder. The orchestra plays a gay mocking tune, and the curtain falls.*

END OF PLAY

EVER SINCE PARADISE

*A Discursive Entertainment,
chiefly referring to Love and
Marriage, in Three Acts*

CHARACTERS

The Musicians	The Commentators	The Example
PHILIP	WILLIAM	PAUL
JOYCE	HELEN	ROSEMARY

The Action is in many different places, and the time is the Present, but between Wars.

Ever Since Paradise—Copyright, 1946, *by John Boynton Priestley.*

First produced at the New Theatre, London, on June 4th, 1947, with the following cast:

PHILIP	DENNIS ARUNDELL
JOYCE	JANE CARR
WILLIAM	ROGER LIVESEY
HELEN	URSULA JEANS
ROSEMARY	JOY SHELTON
PAUL	HUGH KELLY

ACT I

The main curtain may or may not be used, according to the size of the stage. On each side of the stage, as far apart as possible, is a grand piano, each exactly alike, with the keyboard downstage, at an angle of about sixty degrees to the footlights. Near each piano, a little farther upstage, is a chair for each commentator. These are backed by dark curtaining, hiding the stage behind, and there is an entrance through this curtaining at each side, used only by WILLIAM *and* HELEN. *Set a little farther back, occupying all the centre of the stage, with a small proscenium formed by a continuation of the curtaining behind the platforms, is a separate little stage, which may or may not be raised on a small rostrum, and is eight or nine feet deep. This inner stage has its own curtain in front, about nine feet high, and it is essential that this can be pulled up or drawn along very easily, apparently at a touch. At the opening this curtain is down, and the inner stage cannot be seen.*

House lights go down and both pianos are lit. PHILIP *and* JOYCE, *two youngish people in simple evening dress (*PHILIP *in dinner jacket) are seated at the pianos.* PHILIP *at the right and* JOYCE *at the left. They begin playing the overture, which goes along splendidly for two or three minutes, both keeping perfect time. Then they begin to sound ragged and look worried. He wants to increase the tempo and she is lagging behind. Finally, with a discordant crash, they stop, glaring at each other.*

PHILIP (*rising angrily*): There you are, you see!

JOYCE (*rising angrily*): It's not my fault.

PHILIP: Of course it is.

JOYCE: No it isn't, it's your fault.

PHILIP: No it isn't, you were dragging it again.

JOYCE: I wasn't. You were racing away at a ridiculous pace.

PHILIP: I wasn't.

JOYCE: You were. Always the same! Want to rush everything.

PHILIP: I don't want to rush everything.

JOYCE: Yes, you do. Going and taking that cottage!

PHILIP (*very angrily*): What's my taking that cottage got to do with your dragging the time again——?

Enter WILLIAM *in dinner jacket.*

WILLIAM (*reproachfully*): I say, I say, this won't do, you know. You two ought to be playing, not shouting at each other. (*To audience*) I'm so sorry about this. Do excuse us, please! (*To the pianists*) You were playing so well too. I was just remarking to Helen how well you were playing—and then—no more music but another quarrel.

JOYCE: It's his fault. He began to rush it again.

WILLIAM: Now, Philip, you mustn't rush it——

PHILIP: I wasn't. She *will* drag it.

WILLIAM: Now, Joyce, you really mustn't drag it——

JOYCE: I never do. That's just his stupidity.

PHILIP (*rising angrily*): It isn't. It's your——

WILLIAM (*very forcefully*): Stop it, stop it, stop it! Now if one of you would condescend to rush a little less.

PHILIP *and* JOYCE *both sit at their pianos.*

then no doubt you'd keep together, be in time,

HELEN *enters in simple but striking evening dress.*

in exquisite unison, in beautiful harmony, and you'd both be happy and we'd be happy. Whereas——

HELEN: William, you always go on too long.

WILLIAM (*rather annoyed*): How do you mean—I always go on too long?

HELEN: You shouldn't go on with that *Whereas*. Nobody wants your *whereas*. And it's pompous. You're rather inclined to be pompous, you know.

WILLIAM (*horrified*): Pompous! My dear Helen, I'm the least pompous man who ever lived.

JOYCE: You're *all* pompous.

HELEN: Perfectly true, Joyce, dear. They *are* all pompous. But when William has a grievance, I think he's really above the average in pompousness.

PHILIP *audibly guffaws.* WILLIAM *glares across at him.*

WILLIAM: If you're going to snigger and provide her with an appreciative audience, she'll go on for hours.

HELEN: Audience! That reminds me. (*To the audience, with tremendous charm*) I'm so sorry about all this. Do excuse us, please.

WILLIAM (*growling. Pats her on the shoulder*): I've said that already.

HELEN (*sweetly*): Possibly, but perhaps when a little charm is added to the apology——

WILLIAM (*cutting in*): Charm! If there's one quality more contemptible than another in your contemptible bag of tricks, it's this

famous feminine charm. As soon as I see that rotten little piece of
scented silk run up as a flag, I know that honesty and decency are
about to be scuttled.

PHILIP: And I agree.

HELEN (*turning to* PHILIP): Only because you haven't any, Philip
dear.

PHILIP: Oh—I don't know about that.

HELEN (*smiling sweetly at* PHILIP): No, Philip, you don't know
about it.

WILLIAM (*staring at her, then turning her round to face him*): Now
what's the matter with you?

HELEN (*with wide-eyed innocence*): Nothing that I know of,
William. Why?

WILLIAM: Because you're behaving very badly, that's why. You
come on here, looking—I must admit—very delightful, shining and
smiling upon us like a May moon——

HELEN: Thank you, my pet.

WILLIAM: I'm not your pet. And keep away, keep away!

HELEN: Oh—why?

WILLIAM: Because—well, it's less confusing and easier for me to
say what I have to say——

HELEN: Then don't say it. Nobody cares.

WILLIAM: And what I say is that you come on here and instead of
trying to help us out of our little difficulty, you at once make everything worse. Now why—why—do you go and make everything worse?

HELEN: Shall I tell you?

WILLIAM (*exasperated*): I'm asking you to tell me. Though I doubt
if you know.

HELEN: Oh yes, I do. It's perfectly simple. You see, being a
woman I must be noticed and appreciated. We take a great deal of
trouble over our appearance—about twenty times as much trouble
as you do, for instance—and we insist upon first being noticed and
appreciated. Now if you'd said, at once, that I was looking very
nice, or if you'd only smiled at me, that would have been quite enough.
Immediately I'd have felt full of goodwill and kindness and helpful-
ness, and I'd have tried to do my best for everybody. But first of all
I must be noticed and appreciated.

WILLIAM: That seems to me all wrong.

HELEN: Yes, but then you happen to be a man and I happen to
be a woman.

WILLIAM: It shouldn't make so much difference.

HELEN: But it does.

WILLIAM: Well, does it? I know women who aren't like that.

HELEN: Yes, and how much time do you spend with them?

JOYCE *bursts out laughing*.

WILLIAM (*speaking to* JOYCE): I think you'd better start playing again.

HELEN (*rising*): No, not yet.

WILLIAM: Why not?

JOYCE *stops playing*.

HELEN: We ought to look into this a little more, this man-and-woman business.

PHILIP (*with gloomy approval*): Yes, it needs looking into.

HELEN: Of course it does. Now it's no use taking ourselves, is it?

WILLIAM (*brightening at this*): Not a bit. Lot of talk about ourselves—only leads to trouble—scenes, temper and tears—terrible! No use, you see, unless you can be detached.

HELEN: You love being detached, don't you?

WILLIAM: Can't observe properly unless you're detached. That's obvious.

HELEN: All right then, we'll take some other pair.

PHILIP: What about Henry and Muriel?

JOYCE: Dull.

WILLIAM: Very dull.

HELEN: I'm afraid you're right. Well, you suggest somebody.

WILLIAM: Boris and Nina.

HELEN: Oh—no, just a long cat-and-dog fight broken by an occasional orgy.

WILLIAM (*thoughtfully*): True. Though I've always wanted to be in at an orgy. All this writing and talk about orgies, and yet you never seem to catch up with one. Every place I've ever been to, they've always just stopped having them. "You ought to have been here last year," they say. "It was terrible."

PHILIP: I know.

JOYCE: How do you mean, you know?

WILLIAM: Now, Joyce, don't you two start all over again. Look at your music or something——

HELEN (*triumphantly*): I know the very pair. Not too dull, not too wild. Very nice and rather typical. Paul and Rosemary.

WILLIAM: Rosemary and Paul. Yes, they might do. Pleasant pair. As you say, nice people. Not very intelligent, perhaps, but I can supply the intelligence——

HELEN: And you've heard what's happening to them?

WILLIAM: No. Not busting up, are they?

HELEN: Sit down and pay attention. You'll see. Joyce, Philip!

They begin playing some broken, discordant music. Curtains open, to reveal room whose few props suggest waiting-room in a solicitor's office. PAUL, *in middle thirties, with horn-rimmed spectacles and wearing dark overcoat and muffler (to facilitate quick change) is moving about like a man kept waiting for an unpleasant appointment. A noise outside, then* ROSEMARY'S *voice is heard off, saying, "Oh in here. Thank you!" She enters also wearing heavy coat, and looking pale and miserable. She stares at him. He looks very embarrassed.*

PAUL (*with an effort*): I'm afraid this is—er—rather embarrassing —Rosemary.

ROSEMARY (*with similar effort*): Yes—Paul—I'm afraid it is.

PAUL: Well, it's not my fault. . . . I had a note from Coulson asking me to be here at half-past three—to answer some questions about the—the divorce . . .

ROSEMARY (*tiny voice*): Yes, so had I.

PAUL (*restlessly*): Oh, I say—monstrous thing for Coulson to do —asking us both here at the same time. Shows you how blankly insensitive these lawyers are. Typical lawyer's trick, this. Damn Coulson!

ROSEMARY (*faintly*): Oh—I don't think—it's perhaps—(*dies away.*)

PAUL: What?

ROSEMARY: No—nothing . . .

PAUL: Look here, I'll go and wait out there.

ROSEMARY: No—it——

PAUL: Don't mind a bit.

Goes, crossing in front of her. Just as he has passed, she makes a movement as if to halt him, but then sinks back. He goes out and we hear the door closing behind him. She stares after him, then her face begins working, and then she starts sobbing.

WILLIAM: I say, this is too bad.

Curtains close.

Now, Helen.

The curtains have closed and with the broken discordant music as before.

[451]

HELEN (*sympathetically and satirically*): What made it all the worse, of course, is that obviously it was she who had asked their solicitor to send for them both at the same time.

WILLIAM: Yes, but I can't see why she should do that if they were arranging a divorce.

HELEN: Because she was hoping that a miracle might have happened, that, seeing her again, he might have discovered he was still in love with her. We're always hoping for miracles like that. And then—well, you saw.

WILLIAM: Yes, but mind you, if he'd been completely indifferent he'd have stayed in there. He went out chiefly for her sake.

HELEN: She thought he went out because he couldn't even stand the sight of her.

WILLIAM: Quite wrong. What a lot of muddlers we are, aren't we? She ought to be crying over the human race. There *is* something to cry about.

HELEN (*very gravely*): She was crying because once there was love and now there is no love. If we can't cry over the grave of love, what are our tears for? I could cry a little myself.

WILLIAM (*anxiously*): Now, now! Now, now! Don't you start, my dear. Besides, we must keep our detachment, or we'll never learn anything. (*To the pianists*) Play something quiet but cheerful.

They begin to play, HELEN *turns to him and smiles, he takes her hand.*

That's better. Let me see now, how did this begin? Where, when and how did Paul and Rosemary first meet?

HELEN (*slowly, reflectively*): She told me once. Her father gave Paul some architectural job, and asked him to come and dine. You'll have to be Rosemary's father. Go on.

WILLIAM: I thought for a moment you said I'd have to be Rosemary's father.

HELEN: That's what I did say. Go on.

WILLIAM: Certainly. Great pleasure. Only not for long y'know.

Goes out Arch left.

HELEN: It takes some girls months, even years, before they know, but she seemed to know at once.

Curtains open, music swells up, disclosing a corner of a drawing-room. Small table with sherry, cigarettes, etc. No chairs. ROSE-MARY, *looking younger and prettier, is pouring out the sherry.* PAUL, *who looks younger without the spectacles, comes in, followed*

[452]

by WILLIAM, *wearing grey wig and moustache as Rosemary's father.* ROSEMARY *pours out three glasses of sherry.*

WILLIAM (*in older man's voice*): Ah—you haven't met my daughter Rosemary, I think. My dear—Mr. Paul Weybridge.

    They smile and shake hands.

Glass of sherry, eh? (ROSEMARY *hands* PAUL *and* WILLIAM *a glass of sherry.*) Thank you, my dear.

ROSEMARY (*smiling at* PAUL): And how's the bungalow?

PAUL (*smiling back at her*): I think it's going to be grand.

ROSEMARY: I thought your idea for it awfully clever.

PAUL: Thank you.

    They raise their glasses at the same time and smile at each other significantly over the top of them.

WILLIAM (*rambling on without noticing them*): Yes, yes—I think Weybridge realises now exactly what I've always had in mind. Convenient and cosy are my two watch-words. Easy and cheap to run, but snug. Plenty of weather outside, on the top of that cliff (*pours out another glass of sherry*) but none inside, eh, Weybridge?

PAUL (*who is lost*): What? Oh—yes, rather—that's the idea.

WILLIAM: Made a little sketch or two I wanted to show you. Have 'em in my den. This way, my boy.

    WILLIAM *goes out.* PAUL, *obviously reluctantly, hands glass to* ROSEMARY, *there is a pause between them. He turns and goes out. Music plays softly for a moment or two, she stands in a day-dream. Then music stops and she comes forward a pace or two, and speaks to* HELEN.

ROSEMARY: Really I knew then. Or one part of me did.

HELEN (*with sympathy*): I know.

ROSEMARY: That part of me which seems to stand back always and isn't caught up with every moment.

HELEN: Yes, the part that can see far ahead, in a dim sort of way, and seems to know what's coming.

ROSEMARY: That's exactly it, Helen. But how does it work? I mean, it's just as if behind the little *Now* there's this big *Now*, in which all at once you've met a man and loved him for years and lost him. And how can that be?

HELEN: I don't know, darling. I don't believe anybody knows.

    Curtains close. WILLIAM *enters briskly as himself through curtains.*

WILLIAM: I know. It's a question of movement along the fourth dimension——

[453]

HELEN: What is?

WILLIAM: These two Nows—two different kinds of time. Now imagine yourself travelling with the speed of light—a hundred and eighty-six thousand miles a second—along the fourth dimension——

JOYCE: No.

PHILIP: No.

HELEN: No thank you, William.

WILLIAM: I thought you wanted to know.

HELEN: Not just now, thank you. Some other time. Now I wonder when Paul realised he was falling in love with Rosemary?

WILLIAM: Does it matter?

HELEN: Of course it matters.

WILLIAM: Well, he told me it was about the third or fourth time he went there. They were just saying good-bye in the hall.

> *Curtains open.* HELEN *waves* WILLIAM *off rostrum. The inner stage is now set as an entrance hall.* PAUL, *dressed in light overcoat and carrying hat, is about to say good night.*

ROSEMARY (*lightly*): You know, if your taxi is ticking its life away outside, you needn't wait for Father. He may be ages digging out that old photograph, but he can easily post it to you.

PAUL (*rather nervously*): Well, the taxi is there, so I suppose I'd better go. (*He hesitates, then, with a rush*) I wondered—well, the fact is, I've been working too hard lately to go out much, but a—er —client gave me two seats for the Haymarket for next Thursday, and—er—I wondered—whether you'd like to come along with me. We might have some supper afterwards if you like—and—er— dance——

ROSEMARY (*slowly*): Thursday? Yes, I'd love to.

PAUL: We'll have to meet at the theatre, if you don't mind as I'm afraid I shan't have time to dine.

ROSEMARY: No, of course not. We can find out what time it begins, can't we?

PAUL: Yes, I don't think they make any secret of that. Well— Thursday then——

> *They shake hands, he hesitates.*

I suppose your probably go out nearly every night—with fellows who are rolling in money—but to me Thursday will be quite an occasion.

ROSEMARY (*with apparent calm*): Oh—I'm looking forward to it too.

PAUL: I—— Good night.

> *Goes out.*

ROSEMARY (*as he goes*): Good night.

Then, after a short pause talking with great urgency to herself.

Thursday, Thursday, Thursday. I'll have to put Alice off, of course,
but she won't mind. Also the Kershaws can't come to tea because
I may not get back from the hairdresser's in time, but I can easily
put them off. Now if I wear my blue I've time to get another belt
—and—oh!—some shoes—I'll go down on Wednesday with Alice
and buy the shoes. That black bag's filthy but it'll have to do. Unless
I can get a blue one—like Alice's—she said it was quite cheap—
where was it? Somewhere in Regent Street.

WILLIAM *rises, points to* HELEN.

I might look at them while I'm getting the shoes. But perhaps after
all it might be better to wear the white, though it'll be creased in the
theatre and might look terrible afterwards,

WILLIAM *is trying to attract* HELEN's *attention.*

and that means wearing my rotten old red velvet coat—I might have
it cleaned, but they're horribly slow at that place——

WILLIAM: No, no, no.

Curtains close.

Can't have any more of that. Drive a man barmy! (*Looks at*
HELEN, *who is calm and smiling.*) How long would she go on like
that?

HELEN: Hours and hours probably.

WILLIAM: Good God! But the evening she's going to have simply
won't be worth all that agonising. Better to stop at home.

HELEN: Nonsense!

WILLIAM: Did you go through all that?

HELEN: Certainly—still do, sometimes.

WILLIAM *and* PHILIP (*shaking their heads*): Simply isn't worth it.

HELEN: We think it is.

JOYCE: And so—really—do you.

WILLIAM: You know—I believe the secret of you women is—
you've got far less individual conceit than we have.

JOYCE *and* HELEN: But—of course.

JOYCE: That's why we take so much trouble with ourselves.

WILLIAM: On the other hand, as a sex, you seem to have an enormous collective conceit.

HELEN: How do you mean?

WILLIAM: —Well, you're all convinced that though individually
you may not be up to much, Woman herself is a tremendous treat.

That's why if a man starts falling out of love with one of you, you always believe it's because he's falling in love with another one.

JOYCE: And nine times out of ten, at least, we're right!

WILLIAM: It's a sort of trades union conceit. We can't do without a member of the union. And very annoyed you are too when we prove we can.

HELEN: When you can ignore us, you've said good-bye to all hope of magic.

WILLIAM: Magic of a kind. Often a witch's brew. But we can do without your magic, because we're all sons of Adam, who did without it once. But you're all the daughters of poor Eve, who was never by herself, but found Adam already there——

HELEN: And ever since Eve we've felt socially responsible and even as guests we're still anxious hostesses.

PHILIP (*calling out*): Too much talk!

> *He nods to* JOYCE *and they burst into loud dance music, which quietens down as* WILLIAM *speaks.*

WILLIAM (*turning and going upstage with his back to the audience, puts on a pair of spectacles, turns and comes downstage again*): Now this is where I might indulge in one of these philosophical disquisitions on Jazz and the Spirit of the Age, which were so popular a few years ago.

HELEN (*takes off his spectacles, puts them in his breast pocket*): This is a few years ago, but you're not here to philosophise but to dance.

> *Takes his hand, leads him up on to centre of rostrum. The music is loud again.* PAUL *and* ROSEMARY *enter from alcove, they go on to rostrum, both couples start dancing.* PAUL *in dinner jacket,* ROSEMARY *in evening dress.*

WILLIAM (*as they dance*): Having a grand time, isn't she?

HELEN: Yes. So is he. Both of 'em just working up to something drastic. Lovely.

WILLIAM: Might be lovely. (*Pause.*) Might not. Can't tell. (*Pause.*) Never understand why you women always want to help on the biological process. Pairing everybody off as if you were all Mrs. Noah and it had started to rain.

HELEN: We know what life's about.

WILLIAM: My pet, you haven't the foggiest idea.

> WILLIAM *bumps into* PAUL *at the end of the dance.*

WILLIAM (*to* PAUL): Sorry.

> *Music stops and the four stop.* PAUL *and the two women clap enthusiastically,* WILLIAM *perfunctorily. They join up now apparently standing on edge of dance floor.*)

HELEN: You know William, of course, don't you? Paul, Rosemary.

WILLIAM (*to* ROSEMARY): Enjoying yourself, I can see that.

ROSEMARY: Yes, I am, aren't you?

WILLIAM: Not much.

ROSEMARY: Oh, what a shame! I like this place. (*Looks about happily.*)

WILLIAM (*looking about unhappily*): I don't. It frightens me.

ROSEMARY: Some of the people do look pretty awful.

WILLIAM: And some look awfully pretty. But that's not it. Consider the social and philosophical background——

ROSEMARY: I don't think I want to very much to-night.

WILLIAM (*almost as if announcing a lecture*): Jazz, Swing, and the Spirit of the Age——

HELEN (*breaking off talk with* PAUL): No, William, not to-night. And the Cabaret will be starting soon. Naked young women.

WILLIAM (*gloomily*): And the dirty songs at the piano.

> *Dance music again, not too loud.*

PAUL (*happily*): Rosemary!

ROSEMARY (*happily*): Yes, Paul? (*Taking his hand.*)

PAUL: Let's dance.

> *They start dancing round and about.*

WILLIAM: What's the matter with 'em now?

HELEN: It's the first time he's ever called her Rosemary and the first time she's ever called him Paul.

> *Alcove curtain held open, the other two, still dancing, smile and go off.*

And you needn't look so glum about it. That's a very important moment. Don't you remember the first time I ever called you William?

WILLIAM: No. And I think I've had enough of this schoolgirl stuff. It's like being forcibly fed with golden syrup.

HELEN: You're envious really, y'know.

WILLIAM (*horrified*): What—of that—mushy idiocy! (*Burlesquing their eager happy look and tone.*) Paul!

PHILIP: Rosemary!

HELEN (*coolly*): Not of what he's doing, but of his state of mind. And now you're going to see the next stage. Do you remember what the next stage is?

WILLIAM (*cheering up a little*): Yes. Bed.

HELEN: No. These aren't that kind. Think now. He's taken her out for several evenings—dining—dancing, to a play or a film—and they're not shy any longer but are beginning to talk.

WILLIAM: Yes, I know now. They're beginning to talk their heads off, and everything that each of them says, the other thinks is wonderful. The way they have the same tastes, the very same likes and dislikes—it's miraculous.

HELEN: She'll have to cheat a bit, of course.

WILLIAM (*sardonically*): Oh, of course!

HELEN: But not as much as you think.

WILLIAM: Look at the way you pretended to like chess and be interested in politics.

HELEN (*scornfully*): Oh!—chess and politics, there's a limit. But she won't have to cheat very much, she's still an impressionable and rather unformed sort of girl, and his very feeling for her, and her response to it, do really bring her unconsciously into line with his point of view.

> *Curtains open to disclose scene arranged to represent corner of drawing-room.* PAUL *sits in chair,* ROSEMARY *on stool. Both in evening clothes, very eager, inwardly excited.* Note: *During this scene* HELEN *quietly goes out, to make her change.*

PAUL (*eagerly*): I never knew you'd been there.

ROSEMARY (*same*): Yes, I absolutely loved it. I've always been hoping to go there again.

PAUL: So have I. By Jove, if we could only—(*breaks off, then resumes.*) And the castle, you know, is one of the most amusing pieces of baroque I know.

ROSEMARY: Yes, isn't it? I adore baroque.

PAUL: Well, I wouldn't go as far as that. It's *amusing.*

ROSEMARY: That's what I mean, Paul. It's terribly *amusing.* That's all, of course. No more than that. Not like—well——

PAUL: Let's say, Perpendicular Gothic or French Renaissance.

ROSEMARY: Of course not. They're absolutely wonderful. I've nearly finished that book you lent me on the French Renaissance. Completely enchanting. Have you played the Sibelius records yet?

PAUL (*sitting forward*): Yes. I put them on to-night, just before I came out. You're right, of course. He's head and shoulders above all the rest.

ROSEMARY (*joyfully*): Oh—I'm glad you feel like that about him, Paul.

PAUL: Yes, he gives me just the same feeling you described—sort of—you know, cold and stern yet with a kind of deep warmth inside——

ROSEMARY: That's it exactly. It's absurd saying you don't understand music——

PAUL: And it's absurd saying you don't understand architecture, Rosemary. Some people have a natural good taste, a flair, and you're one of 'em. And I haven't met many.

They exchange a smile and lean to each other.

ROSEMARY: Won't you have another whisky and soda——?

PAUL: No, thanks. I must go in a minute.

They look at each other and smile.

WILLIAM (*the interested spectator, after a pause*): Well, what about it? Come on. Everything's all set.

PAUL (*slowly, shyly, looking away from her to out front*): It's queer, you know.

ROSEMARY: What is, Paul?

PAUL: The way you go on perhaps for years not meeting anybody who's really your own kind, who likes the same things you like, who can have fun with you or be serious, just as the mood takes you both, until you begin to think you're an odd kind of bird and almost alone in the world. . . .

WILLIAM: Extraordinary how people can imagine they're so different from the crowd. (*Turns to* PHILIP *at piano.*) *Paul and his odd kind of bird!* One of the most commonplace fellows I know! Scores just like him eating biscuits and cheese in every club dining room.

PHILIP: Sh—Sh—Sh—(*Points to stage.*)

PAUL (*as before*): And then, quite suddenly, you meet somebody. . . .

ROSEMARY (*fervently*): Yes, I know.

PAUL: As we met.

ROSEMARY: Yes. And that's the nicest thing anybody's ever said to me.

PAUL (*putting out a hand*): Rosemary!

ROSEMARY (*giving him her hand*): Dear Paul!

They kiss.

He has pulled her towards him and she is now in his arms and he is kissing her. They are enthusiastic but look a trifle awkward.

Curtains close.

[459]

WILLIAM: Yes, yes! Yes, yes! They'll be hours now excitedly explaining their uniqueness to each other.

JOYCE (*stoutly*): Quite right too!

WILLIAM (*surprised*): Joyce, Joyce!

JOYCE: Well, that's how they feel, and they're quite right.

WILLIAM: Yes, yes, Joyce. Nobody's blaming them. All very natural and pleasant, only of course we don't want to be in at it. All rather cloying and tedious to the onlooker. Where's Helen?

PHILIP: She went out during that last scene.

WILLIAM (*calling*): Helen—Helen.

HELEN (*off, just behind nearest curtain*): Shut up, I'm here.

WILLIAM: What are you doing there?

HELEN: Turning myself into Paul's mother. They're engaged now and Paul is going to introduce Rosemary to his mother. A big moment.

WILLIAM: Undoubtedly a big moment. And I think Rosemary's father ought to put in an appearance.

HELEN (*urgently*): No, that's not necessary. Now don't be silly, darling.

WILLIAM (*with dignity*): There is nothing silly about it.

He goes out.

Curtains open showing scene, corner of another drawing-room with a settee. PAUL *and* ROSEMARY *are standing together, looking rather anxious.*

PAUL: But you dear delightful idiot, what have you to be anxious about? I tell you, she'll adore you. After all, I ought to know. She's my mother.

ROSEMARY: I know, darling. That's just it.

PAUL: The only thing you've got to be afraid of is that very soon, if we're not careful, she'll settle down to tell you what I was like when I was cutting my first teeth or going down with whooping cough.

ROSEMARY: Oh—I don't mind that. In fact, I'd love to know what you were like when you were tiny. That's the point about being in love. You want to know *all* about the other person.

PAUL: I'd hate to know about you at the age of two. I wish mother'd hurry up. Though we were rather early.

ROSEMARY (*nervously*): I think she's here.

He gives her a reassuring pat and she gives him a rather desperate quick smile. HELEN *now enters as* PAUL'S *mother, wearing different dress, grey wig, spectacles perhaps, and proceeds to give a performance as a solemn matron.*

HELEN: I'm so sorry. Well, Paul! (*Smiles and he kisses her cheek lightly.*)

PAUL: Mother, this—is Rosemary.

The two women smile, but stare hard at each other.

HELEN (*with marked change to effusive tone*): Well, well, well! So this is Rosemary. (*Shakes her head and smiles at* ROSEMARY.) You've given me a real surprise, my dear. I'd begun to think Paul was a born bachelor. And now—here you are. (*Embraces and kisses* ROSEMARY.)

ROSEMARY (*shyly*): Yes—and—I'm very, very happy.

HELEN: I'm sure you are. And I know Paul is too.

PAUL: Tremendously happy, Mother.

HELEN (*smiling*): And if he's happy, you may be sure I am, having spoilt him all his life.

ROSEMARY (*smiling*): He doesn't seem very spoilt.

PAUL (*very playfully*): Just you wait! Eh, Mother?

HELEN (*archly*): Yes, indeed. Though I may be able to show Rosemary one or two little tricks—to keep you in order.

Mime talk between HELEN *and* ROSEMARY. *All three smile at each other, rather fatuously.*

PHILIP (*across to* JOYCE): Oh—Lord. I hate this dialogue.

JOYCE: I know. Loathsome! But it's about what they'd say.

Enter WILLIAM *breezily in make-up as before as Rosemary's father.*

WILLIAM: Well, well, well! Here we are, then.

ROSEMARY (*astounded*): But—Father—what are you doing here?

PAUL: This is a surprise, sir.

HELEN (*after glaring at* WILLIAM): *My* surprise this time.

WILLIAM: Yes, yes, quite right. Her surprise. Most amusing!

PAUL: Yes—but—how did you——?

WILLIAM (*bluffly*): Oh, your mother'll explain.

HELEN (*after another glare at* WILLIAM): You see, dear, Rosemary's father and I are old friends.

WILLIAM (*bluffly*): That's right. Old—old—friends.

HELEN: So I told him over the telephone he'd better come along and give you both a surprise.

WILLIAM: And here I am, giving you a surprise. (*To* PAUL) Well,

I expect Rosemary and your mother will have lots to talk about—so suppose we leave 'em to it. Eh?

HELEN: No, no. You men stay here while I take Rosemary with me and get to know her properly. (*Takes* ROSEMARY'S *arm.*) I'm sure you must have a lot to say to each other.

They turn to go together.

WILLIAM (*bluffly*): Yes, yes, naturally. Young man marrying my only daughter.

HELEN: Yes, well—have a nice intimate man's talk together. Come along, Rosemary.

Women go out. WILLIAM *and* PAUL *sit on sofa. Both men look stiff and uncomfortable and should be deliberately wooden in attitude and speech.*

WILLIAM: Humph! All right to smoke?

PAUL: Oh—yes, of course. Sorry. Cigarette?

WILLIAM (*producing case*): No thanks. Never smoke 'em. Cigar?

PAUL: No thanks. Can't cope with cigars. Wish I could.

Both men light up and look straight in front of them throughout following dialogue, which should be slow and wooden.

WILLIAM: I used to smoke a lot of cigars one time.

PAUL: Did you?

WILLIAM: Yes, I did. Used to get 'em by the thousand direct from Cuba. Wonderful cigars.

PAUL: I'll bet they were. Best place for cigars, of course.

WILLIAM: Only place for cigars, really.

PAUL (*pause*): Know much about the South African market, sir?

WILLIAM: No. Never touch it. Why?

PAUL: Nothing really. Just wondered. Client of mine seems to have made a lot out of it, that's all.

WILLIAM: I believe you can. Must be in the know, though. (*Pause.*) D'you ever go out after wild duck——?

PAUL: No. Friend of mine does.

WILLIAM: Does he? (*Pause.*) What's his name?

PAUL: Sanderson.

WILLIAM: Not old Billy Sanderson, used to be out in Malaya?

PAUL: No, this chap's about my age. In the City. He's very keen on wild duck. (*Pause.*)

WILLIAM: It's a wonderful sport. (*Pause.*)

PAUL: I tried my hand at trout—trout last year.

WILLIAM: Did you? (*Pause.*) Dry fly?

PAUL: Yes.

WILLIAM: I never could get on with it. Needs too much practice for me.

PAUL: Does really. I wasn't much good.

WILLIAM: No, neither was I. (*Pause.*)

> HELEN *now appears outside rostrum. If practicable she should look her ordinary self.*

HELEN (*scornfully*): A nice intimate man's talk together, eh? Just like two people made out of wood, sitting there grunting at each other! What do you think you're doing?

WILLIAM (*to* PAUL, *hands his cigar to him to hold for a moment*): Excuse me a moment, my boy.

PAUL (*who doesn't see* HELEN): Certainly.

> *He remains in wooden attitude, while* WILLIAM *comes forward to talk to* HELEN. *He takes off his wig and moustache to show that he is now his ordinary self.*

WILLIAM: What's the matter?

HELEN: Is that your idea of a nice intimate talk between a father and his prospective son-in-law?

WILLIAM: Yes.

HELEN (*indignantly*): But—it's just nothing. Cigars and wild duck!

WILLIAM: A bit impersonal, of course.

HELEN: A bit impersonal!

WILLIAM: You can see the reason, can't you?

HELEN: No, I can't.

WILLIAM: Just shows how insensitive you women are.

HELEN (*aghast*): What?

WILLIAM (*coolly*): Yes, insensitive. We can't get up to your loquacious tricks, pouring out floods of horribly intimate stuff, displaying our underclothes.

HELEN: Who wants you to display your underclothes?

WILLIAM: The fact is, we're shy.

HELEN: But what is there to be shy about?

WILLIAM: This biology we're suddenly caught up in. He's shy because very soon he's going to take my daughter away and share a bedroom with her. And I'm shy because I know he's going to——

HELEN: Yes, yes, yes.

WILLIAM: We're the shy sex, you know. Always were. Now I'll get back and finish this off.

Puts on moustache and wig and goes back to sofa. PAUL *hands back cigar. The two men play just in same manner as before.* WILLIAM *settles down in middle of sofa.* HELEN *goes out to change back into Paul's mother.*

PAUL: How do you like this car you're trying?

WILLIAM: Very comfortable, but find her a bit sluggish so far.

PAUL: Engine needs running in, eh?

WILLIAM: Probably. But don't think she's very nippy. (*Pause.*) You fairly busy now?

PAUL: Yes. We're competing for that big Birmingham job.

WILLIAM: Hope you get it.

PAUL: We stand a fair chance. But that's really my partner's pigeon.

WILLIAM: Yes. I suppose you'll manage to get away all right after the—er—wedding?

PAUL: Yes. I've fixed that all right. Hope to manage a month.

WILLIAM: Good! Any idea where you're going?

PAUL: Not quite decided yet. Might motor across France and end up at the Italian lakes.

WILLIAM: Good trip. Sorry I can't be with you. (*Guffaws awkwardly.*)

They look at each other. PAUL *laughs awkwardly.*

(*Shy and solemn now.*) I know you'll try and make her happy, my boy.

PAUL: It won't be my fault if she isn't, sir.

WILLIAM: No doubt. Won't be hers, though. Happiest little thing you ever saw. Not like some of 'em, always whining and moping. Miss her, y'know, my boy. Miss her like the devil. However, there it is, there it is.

PAUL *and* WILLIAM *rise.* HELEN *as Paul's mother and* ROSE-MARY *enter. They look happy and thick as thieves.*

HELEN (*gaily*): Now, you two. I know you're having a wonderful talk and telling one another all your secrets. Don't stop. But there are drinks in your room, Paul, and I thought you'd like to go along there.

WILLIAM: Good idea.

PAUL: Yes, rather. How's it going, Rosemary?

ROSEMARY: Grand!

HELEN: Passed with honours, didn't you, dear? Now, off you go.

[464]

The men go out, WILLIAM *to change back at once to ordinary self. As* PAUL *passes* ROSEMARY *he pats her arm. The two women get into a feminine huddle, very confidential and close, and talking rapidly.*

HELEN: Yes, dear, I think you're very wise to take a nice little flat at first.

ROSEMARY: I thought a little flat would be best, at first. Afterwards of course——

HELEN: Afterwards, of course, when you've settled down properly then perhaps Paul might build you a house about twenty or thirty miles out. (*Looks to her and smiles.*) But at first, I know you'll both be happier in some convenient little flat in town. Paul's very fond of the country, of course——

ROSEMARY: I am too. I love the country.

HELEN: I'm sure you do. And of course for young children I think the country's perfect. But you've no need to think about that yet. (*Smiles.*) In the meantime, you're quite right to want a nice little flat. Not a service flat, eh?

ROSEMARY: No, I don't think so.

HELEN: Saves trouble with maids, of course. And cooks.

ROSEMARY: But they're so terribly expensive, aren't they?

HELEN: Most of the ones I know are, but there may be cheaper ones now, though what the food and service will be like I don't know. And Paul's rather fastidious about food, you know. Which reminds me, Rosemary, don't try and make Paul give up his club. I know he's so fond of it.

ROSEMARY: Oh—I wouldn't dream of it. Of course not. He'll want to see other men. But I thought if we had a nice little flat somewhere fairly central——

HELEN: Of course, you're absolutely right. You couldn't do better, at first, than start with a nice little flat, preferably somewhere fairly central. If you could find a reasonably cheap service flat, of course——

WILLIAM *enters from alcove.*

WILLIAM: I say!

ROSEMARY: Oh—we'd take it like a shot, if it wasn't too dear. Because after all, it would save trouble with maids and cooks.

WILLIAM: I say!

HELEN: That's the point. As long as the food and service are not too bad. Paul's rather——

WILLIAM (*almost in despair*): Look here!

[465]

HELEN (*after giving him a sharp look*): My dear, I'm sure I've kept you too long from Paul. Run along to his room, where I was showing you the photographs, and you'll find him there.

ROSEMARY (*rising spontaneously*): Oh—I'm so happy.

HELEN: I know you are, Rosemary, and I think you've every right to be, for you're a very lucky girl.

The two women kiss, ROSEMARY *exits.* HELEN *looks at* WILLIAM, *pushes the sofa upstage with her foot, in irritation, the curtains close.*

WILLIAM (*going up on to rostrum and speaking through curtains*): I'm sorry—I say—I'm sorry. (*To* PHILIP) I believe she's annoyed.

PHILIP: I know she was.

JOYCE: She was furious—and quite right too. You deliberately broke into her scene.

WILLIAM: But she interrupted me when I was Rosemary's father. Still I'll try again. I'm sorry. Hearing me, of course, but not answering. I'm sorry. You don't call that conversation, an exchange of views, opinions, ideas, experiences, do you? You were going round and round in a tiny circle. You were simply making cooing noises at each other.

JOYCE (*rather sharply*): Of course they were. They knew that.

WILLIAM: Well, but what's the point of it?

PHILIP: I've been wondering for years.

HELEN *enters from alcove as herself.*

HELEN: Don't be so dense. A girl has just met the mother of the man she's going to marry. A woman has just met the girl her son is going to marry. An ordeal for both of them.

WILLIAM: Yes, I can see that, dense as I am.

HELEN: Well, then they discover, to their great relief, that they're ready to like each other. The ordeal's over. It's going to be all right.

WILLIAM: And so instead of exchanging experiences, opinions, ideas . . .

HELEN: They'll do that much later on.

WILLIAM: They make a lot of nice agreeing noises together, eh?

HELEN: That's it. Women can't jog along on parallel lines as men seem able to do. They're always either going away from each other or coming together. And these two were coming together, and proving it. See?

WILLIAM: Yes. But what a life.

HELEN: Of course, it's ten times harder than being a man. But far more amusing, I fancy. (*Hesitates.*) Now this is rather awkward.

WILLIAM: Why what's wrong.

HELEN: We have to be two different characters soon—guests at the wedding reception——

WILLIAM: Oh, have we? That's all right. I shall be Major Spanner, back from the East and an old friend and admirer of the bride. No trouble about that.

WILLIAM *exits.*

HELEN: Now, Joyce dear, I think we ought to show Paul and Rosemary just for a minute before the wedding. Something romantic—young—touching——

JOYCE (*rising*): Yes.

HELEN: A rainy evening in Spring—wet lilac—and the moon lighting her upturned face——

PHILIP (*rising*): Then you'll want some music.

HELEN: Essential.

HELEN *exits.*

JOYCE: Chopin I think.

PHILIP: Certainly. One of the Nocturnes?

JOYCE: No. The Fantasy Impromptu Middle Section.

PHILIP: All right, but don't go wrong with the triplets in the left hand.

JOYCE: No, of course not. Yes, Chopin coming through some mysterious lighted window. Didn't you always think, when you were young, that there was something magical about those houses where somebody was playing a piano?

PHILIP: No. I didn't.

JOYCE: You didn't? Why, I used to feel there must be something terribly special about the people in that house—that they were living an enchanted life that I'd never know. What's the matter with you?

PHILIP (*sighs*): I suppose the trouble is I just don't think big, beautiful thoughts.

JOYCE: Oh, you're hopeless. (*Joyce goes back and sits at piano left.*)

PHILIP: Well I think we're all set. Lights. (*Sits at piano right.*)

Lights dim on stage. Some moonlight comes on. PAUL and ROSEMARY enter from alcove wearing light raincoats, walking close and lovingly. They stop in a moonlight spot.

ROSEMARY: Darling!

PAUL: What, darling?

ROSEMARY: The lilac.

PAUL: Yes, marvellous.

Softly the Chopin music begins. They listen rapturously.

ROSEMARY: Chopin. Perfect!

PAUL: Perfect. Only three days now, darling.

ROSEMARY: Only three days.

PAUL: I love you.

ROSEMARY: I love you.

They kiss, the moonlight spot fades. They exit.

The Pianists begin a quiet amusing version of the Wedding March. The first Pianist comes up to full strength as the lighting comes up too. The curtain is drawn to reveal the inner stage set as corner of a large room where wedding reception is being held. There are one or two small tables, with champagne, glasses, food, etc. A lot of noise off, both direct and recorded—chatter, noise of plates and glasses.

HELEN *enters as Mrs. de Folyat, a handsome vivacious widow of about thirty-five with an intense arch manner, with champagne glass in her hand.*

WILLIAM *now enters as Major George Spanner, a military rather wooden, bronzed man about forty, who is slightly tight in a rather depressed fashion, and is also busy removing bits of confetti from his clothes.*

HELEN (*shouting*): I beg your pardon?

WILLIAM (*shouting*): Sorry. What did you say?

HELEN (*as before*): I said "I beg your pardon".

WILLIAM (*as before*): Certainly—certainly——

HELEN: What time is it?

WILLIAM: Sorry—can't hear you.

HELEN (*top of her voice*): I said—What time is it?

It happens as she says this that the noise has suddenly stopped, so that it sounds very loud indeed. WILLIAM *glances suspiciously at her before looking at his watch.*

WILLIAM: Twenty to four.

HELEN: What a ghastly hour! Let me see, aren't you Major Spanner?

WILLIAM: Yes. Sorry—I don't remember——

HELEN: No, we weren't introduced. Somebody pointed you out to me. I'm Mrs. de Folyat.

WILLIAM: Oh yes. How d'you do?

HELEN: Do you think it all went off very well?

WILLIAM: Suppose so. No judge really. Don't care for all this business. Beastly functions.

HELEN: Definitely. Let me see, you're out East, aren't you?

WILLIAM: Yes. (*Pause.*) Rubber.

HELEN: That must be wonderful.

HELEN is waving off to somebody again.

WILLIAM: It was once. But ever since the bottom dropped out of the market it's been terrible.

HELEN (*with vague enthusiasm*): Yes, but the life there—the colour, the romance, the mystery! The temple bells. The sense of eternity. Do you practise yoga?

WILLIAM (*horrified*): Good lord!—No! I'm not in India by the way. Straits Settlements. Fifteen hundred miles away from India.

HELEN: Is it really? But then I suppose it's all much bigger out there than one imagines.

WILLIAM: Oh—enormous. People here have not the faintest notion. They ask me to look up fellas who are two thousand miles away from my place.

HELEN (*who has been glancing about her*): Do they really? I wonder why?

She waves as if good-bye to some people who are leaving and makes this very big.

WILLIAM (*disturbed and looking to where she is waving*): Well, because they don't realise these fellas are two thousand miles away.

HELEN (*confidentially*): I think I shall slip away now. This seems a good chance. (*She comes forward to front of rostrum.*)

WILLIAM (*with a quick glance round*): Yes, rather. I was just going out. Join you, I think.

He joins HELEN. The curtains close. Once outside they halt, relieved, as if they had sneaked out of a hotel room. It is now presumed they are in a street.

HELEN (*taking deep breath*): Ah!—it's so good to be in the fresh air again.

WILLIAM: Yes. Frightful row in there. Hate those scrimmages. Taxi!

HELEN (*archly*): Are you bride or bridegroom?

WILLIAM (*astounded, pause*): What?

HELEN: I mean, one of her friends or one of his?

WILLIAM: Oh, one of hers. Don't know him at all. Known little

Rosemary since she was a child. Friend of the family. Rosemary's grown up to be a very fine girl.

HELEN: Has she? Taxi!

WILLIAM (*with genuine enthusiasm*): Yes, decidedly. No doubt about that. Weybridge is a very lucky fella. Hope he realises it.

HELEN: Major Spanner, I do believe—— (*Breaks off.*)

WILLIAM (*intimidatingly wooden*): What?

HELEN: No, no, I don't know you well enough. I mustn't say it. As a matter of fact I don't know her at all. And I've only recently met Paul Weybridge. He's an architect, you know.

WILLIAM: Yes, so I gather.

HELEN: And a very clever one. He's been adding a wing to my little place in the country, *quite* brilliantly.

WILLIAM: He has, has he? Taxi! (*Waving his stick.*)

HELEN: I couldn't help thinking it a pity that a man who has obviously such a tremendous future should go and——

WILLIAM: What?

HELEN: Now, now, Major Spanner, you mustn't tempt me to be indiscreet.

WILLIAM (*bewildered*): Didn't know I was doing so.

HELEN: Besides, it's quite clear I can't expect any sympathy from you.

WILLIAM (*stiffly*): Now look here, Mrs. de Folyat, if you're suggesting he oughtn't to have married because his wife isn't good enough for him——

HELEN: Now I never *said* that. I merely hinted that perhaps——

WILLIAM: Because if so, I'll give you my opinion, as a man who's seen a good deal of the world.

HELEN: And what is your opinion, Major Spanner?

WILLIAM (*stiffly*): That that little girl—Rosemary—is worth ten of him—yes, ten of him. Taxi! Ah, got it. This one, I think.

They step off rostrum and exit.

Lights dim and music begins with final theme of the Act. Curtains open to reveal inner stage set as balcony of hotel in Southern Europe. Moonlight spot comes on. Back of scene is dimly lit, large bedroom window. PAUL in a dressing gown and ROSEMARY in a wrap come out of the long windows, stand close together, looking out into what is obviously a wonderful moonlight night. The music plays softly before they speak, and continues softly throughout.

[470]

ROSEMARY: I feel that you and the night are almost one:
           I seem as near to you when I stare into the night,
           Losing myself in the green ivory world
           The moon has carved, as when I felt your heart
           Dividing each precious moment with my own!
           And when you are so close my eyes have lost you
           To my lips, I seem to float in the wide night
           And behind my eyelids rises another moon.

PAUL (*after a pause*):
           Men are restless and nearly always alone,
           Going off in pursuit, nosing along a trail,
           Following a rumour of gold to the waterless hills.
           Now here comes to an end for me many a trail
           That never had a thought in it of women and love.
           Now there is nothing I wish to find.

     He puts his arms round her.

ROSEMARY: There should be words that ring our joy like bells,
           But I know none. There is sorrow in all words.

PAUL: If my heart still drums it is to stop my ears,
           Because even to-night from somewhere beyond the
             moon
           Still roars into the abyss the cataract of time.

ROSEMARY: Then take hold of this night and keep it fast
           Never, never forget it.

PAUL: I shall not forget.

     He holds her against him, and she leans her head against his
   shoulder. HELEN *enters dressed as herself.*

HELEN (*in happy excitement*):
           Now I'm a woman too, and not a mere voice,
           And blast all supercilious commentating:
           Come on, give me that Mediterranean moon,
           And the right man, and I too can kiss
           And rave the very stars out of the blue.

     Moonlight comes full on her too now. She calls sharply.

William, you idiot!

     Then in soft cajoling tone.

Oh, Bill, my sweet, come on!

     WILLIAM *enters as himself again.*

    WILLIAM (*in fine form*): And here I am. Hey—spill that moonshine!
Spill it and spread it, boys. Ah, that's better.

     With moonlight full on him, he looks across at HELEN.

[471]

God, what a night! And Helen—what a girl.

HELEN: You fat, conceited and adorable fool. You've Paul and Rosemary to thank for this.

WILLIAM (*grandly*): And Adam and Eve and the angel who sometimes nods.

HELEN: And lets us slip under his sword at Eden's Gate.

Music, pause.

PAUL: Rosemary!

ROSEMARY: Paul!

Music, pause.

JOYCE: Philip!

PHILIP: Joyce!

Music, pause.

HELEN (*the light spreading to them*): William!

Music, pause.

WILLIAM: Helen!

They crash into triumphant music. PAUL *and* ROSEMARY *are close together.* HELEN *and* WILLIAM *extend their arms to each other.* PHILIP *and* JOYCE *stare happily across as they play.*

END OF ACT ONE

ACT II

PHILIP *and* JOYCE *begin playing a fairly brisk overture. After about
a minute and a half of it, however, it begins to flag and suddenly*
JOYCE *stops altogether and looks angry. After plodding a bar or
two by himself,* PHILIP *also stops.* JOYCE *rises.*

PHILIP: What's the matter?

JOYCE (*angrily*): You know very well what's the matter.

PHILIP: I don't.

JOYCE: Of course you do.

PHILIP (*annoyed now*): I tell you I don't. All I know is that you
suddenly stopped playing.

JOYCE: And I stopped playing because I couldn't stand it any
longer.

PHILIP: Couldn't stand what?

JOYCE: Couldn't stand the sight of you there, obviously with no
interest whatever in what we were playing, just bored and not making
any effort to hide it. I suppose if it had been Margery Walker you'd
been playing with, your eyes would have been half out of your head
and you'd have been bouncing all over your piano.

PHILIP (*with irritating air of patience, rises*): Would you mind
telling me what on earth Margery Walker has to do with it?

JOYCE: Oh—don't be so pompous!

PHILIP (*with same manner*): I'm not being pompous. I'm merely
asking a reasonable question. What has——

JOYCE (*furiously*): Oh—shut up!

PHILIP (*with injured dignity, sits*): Certainly. Certainly. Only too
delighted.

> *He brings out of his far pocket a copy of a newspaper and very
> ostentatiously leans back and buries himself behind it.*

JOYCE (*after a moment*): How you can sit there—pretending to read
a newspaper——!

PHILIP (*with irritating air of calm*): I'm not pretending to read. I
am reading. I notice here, for instance, that a man called Worsnop
has just found on his estate several Roman coins. The coins, it says,
were in an excellent state of——

JOYCE: I haven't the least desire to hear anything about your
ridiculous coins.

[473]

She goes back to her piano and sits.

PHILIP: Thank you!

He begins reading again. She looks across at him in angry despair. WILLIAM *now enters smoking a pipe and carrying a copy of* The Times. *He looks rather grumpy.* JOYCE *brightens up at the sight of him.*

JOYCE: Hello, William!

WILLIAM (*not interested*): Hello!

JOYCE (*with forced brightness*): Any news?

WILLIAM (*beginning to open paper*): I haven't really looked at the paper yet.

JOYCE: I don't mean in the paper. I mean, have *you* any news?

WILLIAM (*blankly*): Me? Oh—no—nothing at all.

He sits and begins reading his paper. JOYCE *looks in despair from him to* PHILIP *and then plays several hideously-sounding chords.* WILLIAM *and* PHILIP *together appear from behind their papers and look at her with silent reproach. They begin reading again.* HELEN *enters, briskly and cheerfully.*

HELEN (*crossing over to* WILLIAM): William!

WILLIAM (*looking up without interest*): Yes, my pet?

HELEN (*rather like a guide-lecturer*): Pay attention. Now, we're going forward several years in the history of Paul and Rosemary. Last time we saw them, you remember, they were on their honeymoon. Five or six years have passed since then. Rosemary has had a baby, now a very nice little boy between three and four, called Robin.

PHILIP: He doesn't come into this, does he? I mean, you don't show us little Robin bringing his parents together again in the end, do you?

HELEN (*severely*): No, of course not. You see that sort of thing at the films, not here.

PHILIP: Yes, dear, I know, but when you said they now had a nice little boy, I began to be worried.

HELEN: You needn't worry. And by the way, I'm not really talking to you, I'm talking to William.

WILLIAM (*looking up blankly from paper*): Yes, my love, I'm listening.

HELEN: Move your chair round a bit or you won't see anything.

WILLIAM: Certainly, certainly. (*Moves his stool behind piano, preparing to read again.*)

HELEN: So now, after missing these first years of marriage, we now find Paul and Rosemary comfortably settled in London. And here is an average evening.

Curtains open to disclose inner set, as corner of a sitting-room. PAUL *is buried in the evening paper, while* ROSEMARY *is fidgeting between writing a letter, doing a little sewing and reading a book. Both are rather more mature than when we saw them last.* WILLIAM *and* PHILIP *are also reading their newspapers and pay no attention whatever to the scene, to the disgust of* HELEN *and* JOYCE.

ROSEMARY (*after pause*): I saw Diana Ferguson this morning.

PAUL (*muttering*): Don't know her.

ROSEMARY: Yes, you do know her. She says she's expecting her husband back from India at the end of the month.

PAUL *merely grunts. She looks at him in disgust, then tries again.*

ROSEMARY: They're taking a house in South Devon for his leave. Then she wants to go back with him this time. And I must say I don't blame her. Do you? (*Pause. Waits for a reply and doesn't receive one, keeping her temper with some difficulty.*) Is there anything particularly interesting in that paper, dear?

PAUL (*blankly, looking up*): What?—no.

Curtains close.

HELEN *now notices that* WILLIAM *is not looking at all.*

HELEN: William, you're the limit!

She goes over to him and snatches the paper away from him. He stares at her in blank astonishment.

WILLIAM: Now don't be silly, Helen. I'm reading that paper.

HELEN: You were, but now you've stopped. I don't believe you noticed Paul and Rosemary at all, did you?

WILLIAM: Well, I'll tell you——

HELEN: Did you?

WILLIAM: No, I didn't.

HELEN: You were too busy staring at that newspaper. What's in it.

WILLIAM: Nothing. Absolutely nothing to-day. Very dull.

HELEN: I take the trouble to show you Paul and Rosemary having a typical evening——

WILLIAM (*warming as he goes along*): Yes, yes, but I don't want to see them. Let's leave them alone. That's what's the matter with the world now. Everybody interfering with everybody else. Everybody wanting to know what everybody else is doing and saying and thinking. Nobody's left alone. Not for a single half-hour is anybody left

[475]

alone. Well, I say, leave them alone. Refuse to indulge in this universal idiotic and shameless curiosity. Just hand me my paper, will you?

HELEN: Why? It's only crammed with information about other people, news of somebody else's business, all arranged (*hands paper, which she has crumpled, back to* WILLIAM) to satisfy an idiotic and shameless curiosity.

WILLIAM (*with cold dignity and folding his newspaper*): It's one thing to acquaint yourself with what is happening in the world and quite another thing to poke your nose into other people's private affairs. However, if you won't see it, you won't. (*Change of tone*) Now, I suppose you want me to have a look at this pair of yours, several years after marriage, just to show me how dissatisfied she is.

HELEN: If you'd seen and heard——

WILLIAM: I saw and heard enough. She's not really dissatisfied with him—although she thinks she is—but she's dissatisfied because she can't have her cake and eat it——

HELEN (*cutting in, vehemently*): If there's one thing I loathe it's that bit of misery about not being able to have your cake and eat it.

PHILIP: You all do.

WILLIAM: Yes. So she'll begin taking her dissatisfaction out of him. And it's not his fault.

HELEN *and* JOYCE: Of course it is.

HELEN: Just stuck there, with his head in the paper.

WILLIAM: But he has to read the paper some time and probably it happens that's he's been busy all day.

HELEN: And probably not. But that's not the point. The point is he's beginning to treat her as if she weren't really there. All she wants is a little politeness, a little interest, a——

WILLIAM (*cutting in coolly, puts pipe in his mouth and newspaper under his arm*): I know what she'd like. Now I'll show you. (*He claps his hands.*)

Curtains open to same scene as before.

ROSEMARY (*sitting eating chocolates*): I saw Diana Ferguson this morning.

PAUL (*putting aside paper at once*): Did you, darling? When's her husband coming on leave from India?

ROSEMARY: At the end of the month.

PAUL (*brightly astonished*): No!

ROSEMARY: Yes. She's awfully excited.

PAUL: Of course. He must be too. I know *I'd* be almost off my head with excitement if we'd been separated so long. They ought to take a furnished house somewhere for his leave.

ROSEMARY (*triumphantly*): That's just what they have done. In South Devon.

PAUL: In South Devon? Oh, they ought to have a grand time there. I know we should. (*They lean to each other and smile.*)

ROSEMARY: She wants to go back with him this time. And I must say I don't blame her. Do you?

PAUL: No, I don't. Just imagine if it were us. How lucky we are to be able to be together without either of us making any sacrifices. (*Blows kiss to her.*)

ROSEMARY: Yes, darling. (*After smiling at him*) But I'm keeping you from your newspaper.

PAUL: Oh no. (*Throws newspaper over his shoulder.*) I'd much rather have a good talk about *us*, and especially about you. (*Leans forward, regarding her lovingly and kisses her.*)

Curtains close.

WILLIAM: And that's quite enough of that. Now, Helen, that's what she'd like—or what she thinks she'd like, and, honestly, what do you think of it?

HELEN: I've always tried to be honest with you, Bill, haven't I?

WILLIAM: Except when we're quarrelling—yes.

HELEN: So, I'll admit that for an ordinary conversation—not a special occasion, mind you, making it up or celebrating an anniversary——

WILLIAM: No, no—an ordinary conversation at the conjugal hearth.

HELEN: It did strike me as being a wee bit fatuous and sickly.

WILLIAM: Exactly. Like sitting down after dinner and eating two pounds of chocolate creams.

HELEN: But it isn't the absence of that stuff that is making her feel dissatisfied. What she feels is that he's beginning to be bored with her.

WILLIAM: Now why? A man comes home tired at the end of a hard day, and naturally he wants to take it easy and——

HELEN: Yes, yes, we know all about that, and even women can understand it, seeing that they often have even harder days and aren't allowed to take it easy and sprawl and yawn in everybody's face. But what infuriates a wife is this sort of thing.

HELEN *exits*.

[477]   Q*

WILLIAM: What sort of thing?

JOYCE: Watch and you'll see, William.

Curtains open to same scene. ROSEMARY *is reading a book this time.*

ROSEMARY: And I must say I don't blame her. Do you? (*Pause as before.*) Is there anything particularly interesting in that paper, dear?

PAUL (*looking up blankly*): What? No. (*Half stifles a yawn and returns to reading.*)

ROSEMARY (*after another pause*): Did anything amusing happen at the office to-day, Paul?

PAUL (*indifferently*): No, can't remember anything.

She looks at him despairingly but he doesn't even see it. After another pause, to establish atmosphere of boredom, HELEN *marches in, looking very trim and gay.*

HELEN (*briskly*): Hello, Rosemary. 'Lo, Paul! Just looked in to ask you about Saturday.

PAUL: Saturday by all means, Helen. By the way, a most amusing thing happened at the office this morning. We've got a new client, a Mrs. Dowson, who's actually very rich, but looks a queer, shabby old thing. We've also got a new charlady whose name happens to be Mrs. Rowston. (*Laughs.*) Well, this morning this Mrs. Rowston comes in for the first time, and of course the clerk thinks the name she gives is Mrs. Dowson, treats her with enormous politeness, can't understand why she keeps mumbling something about cleaning and keeps apologising abjectly because my partner and I aren't about.

He laughs, so does HELEN. ROSEMARY *does not laugh.*

HELEN (*clearly forcing her appreciation*): What a priceless thing to happen!

ROSEMARY: It doesn't amuse me very much, somehow. The only difference between the two women was that one had a lot of money and the other hadn't any. And I don't think that's funny.

PAUL: Oh—nonsense, Rosemary. (*Pats her on the shoulder.*) That's taking it altogether too seriously.

HELEN: Did you read that extraordinary case of the woman who had two flats and lived a completely different life in them?

PAUL (*eagerly*): Yes. I was just reading about it now. Fascinating business. I don't think she was mad though, do you?

HELEN: No. I believe there was a man in it somewhere.

ROSEMARY: Where *is* this woman?

HELEN: In all the papers to-day.

ROSEMARY (*to* PAUL): And you said there wasn't anything interesting in the paper you were reading.

HELEN (*in ordinary tone*): All right, Rosemary, I think that's enough. You see, that's what I mean. If a man's tired, all right, let him be tired. It's a bit dull for wives, who've been messing about at home all day, if husbands come back in the evening fit for nothing but sprawling and yawning.

ROSEMARY: But we'll make the best of it so long as they *are* genuinely tired, and not simply bored. But you saw what happened. As soon as another woman, an attractive woman, of course, came in, he was up and sparkling, trying to be amusing, ready to show off as hard as he could——

PAUL: I really can't see that just because I show a little ordinary politeness to a friend—a friend of yours as well as mine—you should work yourself up into a jealous fury.

ROSEMARY: I wasn't jealous, and it just shows how stupid you are to imagine I was. I was annoyed because you could take the trouble to entertain Helen when you'd just proved very plainly you couldn't be bothered to entertain me.

WILLIAM (*whistles and beckons them up to him*): I see the point.

HELEN: He sees the point. (*To audience*) We're getting on.

WILLIAM (*turning to* PHILIP): But after all, when somebody calls, you have to exert yourself a little, for the sake of ordinary social decency——

PHILIP: And I agree—— (*He breaks off because both women are shaking their heads.*)

ROSEMARY: I must say, William, I expected something better than that from *you*——

PAUL (*bitterly*): Not from *me*, of course, being only your husband.

WILLIAM: "A wife", said Dostoevsky, after covering himself with glory at a shooting gallery, when his wife had been angry with him for trying to shoot at all—"A wife," he observed profoundly, "is the natural enemy of her husband."

PAUL: And I know exactly what he means.

PHILIP: So do I and I wish I didn't.

HELEN: And I never heard anything more ridiculous. I'm surprised at you, William.

ROSEMARY: So am I.

JOYCE: I thought he was intelligent.

WILLIAM: I am intelligent and so was Dostoevsky.

[479]

ROSEMARY (*bitterly*): The point is, having another woman there he was no longer bored.

HELEN: Perfectly obvious and perfectly maddening.

JOYCE (*rising*): Haven't we all seen it over and over again?

PHILIP (*also rising angrily*): Because you're so childish. You want everything at once.

PAUL: You can't have it both ways.

WILLIAM: You can't have your cake and eat it.

JOYCE (*angrily*): Oh—stop talking rot!

ROSEMARY (*angrily*): What can't we have both ways?

HELEN (*angrily*): Oh—don't begin about that cake.

The men all laugh together at this. The women have all spoken at once, they give each other apologetic little smiles and apologise profusely to each other. Then glare at the men. The women have drifted back and grouped themselves round the piano left. The men begin speaking at once.

PHILIP: It's perfectly simple and I'll explain.

PAUL: What I mean by not having it both ways is——

WILLIAM: Wanting to have your cake and eat it means this——

The women all laugh as the men did at this. The men stop and apologise in a hearty, masculine style to each other.

PHILIP: Sorry, old man! You were going to say——?

PAUL: Not at all, old boy. My fault. Interrupted you both.

The men group themselves round and lean against piano right; they remain in a huddle.

WILLIAM: That's all right, my dear fellow. You go ahead.

JOYCE (*in dry, hard tone*): Lord help us! When you take a good cool look at them, you wonder why you ever bother. They're so damned idiotic. (*Savagely burlesquing them*) No, not at all, old man. Go on, old boy. Urr!

PHILIP: One of us had better speak for the lot.

WILLIAM: Good idea! What about you, Paul?

PAUL: No, you're the chap, William. Your job, old boy.

WILLIAM (*muttering*): All right, old boy.

HELEN (*coolly*): They're like schoolboys who've been allowed to sit up late and guzzle and swill as much as they liked and so have all gone to seed.

ROSEMARY: They don't even try—as we do—to keep young outside while letting themselves grow older inside.

HELEN: Just overgrown, sagging, ruined schoolboys.

WILLIAM (*rising slowly*): Ladies, after we have fallen in love with you we feel that existence would be intolerable if you are not by our sides, so we marry you. What happens then?

ROSEMARY: You take us for granted and are bored.

WILLIAM: That is how you see it, but not how we see it.

PHILIP *and* PAUL: Hear, hear!

WILLIAM: You are now associated in our minds with *Home*, with relaxation, with slippered ease, with all the cosy humdrum of domestic life, with lazy chit-chat——

JOYCE (*bitterly*): And sprawling and yawning.

WILLIAM: If necessary, yes, with sprawling and yawning. With you we feel we need no longer pretend, for we are at home. There is something in most women, however, that feels itself defeated by the ease and familiarity of marriage. (*He stands on stool and assumes the air and deportment of a political speaker.*) It is not that you dislike the cosy domesticity, the slippers and dressing-gown atmosphere. But at any moment when you feel so inclined you think you are entitled to be regarded as a person clean outside this atmosphere, a strange, exciting creature, a figure of romance.

ROSEMARY (*pointing to* WILLIAM): But that's the point. We *are* strange, exciting creatures and what's wrong with you men is that you stop thinking we are, and then you diminish us. We grow angry because there is a light in us and you will no longer let it shine for you.

    She returns to the piano.

PAUL: But the light has been turned into the domestic lamp and firelight. Your trouble is you want to be courted as well as married.

HELEN: And why not?

WILLIAM: Because—and this is one of the cakes you can't both have and eat—to our way of thinking one relationship cancels out the other. Husbands take wives for granted. Of course they do. They married them in order to take them for granted. But wives take husbands for granted just as much, and that, ladies and gentlemen, is our case.

    WILLIAM *drops off stool.* PHILIP *shakes him by the hand,* PAUL *does the same. They go into a huddle round the piano again.*

ROSEMARY: It doesn't *suit* women to be taken for granted. (*Stamps her foot.*) It withers them.

    JOYCE *sits at the piano and plays a few mournful chords.*

HELEN: What's that?

JOYCE: It's the beginning of a lament for women.

JOYCE *plays very softly throughout women's speeches.*

HELEN (*grouped near* JOYCE *with* ROSEMARY): Who was the last to enter the Paradise of Eden—and the first out?

ROSEMARY: The fool who can light up at a single kind word and bleed at a glance.

JOYCE: Who buys a new hat and hopes against hope.

HELEN (*in a grander style and going up on to centre of rostrum*): I sing—after the manner of Walt Whitman, who nevertheless, has always seemed to me an insufferable old bore—I chant the theme Woman. Not Woman and the joys of the open road, for no woman ever had an open road. All roads are narrow, dark, bristling and dangerous to a woman. Not Woman and the happiness of loafing, hanging about, watching other people work and producing nothing but noble platitudes, because no woman is allowed—by herself or by anybody else—to indulge in such idle antics.

Some men are handsomely paid and kept in comfort to prove and preach that the ultimate force in the universe is nothing but Love, and they may or may not believe it. But all women, even the stupidest and ugliest that nobody cares about, act as if this were true. (*Comes down to piano and leans against it.*) And much good it does them.

ROSEMARY: It is terrible to be a woman and know in your heart how dependent you are upon other people, how you wait and wait for some fool of a man, who doesn't happen to have anything better to do, to bring you completely to life.

JOYCE: There are too many of us, that's the trouble.

ROSEMARY: A hurried, indifferent kiss, a hint of a yawn, from some man who isn't really very different from millions of other men, and ice is packed round your heart.

JOYCE: What we need is ice packed round our heads. (*Finish of music.*)

HELEN: After being a woman, to be a man must be like having a long rest, a sort of convalescence——

PHILIP *slides into piano chair and interrupts with some loud, sharp chords while the women look at him.*

PHILIP (*piano silent*): Convalescence! You can't imagine what it's like being a man. It's like this. (*Plays some loud, restless, strident music.*) I tell you—it's hell. (*Plays softly now, but with loud chords between speeches.*)

WILLIAM: In the fields you see the cows staring at nothing with their great soft eyes, placidly grazing and chewing, cosily manufacturing to-morrow's milk. Look further, into some lonely field or dark shed, and you will hear unhappy snorts and grunts and see a majestic but restless form, a creature passionate and bewildered, with a ring through his nose. (*Pause.*) The Bull! And that is Man.

PAUL (*quick leap on to rostrum*): Man, fixed for ever in his terrible dualism, the war between the spirit and the senses that no woman can understand. Man who grasps at the moon, and finds himself eating green cheese. Man, who cannot be lulled by the rhythms of the fat earth and who is haunted by the Paradise you hardly remember.

PHILIP (*sadly*): After all, it is better to buy a hat and hope a bit than to buy dozens of drinks and know there is no hope.

WILLIAM: When a pair of lovers declare themselves, one of them thinks he is juggling with the sun, moon and stars, while the other is busy working out how much it will cost to keep a housemaid in one of those nice new bungalows along Elm Avenue. It is safe to prophesy which one of these two will come a cropper first. The chaps who saw themselves keeping the sun, moon and stars going are bound to come down with a bump. The ladies—God bless them—have never left the ground.

PAUL: Man—alternating between Don Quixote and Don Juan——

PHILIP *points to* WILLIAM *indicating that the women are not listening.*

WILLIAM (*to* PAUL): I don't think they're listening, my dear fellow. Better get back on the job.

PAUL: What? Oh, yes, certainly. (*He goes back into the inner stage, sits in arm-chair.*)

WILLIAM (*crossing to* HELEN *and* ROSEMARY): Come along, you two. Never should have stepped out of the scene like that y'know. Spoils the illusion.

HELEN *and* ROSEMARY *go up on rostrum, take up their former positions.*

HELEN: I'll just say good-bye to you both, and then you show how annoyed you are with him, and we'll carry on from there.

Well, I must run along, children. Oh—what about Saturday? (HELEN *and* PAUL *rise.*)

ROSEMARY (*coldly*): Paul can go if he likes—but I'm sorry—I can't.

PAUL: But you said——

ROSEMARY: I promised to spend the afternoon with Father. You go. I'm sure you'll find it very amusing.

HELEN: Settle it between you and give me a ring, one of you, in the morning. 'Bye, darling.

ROSEMARY: Good-bye, Helen.

PAUL: I'll see you out.

PAUL *goes out with* HELEN. ROSEMARY *now looks furious, takes up her book and hurls it down in chair.*

ROSEMARY (*muttering angrily*): Oh! damn—damn—damn!

These get softer as she drops into chair. PAUL *enters and offers her cigarette box.*

PAUL (*with forced cheerfulness*): Cigarette, darling?

ROSEMARY (*very cold and distant*): No, thank you.

PAUL: Anything the matter?

ROSEMARY: No, why should there be?

PAUL: I dunno—I just wondered. I thought you were very keen on going with them on Saturday.

ROSEMARY (*miles away*): Did you?

PAUL: Well, you said you were.

ROSEMARY: I haven't the least desire to go with them. I loathe the Sunderlands anyhow. I've always thought your friend Helen had a very queer taste in people.

PAUL (*raising his eyebrows*): *My* friend Helen now, eh——?

She does not reply.

She used to be your friend too. In fact you knew her before I did.

ROSEMARY: I only knew her through William. And I *adore* William. I don't dislike Helen, but I think she has some very queer friends and I'd just as soon she didn't bounce in and out like that, even if you have to make such a fuss of her.

PAUL (*very innocently*): Fuss of her! What fuss did I make of her?

ROSEMARY: If you join them on Saturday, you'll be able to have a whole day of it, with funny stories about charwomen and women who live in two flats at once and everything.

PAUL: Look here, I didn't care tuppence about Saturday but if you insist upon taking that tone about it, all right, I *am* going.

ROSEMARY: I should. It'll be a nice change for you after being so bored at home.

PAUL (*angry now*): Now when have I ever said I was bored at home?

ROSEMARY: You didn't need to *say* anything.

PAUL: Well, what have I done then? What's the matter?

ROSEMARY (*stormily*): Nothing. (*Close to tears*) Everything.

She goes out, we hear loud door-slam. Curtains close.

HELEN: Well, there they are then.

WILLIAM: Yes, and I was working out their future. I see three stages waiting for them. First, a stage of constant and bitter quarrelling. Secondly, a stage in which each seeks satisfaction elsewhere. Thirdly, a stage of final separation or a real reconciliation and the beginning of a decent adult life together.

HELEN: Very good, darling. I couldn't have done it better myself.

WILLIAM: You couldn't have done it as well as I did.

HELEN: Yes I could. Actually, you've left out a stage. You see, with some couples like Paul and Rosemary, there's another stage that comes before the constant quarrelling; in this period each partner finds a friend of the same sex that the other partner very much dislikes. It might be called the Unwise Friendship Stage.

WILLIAM: You're right. (*To audience*) She *is* right, y'know. Very clever woman. Most men, especially Englishmen, dislike clever women, but I like 'em. So long as they're reasonably good-tempered, of course. (*Pause.*) An *amiable* clever woman is an absolute treasure. (WILLIAM *takes her hand, brings her downstage.*) Thank you. You've probably been wondering what our relationship is—haven't you? It's very interesting. And perhaps later on—well, we'll see. (*To* HELEN) You're dead right, of course.

HELEN: Rosemary will suddenly become friendly with some terrible woman whom Paul can't stand.

WILLIAM: And Paul will pick up a pal who's poison to Rosemary.

HELEN: It seems accidental—and yet—I don't know——

WILLIAM: The subconscious does it, I think. It deliberately singles out the type that the other partner loathes. (*Pause.*) Well, it's up to us, I suppose.

HELEN: Certainly. What are you going to be?

WILLIAM: I shall be one of those self-made City bachelors. They're always dining in very expensive restaurants and they put up the money for bad musical comedies. Wives hate them, because they imagine that these fellows have flats somewhere crowded with showgirls drinking champagne-cocktails and playing strip poker.

HELEN (*interested*): And have they?

WILLIAM: No, it's all an illusion. Nevertheless, the instinct of the wives is right, because these chaps are fundamentally anti-domestic and try to turn the husbands back into bachelors. That's me, then. And what about you?

HELEN: I shall be Mrs. Ambergate—Gloria Ambergate. I'm separated from my husband—he probably cleared out with his typist —and now I've got a down on all husbands and am very very sorry for the poor wives. And she's gone in for New Thought and Higher Thought and Astral Planes and Auras and Vibrations and she sees

[485]

everybody's personality in terms of colour. And she has a general deep soulfulness from which the coarse scoffing male is excluded.

WILLIAM: I know the type. But Rosemary would never put up with her.

HELEN: Oh yes, she would—for a time. Just because she was sorry for her. It often happens among women. Being members of the gentler and more sympathetic sex——

WILLIAM (*astonished*): Members of the what?

HELEN (*shouting*): The more sympathetic sex—idiot.

WILLIAM: Yes, I see. Well, that's us, then.

HELEN (*to the pianists*): And you two ought to find Leitmotivs for——

WILLIAM: Jimmy Mowbray.

HELEN: Gloria Ambergate.

HELEN *and* WILLIAM *exit*.

PHILIP: Oh, I've got mine. (*Pause.*) This is Jimmy Mowbray. (*He plays snatch of cheerful, rather vulgar dance tune.*)

JOYCE: And this is Gloria Ambergate. (*Plays a snatch of cheaply "soulful" music.*)

PHILIP: Good. Now we can make 'em into something. Short prelude to Scene illustrating this stage of Unwise Friendships.

JOYCE: Alternative title: What on earth Do you See in Him—or Her?

Finish of music they bow to each other. Curtains open to show same set. PAUL *enters with tray with cocktail shaker and glasses. Telephone rings, which* PAUL *answers in dumb show during last bars of music.*

PAUL (*as music ends*): Ha, ha, ha. Of course it's not too early. Come along at once, all right then. Good-bye for now.

ROSEMARY *enters and sits with a book.*

Will you have—er—have a cocktail?

ROSEMARY: No thank you. You know I hardly ever have a cocktail. I think it's an awful waste making them. And why *three* glasses? (*She opens book.*)

PAUL (*uncomfortably*): Well—as a matter of fact—Jimmy Mowbray rang up to say he might look in.

ROSEMARY (*disgusted*): What again? He'd better come and live here, hadn't he?

PAUL (*with great dignity*): Mowbray happens to be a client of mine.

ROSEMARY: That has nothing to do with it, and you know it hasn't. And what you can see in him I can't imagine.

PAUL: Oh—he's not a bad fellow.

ROSEMARY: He's *terrible*. And Sybil Stinnes says he has a flat crowded with chorus girls all drinking champagne-cocktails. Really, Paul, I thought you'd better taste than that.

PAUL (*irritably*): Oh—don't be so snobbish. Jimmy Mowbray may not be your type——

ROSEMARY: My type! He's not anybody's type outside a race-course and non-stop variety. He's——

PAUL (*cutting in sharply*): Jimmy Mowbray's quite a decent, amusing sort of fellow—who might turn out to be a very good client——

ROSEMARY: And then again might not. I wouldn't trust a man like that a yard. Still, I suppose if he wants to turn this house into his cocktail-bar I mustn't complain.

PAUL (*unpleasantly*): Oh—you couldn't complain. You wouldn't know how to.

ROSEMARY: Thank you. (*Giving him a wounded stare.*)

> ROSEMARY *goes to telephone and begins dialling.* JOYCE *plays Ambergate theme softly.* ROSEMARY *speaks into telephone with marked sweetness.* PAUL *sits and picks up paper from table; begins to read it.*

ROSEMARY: Oh—is that you Gloria? Rosemary. . . . Yes, I suppose it might be telepathy.

> PAUL *looks across and snorts.*

No, Gloria, you come here. . . .

> PAUL *throws paper down on table.*

Yes, as soon as you like. . . . Good. (*Puts down telephone.*)

PAUL (*glaring at her*): Was that your dear friend Gloria Ambergate?

ROSEMARY: Yes. She's coming across to spend the evening here.

PAUL (*angrily*): If that awful woman comes here, I'm going straight out.

ROSEMARY (*with mock innocent air*): I thought you were probably going out anyhow, with your nice friend Mr. Mowbray. Weren't you?

PAUL (*rather confusedly*): He suggested our dining somewhere—but I hadn't said definitely I would.

ROSEMARY (*same tone as before*): Well, now you can, and that'll be very nice for you.

PAUL: I warned you before. If you must see that frightful half-baked woman—and what on earth you can see in her beats me—please don't ask her here when I'm about. I *loathe* the woman.

Really, I'm surprised at you, Rosemary. A year or two ago, you couldn't have spent an hour with a woman like that, and now——

ROSEMARY (*vehemently*): Yes, *now*—when I have to watch you being dragged off every other night by that—that——

> *Sharp ring of bell off.* PAUL *rises and hurries out.* ROSEMARY *glares after him, then hastily takes up shaker and smells it in disgust, then hastily puts it down and assumes an air of distant dignity.* WILLIAM *enters as Mowbray.*

WILLIAM (*who has entered laughing*): Ah! Good evening, Mrs. Weybridge.

ROSEMARY (*coldly*): Good evening.

WILLIAM: Wonder if I might snatch your husband—dine with me to meet another friend just back from South America—just the kind of bloke to amuse Paul. Quiet bachelor evening. Steak and a decent bottle o' wine, y'know—an' perhaps finish our cigars at a variety show.

PAUL (*who has been pouring out drinks*): Cocktails? Rosemary?

ROSEMARY (*distantly*): No thank you.

PAUL (*handing one over*): Mowbray?

WILLIAM (*taking it*): Ta! Well, down the hatch!

PAUL: Dry enough for you?

WILLIAM: Oh, yes. Do with a dash p'r'haps. Like a dash myself.

PAUL: Ah—sorry about that.

ROSEMARY (*distantly*): And what is a dash?

WILLIAM: Dash? Don't you know what a dash is? Where have you been? It's absinthe.

ROSEMARY (*condemning it*): Oh—absinthe.

WILLIAM (*not noticing her attitude*): That's it. Absinthe makes the heart grow fonder, eh? (*Guffaws.*) Well, I won't say No to another, old boy.

> PAUL *pours out another drink.*

Had a hard day to-day. Market's all over the place. Still, never say die. (*Gives* ROSEMARY *a hearty pat on the back.*) Met a bloke at lunch to-day who's bringing that musical show over from New York —and blow the expense (*takes drink from* PAUL)—y'know the big smash hit there—*Got What It Takes* or something. Says if he can sneak most of it past the Lord Chamberlain, it'll make London's hair stand on end. He's importing all the original girls. (*Nudging* PAUL *with elbow.*)

ROSEMARY (*coldly*): I would have thought we'd enough chorus girls here without bringing some all the way from New York.

WILLIAM: That's just your innocence, Mrs. Weybridge. These American kids have got something. Ask your husband. Well, down the hatch.

> *Another sharp ring at bell.* PAUL *makes as if to go but ROSE-MARY rises and goes herself.*

PAUL (*dropping his voice*): We'd better push off in a minute, Jimmy. This woman's terrible.

WILLIAM: What woman?

PAUL: You'll see.

WILLIAM: Isn't time for it now, but remind me when we get out to tell you the story of the widow and the piano tuner. It'll kill you. By the way, this bloke you're going to meet—like most of these lads just back from the pampas or whatever they are—is a bit hot and might want to start a pretty thick sort of evening. Have to sit on his head a bit. You don't want any young female society to-night, do you?

PAUL: No, definitely not.

WILLIAM: Same here. Last week-end was bad enough and I've a business to look after. (*Takes another drink which PAUL has poured out.*)

> HELEN *enters as Gloria Ambergate, followed by* ROSEMARY. HELEN *contrives to register her disapproval of the two men and the cocktails at once.*

PAUL: Oh—good evening, Mrs. Ambergate.

HELEN: How d'you do?

ROSEMARY: Gloria—this is Mr. Mowbray.

WILLIAM: How d'you do?

HELEN (*coldly*): Good evening.

PAUL: Cocktail, Mrs. Ambergate?

HELEN (*sitting*): Oh—no, thank you. I can't take alcohol in any form.

WILLIAM (*taking drink offered by* PAUL *to* HELEN): Can't you? It's about the only thing I can take nowadays. (*Laughs.*) Well, Weybridge, better push off, eh?

PAUL: I'm ready. (*Drinks up and puts glasses on table.*)

WILLIAM: Well, the skin off your nose. (*Drinking to* HELEN.) Good night, Mrs. Weybridge.

> WILLIAM *exits.*

ROSEMARY: Don't be too late, Paul.

PAUL: No, I won't be. 'Night Mrs. Ambergate.

HELEN: That man, Rosemary—who is he?

[489]

ROSEMARY: He's a client of Paul's. You can say what you like about him. I loathe him.

HELEN: I'm so glad, dear. I was sure you must. He's a dreadfully undeveloped type. *Earthy*—quite earthy. With a muddy brown aura. I wish you could have been at our lecture last Wednesday. Mdme Rubbishky gave us a *wonderful* talk on I AM THE GREAT ALL——

ROSEMARY: On what?

HELEN (*solemnly*): I AM THE GREAT ALL. And so *profound* —so *stimulating* and yet at the same time so essentially *simple*. We are all of us the Great All. And the Great All is all of us. The whole *thing* was there.

ROSEMARY: I'm not sure I believe in all this, you know.

HELEN: I didn't expect you would, dear, not yet. Perception comes with suffering and loneliness of spirit. You'll see.

ROSEMARY (*dismayed*): But I don't want any suffering and loneliness of spirit.

HELEN: It won't be so bad for you, dear, as it was for me. You'll have friends—certainly *one* friend, darling—who can help and guide. As soon as I saw that man here to-night, and saw him taking your husband away, I knew at once that soon you'll need a friend very badly. I could *feel* a downward, earthward influence——

ROSEMARY: But what kind of influence is that, Gloria?

HELEN: It's downward—earthward, dear—pulling down. I've always been able to feel it, even before I knew what it meant. Chiefly among men, of course. And I've always *known* it was antagonistic. But I myself rejected the influence. I said "You cannot pull me down, I am *all* spirit", I said.—And, of course, I was.

PHILIP: I say, Helen, is there much more of this horrible stuff?

HELEN (*in ordinary tone*): Yes, Philip. Hours and hours.

PHILIP: Then let's cut to midnight. Lights!

Lights black-out. Clock chimes twelve. As lights go on again ROSEMARY *is discovered slumped down in her chair, half asleep, and* HELEN *lying on the floor with her head on a chair.*

HELEN: . . . And four Hindu disciples living in the spare room. Good gracious—twelve o'clock already. We've had such a wonderful lovely satisfying talk, it's just given the evening great golden wings —and—pouf—it's just flown away. (*She rises,* ROSEMARY *giving her a helping hand.*)

ROSEMARY (*stifling a yawn*): Yes, hasn't it?

HELEN (*solemnly*): But I do hope nothing has happened to your husband, dear.

ROSEMARY: Of course not. Why should it? Just a moment, I'll put the light on. (*Exits.*)

HELEN (*moving to door*): It's all very well saying, of course not, my dear. But I can't forget the night I was sitting up late with poor Mildred Fothergill. We heard the ambulance ringing right outside her window, and the telephone went and a voice said, "Come at once, Mrs. Fothergill". But, of course, it was all over by the time she got to the hospital. Mr. Fothergill had departed for the Astral Sphere, and had not even insured himself properly.

Lights on the stage black-out and come up to Full again. We hear the clock strike one o'clock. ROSEMARY *has now changed into a dressing-gown to indicate time lapse. She enters, goes to window and looks out. She seems agitated, now moves to table and is about to pick up telephone but decides not to. Just as she is about to sit down the telephone rings urgently.*

ROSEMARY (*rushing to telephone*): Yes, yes . . .? (*Then sharply.*) No, we're not . . . Well, I ought to know whether we're the gasworks or not. You've got the wrong number, that's all. . . . (*As she puts down the receiver, she mutters to herself*) Silly idiot. . . .

An ambulance bell now rings furiously. This disturbs ROSE-MARY *and she moves restlessly about the stage.*

Enter WILLIAM *from alcove.*

WILLIAM: What's the matter with her?

JOYCE: Paul's late, so now her imagination will get to work. We all do it.

ROSEMARY (*lights fade and* ROSEMARY *picked out in a single pink spot*): . . . the hospital, please driver—and hurry—it's terribly urgent —yes, nurse, I'm Mrs. Weybridge, take me to him—oh!—yes, I'll be brave—I will be brave. (*Then in worrying tone like that in Act One.*) I'd have to ask Father to come up to look after things—and I couldn't let Robin stay here—perhaps he and Nannie could go to Alice's for the week—and as soon as I'd got them off I'd have to order my black —and then when it was all over I couldn't afford to stay on here— I'd have to sell this house—then try to find a little cottage in the country—and then Robin would have to go away to school—but we'd share our little cottage during all his holidays. (*Sighing very dreamily now.*) Yes, dear, it's years ago now, and they realise that my Paul was a great architect—and they want me to unveil a memorial to him—it will be a beautiful experience but, of course, sad too. (*The lights begin to come now,* ROSEMARY *moves upstage to sit down. She is dabbing her eyes with a handkerchief.*)

[491]

We hear PAUL *outside, he is whistling the Mowbray theme, but she does not hear him. He enters.*

ROSEMARY (*with joy and surprise*): Paul! (*Rising.*)

PAUL: I'm sorry, my dear. You shouldn't have waited up——

ROSEMARY (*severely*): Where have you been?

WILLIAM: The eternal question. (*Pause.*) And now I understand why they always put it so angrily.

PAUL: Mowbray took me to his club—and we began playing snooker—and then I couldn't get a taxi. You know how it is, my dear. What have you been doing?

ROSEMARY: Listening to Gloria for hours and hours——

PAUL (*laughing to himself*): Oh! Bad luck.

WILLIAM (*turning to* JOYCE): I wonder if the chump realises this is his chance. He's had as much as he wants of Jimmy Mowbray and she's had far more of Gloria Ambergate. I wonder if he realises this. Oh dear, it doesn't look as if he does.

PAUL *is pouring himself a glass of whisky from the bottle but this bottle only contains sufficient for one glass, therefore he has tipped the bottle up and is draining it.*

PAUL (*drinking*): You know very well, Rosemary, that's a terribly dreary woman.

ROSEMARY: I know—but I'm sorry for her, though I admit she can be an awful bore. But she's lonely. Not like your friend Jimmy Mowbray, who's so pleased with himself.

PAUL: Well I'll admit that Jimmy is a bit much at times. But Oria Glambergate—is a tearily dreary——

ROSEMARY: Paul, I believe you're tight.

PAUL (*swaying about and toying with his glass*): If I say I am, you'll believe I'm not, which wouldn't be quite true. But if I say I'm not, then you'll think I'm very tight, which would be quite wrong. Better ignore the whole thing.

WILLIAM: Now, what's her reaction going to be? She might burst into tears. She might lose her temper and throw something at him. She might rise haughtily and sweep out of the room. Or she——

ROSEMARY *suddenly bursts out laughing. It is quite warm and friendly laughter. He seems to her, at this moment, very funny.*

JOYCE (*as* ROSEMARY'S *laughter is quieter*): This is his chance.

WILLIAM: Of course it is. He's only to drop down and put his arms round her and babble any nonsense and she's his again.

JOYCE (*scornfully*): But he isn't going to. (*Pause.*) You men!

WILLIAM (*sadly*): Pompous vanity is our weakness.

PAUL (*with foolish dignity*): Glad you're amused.

ROSEMARY (*still ready to be reconciled*): Paul, don't be silly.

PAUL: After spending five hours exchanging idiocies with that woman, you can ask me not to be silly!

ROSEMARY: Oh—you are a fool!

Exits. We hear door being slammed. He stares after her half bewildered, half angry, then stares blankly out front. There is a little broken music.

WILLIAM: Let's hide the poor chump.

Curtains close.

HELEN *enters from alcove as ordinary self.* WILLIAM *takes her arm and brings her downstage.*

HELEN: We shall have to look at them now, somewhere in the middle of the next stage.

WILLIAM (*reflectively*): Now wait a minute. Constant quarrelling is bad for both, of course, but I think that in this quarrelling stage the woman is better off than the man.

He says no more because HELEN *begins straightening his tie, brushing his hair back and generally trying to smarten up his appearance. She takes him by left ear and turns him to* JOYCE.

HELEN: And that's supposed to be a clever one. Imagine what some of the rest are like!

JOYCE: He just doesn't know, dear. How could he?

WILLIAM (*severely and rather annoyed*): Instead of indulging in idle antics, I will produce a reason or two for my statement. The woman is better off because—first—an emotional outburst, a *scene* is less repugnant to her than it is to the wretched man, who will go to almost any length to avoid one. Secondly, the woman has a superior technical equipment and knows instinctively how to put the fellow in the wrong and keep him there, and has a diabolical skill in detecting the weak joints in his armour.

HELEN: The said armour consisting of solid plates a foot thick of masculine vanity, conceit and self-complacency. While the poor woman, her heart thumping away, her tummy tying itself into knots, has no armour and feels completely naked.

PHILIP: But I thought you liked to feel naked.

HELEN (*doing a funny walk*): Five minutes after he has stamped out of the house the man begins to forget about the quarrel, and by the time he has plunged into the day's business it no longer exists for him. But the woman lives with the quarrel all day and half the night, as if she were wrestling with a giant scorpion. She hears the angry voices hour after hour. Her whole world looks as if it has been torn into quivering strips by an earthquake. The very chemistry of her entire being . . .

WILLIAM (*catching hold of her hand and kissing it*): Yes, yes, yes, my pet. An excellent speech. How well you do these things. We all enjoyed it. But I think we ought to be getting along. Let's have another look at them.

HELEN: Here they are then. Typical!

> *Curtains open. We now see the same room, but the table has been removed and in its place is a modern desk. There is a different picture on the wall, something which suggests the study of an architect.* PAUL *is sitting at his desk and making a few casual notes; he is not working very hard and after a moment or two* ROSEMARY, *looking rather pale and strained, enters and begins rather elaborately looking for something.*

ROSEMARY (*after a moment, very politely*): I'm sorry to disturb you.

PAUL (*with strained politeness*): No, that's all right. Can I——?

ROSEMARY (*still looking vaguely*): No. No. (*They get weaker.*)

> *She exits and after a moment or two she returns. This time she comes to centre, looking as if she has been in the room for hours.*

You haven't seen my scissors—the large pair—have you?

PAUL (*half rising, very politely*): No, I'm afraid I haven't. Can I——?

ROSEMARY (*looking round vaguely*): No. No. Sorry to disturb you, that's all.

PAUL (*sitting down again*): No, that's all right. (*Goes on with his work.*)

> ROSEMARY *gives him a sharp contemptuous look and goes out.*

WILLIAM: I don't quite see the point of this dodging in and out.

HELEN: She's giving him a chance to be human again and to say he's sorry, and then of course she'll say it's all her fault. But meeting this heavy politeness, she knows that the quarrel is still on.

WILLIAM: Why has the man to say he's sorry first? He nearly always has, you know.

HELEN: Yes, but once he does, the woman is nearly always ready to be downright abject.

WILLIAM: Quite so. But why has he to start the ball rolling?

HELEN: It's a kind of tradition with us.

WILLIAM (*pause*): That is very curious.

[494]

ROSEMARY *enters again and this time stands rather rigidly looking at him.*

Back again. Different technique this time.

HELEN: Yes. She's still giving him a chance, but now she's hardening rapidly. The excuse to talk to him will be a telephone conversation that she's saved up for this moment.

ROSEMARY (*in cold, polite tone*): I forgot to tell you that Mona Roberts rang up to ask if we'd dine with them on the fifteenth. Do you want to go?

PAUL (*rising slowly and taking off his spectacles*): Not particularly, I think he's rather a bore. But—you like her, don't you?

ROSEMARY (*same tone*): Yes, but I can see her some other time. It's not essential that you should go and be bored.

PAUL: No, if you want to go——

ROSEMARY: I know how easily you are bored.

PAUL (*heavily*): Was that necessary?

ROSEMARY (*furious*): Oh—don't be so pompous.

PAUL (*still heavily*): Really, I don't see why I should be accused of being pompous just because I try to be decently polite.

ROSEMARY (*cold, contemptuous*): Don't you?

PAUL (*with more warmth*): No, I don't.

ROSEMARY: Well, what am I to say to them about the fifteenth?

PAUL (*impatiently*): Oh—say what you like. What do I care!

ROSEMARY: What do you care about anything?

PAUL: What does that mean?

ROSEMARY (*contemptuously*): What do you think it means?

PAUL: I don't know.

ROSEMARY: No, of course, *you* wouldn't.

PAUL *and* ROSEMARY *turn their backs to each other.* WILLIAM *and* HELEN *rise. They look at* PAUL *and* ROSEMARY *in astonishment.*

WILLIAM (*to* HELEN): Y'know what's wrong with this is our horrible modern poverty of language. It's sheer misery to feel such sudden hate and despair and yet be so inarticulate.

HELEN: I agree. They'd feel ever so much better if they could let it rip.

WILLIAM: Then we'll let it rip for them. We'll make an Elizabethan job of it. Hold tight, girl! Blow, winds, and crack your cheeks.

HELEN: Rage, blow! You cataracts and hurricanoes——

[495]

There is a roll of thunder and a black-out. HELEN *and* WILLIAM
exit. PAUL *and* ROSEMARY *come downstage. Curtains close.* PAUL
sits stool right and ROSEMARY *on stool left. There are now lightning flashes and thunder.* WILLIAM *and* HELEN *enter from their
respective alcoves with cloaks. They come to centre on rostrum,
the lightning and thunder stops and two blue spots come on them.*

HELEN (*in grand manner*):
    Oh—that I should be tied to such a pudding bag
    Of dreary Vanity and duller wit. A thing
    Made up of braces, collar studs and starch,
    With hardly more red blood in it than drips
    Out of the poor frozen joint from Argentine.

WILLIAM:
    Imagine a cat five feet four inches high,
    Take away dignity and let it rage
    With deep inferiority—and that's a wife.

HELEN:
    Why—hot-water bottles of the cheaper sort,
    Bargains from Boots, bring me more comfort.
    Two and fourpence at the nearest Odeon
    Bring more romance or cheerful entertainment.

WILLIAM: (*pointing to* HELEN):
    You're Madame Nature's grim old conjuring trick.
    Every man's disappointment—girl into wife.
    I married a loving, ripe and merry lass,
    To find myself keeping, at a rising cost,
    A bitter woman who hates the sight of me.

HELEN (*coming to centre and standing in front of* WILLIAM):
    And why? Because I had a lover once
    And now he's disappeared, and in his place,
    For me to live with, are a costing clerk, a
    Lecturer, a stomach and a thirst.

HELEN *comes down to piano left.* WILLIAM *comes down to piano
right.* PAUL *and* ROSEMARY *rise.* JOYCE *and* PHILIP *rise.*

HELEN (*pointing to* WILLIAM): Oh, hateful, pompous clown!

WILLIAM (*pointing to* HELEN): Oh, damned, malicious shrew!

ROSEMARY *and* PAUL *point at each other also* JOYCE *and* PHILIP
do the same, all bitterly quarrelling.

*There is a crash of thunder and the lighting is held until the
curtain has fallen.*

END OF ACT TWO

ACT III

PHILIP *and* JOYCE *begin playing and go on brilliantly for a minute or so. Then he stops and, after a moment or so, she stops too.*

JOYCE (*annoyed, leaning on piano*): What's the matter, darling?

PHILIP: Well, nobody's coming on or anything. What happens now? You see, it's exactly what I said. They can't make a third act out of it. All the critics will say, "Not really a play at all, and even so it goes to pieces in the third act."

JOYCE: Well, you're quite wrong. (*Sits at piano again.*) The third act's all right and it's starting now. Listen!

Plays a few bars of pseudo-Oriental, mystical music.

PHILIP: What's that muck for? (*Pause.*) Are they bringing on a bogus Oriental illusionist?

JOYCE (*as she plays softly*): No, this is the fortune-telling music. Madame Aurora who's just returned from the East——

PHILIP: Probably Clacton-on-Sea.

JOYCE: —to read palms and gaze into crystals.

PHILIP: Rosemary's consulting her, I suppose?

JOYCE: Yes. (*Music stops.*) She and Paul have now arrived at the third stage, when each feels the other is hopeless and is ready to be consoled by somebody else. And so of course Rosemary's having her fortune told.

PHILIP: Using her husband's money to find out if there is any other chap on the way.

JOYCE: What a noble mind you have, maestro!

JOYCE *commences to play again in which* PHILIP *joins her in a mocking manner and curtains open to disclose corner of Mdme Aurora's sitting-room, with a few cheap pseudo-mystical decorations.* ROSEMARY *in outdoor clothes sits at small table with crystal on it, opposite* HELEN *as Mdme Aurora. She wears Oriental shawl, with grey hair showing under it, probably large spectacles. Music dies away.*

HELEN (*in thick common voice, looking at* ROSEMARY'S *hand*): Yes, dear, I see you're married. Two children——

ROSEMARY (*hastily*): One.

HELEN (*quickly*): That's right, dear. One. I'm afraid you're not

[497]

very happy. Nothing like so happy as you thought you was going to be. Of course, dear, your trouble is you're a lot more sensitive than people think—you're a very loving, sensitive nature, it's 'ere as plain as a pikestaff—an' what's the result? The result is people close to you 'urt your feelings when they 'ardly know they're doing it. An' what else? You go an' trust people—for you've a trusting nature. I can see that—an' then they go an' let you down. Isn't that right?

ROSEMARY: Yes, it is. I can't imagine how you can see me so clearly.

HELEN: It's a gift, dear. Very few 'ave it, an' even then it needs a lot of development. (*Coughing.*)

ROSEMARY: Could you—tell me what's going to happen?

HELEN (*taking and staring at* ROSEMARY'S *right hand*): I see a tall man coming over the sea with love for you in his 'eart. You'll meet 'im soon, quite soon, an' he'll make you very 'appy. I see a journey —and a strange bed.

ROSEMARY: What sort of strange bed? (*Withdraws her hand.*)

HELEN (*darkly*): Never you mind about that, dear. (*With marked change of manner*) And that'll be seven-and-sixpence, thank you, Mrs.—er——

ROSEMARY (*hastily*): Oh yes—of course. (*Rises and exits right.*) Thank you so much. Good morning.

HELEN (*rising as* ROSEMARY *goes*): Good morning.

Curtains close. PHILIP *with one hand plays quick harsh music.*

PHILIP (*pleased with himself*): Not bad, eh? Taxis. Street scene.

JOYCE: What about this? (*Plays a heavy thumping tune in march time.*)

PHILIP: Now what's that?

JOYCE: Major Spanner on the way.

PHILIP: Who's Major Spanner?

JOYCE (*loudly and cheerfully*): He was the wedding guest, you remember, who'd known her for a long time and didn't think Paul good enough for her. An awful chump, if you ask me, but nearly every woman's got one of these faithful hounds tucked away somewhere. Keep the street music going.

As he does, ROSEMARY *enters. She goes to centre below rostrum, looks at her watch, then glances at the space above footlights as if it were a shop window, catches sight of something that interests her, tries it on, so to speak, then rejects it and is just turning away, giving another glance at her watch, when* WILLIAM *enters as Major George Spanner, bronzed and trim, just back from the East. He*

[498]

you were happy. But now I know you're not, it's different. (*Pause. Fiercely, leaning back in chair.*) Good God, a wonderful little girl like you not being happy!

ROSEMARY (*half-laughing*): But you're forgetting. I'm not a little girl and haven't been for years. Not only am I married but I'm a mother—nearly a matron.

WILLIAM: Nonsense! To me you're a little girl—(*pats her hand*) —*my* little girl.

ROSEMARY: Really, George (*pats his hand*), I believe you've been taking a course of something. You say all the nice things I want to hear.

WILLIAM (*taking his hands from under hers, pats her hands again*): You won't like this, though it's got to be said. You're not happy, are you? Weybridge doesn't realise what a lucky fella he is.

ROSEMARY (*quietly, sincerely now*): It doesn't seem to be working, somehow.

WILLIAM: Queer thing. At your wedding do, some fool of a woman —a friend of *his*, of course—told me what a clever fella the bride-groom was. And I as good as told the woman there and then that in my opinion you were worth ten of him, ten of him. (*Pause.*) I've been uneasy in my mind ever since.

ROSEMARY (*affectionately*): Poor George!

WILLIAM (*fatuously*): Well, that's something. But—er—is that the best you can do?

ROSEMARY (*in half-comical whisper*): No.

WILLIAM (*doglike devotion in his stare, takes her hand and kisses it*): A wonderful little girl.

> *Curtains close.* HELEN *enters wearing no hat and a light coat or something to suggest outdoors.* PHILIP *plays some music.*

HELEN (*near entrance, calling*): Here I am, Paul.

> PAUL *enters in ordinary lounge suit without hat or overcoat. He carries a note-book with him. It is essential she should look a rich, attractive woman.*

HELEN: Now then, this is what I mean. Would it be possible to enlarge the wing that way? No, you can't see it properly from here. This is better. (*Takes his arm and leads him a few paces, keeping her hand inside his arm.*) Now you see what I mean?

PAUL: Yes, it could be done.

HELEN: Mind you, Paul, I wouldn't *dream* of letting anybody but you lay a *finger* on the house. You do understand that, don't you?

PAUL: Yes. That's very good of you.

HELEN (*turning so they face each other*): Paul—don't be so *professional*.

PAUL (*smiling*): Sorry, Frances. But you see, it was a professional question you were asking me.

HELEN: Oh—but I can't divide relationships into compartments like that. Don't forget (*moves closer and smiles seductively at him*) I'm a woman.

PAUL (*smilingly*): I'm not likely to forget that, my dear Frances. (*In mock whisper*) In fact, if I didn't think there were at least a couple of your housemaids watching us through a bedroom window, I'd probably behave—this very moment—very unprofessionally indeed.

HELEN: You talk as if architects could be struck off the register, like doctors.

PAUL: Oh—no, we can be trusted. If you don't make it too hard for us.

HELEN (*with change of attack*): Paul, I think you're looking tired.

PAUL: I have been rather hard at it lately.

HELEN: Of course. A man in your position and with your genius has to *give* and *give*. We all understand that. But it's obvious that wife of yours isn't looking after you at all.

PAUL: Well, as you know, we don't get on—and of course, now she isn't very much interested in my welfare.

HELEN (*with fine show of indignation*): Paul, I think it's *monstrous*! To have no *intellectual* companionship, no deep store of sympathy, at home—that's bad enough—in fact, for a man of your kind it's the worst thing of all—but on top of that simply to neglect the most obvious duties a woman has towards a man—oh!——

PAUL (*uncomfortably*): Well—there it is. (*About to change the subject.*) Do you think you'd like——?

HELEN (*breaking in, impressively*): Paul, I think I ought to meet your wife. Remember I haven't seen her since your wedding and don't know her at all. You ought to bring us together.

PAUL (*alarmed*): I don't think that would work very well, would it?

HELEN: My dear. *Please* remember I'm a sensible woman of the world—and don't get into a silly masculine panic. There won't be any scenes. I'm a client—we've something to talk over—so you ask me to your house. (*Taking his arm again.*)

PAUL: All right, only don't blame me if you don't enjoy yourself.

HELEN: Of course, I'll enjoy myself. Better make it lunch, though, not dinner. Just the three of us. I'll look at my book and see if we can fix a date.

They go out the way they came in. JOYCE *plays a few harsh chords.*

PHILIP: What on earth is that?

JOYCE (*grimly*): Just a brief sketch of the music for that lunch.

PHILIP: Is it going to be like that?

JOYCE: It'll be worse than that.

Enter WILLIAM *as himself.*

WILLIAM: Getting a bit tired of Major Spanner. Not a character that gives a fellow much scope. Where's Helen? Still doing Mrs. What's-her-name?

PHILIP: Yes. Mrs. de Folyat wants to meet Rosemary, so Paul's got to arrange a lunch.

JOYCE: If he'd any sense, of course, he'd have refused. The two women'll sit there, hating each other, and he'll be wretched. However, I like this third stage, with philandering just round the corner. I'm getting quite interested now.

WILLIAM (*addressing audience*): Not enough comment now, in my opinion. It's rapidly degenerating into ordinary theatrical muck.

PHILIP: That's what she likes.

JOYCE: It's what everybody likes. Let's see how they're getting on at that lunch.

WILLIAM: I'm against it. Leave 'em alone.

JOYCE: Just have a peep.

WILLIAM *jumps up on rostrum and stealthily peeps through curtains into inner scene, then comes away.*

How's it going?

WILLIAM (*sombrely*): Light thickens and the crow makes wing to the rooky wood.

PHILIP: Hamlet?

WILLIAM: Macbeth. And it's extraordinary—the way Shakespeare——

JOYCE (*impatiently breaking in*): Oh, never mind about Shakespeare now—I want to see what's happening at that lunch. It'll be over soon.

WILLIAM: Over now, I think.

WILLIAM *exits. Curtains open and show corner of dining-room.*

HELEN *is just going.* PAUL *is in centre standing.* ROSEMARY *and* HELEN *both have their backs to each other.*

[503]

HELEN (*with false gush*): Thank you *so* much, Mrs. Weybridge. It's been such a pleasure coming here and meeting you, especially after I've heard so much about you from your clever, clever husband.

ROSEMARY (*with obvious false geniality*): Awfully good of you to come, Mrs. de Folyat. I hope you'll come and dine with us sometime.

HELEN: That would be *lovely*.

PAUL: I'll see you down to your car (*crossing after her to left*) and then I must get back to the office. 'Bye, darling.

Follows HELEN *out*.

ROSEMARY: 'Bye, darling.

ROSEMARY *watches them go*.

Of all the false, faked-up, smarmy, poisonous man-hunters! It wouldn't be so bad if he'd found himself a *decent* woman.

PHILIP (*turning to* JOYCE): You women always say that, don't you?

JOYCE: Yes. We do——

ROSEMARY *has now gone to telephone and is dialling*.

ROSEMARY: Is that the Sahibs Club? Is Major Spanner there, please?

Curtains close. PHILIP *is playing de Folyat music.* JOYCE *comes in with the Spanner tune.*

PHILIP: Don't come in with that awful Major Spanner tune now. I'm playing the Mrs. de Folyat music.

JOYCE: I know you are, dear. But I don't particularly like the way you are playing it.

PHILIP: I was playing it very well.

JOYCE: Rather too well, I thought. I believe you are beginning to take an interest in that frightful woman.

PHILIP: I am. Very attractive type. And probably cleverer than she looks.

WILLIAM *enters*.

WILLIAM: Well, I lay six to four against her.

PHILIP: I'll take you. It's money for nothing. Paul hasn't a chance against that woman.

WILLIAM: Hasn't he? Well, I think she's going to learn that the situation is not quite as simple as she imagines. The relation between a husband and wife, even though they may be quarrelling all the time, is never simple, and I think we'll find that Mrs. What's-her-name—de Folyat—doesn't realise that and so plays the wrong card.

JOYCE: I am delighted to hear it.

WILLIAM: Well, let's see. But give her every chance. (*To pianists*) Music, atmosphere.

Curtains open. WILLIAM *exits alcove.* PHILIP *and* JOYCE *play de Folyat music.*

Scene shows corner of Mrs. de Folyat's sitting-room, similar to ROSEMARY'S, *but harder, brighter colours.* HELEN *as Mrs. de Folyat, in loose, semi-evening gown, is seeing that the right drinks —brandy, whisky, etc., are on low table and is all-expectant. She has a final glance at herself, and* PAUL *enters dressed as before.* JOYCE *leans on her piano.* HELEN, *arranging flowers, turns to meet him.*

PAUL: I came along as soon as I could. I was kept at the office until nearly nine.

HELEN (*all solicitude*): Poor boy! But have you had anything to eat?

PAUL: Yes, I had a quick bite at the club on the way here.

HELEN (*moving to table*): Drink then, eh? Whisky, brandy? This brandy's supposed to be rather wonderful. (*Pours out glass.*) Let me give you some. And sit back and relax. You poor boy, you must be so tired.

    PAUL *relaxing, while she gives him a liberal helping of brandy.*

HELEN: There, darling! (*Coming to behind sofa with the glass.*)

    Puts cushion behind PAUL. *As she stands near him, he takes her hand and she immediately leans over and kisses him, then fondles his face for a moment and lifts glass for him to drink. She sits centre of sofa.*

PHILIP: She knows her stuff all right.

JOYCE (*sharply*): Sh—sh. (PHILIP *stops playing.*)

    PHILIP *leans on his piano. They now look very cosy and relaxed.* PAUL *sips his drink.*

PAUL: You're perfectly right, Frances. This is a wonderful brandy.

HELEN: Well, my dear, I always take a little trouble and try and get the best of everything. I may not always look it, but, believe it or not, I'm rather a clever woman.

PAUL (*smiling, takes her hand*): You're a fascinating woman, and that's even more important. (*Kissing her hand.*)

    HELEN *puts her head on* PAUL'S *shoulder who is lying back with his arm round her.*

HELEN (*smiling at* PAUL): Well, we had our lunch.

PAUL (*not quite happily*): Yes, we had our lunch.

[505]

HELEN: And of course, being a man, you loathed every minute of it, didn't you?

PAUL: Yes, 'fraid I did.

HELEN (*soothingly*): Never mind. All over now. But, of course, I had to see for myself.

PAUL: And what did you see? (*Into his glass.*)

HELEN: My dear! Why, of course, you're quite right.

PAUL (*rather stiffly, lowering his glass*): What do you mean? About Rosemary?

HELEN: Of course. Everything you told me about her—as well as everything you meant to infer—was, of course, absolutely right. She's completely wrong for you.

PAUL (*tonelessly*): Yes. (*Puts glass on floor left of sofa.*) I suppose she is.

HELEN: But—I mean—I saw that in two minutes. I can quite see how it all began, of course. A nice, fresh, little thing. But now, you're quite right. You're growing all the time. She can't develop. In fact, like most women of her type, she's narrowing instead of broadening. It's not even a matter of being really *aware*—of being shall we say—intellectual—but, of course, she's not even moderately intelligent. In fact, let's admit it, she's *stupid*.

PAUL (*who has liked this less and less*): You know, you really saw Rosemary at her worst to-day. I mean, we've been having rows and so on—and then I think she spotted something.

HELEN: Oh—but then—as I say, it didn't take me two minutes to *see*. She *is* stupid.

PAUL (*angrily*): She isn't stupid.

HELEN: My dear Paul, there's no need to be cross merely because I'm agreeing with everything you've told me about her.

PAUL (*sulkily*): I never said she was stupid.

HELEN: Not in so many words, perhaps. It takes a woman to do that. But you've told me she doesn't make an effort to understand you—she doesn't try to develop. And now that I've seen her for myself I'm merely telling you in one word—why—because she's——

PAUL (*crossly*): Yes, yes, yes. You said it before.

HELEN: Paul. What's the matter?

PAUL (*turning to face her*): I suppose the matter—is that I don't enjoy listening to you sneering at my wife.

HELEN (*annoyed herself now*): Sneering! When I'm only——

PAUL (*cutting in sharply*): I know. You said that before too. Well, no doubt it's all very illogical, inconsistent and absurd, after the rot I've talked, but there it is—*I don't like it.* (*With forced change of manner*) I'm sorry, Frances, I've had a long day and I'm probably rather tired. I think I'd better go.

HELEN (*cooling rapidly*): I think you had. I also think you're behaving very stupidly.

PAUL: No doubt that's the trouble with us Weybridges—we're *all* stupid people. Thank you for the brandy. Good night.

> *He hurries out. Curtains close.* WILLIAM *exits.* PAUL *wearing light overcoat enters as if walking home. We hear him muttering angrily to himself.* PAUL *goes up on to rostrum. Moonlight spot comes on.*

PAUL: Damned cheek talking about my wife like that! Just damned cheek. Rich, spoilt woman—say anything.

> PAUL *takes same position in moonlight spot as in Act One, then listens.*

ROSEMARY (*voice off*): Darling . . . the lilac . . .

> *Chopin music as before.* PAUL *hears it.*

ROSEMARY (*voice off*): Chopin . . . perfect . . . only three days . . . I love you.

PAUL: Rosemary!

> *Lights stay down but music soars as he hurries out. Curtain draws on right alcove, where* PAUL *is discovered still in his rain-coat. Holding telephone, he is speaking into it eagerly.*

PAUL: Rosemary, listen, darling. . . . Oh, it's you, Nannie. Could I speak to Mrs. Weybridge, please. Gone away, well, if there's a note you'd better read it to me. . . . Gone away for the week-end, perhaps longer, all right then, Nannie. If she does ring up would you tell her I've gone away too, and I might be back on Monday, and I might not.

> *Some music. Curtain closes on alcove. Fade-in ordinary lighting.*

PHILIP: It's too bad she wasn't there, just when he was ready to make it up.

JOYCE (*rising*): Doesn't surprise me, though. That woman at lunch was the last straw, so she telephoned Major Spanner to take her away somewhere, for a nice little bit of consoling romance.

PHILIP (*showing more interest and rising*): Oh—that's it, is it? They've taken to the road, have they, probably under a false name? Fun in a Tudor Trust House, eh? Though I have my doubts about the Major.

JOYCE: Oh, I don't know. I'm beginning to fancy the Major, though I think he'd need a lot of training. Not a week-end man at all.

PHILIP: The blatant cynicism of you women—ugh!

JOYCE (*indignantly*): And after the things *I've heard you say*——

> *Curtains open showing corner of private sitting-room in very Olde Worlde Inne.* ROSEMARY *in day clothes is sitting on sofa, looking rather forlorn and dubious. She sits still throughout outside dialogue.*

PHILIP: There we are. Ye Olde Tudor Inne with plaster beams.

JOYCE: And he's taken a private sitting-room with the best double bedroom adjoining it. Well, well, well!

> WILLIAM *enters as Major Spanner, in dinner jacket.* PHILIP *and* JOYCE *retire to pianos and sit. Spanner has traces of a cold, which gets worse throughout the scene.*

ROSEMARY: But, George, you've changed.

WILLIAM (*startled*): Changed? Same man you've always known. Loved you for years.

ROSEMARY: No, I mean your clothes.

WILLIAM: Oh yes. Always like to change. Make a habit of it. Keeps a fella from getting slack, y'know.

ROSEMARY (*half vexed, half laughing*): But we want to *be* slack. That's why we've come here. Besides I didn't bring any evening things with me.

WILLIAM: Oh—I see. Look odd, will it?

ROSEMARY: Of course it will. We'll have to have dinner up here.

WILLIAM (*rather disconcerted*): Oh—will we? Oh, I say, I've just commandeered a good table down there. Slipped down for a short drink before feeding. (*Sneezes, then sniffs a little.*) Fact is, that bathroom's damned draughty and I didn't notice it in time. Have to be careful after all these years in a hot climate.

ROSEMARY (*vaguely*): Yes, of course. Well, you'd better slip down again and tell them we'll dine up here.

WILLIAM: You don't think it would look odd, do you? I mean, you know what these people are. (*Pointing to the door.*)

ROSEMARY (*rather impatiently*): Well, if you like you can dine down there by yourself and I'll just have something on a tray up here. I'm not very hungry anyhow.

WILLIAM: Oh, aren't you? Oh, I say, that's rather a shame. Food here's pretty good, too. That's how I remembered the name of the place.

ROSEMARY: I don't care. I didn't come here for *food*.

WILLIAM (*rather embarrassed at this*): No, of course not. Neither did I, of course. Happy, little girl?

ROSEMARY: Yes, of course, darling. I've been enjoying the lovely peace of it. To be quiet—with peace all around—lovely.

WILLIAM (*dubiously*): Yes, quite. Mayn't last, though.

ROSEMARY (*startled*): Why?

WILLIAM: Got a big table all laid out down below (*leaning towards her*) and the head waiter told me it's for a crowd of Air Force blokes who make a night of it here every Friday. Probably won't be much peace and quiet when those lads get started. Ho—ho!

ROSEMARY: Yes, but I didn't mean *that*.

WILLIAM: No, of course not. Quite understand what you mean.

ROSEMARY (*after pause, wistfully*): George, do you really love me?

WILLIAM: Why, Rosemary, little girl, you know I do. Haven't I carried that photograph of you with me everywhere for years? Got it here now, matter of fact. (*Pats his back pocket.*)

ROSEMARY: You don't want it now because you've got me. (*After staring at him speculatively*) You know, George, darling, I hope you realise that a photograph is one thing and a real live person is quite a different thing. I mean, are you quite sure it's me—me myself—you really want?

WILLIAM: Why of course, Rosemary darling. I tell you, I've dreamed of this for years.

ROSEMARY (*stifling all doubts*): Darling! (*Holding up her face*) Kiss me!

WILLIAM (*moving to her*): By Jove, yes. Just a second. (*Suddenly stops and turns away, then violently sneezes.*) Oh—damn! Sorry! (*Sniffs and blows his nose hard.*)

ROSEMARY (*not holding up her face now*): Have you got a cold?

WILLIAM (*annoyed and apologetic*): Yes. Beginning to look like it. Damn that bathroom! Felt a touch somewhere too, coming down in the car. That's why I wanted the window closed, but you wouldn't hear of it.

ROSEMARY (*rather coldly*): I'm sorry. I didn't realise you were so susceptible to colds.

WILLIAM: Well, a fella can't be years in a hot climate and then come back to this cold, damp hole—without—— (*Just catches another sneeze, then sits on sofa and looks at her gravely.*)

ROSEMARY (*after a pause*): What's the matter, George? Is it—something about *us?*

WILLIAM (*solemnly*): Oh—no. But I've just realised I didn't pack my little glass thing. For the nose, y'know.

ROSEMARY (*sadly*): No, George, I don't know.

WILLIAM (*solemnly, sitting very close to her*): Sort of nasal douche, y'know. Harley Street fella told me never to be without it here at home. First sign of a cold you fill it with a solution of common salt and bicarbonate, then use it night and morning. (*Goes through motions of douching.*) Loosens and dissolves the mucus, he said.

ROSEMARY (*in a tiny voice*): Did you say the mucus, George?

WILLIAM (*solemnly*): Yes, Rosemary. And I've gone and forgotten the thing and it's too late now to buy one.

ROSEMARY (*sadly*): Yes, George, it's too late now to buy one.

> *He gives another violent sneeze, fiddles with his shirt cuff, takes out his handkerchief, mops his face, and now she suddenly bursts into a fit of hysterical laughter, rocking and sobbing with it while he sniffs and pats his nose and stares in amazement at her. After several moments of this——*

WILLIAM (*puzzled*): Look here, are you laughing or crying?

ROSEMARY: Both! Both! (*Rising with decision.*) Listen, George, do you know what we're going to do?

WILLIAM (*surprised sniffing*): Well, yes, I suppose——

ROSEMARY (*briskly*): No, you don't, so I'm going to tell you. One of us is going to drive back to town to-night, *now,* and the other is taking the early train back in the morning. Now, if you like you can stay here and enjoy your cold and let me go back in the car now. Or——

WILLIAM: But—but—(*just stifling a sneeze*)—I mean to say—what —I thought we were——

ROSEMARY: No, we're not, my dear. I like you very very much, but all the rest of it is simply off. My mistake. And don't pretend not to be relieved because I know very well you are and not just because you've got a cold either. And if we both stay we'll only quarrel and feel silly afterwards. Now, do I go back in the car to-night or do you?

WILLIAM: Well—if it's all the same to you—I think I'd like to get back—because if my cold——

ROSEMARY: I know—your little nose thing. That's settled then. Run down and get something to eat and I'll pack for you. Go on, there's a lamb. (*As she almost bustles him out*) And George! Remember! We've never been here. It never happened. All a dream! Oh—what name did you put in the hotel register?

[510]

WILLIAM (*almost off, still trying to sneeze*): All I could think of was the name of an old C.O. of mine—terrible old stickler (*sneezes*) Smith.

> WILLIAM *goes out.* ROSEMARY *sits on sofa, half-laughing, half-crying. Curtains close. Bar or two of music with Spanner theme suggested.*

JOYCE: All he wanted was to go on with his nice, safe little doglike devotion. A photograph to wag his head over when he'd had a few drinks, and not a real woman.

PHILIP: He's probably got two or three little brown wives in Banji-Banji. But I thought that bogus romantic devotion was just what you women wanted.

JOYCE: Not at all.

> HELEN *enters through curtains and comes to centre of rostrum.*

HELEN: What we women want is something quite simple, and it's you men who make it all seem complicated. What we want is simply to be intensely real living people to the men we love. Nothing fancy at all—we get over that a year after we've left school—not strange, romantic, glamorous figures—but just attractive and desirable *real people.* And your trouble is, whether you're romantics, sensualists, Don Quixotes, Don Juans, it's all the same—you won't let us be real people. You'll turn us into anything, dolls, goddesses, drudges, symbols, phantoms, rather than recognise us as our simple selves. And that's the honest truth.

> *Lights are now fading. Curtain on alcove left draws, showing* ROSEMARY *telephoning like* PAUL *in the previous scene.* JOYCE *plays.*

ROSEMARY (*at telephone*): Oh, Nannie, is Mr. Weybridge there? I see. . . . All right, Nannie. . . .

> *She begins dialling savagely to the sound of staccato music; playing stops.*

Is that Fletcher, Fletcher and Coulson. Is Mr. Coulson there, please? Mrs. Weybridge. Say it's rather important. . . . Oh, Mr. Coulson, could I see you as soon as possible? Well, it is, really. . . . Well, it's —it's—(*hurriedly, but rather louder*)—it's about a divorce——

> *Music starts a little mournful. Close of curtain alcove left.*

HELEN: And there you are. That separated them.

> *Playing stops.*

JOYCE: It's just the sort of dam' silly thing that would.

PHILIP: No doubt. But may I point out one important fact? If she hadn't been in such a hurry to ring up that solicitor——

JOYCE (*cutting in*): Yes, yes, we know. But she felt she had to do *something*. I understand exactly how she felt.

PHILIP: There you are. You women——

HELEN (*cutting in*): Yes, we'll admit it's when we feel thoroughly upset, we *are* inclined to do the first thing that comes into our heads.

JOYCE: Oh Lord—yes!

PHILIP: Quite so. Whereas—if you'd only take it easy, just turn things over, enjoy a little quiet reflection——

JOYCE (*cutting in*): You've been taking it easy, turning things over, and enjoying your little quiet reflection ever since I've known you.

PHILIP: I prefer to ignore that type of remark.

JOYCE (*mocking his tone*): He prefers to ignore that type of remark.

PHILIP (*annoyed*): Oh—shut up!

HELEN: Hoy, hoy! It's not you two we're doing but Paul and Rosemary. Now of course, it was months—and horribly dreary months—before they found themselves together in the solicitor's office.

JOYCE: Yes, it would be. But don't show us any of those dreary months.

WILLIAM *now enters as himself.*

WILLIAM: No, no, we can imagine. (*Sits on rostrum.*)

HELEN: In any case, they ought to be back in that solicitor's office by now. Joyce—Philip.

HELEN *joins* WILLIAM. *Curtains open to reveal exactly the same solicitor's office scene as in Act One.* PAUL *moves about as before.* ROSEMARY'S *voice is heard off, as before, saying "Oh, in here. Thank you!" and she enters as before, wearing the same clothes.* PAUL *is looking out of window and turns. She stares at* PAUL. *He looks embarrassed. All as before.*

PAUL (*with an effort*): I'm afraid this is—er—rather embarrassing —Rosemary.

ROSEMARY (*with similar effort*): Yes—Paul—I'm afraid it is. . . . (*Sits and looks away.*)

PAUL: Not my fault. . . . I had a note from Coulson asking me to be here at half-past three—to answer some questions about the— the divorce. . . .

ROSEMARY (*tiny voice*): Yes, so had I.

PAUL (*restlessly*): Oh, I say—monstrous thing for Coulson to do —asking us both here at the same time. Shows you how blankly insensitive these lawyers are. Typical lawyer's trick, this. Damn Coulson!

ROSEMARY (*faintly*): Oh—I don't think—it's perhaps—(*Dies away.*)

PAUL: What?

ROSEMARY: No—nothing. . . .

PAUL: Look here. I'll go and wait out there.

ROSEMARY: No—it . . .

PAUL: Don't mind a bit . . .

They stare at each other uncertainly and miserably. Lights on inner stage and pianos and fore-stage now begin to fade. JOYCE *rises from piano and begins to move towards back.* PHILIP *does same.*

JOYCE: It's just as it was before. In another minute he'll go out, and that poor girl will start crying——

PHILIP: And if we're not careful, we'll find ourselves arguing about it as before, and then we'll be shown how they first met, and it'll all go round and round.

JOYCE: It's not good enough.

PAUL (*quietly but indignantly*): I couldn't agree with you more.

ROSEMARY (*rising, same tone as* PAUL): It's really Helen's fault—and William's——

PHILIP (*voice beginning to fade*): Well, my dear, let them settle it.

Moves to right alcove, and exits.

JOYCE (*voice fading*): And themselves—if they can.

She exits from alcove left. Curtains close. WILLIAM *and* HELEN *are now lit as if in firelight, with the rest of the stage dark.* HELEN *speaks quietly, as if concluding a long story.*

HELEN: So there they were. Paul, like a fool, went out, and poor Rosemary sat there crying. Of course, she'd asked the solicitor to send for them both at the same time, in the hope that seeing her again he might have discovered he was still in love with her. (*Pause.*) William, are you listening?

WILLIAM: Yes, I'm listening. But I'm thinking too.

HELEN: No doubt. But I don't believe you were listening.

WILLIAM: Yes, I was. The last thing you said was that she hoped he was still in love with her. Well, he is. And he's only got to run into her anywhere outside that solicitor's office, and he'll show her he is.

HELEN: I'll tell her about that. Then she'll make sure he does run into her. But what were you thinking about—those two?

WILLIAM: No. About two other people.

HELEN (*who knows at once*): Oh!

[513]

WILLIAM (*slowly*): Two people—rather older and more mature—and perhaps cleverer in some ways—than those two, who also fell in love, got married, and went galloping away to happiness—only, of course, to find the usual hurdles and jumps and obstacles—losing the first excitement of possession, disagreeing about friends . . .

HELEN (*quietly*): Complaints about being taken for granted or neglected, and jealousy when other men and women were specially attentive——

WILLIAM (*quietly*): And then a whole fog of cross-purposes——

HELEN: And each of them wearing their pride like blinkers——

WILLIAM: And so, instead of clearing the hurdles and reaching the long flat stretch where they could canter home in trust and affection, they turned aside, they broke—they got divorced.

HELEN (*with controlled emotion*): One of them—didn't seem to mind very much—behaved as if it were true what he'd said when—when they were quarrelling—that marriage wasn't right for him——

WILLIAM: He was a fool—and a liar. But he didn't know enough then. And those were the silly easy days when people were busy deceiving themselves. Now he knows that life is hard, and the years are slipping by, and soon the nights will be longer and lonelier and friends will vanish and where there might have been love to the end, not excitement and passion and possession, not rockets and stars but the steady glow of the fire, there will be darkness—and nothing. (*Pause.*) She can't understand that yet.

HELEN (*half-laughing, half-crying*): Oh, can't she? You ask any woman living alone!

WILLIAM: But she needn't live alone.

HELEN: She prefers to.

WILLIAM (*pause, turning to* HELEN): I'm giving myself a last chance, Helen.

HELEN: Why do you say that?

WILLIAM: Because—this being friends, all so gay and matey and cool—doesn't work any longer for me. I've tried hard but I can't make it work. So if this is all, I'm going away.

HELEN (*hastily*): You're not going without me.

WILLIAM (*joyfully*): Helen! (*Turning to her.*)

HELEN: No, wait, William. I agree with everything you've said, and I've felt it too. But it's not good enough. I'm a woman—and not an insurance against a lonely old age. Say it—or never talk like this again.

WILLIAM (*with great sincerity. Pause*): My dear, I love you—I love you with all my heart—and I ask you to forgive me—and marry me again——

HELEN: Oh—my darling—there's nothing to forgive—and I love you too—and, of course, I will——

They embrace, and then after a moment she withdraws and looks at him, half laughing, half crying.

But darling, making all that fuss and getting divorced—and then marrying again—they'll say we don't know our own minds——

WILLIAM (*sturdily*): Well, we do.

HELEN (*same tone as before*): They'll laugh at us.

WILLIAM (*roundly*): Let 'em laugh.

They rise. Curtains open on inner stage. Great burst of laughter from all four on inner stage, with all lights coming on full—showing a back wall of drawing-room and a buffet table, with drinks, food, and the four—PAUL, ROSEMARY, who are now in evening dress standing in front of it. The side curtains of alcoves are also drawn aside to show flowers or lighted decorations. The laughter is friendly and not at all malicious.

PAUL: Well, you're a bright pair. Ask us here to celebrate with you—and then go off into a corner.

He gives WILLIAM a glass, PHILIP hands glass to HELEN.

WILLIAM (*grinning*): Sorry, old boy!

ROSEMARY: And you haven't even congratulated Joyce and Philip.

HELEN (*to PHILIP*): I hope you'll be very happy, Philip. I'm sure you will.

PHILIP: Thank you, Helen. I had to do something to make her play in tune.

WILLIAM (*after drinking*): I don't know that in the long run marriage makes anybody very happy. But then the single life doesn't make anybody very happy either. The fact is, nobody in his senses *can* be happy.

HELEN: Don't start philosophising now.

WILLIAM: No, my love. (*To JOYCE*) My congratulations, Joyce!

JOYCE: Thank you, William! I'm so tired of seeing him look bleary-eyed that I decided I'd better marry him to try and clean him up.

WILLIAM (*sternly*): For that, get back to your piano.

JOYCE *comes down to piano left.*

HELEN (*to PHILIP*): And you to yours.

PHILIP *comes down to piano right. They all have drinks now.*

[515]

ROSEMARY (*holding up glass*): Well, here's to all of us!

JOYCE, PHILIP and PAUL: Well, here's to all of us.

They all toast each other and drink, the three couples look and smile at each other.

WILLIAM: Mind you, the sexual life, as even Shelley had to admit, is a cheat.

JOYCE (*sardonically*): Are you telling me?

WILLIAM (*munching away at a sandwich which* ROSEMARY *has handed him*): It's been a cheat ever since Paradise.

PHILIP: It has.

HELEN: It takes us women in, just as it does you men.

ROSEMARY: Worse, I suspect.

WILLIAM (*broadly now*): But to share the cheat together—with humour and kindness——

HELEN (*smiling at him*): With trust and deepening affection——

WILLIAM: Is to put up a tent not too far from the shining gates.

ROSEMARY: That's true. And I only hope you'll all be as happy as Paul and I have always been.

PHILIP *and* WILLIAM *take a drink.*

PAUL (*too heartily*): Well, I suppose we've been extraordinarily lucky—but there it is—never even a really serious misunderstanding.

ROSEMARY (*sweetly*): We said from the first we'd take care never to quarrel——

HELEN: Well, I must say, my dears . . .

WILLIAM (*to* HELEN *with irony*): I don't think we can do better than follow their wonderful example.

At this PHILIP *and* JOYCE *sit at their pianos and begin playing, while* HELEN *and* WILLIAM *toast each other and move up on to the rostrum to meet* PAUL *and* ROSEMARY.

END OF PLAY